▽△▽△▽△▽△▽△▽△

Indian Traders of the Southeastern Spanish Borderlands

Indian Traders of the Southeastern Spanish Borderlands

Panton, Leslie & Company
and
John Forbes & Company,
1783–1847

William S. Coker
Thomas D. Watson
Foreword by J. Leitch Wright, Jr.

University Presses of Florida
University of West Florida Press/Pensacola

UNIVERSITY PRESSES OF FLORIDA is the central agency for scholarly publishing of the State of Florida's university system, producing books selected for publication by the faculty editorial committees of Florida's nine public universities: Florida A&M University (Tallahassee), Florida Atlantic University (Boca Raton), Florida International University (Miami), Florida State University (Tallahassee), University of Central Florida (Orlando), University of Florida (Gainesville), University of North Florida (Jacksonville), University of South Florida (Tampa), University of West Florida (Pensacola).

ORDERS for books published by all member presses of University Presses of Florida should be addressed to University Presses of Florida, 15 NW 15th Street, Gainesville, FL 32603.

Library of Congress Cataloging in Publication Data

Coker, William S.
  Indian traders of the southeastern Spanish borderlands.

  Bibliography: p.
  Includes index.
  1. Panton, Leslie & Company. 2. John Forbes & Company.
3. Indians of North America—Southern States—Trading posts. 4. Indians of North America—Southern States—Commerce. 5. Southern States—Commerce—History.
I. Watson, Thomas D. II. Title.
E78.S65C65 1985   381'.1'0975   84-25806
ISBN 0-8130-1854-4 pbk.

Copyright © 1986 by the Board of Regents of the State of Florida
All rights reserved
Printed in the U.S.A.

Contents

Maps and Illustrations	vii
Tables	viii
Foreword, by J. Leitch Wright, Jr.	ix
Acknowledgments	xv
Abbreviations Used	xvii
Introduction	1
1. The Partners: Scotsmen All	15
2. Loyalists All	31
3. Establishing the Indian Trade, 1783–1785	49
4. Keeping the United States at Bay, 1785–1787	73
5. Conflict and Confusion in the Indian Country, 1787–1788	93
6. Adversaries to Trade	114
7. McGillivray: Wooed by Washington, Threatened by Bowles	135
8. Carondelet and Panton Take the Offensive	157
9. Beset by Friend and Foe Alike	182
10. War and Business	203
11. The Deaths of Panton and Bowles	226
12. Resolution of the Indian Debts	243
13. The Company and the War of 1812	273
14. The Aftermath of the War of 1812: Slaves and Negro Fort	292

15. The First Seminole War Destroys Trade — 310
16. The Vidal Case — 330
17. Years of Litigation — 350
Summary and Conclusions — 363
    Appendix: The Papers of Panton, Leslie and Company — 371
    Bibliography — 375
    Index — 395

Maps and Illustrations

The Reverend William Leslie	facing page 172
John Innerarity	facing page 173
Lands in dispute between the United States and Spain, 1783–95	3
Indian nations of the southeastern Spanish borderlands, 1780–1820	6
Scottish towns and villages associated with members of Panton, Leslie and Company and John Forbes and Company, 1740–1800	20
Little Tallassee and the Hickory Ground, ca. 1790	22
Colonies of South Carolina, Georgia, and East Florida during the American Revolution	40
Panton, Leslie and Company headquarters, ca. 1796–1848	66
The Forbes purchase, 1804–11	253
Indian lands acquired by the United States with the assistance of John Forbes and Company, 1805	264
Forbes Island, 1839	269
Locations of Forbes's East Florida slave problems, 1812–15	294
Apalachicola-Suwannee Area, 1816–18	322
Land grants to Panton, Leslie and Company and John Forbes and Company, 1804–18	328
Panton, Leslie and Company and John Forbes and Company stores and trading posts, 1783–1821	front endleaves
Panton, Leslie and Company and John Forbes and Company stores and trading posts, 1785–1847	rear endleaves

Tables

1. Tariff of commerce of Creek and Talapoosa Nation, 1784 60
2. Losses sustained by the plundering Indians at Apalachee, 1792 155
3. Losses sustained by Panton, Leslie and Company from increased insurance premiums and vessels captured during the war between France and Great Britain, 1793–97 222–23
4. Debts due Panton, Leslie and Company by Indian nations, 1797 and 1803 228
5. Losses sustained as a result of Bowles's capture of the St. Marks trading post, May 1800 234
6. Debts settled by the Creek-Seminole cession of the Apalachicola lands in 1804 252
7. Indian land cessions to the United States influenced by John Forbes and Company 265
8. Summary of debts collected by John Forbes and Company, 1804–14 271
9. Panton, Leslie and Company and John Forbes and Company, stores and trading posts 365

Foreword
J. Leitch Wright, Jr.

THE American Revolution, which convulsed Britain's New World colonies, led to the founding of the great Indian trading firm of Panton, Leslie, and Company. Most of the area below the Ohio River had long been inhabited by Indians—Creek, Cherokee, Chickasaw, Seminole, Choctaw, and small remnant tribes—and this was the region of the firm's primary interest.

Since the days of first contact in the sixteenth century the natives had traded with Europeans, and they offered mainly two articles—peltry and Indian slaves. After the 1730s the Indian slave trade was constricted because the pool of potential captives was so reduced, but the peltry trade continued. Before the Revolution, trains of packhorses of ten to a hundred or more animals were outfitted in Charleston and Augusta and made their way hundreds of miles into the interior to appropriate Indian villages. After bargaining and trading were completed, the animal trains returned with packs of skins and furs. Deerskins were the mainstay. Manufactured goods customarily were valued in so many pounds of skins, and Charleston, the port most involved in the Indian trade, annually exported thousands of pounds of deerskins.

During the American Revolution, leading Indian merchants from South Carolina and Georgia fled to British East Florida for protection. William Panton escaped to St. Augustine in 1776, subsequently returned to Georgia after royal troops regained control of the colony, and at the end of the

Revolution again sought refuge in East Florida. Whether he was in East Florida or not, during the Revolution he had a contract with East Florida to furnish goods for the Indians, and in 1782–83 he and four other exiles joined to form Panton, Leslie, and Company. Regardless of which flag might fly over the two Floridas after the Revolution ended, these partners resolved to continue trading with the southeastern Indians.

American patriots branded Panton and his partners as Tories. The label is misleading because Panton and his associates espoused representative government and denounced taxation without representation and arbitrary rule by the mother country. They believed, however, like most Scotsmen in America, that by remaining in the empire and not drawing their swords against their lawful king, they could best protect and guarantee traditional liberties and their financial well-being. It was difficult for those in the upper class to remain neutral during the passionate revolutionary years. Those who were not ardent friends of the patriots were considered enemies and labeled Tories, though a more accurate term is "loyalist."

Spain won title to both East and West Florida in the Treaty of Paris in 1783, and with Spain's approval the firm remained in East Florida. But it did not confine its activities to that province. In addition to its warehouses in St. Augustine and on the St. Johns River it established new ones in the west—at St. Marks in Apalachee, at Pensacola and Mobile, and eventually at Chickasaw Bluffs and elsewhere on the Mississippi. During the Revolution, Pensacola had replaced Charleston as the most important port in the southern Indian trade and was the reason that William Panton moved from St. Augustine in East Florida to Pensacola in West Florida at the end of the Revolution. It became the firm's principal establishment on the American mainland. Packhorse trains loaded with munitions, rum, and an assortment of goods were outfitted here and at the company's other warehouses and made their way to Indian villages in the interior, returning with deerskins, furs, bear oil, honey, and foodstuffs. The company's agents, or factors, maintained truckhouses (stores) in Indian villages scattered from the Florida peninsula to the Mississippi River and from the Gulf coast to Lookout Mountain, Tennessee. These factors might be white, Indian, Negro, or some combination thereof. More often than not they were whites or mestizos. Whatever their ethnic background they usually obtained their merchandise from Panton, Leslie and Company.

After 1783, Spain expected Panton, Leslie and Company at St. Augustine and Pensacola to furnish goods to the Creek and Seminole and other British merchants at Mobile and New Orleans to supply the Choctaw and Chickasaw. As Panton, Leslie and Company thrust westward from

St. Augustine to St. Marks, Pensacola, Mobile, and eventually the Mississippi River, it took over more and more of the southern Indian trade and eventually all of it that passed legally through Spanish territory. Spain did not officially grant the company a commercial monopoly, but by the late 1780s Spain made arrangements only with Panton and no one else, the effect of which was to give the firm the whole of the southeastern Indian trade.

To be sure, the firm had competition—primarily from Americans in Georgia and South Carolina and from other British merchants who were not members of Panton, Leslie, and Company, and who were legally excluded from trading with the Indians by virtue of the firm's de facto Spanish monopoly. With limited success Georgians and South Carolinians after 1783 continued some of their prewar commerce, and in 1796 the United States established the first of its "factories" (subsidized warehouses) designed to capture the Indian market. British loyalists who were not members of Panton, Leslie and Company but who had traded with the southern Indians before 1783 were determined to continue their commerce with the Indians despite opposition from Panton and from Spain. Foremost in this group was John Miller, a member of the West Florida assembly, who had fled from Pensacola in 1781 and at the end of the Revolution established himself in Nassau. Associated with him was young William Augustus Bowles, a Maryland loyalist officer who was serving in the British garrison at Pensacola when Spain captured it in 1781. Miller, Bowles, the Bahamian governor Lord Dunmore, and other uprooted loyalists hoped to make the Southeast a British protectorate or colony. Whether or not they succeeded in these political objectives, they expected to profit from trafficking with the Indians.

Despite competition from British and American merchants, and the fact that Spanish officials distrusted loyalists associated with Panton, Leslie, and Company, the firm prospered. Panton and his partners were shrewd, opportunistic businessmen, sparing no pains to ensure that factors in interior villages sent their skins to company warehouses. Partly, they were successful because they and their British correspondents afforded factors and individual hunters long-term credit and also because they had close contacts with London and Glasgow merchants who were experienced in meeting the needs of the southeastern Indians.

As far as Spain was concerned the company's raison d'être was to supply the Indians with sufficient manufactures and to keep them contented and acting in Spain's interest. It is misleading, however, to assume that the company did no more than traffic with Native Americans. It also sold foodstuffs, salt, cattle, and a wide assortment of goods to the Spanish populace in St. Augustine and Pensacola and gave presents to Spanish officials, some of whom suddenly became enthusiastic company supporters. The firm also became one of the largest landowners and real estate speculators in the Southeast. It owned lots in towns and cities scattered throughout the Spanish Floridas, plantations and cowpens in the countryside (frequently adjoining company warehouses), and enormous tracts acquired from the Indians. The Forbes Purchase, hundreds of square miles in extent between the Apalachicola and Wakulla rivers, was the most conspicuous example.

Nor did Panton, Leslie, and Company confine its activities to the American mainland. It had a warehouse in Nassau, managed by Thomas Forbes, one of the original partners. Goods for the Indians and peltry from the Southeast often were funneled through this Bahamian entrepôt. In addition, the company traded with settlers on New Providence Island and on the Bahamian out-islands, and this aspect of the firm's business is one that is least understood. The company traded with the Spanish colonies of Yucatán, Texas, and Louisiana, and also with the United States, but the Southeast always remained the center of the company's interests and the source of its greatest profits.

The far-flung commercial activities of Panton, Leslie and Company and its successors generated large amounts of legal, political, and diplomatic correspondence, bills of lading, insurance and customs reports, and the like, in a variety of languages. These documents today are to be found in public and private archives in Spain, Cuba, Mexico, the United States, Canada, England, Scotland, and even in Australia and the Philippines. It is asking too much that the Panton, Leslie Project collect, preserve, and calendar all surviving records, but its copies of more than 200,000 pages of documents are an invaluable resource for understanding the history of Florida, the greater Southeast, Indian affairs, international trade, and foreign relations. So much of the internal, domestic history of the Floridas during the second Spanish period is buried in these documents. The firm dominated the southeastern Indian trade for almost a half century, and the Panton, Leslie papers probably are the best ethnographic collection available for the southeastern Indians during the late eighteenth and early nineteenth centuries. Better than anywhere else, this collection holds the key to the origins and early development of the Seminoles, and there also is much information on the Creek, Cherokee, Choctaw, Chickasaw, and other Native Americans.

While Panton, Leslie, and Company and its successors flourished, the Floridas were deeply involved in international controversy and diplomacy. Even a cursory glance at material in the U.S. National Archives and in many foreign archives makes this apparent. The partners closely followed diplomatic negotiations relating to the Treaty of Paris in 1783, the Anglo-Spanish Nootka Sound controversy in 1790, the United States–Creek Treaty of the same year, the Spanish-American Pinckney Treaty in 1795, the Anglo-American Treaty of Ghent ending the War of 1812, the Adams-Onís Treaty of 1821 by which the United States acquired the remainder of the Spanish Floridas, and many similar compacts.

From the American Revolution until well into the nineteenth century, much of the history of the southeastern borderlands remains obscure or is totally unknown—yet it is contained in these documents. A guide and calendar will be published in the future, directing investigators to appropriate documents in this outstanding borderlands collection. For these and many other reasons, scholars from many disciplines and the general reader alike will welcome this narrative history.

Acknowledgments

THIS history of the Indian traders of the southeastern Spanish borderlands is an outgrowth—at least in part—of the documentary project "The Papers of Panton, Leslie and Company," which includes also the papers of John Forbes and Company, its successor firm. Without this comprehensive collection of documents, it would be extremely difficult to write a detailed history of these two Indian trading companies. Nevertheless, the narrative history and the documentary collection are two distinct projects. For example, the National Historical Publications and Records Commission (NHPRC) funded the collection and microfilm phases of the documentary project, but funds for the publication of the narrative history came from the Florida Bicentennial Commission and the Ford Foundation. Because there were two projects, it was decided to treat them separately in this volume. Those interested in a brief history of the documentary and microfilm phases (with appropriate acknowledgments to those primarily concerned with that project) are referred to the appendix. This section is reserved for those directly involved in the narrative history. Of course, no clear line can be drawn between the two and some names will appear in both places.

Originally, David Hart White, associate professor of history at the University of Alabama, Birmingham, was scheduled to be a coauthor, but his death in December 1979 precluded that possibility.

Thomas D. Watson, professor of history, McNeese State University, Lake Charles, Louisiana, prepared the introductory chapter and chapters three through ten. Watson and William S. Coker, professor of history and director of the Papers of Panton, Leslie and Company, University of West Florida, Pensacola, shared the work on chapter eleven. Coker wrote chapters one and two and twelve through seventeen and assumed responsibility for the illustrations, bibliography, and other parts of the study.

Professors Robert R. Rea of Auburn University and J. Leitch Wright, Jr., of Florida State University both read this manuscript for the University of West Florida. Not only did their criticisms, comments, and recommendations improve this work in many ways, but Professor Wright also consented to write the foreword for the book.

The University of West Florida editorial committee—James A. Servies, chairman, and John L. Cox, Ralph T. Eubanks, and Stanton Millet, critics—offered valuable editorial suggestions for improving the manuscript, as did Ronald V. Evans, who read an early draft.

Sally Savage in the project office typed part of the manuscript, with additional typing assistance from the office of UWF Vice-President for Academic Affairs Arthur H. Doerr. In particular, we thank Evelyn C. Grosse, Stacy B. Kosmas, Sandra Zepp, and Theresa Bradford from that office and Marianna McDaniels from the history office.

Tamara West Harrell and Gary N. Ives also helped either editorially or with the notes and bibliography.

Professor Jerome F. Coling of UWF deserves acknowledgment for the preparation of the maps.

Special thanks go to the Florida Bicentennial Commission and its executive directors, Shelton Kemp and William R. Adams, and to the Ford Foundation Venture Fund and its representatives, Erma Bischoff and Howard R. Dressner, for the generous financial contributions that made publication of this volume possible.

We also wish to acknowledge the work of those many scholars who literally plowed the way for us over the years. The number of theses, dissertations, articles, and books from which we so liberally borrowed made our job much easier. We refer the reader to the notes and bibliography—because it would take far too much space to list them all here—in showing our gratitude. If we have overlooked anyone, it was unintentional, and we accept sole responsibility for errors and omissions.

We would be remiss if we did not pay particular tribute to two women who helped not only in typing the manuscript and in many other ways but managed by one means or another to endure the long and often frustrating hours which their husbands spent working on it: Polly Coker and Carol Watson.

To the staff of University Presses of Florida go our thanks for their hard work in seeing the volume through the final editorial and production stages.

Abbreviations Used

AGI	*Archivo General de Indias* (Sevilla, Spain)
AGI PC	*Papeles de Cuba* in *AGI*
AGI SD	*Audiencia de Santo Domingo* in *AGI*
AGM	*Archivo General Militar* (Segovia, Spain)
AGS	*Archivo General de Simancas* (Simancas, Spain)
AHI	*American History Illustrated*
AHN	*Archivo Histórico Nacional* (Madrid, Spain)
AHQ	*Alabama Historical Quarterly*
AHR	*American Historical Review*
ANC	*Archivo Nacional de Cuba* (Havana, Cuba)
AR	*Alabama Review*
ASP FR	*American State Papers, Foreign Relations*
ASP IA	*American State Papers, Indian Affairs*
ASP M	*American State Papers, Miscellaneous*
ASP PL	*American State Papers, Public Lands*
BSC	Buckingham Smith Collection, New York Historical Society (New York, New York)
BSL	Bureau of State Lands (Tallahassee, Florida)
CP	Cruzat Papers, Florida Historical Society (Tampa, Florida)
DS	*Dow v. Sanchez* (see "Court Cases" in Bibliography)
EF	East Florida Papers, Library of Congress
ETHSP	*East Tennessee Historical Society Publications*

Abbreviations Used

FHQ	*Florida Historical Quarterly*
FP, MPL	Forbes Papers, Mobile Public Library (Mobile, Alabama)
GHQ	*Georgia Historical Quarterly*
GHS	Georgia Historical Society (Savannah, Georgia)
GP	Greenslade Papers, Florida Historical Society (Tampa, Florida)
HWP	Henry Wilson Papers, Louisiana State University (Baton Rouge, Louisiana)
IHP	Innerarity-Hulse Papers, University of West Florida (Pensacola, Florida)
JIP	John Innerarity Papers, Louisiana State University (Baton Rouge, Louisiana)
JMH	*Journal of Mississippi History*
JSH	*Journal of Southern History*
LC	Library of Congress
leg.	*legajo* ("bundle" or "batch," equivalent to a file)
LDS	The Library of the Church of Latter Day Saints (Salt Lake City, Utah)
LH	*Louisiana History*
LHQ	*Louisiana Historical Quarterly*
LPBL	*Documentos relativos a la Luisiana*, The Bancroft Library (Berkeley, California)
LS	*Louisiana Studies*
LSSC	Louisiana State Supreme Court (New Orleans, Louisiana)
LSU	Louisiana State University (Baton Rouge, Louisiana)
MC	Mitchel Case (see "Court Cases" in Bibliography)
MHS	Maryland Historical Society (Baltimore, Maryland)
MPL	Mobile Public Library (Mobile, Alabama)
MVHR	*Mississippi Valley Historical Review*
NARG	National Archives record group
NCHR	*North Carolina Historical Review*
NLS	National Library of Scotland (Edinburgh, Scotland)
NOPL	New Orleans Public Library (New Orleans, Louisiana)
NYHS	New York Historical Society (New York, New York)
PHS	Pensacola Historical Society (Pensacola, Florida)
PLP	Papers of Panton, Leslie & Company, University of West Florida (Pensacola, Florida)
PROL	Public Record Office (London, England)
PRON	Public Record Office (Nassau, Bahamas)
SCAH	South Carolina Department of Archives and History (Columbia, South Carolina)
SCHGM	*South Carolina Historical and Genealogical Magazine*
SCHM	*South Carolina Historical Magazine*

THSA	*Tallahassee Historical Society Annual*
WP	Elizabeth Howard West Papers, P. K. Yonge Library of Florida History, University of Florida (Gainesville, Florida)
WPA	Works Progress Administration (also Work Projects Administration)
WTHSP	*West Tennessee Historical Society Papers*

This volume is dedicated to
Gilbert Courtland Fite,
Max Leon Moorhead, &
David Martell Vigness,
    who guided and inspired us as students
    and in the years beyond.

Introduction

*T*HE fortunes of war and the processes of diplomacy following the American Revolution produced mixed results for the Spanish empire in North America. The final peace terms gave Spain possession of British East and West Florida, a concession that seemingly made possible the realization of a high-priority war aim—the reestablishment of the Gulf of Mexico as a Spanish lake.[1] British merchants in West Florida would no longer inundate Spanish Louisiana with contraband goods or pose a threat to the closed commercial regimes of Cuba and New Spain. Nor would either Florida menace the security of Spanish America by providing an offensive staging area for some future Anglo-Spanish encounter.

Spanish diplomacy, however, failed to curb the expansionist tendencies of the newly independent United States. During the course of the preliminary peace discussions in 1782, Spain, with French assistance, attempted to confine the western boundary of the United States as near to the Appalachians as possible.[2] The representatives of the United States frustrated Spanish designs by entering into confidential negotiations with British agents that produced quite generous terms for the young republic: cession to the United States of the territory in the interior of North America east of the Mississippi River and south of the Great Lakes. Because

1. Wright, *Anglo-Spanish Rivalry*, 124.
2. Morris, *Peacemakers*, 306ff.

Spain received West Florida, the southern boundary was established at 31° north latitude. In addition, the citizens of the United States received the coveted right to navigate the Mississippi throughout its entire length.

Strangely, Spanish officials never questioned these terms during the subsequent treaty negotiations. Accordingly, these territorial limits, so advantageous to the United States, became a part of the definitive peace accords signed at Paris in 1783. Perhaps as the Spanish foreign minister, the Conde de Floridablanca, later alleged, Spanish inaction stemmed from formal British acceptance of Spain's claim to West Florida by virtue of its conquest by Bernardo de Gálvez, governor of Louisiana. Reasoning that Great Britain could scarcely give away lands and navigational privileges in 1782 that it had earlier forfeited to Spanish arms, Floridablanca apparently reserved the right to challenge the pretensions of the United States at a time and place of his own choosing.[3]

The confrontation that initiated the Spanish struggle with the United States for mastery of the Old Southwest was hastened by disturbing reports filed by Spanish agents in London, Philadelphia, and New Orleans. A common theme ran through numerous dispatches reaching the Spanish foreign ministry: the Anglo-Americans, it was believed, were scheming feverishly to occupy sundry portions of the western lands acquired by the United States at Paris.[4] Ready or not, circumstances compelled Floridablanca to draw up policies for blunting a North American advance that would, it was feared, overrun Louisiana, and quite likely New Spain, if left unchallenged.

Consequently, by the summer of 1784, the Spanish court had completed its plans. On June 26, José de Gálvez, president of the Council of the Indies (or, more commonly, minister of the Indies) issued orders forbidding U.S. citizens to navigate the Mississippi under pain of arrest and confiscation of their property. Three days later Floridablanca announced Spain's own definition of the U.S.–West Florida boundary. Beginning at the mouth of the Apalachicola, the line followed the river northward to its confluence with the Flint, then up the latter to its source. From this point, the boundary proceeded northward in a straight line to the headwaters of the Hiwassee and followed that river to its juncture with the Tennessee. From there, it continued along the course of the Tennessee to the point where it joins the Ohio, which formed the remainder of the dividing line to the Mississippi.

3. Whitaker, *Spanish-American Frontier*, 9–13. On the Spanish conquest of British West Florida, see Caughey, *Gálvez*, 149–214; Starr, *Tories*, 142–224.
4. Whitaker, *Spanish-American Frontier*, 63–67.

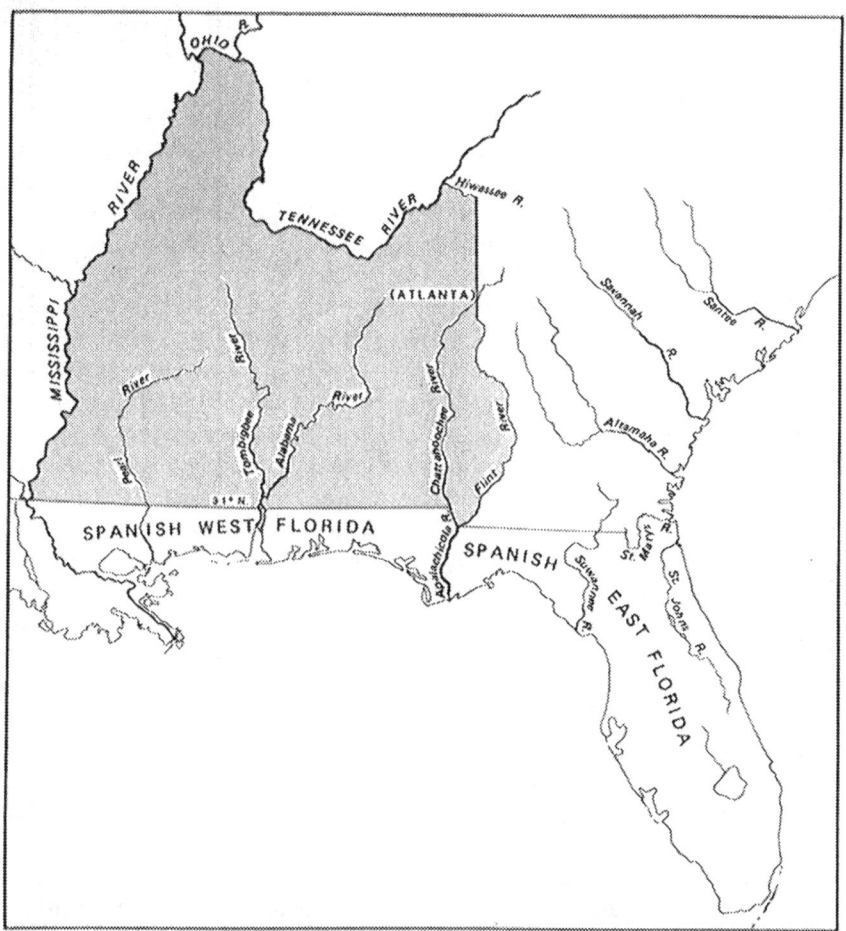

Lands in dispute between the United States and Spain, 1783-95

Having thus denied the validity of the U.S. claim to a considerable segment of contested territory and having restricted American access to the Mississippi River, an indispensable commercial artery, the Spanish court appointed Diego de Gardoqui chargé d'affaires to the United States. Gardoqui departed on his mission bearing instructions to reach an agreeable settlement on these and other matters in dispute with the United States. While granting him latitude to make adjustments on the boundary issue as an inducement in gaining American acceptance of a favorable treaty, Floridablanca strictly enjoined the Spanish envoy to hold the closure of the Mississippi as a nonnegotiable item.[5]

Disputing American claims to the Old Southwest was one matter; imposing effective Spanish control was another. Apart from the few inhabitants, most of English ancestry, who dwelled in small settlements along the east bank of the Mississippi within the Natchez district, the southern Indians occupied most of the territory embraced by Floridablanca's claim. The attitude of these 50,000 or more natives had a significant bearing on the ultimate disposition of the contending claims.

In the northwestern portion of the disputed region, the warlike Chickasaw lived in about a half dozen towns nestled between the upper reaches of the Yazoo and the Tombigbee rivers in what is now northern Mississippi. They claimed hunting lands stretching northward into the bulge of land formed by the Mississippi, Ohio, and Tennessee rivers. Bounded roughly by the Mississippi to the west and the Tombigbee in the east, Chickasaw territory stretched southward toward the Yazoo until it abutted Choctaw lands. In contrast with this extensive landholding, attrition from endemic warfare had reduced the Chickasaw population, which by the end of the American Revolution numbered probably fewer than 2,200.[6]

To the south, the relatively docile Choctaw occupied about seventy villages situated along the upper reaches of the Pearl, spreading to the southeast along the Pascagoula and Chickasawhay rivers. The Choctaw Nation, composed of the Six Towns, the Upper Towns, and the Lower Towns, were the least warlike of all southern Indians. They were noted for their devotion to agriculture, their incredible fondness for alcoholic beverages, and their guile in extorting gifts. About 1785, estimates placed the entire Choctaw population at 15,000.[7]

East of the Choctaw and Chickasaw lay the hunting grounds of the Creek. Although predominantly Muskhogean in ethnic background, and thus distantly related to the Choctaw and Chickasaw, this southern Indian polity was actually a confederation containing important enclaves of Alabama, Euchee, Hitchiti, and Shawnee. Eighteenth-century English traders had earlier divided the Creek into Upper and Lower. The Upper Creek inhabited about twenty-five principal towns scattered along the

---

5. Ibid., 68–72.
6. Gibson, *The Chickasaws*, 3–79, and maps, pp. 5, 143; Swanton, *Creek Indians*, 414–20, 449; Romans, *Natural History*, 39–41; Cotterill, *Southern Indians*; see also De Vorsey, *Indian Boundary*; Fairbanks and Goff, *Cherokee and Creek*, 28–30.
7. Debo, *Choctaw Republic*, 1–36, esp. map of Choctaw land, p. 35; Swanton, *Creek Indians*, 450–51; Cotterill, *Southern Indians*, 6–7. Since almost every historian writing about the Choctaw has his own nomenclature for the three subgroups of the nation, each group may be known by as many as six or eight other names.

Coosa and Tallapoosa rivers where they joined to form the Alabama. The twelve major settlements of the Lower Creek were located to the southeast, on or near the banks of the Chattahoochee and Flint rivers. The Creek confederation claimed hunting grounds spreading outward from their centrally located settlements to the Gulf of Mexico, the Tombigbee, the Tennessee, and most of present-day Georgia west of the Atlantic seaboard. There were slightly more than 15,000 Creeks in the 1780s.[8]

Southeast of the Creeks, seven Seminole villages lay within undisputed Spanish territory, extending east of the Apalachicola well into the interior of East Florida. Often, under certain circumstances, the Seminole were considered part of the Creek confederation, since they were closely associated with the Lower Creek. At the beginning of the second Spanish period they may have numbered about 2,000.[9]

The lands occupied by the Cherokee sprawled across the mountainous terrain where the modern states of Tennessee, Georgia, and the Carolinas meet. Their towns, about forty in all, had been classified before the American Revolution into several groups: Lower, Middle, and Upper (Overhills). During the hostilities an anti-American faction, the Chickamauga, broke away and formed new villages to the west of the major settlements. The 15,000 Cherokee suffered more heavily than any other southern Indian tribe from encounters with U.S. forces. Because their lands lay along the perimeter of the Floridablanca claim, and because of land cessions to the United States in the Treaty of Holston in 1791, the Cherokee became the object of renewed Spanish concern.[10]

The life-styles of the five southern Indian nations bore marked similarities. Tribal members congregated in more or less permanent villages along streams and were primarily agricultural, corn, beans, squash, melons, and pumpkins being their principal crops. Indian families also kept hogs, and the herds of cattle and horses that grazed on the open range surrounding Indian settlements were of some economic importance.

Within each nation, the town was the basic social and political unit, having both a town chief and a war chief at its head. Town meetings were frequent, and the whole tribe had a voice in discussing affairs of common concern. In addition, town chiefs customarily participated in a general tribal council twice a year, in the late spring and fall, where issues of

---

8. Corkran, *Creek Frontier*; Swanton, *Creek Indians*; Cotterill, *Southern Indians*, 8–9; Doster, *Creek Indians*; Fairbanks and Goff, *Cherokee and Creek*, 24–27.

9. McReynolds, *Seminoles*, 3–51; Cline, *Florida Indians*, 1:111–287 and related maps in vol. 2; Doster, *Creek Indians*, 1:275–96.

10. Corkran, *Cherokee Frontier*, 3–12 and map, p. 7; Fairbanks and Goff, *Cherokee and Creek*, 21–22; Whitaker, "Spain and the Cherokee."

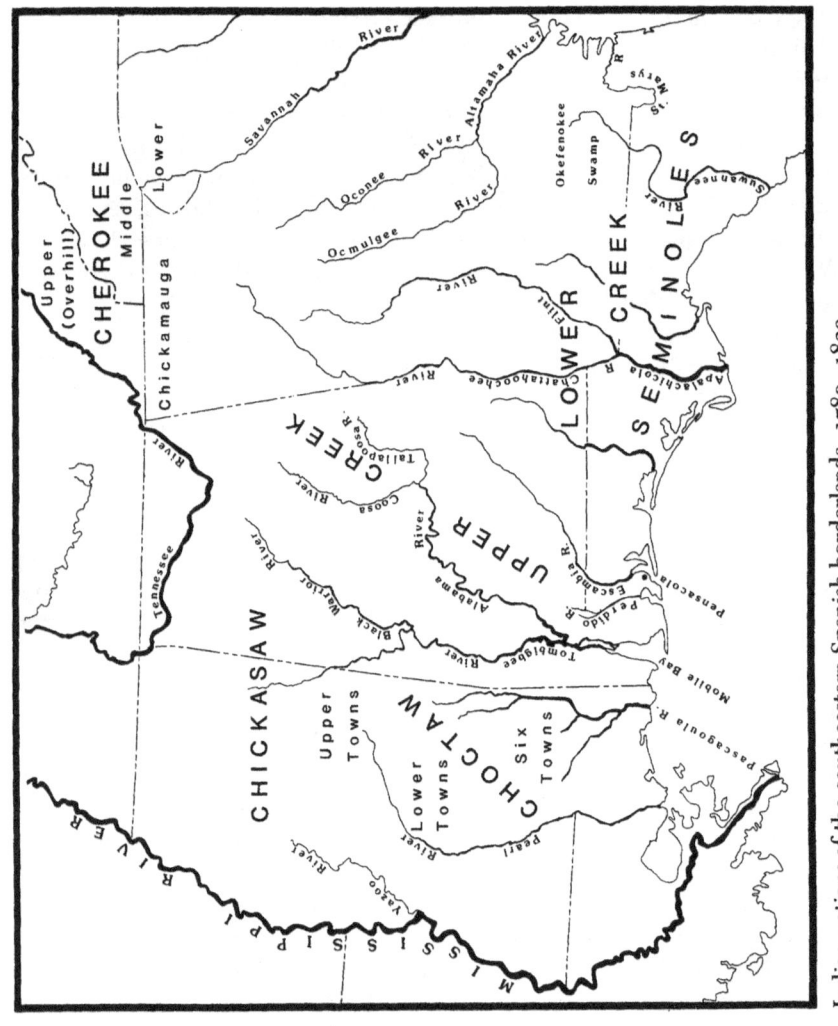

Indian nations of the southeastern Spanish borderlands, 1780–1820

Introduction 7

greater general importance, such as war and peace, were deliberated. Indian leadership depended on personal stature and persuasive ability to gain a consensus in support of a given course of action. But it was impossible for the majority to coerce even a tiny minority into compliance. The political structure of the southern Indians was individualistic in the extreme, even approaching anarchy.

The concept of private property among the southern Indians extended only to immediate personal belongings. Included among these were the crops produced through personal labor (less a portion placed in common storage for emergency use), dwellings, clothing, weapons, household effects, and livestock. Land belonged collectively to the entire nation and could be bargained away only by unanimous consent.[11]

Although the southern Indians traditionally had hunted only to augment their subsistence, hunting grew enormously in economic importance beginning in the late seventeenth century. It provided not only food but also pelts, which could be exchanged for European goods. Englishmen operating out of Charleston opened the southern Indian trade in 1685.[12] The French, from Mobile and other Louisiana outposts, followed after their establishment on the Gulf coast in 1699. Tools, implements, guns, housewares, blankets, textiles, clothing, rum—these and other items of European manufacture soon became almost indispensable to the Indians.[13] By the time of the American Revolution, the number of Indian artisans who produced tools, weapons and similar articles had declined significantly.[14] In these same years, the English, the French, and, to a lesser extent, the Spaniards introduced trade and judicious distribution of presents as elements of Indian diplomacy, employing them regularly to pit tribe against tribe or faction against faction.

In 1763, the struggles culminated in a British triumph. Control over the Floridas enabled Great Britain to establish an exclusive hegemony over the southern Indians. Annual distribution of presents and the availability of English goods peddled by resident traders and renegades in the Indian villages kept the tribes reasonably tractable. Yet occasionally, greedy traders engaged in sharp dealings, became excessively lewd, or perpetrated some other outrage that incited an outbreak of violence and

11. See nn. 6–10 above.
12. Dated but still excellent for the development of the southern Anglo-Indian trade is Crane, *Southern Frontier*. See also Wright, *Florida*, 34–36; Johnson, *British West Florida*, 190–91; Born, "British Trade."
13. For the development of the French and Indian trade see Clark, *New Orleans*; Giraud, *Louisiàne française*; Giraud, *French Louisiana*.
14. Bartram, "Observations," *Transactions*, 1:29.

mayhem.¹⁵ To quell such disturbances, representatives of the southern Indian department usually had to do little more than threaten to suspend all Indian trade. The utter dependency of the southern Indians on European goods was sufficient to keep them subservient to British authority.

Economically, deerskins dominated all other peltry bartered in the southern Indian trade. The bulk of the business flowed through Charleston and Savannah in the 1760s. Deerskins exported from Georgia alone during the decade beginning in 1763 averaged more than 240,000 pounds annually.¹⁶ However, because of overhunting in the east and the onset of disturbances that preceded open rebellion in the Anglo-American colonies along the Atlantic seaboard, Pensacola and Mobile assumed importance as fur trading centers in the 1770s. In 1779, for example, Pensacola alone exported peltry valued at £40,000.¹⁷

Veterans of Spanish service in Louisiana and pre-1763 residents of Spanish Florida fully appreciated the importance of trade in establishing and maintaining good relations with the Indians. From the outset, Indian diplomacy in Spanish Louisiana had been patterned after the Franco-British approach. Within weeks of accepting the surrender of Pensacola, the last British stronghold in West Florida, Governor Bernardo de Gálvez ordered the commandant-designate, Lieutenant Colonel Arturo O'Neill, to use a program of friendship and trade to secure the goodwill and cooperation of the tribes who had served so valiantly in its defense.¹⁸

Gálvez knew full well the importance of the Indian trade to the security of Spanish West Florida. He was equally aware of the potential for substantial profits. His father-in-law, Gilberto Antonio de Maxent, was a wealthy New Orleans fur trader and a veteran of the Louisiana trade. José de Gálvez, Bernardo's uncle and benefactor, had no peer other than Floridablanca in the esteem of Charles III. This family connection, along with the royal gratitude he had earned in the conquest of West Florida, encouraged the Louisiana governor to intertwine his family's pecuniary interests with Spanish diplomacy toward the southern Indians.

Bernardo de Gálvez actually initiated his southern Indian strategy in a letter to his uncle. From the earliest days of his governorship, Gálvez declared in his letter, he had labored constantly at cultivating the friendship

15. Bartram, *Travels*, 51; Romans, *Natural History*, 40–41, 49–50.
16. Romans, 74–75.
17. Phillips, *Fur Trade*, 1:636.
18. Caughey, *Gálvez*, 213; Nasatir, *Borderland in Retreat*, 9; Beerman, "Arturo O'Neill."

of the many Indian tribes dwelling within and adjacent to Louisiana. The task had been both difficult and frustrating because of the constant shortage of Indian trade goods. Merchandise requisitioned for Indian presents more than eighteen months earlier still had not reached Louisiana. Yet British supply sources in East Florida furnished ample inventories for gifts and trading purposes, and British officials and traders were successfully tempting many Indians to cut their ties of loyalty to Spain. Since these conditions posed a serious threat to the security of West Florida and Louisiana, Don Bernardo informed his uncle that Maxent, an experienced man in all aspects of Indian affairs, was being dispatched to Spain immediately with advice that would prove invaluable in the formulation of a sound postwar Indian policy.[19]

A native of Lorraine, Maxent migrated to Louisiana in his early twenties, destined for a long and varied career. In August 1749, he married Isabel La Roche, a Creole of New Orleans, and parlayed her dowry into a fur trade fortune. During the early 1760s Maxent had sided with the French governor, Chevalier Louis Billouart de Kerlérec, in an acrimonious feud with the intendant, Vincent de Rochemore. Kerlérec repaid Maxent's loyalty by granting him in 1763 the exclusive concession of all Indian trade along the Missouri River. Maxent took as a partner Pierre La Clède Liguest. Incidental to opening the partnership's Missouri concession, La Clède founded St. Louis. With La Clède in the field and Maxent directing the headquarters in New Orleans, the partnership was successful until its dissolution in 1769. The association ended primarily because the jealousy of rivals had prompted the revocation of the Missouri trade monopoly. Maxent then chose to serve as a factor for a number of traders operating in Upper Louisiana.

Maxent differed from many of his fellow French colonists in the ease with which he adjusted to the Spanish occupation of Louisiana. In 1766, Martín Navarro, later the colony's first Spanish intendant, became the godfather of one of Maxent's infant daughters; the next year Governor Antonio de Ulloa served in the same capacity for another Maxent child. During the ill-fated rebellion of October 1768, which culminated in Ulloa's ouster from the colony, Maxent took the Spanish side. After reestablishing Spanish control the following year, General Alejandro O'Reilly generously demonstrated Spain's appreciation of Maxent's loyalty with a commission to oversee the transfer of French government property to Spanish control, a captaincy in the newly created militia, and a position as offi-

19. B. de Gálvez to J. de Gálvez, May 26, 1781, AGI, leg. 86-6-12, doc. no. 29, box no. 54, Stetson Collection; Peña y Cámara, Catálogo, 1:173.

cial purveyor of Indian presents for the colonial government. The marriage of two of Maxent's daughters, María Isabel and María Felicitas, to O'Reilly's immediate successors as governors of Louisiana—Luis de Unzaga y Amezaga and Gálvez, respectively—further cemented his ties to Spanish officialdom.

Maxent also became deeply involved in his son-in-law's campaigns against the British in 1779–81. Gilberto himself received the honor of leading the surprise assault that captured the weakly defended Fort Bute at Manchac. He also saw action at Baton Rouge, Mobile, and Pensacola, after having advanced the Spanish government 76,000 pesos from his personal fortune to help finance the campaign.[20]

By the fall of 1781 Maxent had reached Madrid, where on October 4 he presented a memorial to Charles III asking for Louisiana and West Florida to be opened to direct commerce with France and "other friendly ports" for a ten-year period following the establishment of peace. In support of his request, Maxent emphasized the paramount importance of the fur trade as a catalyst in the economic and population growth of the two provinces. He painted a gloomy picture of the languor and decay they would endure unless the prevailing official impediments to the fur trade were removed. Under existing regulations, Maxent pointed out, exporters of peltry were required to ship their cargoes to Spanish peninsular ports. This practice sharply increased the expenses of the fur trade, since the pelts were usually reexported to northern European markets, requiring additional shipping costs, harbor fees, and customs charges. Moreover, the delay greatly increased the risk of spoilage, as peltry was highly susceptible to deterioration and insect damage. The procurement of merchandise suitable for barter with the Indians, Maxent complained, also hampered the fur trade. Under existing rules, foreign-produced trade goods were required to enter Louisiana indirectly through Spanish commercial channels. This practice increased their cost to nearly prohibitive levels, since the Spanish economy produced few items suited to Indian tastes.

Without the prompt removal of these commercial impediments, Maxent predicted, the otherwise potentially profitable fur trade of Louisiana and West Florida would lapse into decay. He even conjectured that the commerce would pass by default to English or Anglo-American merchants, whose traffic with the Indians was unencumbered by such burdensome restrictions. But without them, Maxent foresaw prosperity, a population increase in West Florida, and a significant improvement in customs reve-

20. On Maxent's career, see Coleman, *Maxent*; Whitaker, *Documents*, 225; Watson, "A Scheme Gone Awry."

nues—a major consideration, given the enormous subsidies that administering and defending the provinces would otherwise entail.[21]

Impressed by Maxent's arguments and the observations of others, the Spanish court granted special commercial dispensation to Louisiana and West Florida for the express purpose of stimulating their growth and development. As set forth in the royal *cédula* of January 22, 1782, the new trade regulations opened direct traffic, at a 6 per cent ad valorem duty, between the two provinces and designated French ports for a ten-year postwar period.[22] As Maxent had requested, this feature was largely intended to facilitate the Indian fur trade. The decree, however, stopped short of opening trade with "other friendly ports," as Maxent had desired. In all likelihood, such a radical concession was considered an unwarranted and dangerous loosening of the time-honored closed Spanish mercantilist system.

Having consented to commercial changes to develop a thriving traffic in peltry, Charles III further consented to arrangements intended to make Maxent its prime beneficiary. Maxent was appointed supreme director of Indian affairs for Louisiana and West Florida and received an advantageous contract with the crown to procure and deliver to New Orleans Indian trade goods valued at 380,000 pesos. Under the terms of this agreement, Maxent and a partner, Miguel Fortier of New Orleans, received permission to buy 200,000 pesos worth of goods for reopening the Indian trade of the two provinces. Maxent also committed himself, on behalf of the Spanish government, to purchase presents in the amount of 80,000 pesos for distribution at treaty congresses to be conducted with the southern Indian tribes and to maintain a reserve inventory valued at 100,000 pesos in royal warehouses at New Orleans as a safeguard against future wartime supply disruptions. He was to assemble and transfer all the goods to Louisiana on his own account and risk; reimbursement for the government's portion was to be made after their safe delivery. Although it was anticipated that the bulk of the merchandise would necessarily be purchased from French sources, Maxent was enjoined to give first preference to products of Spanish origin.

Maxent also received liberal financial support from the crown. The king advanced Maxent 50,000 pesos in cash and supplied him with drafts

21. Summary of a representation by Maxent, October 4, 1781, *AGI SD*, leg. 2667, WP. See also, Whitaker, *Documents*, 23–29.
22. *Real Cédula . . . para fomento del comercio de la Luisiana*, January 22, 1782, in Whitaker, *Documents*, 31–39. A royal *cédula* was a written document authorized by the king and dispatched by the court. It was less formal than a royal letter, but was always signed by the monarch himself with the words, "I the King" ["*Yo el Rey*"], with his rubric, Peña y Cámara, *Catálogo*, 2:455.

for an additional 330,000 pesos against the treasury of New Spain.[23] Moreover, José de Gálvez persuaded a Cádiz merchant, Francisco Fernando de Ravago, to help finance the Indian trade project.[24]

The money advanced in Spain went toward the purchase of merchandise later valued at 278,000 pesos that Maxent gathered for export from Bordeaux and Ostend. The cargo included a large quantity of the English-made goods so highly prized by the Indians. Late in 1782, with the merchandise in his charge securely aboard his vessels, *La Margarita* and *La Felicidad*, Maxent sailed for Louisiana. But misfortune occurred en route: British cruisers captured both of Maxent's ships and sent them as prizes to Kingston, Jamaica. Confined as a prisoner of war, the resourceful Louisianian enlisted the services of a local business partnership, Phillip Allwood and Henry Ludlow, to salvage what he could from his disaster.

With 66,739 pesos borrowed from Allwood and Ludlow, Maxent recovered *La Margarita* and purchased sundry provisions. Apparently, he also managed to acquire a valuable cargo of merchandise consigned to St. Augustine via Jamaica to be used by the British government as Indian presents.[25] The terms of the loan called for repayment upon Maxent's release and arrival in Havana as a paroled prisoner of war.

Maxent reached Cuba before mid-1783 and remained there for several weeks before returning to Louisiana. He spent some of his time in Havana perfecting plans for the long-delayed treaty congresses that had been promised the southern Indian tribes. By August, Maxent was safely in New Orleans following his unexpected delay of almost two years. Yet he scarcely had time to take up his official duties as the chief Spanish Indian official before disaster struck again.

An investigation conducted in Havana in September of that year indicated that Maxent had not limited his concerns exclusively to Indian affairs. He and Allwood, together with Juan Manuel de Cagigal, a former captain general of Cuba, and Francisco de Miranda, whose subsequent activities would win him fame as "*el Precursor*" of Latin American independence, were accused of smuggling and other illegal activities. The evi-

23. J. de Gálvez to Intendant of Louisiana [Martín Navarro], March 18, 1782, ANC, *Cédulas y Órdenes*, 286.
24. Whitaker, *Documents*, 225. Maxent's debt to Ravago officially amounted to 147,241 pesos, 6 1/2 reales.
25. Thomas Brown to Sir Guy Carleton, January 12, 1783, in Great Britain, *Report on American Manuscripts*, 3:325–27. *La Margarita* had two other names: *Santa Margarita* and *Frau Margarita*. In 1782 and 1783, her captain was Juan Lino de Gortare. It is entirely possible that this is the same ship that was captured by the British brig *Ranger* in 1779. William Alexander and John Leslie, later members of Panton, Leslie and Company, served as agents for *Ranger* in that episode. A brief mention of this occurs in chap. 2. For information on *La Margarita*, see *AHN Indias*, leg. 21067.

dence indicated that Maxent, among other misdeeds, had delivered 27,000 silver pesos and bills of exchange valued at 1,000 pesos to Allwood aboard a British cruiser at anchor in Havana harbor.[26] After Maxent left Havana for New Orleans, Allwood had remained in Havana awaiting the arrival of silver from Mexico which was due Maxent's account and expected in August.[27] In December, a royal decree was issued placing Maxent under house arrest and suspending him from all official duties. With his personal assets impounded, Maxent's ambitions for fame and fortune in Spanish Indian diplomacy ended abruptly.

From Spain, Bernardo de Gálvez, who had traveled to the court for consultations on postwar policy, ordered Esteban Rodriguez Miró, acting governor of Louisiana, to assume Maxent's responsibilities for Indian affairs.[28] Miró pondered the assignment with foreboding. Maxent's protracted absence, and especially his failure to deliver more than a modest quantity of the goods he had promised, seriously threatened Spanish plans for gaining exclusive influence over the southern Indians. Further postponement of the long-promised treaty congresses would have alienated the Indians even further, as a show of bad faith, since the presents on hand from Maxent were but half of the amount promised. Ironically, supplemental items were unavailable on the New Orleans market at any price; local merchants there had become wary of including Indian trade goods in their inventories because of the royal concessions Maxent had obtained in Spain.

Aside from the shortage of gifts and the adverse effect it had on Indian diplomacy, Miró was even more concerned with getting the Indian trade on a solid footing. Spokesmen for the tribes had repeatedly clamored for the Spaniards to open the trade, only to be put off with promises that satisfactory commercial arrangements would be made at the pending treaty congresses. Any significant further delay in solving the trade question, Miró feared, would force the Indians into the hands of the Anglo-Americans.[29]

The Spanish governor's apprehensions were not unreasonable; the ouster of the British from the Atlantic seaboard and the Gulf of Mexico had virtually halted the southern Indian trade. British posts on the St. Johns River in East Florida afforded the only remaining outlets, and they were much too remote to serve as adequate sources of supply. Neverthe-

26. Maxent, receipt of May 16, 1783, *AHN Indias*, leg. 21067; Coleman, *Maxent*, 96–101.
27. Allwood to Ludlow, July 11, 1783; Allwood to Maxent, July 31, 1783, *AHN Indias*, leg. 21067.
28. Miró to Conde de Gálvez, April 15, 1784, *AHN Estado*, leg. 3885.
29. Ibid.; Miró to Navarro, April 15, 1784, *AGI PC*, leg. 633.

less, in their abject need, Indian parties visited St. Augustine from as far away as the Yazoo River to obtain necessities and to complain about the lack of a convenient supply source.[30] The news of the imminent departure of the British from East Florida caused great despair. The southern Indians did not relish the prospect of resorting to their recent Anglo-American foes for relief. Some way had to be found quickly to offset the blow that Maxent's misfortunes had dealt to Spanish postwar policy. Otherwise, Miró would be powerless to turn the Indians' predicament to Spain's advantage. Fortunately for Spain, however, a British firm already experienced in the Indian trade—Panton, Leslie and Company—wanted to remain in the Floridas. Spanish influence could thus be continued through this seemingly "unholy alliance" with their former enemies.

30. Allevin et al., to Miró, March 9, 1783, Miró Correspondence, LPBL; Kinnaird, *Spain in the Mississippi Valley*, 2:71–73.

1
The Partners: Scotsmen All

*T*HE history of Panton, Leslie and Company is more than the story of a company. It is also a history of people—principally, but not exclusively, of those Scotsmen who were with the company during its formative years. These include the original partners, William Panton, John Leslie, Thomas Forbes, Charles McLatchy, and William Alexander, and their associates, friends, and relatives in both Scotland and America during the second half of the eighteenth century.

William Panton's apprenticeship began in 1765, with John Gordon and Company of Charleston, where he served as a clerk until 1772.[1] John Gordon was the maternal uncle of Thomas and John Forbes; his birthplace in Scotland is unknown. He is probably the same John Gordon who was at Frederica, St. Simons Island, Georgia, and at Beaufort, South Carolina, prior to his presence in Charleston in 1760 as a partner of John McQueen in McQueen, Gordon and Company.[2]

It may have been through Gordon and others that Panton acquired an interest in the Frederica store. Gordon's brief association with McQueen

---

1. Affidavits from William Panton, June 5, 1788, Miscellaneous Records, vol. ZZZ (1807–9), 24–27, SCAH.
2. Tonyn to Lord Germain, January 27, 1781, CO 5/560:73–74, PROL; Candler and Knight, *Colonial Records of Georgia*, 6:215, 8:280–81, 369, 400, 9:398, 10:118, 268; Hamer, *Papers of Henry Laurens*, 3:456n8, 498.

ended with McQueen's death in 1762.³ Gordon then entered into partnership with Grey Elliott at Beaufort, South Carolina, and at Sunbury, Georgia, but this business arrangement ended in 1767.⁴ During the years 1764–65, Gordon also engaged in the slave trade, handling at least three cargoes of Negroes for which he paid a duty of £540.⁵

Gordon's merchandising similarly covered a wide variety of goods. For example, in 1764 he offered to sell maps by William de Brahm and Thomas Jeffreys depicting the southern colonies, including the Cherokee and Creek nations.⁶ Gordon next joined with Thomas Netherclift of Savannah, who had married John McQueen's daughter, Ann, to organize the firm of Gordon and Netherclift, with offices in Charleston and Savannah. Two London merchants, William Greenwood and William Higginson, extended £20,000 credit to the new partnership for goods and merchandise shipped to Savannah.⁷

John Gordon is known to have been in the Indian trade at least by 1763, for he was handling Indian trade goods by that date.⁸ By February 1769, he had entered the East Florida Indian trade with shipments of goods to St. Augustine.⁹ Surviving records suggest that the company's largest East Florida customer between 1769 and 1771 was the fledgling Greek settlement at New Smyrna, which received shipments of axes, nails, saws, salt, and Indian corn. One cargo alone was valued at more than £3,445, and it is likely that supplies from Gordon and Netherclift helped keep the colony at New Smyrna from starving during those years.¹⁰ But Gordon's interest in East Florida was not restricted to trade goods.

Following the transfer of Florida from Spain to Great Britain in 1763, Gordon and his friend Jesse Fish of St. Augustine purchased large tracts of land from the departing Spaniards. The lands subsequently claimed by Gordon and Fish exceeded four million acres, though some observers thought that the total approached ten million acres. For the next fifteen years, Gordon unsuccessfully pursued his Florida land claims.

Convinced that he could not win his case in America, Gordon returned to England in 1772 to appeal to the crown in person.¹¹ On June 1, 1772,

3. Hamer, *Papers of Henry Laurens*, 4:140; Hartridge, *Don Juan McQueen*, xxi.
4. *Georgia Gazette*, October 21, 1767, 2:2.
5. Higgins, "Negro Trade," 210; Hamer, *Papers of Henry Laurens*, 4:140.
6. *Georgia Gazette*, April 12, 1764, 1:1.
7. Bond signed by Gordon and Netherclift, Miscellaneous Records, February 27, 1767, vol. KKK, 210–12, SCAH; Smalley, *Marriage Notices*, 8; "Records Kept by Colonel Isaac Hayne," 32; Hartridge, *Don Juan McQueen*, xxii n3.
8. McDowell, "Directors of the Cherokee," *Colonial Records*, 529–30.
9. CO 5/550:47, PROL.
10. CO 5/552:23; Audit Office Records AO 1/1261:152–55, PROL; Panagopoulos, *New Smyrna*, 83–84.
11. The literature on the Gordon and Fish land ventures in Florida is extensive. For a

Gordon appointed Netherclift and Panton his attorneys.[12] Thus, after seven years in Gordon's employ, William Panton emerged into the business world. The mercantile experience and the friends he acquired while in Gordon's service helped to launch Panton on his career as a "merchant-adventurer."[13]

Panton's early career in Charleston during the prerevolutionary years is obscure. His own statement, made years later, provides the date he arrived in Charleston—1765—and the nature of his employment with John Gordon.[14] He is known to have acquired 300 acres of land near Wilson's Creek, a small branch of the Saluda River, in 1769-70.[15] But before Panton left South Carolina, he had acquired nearly 2,000 acres of land valued at £1,250.[16] The account book of Thomas Elfe of Charleston shows that Panton did business with him from 1769 to 1775, and there is even an entry recording payment to Panton for "schooling the children."[17] After John Gordon had appointed Panton and Netherclift his attorneys in 1772, they continued in the mercantile business and supervised the operation of Gordon's plantation and his other interests.

William Panton's father, John, was a native of the Scottish parish of Monquhitter (also spelled "Montwhitter") in northern Aberdeenshire, about six miles east of Turriff and a dozen or so miles from the North Sea. Parish records indicate that there were at least thirteen Pantons living there in 1696.[18] John Panton married Barbara Wemyss in the nearby parish of Aberdour on April 25, 1738.[19] For the next two years the couple lived at Sealscrook, a farm about a half-mile from the parish church at Monquhitter. A daughter, Christian, was baptized in the church there on

---

convenient summary, see Gold, "Transfer of Florida." A list and map of the Gordon-Fish claim is in Covington, *British Meet the Seminoles*, 15-16, 30-31. After Gordon's death, Thomas Forbes filed a claim for £32,200 on Gordon's behalf. Included in the claim was the value of Gordon's East Florida property and expenses incurred by Gordon in pursuing the title to it. The government eventually allowed £1,250 on the claim: Siebert, *Loyalists*, 2:277, 307. For Jesse Fish in East Florida, see Pickman, "St. Augustine, Florida."

12. Miscellaneous Records, vol. PP, 519-20, SCAH.

13. "Merchant-adventurer," now an obsolete term, was commonly used in the eighteenth century to describe merchants who engaged in foreign trade and who established posts in foreign lands: *Oxford English Dictionary*, 6:348. More precisely, the term denotes a trader independent of a chartered company. See also Watson, "Merchant Adventurer."

14. See note 1 above.

15. *Index to Land Surveys or Plats* (February 15, 1769), 11:12, SCAH; *Royal Grants* (1770-73), 21:209 (October 12, 1770), SCAH; *Memorial Book*, 10:279 (October 17, 1770), SCAH.

16. Audit Office Records, AO 13/100:320, PROL.

17. Webber, "Thomas Elfe Account Book," 35:98, 158; 38:132; 41:152.

18. Spalding Club, *List of Pollable Persons*, 2:364, 75.

19. Old Parish Register 169/1, Aberdour, April 25, 1738, General Registry Office, Edinburgh, Scotland.

March 25, 1739.²⁰ Before their next child was born, the Pantons moved to the Mains of Aberdour, a farm overlooking the North Sea, about eight miles west of Fraserburgh. They returned to Monquhitter for the baptism of their second daughter, Magdalene, on November 19, 1740.²¹ Of the other five children born to John and Barbara Panton, only the baptisms of Robina (May 30, 1758) and John (July 2, 1760) are recorded; these two children were baptized in the parish of Aberdour.²² No records show the birth or baptism of Catherine, Henrietta, or William, though William was probably born in the early 1740s at the farm on the Mains of Aberdour. Nothing further is known about William Panton's life in Scotland, though he lived there until 1765.

Of the Panton family, apart from William, only his sister Henrietta's family played any significant role in the history of the Panton, Leslie and Forbes companies in the Floridas. Her husband was John Innerarity (spelled "Inverarity" then), a tanner, from Brechin, in the County of Angus. They married in Brechin on July 26, 1776.²³

Innerarity preceded his sons to America, but the date of his arrival is not known. On June 24, 1792, however, it is certain he was at St. Marks (San Marcos de Apalache), where he signed a statement of company losses incurred at the nearby trading post.²⁴ The following January, Panton wrote to Robert Leslie, who was also at St. Marks, that John Innerarity was not suited to manage the store there. He instructed Leslie to inform Innerarity that he should come to Pensacola on the next available vessel.

Whatever the reason for Panton's comment about his brother-in-law's unsuitability, Innerarity agreed with it.²⁵ From Pensacola, he apparently went to Savannah, where he spent some time. But by January 1798, or perhaps earlier, he was in London, where he worked diligently on Panton's behalf.²⁶ He died at Stockwell, a London suburb, in 1805.²⁷ James In-

20. Old Parish Register 223/1, Monquhitter, March 25, 1739, ibid.
21. Ibid.
22. Old Parish Register 169/1, Aberdour, ibid.
23. John Innerarity was christened August 7, 1749. He and Henrietta had five children: James (b. August 18, 1777; d. October 3, 1847); Barbara (b. March 6, 1779); Jean (b. September 29, 1780); Henrietta (b. May 1, 1782; d. July 28, 1833); and John (b. November 11, 1783; d. July 28, 1854). All except James were born in St. Nicholas Parish, Aberdeen, Scotland; James was born at Brechin. Mrs. Jean Innerarity Beattie compiled this information from LDS microfiche files of Scottish Parish Registers and kindly furnished it to the authors. John Innerarity, Sr., was listed as a tanner on the baptismal certificate of his son, John (certified copy in GP).
24. "A Statement of the Loss Sustained by the Plundering Indians at Appalachy on the 16th of January 1792," dated June 24, 1792: NARG 94, copy in Federal Records Center, East Point, Georgia. Compare with copy in ASP PL, 4:161–62.
25. Panton to Leslie, January 1, 1793, BSC, NYHS.
26. John Innerarity to William Panton, January 8, 29, June 2, 1798, GP.
27. Probate Records, PROB 6, 1805, vol. 181, f.69, PROL. The statement that "his

nerarity, the eldest of John's children, came to West Florida in May 1796, while the other son, also named John, did not arrive until January 1802.[28] They both became inextricably involved in the businesses of Panton, Leslie and Company and John Forbes and Company.

The second of the two names by which the firm of Panton, Leslie and Company became known was John Leslie. His father, Alexander Leslie, became proprietor of the lands of Balnageith in the Scottish county of Moray in the early part of the eighteenth century. These farmlands were located about a mile southwest of Forres in the parish of the same name. Alexander Leslie married Anna Duff of Elgin and, as so often happened, most of their children were baptized in the parish church at Rothes, to which the Leslie family traced its roots.[29] John was the couple's second son and was baptized at Rothes on October 13, 1749.[30] Of the Leslie family's nine children, two besides John are of interest. Robert, baptized at Rothes on February 3, 1758, came to the Floridas and by 1792 had been admitted as a junior partner in the firm of Panton, Leslie.[31] The Leslies' oldest child, William, though he never came to America, became perhaps the best-known member of the family.

Like most of his brothers and sisters, William Leslie was born at Balnageith and was baptized at Rothes on September 11, 1748.[32] Educated at King's College, Aberdeen, William received an M.A. degree in 1768. He was ordained minister of Auchindoir, Aberdeenshire, in 1774, and moved to St. Andrews parish, Elgin, in 1779. In 1781, the parishes of St. Andrews and Lhanbryd were united under Leslie. After his father's death, William became proprietor of Balnageith, but he continued to serve as minister of St. Andrews/Lhanbryd until his death in 1839. At the time, because of his sixty-five years in the ministry, he was called the "Father of the Church of Scotland." While he had the reputation of being "a little eccentric," he was much beloved by his parishioners.[33] In addition to his

---

death is reported as having occurred on the River Tamoka, near St. Augustine" is incorrect: *FHO* 10 (1932): 186n.

28. Certificates of Spanish Citizenship for James and John Innerarity, October 6, 1812, GP; Greenslade, "John Innerarity."

29. McWatt, "Parish of Rothes," 3:232–33; McDonnel, "Parish of Forres," 448.

30. Old Parish Record 141/2, Rothes, General Registry Office, Edinburgh, Scotland. The Spanish censuses of St. Augustine for 1786 and 1793 give Leslie's age as 35 and 40 years old, respectively. Obviously, the entries were incorrect. See Letters of Eugenia Price of April 29, May 12, 1972, in St. Augustine Historical Society.

31. Old Parish Record 141/2, Rothes, General Registry Office, Edinburgh, Scotland; Memorandum of John Leslie regarding the members of the firm as of August 31, 1792, dated December 31, 1792, exhibit in *Johnson et al. v. Innerarity et al.*

32. Old Parish Record, ibid. Even though not all of the Leslie children were baptized at Rothes, their names are entered in the Rothes Parish record.

33. Obituary in *The Elgin Courant*, April 19, 1839, 3:1. *Churches of the Parish of St.*

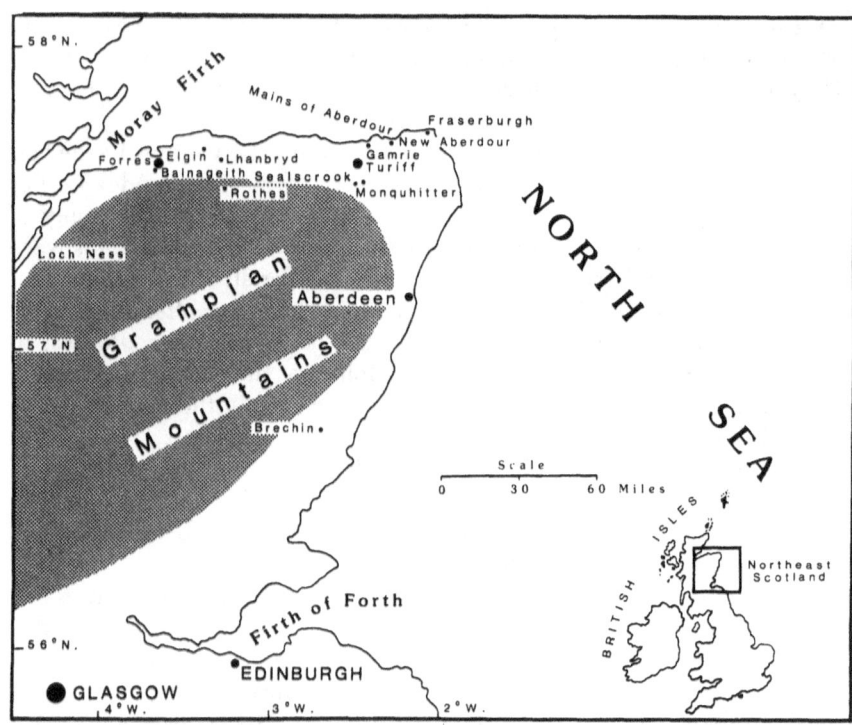

Scottish towns and villages associated with members of Panton, Leslie and Company and John Forbes and Company, 1740–1800

ministerial duties, the Reverend Mr. Leslie also wrote on a variety of subjects. He was the author of three books, one of which, *An Account of the Antiquities, Modern Buildings, and Natural Curiosities, in the Province of Moray, Worthy of the Attention of the Tourist; with an Itinerary of the Province*, first published in 1813, went into a second edition in 1823.[34] He also contributed chapters about his parish in other publications.[35] Leslie's observations on education in Moray were deemed sufficiently noteworthy to be quoted in 1976 in a book about that county.[36] Of the Reverend Mr.

Andrews/Lhanbryd-Cramond, 23–38, contains a delightful sketch of the Rev. Leslie's ministry. See also Scott, *Fasti ecclesiae scoticanae*, 6:397–98; *Sasines Elgin Forres 1781–1860* (294) and (629); see references to Rev. William Leslie in *Miscellaneous Contents in a Bound Volume*, Scottish Collection, County Library, Elgin, Scotland.

34. He also wrote *General View of the Agriculture in the Counties of Nairn and Moray, with Observations on the Means of Their Improvement* and *A Letter to William IV on Church Patronage*.

35. See, for example, Sinclair, *Statistical Account of Scotland*, 172–83.

36. Omand, *Moray Book*, 166–67.

Leslie's numerous progeny—there were fourteen children—one, Alexander, died at Matanzas, Cuba, in 1820.[37] He was undoubtedly in Cuba to secure some portion of the family inheritance from his Uncle John's estate.

Other prominent members of Panton, Leslie and Company were the Forbes brothers, Thomas and John, sons of James and Sarah Gordon Forbes of Scotland.[38] Thomas, the elder, died in 1808; an obituary gave his age at the time of death as fifty.[39] He was surely ten or more years older, since in 1783 he claimed to have been in the Indian trade for sixteen years,[40] and it seems highly unlikely that he would have been in business at the age of nine or ten years. John Forbes, his brother, was christened on December 20, 1767, in the village of Gamrie, County of Banff. John apparently left Scotland for St. Augustine in 1784 and subsequently went to the Bahamas. In 1785, John returned to the Floridas with William Panton.[41] The Forbes family also had two daughters, Anne and Sophia.[42] Sophia was the second wife of Alexander Glennie, who became associated with Panton, Leslie's London factors, Strachan, MacKenzie and Company. Glennie later headed his own firm, A. Glennie, Son and Company.[43]

Of the original partners, little is known about the backgrounds of Charles McLatchy and William Alexander. McLatchy definitely came from Scotland, for he is known to have left two illegitimate children there.[44] Presumably, William Alexander also came from Scotland, but the first definite mention of him was in East Florida in 1771.[45] All five of the

37. Scott, *Fasti ecclesiae scoticanae*, 6:397–98. Certificate of Alexander's death, November 1, 1820, DS, pp. 102–3.
38. John Forbes's Will, October 2, 1820, Will Book I, Mobile County Court House.
39. *Gentleman's Magazine and Historical Record* 78 (1808): 364.
40. Thomas Forbes to Messrs. Davis Strachan & Co., September 20, 1783, AGS Estado, leg. 8138.
41. On John Forbes's christening, see International Genealogical Index, Scotland, card EO141, LDS; information supplied by Mrs. Jean Innerarity Beattie to William S. Coker, November 17, 1982. On John Forbes's departure from Scotland, see John Forbes to John Forrester, August 25, 1807, Testamentory Records, 1808/14, EF leg. 311Q10. Panton to Forbes, May 21, 1785, EF leg. 116L9.
42. John Forbes's Will, October 2, 1820, Will Book I, Mobile County Court House.
43. Ibid. For Glennie as member of the firm of Strachan, MacKenzie and Company, see their petition to Privy Council, March 23, 1798, PC 1/41 A 137, PROL; James Innerarity to John Forbes, August 12, 1815, GP. Alexander (d. April 21, 1830) and Sophia Glennie (d. April 18, 1825) and several of their children are buried in the Glennie family vault, St. Paul's Churchyard, Clapham, London.
44. Luis de Bertucat to [O'Neill], October 14, 1787, *AGI PC*, leg. 37. Some years later, John Leslie referred to a former "Miss McLatchy," by then Mrs. Campbell, who had accompanied John Forbes's mother to London: Leslie to John Forbes, London, July 15, 1802, JIP, LSU. See also *FHQ* 14 (1935): 118–19.
45. Parrish, "Southern Loyalists," 55–56. Spencer Man and William Alexander, Agents for the Contractors, to General Gage, St. Augustine, January 24, 1771, Gage Papers. Numerous references to William Alexander, John Gordon and John Leslie appear in the colonial records of South Carolina and Georgia, but it is impossible to determine whether they are the same persons as the subjects of this study.

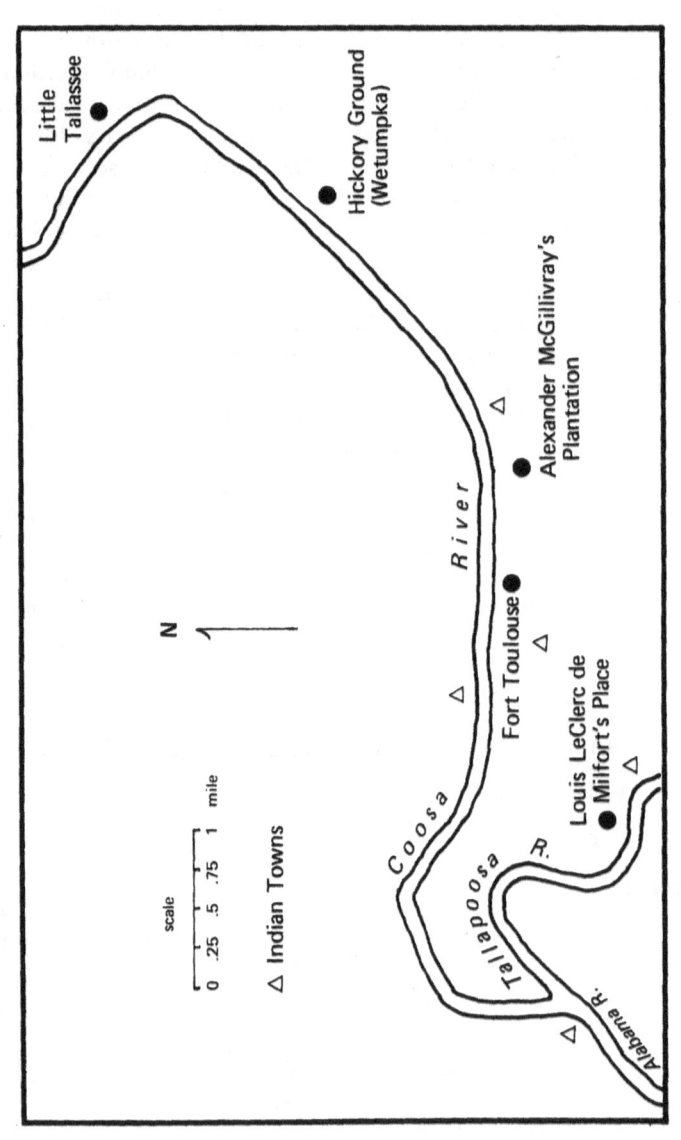

Little Tallassee and the Hickory Ground, ca. 1790

partners—excluding John Forbes, who did not become a partner until 1792—were Scottish merchants and in various ways were connected with the southern Indian trade before the American Revolution. The future partners all met in Charleston, Savannah, or St. Augustine prior to or during the Revolution. Ships plied the waters between those ports with great frequency, and these men either lived in or visited these cities where their business interests required their presence.

By 1783, Thomas Forbes had spent considerable time in Charleston and St. Augustine, where he had been involved in the Indian trade.[46] In Charleston, in February 1767, Thomas witnessed the bond signed by Gordon and Netherclift to Greenwood and Higginson.[47] Later, Gordon appointed Thomas Forbes, William Panton, and others executors of his will.[48] Thomas Forbes also acted on behalf of John Gordon to secure compensation for some church property that Gordon had acquired from the Spaniards in St. Augustine.[49]

The other three original partners, William Alexander, John Leslie, and Charles McLatchy, spent most of their time during the years prior to 1783 in East Florida. In 1771–72, Alexander served as a contractor's agent, victualling and paying His Majesty's forces in East Florida.[50] About the same time, Alexander supplied two hundred bushels of Indian corn to the distressed settlers on the St. Marys River, and also provided pork, flour, peas, rice, and rum for the Indian trade.[51] It was not until 1781, however, that Alexander and John Leslie opened an office in Charleston,[52] even though John Leslie made his first known appearance in St. Augustine in 1777.[53] There is no evidence that John moved to Charleston after he and Alexander established an office there. The first reference to Charles McLatchy in America identified him in August 1773 as agent in charge of James Spalding's store on the St. Johns River.[54] If McLatchy ever visited Charleston or Savannah, the records do not reveal it. While there is no substance to the claim that several of these men were related by blood,[55]

46. Forbes to Messrs. David Strachan & Co., September 20, 1783, AGS Estado leg. 8138.
47. Miscellaneous Records, vol. KKK, 210–12, SCAH.
48. John Gordon's Will, Charleston Wills, vol. 21:792–95, SCAH.
49. Siebert, *Loyalists*, 2:277.
50. Spencer Man and William Alexander, Agents for the Contractor . . . January 24, 1771, to General Gage; Thomas Gage to Messrs. Spencer Man and William Alexander, March 3, 1771; William Alexander, Memorial of February 20, 1772, Gage Papers.
51. CO 5/552:124, 145, PROL.
52. *Royal Gazette*, November 7–10, 1781, 4:2; November 14–17, 1781, 3:3; Smith, "Josiah Smith's Diary," 110.
53. Address of the Inhabitants of East Florida to Gov. Patrick Tonyn, December 1777, CO 5/558:299–301; PROL; Nimnicht, "Willian Panton," 47.
54. Bartram, "Travels in Georgia and Florida," 181.
55. Greenslade, "William Panton," 108. Referring to Panton, Thomas Forbes, and John

they had a common Scottish ancestry and a common spirit of enterprise. Four of them, Panton and Forbes, and Alexander and Leslie, had formed other partnerships before 1783.

Panton may have met others before the Revolution who would be influential in helping Panton, Leslie and Company to succeed during its early years. Alexander McGillivray, the future Creek chief, came to Charleston and resided with his cousin, the Reverend Farquhar McGillivray, to be educated in the local schools. Lachlan McGillivray, Alexander's father, was an Indian trader and merchant, and it is probable that Panton and the McGillivrays first met in Charleston or Savannah in the late 1760s or early 1770s.[56]

John Stuart, superintendent for the Southern department—and, as such, responsible for all Indians south of the Ohio River—spent much of his time between 1765 and 1775 in Charleston. Stuart was indebted to Gordon and Netherclift and Company for over £7,600 by 1771 and certainly would have been acquainted with Panton.[57] Indeed it is entirely possible that Stuart may have been responsible for Panton's entry into the East Florida Indian trade in 1775.

William Panton remained in Charleston between 1772 and 1774, where he was occupied primarily with the Gordon interests. His first appearance as a merchant was in May 1774, when Panton and Philip Moore offered to sell a newly arrived cargo of sixty-five Negroes. Moore and Panton established an office on Broughton Street in Savannah, but there is no indication that Panton actually moved to Savannah. The company's advertisements in the *Georgia Gazette* suggest that they sold a wide range of merchandise. They began in the dry goods business, and between May

---

Leslie, she wrote: "These young men, who were all related by ties of blood, were very much at home in the new land. . . ." There is no evidence that they were related either by blood or marriage.

56. Caughey, *McGillivray*, 9–13, 15. James Doster to William Coker, September 9, 1977, wrote that Alexander McGillivray was born "December 15, 1750, and the information comes from Alexander's father, Lachlan McGillivray in a document which is a matter of legal record in 1767." For a brief discussion of several possible birth dates for Alexander McGillivray, see Watson, "Strivings for Sovereignty," 401n5. To complete the record, Alexander was born at Apple Grove, on the east bank of the Coosa River, about five miles upstream from the plantation where he lived in 1790: Willett, *Narrative*, 104. In 1791, a visitor noted that McGillivray "was superintending some Workmen in the Erection of a Log House embellished with dormer Windows, on the very Spot where his Father resided whilst a Trader in the Nation. Here are some tall old Apple-trees planted by his Father": Pope, *Tour Through the United States*, 47–48. Owen, *History of Alabama*, 401–2, stated that the Apple Grove and Little Tallassee were one and the same place and were "five miles above the Hickory Ground."

57. Alden, *John Stuart*, 211–313. On Stuart's debt, see John Gordon and Thomas Netherclift, Stock in Trade, etc., August 22, 1773, *Mortgages*, vol. FFF (1775–90), 78, SCAH.

1774 and January 1776 offered to sell slaves, horses, wine, butter, and even a brigantine of "600 barrels burthen, completely fitted for sea."[58] Moore and Panton also acquired several town lots in Brunswick and three hundred acres of land in St. Matthew's Parish, Georgia, in 1774.[59] By August 1776, Panton was associated with Thomas Forbes in a separate partnership. At that time, Moore signed a bond on behalf of Moore and Panton in favor of Robert Powell and John Hopton of South Carolina and Samuel Brailsford of Bristol, England, for £18,668 in lieu of £9,334 credit, to be repaid by October 1, 1776.[60] (It was not unusual to use this form of obligation, by which a merchant agreed that if the loan were not repaid on time, he would pay twice the sum of money or credit originally advanced.) Moore remained in Georgia doing business until at least January 1777, when he was threatened with arrest for withholding publicly owned indigo.[61]

The partnership must have been formally dissolved shortly thereafter, for Moore and Panton named Samuel Farley and Thomas Netherclift attorneys to try to collect their outstanding debts. In 1781, Farley and Netherclift advertised for the payment of all obligations due Moore and Panton, warning that those who failed to settle their accounts would be sued. This was no idle threat, as a suit was brought on behalf of Moore and Panton against William Candler for lands, goods, chattels, and monies owed several weeks after the notice first appeared.[62]

In the long run, however, the Moore-Panton partnership met financial disaster. Some years after the Revolution, their American and British creditors sued in the British courts and recovered over £13,000, plus interest, from the former company of Moore and Panton. Panton complained bitterly that he was unable to collect any of the Georgia debts due Moore and Panton. His claim that these obligations exceeded the amount they owed was apparently correct, for in 1798 the total bonds and notes due Moore and Panton, with interest, amounted to £19,585.[63] The failure

---

58. *Georgia Gazette*, May 25, 1774; 1:1; August 3, 1774, 3:2; October 19, 1774, 3:1; January 11, 1775, 2:2; January 25, 1775, 4:1; June 14, 1775, 2:1; June 28, 1775, 3:1; January 3, 1776, 3:1.

59. "Grants, Register of 1772–75," Book L, pp. 196–97 (Reel 52/19); Book M, p. 708 (1774–75; Reel 52/20), Georgia Surveyor General Dept., Office of the Secretary of State, Atlanta, Georgia.

60. Bond, Philip Moore and William Panton, August 1, 1776, *Mortgages*, vol. HHH (1789–95), 224–25, SCAH.

61. Candler, *Revolutionary Records*, 1:221–23.

62. *Royal Gazette of Georgia*, January 11, 1781, 2:1; February 1, 1781, 2:1; August 9, 1781, 6:3.

63. Case of *Johnson et al. v. Innerarity et al.*; Panton to William Moore Smith and others, April 18, 1799; Certified List of Bonds and Notes due Moore and Panton, February 9, 1798, WP; Panton's Will, June 6, 1793, original in PHS.

of Moore and Panton to collect their debts stemmed from the position they took toward relations between the colonies and the mother country.

On June 13, 1775, Panton and Moore attended a meeting in Savannah called to protest the highly unpopular revenue bills imposed on the American colonies by Great Britain. Those present resolved that the utmost effort should be made to preserve peace and good order. Since they considered the interests of Georgia inseparable from those of England, they urged that every legal means should be used to secure the restoration of liberties to the colonies, and they recommended that the Provincial Congress of Georgia prepare a petition for submission to the king, to be signed by every man in the province. Such action, they believed, would bring the desired relief. However, the Provincial Congress received the resolutions and ordered them laid on the table. This was the last effort of the two opposing parties in Georgia to reach a compromise before it was too late to turn back. The resort to a petition did not succeed and a recourse to arms followed.[64] Both Panton and Moore elected to remain loyal to the mother country.

While no date can be determined for the formation of Panton, Forbes and Company, the partnership must have originated before June 28, 1775, for on that date it was announced that Forbes had sailed for England on the *Georgia Packet*. His mission was to secure gunpowder and other goods for the company's trade. On July 6, eight days after Forbes's departure, the Second Provincial Congress banned trade with Britain and the West Indies. Forbes's reception in England was not to his liking either. British officials temporarily dashed his efforts to purchase gunpowder and goods for the Indians by prohibiting the exportation of ammunition and guns to America for fear they would fall into rebel hands.[65] At the same time that Forbes was in England—he had not returned by January 1776—Panton journeyed to East Florida to seek favor with Governor Patrick Tonyn.[66]

Among the stream of loyalists evacuating to East Florida in 1775 was John Stuart, superintendent of Indian affairs. Accused by the Americans of conspiring to keep the Indians loyal to the British, Stuart had been forced to flee to St. Augustine in June to avoid arrest.[67] While the patriots of South Carolina and Georgia determined to woo the Indians to their

---

64. White, *Historical Collections of Georgia*, 66–67; Coleman, *American Revolution*, 55; Candler, *Revolutionary Records*, 1:232–34.

65. *Georgia Gazette*, June 28, 1775, 3:1; Panton to Gov. Tonyn, January 18, 1776, CO 5/556:126–27, PROL; Roberts, "Losses of a Loyalist Merchant," 270.

66. Panton's trip to Florida can only be inferred from his letter to Governor Tonyn, January 18, 1776, CO 5/556:126–27.

67. O'Donnell, *Southern Indians*, 18–19.

cause, Governor Tonyn and Superintendent Stuart made plans to counteract the strategy of the patriots. Not only did the British wish to keep the Indians loyal, they also hoped to use them to help defend East Florida in the event the patriots decided to attack the province, as they threatened to do in late 1775. Therefore, Tonyn and Stuart met with a delegation of Creeks at the Cow Ford—present-day Jacksonville, Florida—in early December 1775.[68] There the British officials and the Indians agreed upon the location of trading posts in East Florida, and Tonyn appointed Panton to manage the Indian trade.[69]

In a letter written by Panton at Frederica on January 18, 1776, he implied that he had recently been in Florida and perhaps at the meeting with the Indians at the Cow Ford.[70] It was one of the few meetings in which Tonyn and Stuart had agreed upon Indian matters, and it would not be surprising to discover that Stuart had recommended Panton as manager of the Indian trade. Panton certainly met with Tonyn's approval, for the governor himself lent Panton enough gunpowder to open trade. In January, Panton wrote Tonyn and apologized for not being able to repay the gunpowder as promptly as he had anticipated. First, he explained, Thomas Forbes had written that gunpowder from England had been detained by British officials. Furthermore, the patriot Council of Safety had seized a large quantity of powder belonging to the Indian traders, of which 2,000 pounds was Panton's. When the council decided to return some of the powder to the traders, Panton's supply was omitted. After inquiring about this treatment, Panton was told "that as I was known to be disaffected to their Cause, and supposed to be under your [Tonyn's] influence, they thought it inconsistent with the Safety of the Province that I should be supplied." Not only did the council refuse Panton his powder, but it also prohibited him from shipping anything to Florida. The council stopped a Panton sloop carrying a cargo of rice, rum, salt, and strouds (coarse woolen cloth, garments, and blankets) in Savannah harbor. Panton appealed to Tonyn and Stuart to intercede with Lord Dartmouth, British secretary of state for the colonies, to lift the embargo and to authorize his London suppliers, Greenwood and Higginson, to ship to him at St. Augustine 3,500 pounds of powder, with sufficient bullets and flints, and 200 guns for the Indian trade.[71] Tonyn complied with Panton's wishes and urged Dartmouth

68. Ibid., 18–32; Wright, *Florida*, 24–29.
69. Tonyn to Earl of Dartmouth, December 18, 1775, CO 5/556:71–73, PROL: Carter, *Territorial Papers*, 4:297–98. In the latter source, Governor William Blount credited Panton's friendship with Colonel Brown as the key to Panton's monopoly of the Indian trade during the Revolution. "Cow Ford" is also spelled "Cowford."
70. Panton to Governor Tonyn, January 18, 1776, CO 5/556:126–27, PROL.
71. Ibid.; Candler, *Revolutionary Records*, 1:90; Alden, *John Stuart*, 15–19.

to permit the Indian supplies to be sent to East Florida, where they were desperately needed.[72] The shipment to St. Augustine would eliminate the problems that Panton was having with the patriot councils of Georgia and South Carolina.

About two weeks after the Georgia Council of Safety refused Panton permission to export goods to East Florida, the South Carolina Council of Safety lodged a complaint against Panton over the exportation of some flour from John Gordon's plantation in South Carolina to East Florida. The council ordered Panton to be apprehended and sent to Charleston since, it warned, he was dangerous to the public safety.[73] In spite of the determination of these two councils to forbid Panton's trade with East Florida, he persisted. But soon he became involved with a shipment that had even more serious repercussions.

In May 1776, Panton brought a quantity of goods into Sunbury, a port on the Medway (Midway) River about thirty miles north of Frederica, which then rivaled Savannah as a seaport.[74] Included in the shipment were planes (tools), osnaburgs (heavy, coarse cloth), salt, and sugar. Panton discovered that there was a great demand for the goods at Sunbury and asked permission from the local committee of safety to trade them for rice. The committee agreed to the transaction, provided that the rice not be shipped to any port under British control. At the same time, George McIntosh, Patrick Houstoun, and George Bailie also obtained permission to ship rice to Surinam, giving bond and security that it would not be landed in a British port. These merchants had also purchased a considerable quantity of goods from Panton, to be paid for by their consignee at Surinam. The three ships cleared Sunbury, but when they reached the mouth of the Sapelo River, Panton boarded the vessels, showed the ships' masters the bills of exchange signed by Houstoun and Bailie, and ordered a change in destination. Panton redirected one ship to St. Augustine, another to the St. Johns River, and the third to the West Indies.

In July, Governor Tonyn wrote Lord George Germain, Dartmouth's successor, complimenting Panton for having succeeded in getting supplies into East Florida where others had failed. Panton had already brought 400 barrels of rice to the St. Johns River, and Tonyn expected the arrival of a thousand more barrels. Tonyn wrote that Panton had done this at great hazard to his own life and property, adding that George McIntosh had greatly assisted Panton. Although McIntosh was a member of the rebel congress of Georgia, he was a loyalist at heart and would do any-

---

72. Tonyn to Earl of Dartmouth, February 26, 1776, CO 5/556:124, PROL.
73. "Journal of the Second Council of Safety," 217–19.
74. Krakow, *Georgia Place-Names*, 219–20. For Panton at Sunbury, see note 75 below.

thing he could to assist the British cause. Tonyn warned that McIntosh would be in danger if his loyalist sentiments became known. But Tonyn's letter was intercepted and delivered to the Continental Congress, whereupon President John Hancock ordered McIntosh's arrest.

Button Gwinnett, president and commander-in-chief of Georgia (and a signer of the Declaration of Independence) directed on January 8, 1777, that McIntosh be placed in irons on a charge of treason against the United States. Gwinnett and the McIntoshes had had other differences. McIntosh, as a member of the Georgia congress, had refused to sign Gwinnett's commission and had declared that Gwinnett was the last person he wanted to see as president of Georgia. Furthermore, George McIntosh's brother, General Lachlan McIntosh, was an avowed political opponent and critic of Gwinnett. General McIntosh, embittered over what he felt was Gwinnett's persecution of his brother, rejoiced too warmly at Gwinnett's failure to be reelected the following May. Gwinnett challenged the general to a duel, which resulted in both men receiving wounds; unfortunately for Gwinnett, gangrene set in and he died within a few days.[75]

After the duel, George McIntosh wrote to Panton at St. Augustine, calling upon him to help clear his name. The new president of Georgia, John A. Truetlen, learned that McIntosh had asked for Panton's assistance and sarcastically informed President Hancock:

> Mr. Panton an open & bitter Enemy to the American Cause, an Inhabitant of East Florida, the greatest Tool of Governor Tonyn, to procure Supplies for the Indians our Savage Enemies, Mr. Panton who had fled from the Vengeance of the Sons of Liberty in South Carolina, & Georgia this well known Mr. Panton is to clear up Mr. McIntosh's Character, & to satisfy the public that he is a disinterested Friend to the United States.[76]

On George McIntosh's behalf, John Perroneau and George Bellenger went to St. Augustine and consulted Panton. Panton told them that he sincerely lamented McIntosh's unfortunate situation and believed him completely innocent of the charges. Furthermore, Panton informed them that in talking with Governor Tonyn he had mentioned that McIntosh was "a man of honour and principle, and that he believed him to be sincerely

---

75. Tonyn to Germain, July 19, 1776, CO 5/557:91–92, PROL; Resolution of Continental Congress, January 1, 1777, ibid., 193, 388–89. For the McIntosh affair, see Jenkins, *Button Gwinnett*, 130–40, 150–57; M'Call, *History of Georgia*, 2:332–37; Jones, *History of Georgia*, 278–80; Coleman, *American Revolution*, 88–89. A recent account of the Panton-McIntosh affair is in Jackson, *Lachlan McIntosh*, 56–57, 169nn16–20; Jackson, "Button Gwinnett," 23–24.

76. Jenkins, *Button Gwinnett*, 248.

attached to the rights and liberties of America." Panton's deposition, and others testifying to McIntosh's loyalty, were submitted to counteract the comments in Governor Tonyn's intercepted letter. Despite such testimony, the charges against McIntosh remained. There is little doubt that McIntosh was a victim of Georgia's revolutionary politics. After suffering loss of property and a stay in jail, he was finally freed on bail. Eventually, McIntosh presented a memorial to the Continental Congress asking that his case be examined. A committee looked into the matter, and on October 10, 1777, Congress passed a resolution that the charges against him be dropped.[77]

It might not be fair to blame Panton either for McIntosh's misfortunes or for the death of one of the signers of the Declaration of Independence, but the chain of circumstances that brought these events about can be traced both to the shipments of rice to East Florida and to existing political factionalism in Georgia. Because of Panton's part in the rice shipments, the Georgia Council of Safety declared Panton "dangerous to the liberties of America," and its resolution also named several of Panton's friends and business associates.[78]

77. M'Call, *History of Georgia*, 337–39.
78. Candler, *Revolutionary Records*, 1:146–47.

2
Loyalists All

THERE was never any reason to question the loyalty to Great Britain of any of the five Panton, Leslie partners. After being declared "dangerous to the liberties of America," the future partners spent most of their time in East Florida, where they actively supported Governor Tonyn and in other ways served the loyalist cause.

In February 1776, some of the inhabitants of East Florida met to draw up a petition of loyalty to the crown, but there was disagreement about the method of presentation of the memorial. The question was whether to submit the petition directly to the king or to send it through Governor Tonyn. William Alexander was among those who felt it should be sent through the governor. Accordingly, at a second meeting held at St. Augustine on March 11, Alexander was among those who signed the address. They pledged allegiance to His Majesty and to Parliament, thanked the governor for having established a haven in East Florida for loyalist refugees, and expressed hope that His Majesty's reign might again be established over America.

In November 1776, Panton, among others, signed a memorial in appreciation of the assistance Governor Tonyn had rendered the loyalist refugees. On the same day, Panton and others also signed a memorial submitted through Tonyn to the King. In addition to proclaiming their loyalty, the memorialists related their attempts to restore peace in Georgia and the persecution that they had suffered as a result. They thanked the

King for the haven established in East Florida and for the generous land grants given to the refugees. They also stated the need for more land to be ceded by the Indians to the government in order to provide for additional refugees from the rebellious colonies. The following year Panton, Alexander, and Leslie signed a memorial renewing their fidelity to the King and offering to cooperate with the royal officials in the defense of East Florida. At the same time, they expressed their discontent with another petition presented to the throne which cast a serious reflection upon Governor Tonyn's reputation. They defended Tonyn's efforts to provide a proper defense for the colony and vowed to stand behind the governor.[1] Although Forbes did not sign any of these memorials, his actions upon his return to Florida left no doubt about where his loyalties lay.

During the next several years Panton and Forbes operated out of East Florida, for it was not until after the Revolution that the company opened stores in Apalachee or West Florida. One matter that has never been satisfactorily resolved is the location of the trading post sites selected by Tonyn for the Indian trade. There are references to a Panton store on the St. Marys River, which did not open until 1791. John Leslie opened the St. Marys River store on behalf of Panton, Leslie and Company in November 1791 and sent John Forrester to manage the post. Forrester also served as *comisionado*, or *alcalde*, for the district after the departure of the previous alcalde, Richard Lang. The exact location of the trading post has not been ascertained, although it was within a league of Lang's house and occupied the buildings abandoned by Leonard Marbury in early 1791. Thus it would probably have been a mile or so east of Kings Ferry. Governor Juan Nepomuceno de Quesada of East Florida authorized Forrester to close the store on November 6, 1792, primarily because of threats from Georgia vagabonds and William Augustus Bowles and his Indian followers and a request from nearby settlers that the post be moved. Although Forrester made periodic trips to the St. Johns River and to St. Augustine in the ensuing months, the post was closed by March 1793. A few months later Forrester opened a new Panton, Leslie Indian trading post on the west bank of the St. Johns River, opposite Picolata. Forrester located the new store on or near the site of the old Spanish fort, San Francisco de Pupo, which originally had been constructed there in 1734 and was captured by General James Oglethorpe of Georgia in January 1740. The new trading post, however, became known as the Almacén de San Fernando [de Pupo].[2]

1. CO 5/557:22–25; CO 5/558:299–301, PROL.
2. On the fort, San Francisco de Pupo, see TePaske, *Governorship of Spanish Florida*, 134–35; *Impartial Account of the Late Expedition*, xxi, 31–32. On the St. Marys and St.

One student of the company believes that a store was located on the St. Johns River near the Cow Ford.[3] Governor Tonyn referred to this store in 1778 when he wrote Superintendent Stuart about the defensive measures taken against patriot attack: "I had fortunately succeeded in well guarding St. John's River by a Naval Force from the Mouth of it to Panton's store."[4] This may also have been the store that a party of plundering rebels robbed in June 1782.[5] Perhaps it was the same place where Panton "established a trading post on St. Johns River, with its wharf, naval storehouse, two warehouses, four 'shades for naval stores,' and various tracts of land principally on the same river."[6]

Two well-established trading posts on the St. Johns River (known as Spalding's lower and upper stores) came into possession of the company, but the details are only speculative.[7] James Spalding and Donald McKay engaged in the Indian trade in the early 1760s and initially operated out of Frederica, on St. Simons Island. In 1768, with McKay's death, Spalding and Roger Kelsall formed a partnership which lasted until the Revolution. They prospered and eventually established trading posts from Sunbury, Georgia, to present-day Volusia County, Florida.[8] In January 1776, Panton purchased some goods from Kelsall and Company, and by November he had rented from Kelsall and Spalding a brig, the *Beaufort*, which he used to carry supplies to St. Augustine.[9] With those facts the record ends. Panton's periodic presence at Frederica, beginning in January 1776, suggests some undefined connection with the Spalding-Kelsall firm. But if Panton was ever a member or employee of the firm, or if Spalding and Kelsall were ever indebted to Panton, the evidence is lacking. By what means Panton and Forbes succeeded to the Spalding-Kelsall trading posts in East Florida remains a mystery.[10]

Spalding's lower store was located at present-day Stokes Landing,

---

Johns stores see [Governor of East Florida] to Commissioner on the St. Marys River, November 3, 1791, *EF* leg. 121D10; John Forrester to John Leslie, November 23, 1791, Leslie to Quesada, October 2, 5, 1792, Quesada to Leslie, October 4, 1792, *EF* leg. 116L9; Quesada to Forrester, April 24, November 6, 1792, *EF* leg. 122E10; [Quesada] to [?], August 3, 1793, *EF* leg. 124G10.

3. Nimnicht, "William Panton," 42.
4. Tonyn to Stuart, July 18, 1778, CO 5/558:227–28, PROL.
5. Nimnicht, "William Panton," 43.
6. Siebert, *Loyalists*, 2:365.
7. Nimnicht, "William Panton," 43; Bartram, "Travels in Georgia and Florida," 223.
8. Nimnicht, "William Panton," 43–46; Lovell, *Golden Isles*, 64–65.
9. Candler, *Revolutionary Records* 1:90; In July 1776, Spalding and Kelsall owed a small sum of money to Gordon and Netherclift: Loyalist Claims, AO 13, Bundle 36, Drawer 40, Box 45, PROL; Nimnicht, "William Panton," 27–28.
10. Wright, "Diplomacy of Trade," 21–23. Wright has brought together several explanations of how Panton acquired the Spalding-Kelsall trading posts in East Florida.

about six miles south of Palatka, on the west bank of the St. Johns River. In 1773, Charles McLatchy operated the post for Spalding and Kelsall. William Bartram visited the site and recorded that the lower store was to be a central depot for supplying three additional trading houses which Spalding's men planned to build that year.[11] The second post, Spalding's upper store, was located on the east bank of the St. Johns River, about five miles south of Lake George.[12]

The Spanish governor of East Florida, Vicente Manuel de Zéspedes, visited the lower store in 1787, which by that date was a thriving Panton, Leslie enterprise. He found the overseer, John Hambly, his wife, María, and fifty or sixty slaves working the cornfields and vegetable gardens and tending a herd of several hundred cattle. The post then provided beef for the St. Augustine garrison; the skins and hides received from the Indian trade were cured and tanned by Hambly before being shipped downriver for the trip to England. Zéspedes thought the post so important that he stationed eight well-equipped, and well-armed soldiers there to protect it. In December 1787, the governor officially designated the site the Almacén de Nuestra Señora de la Concepción, more often referred to simply as Concepción.[13]

The Panton and Forbes trading posts sold a wide variety of merchandise to the Indians. Thomas Forbes prepared a list in 1783 of "Articles of British Manufacture absolutely necessary for the Indians inhabiting the Western frontier of East & West Florida in North America." Included, under coarse woolen goods, were blue and red strouds, blankets of various kinds, Welsh plain or Negro cloth and flannels, coarse Yorkshire broadcloths, and a variety of garters. Linen and cotton goods consisted of Irish and coarse white linens; checked and striped linen and cotton cloth, low-priced printed cotton and linen cloth; printed, checked and silk handkerchiefs; Scotch osnaburgs and threads. Other trade items included coarse saddles, men's strong leather shoes, very cheap rifles and smooth-bore muskets, gunpowder, lead in bars and bullets, and gun flints. In addition, there were brass and tin kettles, cannisters, and mugs; iron pots, pans, axes, and hatchets; carpenters' and coopers' tools; locks and hinges; nails,

---

11. Lewis, "Spalding's Store"; Bartram, *Travels*, 61–63.

12. Most accounts locate Spalding's upper store on the west bank of the river, at present-day Astor. Bartram does not specify that it was on the west bank, but the editor of Bartram's travels, Francis Harper, puts it on the west, or Indian side, of the river. However, according to stoutly defended local tradition, the post was situated on one of several huge shell mounds on the east bank of the river at Volusia: conversation between Coker and Mrs. Lillian Gibson, Volusia, Florida, December 1976. Since the shell mounds have been destroyed, on-site investigation is useless.

13. Tanner, *Zéspedes*, 133; according to Bruce Chappell, Zéspedes visited the lower, *not* the upper store. Governor to Sgt. Angelo Cufareli, December 9, 1787; W. A. Bowles to Carlos Howard, November 15, 1788, *EF* leg. 119B10.

needles, fishhooks, scissors, knives, razors, and gimlets; ribbons of the cheapest kinds; silver trinkets for the ears, arms, neck, etc.; vermillion and lamp black; small dressing glasses, coarse tobacco and pipes for smoking, coarse hats for men, low-priced rum or brandy, and salt.[14]

The most important item in the Indian trade was gunpowder. Panton lamented that carrying goods into the Indian country without also carrying gunpowder was useless because the Indians needed the gunpowder.[15] The major item that the company received in trade was deerskins, and without gunpowder the Indians could not kill enough deer to pay their bills. In September 1776, Panton had 32,000 deerskins on hand. Had he the supplies, he commented at the time, he could just as easily have had 100,000 skins and could have secured the Lower Creek trade to Panton and Forbes forever.[16] Panton feared that if the company could not obtain sufficient goods, other merchants would be permitted to engage in the Creek trade. He felt encouraged that Governor Tonyn had thus far refused to license anyone else in the trade, but he knew the governor would not continue to refuse if Panton could not secure the required merchandise.[17] Two months later, in November 1776, Governor Tonyn implored Lord Germain to permit Davis, Strachan and Company of London to load Panton's brig with ammunition for the Indian trade.[18]

Other general trade seems to have been carried on by Panton and Forbes. The company handled naval stores and lumber, of which some was sold to the provincial government and some perhaps exported.[19] In July 1776, Panton sent to London a cargo of indigo valued at £544.[20] The Panton and Forbes Company also handled bills of exchange, which they passed on to their London factors or to other merchants, and advanced cash and credit as circumstances dictated.[21] Thus, like other merchants, the company often functioned as "bankers" to the frontier economy.

In 1778, the assets of Panton and Forbes began to increase. Each partner received a grant of 1,000 acres of land in East Florida.[22] They acquired

14. The provincial expense account of the government of East Florida with Panton, Forbes and Company for Indian supplies, June 25, 1775 to June 24, 1782, may be found in CO 5/557:3-5, 289-90; CO 5/559:35-36, 268; CO 5/560:30, 286, PROL. Except for the term "sundries," the provincial expense accounts reveal only "duffles" and "Negro cloth" purchased from Panton and Forbes. See Forbes's list of September 28, 1783, AGS Estado, leg. 8138; compare it with that in Tanner, Zéspedes, 90.
15. Panton to Tonyn, January 18, 1776, CO 5/556:126-27, PROL.
16. Panton to [?], September 13, 1776, MHS, WP.
17. Ibid.
18. Tonyn to Germain, November 27, 1776, CO 5/557:30, PROL.
19. CO 5/556:30, PROL; Siebert, Loyalists, 2:365.
20. Panton to [?], September 13, 1776, MHS, WP.
21. Ibid.; Siebert, Loyalists, 2:107.
22. CO 5/559:22-24, PROL; Siebert, Loyalists, 2:269.

a rice and indigo plantation, complete with dam, located about seven miles west of Palatka at a place called Cedar Swamp, now Rice Creek Swamp.[23] They owned a plantation called "Oak Forest," four and one-half miles from St. Augustine, which they sold in 1780 to James Hume, chief justice of East Florida. The plantation was aptly named, as it included a good stand of oak. It was described at the time of sale as having a neat wooden dwelling house, a kitchen, storehouse, dairy, and forty to fifty acres of corn land.[24] In October 1779, Panton and Forbes purchased a tract of land and sundries from the estate of Colin McKenzie, though the size of the purchase was not recorded. William Alexander served as executor of the McKenzie estate.[25] And in the years 1780–82, Panton received 3,500 acres and Forbes 3,250 acres in East Florida from the provincial government. After Panton and Forbes had joined Alexander, Leslie, and McLatchy in the partnership of Panton, Leslie and Company, the new firm acquired some of the former Panton and Forbes property. A few years after the transfer of East Florida to Spain, John Leslie testified that the company owned 72,820 acres of land, all presumably obtained in East Florida by grants from the British.[26]

Periodically, Governor Tonyn was forced to use private vessels for the government's service, and occasionally he turned to Panton and Forbes. The company leased two armed schooners, the *Polly* and the *George*, to the government in 1777 and 1778. They received £100 for the use of the *Polly* and £425 for the *George*.[27] Although it is not entirely clear what assistance was rendered, Panton and Forbes were paid in excess of £100 for "sundry naval services" performed between 1778 and 1780.[28] Whether the appointment of Philip Moore, Panton's earlier business partner, as a naval officer in 1779 had any direct bearing on the government's patronage of Panton and Forbes is unknown.[29]

In November 1780, Governor Tonyn hired the sloop *Hornet*, owned by Panton and Forbes, to bring Thomas Forbes to Havana as commissary for the exchange of prisoners of war.[30] This was not the first time that Forbes acted in this capacity, for in 1778 Tonyn had sent him to Georgia to negotiate an exchange of prisoners with the rebel government of that

23. Siebert, *Loyalists*, 2:179–81.
24. Ibid., 2:37–41, 47.
25. *Moses v. Alexander*, 401A–3B only, 401A–3² F&B, 401A–6F&B, SCAH.
26. Siebert, *Loyalists*, 2:276; ASP PL 6:110–11.
27. CO 5/559:59–61, PROL.
28. CO 5/559:278; CO 5/560:67–68, PROL.
29. Mowat, *East Florida*, 113. Moore replaced Alexander Skinner, who was killed by Indians in March 1779, as naval officer and as commissary and keeper of Indian presents: ibid.
30. CO 5/560:69, PROL; Tonyn to Germain, January 27, 1781, CO 5/560:73–74, PROL.

province. Forbes reached Havana on November 6, 1780, and remained there until January 7, 1781.

Soon after his arrival he heard reports of the ill-fated Spanish armada that had been destined for an attack on Pensacola. The fleet had encountered a severe storm in the Gulf en route to the Florida coast. Forbes noted the number of ships lost or damaged, the size, armament, and number of each vessel, the troops returning to Havana or landing elsewhere, and other details which he believed might be of value to the British. In his intelligence report, Forbes also described the two new forts being constructed for Havana's defense and noted the repairs to El Morro, the famous fort that guarded the harbor's entrance. He even managed to go aboard several of the men-of-war anchored in the harbor in order to make a firsthand evaluation of those ships. Forbes overheard information from the recently arrived *flota* from Spain that indicated that the Spaniards intended to remain in the war at least one more year. By then, they believed, Great Britain's financial condition would be so bad that the British would be forced to sue for peace. Nevertheless, Forbes indicated, the people were tired of the war and of its disastrous effects upon commerce in Havana.

More important, however, Forbes also prepared a detailed report for Governor Tonyn about Spanish preparations to send a second fleet against Pensacola, warning that the fleet would probably sail about mid-January. He informed Tonyn that the Spaniards planned to attack East Florida and the Bahamas, if they completed the conquest of West Florida by taking Pensacola.[31] Tonyn quickly responded to the intelligence provided by Forbes and immediately dispatched a letter to Admiral Marriot Arbuthnot, in command of the North American station, to be forwarded to Lord Germain in London.[32] Although the fleet commanded by General Bernardo de Gálvez did not depart Havana until February 28, Pensacola's fate already had been sealed.[33] In April, Lord Germain informed Governor Tonyn that any assistance to Pensacola would have to come from Jamaica and advised him to inform the British officials there about the Spanish plans. Germain was confident, however, that General John Campbell, in charge at Pensacola, had long anticipated the attack and was sufficiently prepared to withstand it. Germain also doubted the possibility of a Spanish campaign against East Florida and the Bahamas.[34] Subsequently, however, the Spaniards captured both Pensacola and the Bahamas.[35]

31. CO 5/560:75-80, PROL.
32. CO 5/560:73-75, PROL.
33. Caughey, *Bernardo de Gálvez*, 200.
34. Germain to Tonyn, April 4, 1781, CO 5/560:81-83, PROL.
35. Caughey, *Bernardo de Gálvez*, 211, 245.

Forbes's primary purpose on the Havana mission, however, had been to exchange prisoners. He had taken sixteen prisoners of war to Cuba with him on the *Hornet*. The ship ran into a storm, and after it reached Cuba, it was declared unusable. The captain general of Cuba, Diego Joseph Navarro, furnished Forbes with a vessel, the *Industrious*, for the return trip to St. Augustine. The Spaniards had released forty-one English prisoners of war—sixteen for the prisoners brought by Forbes, and twenty-five additional prisoners who were sent along "upon good faith" that corresponding Spanish prisoners of war would be exchanged in the future.

After Forbes returned to East Florida, Governor Tonyn sent him to Charleston to secure the prisoners of war needed for the extra prisoners released. Forbes made the trip and was back in St. Augustine by mid-July with eighty-two prisoners of war. Tonyn detained the *Industrious* until November, in part because the ship needed repairs. Finally, in November 1781, he permitted the ship to sail for Havana with the prisoners of war and a bill for £730 for repairs to the ship.[36]

While Forbes was performing his services for Governor Tonyn, Panton had returned to Georgia in spite of the fact that the state, in March 1778, had passed a bill declaring him guilty of high treason. The same act ordered the confiscation and sale of his estate, and sentenced him to death if he were caught.[37] Panton's return to Georgia had been made possible only by the British victory over the patriots at Savannah in December 1778.[38] It is not known exactly when Panton arrived in Georgia, but on March 11, 1779, he advertised for two coopers in the *Royal Gazette of Georgia*.[39] By 1780 he represented Frederica and St. James Parish in the Loyalist Commons House of Assembly.

The election for the loyalist assembly was held on May 5, 1780. There are no records of the vote, and there is a distinct suspicion that some members either may have been elected by only a handful of voters or were even "selected" by loyalist officials. At this time, Frederica was nearly deserted and Panton may, in fact, have cast the only vote in his election. In order to qualify for his seat in the assembly, Panton had to own at least 500 acres of land or have property worth £500 in the province. Although he owned nearly 2,000 acres in South Carolina, his Georgia holdings amounted only to 300 acres, together with a few lots in

---

36. Juan Manuel de Cagigal to Tonyn, October 18, 1781; Tonyn to Board of Commissioners for the Sick and Hurt, November 24, 1781; Tonyn to Cagigal, November 30, 1781, CO 5/560:161–67, PROL. Spanish documents relating to the exchange of prisoners of war are in *AGI PC*, leg. 1301, 1304, 1309, 1318.
37. Jones, *History of Georgia*, 2:420–21.
38. Ibid., 2:315–22.
39. *Royal Gazette of Georgia*, March 11, 1779, 2:3.

Brunswick. Technically, unless Panton's South Carolina and Florida property was also taken into consideration, he does not appear to have fulfilled the requirements for election to the assembly.

Nevertheless, Panton journeyed to Savannah for the assembly meeting and was appointed to several committees. He helped draw up a letter of thanks to His Majesty for the return of Georgia to the loyalist ranks, and he served on the committee that decided upon the proper method of selecting jurors and on the one that drafted a bill regulating public auctions. Panton then turned his attention to the important business of the assembly.

In retaliation for the act of attainder passed by the rebel congress in March 1778, the loyalist assembly entertained two bills: an act of attainder and a disqualification act. Panton participated in the vote to add and delete certain names from the act of attainder. It is not known why he voted to keep the rebel paymaster's name on that list or why he opposed adding the name of the rebel chief justice. In any event, both names appeared in the final act, which included every prominent person in the state known to sympathize with the rebels. Panton also served on the committee entrusted with the disqualification act. That bill disqualified rebels from holding any office of trust, honor, or profit within the limits of Georgia.[40] According to one Georgia historian, the activities of the assembly after the passage of the attainder and disqualification acts were largely "spasmodic, partial, feeble, and futile."[41] Meeting in Augusta on May 4, 1782, the rebel congress also passed a bill of attainder, banishment, and confiscation, in which the names of William Panton, Thomas Forbes, and Philip Moore appeared prominently.[42] But by January 1781, Panton had already returned to East Florida.[43]

In 1779, during Panton's absence, two of his future partners, William Alexander and John Leslie, formed their own company. The East Florida provincial expense accounts for 1779–82 show that Alexander and Leslie furnished naval supplies and services to the government, as well as supplies for the Indians.[44] The company also served as agent for the owners of the brig *Ranger* which had captured a Spanish schooner, the *Santa Margaritta* [sic], which His Majesty's Court of Vice Admiralty condemned.[45] Although Charleston had fallen to the British in May 1780, it was Novem-

---

40. Nimnicht, "William Panton," 30; Audit Office Records AO 13/100:320, PROL. Jones, *History of Georgia*, 2:418–24; Candler, *Colonial Records*, 15:562–94.
41. Jones, *History of Georgia*, 2:425.
42. *Georgia Gazette*, September 11, 1783, 2:1; Candler, *Revolutionary Records*, 1:373–97.
43. *Royal Gazette of Georgia*, January 18, 1781, 1:3. In this issue, Panton advertised for the apprehension of a Negro slave who had run away from East Florida.
44. CO 5/560:67–69, 286, PROL.
45. Office of the Registrar General, Book M, 73, PRON.

Colonies of South Carolina, Georgia, and East Florida during the American Revolution

ber 1781, before notices began to appear in the Charleston *Royal Gazette* indicating that Alexander and Leslie had opened an office at No. 51 on the Bay, Charleston. The last notice of the company in the Charleston *Gazette* appeared on May 22, 1783. How long the Alexander and Leslie partnership continued is not recorded, but for all practical purposes it terminated with the formation of Panton, Leslie and Company sometime in late 1782 or early 1783. Thirteen years later, however, John Leslie intimated that he should go to Nassau to settle accounts with Alexander.[46]

46. *The Royal Gazette*, November 7–10, 1781, 4:2; November 14–17, 1781, 3:3; May 18–22, 1782, 3:3; Rogers, *South Carolina Chronology*, 40; John Leslie to Robert Leslie, August 21, 1796, GP.

Besides their collective contributions as merchants, the members of the two companies also served the government and people of East Florida in other capacities. Thomas Forbes and John Leslie were elected to the Commons House of Assembly for East Florida in March 1781. As in many other colonial assemblies, only a brief time passed before the assembly and the council, the lower and upper houses, respectively, became involved in bitter feuds. In East Florida, the assembly defended the right of justices of the peace to try Negroes in capital cases because it eliminated the delays, inconveniences, and expenses of a jury trial in St. Augustine; the council insisted on trial by jury. Within a few months a stalemate existed, as neither house would change its stand. Governor Tonyn, weary of the bickering, dissolved the two houses on November 12, 1781. Presumably, Forbes and Leslie were reelected to the second assembly, which met from January 1782 until March 1784. No list of the members elected has survived, but Tonyn earlier had predicted that a new election would return the same persons to the assembly. For the personal satisfaction that the members of the assembly must have experienced, the Board of Trade agreed with the lower house in its stand on the trial of Negroes and rebuked the governor and the council for their opposition. A bill embodying the assembly's position on the subject became law on May 31, 1782.

The law went far beyond the dispute over the trial of slaves and became virtually a Black Code for East Florida.[47] Forbes's introduction to political factionalism during the March 1781 assembly was to be useful in his future role in Bahamian politics. He did not serve the entire second session, however, because he was in London in 1783–85 on behalf of Panton, Leslie and Company.

Alexander and Thomas Forbes acted as attorneys for the estates of several loyalists. Forbes himself represented such notables as the Reverend John Forbes, James Grant Forbes, and John Gordon.[48] In February 1779, Panton was still listed as an attorney-at-law and in 1783 served as justice of the peace in St. Augustine.[49] Panton assisted in the evaluation of some of the property that departing loyalists were forced to leave behind.[50]

---

47. Siebert, *Loyalists*, 1:91–100; 2:269n160, 276n170; Mowat, *East Florida*, 127–34, 160–61, 164.

48. Siebert, *Loyalists*, 2:207, 270–71, 360. Both the Rev. John Forbes and John Gordon were deceased by this date, and Thomas Forbes acted for the heirs. Siebert suggests that Thomas was a brother of the Rev. John Forbes, but no proof of this relationship has ever been produced: ibid., 360.

49. "A List of the Officers of His Majesty's Province of Georgia and their Present Places of Residence," *Collections of the Georgia Historical Society*, 3:251, 253; for Panton as Justice of the Peace, see Loyalist Claims, AO 13, Bundle 36, Drawer 40, Box 46, PROL.

50. Siebert, *Loyalists*, 2:38–39, 41–43, 209.

Governor Tonyn also appointed Leslie and David Yeats to supervise the registration of property sales and transfers from British to Spanish subjects. Because sales seldom exceeded one-fourth of the value of the property, these records served as the basis for subsequent claims against the British government.[51]

After his accession as the Spanish governor, Manuel de Zéspedes also appointed Leslie one of the judges to settle disputes involving British subjects. Several departing British couples even requested that the Spanish governor permit Leslie to marry them in a civil ceremony. But Zéspedes saved Leslie the trouble by urging the couples to hurry their departure instead. After all, as vice-patron of the Catholic Church, Zéspedes could hardly permit civil marriages.[52]

It is impossible to assess the profits of the two partnerships—Panton and Forbes, and Alexander and Leslie—or, for that matter, the profits of Panton, Leslie and Company from its formation some time in late 1782 or January 1783 until the end of British rule in East Florida in 1784. No account books for that period have survived. If the success of the companies is judged by the claims submitted to the British government, they were far from profitable. Those claims, however, must be examined critically, and since some information is not available conclusions must perforce be tentative. After the Revolution, Panton and Forbes claimed losses of £3,990; the British government allowed them £2,295. Since no itemized list has been discovered, the claim might have been for losses either in South Carolina or in Georgia. Alexander and Leslie presented no claims for their partnership, but they joined the other partners in filing three claims. Two were filed on behalf of Panton, Leslie and Company. One amounted to £1,755 for the loss of land, warehouses, stores, and a wharf in East Florida; the government paid the company £1,178 for this claim. The second claim of £2,740 was settled for £1,403, but there is no indication of what losses that claim represented.[53]

The third claim submitted for the five partners, but under the general head of Thomas Forbes and Company, came to £17,367. Some question was raised about its validity since the claim combined personal and real property, the implication being that the government would reimburse the partners for the value of real property left behind but not for personal property, which could be removed from East Florida. The record does not indicate what amount, if any, the government paid on this claim.[54] The

---

51. CO 5/561:149–51, PROL; Siebert, *Loyalists*, 1:168–69; *Bahama Gazette*, October 2–9, 1784, 2:1; October 9–16, 1784, 3:3.
52. Tanner, *Zéspedes*, 49, 68.
53. Siebert, *Loyalists*, 2:276, 307, 366.
54. "Appraisement of Losses sustained in East Florida by William Panton, William Al-

tenor of the query about the claim raises another point. Three of the five partners—McLatchy, Leslie, and Panton—remained in the Floridas, although Panton temporarily went to the Bahamas. Only Thomas Forbes and William Alexander left permanently with the departing loyalists. Thus it appears that the claim under the name of Thomas Forbes and Company was intended to reimburse the partners for their East Florida lands—a questionable act since three of the five stayed in Florida. Although Panton later wondered whether Spain would recognize his title to lands granted him by the British, he left little doubt that the titles would be confirmed. Apparently, Spanish officials never questioned whether the British government had paid compensation for the lands.[55] Personal property losses were another matter. For example, if the store on the St. Johns River, which was robbed by the rebels in 1782, belonged to the company, then reimbursement for those losses would seem to have been reasonable. In all the partners claimed losses totaling £25,852. Some of their claims may have been questionable. Nevertheless, the problems of securing supplies, the risks of shipping, and the hazards of war made business difficult, if not unprofitable. But patronage of the firms by the government of East Florida and the direct assistance of Governor Tonyn undoubtedly enabled them to show a profit at a time when other loyalists were completely ruined.[56]

We can only speculate why these men established Panton, Leslie and Company. Certainly, the combination of the two partnerships, and the addition of McLatchy as a fifth member, enabled them to pool their resources and to expand their enterprise. The company was formed before the partners knew that East Florida was to be ceded to Spain. Plans were already being made to open a new trading post several hundred miles to the west, to accommodate the Creek trade more readily.

McLatchy, with a decade or more of experience in operating the lower store on the St. Johns River, was the logical choice to take charge of this new post. Once the cession of the Floridas became official—the partners

---

exander, John Leslie, Thomas Forbes, and Charles McLatchy," Claim no. 7 [undated], Treasury T 77/1, PROL, from notes in WP.

55. It appears that lands for which the company was reimbursed were later confirmed to the company either by Spain or by the United States. After the United States acquired the Floridas in 1821, a number of land grants totaling 6,750 acres in East Florida were confirmed to the heirs of Thomas Forbes and William Panton. All of these grants were based on British land grants to Forbes and Panton between 1780 and 1782. See *ASP PL*, 6:110–11, and corresponding claims in Bureau of State Lands, Tallahassee. In his will, dated June 6, 1793, Panton specifically mentioned his claims to land in East Florida which dated from the British period. He recognized that Spain might not concede his title to those lands but expressed a conviction that his claims would be allowed: Panton Will, PHS.

56. Nimnicht, "William Panton," 38.

protested the transfer in vain—Leslie, Panton, and McLatchy hoped to remain in the Floridas, while Forbes and Alexander decided to move to the Bahamas.[57]

Alexander preceded his partner to the islands, and from his move we can learn something of his family. He arrived in Nassau in the summer or fall of 1783 with his wife, Mary Cleland, and four unmarried daughters: Hunter Dick, Georgiana Sally Leslie, Rachel Louisa, and Louisa Janet. He also was accompanied by a married daughter, Mary, wife of William McLeod, and two sons, Theodore George and William Keith.[58] Alexander remained a partner with Panton, Leslie and Company for only a few years, until his own prosperity enabled him to withdraw from the firm in February 1788.[59] Alexander and his sons continued in the mercantile business. The father owned 500 acres of land on Great Exuma and a large plantation on Long Island; the sons took turns operating the plantation, which was named "Bon Esperance." An inventory of the property in 1799 showed 42 slaves and 30 head of cattle plus tools and equipment. A separate inventory taken at the same time indicates that the father had a good supply of household furniture, ten slaves, a horse, 155 ounces of silver, and other goods valued at £1,419 16.[60] Alexander served as a member of the Bahama General Assembly for the Eastern District in 1791–93.[61]

Neither Mary nor William Alexander lived to the end of the century. Mary died in October 1797, in her fifty-sixth year. She was described as a "lady of exemplary piety and worth; cheerful, affable, benevolent, and hospitable; she was respected and esteemed by her relations, friends, and acquaintances."[62] Panton in his will had provided £300 sterling to William Alexander "in testimony that I die his friend,"[63] but Alexander preceded Panton to the grave. John Wells, editor of the *Bahama Gazette*, wrote on

57. The company was formed prior to January 15, 1783, and it was not until April 21, 1783, that Governor Tonyn posted the proclamation announcing the cession. There was still hope that the cession might be abrogated, until the definitive orders were received in the spring of 1784: Mowat, *East Florida*, 142–44; "Address of the Principal Inhabitants to Governor Tonyn," June 6, 1783, CO 5/560:313–15, PROL. In 1783, McLatchy was at the St. Marks store, the site selected for the new trading post: McLatchy to O'Neill, December 15, 1783, AGI PC, leg. 196.

58. Parrish, "Southern Loyalists," 55–59; William Alexander's Will, September 30, 1796, PRON.

59. In memorial by Subscribers, Merchants, and Planters of the Bahama Islands to Earl of Dunmore, February 29, 1788, CO 23/27:103, PROL, there was a notation next to William Alexander's name: "late of the House of Panton & Leslie."

60. Parrish, "Southern Loyalists," 55–59; Office of the Registrar General, November 9, 1799, Book Z, 128–30, PRON.

61. Minutes of the Council, 1790–1793, PRON.

62. *Georgia Gazette*, December 8, 1797, 4:2.

63. Panton's Will, PHS.

October 8, 1799: "Died on Sunday at an advanced age, William Alexander, formerly of East Florida. As a merchant he had few equals. . . . he possessed an uncommon cheerfulness of temper, was ever distinguished by hospitality and benevolence, and in the relative situations of both private and public life was highly respectable."[64]

The other member of Panton, Leslie and Company who made the Bahamas his home was Thomas Forbes. Forbes reached Nassau in 1783, where he directed the construction of the company warehouses to be used in the Florida Indian trade, before leaving for London.[65] The company wharf extended into the bay from their lot (no. 31) at the end of Union Street, now Elizabeth Avenue.[66] Forbes returned to Nassau in December 1785, and immediately joined in the fight between the "New Settler" and "Old Settler" factions.[67] Before long he was known as one of the "outspoken leaders of the New Settler faction" and, as such, became involved in the turmoil of Bahamian politics following the arrival in 1787 of Lord Dunmore, former governor of Virginia.[68] In 1789, Forbes was elected to the assembly and represented the island of Abaco until 1794, when he represented Nassau. He served in the assembly until 1795. The new governor, John Forbes—no relation to Thomas Forbes—appointed Thomas to the council, where he remained from 1797 to 1807.[69] He also served as a vestryman for the parish of Christ Church.[70]

During the ensuing years, Forbes successfully conducted the business in Nassau, which served as an entrepôt for the company. Forbes owned several thousand acres of land scattered among the islands and keys in the Bahamas.[71] He was obviously one of the most successful businessmen in the islands.

64. Parrish, "Southern Loyalists," 55.
65. Petition of Thomas Forbes to Board of Trade, London, July 15, 19, 26, 1785, Chatham Papers, 30/8/344:13–15; PC 2/130:315–16, PROL. Forbes journeyed to London via Charleston.
66. "Plan of the Town of Nassau and Environs of the Island of New Providence Surveyed by Order of the General Assembly of the Bahamas by Captain Andrew Skinner, 1788," PRON.
67. *Bahama Gazette*, December 3, 1785; Parrish, "Southern Loyalists," 56.
68. Wright, *William Augustus Bowles*, 28. See especially former Chief Justice Matson's account of the situation in the Bahamas, 1784–88, for much on the quarrels between the two factions, CO 23/28, PROL. Dunmore to Evan Nepean, March 4, 1788, CO 23/27, PROL.
69. See Journal of the General Assembly, and Minutes and Journal of the Council, Bahamas, 1789–1807, PRON. He last attended the council on November 25, 1807: Journal (October 29, 1805, to December 28, 1810), 85, PRON.
70. Office of the Registrar General, January 14, 1797, Book Z, 329, PRON.
71. Forbes's land in the Bahamas, see Grant Books A–C, I, K, Z, Lands and Surveys Dept., Nassau.

On July 9, 1789, Thomas Forbes married Elizabeth Ann Yonge, daughter of Henry Yonge, bookkeeper for Forbes, Munro and Company. They had four children: William Henry, John Gordon, Mary Sophia, and Thomas Irving, who died in infancy.[72] Elizabeth Forbes died in 1798 at thirty years of age.[73] Thomas died February 13, 1808, and was buried near his friends, John Kelsall and John Wells, in the graveyard northeast of St. Matthews Church, Nassau.[74]

John Leslie, who elected to remain in St. Augustine to supervise the business in East Florida, made his home on Avenida Menéndez, a block north of the city's main plaza and market, which afforded him an excellent view of the waterfront and Matanzas Bay.[75] In April 1787, John left the St. Augustine operation in the hands of his brother Robert while he ventured to Nassau on a brief business trip.[76] If Robert had a family, no record of it has survived, though Robert and John Leslie carried on an extensive correspondence.[77]

In 1789, John Leslie married seventeen-year-old Elizabeth Cain, a native of East Florida. She styled herself Eliza, but her name is consistently spelled "Isabel Kean" in the Spanish records.[78] The record notes that she

72. Baptism and Marriage Register, Christ Church, Nassau, 1733–1805, 51, 89. Baptism Register, Christ Church, Nassau, 1791–1840, 2, 6. Henry Yonge was bookkeeper for the company, but the dates of his employment are not known. He certified the list of bonds and notes due Moore and Panton, Nassau, February 9, 1798, copy in WP. Obituary of Thomas Irving Forbes in Card Index Room, Society of Genealogists, London. Some intimate glimpses of Thomas Forbes may be found in an unpublished manuscript by Armbrister, "Henrietta my Daughter," 3, 36, 44, 59–62, 70–71, 75, 78, 83. The Armbrister ms was put in final form by her daughter, Mary K. Young, who provided the authors with a copy.

73. Elizabeth's death is noted in *Georgia Gazette*, November 8, 1798, 3:2.

74. Inscription on tomb of Thomas Forbes: "Sacred to the memory of Thomas Forbes, Esq," *Gentlemen's Magazine and Historical Record* 78 (1808): 364.

75. Plan of the City of St. Augustine, April 25, 1788, by Mariano LeRocque, as modified by Helen Hunt Tanner for frontispiece in *Zéspedes*. Streets are not named in the LeRocque map, but the street on which Leslie lived is now *Avenida Menéndez*.

76. Robert Leslie to James Taylor, April 19, 1787; John Dilworthy to John Leslie, January 23, 1788, BSC, NYHS.

77. John Forbes to Brigadier General O'Neill, November 4, 1790, *AGI PC*, leg. 2371, identifies Robert Leslie as the company agent at Mobile. Robert was at St. Marks by January 1792: Francisco Xavier Guessy to Arturo O'Neill, January 30, 1792, *AHN, Indias*, leg. 21067, No. 507. John Hambly and Robert Leslie both died at St. Marks in the spring of 1798: John McQueen, Jr. to Eliza Anne McQueen, May 19, 1798, in Hartridge, *Don Juan McQueen*, 47. Wright, "Diplomacy of Trade," 145n34, states that Robert died on September 30, 1798. A number of letters between Robert and John Leslie have been preserved in the BSC, NYHS.

78. Since the marriage does not appear in the records of the Catholic Church in St. Augustine, there has been speculation that he never officially married. On October 29, 1789, John Wells wrote to Leslie, congratulating him on his recent marriage: BSC NYHS. On Elizabeth Cain's name, see Will of John Leslie, Prob. 11, vol. 1411, no. 487, folios 364–66 (proved July 16, 1804), PROL. It is also evident that Leslie had a mulatto son, Billi, whom he left well provided for: ibid.

was the daughter of John Cain and Rebecca Downing of York, England.[79] John and Eliza Leslie had three children: Anna, Elizabeth Rose, and Helena. Two of the children died in infancy, while Elizabeth Rose, "little Bet" as John called her, was only about five years old when she died.[80] John and Eliza separated in May 1797 because, according to John, of the bad habits and customs which she had acquired. In spite of this, in the following year when John wrote his will, he provided an annuity of $1,500 (Mexican money) for her, as long as she did not remarry.[81] Eliza remained in St. Augustine where she died on October 7, 1805, outliving John by nearly two years.[82]

The other partners in Panton, Leslie and Company—Charles McLatchy and William Panton—made their homes in the Floridas, although Panton did spend about six months in Nassau, September 1784 to March 1785, where he purchased a home.[83] During those months notices appeared in the *Bahama Gazette*, in which Panton, Leslie and Company advertised porter, beef, pork, tongue, and so on for sale at their store on the bay.[84] Shortly before he left the Bahamas, Panton, among others, signed a letter of protest regarding the possible return of the former governor John Maxwell, who had been recalled because of his arbitrary stand over elections to the Bahamian Assembly. Although Panton's home in Nassau served as the gathering place for the new settler faction, there is nothing to suggest that Panton was involved in that political struggle beyond his part in

79. For her parents, etc., see *Deaths (White)*, 1784–1809, vol. 1, no. 372; 133, Catholic Church, St. Augustine. Testamentary Records 1794/25, *EF* leg. 303. See documents file Conf. K10, Zephaniah Kingsley, doc. 3, Rebecca Pengree, November 10, 1803, and doc. 10, Rebecca Pengree, November 26, 1803, Bureau of State Lands, Tallahassee, in which she states that her daughter, Isabel, had married Juan Leslie and signed herself "Eliza."

80. Anna Leslie, born November 9, 1790, *Baptisms (White)*, 1784–1792, vol. 1, no. 420, Catholic Church, St. Augustine, died May 29, 1792: *Deaths (Infant White)*, 1784–1826, vol. 72, ibid.; Isabel Rosa Leslie, born October 24, 1792, *Baptisms (White)*, 1792–1799, vol. 2, no. 28, ibid., died before 1798: see John Leslie to Robert Leslie, May 9, 1796, GP.; Will of John Leslie, Prob. 11, vol. 1411, no. 487, folios 364–66, PROL. Helena Leslie died May 11, 1795, at the age of ten months and eleven days: *Deaths (Infant White)*, 1784–1826, no. 125, Catholic Church, St. Augustine.

81. See Will of John Leslie, Prob. 11, vol. 1411, no. 487, folios 364–66, PROL.

82. *Deaths (White)*, 1784–1809, vol. 1, no. 372:133, Catholic Church, St. Augustine. John Leslie died in London in December 1803. No notice of his passing appeared in the London papers, and it is only by inference that the month of his death has been determined. John Forbes went to London in 1804, to assist in the execution of the will, and obtained possession of goods, chattels, and credits from Leslie's estate. Forbes's presence is noted in the probate of John Leslie's will, Prob. 11, vol. 1411, no. 487, folios 364–66, PROL.

83. Panton went to the Bahamas in the *Sally* as noted in *Bahama Gazette*, September 25 to October 2, 1784, 3:2. Panton's stay in Nassau can be verified further by a series of letters he wrote between October 1784 and March 1785, in the Chatham Papers, 30/8/344, PROL.

84. *Bahama Gazette*, October 9–16, 1784, 2:1; the ad last appeared in the issue of March 26–April 2, 1785.

the Maxwell dispute. After Lord Dunmore impounded several thousand *piastres* from one of the company vessels, Panton brought suit against the governor and recovered the money. Thus began the bitter feud between Dunmore and the company that later had serious repercussions in the Floridas.[85] By April 1785, Panton had moved to Pensacola, where he lived for the next fifteen years. Panton remained a bachelor.[86] McLatchy went to St. Marks in 1783 and spent the rest of his life there, until his death on October 14, 1787.[87]

    85. Parrish, "Southern Loyalists," 38–42, 148–49; Wright, *William Augustus Bowles*, 28; *Bahama Gazette*, March 5–12, 1785, 3:1; May 7–14, 1785, 3:3.
    86. Panton arrived in Pensacola from St. Marks with a cargo of goods aboard the *Mary* on April 6, 1785, Francisco de la Rua, Official Report, April 27, 1785, *AGI PC*, leg. 613A; Panton to O'Neill, April 15, 1785, *EF* leg. 116L9.
    87. Luis de Bertucat to O'Neill, October 14, 1787, *AGI PC*, leg. 37.

3
Establishing the Indian Trade, 1783–1785

*T*HE withdrawal of British forces from Savannah and Charleston in 1782 created deep anxiety among the southern Indians. Creek, Cherokee, Chickasaw, and Choctaw war parties had served as British auxiliaries against both Spanish and Anglo-American forces during the American Revolution. With Mobile and Pensacola firmly under Spanish control, the British evacuation of Georgia and South Carolina caused the Indians to fear that they were being abandoned to their Anglo-American foes. Accordingly, in late 1782, large bands of southern Indians, accompanied by representatives of northern tribes from as far away as the Great Lakes, descended upon St. Augustine to seek reassurances from British officials about their future security. Indian spokesmen protested against the relaxation of British military activity and requested support for a grand Indian confederacy, which they hoped would stem American westward expansion.[1]

These demands placed Governor Tonyn and Lieutenant Colonel Thomas Brown, who had succeeded Stuart as superintendent of Indian affairs in East Florida, in a quandary. They did not know what British officials had in mind for a peace settlement in North America. They prudently resolved, therefore, to exhort the Indians to remain faithful British

1. Patrick Tonyn to Sir Guy Carleton, December 23, 1782, in Great Britain, *Report on American Manuscripts*, 3:276–77.

allies while cautioning them against further aggression. At a congress held at St. Augustine in January 1783, Brown assured the Indians of the King's gratitude for their steadfast loyalty, but urged them for the moment to resume the peaceful pursuits of hunting and trading. Responding to the complaints of the southern Indian delegations concerning their severely disrupted trade, the superintendent promised to devise remedies as quickly as possible.[2]

Many of the Indians returned to their homelands, apparently content with the outcome of their visit. As early as February 1783, Spanish authorities in West Florida and Louisiana received reports that English traders were en route with supplies for Choctaw and Creek villages. Indeed, rumors circulating among the Choctaw implied that the restoration of Pensacola and Mobile to British control was imminent.[3] Some 3,000 Creek, however, persisted in staying in East Florida. Superintendent Brown ordered them to return home to hunt, but the Creek refused, pleading poverty and professing friendship.[4]

To allay the fears of the Creek, as well as to enhance the flow of goods to the other southern tribes, Tonyn and Brown, at the request of the Indians meeting in St. Augustine in early January, granted a license to Panton, Leslie and Company on January 15, 1783, to continue in the Indian trade. In return, Panton pledged to locate a trading post on the Apalachicola River nearer the Creek settlements.[5] Instead of a store on the Apalachicola, however, in March the company selected a site on the west bank of the Wakulla River about four miles from the abandoned Fort St. Marks. In the fall of 1783, the trading post opened for business under the direction of Charles McLatchy.[6]

Meanwhile, in April 1783, Governor Tonyn received official notification of the retrocession of East Florida to Spain. The final details of the transfer, however, did not reach East Florida for nearly a year. The hapless Florida tories, most of whom were refugees from the rebellion to the

2. Thomas Brown to Sir Guy Carleton, November 15, 1782, ibid., 222–23; O'Donnell, "Alexander McGillivray," *GHQ*, 181–82.

3. Arturo O'Neill to Luis de Unzaga, February 15, 1783, *AGI PC*, leg. 1336; WP; Allevin et al. to Miró, March 9, 1783, Miró Correspondence, LPBL; Kinnaird, *Spain in the Mississippi Valley*, 2:71–73.

4. Thomas Brown to Sir Guy Carleton, January 12, 1783, in Great Britain, *Report on American Manuscripts*, 3:325–27.

5. Tonyn, et al., License to Panton, Leslie and Co., January 15, 1783, Exhibit 26AA in MC; 9 Peters 711.

6. Panton to McGillivray, February 9, 1792, *AGI PC*, leg. 203; McGillivray to O'Neill, March 26, 1784, *AGI PC*, leg. 197; McLatchy to O'Neill, December 15, 1783, *AGI PC*, leg. 196; Corbitt, "Papers from the Spanish Archives," 9:112–13.

north, discovered that they had only until March 1785 to settle their affairs and relocate in other British possessions.[7]

Not all East Floridians, however, resigned themselves to participating in the British exodus. Panton and Leslie, for example, had faith in their ability to convince Spanish authorities that their services were indispensable to the security of both Floridas. They hoped to argue convincingly that Spain possessed neither the resources nor the expertise to conduct the Indian trade, and that, without the company's support, the southern tribes would eventually be drawn into the orbit of the United States. In keeping with their expansionist practices, the United States could be expected to incite the Indians into raiding and harassing settlements in the Floridas and Louisiana, making the Spanish position untenable.

Governor Tonyn made the first overture to the Spanish government on behalf of Panton, Leslie and Company in September 1783. In a letter addressed to the Spanish governor of East Florida, Tonyn apprised his successor of the company's past contributions to the province's well-being through "maintaining cordial harmony and trade with the Indian nations." Since the firm wished to remain in East Florida, Tonyn recommended that the Spanish governor extend to its members "protection and patronage so that they may continue their business for the public good." Tonyn also conveyed the company's intentions to implement its plans to open a trading post on the Apalachicola, a decision he hailed as most important in keeping the Indians from trading with the United States. The Georgians and the Carolinians, Tonyn pointed out, were eager to "conciliate the Indians" and to "cause them to imbibe notions extremely dangerous to the peace of this province."[8]

In the same month, Thomas Forbes was in London seeking the support of Bernardo del Campo, the Spanish ambassador, for the company's designs. Forbes described to the Spanish diplomat both the economic potential of East Florida and the existing state of Indian affairs. Interrelating these matters in his description, Forbes maintained that the growth, prosperity, and continued peace in the province depended on the ability of Spain to adopt the British approach toward the management of the Indians.

The most certain method for frustrating the U.S. bid for hegemony over the southern Indians, Forbes argued, was to allow the company's

---

7. Mowat, *East Florida*, 142–46.
8. Tonyn to O'Neill, September 19, 1783, enclosure no. 1 of Vicente Manuel de Zéspedes to José de Gálvez, March 22, 1784, *AHN Estado*, leg. 3901, Exp. 5; Lockey, *East Florida*, 190.

trade to be conducted on a regular basis directly between Florida ports and Great Britain. English goods in steady supply should flow into the Indian villages through the agency of the established resident-traders with whom the Indians were accustomed to dealing. Goods should be exchanged for peltry at prearranged prices, agreed upon by the Indians. Any other arrangement, Forbes stated, would give U.S. merchants a competitive edge over the Spaniards. Many items employed in the Indian trade, he observed, were manufactured only in England and thus were purchased more cheaply in London than in other European markets. Furthermore, the Spanish economy was incapable of absorbing the enormous quantity of perishable deerskins that constituted the bulk of the returns of the southern Indian trade. This meant that Spanish merchants would face the added costs and delays of re-exporting bulky deerskins while risking losses through spoilage. The British merchant warned that this would allow the Americans, with ready access to British trade channels, to undersell the Spaniards.

On the other hand, as long as Panton, Leslie and Company remained in the East Florida trade, the United States would have little or no success in winning over the Indians. The Indians fully understood the avarice of the Georgians and Carolinians, who wished to dispossess them of their hunting grounds. The company, Forbes maintained, had all the assets—credit, experience, and goodwill—required to keep the Indians adequately supplied and loyal to Spanish interests. Thomas Forbes asked Campo to recommend that the company receive the protection of the Spanish governor of East Florida and also intimated the firm's interest in the West Florida trade, provided it was conceded for a period of five to seven years. Such an arrangement, he implied, would buy time for Spanish artisans to master the task of duplicating the favored English-made items. Meanwhile, whatever course the Spaniards might eventually take in furnishing the Indian trade, they must accept the necessity of employing large quantities of English manufactures.[9]

9. T. Forbes to Campo, September 22, 28, 1783; Thomas Forbes to Messrs. Davis Strachan & Co., September 20, 1783; "Articles of British Manufacture Absolutely Necessary for the Indians Inhabiting the Western Frontier of East & West Florida in North America," September 28, 1783, *AGS Estado*, leg. 8138. By May 1784, Forbes had heard nothing from his appeals to Campo. He then opened a new channel of communication by writing to Robert Edmonston of Berwick, England, and requesting the aid of Edmonston's brother-in-law, who held an "elevated position in the Council of Spain": Forbes to Edmonston, London, May 3, 1784; a summary of this letter appears in Catalog no. 202, Howard S. Mott, Sheffield, Mass., p. 17, entry no. 66. There is nothing to suggest that Forbes's efforts in London had any bearing on the company's request to remain in the Floridas, but he did succeed in securing permission from the Board of Trade for commerce with the Spanish Floridas. See note 62 below.

Both Tonyn and Forbes stressed the importance to Spanish Indian policy of gaining the friendship of the Creek confederation. Creek hunting grounds abutted the western fringes of settlements in Georgia and South Carolina, and Creek leaders were justifiably wary of American intentions. Unlike their Cherokee neighbors to the north, whose lands were also threatened by American expansion, the Creek had not been demoralized by the patriots' punitive expeditions during the southern campaigns.[10] Indeed, given encouragement, they possessed the fighting capabilities for resisting U.S. encroachment. Furthermore, the Creek could rely on the capable leadership of the astute, politically adept Alexander McGillivray, who had worked energetically against the American cause.

Alexander was born of a union between Lachlan McGillivray, a native of Scotland who had prospered in the Indian trade, and Sehoy Marchand, a half-French Creek woman of the prestigious Wind Clan. After spending a few years in Charleston studying under the tutelage of his cousin, the Rev. Farquhar McGillivray, Alexander interrupted his studies to become a clerk in the Savannah-based mercantile house of Samuel Elbert, who later became governor of Georgia.

By the beginning of the Revolution, or perhaps earlier, Alexander McGillivray had returned to the Creek country, bringing with him slaves and other property from the family estate. His loyalist convictions were strengthened by the confiscation of the McGillivray holdings in Georgia, property valued at more than $100,000. In 1777, McGillivray became an agent in the southern Indian department and within two years achieved the rank of British commissary to the Creek. He worked diligently at stirring up resentment against the Americans among the Indians, and he dispatched warriors to serve with British units. In May 1783, the Creek elevated McGillivray to the position of head warrior to succeed Emistisiguo, who had been killed in 1782 at the siege of Savannah.[11] McGillivray immediately placed the Creek on a war footing as a defensive measure against the schemes of Georgia and South Carolina for annexing Creek lands.

Shortly afterward, the defensive preparations of the Creek received a serious blow. In the spring of 1783, Superintendent Brown advised McGillivray that the southern Indian department had been ordered to begin preparations for evacuating East Florida; all agents were to withdraw

10. O'Donnell, *Southern Indians*, 48, 52, 107, 111.
11. On McGillivray's formative years and activities during the American Revolution, see Caughey, *McGillivray*, 3–17; O'Donnell, "Alexander McGillivray." "Emistisiguo," like most Indian names, is variously spelled, appearing also as "Emisteseguo": Corkran, *Creek Frontier*, 336.

from Indian territory immediately. Disconsolate over this abandonment, McGillivray insisted to Brown that the British must furnish the Creek with arms and munitions needed to withstand the land-hungry Americans. Brown, however, advised against any precipitate action for the moment. Instead, McGillivray should apply to Spanish officials in Pensacola for arms and ammunition, inasmuch as they too were extremely interested in forestalling the American westward advance.[12]

William Panton offered McGillivray similar advice. Panton proposed that he should solicit Spanish protection and also promote Panton, Leslie and Company's interest in the Indian trade. Success would assure the Creek of adequate trade goods, thereby eliminating dependence upon American supply sources. With Spanish support and freedom from commercial dependence on the United States, the Creek could then successfully resist U.S. expansion. As an added inducement, Panton offered McGillivray a share of the company's profits for his assistance in obtaining Spanish approval of the company's plans.[13]

Developments in late 1783 revealed that Panton, Leslie and Company needed all the support it could muster. By December, the representations made by Tonyn and Forbes on the company's behalf had reached the Spanish court, where they came under the scrutiny of the capable Bernardo de Gálvez, who needed no reminders from British subjects on the importance of trade in successful Indian diplomacy. However, mindful of the profits involved and having faith in the feasibility of commerce with the southern Indians under the liberalized commercial provisions of the royal *cédula* of January 22, 1782, Gálvez preferred granting Louisianians the opportunity "to gain and preserve the friendship of the natives—a thing that is not so impossible as the English believe." The following May, Don Bernardo influenced a royal decision permitting Panton, Leslie and Company to remain temporarily in the East Florida trade if the partners agreed to use

12. Corkran, *Creek Frontier*, 322–24; O'Donnell, "Alexander McGillivray," 181–82, 186.

13. McLatchy wrote O'Neill on March 4, 1784, that McGillivray was "partly connected with us in the treading [*sic*] business": ANC F, leg. 1, Exp. 12, no. 1. McGillivray soon after personally confirmed his association with the company: "Since I have taken a share in the interests of your house, I am determined to work with interest and integrity": McGillivray to McLatchy, October 4, 1784, EF leg. 116L9; Caughey, *McGillivray*, 82–83. Panton later wrote that McGillivray shared in the profits of the firm from 1785 to 1787 and formally resigned his interest in the company on September 20, 1788: Panton to Lachlan McGillivray, April 10, 1794; Alexander McGillivray to Panton, September 20, 1788. According to claims against the company years later, the McGillivray heirs claimed that Alexander McGillivray was entitled to a one-fifth share in the company profits to the time of his death. However, McGillivray died on February 17, 1793, and was not a member of the company when it was reorganized on September 1, 1792: memorandum by John Leslie, December 31, 1792. Copies of the last three documents are in *Johnson et al. v. Innerarity et al.*

Spanish goods or those obtainable under the *Reglamento de comercio libre* of October 12, 1778—a measure specifying that trade between Spanish colonies and non-Spanish markets must be cleared through designated Spanish ports, subject to high duties and imports.[14] This concession was probably extended because the Spaniards had no immediate alternative means for supplying the Seminoles (whose trade, at any rate, was of lesser economic importance than that of the other southern Indians).

Meanwhile, Alexander McGillivray was confronted with pressures from Georgia for a cession of all Creek lands east of the Oconee River. Since he was denied British assistance in resisting these demands, he took Superintendent Brown's advice to try his luck with the Spaniards. In September 1783, the Creek leader, accompanied by a coterie of other influential headmen, visited Governor Arturo O'Neill in Pensacola. In apprising the Spanish governor of the plight of his nation, McGillivray declared that the Creek intended to turn their backs on the British, to seek peace and trade with the Spaniards and to frustrate the designs of the Georgians for a treaty and land cession. He offered O'Neill his services in promoting the Spanish interest among the Creek. Impressed with his visitor's influence, bearing, and resentment against the Americans, O'Neill recommended cultivating the friendship of McGillivray and other mixed-bloods who resided among the Creek as the best means for acquiring their trade.[15]

Shortly afterward, Georgia demonstrated its adherence to the almost universally accepted premise underlying U.S. Indian policy: as British allies, the tribes inhabiting U.S. soil were considered conquered nations whose territorial claims were forfeit. In October, two pro-American Creek chiefs led a splinter faction to Augusta to parley with Georgia officials. A treaty signed November 1, 1783, ceded some 800 square miles of Creek lands east of the Oconee to Georgia, required the Creek to honor their past indebtedness to Georgia merchants, and provided for the reopening of trade.[16] McGillivray and his supporters immediately disavowed the Augusta treaty, claiming it had been exacted under duress from a small Creek faction which lacked authority to negotiate for the entire nation. Never-

14. B. de Gálvez to J. de Gálvez, December 20, 1783, *AGI PC*, leg. 1375; Whitaker, *Documents*, 39–41; Conde de Gálvez to Manuel de Zéspedes, June 20, 1784, *AGI SD*, leg. 2670, WP. For a good overview of the negotiations that led to establishment of Panton, Leslie and Company in Spanish East and West Florida, and of the subsequent relations between the company and Spain, see Mirat, *Situación Histórica de las Floridas*, 35–46, 111–47.

15. O'Neill to José de Ezpeleta, October 19, 1783, *AGI PC*, leg. 36; Caughey, *McGillivray*, 62–63.

16. Downes, "Creek-American Relations," 143–46. The text of the treaty appears in DePauw, *First Federal Congress*, 2:165–67.

theless, agents of Elijah Clarke and Samuel Elbert introduced small quantities of sorely needed goods into the Creek villages following negotiations, a development in which McGillivray acquiesced.[17]

The Augusta treaty, coupled with the loss of any hope of success in British bargaining for retention of the Floridas, caused McGillivray to redouble his efforts to seek an accord with the Spaniards. McGillivray corresponded with Governor O'Neill in January 1784, decrying the British action of granting the United States jurisdiction over Creek territory in the peace settlement. As a free nation, he asserted, the Creek could choose their own protector and consequently, he would seek Spanish protection. Since the establishment of peace, the Creek spokesman warned, the United States was in serious financial difficulty and had imposed taxes and duties on the thirteen states, which had been ill received by the people. He anticipated hordes of restless and uncontrollable Americans pouring across the frontiers toward the Mississippi, where they would create a "Western Independency," out of reach of the eastern government. Once established, their removal would be difficult. Furthermore, the southern states were employing goods and gifts in an effort to secure the allegiance of the Creek and to convert them into enemies of Spain. If successful, the Indians would likely be employed in future American designs against Pensacola, Mobile, or elsewhere.

To frustrate the schemes of the United States, McGillivray recommended that Spain permit the introduction of an abundant supply of trade goods into the Creek nation, "for Indians will attach themselves to and serve them best who supply their necessities."[18] Unwittingly or otherwise, McGillivray announced that the terms of peace granted Panton, Leslie and Company the privilege of continuing in the East Florida Indian trade, with the possibility of expansion to Pensacola or Mobile. If the petition received approval, McGillivray was to be given a part interest. The Creek spokesman also offered his services to Spain as an agent for Indian affairs.[19]

Governor O'Neill took the initiative in accepting McGillivray's request for Spanish protection for the Creek, a measure subsequently approved by the Spanish crown. Regarding the trade proposals, however, the Spanish governor, apparently not yet informed of Maxent's fall from grace,

17. Downes, "Creek-American Relations," 145–46; McGillivray to Miró, March 28, 1784, AGI PC, leg. 197; Caughey, *McGillivray*, 73–74.
18. McGillivray to O'Neill, January 1, 1784, AGI PC, leg. 197; WPA, "Creek Letters," Part 1:52B, C; Caughey, *McGillivray*, 64–66.
19. Caughey, *McGillivray*, 64–66; McGillivray to O'Neill, January 3, 1784, ibid., 66–67.

evasively replied that they would be referred to the former superintendent and Miró "at the proper time."[20]

On the other hand, O'Neill gave Charles McLatchy cause for alarm over the company's future status when he responded to McLatchy's request to continue trade operations at St. Marks. The governor surmised that unless McLatchy was joined by a Spanish partner and received the approval of the Indian superintendent, he would be denied the trading privileges he sought. Nor, O'Neill advised, should McLatchy attempt to restock the St. Marks post through British commercial channels. O'Neill concluded by recommending that McLatchy sell his current inventories to some Spanish merchant in Pensacola.[21]

In his reply, McLatchy reminded the Spanish governor that East Florida still remained under British control and explained that Governor Tonyn earlier had approved restocking the St. Marks post. Additional trade goods were expected to arrive momentarily. McLatchy stated that Panton, Leslie and Company fully realized that its future operations required the approval of Spanish authorities in both Floridas. But immediate suspension of the St. Marks trade would cause the company to suffer losses for goods already consigned to traders on credit. Insinuating that rejection of the company's request to trade under Spanish auspices might force it to relocate in "some other Country," McLatchy added that he had suggested that either Panton or Leslie visit Pensacola for direct trade discussions with O'Neill and the superintendent.[22]

McGillivray also protested against the threat to the St. Marks trade, announcing to the Spaniards that the post had been opened at the request of the Indians. With trade goods virtually unobtainable from Pensacola, he declared that the Creek were prepared to defend the St. Marks post against closure at least until the Spaniards made satisfactory trade arrangements. Uninstructed on the firm's change in name, McGillivray reiterated his ties with "Messrs. Panton, Forbes & Co."; declared that he had requested Panton to accompany him to Pensacola in May for the Spanish-Creek treaty discussions; and recommended conceding the entire Creek, Chickasaw, and Choctaw trade to the British concern by joint agreement. McGillivray also forwarded proposals for the consideration of "Monsieur Maxent the Superintendent," who, he suggested, should associate him-

20. O'Neill to Miró, February 17, 1784, *AGI PC*, leg. 36; Caughey, *McGillivray*, 71–72.
21. McLatchy to O'Neill, December 15, 1783, Corbitt, "Papers from the Spanish Archives," 9:112–13; O'Neill to McLatchy, February 6, 1784, *AGI SD*, leg. 2543; *EF* leg. 116L9.
22. McLatchy to O'Neill, March 4, 1784, *ANC F*, leg. 1, Exp. 12, no. 1, WP; *AGI PC*, leg. 196.

self with the Panton firm as the "only means" of forestalling designs by the United States on the Creek trade.[23]

In New Orleans, meanwhile, Miró and Martín Navarro, the intendant for Louisiana, were devising a solution to the trade quandary from resources more immediately at hand. By April 1784, they had acquired assurances from the New Orleans merchant, James Mather, of his willingness to supply the Indians, insofar as his limited resources permitted. Mather also agreed to procure additional merchandise to place the West Florida Indian commerce on a sound basis.[24]

Miró and Navarro clearly understood that gaining the approval of McGillivray for any trade proposal was an inescapable requirement. His warnings that his people, despite their reluctance, might be forced by necessity into succumbing to U.S. offers made the two Spaniards shudder. Accordingly, Miró informed McGillivray that trading arrangements of "all sorts" would be discussed at the pending treaty conference and that James Mather would be on hand with offers of particular interest.[25]

The long-awaited Spanish-Creek treaty congress finally began at Pensacola on May 30, with Miró, Navarro, and O'Neill representing Spain and McGillivray acting as chief spokesman for the Creek. The terms agreed upon established peace between the Creek nation and Spain, with the Creek recognizing His Catholic Majesty as their sole protector. Spain pledged to maintain the Creek trade on a permanent basis at mutually agreeable prices, except for disruptions arising from war. The Creek agreed to prevent whites without valid passports from entering their nation and promised to surrender all Americans detained under this provision to Spanish officials. They promised to honor all debts contracted with traders duly licensed by the Spanish government who offered their goods at the prescribed prices. The Creek also agreed to refrain from engaging in clandestine trade. For its part, Spain guaranteed Creek lands but only insofar as they lay within Spanish territorial limits. However, should warfare or other misfortune deprive the Creek of their lands, the Spanish monarch would provide them with lands of equivalent value elsewhere in his dominions.[26] A separate "tariff" agreement of June 1, 1784, listed each

---

23. McGillivray to O'Neill, March 26, 1784, *AGI PC*, leg. 197; Caughey, *McGillivray*, 72–73.

24. Miró to Conde de Gálvez, April 15, 1784, *AHN Estado*, leg. 3885, Exp. 22, doc. 3; Miró to Navarro, April 15, 1784, *AGI PC*, leg. 633, WP.

25. Navarro to J. de Gálvez, April 16, 1784, *AGI PC*, leg. 633; *AHN Estado*, leg. 3888, Exp. 1; McGillivray to McLatchy, October 4, 1784, *EF* leg. 116L9; Caughey, *McGillivray*, 82–83.

26. Spanish-Creek treaty, June 1, 1784, *AGI PC*, leg. 2360; *AHN Estado*, leg. 3885, Exp. 22, WP. Both Miró and Navarro, with a high respect for Creek prowess, had determined to keep them free of American influence long before the treaty talks began, even if it

item to be employed in the Creek trade and its corresponding value in deerskins (table 1).[27]

Mindful of the extreme importance of keeping McGillivray attached to the Spanish interest, Miró, subject to royal confirmation, appointed the powerful *castizo* as Spanish agent to the Creek at an annual salary of 600 pesos. Subject to O'Neill's supervision, McGillivray's duties included promoting Spanish influence among the Creek, supervising the conduct of the trade, maintaining peace with neighboring tribes, and arresting illegal entrants.[28]

On leaving Pensacola, Miró and Navarro called at Mobile, where on June 22–23 they concluded separate treaties and "tariff" agreements with the Choctaw, Alabama, and Chickasaw. These treaties differed little from the Pensacola treaty, except for their lack of a limited territorial guarantee.[29]

Panton had intended to be at Pensacola for the Indian conference but was detained at St. Marks until after June 4. There he met with several Indian acquaintances and together they celebrated the birth of the British sovereign "with no Small degree of Joy in spite of the melancholly reflection which forced itself on our recollection of its being perhaps the last day of the kind we ever were to spend together." He continued, "You who are acquainted with how much I regard those neglected, unfortunate, brave natives, who so readily assisted Governor Tonyn in the defense of Florida during the war, can guess at my feelings on their acclamations for the long life of our Common Father notwithstanding our enemies have forced him to abandon his Red Children." Panton voiced his own sentiments about the loss of the Floridas in a letter to Thomas Forbes: "I come now to give you some account of the long Journey I took after I reached our Stores at Appalachia, and which our extensive concerns induced me to make over a part of that immense territory which that Simpleton of a Politician, Mr. Oswald, did with so much ease give away."[30] As

---

meant relocating them on lands belonging to Spain: Miró to Navarro, April 15, 1784, *AGI PC*, leg. 633.

27. Creek tariff, *AHN Estado*, leg. 3885, Exp. 22, doc. 8. Although not specifically stated in the tariff, all skins offered for trade were assumed to be "dressed" skins.

28. Miró to B. de Gálvez, August 1, 1784, *AHN Estado*, leg. 3885, Exp. 22, doc. 2; instructions to McGillivray, ibid., doc. 14; Coker and Inglis, *Spanish Censuses of Pensacola*, 3.

29. Navarro to José de Gálvez, July 27, 1784, *AHN Estado*, leg. 3888, Exp. 1; *AGI PC*, leg. 633.

30. Extract of Sundry Letters to Mr. Thomas Forbes, Merchant, from William Panton, New Providence, November 20, 1784, Chatham Papers, 30/8/344 Part 1, PROL. "Mr. Oswald" was Richard Oswald, who, with others, negotiated the preliminary articles of peace between Great Britain, Spain, France, and the American colonies in Paris, in 1782 and early 1783. Although the provision to cede the Floridas to Spain was included in the preliminary

Table 1. "Tariff arranged for the commerce of the Creek and Talapoosa Nation in the general Congress celebrated in Pensacola the days of 31 May and 1 June 1784"

A Limbourg blanket of two Castilian yards	8 lbs. (of 18 oz.) of dressed skins
A blanket of a yard and a half	6 lbs. of dressed skins
A yard of Limbourg [blanket]	4 lbs. of dressed skins
An ordinary striped blanket	8 lbs. of dressed skins
A blanket with only one stripe	6 lbs. of skins
A white shirt with ruffles	8 to 10 lbs. of dressed skins according to their quality
A plain shirt	4 to 6 lbs.
A gingham shirt or one of ordinary ticking	4 to 5 lbs. of skins
A yard of calico	4 to 5 lbs.
The more ordinary Indian handkerchiefs	2 to 3 lbs.
Black silk handkerchiefs	6 to 8 lbs. each
One half pound of gunpowder	1 lb. in skins
Forty balls [of shot]	1 lb. in skins
Twelve gun flints	1 lb. in skins
Knives according to size	1, 2, or 3 lbs. each
Hatchets	1 to 6 lbs. in skins each
Trade guns	16 to 18 lbs. in dressed skins
Looking glasses according to size	1 to 5 lbs. in skins
Four yards of ordinary wool binding	1 lb. of dressed skins
A pair of silver ear-rings	2 lbs.
Broach or silver pin for the shirt	2 to 3 lbs. of skins
Riding saddle	from 30 to 60 lbs. according to quality
Simple bridle	4 to 5 lbs. in skins
Double bridle	6 to 7 lbs.
5 strands of [barley-corn] glass beads	1 lb.
5 strands of common glass beads	1 lb. of skins
10 strands of enameled white beads	1 lb. of skins
A yard of garlic, or ordinary white linen	2 to 3 lbs.
A yard of fine linen	3 to 4 lbs. in skins
Printed handkerchiefs	3 to 4 lbs. of dressed skins
Slightly used scarlet and blue cloth	Will trade according to quality
A yard of white baize [flannel]	2 to 3 lbs.

NOTE:

Thus, as it has been stipulated, the yard is to be the Castilian [Spanish] yard. As it has been determined following ancient usage, the pound will be of 18 ounces. The skins that weigh less than one pound will pass two for one. Those that are less than two pounds will pass for one pound; as it has always been the custom.

Pensacola, 1 June 1784
Estevan Miró
Arturo O'Neill
Martín Navarro
Alexander McGillebrey

Source: see note 27.

a result of his delay at St. Marks, Panton did not arrive in Pensacola until after Miró and Navarro had departed for Mobile.

In Pensacola the Scottish merchant joined McGillivray, who gave a less than candid account of what had transpired. From his colleague, Panton learned only that the governors of New Orleans and Pensacola would recommend placing the Creek trade "on a solid footing" and that McGillivray had obtained immediate permission for the transfer of goods from St. Marks and St. Augustine to Pensacola. After acquiring the necessary passports, Panton left to arrange the transfer, confident that the Spaniards would report the company in a favorable light to Madrid; they appeared too anxious to win over the Indians to do otherwise. Panton was oblivious to the fact that Miró and Navarro considered the transfer of goods to Pensacola as a "one time only" expedient and even then sanctioned it only because of the extreme need of the Creek.[31]

Nor was Panton aware that James Mather had attended the treaty discussions and, supported by Miró and Navarro, had solicited McGillivray's partnership. On mentioning his connections with Panton's firm, McGillivray was advised against flatly rejecting Mather's offer; his influence was too powerful to ignore.[32] McGillivray did not immediately accept Mather's proposition, but by December he had consented to become involved with Mather's firm in the Choctaw-Chickasaw trade at Mobile, while envisioning a similar relationship with Panton at Pensacola.[33] McGillivray indeed had pressed for Pensacola as the locus of the Creek trade and had insisted on the use of English goods. Yet while observing Panton's actions in Pensacola, McGillivray had formed the opinion that the Scot mistrusted the Spaniards, and therefore was hesitant in pressing his case. The Creek leader also expressed concern over Panton's failure to reach an understanding with O'Neill before leaving Pensacola.[34] Possibly McGillivray was hedging his bets.

---

treaty signed January 20, 1783, the cession of East Florida does not appear to have been in Oswald's own best interest. In fact, he owned 20,000 acres of land there—"Mount Oswald," a flourishing plantation—and at least one historian indicates that Oswald actually opposed the cession: Wright, "Dunmore's Loyalist Asylum," 375–76. Davenport and Paullin, *European Treaties*, 4:150; Mowat, *East Florida*, 60–61, 67, 69–70, 140–41; Wright, *Florida in the American Revolution*, 120–21; Stephen and Lee, *Dictionary of National Biography*, 14:1223–24. For an excellent bibliographical note on Richard Oswald, see Robinson, *Richard Oswald's Memorandum*, 53–56.

31. O'Neill to Zéspedes, July 17, 1784, EF, leg. 114J9; Navarro [?] to J. de Gálvez [?], no. 255, August 18, 1784, AGI PC, leg. 633.

32. McGillivray to McLatchy, October 4, 1784, EF, leg. 116L9; Caughey, *McGillivray*, 82–83.

33. McGillivray to McLatchy, December 25, 1784, EF, leg. 116L9; Caughey, *McGillivray*, 84–87.

34. McGillivray to McLatchy, December 25, 1784, and McGillivray to Panton, August 10, 1784, EF, leg. 116L9; Caughey, *McGillivray*, 78–79.

Whatever thoughts McGillivray entertained with respect to Panton, Leslie and Company, the attitudes of Miró and Navarro were clear. They planned to award the entire southern Indian trade to Mather and Strother on a provisional basis, subject to permanent confirmation by the court.[35] On July 24, the governor and intendant reached a contractual agreement with Mather that set forth terms under which he could import enough merchandise to support his trade for one year. The goods were to be transported to West Florida in two vessels, one cargo to be designated for Pensacola and the other for Mobile. He was allowed the discretion of obtaining the necessary Indian trading wares in any English, Dutch, or Danish port. Mather consented to undertake the venture at his own expense and risk and to use his personal credit in purchasing the goods. He was expressly forbidden to remove silver from Louisiana under any pretext whatsoever. He also agreed to pay a 6 per cent ad valorem duty on imported merchandise and peltry exports. In August, Miró granted a passport to Mather authorizing him to send his ship to any neutral or allied island or to any European port in quest of goods for the Indian trade.[36]

The Mather enterprise clearly violated the provisions of the royal *cédula* of January 1782 designed to facilitate Indian trade by opening commerce with designated French ports. Miró and Navarro explained to their superiors that the decision to deviate from established commercial practices was based on the overwhelming necessity for haste. Delay in restoring the southern Indian trade would create ill will for Spain and force the Indians to trade with the United States, thus endangering the security of Louisiana and the Floridas. The Indians had demanded English trade goods, and Mather alone possessed sufficient credit in London to purchase the required wares without delay. Procuring English goods in France would have been both time-consuming and costly. Since many Indian trade articles were produced only in England, and since Maxent earlier had received approval to procure a large quantity of English-made items through Ostend, the Louisiana officials felt their action was appropriate—at least as a temporary expedient. Spain, they observed, would draw no economic benefits from routing the Indian trade through either France or England, making preference in the matter a moot proposition.

Miró and Navarro also submitted suggestions for royal consideration in shaping permanent policies for the southern Indian trade. They suggested that it should be conducted at private rather than public expense

---

35. Miró to Ezpeleta, August 1, 1784, *AGI PC*, leg. 1394; WPA, "Despatches," 13:6–9; Miró to B. de Gálvez, August 1, 1784, *AHN Estado*, leg. 3885, Exp. 22, doc. 2.

36. Mather contract, July 24, 1784; Mather passport, August 4, 1784, *AHN Estado*, leg. 3885, Exp. 22, docs. 12–13.

through permanent stores in Pensacola and Mobile. English manufactures should be employed in the trade because of the stated preferences of the Indians. The merchant selected to conduct the trade should possess adequate financial resources to operate it on a permanent basis. These measures, they observed, would relieve the treasury of burdensome capital outlays for government-sponsored trade, lessen royal expenses for gifts, and keep the southern Indians safely under Spanish influence.[37]

By September 1784, Panton's search for goods for Pensacola had led him back to St. Augustine, where he discovered that the company's inventories were almost depleted. Thus Panton could not keep his promise to Governor O'Neill to send a shipment of goods from the St. Augustine store to Pensacola. Panton quickly approached the Spanish governor, Vincente Manuel de Zéspedes, who had arrived on June 27—but who did not take official possession of East Florida until July 12—for a passport to Nassau. The company expected the arrival in New Providence of a large consignment of goods suitable for restocking the post at St. Marks, with the balance to be sent to St. Augustine. Shortages at St. Marks, Panton told Zéspedes, were causing considerable anxiety among Indians and traders alike. Zéspedes readily granted the passport.[38]

Before Panton's return to St. Augustine, Tonyn, Leslie, and Brown, with special assistance from Indian visitors, had already convinced the East Florida governor that the services of Panton, Leslie and Company were indispensable. Almost from the moment of his arrival Zéspedes found Indian affairs to be among his "greatest cares" of office.[39] Seemingly endless delegations of Indians called at St. Augustine to greet him and to receive the presents customarily distributed on such occasions. Leslie cheerfully rescued the governor from his embarrassment over having failed to include suitable Indian presents among the stores transported from Cuba; his oversight was remedied by advancing the needed articles on credit from company stock. Indeed, by January 1785, Zéspedes owed the company $3,000. Leslie claimed to be the de facto Spanish Indian superintendent for East Florida but hastened to point out that it was not a very lucrative or beneficial appointment. Between November 1785 and November 1786, Leslie advanced on credit to Zéspedes an additional 13,569 pesos worth of goods to be used as gifts to the Indians. Included in

37. Navarro to J. de Gálvez, July 27, 1784, *AGI PC*, leg. 633; Miró to B. de Gálvez, August 1, 1784, *AHN Estado*, leg. 3885, Exp. 22, doc. 2.
38. Panton, Leslie and Co. memorials to Zéspedes, September 7, 10, 1784, *EF*, leg. 116L9 (the latter is also in Caughey, *McGillivray*, 79–80); Tanner, *Zéspedes*, 28–34, 36; Beerman, "Arturo O'Neill," 35.
39. Zéspedes to O'Neill, September 12, 1784, *EF*, leg. 114J9; Lockey, *East Florida*, 271–74; J. Leslie to T. Forbes, July 25, 1784, Chatham Papers, 30/8/344, Part 1, PROL.

the assortment were dry goods, foodstuffs, gunpowder, bullets, brandy, wine, tobacco, honey, and sugar.[40]

The grateful Zéspedes repaid the company's favors in numerous ways. In August 1784, he strongly endorsed a Panton, Leslie and Company memorial to the Spanish crown requesting the privilege of trading "on the same basis as formerly under the British government of this province." The memorial requested direct access to British markets; in return, the partners pledged to take oaths of obedience to the Spanish crown, remain loyal to Spanish interests, obey Spanish laws, and import only those British articles "absolutely necessary for the Indian trade." The memorialists also requested the right to withdraw from the province with their personal goods to any British territory only after formally giving due notice, even in the event of an Anglo-Spanish war. But they promised to refrain from "active personal" involvement in hostile acts against Spain should war occur. The petition also asked Spanish indulgence for the partners' "religious persuasions until perhaps a conviction of the errors of Protestant doctrine" should lead to their conversion. In addition to proclaiming the company's superior capabilities in promoting and preserving Spanish friendship among its Indian clientele, the memorialists acknowledged their marked preference for Spanish protection rather than relocation in a neighboring American state, where they "would be received with open arms."

In supporting the privileges requested in the memorial, Zéspedes emphasized the company's crucial ties with the influential Alexander McGillivray, the abject dependence of Indians on European goods, and the economies to the government from promoting private trade. Under the British system, the governor asserted, the resident trader in each Indian village also served as an effective diplomat in advancing official policy. He observed that in addition to their desires for profit, the partners hated the United States intensely. This combination, Zéspedes believed, would compensate for whatever lack of affection Panton or Leslie bore toward Spain.

The court, Zéspedes suggested, should allow the petition and should also introduce English-speaking Spaniards into the firm. Panton, Leslie and Company would thus provide the means for Spaniards to master the intricacies of the Indian trade. The court should also send young, underprivileged Spanish boys to St. Augustine, where they could train to become part-time residents in Indian villages. They would thereby learn

---

40. J. Leslie to T. Forbes, July 25, 1784, January 25, 1785, Chatham Papers, 30/8/344, Part 1, PROL; Mirat, *Situación Histórica de las Floridas*, 41.

Indian dialects and customs, preparing themselves for careers as resident-traders. Once these ends were attained, the British firm could be replaced. While awaiting the court's decision, Zéspedes stated that he would allow the company to operate under the conditions requested in the memorial.[41] Zéspedes also granted Panton permission to go to New Providence for the goods so badly needed at St. Marks and Pensacola.[42]

On September 26, Zéspedes received a dispatch from Bernardo de Gálvez outlining the restricted conditions imposed upon the company in the royal decision of May 1784. The governor, unwilling to cope alone with the "insatiable greed" of Indians for gifts, deferred executing the decree and explaining to Don Bernardo that he would await the court's disposition of the company's August memorial.[43] The governor withheld the adverse news from Panton and Leslie, partly from fear of losing their cooperation.[44]

Panton arrived in Nassau in late September for an unanticipated six-month stay occasioned by inventory shortages and the late arrival of goods from London. Although he sent cargoes to the St. Marks and St. Johns posts shortly after reaching Nassau, he was forced to delay his departure for Pensacola until new stock arrived. While distressed at being unable to reach Pensacola more quickly, Panton remained confident of arriving at an agreement with O'Neill regarding the West Florida trade. In clinging to this sentiment, Panton chose to disregard the counsel of friends against placing too much trust in the word of Spaniards.[45]

En route to Pensacola, Panton called at St. Marks in mid-March 1785 with supplies for McLatchy, who informed him of the McGillivray-Mather connection and of the Louisiana governor's support of the New Orleans firms. The astonished Panton immediately sent word to McGillivray reiterating his determination to compete for locations at Pensacola and Mobile, a matter the two had discussed fully during the past year. The time had come, Panton concluded, for McGillivray to choose between the contenders.[46]

41. Panton, Leslie and Co. memorial, July 31, 1784, enclosed in Zéspedes to B. de Gálvez, August 16, 1784, *AHN Estado*, leg. 3901, Exp. 5; Lockey, *East Florida*, 254–60; Mirat, *Situación Histórica de las Floridas*, 38–40.
42. Zéspedes to Conde de Gálvez, September 21, 1784, *AHN Estado*, leg. 3901, Exp. 5.
43. Zéspedes to Bernardo de Gálvez, October 21, 1784, *AHN Estado*, leg. 3901; Lockey, *East Florida*, 296–97.
44. Ibid. By January 1785, Leslie seems not to have been aware of the court's decision; J. Leslie to T. Forbes, January 25, 1785, Chatham Papers, 30/8/344, Part 1, PROL.
45. Panton to Zéspedes, December 4, 1784; Panton to Carlos Howard, December 5, 1784; Panton to J. Leslie, January 7, 1785, *EF* leg. 116L9.
46. Panton to J. Leslie, March 21, 1785, ibid.

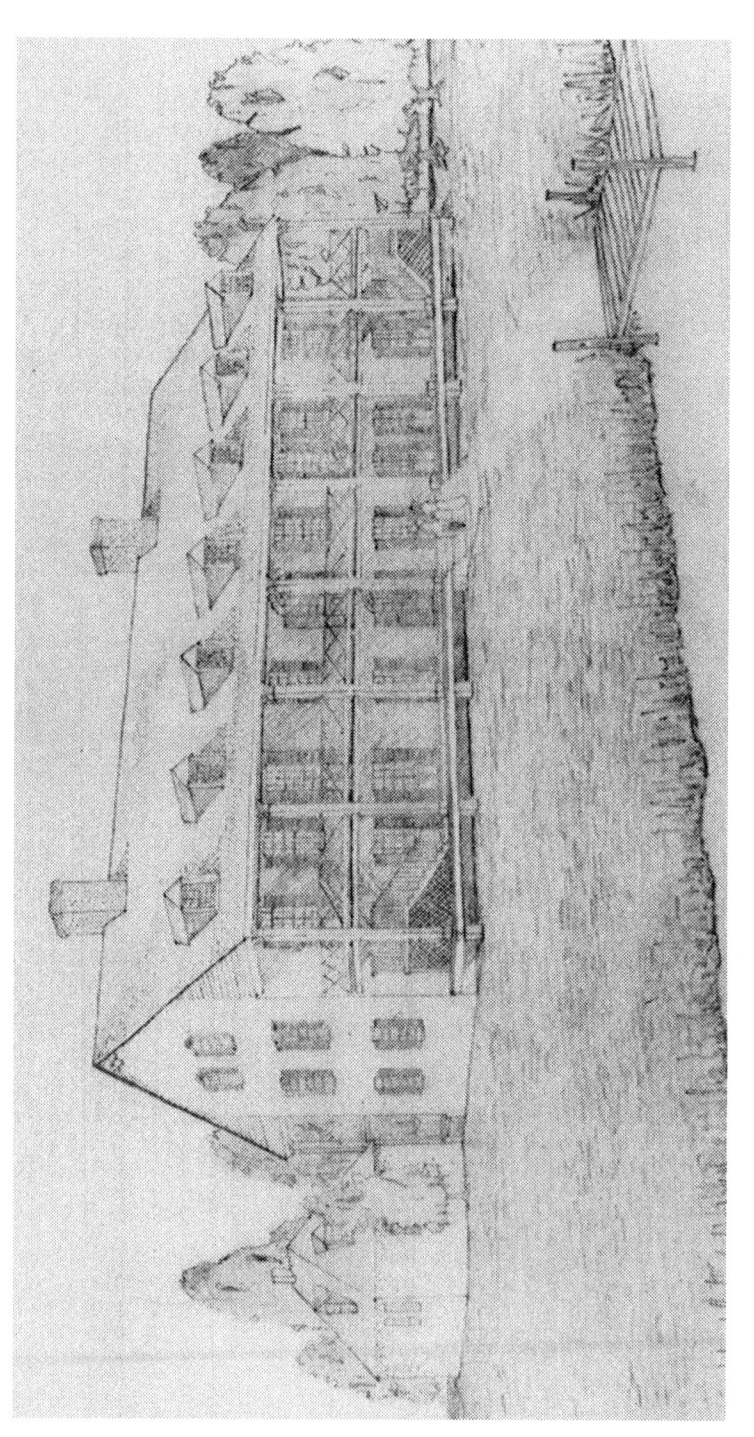

Panton, Leslie and Company headquarters, ca. 1796–1848. Artist's concept based on 1801 bill of materials of the "mansion" built at Pensacola about 1796. Converted into a residence by John Innerarity in 1806, the building and much of Pensacola was destroyed in a fire on the night of September 24, 1848. Sketch by Al See, courtesy of *Florida Historical Quarterly* (vol. 60, July 1981).

While at St. Marks, Panton also saw a copy of the royal decree of May 1784, which, in O'Neill's accompanying explanation, confirmed the company in the East Florida Indian trade on an equal basis with Spanish subjects. No longer completely confident of gaining a foothold in West Florida, the Scot nevertheless prepared orders for his London factors to assemble merchandise for 1786. Spanish concern over Indian friendship and the trade promises made at the treaty congress led Panton to believe that his services would be needed at least for the immediate future. The discoveries at St. Marks, however, made him doubly anxious to reach Pensacola and to confer with Governor O'Neill.[47]

After an agonizingly slow voyage under adverse conditions, Panton arrived in Pensacola on April 6, 1785. To his chagrin, he discovered that O'Neill had sailed to Havana for consultations with Bernardo de Gálvez, who, while retaining his authority over Louisiana and the Floridas, was preparing to embark for Mexico for installation as viceroy of New Spain. Knowing of O'Neill's close ties with Gálvez, Panton wasted little time in writing the West Florida governor of his concern over Miró's arrangements with Mather. In addition to soliciting O'Neill's assistance in advancing his firm's cause, Panton expressed particular interest in discovering whether the Mather concern would be awarded exclusive trading privileges. He also intimated that he had never intended to compete for the Indian trade with naturalized Spanish subjects—certainly not any who enjoyed official support. On the other hand, he expressed bemusement over the proposition of entrusting a matter of such vital concern to persons inexperienced in dealing with Indians. Unless O'Neill could aid in securing for Panton, Leslie and Company terms at least equal to those extended to its competitors, the merchant stated, he wished only permission to dispose of goods on hand before retiring from Pensacola. In the interim, Panton promised his assistance to Mather and Strother in establishing the trade properly.[48]

Panton erred in his estimate of O'Neill's favor. Later, O'Neill displayed an almost pathological distrust of the British. While in Havana he apparently persuaded Don Bernardo to place St. Marks within the jurisdiction of West Florida and to regarrison the abandoned fort. Unwatched British traders in close contact with Indians in such a strategic area made O'Neill uneasy. He returned to Pensacola in June with little information of interest to Panton except that Navarro, as Louisiana intendant, had been given

47. O'Neill to McLatchy, January 24, 1785; Panton to T. Forbes, March 26, 1785, Chatham Papers, 30/8/344, Part 1, PROL.
48. Panton to O'Neill, April 15, 1785, EF leg. 116L9.

discretionary authority to maintain the Indian trade until an official decision was reached about permanent arrangements.[49]

McGillivray journeyed to Pensacola in May to assist in opening the trade. Panton quickly demanded an accounting of his erstwhile partner's dealings with Miró and Mather. McGillivray explained that he had hesitated to reject Mather's offer outright; such a course might have adversely affected the trade discussions. Miró might have disapproved the use of English goods. After all, McGillivray pointed out, the exertions of Miró and Navarro to get the southern Indian trade established quickly, if approved by higher authority, set favorable precedents. Panton, unable to find fault with McGillivray's explanations, agreed to follow along with his plans a while longer.

Panton and McGillivray each speculated on their chances of winning out against Mather and Strother, but their speculations were based on a faulty assumption: they took no account of the fact that West Florida had been made a political appendage of Louisiana. Neither Panton nor McGillivray seemed aware in May 1785 that Miró and Navarro had been given complete authority over southern Indian affairs. The two partners therefore assumed that if the company won the Creek and Chickasaw trade, it would eventually gain that of the Choctaw and Cherokee as well. They counted on the support of O'Neill and Zéspedes—whom they considered resentful of Miró's interference in their respective provinces—in getting Panton, Leslie and Company confirmed in the Creek and Chickasaw trade. Should this materialize, Panton and McGillivray hoped Mather might withdraw from the business. They also took consolation in the knowledge that Mather's trade goods had not yet arrived. In the event of a protracted delay, Panton could make solid ties with the Choctaw and Chickasaw traders. Mather, whom these traders supposedly held in low esteem, would then find the task of supplanting Panton extremely difficult.[50]

Throughout the summer of 1785, McGillivray importuned Spanish officials on behalf of Panton, Leslie and Company. The Creek, Chickasaw, and Cherokee, he reported to O'Neill, were "exceedingly well Satisfied" with Panton's arrival in Pensacola and expected "the Trade thus begun" would "be established on the most permanent footing," as promised at the congresses of 1784. Panton, McGillivray added, not only possessed the experience and means for furnishing "Goods equal to the Demand of

49. O'Neill to Conde de Gálvez, Janaury 9, 1785, *AGI PC*, leg. 37, WP; Conde de Gálvez to Miró, May 6, 1785, *AGI PC*, leg. 11.
50. Panton to T. Forbes, May 21, 1785, *EF* leg. 116L9; McGillivray to J. Leslie, May 22, 1785, *AHN Estado*, leg. 3901, Exp. 5.

the Indians" but also was well disposed to advance the Spanish viewpoint. McGillivray added that he had requested the British merchant to present O'Neill with the terms on which he could "continue to Import Goods for the Support of the Indian Nations in Alliance with his Majesty the King of Spain."[51] To Zéspedes, McGillivray wrote that Panton's arrival had been attended with "the very best effects to his Majestys Interest," whose "goodness," it was hoped, would "secure to us a permanency of trade & Support through the channel it has Commenced in." In his capacity as Spanish Indian superintendent, McGillivray reminded Zéspedes of the expediency of allowing the frequent replenishment of the Panton, Leslie stores at St. Marks and on the St. Johns. Since the company was, he said, "Strictly Speaking . . . a political affair," any extra indulgences afforded to it could only be regarded as in the King's best interest.[52]

The *Condesa de Gálvez* reached New Orleans in June 1785, with a cargo of Indian trade goods valued at 40,000 pesos, all that Mather's credit had been able to obtain. In casting aspersions on Mather's performance, McGillivray complained that the vessel should have arrived eight months earlier and expressed his relief that the Indians, in their dire want, had not been dependent solely on Mather. Despite their reluctance, the Creek would have been forced to sacrifice considerable territory and to acquiesce in other American demands had it not been for the goods supplied by Panton and Leslie.[53]

With Zéspedes, McGillivray's advice produced the intended results. In June, the complaisant East Florida governor issued a passport to Panton, Leslie and Company for the importation of salt and other supplies to St. Marks and, if necessary, Pensacola. Zéspedes granted the passport, even though some weeks earlier he had received official notification of the transfer of St. Marks to West Florida. Indeed, he also issued a safe conduct pass for McLatchy and other company dependents to remain at St. Marks as a preventive measure against any orders for their ouster emanating from New Orleans. Zéspedes then explained to his superiors that his action on behalf of McLatchy had been taken *before* he received news of the transfer, and that, moreover, he was reluctant to countermand it in light of the American threat. The East Florida governor justified his breach of protocol in authorizing the resupply of St. Marks and Pensacola

---

51. McGillivray to O'Neill, July 24, 1785, *AGI PC*, leg. 198; Caughey, *McGillivray*, 93–94.

52. McGillivray to Zéspedes, May 22, 1785, *EF* leg. 114J9; Caughey, *McGillivray*, 87–90.

53. Navarro to José de Gálvez, June 22, 1785, *AHN Estado*, leg. 3901, Exp. 4; McGillivray to J. Leslie, August 22, 1785; McGillivray to Zéspedes, August 22, 1785, ibid., Exp. 5; Lockey, *East Florida*, 682–85.

on the grounds of McGillivray's advice, Mather's inadequacies, Miró's initiatives in establishing the Indian trade through unorthodox channels, and the higher necessity of keeping the Indians attached to Spain.[54] Despite his surprise over Zéspedes' impropriety, Navarro later acquiesced in the fait accompli.[55]

In June and July, Panton forwarded to O'Neill and Navarro the conditions his company sought for continuing in the Indian trade, together with requests for passports to replenish his rapidly diminishing inventory. The Scottish merchant requested immediate permission to bring in $35,000 worth of Indian trade goods from Nassau and St. Augustine to meet autumn requirements, and passports to import an additional $120,000 worth of merchandise for the 1786 trading season. He requested approval to bring the supplies for 1786 to Pensacola on two small vessels as a safeguard against the loss of the entire consignment through some mishap. Panton promised to pay 6 per cent ad valorem duties on all imports and to adhere to the price schedule as stipulated in the "tariff" of 1784. He also asked for the privilege of exporting the peltry and other produce acquired through the Indian trade, even to France or Spain, if necessary. The Spaniards, Panton advised, must permit the ships delivering the goods to depart from Pensacola promptly, to avoid spoilage of the peltry. The ships should also be permitted to return in ballast the following winter to transport to market all skins and other effects received in payment for the cargoes. Panton asked that no other duties be levied except the 6 per cent on imports. Stating that his company's proposals had been submitted candidly and straightforwardly, Panton proclaimed his willingness to abide by any Spanish decision. He was prepared "to remove or to remain" as directed.[56]

The responses to Panton's requests, reaching Pensacola from New Orleans, however, were both tardy and vague. In August, McGillivray, having developed misgivings as to the ardor of Governor O'Neill's support, advised Panton to travel to the Louisiana capital and present his views in person.[57] The Scot agreed, and upon reaching New Orleans, he persuaded Miró to intercede with Navarro concerning the company's requests. The

---

54. Zéspedes to J. de Gálvez, June 20, 1785, *AHN Estado*, leg. 3901, Exp. 5; Lockey, *East Florida*, 562–64; Zéspedes to Carlos Howard, June 14, 1785, *AGI PC*, leg. 40; safe conduct for Charles McLatchy, June 2, 1785, *AHN Estado*, leg. 3901, Exp. 5; Zéspedes to O'Neill, June 15, 1785, *EF* leg. 114J9; *AGI PC*, leg. 40.

55. O'Neill to Zéspedes, September 30, 1785, *EF* leg. 114J9; Lockey, *East Florida*, 726; Zéspedes to O'Neill, January 7, 1786, *AGI PC*, leg. 40.

56. Panton to O'Neill, July 30, 1785, *AGI PC*, leg. 613B; quote taken from Panton to Miró, June 27, 1785, *ANC F*, leg. 1, Exp. 5, no. 1, WP; Corbitt, "Papers . . . Georgia-Florida Frontier," 20:361.

57. McGillivray to J. Leslie, December 10, 1785, *EF* leg. 114J9; Lockey, *East Florida*, 743–44. In August, McGillivray had written Leslie, "Governor O'Neill supports us with all

Louisiana governor based his intercession on McGillivray's alarming descriptions of American machinations to absorb the Indian trade. Out of interest for the security of the provinces, Miró declared, "we should not neglect so favorable an opportunity." Panton, he suggested, should be permitted to import up to 150,000 pesos worth of Indian trade goods at duty levels no greater than those imposed on Mather.[58]

Panton returned to Pensacola in late September 1785 quite pleased with the outcome of his visit to New Orleans. Navarro had licensed him to import into Pensacola from any neutral or friendly port merchandise valued at 125,000 pesos for the 1786 Indian trade. Panton also received permission to export peltry but—along with imports—it was subject to 6 per cent duties. His success undoubtedly stemmed from the fact that Mather and his associates could not adequately provide for the Indian trade at both Pensacola and Mobile. In all likelihood, Panton also offered Miró and Navarro a one-fourth share in the company profits. There is little doubt that the governor, and perhaps the intendant, shared in the profits of Mather's firm too.[59]

Thus, Panton operated out of Pensacola and St. Marks, while Mather and Strother conducted their Indian commerce through Mobile. In West Florida, the trading privileges of Panton and Mather for some time thereafter were extended year-to-year by Miró and Navarro on the basis of the royal directives of October 10, 1785, and May 30, 1786. These gave the governor and intendant discretionary authority to license the importation from any friendly or neutral port of two or more cargoes of goods yearly for the southern Indians.[60] In East Florida, however, a royal decree of

---

his influence and we are much obliged to him": McGillivray to J. Leslie, August 22, 1785, *AHN Estado*, leg. 3901, Exp. 5; Lockey, *East Florida*, 684–85.

58. McLatchy to J. Leslie, December 10, 1785, *EF* leg. 114J9; Lockey, *East Florida*, 742–43; Miró to Navarro, September 16, 1785, *ANC F*, leg. 9, Exp. 1, WP; Corbitt, "Papers . . . Georgia-Florida Frontier," 21:76–77.

59. Navarro permit to Panton, September 16, 1785, *AGI SD*, leg. 2670; Corbitt, "Papers . . . Georgia-Florida Frontier," 21:77. There is no direct evidence from Panton's trip to New Orleans that he offered Miró and Navarro a share of the profits. However, in 1788, when McGillivray formally resigned his interest in the company, he wrote to Panton, "I observe with much satisfaction that the Governor & Intendant of New Orleans have relinquished their claim of one fourth of the profits of your trade": McGillivray to Panton, September 20, 1788, exhibit in *Johnson et al. v. Innerarity et al.* In 1806, James Innerarity stated explicitly that the governor and intendant of New Orleans had been secret partners in the company: Innerarity to John Forbes, November 22, 1806, exhibit in *Johnson & Edwards v. the Inneraritys & Alexander Gordon*. Inferences of Miró's interest in the Mather firm are in Caughey, *McGillivray*, 25, 82–83; McGillivray to McLatchy, October 4, 1784, *EF* leg. 116L9. See also Pitot, *Observations*, 81. There is a secret cipher, called the "Pontalba-Miró Cipher," in the Forbes Papers. The implication is that the cipher was used by Miró, Panton, and Forbes.

60. Marqués de Sonora to Governor of Louisiana, October 10, 1785, May 30, 1786, *AHN Estado*, leg. 3901, Exp. 3; J. de Gálvez to Conde de Gálvez, May 30, 1786, ibid., leg. 3898; Miró passport for Panton, January 23, 1787, *EF* leg. 114J9.

May 8, 1786, temporarily conferred on Panton, Leslie and Company the privileges requested in its memorial of August 1784.[61]

In St. Augustine, John Leslie encountered no major official obstacle in managing the company's Indian affairs. Because the volume of the East Florida Indian trade remained relatively low, Nassau and Charleston ordinarily served as entrepôts for the company's operations. In the summer of 1785, Thomas Forbes requested and received approval from the Privy Council for the company to trade between New Providence Island and the Spanish Floridas.[62] Thereafter, he skillfully directed the company's affairs in Nassau. Still, despite Miró's and Navarro's share of the profits, William Panton, as overseer of the company's West Florida interests, experienced considerable difficulty before gaining final Spanish approval for the status the firm desired in the southern Indian trade.

61. Sonora to Zéspedes, May 8, 1786, *AGI SD*, leg. 2670; Sonora to Conde de Gálvez, May 8, 1786, *AHN Estado*, leg. 3898.

62. T. Forbes, petition to Privy Council, July 15, 1785, PC 2/130: 315–16. See also minutes of the Board of Trade, July 19, 26, 1785; Extracts of Correspondence of Mr. Forbes, July 26, 1785, Chatham Papers, 30/8/344, PROL.

4
Keeping the United States at Bay, 1785–1787

AFTER the moderate success of their initial dealings with the Spaniards, Panton and McGillivray continued working toward their ultimate goal: winning Spanish approval for an expanded Panton, Leslie and Company monopoly over the southern Indian trade. Their endeavors toward this objective, however, were prompted to some extent by considerations over and above purely pecuniary interests. Both men harbored animosities against Americans, and particularly Georgians, for their past sufferings and losses. McGillivray was motivated by considerably more than a tinge of Creek patriotism, as his actions in directing the affairs of the Creek indicate. His influence in channeling the Creek trade exclusively through Panton, Leslie and Company, insofar as it enabled the Creek to remain aloof from Anglo-American influence, afforded the best available means for preserving their lands from Anglo-American encroachment.

What is perhaps less obvious at first glance is that the Creek also had a vital interest in preventing the development of intercourse between the Choctaw and the Chickasaw, who were their neighbors to the west, and the Americans. McGillivray clearly perceived that any American foothold that might be gained in that quarter threatened the Creek with eventual encirclement. Insofar as Creek aggression forestalled American commercial penetration into the southern Indian domains, it constituted a fur traders' war that advanced the interests of Panton, Leslie and Company.

Chapter 4

To Panton and McGillivray, it seemed obvious that to deny the Anglo-Americans access to the Old Southwest, forcibly or otherwise, was also in the Spanish interest. But Spanish officials seemed uncomfortable about leaving the fate of that area to agents whose ultimate loyalties were to Great Britain, whatever their frequently expedient usefulness. Indeed, Panton, McGillivray, and the Creek at times were regarded as dangerous to the security of Louisiana and the Floridas rather than useful pawns in Spanish *política realista*. This basic suspicion about true commonality of interest among Spaniard, Indian, and Scottish merchant continually impeded Panton and McGillivray in pursuing their political and commercial objectives.

Of the three southernmost states claiming western lands as far as the Mississippi, only North Carolina and Georgia made serious efforts to capitalize on their territorial pretensions.[1] Two settlements lay within the trans-Allegheny claims of North Carolina: Cumberland, on the Cumberland River in the vicinity of present-day Nashville, and the stillborn state of Franklin, stretching to the southwest down the valleys that form the headwaters of the Tennessee River. Whereas only about 4,000 hardy settlers had taken up homes in the isolated Cumberland district, the Franklinites numbered about 10,000.

In May 1783, under the aegis of William Blount, that unparalleled political manipulator and land jobber, the North Carolina legislature opened the state's western claim to public sale, reserving only a relatively small tract in present-day southeastern Tennessee for the Cherokee. In the ensuing "great land grab," Blount and other politically influential speculators filed claims to nearly four million acres of choice lands. They then secured passage of an act in June 1784 that ceded North Carolina's transmontane lands to the Congress of the Confederation. The speculators reasoned that Congress would have "the burden of protecting and developing the lands while those who had derived claims from North Carolina could, at the same time, be protected in their rights by the terms of the grant."[2] This legislative measure, though rescinded in November of that year, sparked the separatist movement of the Franklinites. Under the leadership of the inveterate Indian fighter and ardent expansionist John Sevier, the separatists lived in a state of turbulent political dualism until late 1788, when North Carolina regained undisputed control of the west.[3]

---

1. For accounts of Anglo-American involvement in the Old Southwest in the aftermath of the American Revolution, see Whitaker, *Spanish-American Frontier*; Abernethy, *Frontier to Plantation*; and Coleman, *American Revolution*.
2. Abernethy, *Frontier to Plantation*, 49–56.
3. Ibid., 57–90; Williams, *Lost State of Franklin*, 19–291 passim.

Significantly, Sevier's status as a "rebel" previously had interfered little in his connections with Blount and others in attempting to colonize the commercially strategic Muscle Shoals district on the Great Bend of the Tennessee—a project of sufficient interest to Blount that he persuaded the Georgia legislature to create Houston County as a sign of its political substance. Though Sevier kept alive the elusive Muscle Shoals colonization project throughout his tenure as governor of Franklin, it never matured.[4]

To the west, James Robertson, foremost among the founders of the Cumberland settlements, dreamed of establishing a settlement on the equally desirable Chickasaw Bluffs, whose heights dominated the east bank of the Mississippi on the present-day northern outskirts of Memphis. This, too, remained an unattainable object for the duration of the Spanish-American struggle for the control of the Old Southwest.[5]

The vast western claims of Georgia dwarfed those of North Carolina, and the mania for building private empires there equaled, and perhaps surpassed, that prevailing in North Carolina, Franklin, and Cumberland. Colonel Elijah Clarke, Georgia patriot, backwoods political leader, Indian trader, and expansionist, advised Sevier to "open a Land Office as speedily as possible" as a certain means of assuring the prosperity of Franklin.[6] On the other hand, Georgians faced far greater impediments to westward expansion than did frontiersmen to their immediate north. Georgia claimed lands also claimed by Spain. Of more importance, the Georgia backcountry impinged on Creek hunting grounds, whereas the North Carolina and Franklin expansionists contended mostly with the tractable Chickasaw and the dispirited Cherokee. Only the Chickamauga made a serious attempt to resist encroachment at the end of the American Revolution.

As early as May 1783, McGillivray, acting as principal war chief, placed the Creek on a war footing in anticipation of Georgia's demands for lands.[7] The ink on the Spanish-Creek Treaty of Pensacola, signed June 1, 1784, had scarcely dried before McGillivray took steps to undo the Treaty of Augusta (November 1, 1783), in which the Tame King of Tallassee and the Fat King of Cussitah, vexed at McGillivray's ascendancy in Creek councils at their expense, had ceded to Georgia the lands lying between the Ogee-

---

4. Whitaker, "Muscle Shoals," 367–77. This was considered necessary when the original six-man consortium behind the Muscle Shoals project discovered that their chosen site lay below the southern boundary of the North Carolina claim.
5. Whitaker, *Spanish-American Frontier*, 54.
6. Williams, *Lost State of Franklin*, 178.
7. Cotterill, *Southern Indians*, 61.

chee and Oconee rivers.⁸ A "talk" dispatched in June 1784 warned Georgians against trespassing on the Oconee lands. If the admonition went ignored, McGillivray advised, restraining Creek braves from acts of violence would become impossible. He also announced a December 1784 deadline for all traders supplied through Colonel Elijah Clarke's post on the Ogeechee to settle their affairs and leave the Creek country.⁹

With unexpected diplomacy, Georgian leaders initially responded to McGillivray's stern warning in a conciliatory manner. Governor John Houstoun advised the Creek spokesman that the Georgia Assembly had issued strong injunctions against settling on the disputed lands. Clarke intimated that a movement was under way among McGillivray's friends to restore the family holdings confiscated during the war. For a while, McGillivray mistakenly believed that the likelihood of war with the Georgians had subsided appreciably.¹⁰

Early in 1785, however, the Georgians dispelled whatever lingering notions McGillivray might have had about their intention of respecting his version of the Georgia-Creek boundary. A legislative act of February 1785 approved measures for setting the state's limits as established in the Treaty of Augusta. The following month Governor Samuel Elbert (for whose Savannah mercantile firm McGillivray had briefly worked as a clerk in the prerevolutionary years) blithely ignored his former employee's warnings and summoned Creek representatives to assist in running the boundary. McGillivray responded to Elbert's summons by unleashing Creek war parties against backwoods intruders on the Oconee lands, seven of whom lost their lives in the ensuing raids.¹¹

Shortly afterward, Mad Dog, war chief of Tuckabatchee and a trusted follower of McGillivray, traveled to Pensacola and reported the Creek forays to Governor O'Neill. The Indian reminded O'Neill of the Spanish promises to protect the Creek and solicited a gift of ammunition with which to withstand the anticipated retaliatory measures of Georgia. O'Neill complied, donating 400 pounds of powder and 800 pounds of rifle balls to enable the Creek to "defend themselves from the Bears and other fierce Animals."¹² Miró and Gálvez approved giving the Indians ammunition

---

8. Ibid., 57–63; Downes, "Creek-American Relations," 144–46.

9. Downes, "Creek-American Relations," 145–46; McGillivray to McLatchy, October 4, 1784, EF leg. 116L9; Caughey, *McGillivray*, 82–83.

10. McGillivray to O'Neill, November 20, 1784, AGI PC, leg. 197; Corbitt, "Papers from the Spanish Archives," 9:120–21; McGillivray to McLatchy, December 25, 1784, EF leg. 116L9; Caughey, *McGillivray*, 84–87.

11. Downes, "Creek-American Relations," 146–53. According to information given O'Neill, ten Americans and two Indians were killed. See note 12.

12. O'Neill to Conde de Gálvez, May 30, 1786, in Corbitt, "Papers from the Spanish Archives," 10:139–40.

with which to defend themselves, although Gálvez insisted that it be done with the "greatest secrecy."[13] Spain had adopted a policy of using Creek truculence to complement the efforts of Diego de Gardoqui, Spanish chargé d'affaires, who at this juncture arrived in New York on a diplomatic mission to settle Spain's outstanding disputes with the United States.

Shortly before Gardoqui's arrival, the Georgia Assembly had demonstrated its readiness to dispose of lands which were effectively under Spanish control as if they were merely Indian hunting grounds. Responding to the petition of Thomas Green, a disgruntled inhabitant of the Natchez District, the Georgia Assembly on February 7, 1785, organized Bourbon County. Its boundaries stretched from the mouth of the Yazoo River down the middle of the Mississippi to the thirty-first parallel, incorporating all lands relinquished by the Indians to the east (a distance of about sixty miles), thence northward to the Yazoo River, and from that point downriver to its mouth. Bourbon County was coterminous with the 1765 Choctaw cession to the British which the Choctaw later (1801) confirmed to the United States. Much of this area was occupied by former loyalists and had been governed by Spain since 1779. The act of organization designated thirteen justices of the peace to establish the county's government, four of whom were present in Georgia to receive their commissions and instructions—Green, William Davenport, Nicholas Long, and Nathaniel Christmas.

The Bourbon County episode quickly deteriorated into a fiasco. Green, the first of the justices to arrive in Natchez, blatantly ignored his instructions against the use of threats or force if Spanish objections were encountered. Instead, he demanded the surrender of the Spanish garrison and spread rumors of the imminent arrival of American invaders commanded by George Rogers Clarke. Green's actions caused a furor among the settlers, few of whom relished the idea of Georgia citizenship. Yet Governor Miró temporized in dealing with the Georgia commissioners, feeling out their support and waiting for instructions from the Conde de Gálvez. The Louisiana governor eventually ordered the justices expelled, and Gardoqui lodged strong protests with the U.S. Congress, which peremptorily disavowed support for the Bourbon County scheme.[14]

Before their departure from Natchez, Long, Christmas, and Davenport reported on the disposition of the southern Indians. Of all the In-

13. Conde de Gálvez to Miró, May 20, 1786, in Corbitt, "Papers from the Spanish Archives," 10:136–37; Conde de Gálvez to Floridablanca, August 30, 1786, *AHN Estado*, leg. 3886, Exp. 14.
14. Whitaker, *Spanish-American Frontier*, 55–58; Burnett, "Papers," 297–353, contains many of the documents regarding this affair. For a map of Bourbon County, see Jackson and Adams, *Atlas of American History*, 106.

dians whom the commissioners had observed, the Creek were found to be the most unfriendly to the Americans and the Chickasaw the most favorably disposed. The latter had been drawn to the Spanish, to whom they were habitual enemies, because, they said, the Americans had apparently forgotten them. The agents also discovered many Choctaw factions desiring trade and friendship with Georgia, particularly within the Large Party (Lower Towns) under the influence of Franchimastabe.[15] The signs of discontent among the Choctaw and Chickasaw were sufficiently encouraging for Davenport to remain in their midst as Georgia's agent.

The assessments of the commissioners were essentially accurate. Franchimastabe, aside from his proclivities as master extortionist of gifts, held a genuine fondness for Britons and a corresponding dislike for Spaniards. As late as 1783, he was spurning Spanish overtures for a treaty, opting instead for an arrangement with Georgia. The Georgians replied with alacrity, promising to supply the Choctaw, should they arrange safe passage for Georgia traders through the Creek nation—which was an impossibility.[16] Even more steadfast in his strong preference for American friendship was the Chickasaw war chief Piomingo, through whose influence the Chickasaw had dispatched emissaries in 1782 to extend peace feelers to the "Virginians," as they labeled all Americans. Virginia responded by authorizing Joseph Martin and John Donelson to negotiate with the Chickasaw, and the Virginia agents concluded a treaty of friendship in 1783 at French Lick (Nashville). Although the treaty settled the Chickasaw-Virginia boundary, it did nothing about trade.[17]

In early 1785, Piomingo consulted frequently with Sevier in Franklin, seeking out sorely needed trade contacts which, until then, neither the Spaniards nor the Americans had been able to supply. A desire to enjoy Spanish largesse in the form of gifts and rations, and a lack of alternatives, had motivated many Choctaw and Chickasaw to treat with the Spaniards in 1784 at Mobile.[18] Contrary to the Creek, as intermittent enemies whose hunting grounds were in imminent danger of American expropriation, many Choctaw and Chickasaw were less than ardent in their feelings about Spanish protection.

McGillivray, buoyed in spirit by Panton's timely arrival in Pensacola in April 1785 with sorely needed trade goods, responded to the Bourbon County threat with vigor. The Creek leader was among the first to alert Miró to the Georgia scheme.[19] In July, McGillivray orchestrated a general

15. N. Long, Jr., W. Davenport, and Nat Christmas to Governor Elbert, September 13, 1785, in Burnett, "Papers," 335–37.
16. Cotterill, *Southern Indians*, 60.
17. Ibid., 59–60; Cotterill, "Virginia-Chickasaw Treaty," 494–95.
18. Williams, *Lost State of Franklin*, 264–65; Cotterill, *Southern Indians*, 60–61.
19. Whitaker, *Spanish-American Frontier*, 60–61.

council, in which his friends among the Chickasaw and Cherokee joined with the Creek to adopt measures to counter the endemic expansionist tendencies of the Americans. The deliberations of the council produced a memorial to the Spanish crown, denying the validity of the British cession of Indian lands to the United States, calling attention to the recent outbreak of American encroachments, and petitioning His Catholic Majesty to refrain from entering into any boundary agreement with the United States which might be prejudicial to the hunting grounds of the Indians. The Spanish ministers attached great importance to the July memorial, sending it to Gardoqui for use as diplomatic grist in grinding out a favorable boundary settlement.[20]

In March, since some of its membership was perhaps as disquieted as McGillivray and the Spaniards over the turbulent developments along the southern frontier, Congress appointed commissioners to conclude peace treaties with the southern tribes. The following May, three of the commissioners—Joseph Martin, an experienced Cherokee agent; Benjamin Hawkins, destined for a long career in the Indian service; and General Andrew Pickens, Indian fighter and negotiator—met in Charleston to settle details of the treaty talks. They decided to negotiate first with the Creek, inviting them to meet on October 24 at Galphinton.[21] McGillivray at first hailed the peace overtures as long overdue, promised to attend, and expressed confidence that all differences would be settled with "liberality and Justice."[22]

The Georgians, however, in a display of the particularism generally prevalent in those times, shared none of McGillivray's initial enthusiasm for congressional interference in their state's management of its own Indian affairs. Accordingly, Governor Elbert did his utmost to frustrate the proposed treaty talks. He declined to appropriate Georgia's share of the expenses and appointed state commissioners to see that the congressional peacemakers did not interfere in any way with Georgia's prerogatives in regulating the affairs of Indians residing within the state. He also notified the Creek that Georgia intended to use the Galphinton conclave as an occasion for making arrangements to mark the controversial Oconee boundary line.[23]

Governor O'Neill, always suspicious that McGillivray's ultimate loyalties lay with Panton, and with trade, rather than with Spain, urged McGillivray not to negotiate with the Americans. The Creek leader, fore-

20. McGillivray memorial of July 10, 1785, *AGI PC*, leg. 37; Caughey, *McGillivray*, 90–93.
21. Cotterill, *Southern Indians*, 65.
22. Downes, "Creek-American Relations," 150–51.
23. Ibid., 149–50.

warned of Georgia's intentions, readily accepted O'Neill's advice, craftily informing the Spanish commandant that the Creek expected Spanish support in the event that a refusal to negotiate led to war. McGillivray then sent four trusted chieftains to Galphinton with instructions to denounce the Treaty of Augusta and to insist on adherence to the boundaries established in the British-Creek treaty of 1773.[24]

Very few Creek journeyed to Galphinton for the October conference. The congressional commissioners, chagrined at the absence of McGillivray, or any representative group of Creek leadership, and intimidated by the invective of the querulous Georgians, refused to negotiate and departed for the Pickens estate at Hopewell, near Seneca, South Carolina, for talks with the other southern tribes.[25] The Georgia agents then concluded a treaty with the anti-McGillivray Fat King and Tame King which not only reaffirmed the cession of the Oconee lands but also ceded to Georgia additional Creek lands lying between the Altamaha and St. Marys rivers.[26]

McGillivray reacted vehemently to the Treaty of Galphinton. Again repudiating the actions of his dissident Creek opponents, he convened a council of war at the Upper Creek town of Tuckabatchee to deliberate on stronger forms of protest. The Creek spokesman assured his assembled followers that they enjoyed Spanish protection and therefore could expect material support in opposing Georgian rapacity. On April 2, 1786, the council determined to wage general war against all American intruders.[27]

Creek war parties first struck at the Oconee settlements, plundering, razing buildings, destroying crops, and breaking up two Indian trading posts. Other Creek braves who were dispatched against the embryonic U.S. settlement at Muscle Shoals arrived too late; the Chickamauga had laid waste to the site several months earlier. The Creek and Chickamauga then joined forces and launched a series of fierce attacks against the Cumberland settlements.[28]

McGillivray was aware that the Treaty of Pensacola guaranteed Creek territorial integrity only insofar as their lands lay within Spanish dominions—the boundaries of which were yet to be determined. Guilefully, he therefore reported the hostilities to the Spanish authorities after the fact. Writing to Miró in May, McGillivray informed him of the measures un-

24. Ibid., 151; McGillivray to O'Neill, October 10, 1785, *AGI PC*, leg. 198; Caughey, *McGillivray*, 98n46, 106–10; McGillivray to Miró, May 1, 1786, *AGI PC*, leg. 3887.
25. Downes, "Creek-American Relations," 151; Cotterill, *Southern Indians*, 65–66.
26. Downes, "Creek-American Relations," 151–52.
27. Ibid., 152–53; McGillivray to Miró, May 1, 1786, *AGI PC*, leg. 3887; Caughey, *McGillivray*, 106–10.
28. Caughey, *McGillivray*, 106–10; Cotterill, *Southern Indians*, 70.

dertaken by the Creek in defense of their lands, assuring him that the war parties had been strictly enjoined to avoid needless bloodshed in repelling the American intruders. The Creek leader, observing that "the revengefull disposition of the Americans" might lead them to misconstrue their purely defensive measures as a declaration of war, asked for munitions for repelling American retaliation.[29]

Fortunately for McGillivray, the Conde de Gálvez had already determined to employ Spain's "new friends" to chastise the Americans into assuming a more reasonable posture in their territorial pretensions. He instructed Miró to supply the Creek with armaments in quantities adequate for their defense against American encroachment. Gálvez, however, took precautions to impress his subordinate with the need for strict secrecy in effecting their delivery; should Spanish involvement become known, a direct confrontation with the Americans might result.[30] Miró, in compliance with his superior's orders, invited McGillivray to New Orleans, where the two reached an agreement on the delivery through Pensacola of 5,000 pounds of powder and twice that weight in balls to the Creek.[31] The Creek leader obtained similar support from East Florida. Zéspedes donated a significant quantity of ammunition to the Creek from royal stores in St. Augustine.[32]

In the meantime, O'Neill won Panton's consent to cooperate in a clandestine plan for arming the Creek by channeling Spanish munitions through his Pensacola store. Under the arrangement, small bands of Indians called at the Panton establishment at carefully staggered intervals, presented requisitions for ammunition signed by McGillivray, drew their allotments, and returned home.[33] Panton was quite willing to participate in the Spanish subterfuge, since it seemed to be in his interest to forestall the diminution of Indian hunting grounds. Besides, he bore an enduring hatred for Georgians. But of greater importance was the fact that the Creek war had eliminated trade competition. Panton later alleged that his

---

29. McGillivray to Miró, May 1, 1786, *AGI PC*, leg. 3887; Caughey, *McGillivray*, 106–10.

30. Miró to O'Neill, June 20, 1786, *AHN Estado*, leg. 3887, Exp. 1; Conde de Gálvez to Miró, May 20, 1786; Conde de Gálvez to Floridablanca, August 30, 1786, *AHN Estado*, leg. 3886, Exp. 14.

31. Miró to O'Neill, June 20, 1786, *AGI PC*, leg. 37; Caughey, *McGillivray*, 30–31, 117–18.

32. McGillivray to Zéspedes, August 3, 1786; Zéspedes to McGillivray, May 22, 1786; Zéspedes to Sonora, May 25, 1786, *AHN Estado*, leg. 3887, Exp. 1.

33. O'Neill to Miró, October 11, 1786, *AGI PC*, leg. 2353, West work cards (West work cards are notes prepared by Elizabeth Howard West from the documents and are on file in the P. K. Yonge Library of Florida History, Gainesville); O'Neill to Conde de Gálvez, October 11, 1786, Corbitt, "Papers from the Spanish Archives," 10:149–50.

company had lost more than $30,000 in 1784 and 1785 out of the need to undersell its Georgia competitors.[34]

The Georgia Assembly responded to the Creek attacks by selecting Daniel McMurphy, probably on Elijah Clarke's recommendation, as its agent for the incredible mission of restoring order among the Creek. McMurphy arrived in the Creek country before McGillivray returned from New Orleans, but he failed to gain an audience before a general council. On the other hand, he discovered through McGillivray's enemies the Creek leader's newly found access to Spanish arsenals. Writing a formal protest to O'Neill, McMurphy boldly assumed the position that Georgia's right to control the Creek nation was beyond question and feigned disbelief that Spain would actively foment Creek aggression. The Georgian instead chose to blame Creek discord on "persons who were dissatisfied that they Could not get their Ends when the British were at War with the Americans." McMurphy also expressed astonishment at discovering that the Creek traders possessed not Georgia licenses but instead licenses issued by McGillivray who, in collusion with Panton, had ordered them to default on their debts to Georgia suppliers and carry peltry only to Pensacola and St. Marks. He reported that the Creek desired peace and trade "with all who Chuse to Come to their Land." In closing, he hinted that further Indian cruelties could be stopped by bringing the mischiefmakers "under the proper Subordination."[35]

The McMurphy protest produced what became a standard Spanish response to all subsequent accusations against Spanish arming of the Creek. Spanish officials insisted that only token amounts of ammunition were given Creek headmen in the form of presents. Most munitions flowing into Creek towns, they alleged, were acquired through trade sanctioned by formal treaty provisions, and, regrettably, their ultimate use was beyond Spanish control. Spanish denials accomplished nothing more than to arouse great speculation in the Georgia backcountry on whether the Spaniards and the British had combined in a secret anti-American alliance. The collusion hypothesis was made plausible by the toleration that Panton, Leslie and Company enjoyed in the Floridas.[36]

With the failure of the McMurphy mission, the Georgians devised

34. Panton memorial to Campo, April 2, 1788, *AHN Estado*, leg. 3901, Exp. 3, WP.
35. McMurphy to O'Neill, July 11, 1786, *AGI PC*, leg. 37; McGillivray to O'Neill, August 12, 1786, *AGI PC*, leg. 199; Caughey, *McGillivray*, 21, 118–21, 127–28; O'Neill to B. de Gálvez, October 11, 1786, Corbitt, "Papers from the Spanish Archives," 10:149–50; Cotterill, *Southern Indians*, 71–72.
36. Enrique Roche to McMurphy, July 23, 1786, Corbitt, "Papers from the Spanish Archives," 10:146; Zéspedes to Josef de Ezpeleta, November 9, 1787, *AGI PC*, leg. 1395, Pac. 11, doc. 8, Lockey Papers; Zéspedes to George Mathews, December 18, 1787, *EF* leg. 108D9.

elaborate plans for bringing the Creek into submission. The state assembly created still another treaty commission and gave its members discretionary authority either to secure a treaty to which the Creek nation would adhere or, failing this, to precipitate war. In preparing for the latter possibility, Governor Edward Telfair alerted militia units and requisitioned supplies for a sustained campaign. He also invited the state of Franklin to join in the anticipated hostilities, offering to compensate the services of Sevier and his followers with lands at Muscle Shoals. Sevier accepted Telfair's offer and promised to be ready to march in December. The Georgia governor also attempted to recruit Choctaw and Chickasaw warriors, commissioning Benjamin James, a pro-Georgian trader who exerted great influence over Franchimastabe, for this task. As Georgia's commissary, William Davenport, who had worked closely with James after the failure of the Bourbon County scheme, was instructed to deliver the necessary munitions to James's Indian recruits.[37]

With these preparations under way, the Georgia commissioners invited McGillivray to Shoulderbone Creek on the Oconee on October 15 "to remove all causes of discontent."[38] To underscore the importance Georgia placed on obtaining satisfactory results from the meeting, the commissioners' message declared that their state was prepared for peace or war. McGillivray declined the invitation but first prudently granted a truce to the Cumberland settlements until April 1787 to remove the danger of an attack on the Creek from that quarter.[39]

The Georgia commissioners nevertheless proceeded to Shoulderbone Creek under a militia escort of 1,500 men. There they were joined by a small contingent of Lower Creek and a few Upper Creek, led by the Fat King and the Tame King, respectively. On November 3, 1786, the Georgians concluded an agreement which—with somewhat inscrutable logic—they professed to believe averted the need for war. The treaty reaffirmed the cessions made at Augusta and Galphinton and secured Creek promises to fix the boundaries, to restore plunder amassed in past raids, and to atone for the lives of slain Georgians by offering payment in kind.[40]

Apparently, Clarke and other backwoods leaders erroneously placed

37. Downes, "Creek-American Relations," 154–57; Mohr, *Federal Indian Relations*, 153–54. James also purchased goods from Panton, Leslie and Company, but the exact date he began trading with the company is not known. For James and debts owed to Panton, Leslie, see chap. 12.

38. Georgia Commissioners to McGillivray, August 15, 1786, EF leg. 116L9; Caughey, *McGillivray*, 129–30.

39. McGillivray to John Habersham, et al., September 18, 1786, AHN Estado, leg. 3887; McGillivray to O'Neill, October 8, 1786, AGI PC, leg. 199; Caughey, *McGillivray*, 130–34.

40. Downes, "Creek-American Relations," 154–57; Cotterill, *Southern Indians*, 72.

Chapter 4

great store in the "death proviso" as a key measure for settling the Creek problem. While the Creek commonly employed the "eye-for-an-eye" maxim in meting out justice, the political assassination of tribal members was an absolute taboo in their culture. But the Georgians, it seemed, meant to exact the lives of McGillivray and his closest lieutenants in fulfillment of their demands.[41] Assassination was discussed informally during the proceedings, and the Georgians took the Tame King, the Fat King, and a number of Lower Creek hostage to ensure fulfillment of the terms of the treaty.[42] Shortly after the conference ended, McMurphy visited the Creek again, offering substantial rewards for the lives of McGillivray and others.[43]

The proceedings at Shoulderbone Creek ultimately served McGillivray's cause rather than Georgia's, for the resolutions tended to solidify and strengthen Creek resentment toward the Americans. Creek returning home from the parley spread tales of having been subjected to intimidation and insults. The Tame King flew into such a rage on discovering that he was to be held captive that his bemused abductors released him. The news that their leaders had been confined in Augusta as hostages enraged the Lower Creek. McGillivray immediately denounced the treaty and the pressures used to exact it and sent McMurphy scurrying for safety by ordering *his* death. The Georgians discovered all too quickly that their efforts of 1786 had been nothing more than a prodigal exercise in futility.[44]

While the Creek were becoming more resolute in opposing American interests, the Choctaw and Chickasaw were becoming more amenable to American blandishments. Many factions within the latter tribes had not reconciled themselves to Spanish hegemony, and still larger numbers were displeased with Spanish trade arrangements. Thus, compared to their frustrated attempts to negotiate with the Creek at Galphinton, the congressional commissioners encountered few obstacles in dealing with the Choctaw and Chickasaw at Hopewell.

The Hopewell treaty with the Cherokee, concluded November 28, 1785, set the pattern for agreements made with the Choctaw and Chickasaw the following January. Not only were the Cherokee elated on learning that the intent of Congress was to confirm their lands, rather than to deprive them thereof, but they also took immense pleasure in witnessing the restoration of lands extorted earlier by the Franklinites. In this atmo-

41. Cotterill, *Southern Indians*, 61.
42. Downes, "Creek-American Relations," 158.
43. McGillivray to O'Neill, April 18, 1787, *AGI PC*, leg. 202; Caughey, *McGillivray*, 141n79, 149–51.
44. Cotterill, *Southern Indians*, 72–73; Downes, "Creek-American Relations," 157–58; Coleman, *American Revolution*, 245–46.

sphere, the Cherokee readily consented to recognize the United States as their exclusive protector, with sole rights to regulate their trade.[45] The accords reached with the Choctaw and Chickasaw contained similar provisions, but the territorial clauses included noteworthy differences. In addition to defining and confirming the boundary claims of the two tribes, they set aside four small parcels of land for the establishment of American trading centers. The Chickasaw ceded a circular tract five miles in diameter on the Muscle Shoals, at the confluence of the Ocochappo and Tennessee rivers. The Choctaw ceded three six-mile-square tracts, deferring to a later date exact location of the sites.[46]

North Carolinians and Georgians denounced the Hopewell treaties as unwarranted congressional interference in the internal affairs of their states.[47] On the other hand, Governor Miró viewed the Hopewell proceedings with equanimity, reporting to the Conde de Gálvez that those Choctaw and Chickasaw who had participated in the negotiations lacked authority to make valid agreements. Miró had appointed traders to both nations before the Hopewell discussions took place and had ordered the Indians to eject from their midst all traders refusing to swear allegiance to Spain.[48] As an added precaution, he asked McGillivray to verify reports that William Davenport was among the Chickasaw awaiting the return of Piomingo from Hopewell, in order to conclude a treaty with Georgia. If the reports were accurate, McGillivray was to prevail on the Chickasaw to expel the Georgia agent.[49] The Creek leader indicated that he intended to do more: He would force the Chickasaw to avoid further contact with the Americans, and would exterminate the pro-American factions, if necessary.[50] Miró dismissed subsequent reports of Chickasaw complaints against the Mobile trade as mere grumblings to acquire better terms. Both Mather and McGillivray had assured the Louisiana governor that it was impossible for Americans to compete against the prices offered by Panton and Mather.[51]

Aside from the question of whether American enterprise could offer competition to Mather and Strother, Panton's traders did make inroads into

45. Mohr, *Federal Indian Relations*, 148–53; Cotterill, *Southern Indians*, 66–69.
46. The treaties may be found in Kappler, *Indian Affairs*, 2:11–16; Mohr, *Federal Indian Relations*, 151–53.
47. Cotterill, *Southern Indians*, 69.
48. Miró to Conde de Gálvez, June 28, 1786, AHN Estado, leg. 3886, Exp. 14, doc. 7; Benjamin Hawkins et al. to Richard Henry Lee, December 2, 1785, *ASP* 1A, I:38–39.
49. Miró to McGillivray, April 26, 1786, Corbitt, "Papers from the Spanish Archives," 10:130–31.
50. O'Neill to Gálvez, May 20, 1786, ibid., 10:137–38.
51. Miró to Favrot, July 6, 1786, ibid., 10:141; Pedro Favrot to Miró, May 30, 1786, Kinnaird, *Spain in the Mississippi Valley*, 2:173.

the Choctaw-Chickasaw trade by underselling their Mather-sponsored rivals. In September 1786, Miró, displaying solicitude for the New Orleans trading concern, which was not altogether consistent with his obligation to promote harmonious Indian relations, warned Panton that his interference must stop. The Louisiana governor craftily explained that Mather, by virtue of his precedence over Panton in contracting for the Indian trade, had been granted the Choctaw-Chickasaw concession. Each company would thereafter confine its activities to its assigned commercial sphere, thus removing all cause for discord.[52] Miró and Navarro later issued decrees enjoining all traders to confine their dealings to their assigned territories, and authorizing both Mather and Panton to confiscate any goods belonging to his rival which he might discover within his concession.[53] The directives drove many Choctaw and Chickasaw traders to the verge of quitting the business because of Mather's practice of downgrading the quality of Indian pelts and trading his own goods at prices higher than those prescribed by the Choctaw-Chickasaw tariff schedule.[54] All in all, the support of Miró and Navarro for Mather and Strother caused as much muttering among the Choctaw and Chickasaw as American agitation did, and perhaps even more. That the "gentlemen to the westward" would sacrifice "the peace and prosperity of a Colony" to the interest of one company left Panton bewildered and disgusted.[55] Denied the Choctaw-Chickasaw trade, he considered his continued presence in Pensacola an unnecessary extravagance and contemplated a return to East Florida. There the company enjoyed the dual advantages of dealing with the complaisant Governor Zéspedes and of possessing royal confirmation of the trade privileges requested in the company's memorial of July 1784. Accordingly, Panton consulted with McGillivray, John Leslie, and Charles McLatchy on the merits of withdrawing from Pensacola, preferably to St. Marks, if it still remained under the jurisdiction of Zéspedes.[56]

All parties concurred in the desirability of relocating the Creek trade at St. Marks, but in questioning Zéspedes, Leslie learned that the Conde de Gálvez had placed St. Marks under the administration of West Florida in 1785. Yet the East Florida governor advised against abandoning St. Marks until he could obtain clarification from Madrid on the company's status. Leslie surmised that the reply would be favorable, because at the time he submitted the Panton, Leslie memorial, St. Marks had been at-

---

52. Miró to Panton, September 5, 1786, *EF* leg. 114J9.
53. Favrot to O'Neill, March 12, 1787, *AGI PC*, leg. 200.
54. Favrot to O'Neill, June 28, 1787, *AGI PC*, leg. 13, West work cards; Serrano y Sanz, *España y los Indios*, 31–32.
55. Panton to J. Leslie, February 22, 1787, *EF* leg. 114J9.
56. McGillivray to Zéspedes, January 5, 1787; Panton to J. Leslie, February 22, 1787; McLatchy to J. Leslie, March 12, 1787, *EF* leg. 114J9.

tached to East Florida, and the Royal Order of May 8, 1786, had expressly granted the company privileges on the terms solicited.[57] Leslie, therefore, agreed to postpone momentarily any decision on evacuating St. Marks. On March 30, 1787, Zéspedes wrote the minister of the Indies on the company's behalf, explaining the legal ramifications of the case, McGillivray's "evident predilections" for the firm, and the disastrous consequences that would result if the company was forced to abandon St. Marks, given the critical state of Spanish-American relations. Zéspedes included a plea to restore St. Marks to East Florida, thereby freeing the Panton firm from the vexations of dealing with two separate administrations.[58]

Other considerations, apart from Miró's ban on trade with the Choctaw and Chickasaw, also contributed to Panton's desire to withdraw from Pensacola. In January, Miró and Navarro had imposed rules governing the importation of Indian trade goods for 1787, which the Scottish merchant now considered wholly unacceptable. The objectionable import strictures, however, emanated not from the caprice or malice of the governor and the intendant but from developments in London and Madrid.

Throughout 1786, the Marqués del Campo, Spanish ambassador to England, inundated Floridablanca with reports of irregularities and abuses surrounding the Indian trade in Louisiana and the Floridas. Campo expressed alarm over the arrival at London, from Louisiana and Florida ports, of vessels ostensibly under Spanish registry but manned by English crews. According to the ambassador, the cargoes included silver pesos—the worst form of contraband. Furthermore, the captains, contrary to Spanish regulations, had neglected to present themselves at the embassy. He speculated on whether English merchants were using the inconsequential Indian trade for conducting massive smuggling operations in the Indies. Equally ominous, Campo suggested, the English "leeches" probably had worked underhandedly to destroy the Indians' loyalty to Spain, all of which could be eliminated by employing Spanish middlemen to supply Indian trading goods.[59]

Floridablanca passed Campo's intelligence along to José de Gálvez, and the minister of the Indies, in turn, ordered Navarro to exercise vigilance against English abuses and to respond to the ambassador's allegations.[60] The intendant's reply explained that Great Britain's Navigation Acts permitted the importation of peltry and other American produce in

57. Zéspedes to McGillivray, March 27, 1787, ibid.; Zéspedes to J. de Gálvez, March 30, 1787, AHN Estado, leg. 3901, Exp. 5.
58. Zéspedes to J. de Gálvez, March 30, 1787, AHN Estado, leg. 3901, Exp. 5.
59. Floridablanca to Sonora, March 16, 1786; Campo to Floridablanca, September 5, December 29, 1786, AHN Estado, leg. 3885 bis.
60. Sonora to Intendente de Luisiana, March 21, 1786 AHN Estado, leg. 3885 bis. Exp. 8.

English ships only, and infractions subjected the cargoes to confiscation; hence, it was necessary that the captains avoid contact with the Spanish embassy in London.[61] Because of Campo's continuing adverse reports, José de Gálvez warned Navarro in October that, if existing safeguards—which were intended to ensure that vessels engaged in the Louisiana and West Florida commerce returned directly from their destinations to their ports of embarkation—were inadequate, then His Majesty would rescind the commercial privileges granted the provinces under the royal *cédula* of January 22, 1782.[62]

Navarro denied the actual as well as the possible existence of wholesale abuses in the commerce under his supervision. Referring specifically to the Indian trade, the intendant reminded his superior that U.S. traders, not British, posed the immediate threat to Louisiana and the Floridas. This consideration, above all, made the services of Mather and Panton indispensable for the present, he added, emphasizing the connections between the latter and the all-important McGillivray. No Spaniard, Navarro conjectured, would willingly replace the British, given the high risks and low returns brought about by a declining peltry market.[63]

Despite the intendant's disavowal of wrongdoing, the admonitions from above prompted Miró and Navarro to institute safeguards against smuggling on the part of Mather and Panton. On O'Neill's recommendation, the Louisiana officials agreed to refurbish and garrison the abandoned fort at St. Marks—a project which, although approved earlier, had languished for economic reasons. The presence of Spanish troops at St. Marks would serve to check any possible irregularities in the activities of Panton, Leslie and Company in the remote recesses of Apalachee Bay.[64] Miró and Navarro also issued passports to Mather and Panton, for the importations requested for 1787, that were so laden with restrictions as to evoke heated objections from both merchants.[65]

The license given to Panton limited his imports, under pain of confiscation, to goods intended specifically for use in the Creek trade. It also stipulated that the master of the ship and two-thirds of his crew must be Spaniards, and it required the posting of a bond, to be forfeit should the

---

61. Navarro to Sonora, July 22, 1786, ibid.
62. Sonora to *Intendente de Luisiana*, October 5, 1786, ibid.; Navarro to O'Neill, February 16, 1787, AGI SD, leg. 2670.
63. Navarro to Sonora, February 12, 1787, AHN Estado, leg. 3885 bis, Exp. 8, doc. 18.
64. O'Neill to Miró, February 15, 1787, AGI PC, leg. 37; Miró to O'Neill, February 15, 1787, AGI PC, leg. 40, West work cards; Miró to McGillivray, July 13, 1787, Corbitt, "Papers from the Spanish Archives," 11:84.
65. Panton to Miró and Navarro, February 15, 1787; Miró and Navarro to Marqués de Sonora, March 24, 1787; license to William Reid, March 13, 1787, AHN Estado, leg. 3901, Exp. 3.

vessel touch at any other port en route to or from London. The captain was to call on the Spanish consul general in London for instructions and clearance before returning to Pensacola.[66]

Panton curtly rejected the terms imposed by Miró and Navarro, except for the requirement to call on the Spanish consul general. Compliance with the rest, he stated, would subject his firm to the risk of absolute ruin. The Scottish merchant also announced his intention to retire to East Florida, where the company operated without such restraints. The inventory on hand, Panton estimated, would be exhausted by February 1788. In the interim, Miró and Navarro could seek a replacement for the Pensacola trade.[67] On February 28, the company's brigantine *Mary* sailed for London carrying peltry and instructions to return to New Providence Island with a limited quantity of trade goods. A small consignment would suffice, Panton thought, until the future became more certain.[68]

Miró and Navarro, disturbed at Panton's threat, attempted to placate the merchant, protesting that he had misunderstood their intent. They had meant for the vessel to stay away from *Spanish* ports, especially those in the Indies. In case of storms or other mishap, they explained, the vessel would have been completely free to put into any non-Spanish port along its route. As naturalization was available to any crewmen upon request, the governor explained, their crew requirements offered no obstacle. Nor did they understand Panton's objections to their trade limitations, since he had been confined to the Creek trade from the beginning.[69] Should Panton change his mind, the Spanish officials declared, he would still be allowed a passport for London. They also promised to supply a letter to Campo explaining the necessity of conducting the trade through London without undue interference, until a royal decision had been made on a permanent arrangement for the Indian trade. But, they warned, the ambassador's approval would be absolutely essential for the return voyage to Pensacola.[70]

In Panton's case, the offer was moot: The *Mary* had sailed before he received it. On the other hand, Mather, with no place to retreat to, yielded to the impositions; the *Condesa de Gálvez* sailed from New Orleans on March 13, under terms identical to those offered to Panton.[71] Panton, nevertheless, availed himself of the opportunity to effect a rapproche-

66. Panton to Miró and Navarro, February 15, 1787, ibid.
67. Ibid.
68. Panton to [Miró and Navarro], May 9, 1787, ANC F, leg. 1, Exp. 5.
69. Miró and Navarro to Panton, March 9, 1787, AGI SD, leg. 2670.
70. Ibid.
71. License to William Reid, March 13, 1787, AHN Estado, leg. 3901, Exp. 3; Manifest list of *Condesa de Gálvez*, March 12, 1787, AHN Estado, leg. 3885 bis, Exp. 8.

ment, informing Miró and Navarro that he would be pleased to forward their letter to the ambassador, and to Strachan and MacKenzie, his London factors, via the Bahamas. They, in turn, would present the letter to Campo and, if Miró and Navarro desired, they would also request permission for the *Mary* to return to Pensacola. Panton would be satisfied to remain indefinitely, he wrote, if he was granted the same privileges the company enjoyed in East Florida. Among these were the right to supply the Creek with British goods and to export peltry wherever the company pleased, with imports alone subject to 6 per cent duties. Granted these terms, Panton declared, he could compete with the Georgians on equal terms and would be able to "defeat their perfidious views" toward the Indians.[72]

As to the Choctaw and Chickasaw trade, Panton expressed a willingness to wait. Under the prevailing poor market conditions, the Creek were consuming all the goods he cared to risk. He predicted, however, that should Georgia ever make peace with the Creek, Miró and Navarro would "learn the necessity" of granting the Indian trade to persons who sold at the lowest possible prices.[73]

In June and July 1787, the Marqués del Campo received calls from two groups of visitors at the London embassy: Captain William Reid, master of the *Condesa de Gálvez*, and Pat Morgan, London factor for Mather and Strother; and Captain Matthew Forrest, accompanied by James Strachan. The callers bore identical letters from Miró and Navarro requesting the ambassador to relax the formalities in granting the Panton and Mather vessels clearance for West Florida. Both merchants, the letters explained, claimed that the Navigation Acts confined the loading of pelts onto British ships manned by British crews. Furthermore, the letter stated, the very possession of Spanish clearances, if detected by British customs, subjected the outgoing cargoes to possible seizure. Both Mather and Panton, Campo was informed, threatened to quit the West Florida Indian trade if the restrictions were not eased, and replacing those two, the Marqués knew, would prove extremely difficult. The need to preserve Indian friendship called for every available expedient.[74]

Campo thus grudgingly issued the clearances. He was exasperated at only being able to warn the captains that their passports did not cover the landing of contraband along the lonely Florida coastline.[75] His dealings with Morgan and Strachan convinced him more than ever that the mer-

---

72. Panton to Miró and Navarro, May 9, 1787, *ANC F*, leg. 1, Exp. 5.
73. Ibid.
74. Miró and Navarro to Campo, March 14, 1787, *AHN Estado*, leg. 3901, Exp. 3.
75. Campo to Miró and Navarro, August 24, 1787, *AHN Estado*, leg. 3885 bis, Exp. 8.

chants were abusing their indulgences. The ambassador's investigations revealed that the cargo of the *Condesa de Gálvez* had been insured for £30,000, a sum he believed to be greatly in excess of the cargo manifest submitted for clearance.[76] Strachan remarked that the rapidly declining peltry market warranted every possible encouragement to the Indian trade. Campo wondered aloud what motives could cause reasonable men to pursue an unprofitable activity encumbered with such heavy restrictions. Strachan's refusal to send the *Mary* directly to Pensacola, on the grounds that the ship had already taken on cargo consigned to Thomas Forbes at New Providence Island for reshipment to St. Augustine and St. Marks, further aggravated Campo. Without other recourse, the ambassador dutifully passed his misgivings along to Floridablanca once again.[77]

Miró and Navarro had doubted Campo's cooperativeness in issuing the clearances. Accordingly, they had asked the minister of the Indies to intervene, if necesssary, in procuring the return of the ships to West Florida, advancing with their petition all the arguments presented to the ambassador and many more.[78] José de Gálvez, however, died on June 17, perhaps before the petition of his Louisiana subordinates arrived. Addressed to Navarro, a royal directive of August 16, 1787, announced that, while all earlier measures taken in support of the Indian trade were approved, neither he nor Miró should issue any more passports for that purpose without consulting the court beforehand. The decree further directed the intendant to submit a list of the articles required in the Indian trade; the court had resolved to supply the Indians from Spanish sources as soon as practicable.[79] Less than two months later, Antonio Valdés y Bazán—who had assumed many of the duties of the deceased minister of the Indies—while poring over an *expediente* on Panton, Leslie and Company, resolved to terminate its stay in the Floridas.[80]

The pressures behind the court's toughening stance of 1786–87 toward the Indian trade had been building for some time. The powerful Spanish merchant guilds regarded the liberalized commercial privileges granted to Louisiana and West Florida in 1782, sanctioning direct trade with French ports at 6 per cent duties, as a giant sieve through which enormous quantities of smuggled merchandise flowed into other Spanish colonies. In this atmosphere, Campo's alarming reports tended to confirm suspicions. The

76. Campo to Floridablanca, July 13, 1787, ibid.
77. Campo to Floridablanca, August 12, 1787, ibid.; Strachan and MacKenzie to Panton, Leslie and Co., July 26, 1787, *AGI PC*, leg. 37.
78. Miró and Navarro to J. de Gálvez, March 24, 1787, *AHN Estado*, leg. 3901, Exp. 3.
79. Antonio Valdés to Navarro, August 16, 1787, *ANC F*, leg. 9, Exp. 1; Navarro to Valdés [January 8, 1788], *AHN Estado*, leg. 3888.
80. Whitaker, *Documents*, xxxiiin28.

demise of José de Gálvez and the untimely earlier death in Mexico of his nephew, Bernardo de Gálvez, removed two influential advocates of liberal trade policies from the ranks of Spanish decision-makers. A reappraisal of the Indian trade question was but one facet of broader deliberations on the best means of placing Louisiana and West Florida fully within the Spanish mercantilist orbit.[81]

81. Ibid., xl–xliii.

Conflict and Confusion in the Indian Country, 1787–1788

THE Spanish government was not alone in having to come to grips with the problem of relations with the southern Indians. In August 1786, the United States, drawing upon the ambiguous authority granted to Congress for the management of Indian affairs under the Articles of Confederation, divided the western hinterland into northern and southern Indian superintendencies. Under the guidance of the secretary of war, the superintendents had the responsibility of regulating the Indian trade, enforcing U.S. directives, and monitoring the activities of the Indians residing in their districts. By asserting its jurisdictional claims over the Indians, and over their lands as well, Congress expected to restore tranquillity to the southern frontier, which at that time was the greatest source of friction in Indian relations.[1]

Dr. James White, a North Carolinian who later became involved in the so-called Spanish intrigue, was appointed southern Indian superintendent. As his first order of business, White embarked on a peacemaking mission to the Creek. His timing was excellent; he arrived in Lower Creek country in April 1787, just as McGillivray and the other chieftains were assembling to plan new action against Georgia.

White gained permission to address the assembly, and in his harangue

---

1. Prucha, *American Indian Policy*, 35–36.

he entreated the Creek to recognize Georgia's claim to the Oconee lands. But the superintendent's appeal fell upon deaf ears. In reply, the Hallowing King, speaking for the assembly, demanded that Congress uphold the Creek claim to the disputed land. The Creek spokesman also railed against the Georgians for holding hostages against demands for the assassination of McGillivray and other prominent leaders.[2] Confronted with such determination, White found it impossible to settle the Georgia-Creek controversy. He did, however, secure a temporary truce and the release of the Creek hostages before returning to New York to report on the solidarity of Creek opposition to Georgia's acquisitiveness.[3]

Panton's discussion of White's mission aroused Governor O'Neill's apprehensions.[4] After he talked to Panton, but before he received McGillivray's account of the meeting, O'Neill speculated that White might offer flattery and presents in place of the threats and violence of the previous year, in a bid for McGillivray's friendship.[5] The ever-suspicious O'Neill had a premonition that such an approach might succeed, because of the resentment that McGillivray and Panton had so openly demonstrated toward the recently imposed trade restrictions. Access to free Spanish munitions, O'Neill surmised, had greatly enhanced McGillivray's prestige and control over the Creek but without proportionately increasing his attachment to Spain. McGillivray was entirely too independent a thinker for O'Neill's comfort, and might be susceptible to some American proposition to free the Creek trade—and Panton, Leslie and Company—from Spanish control.[6]

O'Neill demonstrated remarkable prescience in analyzing the dangers of White's visit with the Creek. White later reported an interesting proposal offered by McGillivray for settling the Georgia-Creek dispute. The Creek, McGillivray suggested, would cede the Oconee lands to Georgia in exchange for a Georgia cession of the lands south of the Altamaha to the United States. He further promised to become "the first" to swear allegiance to whatever government Congress might choose to create for the new territory. White conjectured that McGillivray was more interested in securing relief from Spanish trade restrictions than in acquiring U.S. citizenship.[7]

2. McGillivray to O'Neill, April 18, 1787, *AGI PC*, leg. 202; Caughey, *McGillivray*, 149–50.
3. Cotterill, *Southern Indians*, 73–74.
4. McGillivray to O'Neill, April 18, 1787; O'Neill to Miró, April 27, 1787; *AHN Estado*, leg. 3887, Exp. 1; Corbitt, "Papers from the Spanish Archives," 11:72–73.
5. Corbitt, ibid.
6. O'Neill to Miró, May 21, 1787, *AGI PC*, leg. 37; Caughey, *McGillivray*, 152–53.
7. White to Henry Knox, May 24, 1787, *ASP IA*, 1:20–21.

The degree of Panton's involvement in McGillivray's proposal is unclear. The Creek leader was certainly aware of Panton's dissatisfaction with the company's status in West Florida well in advance of White's arrival. O'Neill seems to have been convinced that Panton had encouraged McGillivray to seek a settlement that would open an Atlantic coast trade outlet for the company. According to O'Neill, Panton had told McGillivray that if the post on the Atlantic could be obtained, the company would be able to offer goods at lower prices "because no duties would have to be paid."[8] Whether Panton had done so is unknown. Panton was so disappointed with the arrangements in West Florida that he would not have been averse to letting O'Neill *believe* that he was planning to move to the U.S. east coast.

The uneasy truce between the Creek and their frontier adversaries to the north and east did not survive the early summer. In May 1787, James Robertson led a punitive expedition from the embattled Cumberland district against a French trading post at Coldwater Creek, near Muscle Shoals. For some time the French traders, supplied from Canada via the Wabash and Tennessee rivers, had been patronized by Chickamauga and Creek, who also regularly plundered the Cumberland settlements. Robertson's attack surprised and killed several French traders, as well as a number of Creek and Cherokee, and completely leveled the post.[9] The attack inadvertently benefited Panton's own traders, one of whom, John Kelly, had complained about competition from Coldwater.[10] At about the same time, a body of Georgia militia, in pursuit of Upper Creek marauders, ambushed an innocent band of Lower Creek hunters, killed twelve of them, and scalped at least six.[11]

McGillivray immediately sent large war parties against the Cumberland settlements and informed O'Neill of his intention "to give the Georgians a hearty Chastisement" as soon as circumstances permitted.[12] Following Georgia's refusal to give satisfaction "in kind" for the massacre of

8. The principal informant on McGillivray's offer was James O'Keefe, an Indian trader among the Lower Creek whom McGillivray had alienated. See O'Neill to Miró, September 10, 1788, Corbitt, "Papers from the Spanish Archives," 15:101–3.

9. Williams, *Lost State of Franklin*, 170–73; Cotterill, *Southern Indians*, 71, 74; McGillivray to O'Neill, July 10, 1787, AGI PC, leg. 200; Caughey, *McGillivray*, 155–56; Abernethy, *From Frontier to Plantation*, 95.

10. Extract of John Kelley to Panton, January 23, 1787, AGI PC, leg. 37; Corbitt, "Papers from the Spanish Archives," 11:65.

11. McGillivray to O'Neill, June 20, 1787, AGI PC, leg. 200; Caughey, *McGillivray*, 153–55; Coleman, *American Revolution*, 247–48. The number of Indians killed varies in different accounts from eleven to thirteen.

12. McGillivray to O'Neill, July 10, 1787, AGI PC, leg. 200; Caughey, *McGillivray*, 155–56.

the Lower Creeks, McGillivray plunged the Georgia frontier into a state of general warfare.

But McGillivray soon discovered he had chosen a less than propitious moment for renewing hostilities. Governor Miró had already resolved to dissuade the Creeks from engaging in further aggression. Continued provocation, he feared, would bring the U.S. Congress into the fray, escalating the fighting and possibly drawing Spain and the United States into open confrontation.[13] On O'Neill's advice, Miró agreed to send Juan Garçon, the Creek interpreter at Pensacola, to Little Tallassee to inform McGillivray orally of the policy changes. Miró was hesitant to put his instructions in writing, for if they fell into the wrong hands, Spanish complicity in arming the Creek would be exposed.[14] Garçon was ordered to urge McGillivray not to attack the Americans, and to accept the Oconee River boundary as a basis for making peace with Georgia. Miró had been apprised of O'Neill's suspicions concerning Dr. White's visit. Accordingly, he told Garçon to persuade McGillivray to refrain from making commercial concessions in any peace settlement with the United States. McGillivray was to be assured that, if the Creek remained on the defensive, ample supplies of guns and ammunition would be provided quickly, should the United States attack. Meanwhile, they would receive a small gift of arms in return for their promise not to attack the United States.[15] Miró's initiative in curbing Creek aggression later gained full royal approval.[16]

If Garçon complied with his instructions, McGillivray chose to ignore them, for he reported the hostile actions contemplated against Georgia to O'Neill *after* Garçon's departure from Little Tallassee, and later reported the results of the foray.[17] Indeed, the first occasion on which McGillivray acknowledged any awareness whatever of the curtailment of Spanish support came in October, when he visited Pensacola to inquire why the delivery of munitions had been delayed. There he heard from O'Neill firsthand of Miró's decision not to support Creek aggression—a condition that the Pensacola commandant, to McGillivray's relief, believed it would be improper to enforce, since the fighting had already begun.[18] Pretending disbelief, McGillivray wrote to Miró, informing the Louisiana governor of Creek victories, stating that his requests for additional arms and ammuni-

13. Miró to O'Neill, March 24, 1787, *AHN Estado*, leg. 3887, Exp. 1; Caughey, *McGillivray*, 145–46.
14. O'Neill to Miró, April 27, 1787; Miró to O'Neill, May 4, 1787, *AHN Estado*, leg. 3887, Exp. 1. Since Garçon could not read, O'Neill and Miró thought it useless to give him written instructions in any case.
15. Ibid.
16. Valdés to Miró, July 31, 1787, *AGI PC*, leg. 5; *AHN Estado*, 3887, Exp. 1.
17. McGillivray to O'Neill, July 10, 25, 1787, *AGI PC*, leg. 200; Caughey, *McGillivray*, 155–56, 158–59.
18. McGillivray to Zéspedes, October 6, 1787, *EF* leg. 114J9.

tion would be frequent, and professing that his actions flowed from a "desire to promote the Kings interest & Service." Learning whether Miró approved his exertions, McGillivray declared, was extremely important. Without Spanish backing, the safety of the Creek would be endangered.[19] With Zéspedes, in whom he placed greater trust, McGillivray was more forthright. Confiding to the East Florida governor his dismay at Miró's apparently strange conduct, McGillivray asked whether Miró's withdrawal of support actually reflected a change in Spanish policy.[20]

In November 1787, McGillivray concluded with pride that "the American Lads have been pretty well drubbd."[21] Prompted by McLatchy's death, Panton and McGillivray met at St. Marks in January 1788, where McGillivray apparently informed Panton of Creek plans to continue the war.[22] Shortly thereafter, in Cumberland, Creek raiders wrought havoc on crops and buildings, brought commerce and immigration to a standstill, and even caused a partial evacuation of the settlement. The embattled settlers, finding their pleas for outside assistance ignored, sent emissaries to McGillivray in April seeking peace on any terms. The Creek leader granted them a truce.[23]

McGillivray had unleashed the Creek fury against the Georgia frontier several months before he initiated the assault against Cumberland. Fighting in Georgia, which had begun in earnest in the fall of 1787, continued into the summer of the following year. Wave after wave of Creek warriors swept through the Georgia backcountry, killing, plundering, burning, and leaving over thirty dead behind them. Georgians were horrified when, in November, Greensville and the Green County courthouse were reduced to ashes.[24] As the crisis mounted, the Georgia Assembly declared war on the Creek nation and authorized the immediate mobilization of 3,000 militiamen. Because of the deplorable state of public finances, however, Governor George Mathews found himself with a war on his hands but with no means to support it. In November, he appealed to Congress to assist in a full-scale punitive campaign against the "perfidious" Creek, without which no secure and lasting peace could be expected.[25] Mathews also informed Congress that he had reason to believe that the Spanish government of West Florida had supplied the Creek

19. McGillivray to Miró, October 4, 1787, ibid.
20. McGillivray to Zéspedes, October 6, 1787, ibid.
21. McGillivray to O'Neill, November 20, 1787, *AGI PC*, leg. 200; Caughey, *McGillivray*, 163–64.
22. Panton to Zéspedes, January 28, 1788, *EF* leg. 116L9.
23. McGillivray to O'Neill, April 25, 1788, *AGI PC*, leg. 201; Caughey, *McGillivray*, 178–79.
24. Downes, "Creek-American Relations," 160–63.
25. Ibid., 165, 169; Mathews to President of Congress, November 15, 1787, Lockey Papers.

with arms and ammunition, and asked for an official remonstrance against the practice. Estimating the requirements of a Creek war at $450,000 to sustain a 2,800-man militia force for nine months, Secretary of War Henry Knox concluded that it would be an impossible burden.[26]

Governor Mathews, acting on a resolution of the assembly, also requested governors O'Neill and Zéspedes, "agreably to the Law of Nations," to protest the arming of the Creek in their respective provinces.[27] James Seagrove, a Georgian who resided near the St. Marys River, was commissioned to deliver the appeal to Zéspedes in St. Augustine. Zéspedes received the Georgia emissary warmly and officially decried Creek barbarities, but he denied Spanish involvement in arming the Creek, who had received only small occasional gifts of ammunition sufficient for hunting. The gifts, he insisted, were necessary to maintain peaceful relations and thus avert attacks against the Spanish provinces.[28] He reported later that Seagrove showed keen interest in discovering the exact relationship between Panton, Leslie and Company and the Spanish government. Zéspedes, as well as other Spanish officials, began to speculate that filibustering expeditions were likely to be launched by irate Georgians against the remote Panton, Leslie stores at St. Marks and on the upper St. Johns River.[29]

By mid-1788, the threat of U.S.–Creek war of major proportions had subsided. McGillivray, through additional visits from Garçon, a conference with O'Neill, and letters from Miró, had become painfully aware of the Spanish position. He was to make peace while refusing either to recognize U.S. sovereignty over the Creek or to concede their trade to American suppliers.[30] Meanwhile, in late 1787, Congress had formed a treaty commission consisting of one congressional appointee and three delegates selected by Georgia, North Carolina, and South Carolina. In February, Georgia Governor George Handley, seeking relief from Creek depredations in the Georgia backcountry, postponed military action indefinitely. He then urged the former governor, Mathews, and General

26. Mohr, *Federal Indian Relations*, 158–59; Downes, "Creek-American Relations," 169.
27. Mathews to Zéspedes, November 6, 1787, EF leg. 108D9; Mathews to Arturo O'Neill, November 7, 1787, Lockey Papers.
28. Zéspedes to Mathews, December 10, 1787, EF leg. 108D9.
29. Zéspedes to Ezpeleta, November 9, 1787, AGI PC, leg. 1395, Pac. II, Doc. 8, Lockey Papers; Bertucat to O'Neill, November 21, 1787, AGI PC, leg. 2352, West work cards; Zéspedes to Marquez de Sonora, November 9, 1787; Zéspedes to Valdés, January 10, 1788, AHN Estado, leg. 3887, Exp. 1.
30. McGillivray to O'Neill, March 28, April 15, 1788; McGillivray to Miró, June 12, 1788, AGI PC, leg. 201; Caughey, *McGillivray*, 172–74, 176–77, 183–85; Miró to O'Neill, April 1, 1788, AGI PC, leg. 5, WP.

Pickens, who represented Georgia and South Carolina on the treaty commission, to arrange a Creek truce. They, in turn, sent George Whitefield, a South Carolina trader, to confer with McGillivray. In June, the Creek spokesman, succumbing to Spanish pressures and American entreaties, agreed to end the fighting. But to the consternation of the commissioners, McGillivray insisted on an evacuation of the Oconee lands as an indispensable preliminary to any treaty negotiations.[31] This demand, together with Georgia's insolvency and the general preoccupation with launching the newly established U.S. federal government, led to a mutual agreement to postpone discussions until the summer of 1789. McGillivray was predictably amenable to such a postponement.[32]

Aside from checking the westward advance of the American frontier, the sporadic warfare of 1786-88 served as a barrier against American commercial penetration into the Choctaw and Chickasaw nations. However, the hostile actions of the Creek and Chickamauga scarcely diminished the persistence of important factions within the westerly tribes from seeking American trade contacts, particularly the adherents of Franchimastabe and Piomingo. The favoritism of Miró and Navarro for the operations of Mather and Strother in Mobile exacerbated the Indians' discontent with their dependency on Spanish trade and prompted their leaders to seek remedies through U.S. contracts.

In May 1786, a Chickasaw chieftain visiting Mobile disclosed that he could "well see" why the Spaniards refused to allow the United States to trade with his people; he had discovered that furs had "no value" in Spanish trading posts. He also reported that "an American" from Natchez (probably William Davenport) had offered a bounty of gifts in exchange for a treaty with the Chickasaw, and he declared his intention to accept the offer as soon as the promised goods arrived.[33]

Early the following year, Piomingo harangued Joseph Martin, complaining that the Chickasaw had seen no American trade goods since making the land cession at Hopewell in exchange for opening a trading post at Muscle Shoals. The failure of the United States to meet its obligations, Piomingo asserted, had led the Chickasaw to wonder whether the Americans merely intended to "jockey" the Indians out of their land.[34] About the same time, Chief Taboca, a close follower of Franchimastabe, led a delegation of Choctaw and Chickasaw to New York in a futile attempt to prod

31. Downes, "Creek-American Relations," 170–71; McGillivray to Pickens and Mathews, June 4, 1788, *AGI PC*, leg. 201; Caughey, *McGillivray*, 180–83.
32. Downes, "Creek-American Relations," 171–72.
33. Favrot to Miró, May 30, 1786, Kinnaird, *Spain in the Mississippi Valley*, 2:173.
34. Piomingo "talk" to Joseph Martin, February 17, 1787, Williams, *Lost State of Franklin*, 142.

Congress into complying with the promises made at Hopewell.[35] Of greater immediate concern to Miró, Davenport attended a March conference on the banks of the Yazoo with disgruntled Choctaw and Chickasaw chieftains and traders.

Fortunately, from the Spanish viewpoint, Pedro Juzan and Simon Favre, Spanish Indian agents at Mobile, became unexpected participants in the conference. Their presence apparently had a moderating effect on the proceedings. Ben James, who was Davenport's close collaborator, a Georgia agent and also a licensed Spanish trader, embarrassingly disavowed his American connections. He was present, he declared, merely to observe. Davenport informed the assembled Indians that the Americans wished only to extend to them the peace and prosperity they formerly had enjoyed under the British. But the warfare perpetrated by the Creek, Davenport explained, had actually delayed the delivery of merchandise for the Choctaw and Chickasaw trade. His listeners, however, would see goods in abundance once the Creek were defeated. Juzan told the assembly that he had come not to make promises but to listen and to deliver the Indians' complaints to New Orleans. As neither side offered tangible improvements, the Indians—at least in Juzan's presence—adopted a "wait and see" position.[36]

Franchimastabe and the Chickasaw king (Taski Etoka) availed themselves of Juzan's offer to place before Miró their grievances in writing. Both chiefs complained that peltry had been arbitrarily undervalued at Mobile and that goods were being priced in excess of the tariff rates governing the Choctaw and Chickasaw trade. Without changes, their traders would quit, and the Indians, reduced to extreme want, would likely resort to American suppliers. The Chickasaw king requested a reply without delay.[37]

The complaints stirred Miró into taking modest corrective action. James received a stern warning to stay clear of American contacts. The Louisiana governor also questioned Mather and Panton on their pricing policies. Both men complained of suffering losses in 1786 because of falling prices on the London fur market. Mather said that his losses made it impossible to adhere to tariff prices. Panton, however, had followed the established prices—at least partly because the proximity of the Creek to the Georgians precluded overpricing.[38] Accordingly, during the summer

---

35. Williams, ibid., 141–42; Knox to President, July 7, 1789, *ASP IA*, 1:48–49.
36. Serrano y Sanz, *España y los Indios*, 33–34; Benjamin James to Mather and Strother, July 23, 1787, McGillivray to Miró, July 25, 1787, Corbitt, "Papers from the Spanish Archives," 11:85–87, 88–89.
37. Serrano y Sanz, *España y los Indios*, 31n2.
38. James to Mather and Strother, July 23, 1787, Corbitt, "Papers from the Spanish Archives," 11:85–87; Miró to J. de Gálvez, June 1, 1787, *AHN Estado*, leg. 3887, Exp. 1.

of 1787, Miró flirted briefly with the idea of conceding the Choctaw and Chickasaw trade to Panton. But the Spaniard changed his mind after Mather agreed to meet the prices at which Panton had offered to supply the Mobile trade. Assured of Mather's cooperation, Miró made plans to send Captain Juan de la Villebeuvre (who later distinguished himself as foremost among Spanish Indian diplomats) to the Yazoo to mollify the disaffected Indians.[39]

In 1786, while Panton was under consideration for the Mobile trade, McGillivray sent a party of Coushatta to verify reports that American merchants were actually erecting trading posts in Chickasaw territory. The war party discovered Davenport and a small group of Americans indeed busily engaged in constructing a post within thirty miles of the Chickasaw villages. The Coushatta attacked, killing Davenport and three other Americans, wounding three others, and taking a young boy as prisoner. The plunder acquired in the raid included seventy rifles. McGillivray later observed that the death of the troublesome Georgia agent would deter the Americans from meddling with the Choctaw and Chickasaw.[40] The Spanish chided McGillivray for the violent attack on the Davenport party, and this prompted him to cancel an attack on a group of Davenport's collaborators who had reportedly established themselves on the Chickasaw Bluffs. Nevertheless, Miró believed the Creek leader's display of force furthered the interests of Spanish policy. He also interpreted the failure of the Chickasaw to retaliate against the Coushatta party as evidence that most Chickasaw were content with their Spanish ties. Chickasaw restraint, however, more likely indicated a shortage of ammunition.[41]

Miró accurately concluded that the Davenport incident had created a propitious moment for countering American influence among the Choctaw and Chickasaw. The Creek violence left their westerly Indian neighbors in a more tractable mood, thus contributing to the success of Villebeuvre's October Yazoo conference. The Spanish officer promised a favorable adjustment of prices at Mobile but also explained the deteriorating trade atmosphere in London. He admonished the Indians against accepting any more unauthorized intruders into their villages. They were to be expelled but were not to be killed or otherwise molested.[42]

39. Miró to Ezpeleta, September 24, 1787, *AGI PC*, leg. 1394; Miró to McGillivray, October 16, 1787, *EF* leg. 114J9.
40. McGillivray to O'Neill, July 25, 1787, *AGI PC*, leg. 200; Caughey, *McGillivray*, 158–59; John Sevier to Gov. Franklin, September 12, 1787, Williams, *Lost State of Franklin*, 168.
41. McGillivray to Miró, October 4, 1787, *EF* leg. 114J9; Miró to O'Neill, August 12, 1787, *AGI PC*, leg. 40; J. Robertson to Sevier, August 1, 1787, Williams, *Lost State of Franklin*, 171–72.
42. Serrano y Sanz, *España y los Indios*, 35–40.

The Chickasaw king and other Indian leaders accompanied Villebeuvre on his return to New Orleans, where they were warmly received and feted by Miró. The Indians expressed their satisfaction with Spanish overlordship and their pleasure at the changes to be made at Mobile. They disavowed the Hopewell treaties, claiming that the United States had used chicanery and alcohol to secure approval of those treaties. The Chickasaw king, acting also as spokesman for the absent Franchimastabe, who pleaded that ill health prevented him from making the journey, presented the Choctaw leader's English medal and flag to Miró and asked for Spanish replacements. By 1788, only the Chickasaw chief and about a hundred followers of Piomingo openly resisted detente with the Spaniards.[43]

Miró's withdrawal of the tendered Mobile concession disappointed Panton and McGillivray. But this was a mild setback, compared to the restrictions imposed in 1787 on the company's operations at St. Marks. In July, Miró advised McGillivray that, in line with his request, the St. Marks post would be renovated to protect the Indian trade.[44] The Creek spokesman immediately arranged a favorable reception from neighboring Seminole villages for the Spanish troops. Panton cooperated in the venture by transporting Captain Luis de Bertucat, the St. Marks commandant, and his troops to their new post. By November 1787, the decaying installation had been restored to serviceable condition without mishap or incident.[45] Meanwhile, following Charles McLatchy's death, Panton and McGillivray journeyed to St. Marks to put the company's affairs there in order. Upon arriving, they learned to their astonishment that Bertucat had impounded a company vessel bringing trade goods from Nassau to replenish the company's St. Marks inventories.[46]

Bertucat explained that he had standing orders from Miró to require all ships entering or leaving St. Marks to clear through Pensacola customs. Since St. Marks had been attached to West Florida, its imports and exports were henceforth subject to the required duties, which would be levied at Pensacola.[47]

Panton and McGillivray quickly registered complaints against the altered commercial regulations at St. Marks, appealing first to Zéspedes. McGillivray declared it a "pitiful Policy" to burden the Creek trade while

43. Ibid., 40; Miró to Ezpeleta, April 1, 1788, Lockey Papers.
44. Miró to McGillivray, July 13, 1787, Corbitt, "Papers from the Spanish Archives," 11:84.
45. McGillivray to Zéspedes, January 5, 1788; Panton to Zéspedes, January 8, 1788, *EF* leg. 116L9; Caughey, *McGillivray*, 165–66.
46. Panton to Zéspedes, January 8, 1788, *EF* leg. 116L9.
47. Panton to Miró and Navarro, January 28, 1788, *AGI PC* leg. 203, doc. 2, WP; Panton to Campo, April 2, 1788, *AGI PC*, leg. 6.

the Indians were at war and had little time for hunting. He also claimed to have received assurances that the garrisoning of St. Marks would not affect the commercial privileges enjoyed there.[48] In a more abrasive letter to the East Florida governor, Panton fulminated against the latest "Miserable and wretched" impositions of the "Western Masters." The Scot estimated that his company already had suffered losses of nearly $25,000 from 1784 through 1786 in luring the Creek away from Georgian influence. Subsequent profits had been "too inconsiderable" to compensate for the time, effort, and risk expended in the task. "If I mistake not," he continued, the royal order confirmed his company in the St. Augustine and St. Marks trade "on the *terms proposed by ourselves.*" Panton threatened that unless the company's former privileges at St. Marks were restored, he and his partners would "retire to our own Native Government," and he appealed for Zéspedes to assist in rectifying the matter.[49]

In a similar but more subdued letter to Miró and Navarro, Panton again argued the applicability of the company's East Florida privileges to St. Marks but raised the 1784–86 loss figures to $30,000. He asked the governor and intendant either to remove their impositions on the St. Marks trade or to grant him permission to withdraw.[50] Miró, however, declared that he was unfamiliar with the May 1786 royal order and therefore could do nothing more than forward Panton's complaint to the Spanish court for resolution. The only immediate relief measure afforded Panton was exemption from the requirement of clearing peltry exports from St. Marks through Pensacola customs. It was granted in recognition of the scarcity of safe anchorages along the route and of the dangers of storm damage to cargo. The 6 percent duty, however, was to be collected at St. Marks.[51]

However annoying Panton's grumblings may have been, Miró and Navarro understood the danger inherent in dismissing the recalcitrant Scot. McGillivray's ties with Panton made even his voluntary withdrawal extremely delicate.[52] But to complicate matters still further, Mather and Strother also had developed strong misgivings about remaining in the Indian trade. The New Orleans merchants, plagued with high risks and low profits and upset over the royal ban of August 1787 against the issuance of further passports for London, were reluctant to restock their rapidly

48. McGillivray to Zéspedes, January 5, 1788, *EF* leg. 116L9.
49. Panton to Zéspedes, January 8, 1788, ibid.
50. Panton to Miró and Navarro, January 28, 1788, *AGI PC*, leg. 203, doc. 2, WP.
51. Miró to Valdés, April 7, 1788, *AHN Estado*, leg. 3888, Exp. 1; O'Neill to Gabriel Marín Pizarro, March 8, 1788, *AGI SD*, leg. 2670.
52. Navarro to Valdés, January 8, 1788, *AHN Estado*, leg. 3888, Exp. 1; Miró to Valdés, July 13, 1788, *AHN Estado*, leg. 3901, Exp. 3.

dwindling inventory at Mobile. Furthermore, because of past collection difficulties, Mather and Strother drastically curtailed the consignment of goods on credit. To relieve the company's problem of rapidly dwindling capital resources, Miró and Navarro had permitted the Mather firm to sell "surplus" goods in New Orleans during the summer of 1787 for the Upper Louisiana Indian trade. But this measure proved inadequate; in the spring of 1788, Mather and Strother informed Miró that they faced ruin if they could not secure assistance from Spain.[53]

In response, the governor and the intendant endorsed a Mather and Strother petition to the crown seeking financial assistance to remain in the Choctaw-Chickasaw trade. The merchants requested permission to deposit 50,000 pesos in paper money in New Orleans (worth only thirty per cent of its face value) to be exchanged for 50,000 silver pesos from the royal treasury in Vera Cruz. Miró and Navarro supported the proposal on the grounds that the company's resources were inextricably entangled in credit. In addition, they exaggerated the danger of losing the Choctaw and Chickasaw to the United States should Mather and Strother be unable to supply them with goods.[54]

Both Panton and Mather received permission early in 1788 to ship peltry collected during the previous trading season directly to London. Although these voyages clearly violated the royal directives of August 1787, Miró and Navarro hoped that their disobedience would be forgiven because of an overriding Spanish interest in maintaining the southern Indian trade. However, they took the precaution of advising Valdés that their ships could not return to West Florida without royal permission. Miró and Navarro expressed confidence that Valdés would assist in obtaining a speedy decision on conducting the Indian trade, since goods on hand in Pensacola and Mobile would be exhausted by November. It made little difference, they said, how the matter was resolved, as long as the Indians obtained the preferred English wares at favorable prices such as Mather and Panton offered.[55]

On his outbound vessel, the *Mary*, Panton traveled from Pensacola to St. Marks, where he addressed a rambling memorial to Bernardo del Campo outlining the company's present difficulties, specifying the terms it required to remain in West Florida, and requesting immediate withdrawal should the terms be denied by the court. In the memorial he again

---

53. Miró and Navarro to Valdés, April 1, 1788, *AHN Estado*, leg. 3901, Exp. 3; Vicente Folch to Miró, April 26, 1788, Corbitt, "Papers from the Spanish Archives," 14:97–98, 100–101.

54. Mather and Strother memorial to the King, March 30, 1788; Miró and Navarro to Valdés, April 1, 1788, *AHN Estado*, leg. 3901, Exp. 3.

55. Miró and Navarro to Valdés, February 22, 1788, *AGI PC*, leg. 633.

recited the burdens added to the St. Marks trade contrary to the royal order of May 1786, all of which subjected "the whole business to such intollerable risks, expenses, and delays" that if they continued, the company's "ruin would in a little time be perfectly Compleat." As Miró and Navarro claimed that they were powerless to rectify matters, he continued, it had become necessary to appeal to His Catholic Majesty, as well as to Campo, to learn whether and on what terms the *Mary* would be permitted to return with supplies.[56]

Panton left it to Campo to determine the value of the company's services to Spain, asking him merely to compare the tranquillity prevailing along the Spanish frontier with conditions in Georgia and the American settlements on the branches of the Ohio. The favorable state of Indian affairs, Panton asserted, had been obtained through the "utmost exertion of all the Connections of this House," at an expense of $30,000 in losses before the American traders were expelled from the Creek nation. Past losses and current low profits made it impossible to maintain so unprofitable a business unless the onerous restrictions were removed and the company enjoyed the liberty of importing "freely whatever is necessary for the Indian Trade."[57]

But, Panton declared, the company did not seek the privilege of importing more goods into West Florida. It desired, instead, passports for two vessels to remove the company's property from Pensacola and St. Marks. However, should His Majesty see fit to remove the restrictions complained of and grant the company exclusive trading privileges with the Choctaw and Chickasaw, the company would be pleased to remain.

The Choctaw-Chickasaw concession was necessary, Panton explained, to offset the losses incurred in underselling Georgia merchants in the Creek trade. If the competition from Georgia were not met, the Creek "Country would be opened, thro' which the American Merchants would pour their Traders & Goods to the Chickesaws and Choctaws." The Scot concluded his argument for the Mobile concession by questioning the logic of compelling his firm to "stand for ever on the outpost, while others are securely at our Expense enjoying a feast within."[58] Speedy action was required, as the United States had exempted the Indian trade from all duties and imposts. Without timely adjustments, the southern Indian trade would "Revert back to the Georgians from whom it could only be Wrested by the unwearied Exertion of this House."[59]

56. Panton memorial to Campo, April 2, 1788, *AGI PC*, leg. 6, WP.
57. Ibid.
58. Ibid.
59. Ibid.

Before returning to Pensacola, Panton traveled to Little Tallassse to apprise McGillivray of the action he had taken. Quite likely the Scottish merchant also believed it necessary to calm the Creek leader, who in February, according to an informant of O'Neill's, had entertained notions of ridding himself of the torments of the Spanish "wasps" even if it meant accepting a commercial agreement with the United States.[60] Panton's sojourn among the Creek apparently coincided with the peace-seeking mission of George Whitefield. Panton and McGillivray seized the opportunity afforded by the American overtures to pressure the Spaniards into favorable action on the April memorial to Campo.

Panton returned to Pensacola bearing a letter for Miró from McGillivray, in which the latter reported accepting the request for a treaty conference from commissioners Pickens and Mathews. The Creek leader then informed the Spanish governor that he had delayed the talks until September in order to obtain beforehand firm advice on dealing with the "crafty, cunning, republicans." With respect to commercial matters, McGillivray observed that the United States would likely attempt to recover the southern Indian trade that "the absurd & blind policy of the Georgians . . . had so foolishly lost." The Creek leader asked Miró to believe that while his fellow headmen could be managed with ease in political affairs, they were not so easily controlled in questions of trade. The American traders, McGillivray observed, understood this well and had continually made tempting trade offers as bargaining leverage. However, should Panton's trade be placed on the terms he had solicited, there would be no cause for the Creek "to desire another market," as Panton then would be able to "furnish Goods as cheap as the Georgians." On the other hand, if the current restrictions were retained, the Scottish merchant would likely "leave off a traffic which has much hurt him." Should this occur, McGillivray declared, he was "ignorant" of what arrangements had been made to replace Panton.[61]

Panton, learning that Navarro's voluntary resignation of the Louisiana intendancy had been accepted, forwarded to Miró and Navarro in New Orleans a copy of his memorial to Campo. Informed of its terms, Miró and Navarro could use the occasion of the latter's departure for Spain to make whatever representations they wished on Panton's proposals to the Spanish court.[62]

60. O'Neill to Miró, July 28, 1788, *AGI PC*, leg. 38; O'Neill to Miró, June 22, 1788, *AHN Estado*, leg. 3901, Exp. 3.
61. McGillivray to Miró, June 12, 1788, *AGI PC*, leg. 177; Caughey, *McGillivray*, 183–85.
62. Panton to Miró and Navarro, June 18, 1788, *AGI PC*, leg. 6, doc. B, WP.

Miró felt the U.S.–Creek negotiations scheduled for September required his prompt attention. He therefore dispensed with the established procedure of referring the matter to the captain general of Havana before advising McGillivray of the Spanish position toward any resulting treaty. The governor quickly forwarded to the Creek spokesman excerpts from a copy of a royal order sent to Gardoqui the preceding year, declaring the Creek to be under the protection of the Spanish crown. McGillivray should show the royal order to the U.S. commissioners, Miró advised, and also should read them the articles of the Treaty of Pensacola, establishing Spanish protection on condition that the Creek trade exclusively under Spanish auspices. If McGillivray deviated even slightly from the stipulations in the Pensacola agreement, Miró warned, the Spaniards would regard the Creek as having used Spanish protection and trade support merely to secure better terms from the United States. McGillivray, in short, was limited to agreeing to a peaceful settlement of the boundary dispute. As to Panton's affairs, Miró informed McGillivray that the susceptibility of the Creek to U.S. trade offers indicated that Panton was not adhering to the Pensacola tariff prices. Furthermore, the duties collected on Panton's commerce were inadequate to cover Spanish outlays for Indian gifts.[63]

Governor Miró attributed McGillivray's unswerving support of Panton's pretensions to the Indian leader's pecuniary self-interest, and to the realization of his extreme difficulties in finding a suitable replacement. Yet the governor was equally convinced that maintaining the all-important Creek barrier against the United States required the cooperation of McGillivray and, at least temporarily, of Panton. Accordingly, Miró was inclined to reach an agreement with Panton that would improve his profits.[64]

Much to Miró's consternation, by mid-year 1788, his subordinate at Pensacola, Governor O'Neill, shared none of his convictions of the usefulness of either McGillivray or Panton. Never much at ease with the influence that the two wielded over the Creek, the Pensacola governor took umbrage at the reaction of McGillivray to the arms curtailment. O'Neill was especially piqued by the vociferous complaints of Panton and McGillivray about the altered trade regulations for St. Marks. Moreover, the garrisoning of the remote outpost at Apalachee Bay represented the fulfillment of one of O'Neill's foremost objectives. In February, when officials in Pensacola were notified of a possible rupture in Anglo-Spanish relations, O'Neill placed McGillivray and Panton under close surveillance.

63. Miró to Valdés, July 13, 1788; Miró to McGillivray, July 8, 1788, *AHN Estado*, leg. 3901, Exp. 3.
64. Miró to Valdés, July 13, 1788, ibid.

In the Spanish officer's mind, these two suspects would have been elated at such a development.[65]

On June 4, 1788, O'Neill informed Miró that both Panton and McGillivray had become noticeably recalcitrant in their dealings with Spanish officials. As evidence, the Pensacola governor cited the grumblings of both men concerning commercial restrictions. Panton had insisted on retaining his British citizenship, apparently believing that he had indeed sworn only fidelity and obedience to the Spanish crown, while McGillivray maintained a surly independence despite his Spanish pension. In the interest of security, O'Neill suggested, Miró should replace McGillivray and Panton with loyal subjects of the King.[66] Then, after Panton's return to Pensacola in June from his consultations with McGillivray, O'Neill learned the terms of the April memorial to Campo and of Panton's threat to withdraw if the privileges solicited were not forthcoming. The Pensacola governor informed Miró that he did not doubt in the least that McGillivray and Panton held the Indians in attachment to Spain only because of Spanish tolerance of Panton's trade. Since the two would detach the Creek in the event of an Anglo-Spanish break, O'Neill predicted that, with time and reflection, Miró would find it convenient to destroy their power over the Creek.[67]

At first, Miró replied mildly to O'Neill's suspicions. Although the question of Panton's loyalty was not without significance, his precipitous removal was a matter of delicacy. Moreover, the court apparently was devising plans to conduct the Indian trade through loyal Spaniards. In the meantime, Miró advised, O'Neill should determine the precise nature of McGillivray's interest in the Panton firm. Then the influential Creek leader must be offered a similar relationship with whoever assumed control of the Pensacola trade. Given McGillivray's position as the principal Creek spokesman, O'Neill's grounds for suspicion were insufficient. A certain degree of independent-mindedness on his part seemed natural enough to Miró. Furthermore, any attempt to undermine McGillivray's authority would involve too great a risk. Therefore, Miró ordered, O'Neill must refrain from initiating any unusual actions against either McGillivray or Panton.[68]

In July, irritated by O'Neill's unabated urgings that he sack McGillivray and Panton immediately, Miró angrily informed O'Neill of the

---

65. O'Neill to Miró, July 28, 1788, *AGI PC*, leg. 38.
66. O'Neill to Miró, June 4, 1788, *AHN Estado*, leg. 3901, Exp. 3; Caughey, *McGillivray*, 180.
67. O'Neill to Miró, June 22, 1788, *AHN Estado*, leg. 3901, Exp. 3.
68. Miró to O'Neill, June 18, 1788, ibid.

great embarrassment caused by his suspicions, particularly as they were grounded on no firmer evidence than that the accused possessed "British hearts." If O'Neill knew of means for replacing Panton, he should submit his ideas for consideration. Meanwhile, Miró contemplated no action unless tangible evidence of wrongdoing was forthcoming.[69]

In reporting to Valdés, Miró stated that he found nothing extraordinary in the British loyalties of O'Neill's suspects. These very loyalties made Panton and McGillivray implacable foes of the United States and thus useful to Spain. Miró described Panton's conduct as cooperative, except for his refusal to take the full oath of Spanish allegiance. The Louisiana governor even stated that Panton's request for duty exemptions was reasonable, given the declining profits of which even Mather complained. Even should Panton be replaced, Miró considered that the risks were too grave to supplant McGillivray, as the Creek would surely be alienated.

Miró informed Valdés that Panton might be assuaged if offered the privilege of importing one-fifth of each cargo "in goods not destined for the Indian trade." Miró believed Panton might then be willing to pay duties on everything. The plan, Miró declared, not only would improve the Scottish merchant's profits, but the duties levied on his commerce would also continue to flow into the royal treasury.[70] What Miró left unsaid was that Panton's acceptance also would cancel his demands for the Choctaw-Chickasaw trade.

Miró indeed suggested the alternative plan to Panton, but to the governor's chagrin, the Scot politely declined the proposal. In addition to his request for duty-free status, Panton asserted that he also should be permitted to assign one-fourth of each cargo to the Louisiana market. This, he explained, would place his company on equal footing with the Georgia merchants, since their commerce was not limited solely to the Indians.[71]

In August, the rebuffed Miró unfavorably represented Panton's demands as expressed in the April memorial to Valdés. Mather and Strother were faithful subjects who had paid duties at Mobile without complaint and who, therefore, should not be displaced involuntarily. Moreover, since Panton had refused to take a full oath of allegiance, perhaps his services should be dispensed with.[72]

Meanwhile, in July, James Strachan and Captain Matthew Forrest presented Ambassador Campo with Panton's memorial and with letters from Miró and Navarro for himself and Valdés. The Louisiana officials pleaded

69. Miró to O'Neill, July 8, 1788, ibid.; Caughey, *McGillivray*, 186-87.
70. Miró to Valdés, July 13, 1788, *AHN Estado*, leg. 3901, Exp. 3.
71. Panton to Miró, Aug. 5, 1788, ibid.
72. Miró to Valdés, Aug. 28, 1788, ibid.

the expediency of allowing the *Mary* to return to Pensacola with sorely needed Indian merchandise if the court had not settled on other means of supply. The Spanish ambassador remained unconvinced. He suspected that Panton's representations of hardship and his request to retire from West Florida were ploys to pressure the court into favorable action. He therefore feigned great reluctance in issuing a passport for the return voyage to Pensacola. Subsequently, Campo declared that the practice of Panton's vessels calling first at New Providence Island while en route to West Florida caused him to suspect rampant smuggling activity. Strachan and Forrest denied the accusation and promised that the *Mary* would not call at the Bahamas. Campo then announced that, despite his misgivings, he would permit the dispatch of a moderately valued cargo of Indian merchandise directly to Pensacola.[73]

Strachan and Forrest stated that the depressed prices of deerskins made duty relief absolutely necessary. To this, Campo replied that it seemed all the more strange for merchants to employ a ship to carry 100,000 items of such dubious value, unless it was to enjoy the recently enacted English subsidy on prepared hides. He terminated the interview by saying with pretended candor that if Panton, Leslie and Company had at least attempted to use *some* Spanish manufactures, it might have enjoyed greater confidence.[74]

The Spanish ambassador adamantly refused a subsequent request from Strachan and MacKenzie to send a second ship in ballast to St. Marks to transport peltry to London. Irritated at Campo's indifference to their explanations that one vessel could not possibly return with the voluminous quantity of deerskins collected at Pensacola and St. Marks, the London correspondents asked for passports to remove the company's assets from West Florida. It was apparent, they declared, that the ambassador disapproved of Panton, Leslie and Company. Furthermore, denying permission to return the deerskins to London was equivalent to denying the firm's trade altogether.[75]

Campo, however, was temporarily absent in Spain, and his subordinate in charge, Francisco Mollinedo, lacked instructions for handling the request. An answer to the London merchants was thus postponed until he received instructions from Floridablanca.[76]

In Spain, Valdés was in the process of considering the Indian trade policy of the Floridas when Mollinedo's dispatches to Floridablanca ar-

73. Campo to Floridablanca, July 4, 1788, ibid.
74. Ibid.
75. Campo to Strachan and MacKenzie, July 13, 1788; Strachan and MacKenzie to Campo, July 21, 1788, *AHN Estado*, leg. 3885, bis, Exp. 8.
76. Mollinedo to Floridablanca, July 22, 1788, ibid.

rived. On August 29, after some deliberation, the court decided to extend trading privileges for another year. In the interim, the Supreme Council of State would reach its final decision on the future of the trade. Accordingly, Floridablanca ordered Mollinedo to issue the two passports requested by Strachan and MacKenzie.[77]

In Pensacola, meanwhile, O'Neill, undaunted by Miró's rebuffs, had been busily engaged in compiling incriminating dossiers on McGillivray and Panton. For this work, O'Neill had assembled an elaborate network of informants. It included Timothy Lane and James O'Keefe, both Creek traders with grudges against McGillivray, and John Maypother, a protégé of O'Neill's, whom he had placed in Panton's hire. All three assisted the Pensacola governor in his task. Rumors—accurate and inaccurate—supplied by these three and other sources, coupled with McGillivray's known resentment at the Spanish curtailment of support and Panton's open demands and threats to leave West Florida, were incriminating enough.[78] But, above all, McGillivray's belated report of the arrival of a "strange man" among the Creek who mysteriously promised a "good supply of arms & ammunition from a Society of certain charitable people" led O'Neill to conjecture that Panton and McGillivray were involved in some conspiracy of massive and sinister proportions.[79]

Long before the appearance of the purported stranger, Maypother had informed O'Neill of McGillivray's irritation over Spanish trade restrictions and of his notions of turning the Creek trade over to the United States. Maypother also had reported John Forbes, Panton's chief clerk, as having said that, beyond doubt, Creek valor would eventually win a free port for the nation.[80] From O'Keefe, the Pensacola governor learned of the offer McGillivray had made to Dr. James White in 1787 regarding the exchange of the Oconee lands for a newly created American state south of the Altamaha.[81] O'Neill also heard that McGillivray had spread rumors among the Creek traders that Panton would shortly close his Pensacola store to relocate in a more advantageous place, one where he would be exempt from duties.[82]

77. Valdés to Floridablanca, August 29, 1788, ibid.; Valdés to Zéspedes, August 9, 1788, AHN Estado, leg. 3901, Exp. 5; Mollinedo to O'Neill, October 22, 1788, AGI PC, leg. 6, WP.
78. O'Neill to Miró, June 10, 1788; O'Keefe to O'Neill, ca. July 10, 1788, AGI PC, leg. 1394; O'Neill to Miró, July 21, 28, August 22, 1788, AGI PC, leg. 38.
79. McGillivray to O'Neill, August 12 1788, AGI PC, leg. 201; Caughey, McGillivray, 191–93, 197–98; O'Neill to Miró, September 10, 1788, AGI PC, leg. 38; O'Neill to Miró, August 22, 1788, AGI PC, leg. 1394.
80. O'Neill to Miró, July 28, 1788, AGI PC, leg. 38.
81. O'Neill, to Miró, September 10, 1788, ibid.; Corbitt, "Papers from the Spanish Archives," 15:101–3.
82. Corbitt, "Papers from the Spanish Archives," ibid.; O'Neill to Miró, July 28, 1788, AGI PC, leg. 38.

Before the appearance of the unexpected visitor, O'Neill's evidence strongly suggested that Panton and McGillivray were not prepared to submit gracefully to an adverse Spanish ruling on the status of Panton, Leslie and Company in the Floridas. However inchoate their plans may have been, either or both of the formerly staunch British loyalists apparently was not above bidding, at least within limits, on a commercial arrangement with the United States should their dealings with the Spaniards turn sour.

In July, O'Neill learned still more about the intruder. O'Keefe, Lane, and others declared that McGillivray had met with a certain Bowles, who had traveled from New Providence Island, offering the Creek the wherewithal to continue resisting their enemies. McGillivray, the reports said, had dispatched a caravan of 150 packhorses to the mouth of the Indian River below St. Augustine to retrieve a substantial quantity of free ammunition.[83] That much McGillivray later freely admitted to the Spaniards. He also informed Panton that he could see no grounds for Spanish objection if the Creek accepted free arms from the "Grand Turk or any other power . . . not at war with Spain."[84]

Unsubstantiated rumors and reports from the Creek country drew O'Neill into a flurry of speculation on the intentions of McGillivray and Panton. At one point, the Pensacola governor conjectured that McGillivray, with the assistance of sundry adventurers, was planning an all-out attack on Georgia.[85] O'Neill soon abandoned this conclusion only to theorize that the two suspects had formed a plot with Colonel Thomas Brown and other Bahamians to establish a port on the Florida peninsula. Then, with volunteers recruited from Cumberland and elsewhere, the conspirators intended to build a fort on the east coast and to establish an independent nation under British patronage.[86] Although O'Neill's musing shifted frequently, he remained convinced that Panton was somehow involved with the mysterious visitor to the Creek. At the very least, the Pensacola governor believed, the plotters were maneuvering to exact Panton's trade demands from the Spanish crown.[87]

Panton, however, quickly disavowed any connection with the intruder. Indeed, he informed both O'Neill and Miró that what scant information he had indicated that Bowles's visit constituted more of a threat to Panton, Leslie and Company than to Spain. When Miró requested Panton to urge

---

83. O'Neill to Miró, August 22, September 10, 1788, *AGI PC*, leg. 38; Corbitt, "Papers from the Spanish Archives," ibid.
84. McGillivray to Panton, September 20, 1788, *Johnson et al. v. Innerarity et al.*
85. O'Neill to Miró, July 23, 1788, *AGI PC*, leg. 38.
86. O'Neill to Miró, July 28, 1788, ibid.
87. O'Neill to Miró, July 31, 1788, ibid.

McGillivray to refrain from any action that might jeopardize Creek-Spanish relations, Panton readily agreed.[88]

Despite Miró's orders to exercise restraint, O'Neill, obsessed with suspicion, encouraged the Tame King—McGillivray's implacable adversary—and other Creek headmen to oppose Bowles's overtures and to undermine McGillivray's influence. In Pensacola, several drunken Indians were questioned, and McGillivray's retainers, relatives, and followers were incarcerated and otherwise harassed.[89] O'Neill's behavior created a furor among the Upper Creek; McGillivray's supporters were so reluctant to visit Pensacola that Panton's business temporarily dwindled to a near standstill. On August 20, 1788, enraged at O'Neill's accusations of duplicity, McGillivray resigned his Spanish commission.[90] Shortly afterwards, he relinquished his assigned share in Panton, Leslie's profits—possibly, as Panton believed, to remove Spanish suspicion of any complicity on his part in McGillivray's activities.[91]

McGillivray indeed regarded Bowles's offer as heaven-sent. The Georgia backwoodsmen had learned that the flow of Spanish munitions to the Creek had been halted. Stirred up by Elijah Clarke and a close friend, Colonel James Alexander, the Georgians had broken the truce by announcing that there would be no peace without full Creek satisfaction of Georgian demands. The congressional peace commissioners informed McGillivray that the meeting to negotiate a peace treaty had to be delayed until spring because they had not received enough money to buy the needed presents and because they anticipated additional instructions from the new congress.[92] More pessimistic than ever about the likelihood of diplomatic success, McGillivray was preparing to wage war even if, as he informed Miró, it meant turning to "other resources" for arms. To Panton, he explained that the Creek had every intention of remaining an independent nation.[93]

88. Panton to Miró, August 5, 1788, *AGI PC*, leg. 2361; Panton to [O'Neill] January 22, 1789, *AGI PC*, leg. 202, WP.
89. O'Neill to Miró, July 21, 1788, *AGI PC*, leg. 38; O'Neill to Miró, August 23, 1788, *AGI PC*, leg. 1394, Lockey Papers; McGillivray to Panton, September 20, 1788, *Johnson et al. v. Innerarity et al.*
90. McGillivray to Panton, September 20, 1788, *Johnson et al. v. Innerarity et al.*; McGillivray to Miró, August 20, 1788, *AGI PC*, leg. 2361; Caughey, *McGillivray*, 195–96.
91. McGillivray to Panton September, 20, 1788, *Johnson et al. v. Innerarity et al.*; extract of Panton to J. Leslie, November 20, 1788, *EF* leg. 116L9.
92. Ibid.; McGillivray to Miró, September 20, 1788, *AHN Estado*, leg. 3887, Exp. 1; Caughey, *McGillivray*, 199–202.
93. Caughey, *McGillivray*, 199–202; McGillivray to Panton, September 20, 1788, *Johnson et al. v. Innerarity et al.*

6

Adversaries to Trade

*T*HE visit of William Augustus Bowles to the Creeks in the summer of 1788 was not his first and it would not be his last. On the other hand, it is noteworthy because it marked his entry into the intrigue-ridden affairs of the Spanish-American frontier. Brash, persuasive, and theatrical, Bowles possessed a degree of self-confidence and personal magnetism that enabled him to deceive both himself and others into believing in his ability to accomplish the impossible. His many detractors—William Panton was one of the foremost—called him many epithets, but his biographer has noted that none ever called him dull.

Born in 1763 on the Maryland frontier, Bowles served the Tory cause in the American Revolution, eventually attaining the rank of ensign in a Maryland Loyalist regiment. In 1778, his unit was deployed at Pensacola where, after a clash with a superior, he abruptly left the service. Shortly afterward, he drifted into the Lower Creek country, where he acquired two wives—one Creek, one Chickamauga—and settled on the Chattahoochee near his half-Creek father-in-law, Chief Thomas Perryman. When the Spanish conquest of Pensacola looked imminent, Bowles returned there, regained his commission, and acquitted himself well in the ensuing action. Following the capitulation of Fort George, Bowles's regiment was eventually paroled to New York. At the war's end, Bowles was mustered out at half-pay and joined the Loyalist exodus to the Bahamas.

Lacking both the temperament and the means to become a planter,

Bowles shuttled between the Bahamas, Georgia, and the Creek country, keeping fully abreast of the Georgia-Creek disturbances. The Creek crisis, together with political conditions in the Bahamas, presented Bowles with a possible opportunity for immense personal gain.[1]

After the influx of Loyalist refugees into the Bahamas, the islands became a hotbed of intense factional strife. One group, the Board of American Loyalists, consisted mostly of affluent refugees from East Florida, Georgia, and the Carolinas; William Panton, Thomas Forbes, and their sympathizers belonged to this group. Their opposition included the original "Conch" settlers and poorer West Florida refugees, all of whom the "board" adherents viewed condescendingly. The governor at that time was the rapacious Earl of Dunmore, whose earlier political career in the North American colonies had merely whetted his appetite for wilderness empire building. He had sided with the Conch faction[2] and was thwarted in an attempt to seize as contraband 6,000 piasters (Spanish dollars) remitted by Panton to Nassau; ever after, he covertly schemed to destroy Panton, Leslie and Company.[3] John Miller, who was a merchant-partner of Broomfield Bonnamy, a close friend of Dunmore, and himself an exile from West Florida, hated the Spaniards both for having forced him to abandon a large plantation on the Tensaw River and for the abuse he suffered during the brief Spanish occupation of the Bahamas. As a Conch and a merchant, Miller resented (and at the same time envied) Panton and his partners.[4] It was, then, natural for Bowles, Dunmore, and Miller to gravitate together for mutual benefit.

Bowles appreciated the lingering affinity of the Indians for British rule. At that time, there was much talk in the air in the Bahamas about McGillivray and the Creek joining the northern tribes in a grand, antiexpansionist Indian confederation. Bowles and his associates knew of the support the British had extended the Indians in the Great Lakes region. Dunmore and his supporters apparently believed that the time was ripe for a bit of filibustering, so they determined to employ Bowles's professed influence with the Creek to supplant Panton, Leslie and Company in the

---

1. Wright, *William Augustus Bowles*, vii, 1–29. While Wright declines to state positively that Bowles's father-in-law was Thomas Perryman, James F. Doster has no such reservations: *Creek Indians*, 1:250. A brief autobiographical sketch by Bowles, translated into Spanish, differs somewhat from the details in Wright's biography. See *A la Causa contra el Aventurero Guillermo Bowles, y Guillermo Cunningham*, AHN Indias 21067, no. 507, folios 28–34.

2. Peters, "American Loyalists," 229–31.

3. "Hearing of Appeals Committee from Plantation," PC 2/134, PROL; J. Leslie to Zéspedes, October 3, 1788, EF leg. 116L9, WP; Milfort, *Memoirs*, 60–61.

4. Peters, "American Loyalists," 231–32; Wright, *William Augustus Bowles*, 27; Wright, "Queen's Redoubt Explosion," 177–93.

Creek trade.⁵ Upon reaching the mainland, Bowles proceeded to Coweta, the council town of the Lower Creek, with presents from Dunmore and an invitation to McGillivray to confer on the Creek crisis. McGillivray agreed and at Coweta accepted Bowles's offer of munitions and men as a godsend.⁶

The desperate McGillivray was apparently too pleased with his newly found succor to take exception to Bowles's activities in undermining Indian confidence in Panton, Leslie and Company. The artful adventurer, posing as an official English emissary, alleged that the Panton firm had gone bankrupt and consequently was gouging its customers with high prices. According to Bowles, King George III and Lord Dunmore had determined to halt the company's trade with the Indians. Standing orders had even been issued to confiscate Panton, Leslie vessels and cargoes in all British ports. Furthermore, Bowles said that Panton and his partners had become naturalized Spaniards and no longer merited trust. But all of this would be rectified shortly, he promised. Other merchants from the Bahamas would soon replace the discredited Panton firm.⁷

Even if Bowles made these assertions beyond earshot of McGillivray, such lurid slanders could not have escaped the attention of the Creek leader. McGillivray's acquiescence in Bowles's attacks on Panton explains in part why he voluntarily terminated his claim to a share in the company's profits, an action Panton diplomatically chose to overlook.⁸ McGillivray's support was crucial to the successful outcome of Panton's efforts to acquire permanent and improved trade conditions in West Florida. McGillivray's loyalty to Panton was not completely steadfast, but his defection stemmed in part from his deep bitterness over Spanish policy shifts. He never made a deliberate decision to abandon Panton as a friend and benefactor. Panton understood that McGillivray had succumbed to the blandishments of Bowles from despair at the withdrawal of Spanish support and uncertainty about the future status of the Creek trade. Concerning the latter, McGillivray believed Panton had resolved "to throw up that trade" if the Spaniards refused to accede to his terms, and the Creek leader wanted assurances of an adequate replacement should this occur.⁹

5. Wright, "British Designs," 271–74; Wright, *William Augustus Bowles*, 29; For an explanation of why Dunmore supported Bowles, see Wright, "Dunmore's Loyalist Asylum."

6. Wright, *William Augustus Bowles*, 28–30; Milfort, *Memoirs*, 61; McGillivray to O'Neill, June 22, August 12, 1788, *AGI PC*, leg. 201; Caughey, *McGillivray*, 185–86, 191–93.

7. J. Leslie to Zéspedes, October 3, 1788, *EF* leg. 116L9, WP.

8. McGillivray to Panton, September 20, 1788, *Johnson et al. v. Innerarity et al.*; Pickett, *History of Alabama*, 385–88; Panton to J. Leslie, November 20, 1788, *EF* leg. 116L9.

9. O'Neill to Miró, January 10, 1789, *AGI PC*, leg. 38; McGillivray to J. Leslie, November 20, 1788, *EF* leg. 114J9; Caughey, *McGillivray*, 205–8.

The Spanish abandonment of the Creek had caused the bewildered McGillivray to perceive his nation as caught in the jaws of a vise, squeezed between devious Spaniards and land-hungry Georgians. The Spanish-inspired coercion of Panton and John Leslie to induce a Creek-American settlement also irritated McGillivray and made him more independent of mind.[10] If Bowles were to provide the wherewithal to secure not only a better peace with the Georgians but also more dependable trade conditions, McGillivray could do little else but cooperate, within calculated limits.

Whether McGillivray and Bowles reached an understanding is unclear, but if they did it was not an agreement between strangers. Their acquaintance dated from Bowles's military tour at Pensacola, and consequently McGillivray at first set great store in his promises "of Succor & aid, besides many other fine things which wore rather an Improbable face."[11]

The two men apparently discussed ways and means to secure a free port for the Indian trade. Perhaps McGillivray was the first person to impress Bowles with the advantages to be gained from an independent commercial outlet, thus inspiring Bowles in his ambitious pursuit of that objective later in his career. Shortly after his discussions with Bowles, McGillivray reaffirmed to Miró that the British had formally restored the St. Marks district to the Indians long before Spain regained the Floridas. As a consequence, they expected the St. Marks trade to be free from Spanish imposts "as it was our own unoccupied port," despite the fact that the Spaniards had refurbished and garrisoned the abandoned outpost.[12]

Later, however, McGillivray disclosed to John Leslie that Bowles had vaguely insinuated "the necessity of opening a port in one of the many channels or bays with which the coast abounds." The port would facilitate the influx of an abundance of presents to attract recruits for a continental Indian alliance under McGillivray's leadership. The Creek leader believed that the project was quite plausible.[13]

Bowles returned to Nassau vaguely convinced of having received McGillivray's blessing for Miller and Bonnamy to supplant Panton, Leslie and Company in return for "Succor & aid." Probably, McGillivray had done nothing to discourage such a belief, though, as he later insisted, Bowles

10. McGillivray to Panton, September 20, 1788, *Johnson et al. v. Innerarity et al.*; McGillivray to J. Leslie, November 20, 1788, *EF* leg. 114J9; Caughey, *McGillivray*, 205–8.
11. Caughey, ibid.
12. McGillivray to Miró, August 12, 1788, *AGI PC*, leg. 2361; Caughey, *McGillivray*, 193–95.
13. McGillivray to J. Leslie, February 8, 1789, *EF* leg. 114J9; Caughey, *McGillivray*, 222–23.

likely had been reticent and evasive when asked about the identity of his sponsors, denying only a connection with Dunmore.[14] McGillivray presumably believed that, if necessary, matters such as trade concessions could be resolved after the safe delivery of the arms and assistance Bowles promised. In fact, emboldened by the expectation of massive outside assistance, McGillivray hinted to Miró that should Panton be denied the commercial privileges he sought in West Florida, the highly esteemed and influential Scot held "the power to carry the greater part of the trade to where he wishes." Thus, in McGillivray's thinking, if subsequent developments made it either necessary or desirable to coerce the Spaniards into yielding a free port to the Creek, Panton would at least share in its commerce—Bowles and his mysterious supporters to the contrary notwithstanding.[15]

Once back in the Bahamas, Bowles and Miller—with covert assistance from Dunmore—feverishly organized a return expedition. The merchant contributed two ships, arms, and supplies to the cause, and the governor allegedly furnished muskets and powder from the royal arsenal. With some difficulty, Bowles, masquerading as a commissioned English officer engaged in an officially sanctioned enterprise, raised about fifty recruits, with Dunmore even countenancing the enlistment of prisoners and deserters from the crew of the *Sherborne Castle*. Finally, in early October, the self-styled "Colonel" Bowles and his party found harbor in the mouth of the Indian River, well to the south of St. Augustine.[16]

While encamped at Indian River, the rank-and-file overheard conversations among Bowles, Broomfield Bonnamy, and the officers that exposed the true objectives of their mission: the pillage and destruction of the Panton, Leslie stores on the St. Johns and at St. Marks. "Colonel" Bowles blatantly declared that McGillivray had conferred upon him the mantle of Creek leadership and that hundreds of Indians were at his beck and call to assist in the project.

The forces under Bowles would first assault and plunder the Panton, Leslie and Company lower store, Concepción, on the St. Johns, while Bonnamy returned to Nassau, engaged an armed schooner, and proceeded to Apalachee Bay. After leveling the St. Johns store, Bowles would march overland to Apalachee and join Bonnamy in attacking the Spanish fort and looting and destroying the company's St. Marks store. The way

14. McGillivray to Leslie, November 20, 1788, *EF* leg. 114J9; Caughey, *McGillivray*, 205–8.
15. McGillivray to Miró, August 12, 1788, *AGI PC*, leg. 2361; Caughey, *McGillivray*, 193–95.
16. Wright, *William Augustus Bowles*, 30–31.

then would be prepared for Miller and Bonnamy to monopolize the Creek trade.[17]

Within a few days Bowles broke camp, coasted northward, and made a rendezvous with a horse pack train led by John Galphin, which had been dispatched earlier by McGillivray to secure the armaments. After disembarking and transferring the baggage to Galphin's care, Bowles marched off to destroy Panton's St. Johns store, but to his discomfiture his plans rapidly disintegrated. The hungry, cold, wet band of adventurers attracted few Indian followers and little hospitality. Erroneously informed by the Indians that a large troop of Spanish soldiers had been stationed at the Panton, Leslie store at Concepción to ambush his party, Bowles elected not to attack the post. Actually, there were only a corporal and a few soldiers at Concepción. Instead, Bowles headed for Alachua, where the Indians gave him no more encouragement than he had received previously. Worse, he could secure but few provisions for his hungry army.

While he was trying to make up his mind whether to proceed to Apalachee Bay or to return to the St. Johns store, many of his followers deserted. A dozen of them even surrendered to the small detachment commanded by Corporal Mateo Martín at Concepción. Bowles pursued this little band to Concepción but failed to recover any of the deserters. In spite of earlier threats, Bowles made no move to harm John Hambly or to take over the Panton, Leslie store. Because of the few soldiers at his command, Martín similarly made no attempt to take Bowles captive. During his brief stay at Concepción, Bowles wrote Captain Carlos Howard, Governor Zéspedes's secretary, attesting that he meant no harm to the Spaniards. His plans, he explained, were only to lead his army against their common enemy—the Georgians. Crestfallen by the desertions, however, Bowles left Concepción and by December 1788 had returned empty-handed to the Lower Creek.[18]

Meanwhile, Colonel Thomas Brown and other Panton, Leslie and Company supporters in the Bahamas had alerted Governor Zéspedes and

---

17. "Substance of a Voluntary Declaration Made by Sundry of Bowles's Banditti," St. Augustine, November 21, 1788, ANC F, leg. 1, Exp. 24, no. 2, WP; also appended to Kinnaird, "International Rivalry," 79–85. The Panton, Leslie store that Bowles intended to plunder was the so-called lower store, or Almacén de Nuestra Señora de la Concepción, at present-day Stokes Landing, near Palatka: Ross and Chappell, "Diary of Hambly," 60–61.

18. Ross and Chappell, "Diary of Hambly," 60–61; Wright, *William Augustus Bowles*, 31–32; John Hambly to John Leslie, September 28, 1788; Galphin to Bowles, September 17, 1788, EF leg. 116L9; Bowles to Howard, November 15, 1788; Corporal Mateo Martín to Zéspedes, November 18–20, 22, 1788, EF leg. 119B10; William Pengree to John Leslie, November 16, 20, 1788, BSC, NYHS; Zéspedes to Ezpeleta, November 24, 1788, EF leg. 21H2; Gov. Quesada to Luis de Las Casas, August 9, 1790, EF leg. 22I2.

John Leslie to the Bowles-Dunmore-Miller conspiracy. This intelligence, together with confessions made by the deserters, was hastily dispatched to McGillivray. Leslie, Zéspedes, and Howard urged the Creek leader to arrest and deliver the upstart adventurer to Spanish authorities or to dispose of him otherwise.[19] McGillivray, however, estimated that Bowles was temperamentally incapable of carrying out grand designs and thus was no threat to the security of Panton, Leslie and Company. The Creek leader promised only that Bowles would "be exposed before the Indians & dismissed for a Needy Vagrant." Any armaments Bowles delivered would be seized beforehand, McGillivray advised.[20]

As these events were transpiring in East Florida, Governor Miró had assessed his intelligence about the activities of Bowles submitted by O'Neill. This, together with information received from McGillivray and Panton, led Miró to conclude that the entire affair was a private adventure that possibly enjoyed Dunmore's unofficial support and that had been instigated on McGillivray's initiative. The governor, unlike O'Neill, believed that the English intrusion posed no threat to the security of Pensacola and that McGillivray's behavior was attributable to disgruntlement over the arms curtailment in the face of the recent truculence of the Georgians.[21]

Both Panton and McGillivray reported to Miró that Georgia had broken the truce. Panton even proffered the unsolicited advice that, in the light of this development, it would be in the interest of both humanity and good politics to regain Creek friendship. Although he did not say so, it was clear that gifts to the Creek should include Spanish munitions.[22] Weighing this suggestion against McGillivray's remarks that the Creek "must have recourse to every means" for their defense, Miró recommended to Havana the wisdom of restoring Spanish assistance. Then, thought Miró, should McGillivray continue to hold himself aloof, it would become necessary to call a Creek congress in Pensacola for the purpose of discrediting his leadership.[23]

19. Zéspedes to McGillivray, October 8, 1788, *EF* leg. 114J9; Caughey, *McGillivray*, 202–4; Leslie to McGillivray, December 11, 1788, ANC F, leg. 1, Exp. 5, no. 3, WP. As desperately as Zéspedes wanted Bowles captured, the governor fully concurred with Martín's decision not to provoke a fight with Bowles when he was at Concepción in mid-November: Zéspedes to Martín, November 20, 1788, *EF* leg. 119B10.
20. McGillivray to J. Leslie, November 20, 1788, *EF* leg. 114J9; Caughey, *McGillivray*, 205–8.
21. Miró to Ezpeleta, July 28, 1788, *AGI PC*, leg. 1394; Miró to Ezpeleta, August 16, 1788, *AGI PC*, leg. 1394; WPA, "Despatches," XVI, Book 4:10–12.
22. Panton to Miró, August 5, 1788, *AHN Estado*, leg. 3901, Exp. 3; McGillivray to O'Neill, July 14, 1788, *AGI PC*, leg. 2361; Caughey, *McGillivray*, 190.
23. Caughey, ibid.; Miró to Ezpeleta, August 16, 1788, *AGI PC*, leg. 1394, Lockey Papers; WPA, "Despatches," XVI, Book 4:10–12.

Captain General José de Ezpeleta concurred in Miró's suggestions, and in December the governor assured McGillivray that it was "needless for [him] to look after extraordinary means" to acquire arms and ammunition. These would be made available free, through Pensacola. Miró even revealed that he and the captain general both believed that McGillivray should insist on the removal of the Americans from Creek lands before any treaty could be concluded. Elated at Miró's offer, McGillivray immediately demanded 6,000 pounds of powder, 12,000 pounds of musket balls, and 1,500 English trade guns—which were much more serviceable than the guns the Spaniards had given him earlier—to be delivered by April 20, 1789.[24] Expressing his satisfaction with the renewal of Spanish support, McGillivray added that the "happiness & contentment" of the Creek would be complete should His Catholic Majesty place their West Florida trade on the same footing as the privileges they enjoyed in East Florida.[25] Panton thought that since McGillivray had been "fully informed . . . of the wicked Views" that Bowles and his supporters held "for entering on this business," and since Miró had resumed support of the Creek, McGillivray would see the threat that Bowles posed to his leadership and would return to the Spanish fold.[26]

Despite the return of surface cordiality in relations between McGillivray and the Spaniards, mistrust persisted on both sides because of a number of outstanding differences. McGillivray remained bitter toward O'Neill for the latter's attempts to undermine the former's influence, and O'Neill was not inclined to a change of heart toward McGillivray. The Pensacola commandant continued to harbor Timothy Lane, whom McGillivray had marked for extinction for spying and heaping insults on his family and retainers. Because of Lane's presence, McGillivray avoided visiting Pensacola until coaxed down by Panton. While in Pensacola, McGillivray severely upbraided Lane for his past iniquities, and Miró subsequently may have had the discredited former Creek trader removed to Mobile. As O'Neill was absent from Pensacola during McGillivray's visit, the opportunity for a personal reconciliation passed.[27]

Of greater consequence for Creek-Spanish relations, Vicente Folch y Juan, commandant at Mobile and Miró's nephew, accused McGillivray of

---

24. Miró to McGillivray, December 13, 1788, *AGI PC*, leg. 201; Caughey, *McGillivray*, 209–11, 215–20; McGillivray to Panton, February 1, 1789, *AGI PC*, leg. 202, 2361.

25. McGillivray to J. Leslie, February 8, 1789, *EF* leg. 114J9.

26. Panton to Miró, January 9, 1789, *AGI PC*, leg. 6, doc. C, WP.

27. On the McGillivray-Lane dispute, see Caughey, *McGillivray*, 34, 37, 154–55, 196; McGillivray to Panton, January 12, 1789, *EF* leg. 116L9, WP; Miró to Panton, February 28, 1789, *AGI PC*, leg. 6, WP; McGillivray to Cruzat, July 2, 1789, *AGI PC*, leg. 15B, doc. M, WP; Panton to Miró, April 7, 1789, *ANC F*, leg. 1, Exp. 5, no. 5, WP.

encouraging Indian attacks against the Tensaw-Tombigbee settlements north of Mobile, a charge McGillivray vehemently denied.[28] The controversy arose from Spanish policy changes following the breakdown of the Jay-Gardoqui negotiations in 1786, and the ensuing "separatist" intrigues initiated by James Wilkinson, Dr. James White, James Robertson, and John Sevier. The overtures made by Robertson and Sevier to Spanish officials, it should be noted, were inspired in large part by a desire to escape the Creek-Chickamauga fury.[29] These overtures prompted Floridablanca and other high-ranking Spanish policy makers to encourage American immigration to Spanish territory and to open the navigation of the Mississippi to the American frontier settlements, subject (at Miró's discretion) to a 6 to 15 per cent duty. These policy changes were intended primarily to placate the American frontiersmen and thus to forestall aggression against Louisiana and West Florida. Building up the population of the Spanish provinces was a secondary consideration.[30]

But above all else, in the light of deteriorating relations with Great Britain, Floridablanca desired to conclude a treaty with the United States. A proposal drafted in September 1787 instructed Gardoqui to secure an agreement with the United States by offering to recognize American territorial claims as far as the thirty-first parallel, excepting the Natchez district. With respect to the Mississippi question, the Spanish chargé d'affaires could propose the establishment of a joint commission to study the validity of American claims. Had Gardoqui received these instructions before the movement for ratification of the federal constitution began, he might have succeeded in carrying out Floridablanca's orders. In short, the absence of competent authority with whom to negotiate indirectly granted McGillivray, the Creek, and Panton, Leslie and Company a reprieve from abandonment.[31]

Fortunately for the Spanish interest, neither Panton nor McGillivray ever became aware of Floridablanca's diplomatic shift. Miró explained to both that Spain was encouraging American immigration to Louisiana in order to erect a bulwark against U.S. penetration into New Spain. According to Panton, McGillivray compared the policy to "placing a common thief as Guard on Your door & giving [him] the key in his pocket."[32] But the Creek leader seemed not to object too greatly to settling Americans west of the Mississippi—a solution he indeed wished that the Creek

28. McGillivray to O'Neill, March 1, 1788, *AGI PC*, leg. 201; Caughey, *McGillivray*, 168–70; McGillivray to Panton, May 20, 1789, *ANC F*, leg. 1, Exp. 5, no. 6, WP.
29. Whitaker, *Spanish-American Frontier*, 108–13.
30. Ibid., 101–2.
31. Ibid., 83–85.
32. Panton to Miró, July 3, 1789, *AGI PC*, leg. 120, doc. B, WP.

had the power to impose. His major objection was to the introduction of American immigrants along the rivers north of Mobile, a practice that in 1789 almost touched off a second crisis in Spanish-Creek relations.[33]

Throughout 1788, a number of Indian depredations occurred in the settlements in the Tensaw-Tombigbee district, which the Choctaw and pro-American traders informed Folch had been fomented by McGillivray. The Creek leader, however, denied the charges, retorting that disgruntled Choctaw and Alabama had perpetrated these hostile acts. Yet McGillivray made it clear that he sympathized with the aggrieved Indians who, he implied, were only venting their displeasure at American encroachment on Indian lands, made despite Spanish promises of protection. McGillivray also warned that he was powerless to keep the Alabama completely in check, since their ties with the Creek confederation were too loose.[34] Folch remained unconvinced of McGillivray's sincerity, preferring to believe that the incidents were committed by Creek, a belief that set off acrimonious exchanges between the two.[35]

At first, Miró sided with McGillivray. Although the Louisiana governor publicly discounted Choctaw involvement in the raids, he personally believed the Alabama were culpable, and acting without McGillivray's orders. In May 1789, however, Miró received reports from Carlos de Grand Pré, commandant at Natchez, of a rumored impending Creek attack in that district. Miró subsequently informed McGillivray of the rumor but adroitly suspended judgment, as it would be impossible to undertake such an outrage without McGillivray's knowledge. Miró then urged McGillivray to try to disabuse the Alabama and the Creek of apparent misinformation about treaties. Further, Miró warned, should the attacks go unchecked, he would suspend the Creek trade, halt the distribution of Spanish arms, and prepare for war.[36]

Later, Miró even called on Panton to use his influence in bringing McGillivray around, and the Scottish merchant readily complied. His approach was conciliatory in that he strove as an "honest broker" to allay the suspicions of both Indian and Spaniard. Meanwhile, McGillivray had acted to restrain the Creek and to arrange a meeting between spokesmen for the Alabama and Folch before receiving Miro's stern warnings. Miró

33. McGillivray to Panton, August 10, 1789, *Johnson et al. v. Innerarity et al.*
34. McGillivray to Folch, April 22, 1789, *AHN Estado*, leg. 3887; McGillivray to Folch, May 14, 1789, *AGI PC*, leg. 52; Caughey, *McGillivray*, 226–28, 230–32.
35. Caughey, *McGillivray*, 226–28, 230–32, 236–38; Folch to McGillivray, June 14, 1789, *AGI PC*, leg. 52, doc. J; McGillivray to Panton, August 10, 1789 (in which McGillivray refers to Folch as a "madman"), *Johnson et al. v. Innerarity et al.*
36. Miró to Folch, May 10, 1789, *AHN Estado*, leg. 3887; Miró to McGillivray, May 22, 1789, *AGI PC*, leg. 2352; Caughey, *McGillivray*, 232–33.

also worked toward a resolution of the crisis, ordering Folch to erect a fort on the settlement line as a buffer between the Tensaw-Tombigbee settlers and the Indians. In the interest of harmony, Miró later forbade Folch to correspond further with McGillivray. With the completion of Fort San Esteban de Tombecbé, and with Miró's promise not to relocate additional immigrants from the American frontier in the Natchez area, the crisis subsided—if not the mutual distrust it had engendered.[37]

Another source of irritation between McGillivray and the Spanish arose from the difficulties Miró encountered in meeting the Creek leader's demands for high-quality English trade muskets for the defense of his nation. Miró promised to deliver 1,200 of this superior type of weapon, 300 less than McGillivray originally had requested. Even so, the governor could immediately procure no more than half the total number pledged through Panton and Mather. Miró, therefore, authorized Panton to import additional weapons from the British West Indies, though the search for muskets there was to prove largely unsuccessful. By November, the Creek still had only half the pledged allotment, and their persistent visits to Pensacola for arms were severely straining Spanish hospitality. McGillivray suspected Miró of deliberate dilatoriness in honoring the Creek weapons requests, while Miró, in turn, believed the Creek leader's professions of renewed friendship stemmed only from expediency.[38]

Contrary to his promises, McGillivray permitted Bowles to linger unmolested among the Lower Creek, perhaps so the adventurer and his contacts would be available as insurance of British support, should the Spaniards deceive him. On his own initiative, Bowles left for the Bahamas in the spring of 1789, accompanied by a few Lower Creek and Chickamauga retainers. After a brief sojourn there, the adventurer wrote to Spanish officials in St. Augustine, Havana, and Madrid, lodging formal complaints against the "economic stranglehold" that Panton, Leslie and Company had imposed on the Creek. Thereafter, Bowles and his small entourage left in quest of British assistance.[39]

37. Panton to McGillivray, June 6, 1789, ANC F, leg. 1, Exp. 12, no. 8; Panton to Miró, June 9, 1789, ANC F, leg. 1, Exp. 5, no. 8; Miró to Panton, June 19, 1789, AGI PC, leg. 6, doc. G; Panton to Miró, July 3, 1789, AGI PC, leg. 120, doc. B, WP; McGillivray to Miró, May 26, 1789, AGI PC, leg. 52; Miró to Folch, June 29, 1789, AGI PC, leg. 56; Caughey, *McGillivray*, 234–35, 241; McGillivray to Panton, August 10, 1789, *Johnson et al. v. Innerarity et al.*; Holmes, "Notes on Fort Tombecbé," 282.

38. Miró to Cruzat, February 28, 1789, AGI PC, leg. 5, WP; Miró to Cruzat, March 12, 1789, AGI PC, leg. 6, West work cards; Cruzat to Miró, March 31, 1789, AGI PC, leg. 15B, doc. G, WP; McGillivray to Miró, March 31, 1789, AGI PC, leg. 202; Enrique White to Miró, November 6, 1789, AGI PC, leg. 15B doc. Q, WP; McGillivray to Miró, May 26, 1789, AGI PC, leg. 52; Caughey, *McGillivray*, 225–26, 234–35; Miró to Cruzat, June 20, 1789, AGI PC, leg. 6, doc. H, WP.

39. Bowles to Zéspedes, August 21, 1789; Bowles to Ezpeleta, August 21, 1789, AGI PC, leg. 1425, Lockey Papers; Wright, *William Augustus Bowles*, 34, 38–40.

Bowles and his followers eventually reached London in October 1790 after completing an itinerary that even included a brief visit to Quebec. They had been hurried to England by news of what seemed to them a propitious development. At Nootka Sound, located on the remote northwestern Pacific coast of North America, a Spanish officer had seized several English ships engaged in the sea-otter trade. In the ensuing diplomatic controversy, the British government challenged Spain's pretensions to exclusive control over the region. War talk briefly pervaded Whitehall, but Spain finally yielded to Britain's insistence on applying the principle of effective occupation along the Pacific coast.[40] For a while, however, it appeared that Bowles's determination would be amply rewarded by coveted official support.

Meanwhile, the Panton, Leslie and Company vessel, *Mary*, reached Pensacola in December 1788 on its return voyage from London. Its hold, however, contained considerably smaller quantities of merchandise than Panton had originally ordered for the coming trading season. The company's London factors had decided on a smaller cargo because the Spanish court had not yet reached a decision on Panton's memorial of the preceding April. Panton, concluding that his stay in West Florida would soon be terminated, made plans for the collection of debts owed the company.[41]

Panton's cautious pessimism disturbed Miró. Bowles's continued presence presented an ominous threat to Spanish hegemony over the Creek, a circumstance that made the Louisiana governor unusually solicitous of harmony, in order to avoid any disruptions to their trade. Encouraging Panton to adhere to his usual business practices, Miró advised patience, intimating that Madrid would discover soon enough the difficulties involved in finding a suitable trading replacement. The King's ministers, after sober reflection, he said, would never risk the consequences of assigning so politically important a matter as the Creek trade to inexperienced Spaniards.[42]

As an added inducement, Miró promised to represent the April 1788 memorial favorably to Valdés. The governor even went so far as to pledge himself to ask that the duty exemptions Panton sought be made retroactive for 1788. Predicting an agreeable outcome, Miró reminded Panton that reasonable persistence on his part would enable him to recoup the company's previous losses.[43]

40. Wright, *William Augustus Bowles*, 41–48; Cook, *Flood Tide of Empire*, 217–43.
41. Panton to Miró, January 9, 1789, *AGI PC*, leg. 6, doc. C, WP; Miró to Valdés, February 12, 1789, *AHN Estado*, leg. 3901, Exp. 3; Panton to Miró, February 12, 1789, *ANC F*, leg. 1, Exp. 5, no. 4, WP.
42. Miró to Valdés, February 12, 1789; *AHN Estado*, leg. 3901, Exp. 3; Miró to Panton, December 22, 1788, *AGI PC*, leg. 54.
43. Miró to Panton, December 22, 1788, *AGI PC*, leg. 54.

Panton's spirits were only partially buoyed, however, by Miró's support. He informed the governor that poor prices for peltry in Europe made him quite indifferent to remaining in the trade, and he stated his willingness to assist in the establishment of a Spanish replacement for his company. Meanwhile, the prevailing uncertainties not only made ordering goods for the 1790 season problematic but also raised the specter of losing the Creek trade to U.S. commercial interests in the interim.[44]

At this juncture, Miró's dependence on Panton's goodwill increased markedly. Before returning to New Orleans, the *Condesa de Gálvez* had called at Cádiz, where Pat Morgan, the London correspondent for Mather and Strother, had disembarked and journeyed to Madrid to expedite the partnership's loan request. But the court disapproved the loan, a decision that led Morgan to limit the heavily extended Mather and Strother to 10,000 pesos in goods for the 1789 trading season. The beleaguered partners, unable to restock their Mobile inventories adequately, made alternate proposals to Miró for securing more trade wares, but to no avail. On February 28, 1789, the Louisiana governor offered Panton the long-sought-after Choctaw-Chickasaw concession, advising him that acceptance might be looked on favorably by the Spanish court.[45]

Panton accepted with reservations. It was unfortunate, he informed Miró, that the Mobile concession had been tendered before learning of the court's disposition toward the memorial of April 1788. Although agreeing to dispatch vessels to the Bahamas, Jamaica, and Nova Scotia in search of goods for Mobile, Panton reiterated his intentions of withdrawing from West Florida unless Spain agreed to the privileges he sought and also granted Panton, Leslie and Company some degree of tenure. He could not resist observing how incomprehensible it was for the Spanish government to object to the loss "of a few thousand Dollars in duty's," which hardly defrayed collection expenses when compared to the advantage of "keeping the Indians contented & seperated from Georgia . . . which with good management would last for ages."[46]

In May 1789, Miró advised Valdés of the arrangements he had made for sustaining the Choctaw-Chickasaw trade, describing them as a momentary solution to an urgent problem. The Louisiana governor also transmitted Panton's terms for continuing: no duties, and guarantees of tolerance for a fixed period of time. Of all his terms, Miró observed, Panton's insistence on some degree of permanency was of the greatest importance, due to the heavy credit demands of the Indian trade. Should the court

44. Panton to Miró, February 12, 1789, ANC F, leg. 1, Exp. 5, no. 4, WP.
45. Miró to Valdés, May 20, 1789; Miró to Panton, February 28, 1789, AHN Estado, leg. 3901, Exp. 3; Miró to Cruzat, February 28, 1789, AGI PC, leg. 5, WP.
46. Panton to Miró, April 7, 1789, ANC F, leg. 1, Exp. 5, no. 5, WP; Panton to Miró, April 7, 1789, AGI PC, leg. 202, doc J, WP.

deny Panton's terms, justice dictated that he be allowed to liquidate his affairs in West Florida in an orderly fashion.[47]

By the time Miró wrote Valdés, however, the matter had been resolved. In September 1788, the Supreme Council of State turned its full attention to the Indian trade problem of the Floridas, having before it the many advisements of Miró, Navarro, Zéspedes, and the Marqués del Campo. On numerous occasions, Miró and Navarro had listed among the major liabilities in dealing with the Indians the enormous credit demands, the attendant risks of recovery, and falling peltry prices. Consideration of these, they advised, should lead the court to exercise special care in seeking a Spanish replacement for the British Indian merchants. Any Spaniard who contemplated assuming the concession should first travel to Louisiana to gain firsthand knowledge of the difficulties involved. Otherwise, Miró and Navarro predicted, any Spanish venture into the Indian trade would likely be abandoned quickly, and the Indians would resort to U.S. supply sources. They also stressed the necessity of granting McGillivray an interest in any consortium that should replace Panton, Leslie and Company.[48]

Zéspedes had forcefully pointed out to his superiors that it was in the Spanish interest to wean the Indians away from their pro-British tendencies, but at the same time he had insisted that this objective must be achieved gradually. To do otherwise, he feared, involved the grave risk of alienating the Indians from Spain. To avoid such a disaster, Zéspedes suggested introducing a Spaniard into the Panton, Leslie partnership, thereby affording him the opportunity of mastering the intricacies of the Indian trade. In addition, young Spanish cadets should be assigned to reside among the Indians, not only to learn their dialects and customs, but also to gain their confidence and respect. Such an approach would provide for an orderly transition from British to Spanish ascendancy over the Indians.[49]

Despite his conviction that the Indian trade in the Floridas served as a grand subterfuge for wholesale smuggling, the Marqués del Campo also had stated his misgivings about making abrupt changes. In July 1788, he grudgingly admitted the political folly of rooting out the British merchants too hastily and took pains to communicate his doubts to Floridablanca.[50]

Against these precautionary observations the council weighed the demands of the Spanish merchant guilds to Hispanicize the commercial re-

47. Miró to Valdés, May 20, 1789 and enclosures, *AHN Estado*, leg. 3901, Exp. 3.
48. Decision of *Junta Suprema de Estado*, September 22, 1788, *AHN Estado*, leg. 3885 bis, Exp. 8; Whitaker, *Documents*, 99–103; Miró to Valdés, July 13, 1788, *AHN Estado*, leg. 3901, Exp 1; Navarro to Valdés, January 8, 1788, *AHN Estado*, leg. 3888, Exp. 1.
49. Zéspedes to Valdés, March 24, 1788, *AHN Estado*, leg. 3901, Exp. 5; Corbitt, "Papers from the Spanish Archives," 14:86–94.
50. Campo to Floridablanca, July 4, 1788, *AHN Estado*, leg. 3901, Exp. 3.

gime of Louisiana and the Floridas. In October, the council resolved to call on the expertise of the former intendant Martín Navarro in devising an acceptable solution.[51] Navarro denied the charges made by Spanish merchant guilds that the liberalized trade privileges granted Louisiana and West Florida encouraged rampant smuggling, thus causing a decline in Spain's trade with the Indies. Yet he agreed on the feasibility of converting the Spanish economy to complement the trade requirements of the suspect provinces. Indeed, Navarro observed, Spain possessed latent potential for producing almost all the items required in the Indian trade, and the few products unobtainable in Spain could be acquired in France. But, he warned, until the necessary measures were implemented to stimulate Spanish production, the court must permit the Indian trade to continue in its present channels.[52]

Out of Navarro's proposals grew an ambitious project in which the former Louisiana intendant toured French and British manufacturing centers, gathering products and tools to provide patterns and models for duplication by Spanish artisans. The Spanish court hoped to achieve adequate production levels by early 1794, the time when the royal *cédula* of January 1782 governing the trade privileges of Louisiana and West Florida would expire.[53] As Spanish ministers became increasingly preoccupied with the calamitous events spawned by the French Revolution, however, the project slipped into oblivion. But in approving Navarro's undertaking, the Spanish government unknowingly granted Panton, Leslie and Company the permanency its partners had so long desired.

On March 16, 1789, in order to give Navarro time to complete his assignment, the Supreme Council of State recommended that Panton and Mather be exempted from all export and import duties in conducting the Indian trade.[54] The recommendation led to the promulgation of a royal order on March 23, sanctioning duty exemptions as a means for His Catholic Majesty to supply the treaty Indians with their necessities at lower costs. Its terms required Miró, who had assumed the duties of intendant on Navarro's departure, to prepare a list of all items required in the Indian trade, and these items alone were to be imported by the Indian merchants. Imports were to be limited to two cargoes per year, one for Pen-

---

51. Decision of *Junta Suprema de Estado*, September 22, 1788, AHN Estado, leg. 3885 bis., Exp. 8; Whitaker, *Documents*, 99–103.

52. Navarro to Valdés, June 12, 1789, AHN Estado, leg. 3885 bis, Exp. 8, doc. 57, WP; *Informe* of Navarro, January 15, 1789, AGI SD, leg. 2665, WP.

53. Navarro to Valdés, April 26, December 8, 1789, AGI SD, leg. 2665; Whitaker, *Documents*, xliii–xliv, 102–17.

54. Decision of *Junta Suprema de Estado*, March 16, 1789, AHN Estado, leg. 3888, doc. 23.

sacola and one for Mobile. The merchants were to adhere to the tariff prices as established in 1784. Goods intended for use in the Louisiana Indian trade were specifically excluded from duty-free status. The directive also required the merchants at Mobile and Pensacola to obtain their rum and salt only from Havana.[55]

In late July, when Miró informed Panton of the court's favorable action, the elated merchant expressed general satisfaction with the stipulations set forth in the royal order. Omissions, however, required the two to negotiate clarifications of and additions to the original provisions, and in January 1790 these were approved by the court. For instance, St. Marks, not mentioned in the original royal order, was given the same status as Pensacola and Mobile. Panton, Leslie vessels gained permission to enter the Mississippi, to take on cargoes of sugar crates produced by the sawmills along the river, before voyaging to Havana for salt and rum. In the event of war or of a desire to withdraw voluntarily, the company was entitled to a twelve-month period of grace in which to settle its affairs. Should the partners or associates of Panton, Leslie and Company die in the Spanish provinces, their estates would be exempt from confiscation (*droit d' aubane*). The company, also by this order, received permission to cater to the immediate needs of the inhabitants and garrisons at Mobile, Pensacola, and St. Marks, but the merchants were warned strictly not to abuse this privilege. By no means must duty-free goods find their way into New Orleans, inadvertently or otherwise. Reminded by Panton that his request for relief from duties was submitted during 1788 and intended for that year, the court made the exemptions retroactive as well.[56]

Apparently, Floridablanca had been remiss in informing Ambassador Campo of the commercial privileges granted Panton, Leslie and Company—an oversight that for two years frustrated the efforts of Strachan and MacKenzie to fill Panton's orders. By late September 1789, the Spanish embassy had heard nothing from Madrid on Panton's memorial, leading the company's London correspondents to fear the worst and to request permission to remove the company's effects from West Florida.[57]

Shortly afterward, however, Strachan and MacKenzie learned through correspondence received from John Leslie in St. Augustine of the Spanish court's favorable action and of the company's having received the Mobile

---

55. Copies are included in Domingo Cabello to Zéspedes, June 26, 1789, *AGI PC*, leg. 1792, and Valdés to Miró, March 23, 1789, *AGS Estado*, leg. 8148.

56. Panton to Miró, July 31, 1789; Miró to Panton, August 20, 1789; Valdés to Governor of Louisiana, January 25, 1790, *AHN Estado*, leg. 3901, Exp. 3; Miró to White, August 24, 1789, *AGI PC*, leg. 6, WP; Miró to Valdés, October 1, 1789, and enclosures, *AHN Estado*, leg. 3901, Stetson Collection.

57. Strachan and MacKenzie to Campo, September 25, 1789, *AGS Estado*, leg. 8137.

concession as well. Strachan and MacKenzie immediately apprised Campo of their information and furnished the ambassador with a copy of the royal order, which Leslie had enclosed with his letter.[58] But their pleadings with Campo to authorize two cargoes for West Florida on the strength of the evidence provided came to naught. Lacking directives from the Spanish court, the obdurate diplomat consented to allow only one cargo of moderate value for Pensacola, justifying his action as necessary to avoid disrupting the commerce of the Indians.[59]

The harried merchants worked feverishly to fit out the frigate *Raikes* and to assemble whatever Indian trade wares they could on such short notice. In late October, the *Raikes*, Captain Matthew Forrest commanding, left London. Shortly before the vessel's departure, the merchants and the ambassador engaged in a series of mild recriminatory exchanges. Strachan and MacKenzie deplored the costly haste entailed by Campo's procrastination; Campo, in turn, accused them of having smuggled specie and of having consigned goods to West Florida which were suited to the tastes of persons other than Indians.[60]

Strachan and MacKenzie, fortunately for Panton, had partially offset the adverse consequences of Campo's refusal to issue passports by consigning a small quantity of Indian merchandise to Nassau. This contingency supply would be available should the Spaniards, for some reason, approve the terms Panton had requested. Panton received notice of their action late in December, and the *Raikes* arrived in Pensacola shortly afterward with an account of the arduous dealings with Campo and the uncertainties of Strachan and MacKenzie due to the confusion over the company's status in West Florida.[61]

Panton took steps to resolve the immediate supply problem and also to allay the misgivings of his London correspondents. With Miró's approval, the resourceful Scot arranged the immediate transfer of the merchandise deposited at Nassau to Pensacola, ordered Strachan and MacKenzie to dispatch an additional cargo to Nassau by June for re-exportation to Pensacola, and obtained two passports from the Louisiana governor-intendant for return cargoes from London in the fall of 1790. The latter measure, Panton told Miró, would obviate further dependence on the whims or doubts of the intractable Campo. Later, Miró also furnished the Pensacola

58. Strachan and MacKenzie to Campo, October 3, 1789, ibid.
59. Campo to Strachan and MacKenzie, October 9, 1789, ibid.
60. Strachan and MacKenzie to Campo, October 12, 23, 1789; Campo to Strachan and MacKenzie, October 23, 1789; [Campo?] to Floridablanca, October 1789, *AGS Estado*, leg. 8137.
61. Panton to Miró, December 29, 1789, January 14, 1790, *AGI PC*, leg. 203; Panton to Miró, January 14, 1790, *AGI PC*, leg. 203, Stetson Collection.

tradesman with official copies of the royal orders, confirming the company's commercial privileges in Mobile, for transmittal to Strachan and MacKenzie, a measure required to buttress their confidence in extending credit to the Panton, Leslie concern.[62]

Strachan and MacKenzie complied with Panton's instructions, and in September they informed Campo that they had prepared a cargo for shipment to Pensacola for the 1791 trading season. The goods, they declared, would be freighted on the *Mary*, and they assured the ambassador that they and Captain Forrest would call to receive his orders before the vessel sailed.[63] Campo, however, irately admonished the London merchants for their breach of established procedure. Without express approval from the Spanish court, he protested, neither he, they, nor even Miró could authorize direct sailings to West Florida. If Strachan and MacKenzie persisted in their intentions, Campo would disassociate himself entirely from the affair.[64]

The London merchants apologetically explained that they had acted out of concern to prevent disruptions to the Indian trade and had done so on the strength of the royal orders and passports supplied by Miró, never intending to circumvent Campo's authority. They had acted in order to have everything in readiness for the time when the embassy received the court's instructions on sailing to West Florida. As these were still lacking, Strachan and MacKenzie begged the ambassador's indulgence to permit the ship to sail, despite the absence of court directives. The dispatch of the second vessel, the traders explained, could be safely deferred until the king's instructions arrived. Campo permitted the voyage, taking the occasion to dispatch a letter to Miró, upbraiding him for issuing the controversial passports.[65]

Because of the war scare that grew out of the Nootka Sound crisis, and possibly because Campo's disdain made him indifferent to soliciting his court's advice on governing the Indian trade, the *Mary* was the only vessel dispatched to Pensacola in the fall of 1790. As the limited cargo space of the *Mary* was inadequate for transporting the voluminous bales of peltry on hand in Pensacola and Mobile, Panton alleviated the export problem by engaging space in Mather's *Condesa de Gálvez*, which was

---

62. Panton to Miró, October 9, 1789, *ANC F*, leg. 1, Exp. 5, no. 10, WP; Panton to Miró, December 29, 1789, January 20, 1790; Miró Passport, February 20, 1790, *AGI PC*, leg. 203, Stetson Collection; Miró to O'Neill, January 11, 1790, *AGI PC* leg. 40, Stetson Collection.
63. Strachan and MacKenzie to Campo, September 13, 1790, *AGS Estado*, leg. 8137.
64. Campo to Strachan and MacKenzie, September 15, 1790, ibid.
65. Strachan and MacKenzie to Campo, September 21, 1790; Miró to Campo, April 1, 1791, ibid.

sailing to London with deerskins collected against the defunct trading concern's outstanding credit. He also employed a small brig out of Nassau in the summer and fall of 1791 to bring items in short supply to Pensacola and Mobile.[66]

Meanwhile, Panton complained to Miró that Campo's interference had been "very distressing," and, if repeated, would prove "fatal" to his company's affairs.[67]

Miró dispatched a conciliatory letter to the ambassador, explaining that he had believed that the royal privileges granted Panton, Leslie and Company had empowered him to issue passports for return voyages from London. But in the light of Campo's admonitions, Miró declared he would discontinue the practice and also had warned Panton against bypassing the ambassador's authority in the future. Miró, however, impressed Campo with the urgency of fostering a smooth flow of Indian trade goods from London to West Florida, even in the event of an Anglo-Spanish war. To do less would incur the risk of a Creek defection either to the United States or to English adventurers from the Bahamas.[68]

During the course of 1791, Strachan and MacKenzie received positive assurances from Campo that they would no longer experience delays in the issuance of passports. The change reflected in part the decision of the Spanish ministry to encourage the Panton, Leslie trade, even if war with Great Britain became a reality—which in late 1790 loomed as a distinct possibility.[69] The hostile threats emanating from the Nootka controversy were more than vaguely disquieting. They raised both actual and potential problems for carrying on the West Florida Indian trade.

As the war scare mounted in the summer and fall of 1790, Strachan and MacKenzie became wary of risking a large consignment of goods to West Florida, the colony of a potentially hostile nation. Thus, they shipped fewer goods than ordered for the West Florida trade but shrewdly included, in the same cargo for Pensacola, goods intended for John Leslie at St. Augustine, necessitating re-exportation to East Florida.[70] Moreover, British bans against the export of munitions forced Panton to ask O'Neill

---

66. Panton to Miró, December 20, 1790, *AGI PC*, leg. 203, WP and Stetson Collection; Panton to Miró, December 29, 1790, *ANC F*, leg. 1, Exp. 5, no. 16; Panton to Miró, October 23, 1791, *AGI PC*, leg. 203, WP; Miró to O'Neill, January 5, 1791, *AGI SD*, leg. 2670, WP; Passport for *Condesa de Gálvez*, April 1, 1791, *AGS Estado*, leg. 8137.

67. Panton to Miró, April 18, 1791, *AGI PC*, leg. 40, WP.

68. Miró to Campo, April 1, 1791, *AGS Estado*, leg. 8137.

69. Floridablanca to Campo Alange, June 12, 1790, *AHN Estado*, leg. 3885, bis, Exp. 8, doc 60, WP.

70. Panton to Miró, April 18, 1791; Miró to O'Neill, May 23, 1791, *AGI PC*, leg. 40; Panton, Leslie and Company to J. Nepomuceno de Quesada, May 20, 1791. *AHN Estado*, leg. 3888, doc. 33, WP.

and Miró to lend the company powder, musket balls, and flints—indispensable commodities for reaping the deerskin harvest—from Spanish ordnance stores. O'Neill made available for Panton's use 10,000 pounds of powder and 10,204 pounds of musket balls, only half the amount Panton desired, and less than 4,000 of 40,000 flints requested.[71]

The most perplexing consideration, however, was to devise a means to conduct the sea traffic between West Florida and London under wartime conditions. Panton and Miró conferred on the problem, variously considering such possibilities as exporting peltry under flags of truce and using neutral shipping.[72]

The threat of war also complicated the procurement of salt from Havana, as mandated under the royal order confirming Panton, Leslie and Company's West Florida trade privileges. Anxious to avoid a scarcity, the Havana intendancy, the agency responsible for supervising the royal salt monopoly, simultaneously hesitated to release the quantities required in the southern Indian trade and also drastically increased prices. Negotiations between different branches of Spanish officialdom on the company's salt requirements continued at least through mid-1791, but without causing Panton or his partners undue concern.[73] They had operated a salt works on Little Exuma Island in the Bahamas for several years and were pleased at the opportunity to use their own resources.

In August 1790, Panton informed Miró that dwindling salt supplies at Pensacola and Mobile would necessitate dispatching a ship to Turk's Island for a fresh supply. This communiqué was repeated in October by John Forbes, who would soon assume direction of the company's Mobile store, but with an added request. Forbes also asked Miró's approval to export corn and planks obtained in the Tombigbee-Tensaw district, to be bartered for the needed salt—declaring that it was the company's desire to export such products regularly in the interest of promoting the prosperity of the local inhabitants. Miró disapproved the request, explaining that the practice exceeded the privileges granted the company under the royal order of March 1789. The governor-intendant approved, however, the regular export of West Florida produce to the Bahamas, provided that no cargoes were carried on the return voyages.[74]

71. Panton to Miró, August 20, 1790, *AGI PC*, leg. 203, doc. 14, WP and Stetson Collection; Panton to O'Neill, August 20, 1790, *AGI PC*, leg. 196, West work cards; Miró to O'Neill, December 11, 1790, *AGI PC*, leg. 7.
72. Panton to Miró, August 20, 1790, *AGI PC*, leg. 203, doc. 14; Panton to Miró, January 31, 1791, *AGI PC*, leg. 120, doc. D, WP.
73. Panton to Miró, August 6, 1790, *AGI PC*, leg. 203, doc. 13; Panton to O'Neill, May 19, 1791, *AGI PC*, leg. 204, doc. 13, WP and Stetson Collection.
74. Panton to Miró, August 6, 1790, *AGI PC*, leg. 203; J. Forbes to Miró, October 22,

Accordingly, in December, Panton freighted a cargo aboard the brig *Dispatch*, which had called earlier at Pensacola with an emergency shipment of trade goods from Nassau. The following month the resourceful Scot "took the liberty" to bring some 500 barrels of salt into Pensacola on still another vessel he had engaged in the Bahamas to assist with the 1791 peltry exports. In reporting the unsanctioned arrangement, Panton innocently expressed the hope that Miró would not develop suspicions that he had become a *contrabandista* in salt. Miró acquiesced in the fait accompli.[75]

Thus, by mid-1791, numerous exceptions had been made to the commercial limitations imposed on the company's West Florida activities under the royal order of March 23, 1789. Furthermore, the emergencies arising from the Nootka Sound crisis and Campo's uncooperativeness actually tended to broaden the scope of the company's commercial activities. Exports of West Florida products (grain, lumber, and so on) to the Bahamas became routine, as did the importation of salt from the same islands. From time to time, small assortments of manufactured goods were imported from Nassau—all under the discretionary authority granted the Louisiana intendancy in the interest of preventing a breakdown in the Indian trade.[76] By 1793, Panton, Leslie and Company also gained the privilege of drawing credits (*libranzas*) from the Havana intendancy for the purchase of rum, sugar, and coffee regularly obtained in Cuba. These credits were balanced against the amount due the firm for the concession it held in East Florida to supply fresh beef for the Spanish garrison. The carrying of staves and other wood—perhaps even logwood obtained from Campeche—to ballast ships carrying peltry from West Florida also became a standard practice in the company's operations.[77]

1790, *AGI PC*, leg. 203, Stetson Collection; Forbes to Miró, November 4, 1790, *ANC F*, leg. 1, Exp. 9, no. 2; Miró to Folch, November 2, 1790, *AGI PC*, leg. 7; Miró to O'Neill, December 10, 1790, *AGI SD*, leg. 2670, WP.

75. Miró to O'Neill, December 10, 1790, *AGI SD*, leg. 2670; Panton to Miró, January 31, 1791, *AGI PC*, leg. 120, doc. D; Miró to Panton, February 25, 1791, *AGI PC*, leg. 120, doc. E, WP. In 1786, Panton, Forbes and Company reported that company workers had raked 5,000 bushels of salt at the Great Pond on Little Exuma in ten days: CO 37/23:22, PROL.

76. Luis de las Casas to Miró, February 5, 1791, *AGI PC*, leg. 151B, West work cards; Miró passport, June 27, 1791, *AGI SD*, leg. 2670, WP and Stetson Collection.

77. Panton to Las Casas, June 16, 1793; Panton to J. Leslie, August 28, 1793, *EF* leg. 116L9.

7

McGillivray: Wooed by Washington, Threatened by Bowles

*I*N the spring of 1789, while Spain was granting Panton, Leslie and Company status and tenure in the Floridas, the political leaders of the United States were engaged in forming "a more perfect union." The new federal government faced myriad problems, of which poor relations with the southern Indians—particularly the Creek—were by no means the least. In August 1789, President Washington appeared before a secret session of the Senate to solicit advice on Indian affairs. The upper house concurred with the president on the desirability of securing a treaty with the Creek.[1]

The president appreciated the fact that the Creek likely had legitimate grounds for complaint in their past dealings with Georgia. Thus, in the interest of successful negotiation, he replaced the commissioners named by the former government with men he knew and trusted. Named to the new commission were Cyrus Griffin, the last man to serve as president of the defunct Congress, and Benjamin Lincoln and David Humphreys, both old comrades-in-arms. The new commissioners also shared a lack of prior involvement in the Creek-Georgia dispute. Indeed, the president counted heavily on their presumed impartiality as the best assurance of reaching a fair and amicable settlement.[2]

---

1. DePauw, *First Federal Congress*, 2:31–36.
2. Downes, "Creek-American Relations, 1782–90," 176; *ASP IA*, 1:65–68. Brief biographical sketches of the commissioners appear in Caughey, *McGillivray*, 252n224.

Washington's instructions to the commissioners required them to investigate thoroughly the circumstances surrounding the Creek-Georgian treaties of Augusta, Galphinton, and Shoulderbone. If they discovered that coercion or subterfuge had been employed in the earlier negotiations, the boundary claims of Georgia were not to be upheld. But, Washington advised, since the disputed Oconee lands had already been opened to settlers, it would be "highly embarrassing" to allow the land to revert to Creek control. To induce the Creek to accept Georgia's purported boundaries, the commissioners could offer them a "secure port" through which their trade would flow under conditions identical to those enjoyed by American citizens. The Creek also could be offered gifts, and their influential leaders could be presented with bribes and military titles. If absolutely necessary to conclude an agreement, the commissioners could solemnly guarantee that the federal government would uphold the Creek title to all their remaining lands.[3]

McGillivray felt a lingering dissatisfaction with the Spanish, and Washington's peacemaking efforts were timely. In August, while the president labored at forming Creek policy, McGillivray cavalierly dismissed a threat from Miró to suspend the Creek trade unless depredations against the Tensaw-Tombigbee settlements came to a halt. Had a Spanish trade ban materialized, the Creek leader informed Panton, he could have reached a commercial agreement with the United States quite easily.[4] Earlier in the year, when McGillivray's confidence in Spanish support was much lower, he considered ceding the Oconee lands to Georgia for a suitable equivalent. Panton hastily advised against a cession, pointing out that better trade terms were the only possible gain. Any trade advantages thus derived, Panton prophesied, would be quickly negated. Spain's granting of the commercial concessions he had requested seemed imminent.[5]

McGillivray learned of the accuracy of Panton's prophecy in mid-August, shortly before his scheduled departure for the long-delayed discussions with the American peace commissioners. The Creek spokesman also received assurances from Miró of full Spanish support for the Creek

3. The instructions are in *ASP IA*, 1:65–68, and DePauw, *First Federal Congress*, 2:202–10.

4. McGillivray to Panton, August 10, 1789, *Johnson et al. v. Innerarity et al.*; Pickett, *History of Alabama*, 389–95. A slightly different version, obviously edited by Panton to make it more palatable to Miró, is in *AGI PC*, leg. 203, doc. 7, and in Caughey, *McGillivray*, 245–49. Caughey, unaware that two different copies existed, accused Pickett of printing an inaccurate copy.

5. McGillivray to Panton, May 20, 1789, *ANC F*, leg. 1, Exp. 5, no. 6, WP; Panton to McGillivray, June 7, 1789, *ANC F*, leg. 1, Exp. 5, no. 7, WP. See also Mohr, *Federal Indian Relations*, 170, who paraphrases this letter from the copy in Wagstaff, *John Steele Papers*, 1:51.

position in the treaty discussions. The Creek, Miró advised, need only agree to live at peace with the United States. The Spanish crown would stand squarely behind them should the talks come to naught because of U.S. demands for territory, trade, or any abrogation of the Spanish-Creek treaty of 1784.[6]

McGillivray jubilantly informed both Panton and Miró that the news of the Spanish commercial concessions had silenced the grumblings of the pro-American tribal factions for trade with the Georgians.[7] The Creek spokesman vowed to Miró that he would break off the discussions if the U.S. commissioners insisted on a commercial agreement or on any other condition that would impair the treaty obligations of the Creek to Spain.[8] To Panton, however, McGillivray declared his satisfaction in every respect except one: the Spanish distrust of the Indians.[9]

Early in September, McGillivray and about nine hundred Creek arrived at Rock Landing, the designated treaty grounds, only to discover that Washington's commissioners were still en route. The Creek soon became restless and threatened to leave, but the crisis passed when Lincoln and Humphreys arrived on September 20. McGillivray met informally with the two commissioners the following day.

Contrary to his statements to Miró, McGillivray at first gave every indication of a willingness to bargain openly. He told Lincoln and Humphreys that it was more in the interest of the Creek to establish friendly relations with the United States than with any other power. He also stated that the Creek already enjoyed advantageous commercial benefits and territorial guarantees under the Treaty of Pensacola. These Spanish concessions could not be discarded unless the Creek received suitable equivalents from the United States.[10]

Griffin, Lincoln, and Humphreys, however, had accepted the validity of Georgia's claim to the disputed lands.[11] Consequently, in the ensuing informal exchanges, they noticed a shift in McGillivray's mood. He ex-

---

6. Miró to McGillivray, July 22, 1789, Spanish draft in *AGI PC*, leg. 202, WP; McGillivray to Miró, August 12, 1789, ibid.; Caughey, *McGillivray*, 243–44; and *AHN Estado*, leg. 3887, Exp. 1.

7. McGillivray to Miró, August 12, 1789, *AHN Estado*, leg. 3887, Exp. 1; McGillivray to Panton, August 12, 1789, *AGI PC*, leg. 203, Stetson Collection; Corbitt, "Papers from the Spanish Archives," 21:87.

8. McGillivray to Miró, August 15, 1789, *AHN Estado*, leg. 3887, Exp. 1; Caughey, *McGillivray*, 249–50.

9. McGillivray to Panton, August 15, 1789, *AGI PC*, leg. 203, doc. 7, WP; Corbitt, "Papers from the Spanish Archives," 21:88–89.

10. Humphreys to Washington, September 26, 1789, Humphreys, *Life and Times*, 2:6–9; Downes, "Creek-American Relations, 1782–90," 177–78.

11. Downes, ibid.; Whitaker, "Alexander McGillivray," 292.

pressed dissatisfaction with their boundary proposals, as well as other matters. Despite the worsening atmosphere, General Lincoln presented the Creek in formal assembly with a draft treaty confirming Georgia in possession not only of the Oconee lands but also those lying between the Altamaha and the St. Marys. The terms also required the Creek to recognize the United States as their exclusive protector. In return, the United States recognized the validity of the Creek claim to their remaining tribal lands and offered to establish a port through which Creek commerce could flow on equal terms with those extended to U.S. citizens.[12]

The Creek representatives withdrew to confer among themselves on the American proposals. The following day, September 25, McGillivray sent the commissioners a message expressing particular dissatisfaction with the boundary terms. Announcing that the Creek were departing for the fall hunt, their spokesman promised to maintain a truce until hearing "farther . . . on the part of the United States."[13] The startled commissioners immediately sent Humphreys to confer with McGillivray but to no avail. Humphreys's alternating use of bribes, flattery, and intimidation only angered the Creek spokesman. Two days later the Creek broke camp without even announcing their departure. Subsequent entreaties by intermediaries failed to entice them to return.[14]

In reporting the abortive outcome of their mission to President Washington, the commissioners attributed their failure solely to McGillivray's obstinacy. As evidence, they cited his unwillingness to sever his Spanish ties "without obtaining a full equivalent."[15] They also alluded to McGillivray's "frequent intimations" that the Creek must receive "a free and exclusive Port" on either the Altamaha or the St. Marys and his "most positive refusal" either to recognize the Creek as living within U.S. territorial limits or to accept American protection.[16]

These observations on McGillivray's position were accurate as far as they went. Yet the commissioners omitted any elaboration of what McGillivray might have considered a fair bargain for breaking with the Spaniards. Apparently, he was prepared to forgo a firm commitment from Miró—at least on paper—of Spanish material and diplomatic support for

12. Humphreys to Washington, September 26, 1789, *Life and Times*, 2:6–9. The treaty draft is in "Report of the Commissioners for Southern Indians," DePauw, *First Federal Congress*, 2:224–25.

13. McGillivray to U.S. commissioners [September 25, 1789], DePauw, *First Federal Congress*, 2:225–26.

14. Downes, "Creek-American Relations, 1782–90," 179; McGillivray to U.S. Commissioners, September 27, 1789, *ASP IA*, 1:74–75; DePauw, *First Federal Congress*, 2:229; McGillivray to Panton, October 8, 1789, LPBL; Caughey, *McGillivray*, 251–54.

15. DePauw, *First Federal Congress*, 2:235; *ASP IA*, 1:77–78.

16. *ASP IA*, 1:77–78.

Creek territorial claims. Such a move, of course, probably would have meant the end of the Creek commercial channels through the Spanish Floridas. This consideration, however, would not have caused McGillivray great consternation if he could have gained a free and open trade outlet on the Atlantic between Georgia and East Florida.

From the time he learned of the British loss of East Florida, McGillivray had held to the idea of winning formal recognition of complete sovereignty for the Creek nation.[17] In 1787, he openly declared to Dr. James White that he regarded the United States as the "most natural allies" of the Creek. McGillivray then offered to cede the Oconee lands to Georgia, should Congress create a new state between the Altamaha and the St. Marys.[18] Thereafter, while the status of Panton, Leslie and Company in the Floridas remained tenuous, rumors of its imminent removal to an Atlantic site spread throughout the Creek country.[19]

McGillivray obviously pursued the same line of bargaining at Rock Landing that he had first outlined to White. The official report of the U.S. commissioners substantiates this conclusion. Moreover, in May 1789, McGillivray wrote Panton of his inclination to use the Oconee lands as a bargaining wedge. In the same letter, the Creek leader assured his associate that he would counter any American trade blandishments on the grounds "that it would be ungenerous to leave out or desert" Panton, who had been the "only Support" of the Creek during their long years of distress.[20] Many Georgians attended the Rock Landing conference as casual observers, and many expressed an interest in becoming citizens of the new state McGillivray was attempting to establish.[21] General James Wilkinson, Spain's Kentucky informant, reported to Miró that McGillivray's first demand was for "a free Port on the Atlantic exempt from duty of any kind," a concession the commissioners were powerless to accommodate.[22]

Lincoln, Griffin, and Humphreys indeed lacked authority to grant the Creek a free port, much less to recognize their sovereignty and indepen-

---

17. See, for example, McGillivray to [O'Neill], January 1, 1784, *AGI PC*, leg. 197; McGillivray memorial of July 10, 1785, *AGI PC*, leg. 198; Caughey, *McGillivray*, 64–67, 90–93.

18. James White to Major General Knox, May 24, 1787, *ASP IA*, 1:20–21.

19. O'Neill to Miró, July 28, 1788, *AGI PC*, leg. 38; Corbitt, "Papers from the Spanish Archives," 15:95–98.

20. McGillivray to Panton, May 20–21, 1789, *ANC F*, leg. 1, Exp. 5, no. 6; Corbitt, "Georgia-Florida Frontier," 12:283–88.

21. McGillivray to Panton, October 8, 1789, LPBL; Caughey, *McGillivray*, 251–54; McGillivray to J. Leslie, October 12, 1789, *EF* leg. 116L9; extract in Caughey, *McGillivray*, 254–55.

22. Wilkinson to Miró, January 26, 1790, *AGI PC*, leg. 2374; Corbitt, "Papers from the Spanish Archives," 22:133–39.

dence. Their inability to bestow complete commercial freedom on the Creek apparently stemmed from an action of the U.S. Senate. President Washington knew, from the White mission correspondence and from information supplied by Secretary of War Henry Knox, of McGillivray's ties with the British merchants in the Creek trade and of his earlier dissatisfaction with the Spaniards.[23] Accordingly, while consulting the Senate on the forthcoming Creek negotiations, the president asked for advice on forms of compensation to offer for the Oconee lands, should such a step become necessary. Among other considerations, Washington sought approval to allow the Creek "a secure [free] Port on the Altamaha or St. Mary's Rivers."[24] The Senate concurred in principle, but only after Samuel Otis, the Senate clerk, struck out the word "free" and inserted "secure" in its place.[25] While no explanation for this substitution is offered, it appears that objections were raised, possibly by the Georgia delegation, to allowing the establishment of Tory British Indian merchants on the Atlantic, which would enhance both Creek independence and British influence. But McGillivray, armed with both Spanish backing and assurances that Panton, Leslie and Company had just received royal confirmation of its trade privileges, was unwilling to settle for less.

McGillivray explained to Miró and Zéspedes that the negotiations had reached an impasse because of demands that the Creek recognize the United States as their exclusive protector and because the U.S. commissioners insisted on a land cession. He emphasized his objections to accepting U.S. protection, guilefully declaring his determination to honor Creek treaty obligations to Spain as a major consideration behind termination of the talks.[26] Miró also received, compliments of Panton, copies of extracts from the proposed treaty—minus the "secure port" clause—and other official papers of the commissioners. Yet included among these documents was General Lincoln's official harangue to the Creek assembly, in which he pointed out the advantages they would gain from a secure port.[27] But on this subject, McGillivray remained silent. However, both before and after the Rock Landing talks, Miró received information of McGillivray's ambitions for an outlet to the Atlantic.[28] The Louisiana gov-

23. Knox to Washington, July 6, 1789, *ASP IA*, 1:15–16; White to Knox, May 24, 1787, *ASP IA*, 1:20–21.
24. DePauw, *First Federal Congress*, 2:31–35, esp. 34.
25. Ibid., 34nn60, 63.
26. McGillivray to Miró, December 10, 1789, *AHN Estado*, leg. 3887, Exp. 1; McGillivray to Zéspedes, December 1, 1789, *EF* leg. 114J9.
27. These are enclosures with McGillivray to Miró, December 10, 1789, *AHN Estado*, leg. 3887, Exp. 1. The transcriptions are in the hand of Robert Leslie and are endorsed by Panton. John Forbes served as McGillivray's amanuensis for the letter. A typescript copy of McGillivray's letter, in English (less the enclosures), is in WP.
28. Folch to Miró, July 2, 1789, *AGI PC*, leg. 52; extract in Caughey, *McGillivray*, 242;

ernor prudently overlooked McGillivray's silence, and instead approved the stand the Creek spokesman had taken, except for the abrupt manner in which he broke off the discussions. Miró felt that the United States might seize upon McGillivray's leave-taking as a pretext for war; nevertheless, he agreed to the Creek request for additional arms and ammunition.[29]

President Washington was not yet ready to abandon diplomacy for military action. He believed that his commissioners were at least partly responsible for the collapse of the negotiations at Rock Landing.[30] Furthermore, his administration wanted to enlist the assistance of the Creek in dealing with a challenge to federal control over the Old Southwest—a challenge raised by American land speculators rather than by the Spanish.

Much of the opposition to ratification of the federal constitution had stemmed from the objections of southern land-jobbers to the delegation of the Indian treaty-making power to the United States. The territorial guarantees of the Hopewell treaties—concluded in 1785 and 1786 with the Cherokee, Chickasaw, and Choctaw—had generated much vituperation among speculators, who saw in the accords an unwarranted infringement on their liberty to pursue personal happiness at the expense of the Indians.[31] Fully anticipating similar interference from the Washington administration, prominent southerners sought recourse through Georgia, the only state that had not relinquished its western land claims by 1789. In December of that year, the Georgia assembly obligingly made available 15 million acres of land to three land companies at a negligible cost. The enabling legislation deviated from the precedents set in the earlier attempt to create Houston and Bourbon counties; it contained no provisions for establishing local political subdivisions subject to state authority. The oversight was intentional, for it enabled the South Carolina Yazoo Company, the most energetically directed of the three speculative enterprises, to seek Spanish approval to establish its grant as an autonomous buffer state friendly to the Spanish interest.[32]

The South Carolina Yazoo Company lands stretched eastward from the Mississippi to the Tombigbee, and about fifty miles north and south of Walnut Hills (present-day Vicksburg), the company's chosen site for the commercial center of its enterprise. The company's agent, Dr. James O'Fallon, reputedly a defrocked Irish priest, at first avidly courted Zéspedes, Gardoqui, and Miró in search of Spanish support for its colonization

---

Wilkinson to Miró, January 26, 1790, *AGI PC*, leg. 2374; Corbitt, "Papers from the Spanish Archives," 22:133–39.

29. Miró to McGillivray, January 12, 1790, *AHN Estado*, leg. 3887, Exp. 1; Caughey, *McGillivray*, 255–56.
30. Whitaker, "Alexander McGillivray," 293.
31. Whitaker, *Spanish-American Frontier*," 93, 124–25.
32. Ibid., 126–29.

scheme. Company directors, including Alexander Moultrie, former governor of South Carolina, and Tom Washington, later executed for counterfeiting, sought the aid of McGillivray and such prominent settlers in the Natchez district as Colonel Peter Bryan Bruin, to serve as intermediaries with the Spanish. Company officials declared that McGillivray had been won over: this evidently was a deliberate misrepresentation to enhance the company's prestige in the eyes of prospective settlers.[33]

President Washington deplored the manipulations of the Yazoo speculators which, if unchecked, might well precipitate hostilities with Spain or the Indians, or both. At the very least, the jurisdictional claim of the federal government to the Old Southwest would be jeopardized should the South Carolina Yazoo Company carry out its objectives. Accordingly, the president resolved on one final attempt to secure a treaty with the Creek, whose well-known enmity toward usurpers of Indian lands could prove useful. In May 1790, his personal emissary, Colonel Marinus Willett, bearing a peace-or-war ultimatum addressed to McGillivray, together with an assortment of other compelling considerations, appeared among the villages of the Upper Creek. Included among the messages were guarantees that the proposed treaty would prevent encroachment on Indian lands by land-hungry adventurers.[34]

In June, upon gaining the approval of the Indian assemblies, Willett escorted McGillivray and thirty other Creek and Seminole chiefs to New York for direct negotiations with federal representatives. In explaining his decision to parley in New York, McGillivray emphasized that the United States had promised to check the schemes of the land companies. The explanation seemed sincere. Too many Creek adamantly opposed encirclement by American frontiersmen for McGillivray to risk his leadership by espousing the cause of the South Carolina Yazoo Company. In spite of that, Panton had been sufficiently disturbed by the maneuverings of the company's directors to suggest to Miró that McGillivray's pay and allowances should be increased appreciably to keep him from succumbing to the tempting offers of the "lunatic" speculators. The Scot trader also had thought it prudent to embark on a personal tour of the Choctaw and Chickasaw villages, to harden the resolve of the Indians to resist the enticements of the American land-jobbers.[35]

33. Ibid., 129–34; Kinnaird, *Spain in the Mississippi Valley*, 2:27–29. A biography of Peter Bryan Bruin, by William S. Coker, currently in manuscript, includes a chapter on the South Carolina Yazoo Company's plans and efforts to establish a separate state on the Mississippi and its attempts to secure Bruin's assistance.

34. Hawkins to McGillivray, March 6, 1790, AGI PC, leg. 203, doc. 124, WP; McGillivray to Panton, May 8, 1790, AGI PC, leg. 203, doc. 125, WP; Caughey, *McGillivray*, 256–63.

35. Willett, *Narrative*, 105–13; McGillivray to Panton, May 8, 1790, AGI PC, leg. 203,

While visiting the Chickasaw, Panton learned of Willett's presence among the Creek. The merchant immediately made a forced march of more than three hundred miles to Little Tallassee in hopes of counseling his associate on how to deal with the Americans. To his regret, however, when Panton arrived at his destination, McGillivray already had left for New York. Although less confident than McGillivray of the chances of securing a treaty with the United States that would leave intact the Creek commitments to Spain, Panton nevertheless believed that McGillivray would reject any proposal that might be "Considered injurious to Spain or disgracefull to himself and friends."[36]

In New York, the movements of the Creek delegates came under the close scrutiny of both British and Spanish agents. The presence of unwanted intruders caused Secretary of War Knox, the harried chief American negotiator, to isolate McGillivray behind a heavy protective barrier.[37] Indeed, the interference of foreigners well may have prevented the American representatives from driving as hard a bargain as they wished. This, and McGillivray's adroitness, proved Panton's confidence in the Creek leader's trustworthiness to be well founded. The final treaty, signed August 7, 1790, while slightly injurious to Spanish pride, was considerate of the interests of McGillivray's "friends."

The Treaty of New York consisted of both open and secret articles. The open articles established "perpetual" peace and friendship between the Creek and Seminole nations and the United States and recognized the United States as the exclusive protector of all Creek residing within the limits of the United States. The Creek yielded the disputed Oconee lands to Georgia but retained possession of their hunting grounds lying between the Altamaha and St. Marys rivers—a partial victory for both disputants. The new boundaries were to be marked by a joint U.S.–Creek surveying party in October 1791. The United States absolutely guaranteed complete tribal control over all remaining Creek lands. Minor provisions included procedures for maintaining amicable relations, aid for the Creek in adapting themselves to a more domestic life-style, and provisions for assigning American interpreters to Creek villages.[38]

While preparing for the Creek negotiations, President Washington

---

doc. 1, WP; Caughey, *McGillivray*, 256–62; Panton to Miró, May 4, 1790, *AHN Estado*, leg. 3898.

36. Panton to Miró, July 12, 1790, *AGI PC*, leg. 203, doc. 12, WP; Caughey, *McGillivray*, 267–70.

37. Wright, "Treaty of 1790," 388–92; Howard to Quesada, September 24, 1790, *AGI PC*, leg. 1436; Caughey, *McGillivray*, 281–84.

38. The open articles are in *ASP IA*, 1:81–82, and DePauw, *First Federal Congress*, 2:241–48.

and his advisors had hoped, by including generous trade concessions in the treaty, to entice McGillivray into breaking his connections with both Panton and Spain. The American negotiators gave much importance to McGillivray's earlier demands for a free port, assuming that he was interested in monopolizing the Creek trade for himself.[39] Consequently, Secretary of State Thomas Jefferson devised a plan by which the United States might capitalize on the Creek leader's pecuniary interests. However, McGillivray's association with the British merchants would have to be terminated and U.S. citizens would replace them.[40] Jefferson indicated that achieving this purpose almost certainly would require allowing McGillivray to retain absolute control of the Creek trade, which would have to be granted duty-free status. Thus, Jefferson suggested, the treaty should specify that all persons wishing to trade with the Creek must first obtain a special license from the president, and the licenses granted should be strictly limited in number. The treaty also should stipulate that, before receiving a license, an applicant must be approved by the Creek nation. Since the treaty, once ratified by the Senate, would have the full force of law, it would bestow de facto sanction on a duty-free trade monopoly controlled by McGillivray—particularly if it were tacitly understood "that the stipulated number of licenses shall be sent to him blank, to fill up."[41]

But the negotiations failed to detach McGillivray from Panton or, for that matter, from the Spaniards. The Creek spokesman resisted every American inducement to relinquish the Spanish trade connection, even the persuasive argument that the Nootka Sound Crisis portended a war which would be certain to disrupt Spanish commerce. Forewarned of McGillivray's interest in the British mercantile firm, the United States became painfully aware during the treaty conferences of his preference for Panton, Leslie and Company. Washington and Knox even offered, at one point, to extend American citizenship to Panton and his associates, to grant their firm privileges identical to those they enjoyed under Spain, and to allow them access to an Atlantic port. McGillivray replied that he doubted whether the Britons would accept.[42]

As a result, the parties agreed to defer action on any definite U.S.–Creek trade arrangements until agreement could be reached in subse-

39. Fitzpatrick, *Diaries of George Washington*, 4:54; Humphreys to Washington, September 26, 1789, Humphreys, *Life and Times*, 2:6–9; Willett "talks" to "Ositchy" and "Tuckabatchy," May 17, 21, 1790, Willet, *Narrative*, 105–8.
40. Boyd, "McGillivray's Monopoly," *Jefferson Papers*, 17:288–89.
41. Ibid., 289.
42. McGillivray to Howard, August 11, 1790, *AGI PC*, leg. 182; Howard to Quesada, September 24, 1790, *AGI PC*, leg. 1436; Caughey, *McGillivray*, 273–76, 281–84.

quent discussions on or before August 1, 1792. The U.S. Senate ratified this stipulation as part of Secret Article I of the final treaty. Evidently, this provision was intended to give McGillivray time to discuss the commercial offers with Panton and John Leslie. The same articles also gave McGillivray an important option to escape possible dire consequences to the Creek trade resulting from the Nootka Sound incident, as well as from the vagaries of future Spanish policy changes. In case of obstructions rising from "war or prohibitions by the Spanish government," the president was empowered to appoint "persons . . . to introduce into and transport through the territories of the United States to the . . . Creek nation" duty-exempt goods of up to $60,000 in value. This concession, similar in principle to Jefferson's recommendations for handling the trade issue, would remain effective "as long as such obstructions shall continue."[43]

In seeking the advice and consent of the Senate on this article, President Washington reported that "the present arrangements of the trade with the Creeks have caused much embarrassment." Their commerce, he continued, was "almost exclusively in the hands of a Company of British merchants, who, by agreement, [made] their importations of Goods from England into the Spanish ports."[44] Washington conceded the importance of trade control to the "political management" of the Indians, without which the United States might be powerless to hold the Creek to specific performance of their treaty obligations. Yet it could prove even more disastrous to the interests of the United States to leave the Creek commerce liable to interruption "at the caprice of two foreign Powers."[45] Although rechanneling the Creek trade through the United States was a matter of "real importance," Washington resignedly reported that the undertaking would "require time, as the present arrangments cannot be suddenly broken without the greatest violation of faith and morals."[46]

McGillivray divulged the secret trade provisions to Panton, but apparently he and his partners were, at best, lukewarm to the notion of accepting either U.S. sponsorship or U.S. citizenship.[47] They were content with

43. DePauw, *First Federal Congress*, 2:248–50; President Washington sought and received Senate approval of the secret trade article on August 4, 1790, three days before the conclusion of the negotiations. His covering letter implied that the postponement of a commercial agreement with the Creek arose from McGillivray's need to consult Panton and Leslie beforehand. See note 44.
44. Washington's message to the Senate, August 4, 1790, DePauw, *First Federal Congress*, 2:86–87.
45. Ibid.
46. Ibid.
47. McGillivray habitually entrusted Panton with U.S. correspondence and documents for copying and transmittal to Spanish authorities. Many of the originals were retained by Panton. See McGillivray to Panton, February 1, 1789, *AGI PC*, leg. 202; Caughey,

the terms of the commercial concession recently won from the Spanish court, and even more so once the Nootka Sound incident was amicably settled. Besides, the American offer made no mention of the company's status in the Choctaw and Chickasaw trade. In addition, as British citizens, the partners enjoyed important advantages within the framework of British mercantilism. Further, the option of rerouting their trade through the United States gave Panton, Leslie and Company, as well as the Creek, leverage to keep Spanish officials solicitous of their mutual interests. To have exercised the option would have eliminated its greatest immediate advantage.

Another of the secret articles included McGillivray's promise "to cultivate the firmest friendship between the United States and the said Creek nation." In return, McGillivray received an appointment as brigadier general in the American army at an annual salary of $1,200. To qualify for these rewards, the Creek spokesman took an oath of allegiance to the United States.[48]

After his return to the Creek country, McGillivray reported to Spanish officials, with reasonable candor, the developments at New York. Recognition of U.S. protection over Creek villages lying within U.S. territory, the Creek leader explained, could be obviated by Spanish diplomacy in any subsequent boundary agreement with the Americans. The trade article, he first reported, had seemed necessary in the face of the Nootka Sound crisis, but it had become superfluous with the settlement of that problem. He subsequently made known the full ramifications of the trade article. On the matter of his appointment as brigadier general and his pension, however, McGillivray was less than candid, indeed, evasive and untruthful. In one instance, McGillivray reported that he had accepted the military rank with resignation after "being repeatedly pressed to do so." In another, McGillivray stated that he had refused the military commission because of the required oath of allegiance. The pension, he explained, was offered as compensation for the loss of his family estate, which had been confiscated by Georgia.[49]

McGillivray, 215–20. Among these papers was an original copy of the secret articles of the Treaty of New York, which was subsequently submitted as "Exhibit H," *Johnson et al. v. Innerarity et al.*; this copy remains in the LSSC. McGillivray also explained the trade discussions at New York to John Leslie personally in the presence of Carlos Howard: see Howard to Quesada, September 24, 1790, AGI PC, leg. 1436; Caughey, *McGillivray*, 281–84.

48. DePauw, *First Federal Congress*, 2:248–49. For the oath of allegiance, see "Alexander McGillivray's Oath of Allegiance," 47–48.

49. McGillivray to Miró, February 26, 1791, AGI PC, leg. 184; McGillivray to Miró, June 8, 1791, AGI PC, leg. 2371; McGillivray to Howard, August 11, 1790, AGI PC, leg. 182; Caughey, *McGillivray*, 273–76, 288–93.

Miró speculated with remarkable accuracy on Washington's trade strategy. Before receiving McGillivray's report on the discussions at New York, the Louisiana governor shrewdly estimated that the Creek leader might be coaxed into divulging the details of Creek trade connections in the Floridas and perhaps enticed to approach Panton on relocating in the United States.[50] Such an approach, in Miró's view, comported well with the eagerness of the United States to acquire the Creek trade. Perhaps James Wilkinson, Spain's agent in Kentucky, influenced Miró's speculations. While the Creek deputation was en route to New York, Wilkinson passed along the rumor that Panton, Leslie, and McGillivray were seeking citizenship from Georgia, reminding Miró that "Scotchmen throughout the World are governed by the basest Interests."[51]

Despite his growing mistrust, Miró responded cautiously to the new state of affairs. He limited himself to remonstrating with McGillivray against forming close connections with the United States and invited him to New Orleans for consultations. Reversing his earlier position, Miró recommended an increase in salary to 2,000 pesos a year for McGillivray, as the Creek leader had requested before departing for New York. The Louisiana governor also recommended dispatching a Spaniard as agent to the Creek to keep them under close surveillance, stressing the importance of taking advantage of McGillivray's pleas for administrative assistance.[52] The court approved both measures and even instructed Miró to double McGillivray's salary if necessary; retaining the friendship of the powerful Creek spokesman had assumed extreme importance in Spanish policy.[53]

For all the furor it created, the Treaty of New York never went into effect. The Spaniards, apprehensive over its implications for the boundary question, maintained that it infringed on the Treaty of Pensacola of 1784.[54] The Georgians denounced it because of the threat it posed to state land claims and also because it sealed the fate of the Yazoo land companies.[55] Some Creek demonstrated open displeasure when McGillivray explained

50. Miró to Las Casas, October 16, 1790, *AGI PC*, leg. 1440; Caughey, *McGillivray*, 285–86.
51. Wilkinson to Miró, July 20, 1790, Corbitt, "Papers from the Spanish Archives," 24:108.
52. Miró to McGillivray, March 29, 1791, *AGI PC*, leg. 202, WP; Miró to Valdés, August 10, 1790, Miró Papers, NOPL; Miró to McGillivray, November 20, 1790, *AGI PC*, leg. 7, doc. D, WP.
53. O'Neill to [?], March 29, 1791, *AGI PC*, leg. 40, WP; Pedro de Lerena to Miró, December 25, 1790, Caughey, *McGillivray*, 290n265.
54. O'Neill to Las Casas, October 18, 1790, *AHN Estado*, leg. 3898; Corbitt, "Papers from the Spanish Archives," 24:119–21; Miró to Las Casas, October 16, 1790, *AGI PC*, leg. 1440; Las Casas to McGillivray, July 7, 1791, *AGI PC*, leg. 1484; Caughey, *McGillivray*, 285–86; 293n270.
55. Whitaker, "Alexander McGillivray," 299–300.

the terms of the treaty in council, largely because it yielded the Oconee lands to the Georgians.[56] Latent dissatisfaction among the Creek over the treaty paved the way for a serious challenge to McGillivray's authority from William Augustus Bowles who, on returning from London to the Creek country, exploited the treaty's unpopularity.

Bowles and his small entourage of Lower Creek and Chickamauga chiefs arrived in London in October 1790, on the eve of the climax of the Spanish-British war threat. Accordingly, they found in Home Secretary William Grenville a sympathetic listener. Grenville, occupied with planning military action against Spain, welcomed Bowles's petitions for British protection for the Cherokee and Creek in return for their services as British auxiliaries, and he arranged an audience for them with George III. But Spain capitulated to British demands before the appointed time of the audience, and the crisis passed. In the interest of avoiding needless provocation of Spain and the United States, the Indian deputation's appearance before the throne was canceled.[57]

Nonetheless, Bowles and his Indian colleagues remained in London well into the following spring, with Bowles dividing his time between social engagements and salvaging what he could from the unfortunate turn of events. Open British support for the Indians was out of the question for the moment, so the adventurer devised another approach. Boldly proclaiming the existence of the independent state of "Muskogee," and himself as director general of its Creek and Cherokee citizens, Bowles sought British political recognition for his creation. "Director General" Bowles confided to Grenville that Muskogee would establish free ports and seek direct trade with the Bahamas, even if it meant war with Spain. Bowles implied that a victorious Muskogee, by virtue of its mastery of the Floridas and Louisiana, might some day become a valuable British ally.[58]

Seeing merit in Bowles's scheme, Grenville, insofar as decorum permitted, encouraged the "director general" to pursue his ambitions. While advising Bowles against expecting open aid, the home secretary stretched the intent of the Free Port Act of 1787 to assure him that ships flying the Muskogee ensign would be welcome at Nassau. In short, Bowles gained de facto recognition of the sovereign state of Muskogee in return for its possible future value to British adventures in North America.[59]

The "director general" also found ample time for negotiations with His Catholic Majesty's ambassador, the Marqués del Campo, and became

56. Swan, "Muscogee Nation," 5:254; McGillivray to Knox, May 18, 1792, *ASP IA*, 1:315–16.
57. Wright, *William Augustus Bowles*, 48–50.
58. Ibid., 51–54.
59. Ibid., 54.

a frequent guest at the residence of the Spanish emissary. Taking up the ideas expressed to Spanish officials in his letters of 1789, Bowles denounced Panton, Leslie's despoilment of the Indians through arbitrary price gouging, and maintained that a free port for Muskogee was an essential remedy. Bowles also divulged that Great Britain was in no way involved with either Muskogee or himself and that he would open negotiations with the Florida officials immediately upon his return to the Creek country.[60]

Bowles reached Nassau in June 1791, where Lord Dunmore enthusiastically, if not openly, embraced the state-building scheme. John Miller once again fitted out a vessel to take Bowles to the mainland and stocked it with a small quantity of goods intended for opening trade with Muskogee. Sailing out of New Providence in August, the ship first called at Indian River, unloaded a portion of the cargo intended for the Seminole, and then rounded the Florida cape en route to Apalachee Bay. Immediately after landing there, Bowles made his way to the Lower Creek villages for a joyous reception by Chief Perryman, his father-in-law, and Chief Philatouchy.[61]

While Bowles, Miller, and Dunmore were making preparations for Bowles's return to the mainland, Thomas Forbes kept his partners abreast of their rivals' plans. Panton and Leslie in turn alerted the Spanish authorities to the imminent arrival of the "villanous" Bowles.[62] Spanish warships, dispatched from Havana and St. Augustine, failed to intercept their elusive quarry, however. Forbes also warned Panton and Leslie that the rumored first objective of the self-appointed "director general" of Muskogee was an organized Indian attack against St. Marks. It was to be the initial move in a strategy designed to bring the Florida coastline, from the mouth of the Apalachicola to the southernmost tip of the peninsula, under Indian control by right of effective occupation.

Forbes further calculated that Bowles would move quickly to ingratiate himself once again with McGillivray.[63] In this the Nassau merchant was mistaken. Bowles actually intended to break McGillivray's control over the Creek, and to become his successor. McGillivray's complicity in framing the Treaty of New York, Bowles shrewdly surmised, made him vulnerable to attack. With McGillivray pushed aside, Bowles planned to organize the Indians from the Gulf coast to the Great Lakes into a grand

60. Ibid., 53–54.
61. Ibid., 55–57.
62. T. Forbes to J. Leslie, August 1, 1791, *AGI PC*, leg. 2362, WP; Quesada to O'Neill, August 20, 1791, *EF* leg. 114J9, WP; Panton to Miró, October 8, 1791, *AGI PC*, leg. 203; Caughey, *McGillivray*, 295–97.
63. Forbes to Leslie, August 1, 1791, *AGI PC*, leg. 2362, WP.

confederacy, to solicit aid from British outposts in Canada, and to drive the Spaniards out of Louisiana and the Floridas.

Bowles opened his bid for power early in the fall of 1791 at Coweta, before a grand Indian council attended by Upper and Lower Creek, Chickamauga, and Seminole. Addressing the council, Bowles announced that he had come to protect the Indians from their enemies, both within and without. McGillivray, he declared, had betrayed the Creek to the United States at New York, not only by giving away their lands, but also by accepting U.S. pay. Furthermore, he alleged, the traitorous McGillivray was even then in collusion with the Yazoo speculators to deprive Indians of still more of their precious hunting grounds. But, fortunately for the Indians, Bowles, a duly commissioned British Indian superintendent (so he said), would rescue them from all their foes—the land-hungry Americans, the deceitful Spaniards, and Panton, Leslie and Company, who were Spain's willing agents. Asserting that thousands of loyalists waited in the Bahamas for his call to arms, Bowles promised his listeners that he would restore the happy existence they had known before the evil days of 1776. As the preliminary step in bringing about the halcyon years of British dominance, Bowles requested authority to establish two ports, to open direct commerce with the Bahamas. The first, at the mouth of the Indian River, would serve primarily the Seminole. The second, to be located near the mouth of either the Apalachicola or the Ocklochonee river, would be accessible to all the southern Indians.[64]

Shortly after Bowles arrived on the Florida coast, McGillivray informed Panton that Bowles's prime objective seemed to be the ruination of the company. When subsequent reports indicated that an assault on his own power was an equally important goal, the shaken McGillivray attempted to counter the threat. He visited the Lower Creek villages and tried to lure the heavily protected Bowles into capture on the pretext of a desired conference. McGillivray then appointed three assassins, but these found their assignment impossible to carry out. Bowles's persuasiveness made serious inroads into McGillivray's following, especially among the Lower Creek and Seminole but among some Upper Creek as well. Dismayed and dejected by his challenger's erosive tactics, McGillivray declared himself "absolutely worn down" by his responsibilities and journeyed to Pensacola, to seek reassurance from Panton and for his personal safety. The exultant Bowles interpreted his rival's retreat as abdication.[65]

The Spaniards, alarmed at Bowles's ascendancy among the Creek and

---

64. Wright, *William Augustus Bowles*, 58–60.
65. McGillivray to Panton, October 28, 1791, *AGI PC*, leg. 2362; Caughey, *McGillivray*, 298–300, McGillivray to Panton, March 12, 1792, *ANC F*, leg. 1, Exp. 5, WP; Corbitt, "Georgia-Florida Frontier," 22:189–90; Wright, *William Augustus Bowles*, 59–60.

Seminole, considered his renewed presence a definite menace to their weak foothold in the Floridas. They responded ambivalently because they feared the adverse consequences that strong opposition to the "director general" might bring. On the other hand, Panton reported the movements of Bowles and his followers in Nassau and confidently predicted that his downfall was inevitable.[66] Success in maintaining a strong following among the Indians, Panton knew, depended on keeping them adequately supplied with gifts and trade. In Bowles's case, these were slow in coming.

In the fall, meanwhile, George Wellbank, who was Bowles's second-in-command, had supervised the construction of crude facilities for the first free port of Muskogee at a site near the mouth of the Ocklochonee. But the traffic from and to Nassau was light, and only occasionally did small quantities of supplies trickle in. In this critical situation, Bowles, never lacking in audacity, sent runners to obtain provisions from the Panton, Leslie and Company store at St. Marks, asking to be billed as a British director of Indian affairs. Indeed, Bowles and a recent addition to his staff, William Cunningham—a Maryland loyalist and more recently an expatriate of the defunct state of Franklin, whom Bowles "commissioned" as a major—seem to have established friendly relations, at least temporarily, with Edward Forrester, the St. Marks storekeeper.[67]

In New Orleans, meanwhile, Francis Luis Hector, Barón de Carondelet, succeeded Miró as governor-intendant of Louisiana and West Florida. In January 1792, Carondelet began preparations for a coordinated land-sea expedition against Bowles in which McGillivray and Panton were asked to lend assistance.[68] Before the operation could be launched, however, Major Cunningham, supported by Bowles and a party of Indians lying in ambush, repaid Edward Forrester's courtesy by seizing the St. Marks trading post. Bowles had decided that gifts and supplies plundered from Panton, Leslie and Company would preserve his influence better than empty promises of supplies from the Bahamas.[69]

Panton learned of the capture of his St. Marks post early in February and estimated his losses at a minimum of $10,000, excluding the possible plundering of deerskins.[70] Unsuited by temperament to comtemplating

---

66. Panton to Miró, December 11, 1791, *AGI PC*, leg. 203, doc. 20, WP.

67. Wright, *William Augustus Bowles*, 64–66; Bowles to R. Leslie, January 9, 1792, *AGI PC*, leg. 203, WP.

68. Carondelet to McGillivray, January 19, 1792, and to Panton, same date. *EF* leg. 114J9.

69. Statement of Edward Forrester, February 28, 1792, *AGI PC*, leg. 2371; the statement (misdated 1782) is in Kinnaird, "Seizure of Panton's Store," 170–76; Wright, *William Augustus Bowles*, 66.

70. Panton to Carondelet, February 9, 1792, *AGI PC*, leg. 203, doc. 4, WP.

losses, the irate Scot immediately brought to bear all of his influence, his powers of persuasion, and his considerable fortune against his adversary.

Writing to McGillivray, Panton caustically stated that "the vessels which Bowles expected [were] neither more nor less than the Goods in our Store."[71] He called on the irresolute "first chief" of the Creek to bring together the headmen and demand to know what the company had done to merit such treachery. As recompense for supporting the Indians in times of starvation and when they were beset by enemies, Panton fumed, they had "Joined with a Scoundrel to destroy me."[72] He indicated his willingness to forgo restitution but not blood satisfaction and demanded either "the Life of that Villain Bowls" or his delivery to the Spaniards for trial.[73] In a separate "talk" addressed to the Creek nation, Panton reminded the Indians of their "solemn" promise to protect the store at St. Marks as a prior condition of its establishment. Unlike Bowles, he declared, he had not appeared among the Indians "in the Garb of poverty and wretchedness"; nor did he lead them "with lies to the Sea there to gape at the Wind, looking for Vessels that [would] never arrive."[74] Instead, Panton continued, he had supported the Indians in all their troubles. He laid on Bowles the principal burden of blame for the misconduct of the Indians and said that he would be reconciled if they apologized to McGillivray for having deserted him under the calumnious influence of "that Prince of Liars," whom they must punish.[75] Panton also offered incentives to prospective assassins, such as cancellation of debt and lifetime freedom from poverty for the death of Bowles—"a publick Pirate, who it becomes every good man's duty to Hunt down as one would a mad Dog---."[76]

Meanwhile, the looting of the St. Marks store continued unabated. Edward Forrester and John Leslie's younger brother, Robert, who had taken refuge in the Spanish fort, were unable to prevail upon the commandant to take effective action against Bowles's well-armed, superior forces. With fewer than fifty soldiers available, the Spanish officer considered it impossible to do more than defend his post. But the feared Indian assault against the fort never materialized. Bowles developed second thoughts about besieging and capturing the Spanish outpost, deciding in-

---

71. Panton to McGillivray, February 9, 1792, *AGI PC*, leg. 203, doc. 24, WP; Caughey, *McGillivray*, 307–8.
72. Caughey, ibid.
73. Ibid.
74. Panton "talk" to the Creek, February 19, 1792, *AGI PC*, leg. 203, doc. 25, WP; Caughey, *McGillivray*, 308–10.
75. Ibid.
76. Panton to R. Leslie, March 4, 1792, extract in *AGI PC*, leg. 203, doc. 25, WP.

stead that the time was ripe to induce the Spaniards through peaceful negotiations to discard both Panton and McGillivray.[77]

Word of Bowles's depredations at St. Marks, reaching East Florida, terrified John Forrester, Edward's brother, who was then managing the Panton, Leslie Indian trading post on the St. Marys River, near Kings Ferry. Forrester had opened the store there in November 1791, only two months before the events at St. Marks. In addition to running the store, Forrester had been commissioned by Governor Juan Nepomuceno de Quesada to look after new inhabitants in the area. Informed that Bowles had sacked the St. Marks store, Quesada immediately dispatched a sergeant, a corporal, and eight soldiers to the St. Marys, not only to protect the company's property but because the store was the most centrally located point for the defense of the district. A few weeks later, reports reached the St. Marys that Bowles was en route to attack that trading post as well. The nearby settlers quickly gathered at the store and requested a cannon from the governor so that they could better defend themselves. However, in spite of persistent rumors to the contrary, Bowles and his Indian allies did not march on the St. Marys. Instead, he decided, not very wisely, to play his game with the Spanish in West Florida and in Louisiana.[78]

On receiving news of the capture of the Panton, Leslie store, Carondelet immediately dispatched the *Galga*, Captain Pedro Rousseau commanding, and twenty-three soldiers led by Ensign José de Hevia, to augment the St. Marks garrison and to prevent contact between Bowles and the Bahamas. Shortly after his arrival, Hevia succeeded in luring the "director general" into the fort on the pretext of receiving peace offerings from Carondelet. Within the walls of the fort, Hevia carefully nurtured Bowles's hopes of coming to terms with Spain. The ensign declared that while Bowles's desire for free ports and friendly relations with Spain would receive full attention, St. Marks scarcely provided the proper setting for deliberations of such consequence. Hevia suggested that Bowles should therefore accompany him to New Orleans for conversations with Carondelet, offering him safe conduct and a solemn promise that he could return within forty days, whatever the outcome of the talks. Bowles accepted, leaving Wellbank in command during his absence.[79]

77. Wright, *William Augustus Bowles*, 66–67; Robert Leslie to Panton, January 30, 1792, *AGI PC*, leg. 203, WP; Caughey, *McGillivray*, 305–6.
78. Manuel Rodriquez to Fernando de la Puente, February 4, 1792; Quesada to Manuel Rodriquez, February 6, 1792; Quesada to Fernando Medina, February 6, 1792; Fernando Medina to Quesada, February 18, 1792, *EF* leg. 122E10. See chap. 2, note 2, for additional documentation.
79. Wright, *William Augustus Bowles*, 67–69; R. Leslie to Panton, March 9, 1792, *ANC F*, leg. 1, Exp. 5, no. 18, WP; Corbitt, "Georgia-Florida Frontier," 22:184–86.

Panton soon sent McGillivray's brother-in-law, Louis Le Clerc de Milfort, a native of France, at the head of a large war party of loyal Creek against Bowles's "renegade" followers. After lengthy harangues, Milfort talked Wellbank into surrendering the store and dispersing his followers. The losses incurred by the company at St. Marks were reported at over £2,800, not necessarily an inflated figure. Panton advised Carondelet that, everything considered, his losses exceeded $15,000 (see table 2).[80]

Panton at first assumed, mistakenly, that Carondelet would mete out swift justice to Bowles for his misdeeds. The Scottish merchant, therefore, asked Carondelet for evidence obtained from questioning Bowles and Cunningham. The latter had taken refuge in the Spanish post at St. Marks after quarreling with Bowles, only to be arrested. Panton hoped that information exacted from them might be useful against Miller and Dunmore.[81]

Instead, Bowles captivated the baron and in the process discredited Panton and McGillivray in the Spanish governor's eyes. Panton's inflated prices, Bowles claimed, had made the merchant an object of hatred among the Indians. McGillivray, by ceding the Oconee lands and by becoming an American agent, had forfeited the respect of his Creek following. The suspicious Carondelet was convinced of the basic accuracy of Bowles's allegations, despite Panton's advice against placing any trust in "that Jockey . . . [whose] volubility of Speech Can only be equalled by his Empudence, in uttering the grocest falsehoods."[82]

By casting aspersions against Panton and McGillivray, Bowles hoped to gain Carondelet's assent to a Spanish-Muskogee alliance. Toward this end, Bowles also emphasized that it was as much to the interest of Spain as it was to the Creek to foil the designs of the United States in fixing the Oconee boundary. Bowles also declared that, as the supreme leader of Muskogee, he not only held sway over the Chickamauga and Creek but also had a treaty of alliance with the northern tribes. Only Carondelet's recognition of Muskogee and its right to trade freely with the Bahamas

---

80. Panton to Carondelet, April 12, 1792, ANC F, leg. 1, Exp. 5, no. 24, WP; Corbitt, "Georgia-Florida Frontier," 22:289–90; Panton to O'Neill, May 28, 1792, AGI PC, leg. 39; Wright, *William Augustus Bowles*, 70; "Statement of Losses," signed by Robert Leslie, Edward Forrester, and John Innerarity [Sr.], NARG 94. In 1799, Panton stated that the losses amounted to only £2,681, 1s., or $11,915.06 ¼ reales: ASP PL, 4:161–62. It should be noted that the John Innerarity who signed the statement at Apalachee in 1791 was the father of James and John Innerarity, Panton's nephews.

81. Wright, *William Augustus Bowles*, 71–72; Panton to Carondelet, April 12, 1792, ANC F, leg. 1, Exp. 5, no. 24, WP.

82. Panton to Carondelet, March 17, 1792, ANC F, leg. 1, Exp. 5, no. 19; Wright, *William Augustus Bowles*, 73.

Table 2. "A Statement of the Losses sustained by the Plundering Indians at Appalachy in the 16th January 1792, viz."

Amount of inventory of goods existing in Apalachy November 1, 1791, including one-quarter per cent. on the goods	£5,550	16	9			
Amount of invoice of November 1, 1791, with four per cent. to cover charges	1,239	15	3			
				£6,790	12	0
Sold from the store from November 1, 1791, to January 16, 1792, by account taken from the books by R. Leslie, with four per cent., in order to agree with the inventory and invoice	564	11	8½			
Preserved since the robbers were expelled, according to inventory taken the 16th of March by R. Leslie, with four per cent.	623	1	10½			
	1,187	13	7			
In the inventory of November, 1791, were included the cattle, horses, hogs, poultry, negroes &c., of which were preserved—						
60 head of cattle, at 64s.	£ 192	0	0			
10 hogs, at 40s.	20	0	0			
2 dozen hens, at 11s. 3d.	1	2	6			
18 horses, at 90s.	81	0	0			
Negroes, according to inventory	857	0	0			
15 old trunks and a press filled with peltry, according to invoice	42	10	0			
Perogue, boat chalan, &c., per invoice	29	1	0			
All the peltry, per invoice	1,486	12	0			
House furniture, per invoice	5	0	0			
Plate and silks charged to Perryman's wife, with four per cent.	74	14	1			
H. Smith charged to Barnet this sum, recovered according to daybook	135	14	8			
Omissions, &c.	4	3	2			
				£ 4,116	11	0
Loss in pounds sterling				2,674	1	0
By amount of actual loss by the preceding statement				£ 2,674	1	0
100 bushels of corn omitted, bought between the 1st of November and the 16th of January				30	0	0
Expenses incurred at the fort for provisions for Indians and others assisting us, and our own living				100	0	0
				£–2,804	1	0

We certify that the preceding account is a true statement of the loss sustained by Panton, Leslie & Company from the robber Bowles and his followers. Apalachy, June 24, 1792.

ROBERT LESLIE.
EDWARD FOSTER.
JOHN INNERARITY.

Sources: see note 80.

was necessary to forge a formidable Indian coalition that would check American westward penetration from Canada to the Gulf of Mexico.[83]

Although impressed with the abilities of the "director general," Carondelet could see little benefit for Spain in replacing Panton and McGillivray with another set of pro-British agents. Furthermore, yielding free ports to Muskogee would release the southern Indians from dependency on Spanish trade outlets. Meeting Bowles's demands, Carondelet reasoned, would raise the threat of ultimate British dominance of the Mississippi Valley—a poor bargain for removing the immediate threat of U.S. expansion.[84]

Accordingly, to isolate Bowles from the Creek, Carondelet persuaded him to sail to Havana for further negotiations with Captain General Luis de Las Casas. Upon arrival, Bowles discovered that he had been duped by the Spaniards. The adventurer, however, was never brought to justice for plundering Panton, Leslie and Company. Instead, he was held as a political prisoner, incarcerated first in Spain and then exiled to the Philippines, yet always available for possible service to Spain.[85] Meanwhile, Carondelet turned his attention to the more pressing demands of Indian affairs.

83. Wright, *William Augustus Bowles*, 72–73; Bowles to Carondelet, March 13, 1792, *AGI PC*, leg. 2371; Caughey, *McGillivray*, 310–13; Carondelet to Floridablanca, March 22, 1792, WPA, "Despatches," Book 10:80–84; *AHN Indies*, leg. 21067, no. 507.
84. Wright, *William Augustus Bowles*, 72–73.
85. Ibid., 73–94.

8
Carondelet and Panton Take the Offensive

THE Barón de Carondelet governed Louisiana during turbulent times—an unfortunate circumstance in that he was ill suited by temperament to handle crises of state. His lack of insight tended to drive him into forming hasty and often unwarranted conclusions regarding both the security of the provinces under his charge and effective means for their defense. Unlike his predecessor, Miró, or his successor, Manuel Gayoso de Lemos, Carondelet felt compelled to respond with decisive action to every menacing rumor that drifted down the Mississippi or across the Indian country from the American frontier. Consciously or unconsciously, the baron attempted to compensate for a faulty sense of judgment with bustle and energy.

On the other hand, overseeing the defenses of the sprawling, sparsely inhabited provinces of Louisiana and West Florida was a frustrating responsibility. Troop strength was never adequate, and the fortifications of the widely scattered Spanish outposts usually languished in decay because of the miserliness of royal support. The immigration policy implemented during Miró's governorship proved disappointing, partly because only small groups from the United States trickled into the Spanish dominions, and partly because Carondelet doubted that unruly frontiersmen could be converted into tractable subjects of the Spanish crown. The separatist intrigues among the western settlements, never directly encouraged by the Spaniards, had become moribund by the 1790s. Given such limited and unpromising options, Carondelet decided to implement an aggressive Indian policy as the best approach to holding back the American advance. Yet, in opting to employ Indian braves as the first line of frontier defense, Carondelet overestimated both their potential for sustained military operations and their general reliability.[1]

Carondelet's grand strategy for the Indians called for bringing the Cherokee within the Spanish orbit, forging a confederacy among the southern Indians that also would include as many northern tribes as possible, forming an offensive-defensive alliance with this Indian confederation, and inciting the Indians to demand that the United States recognize tribal boundaries as they had existed in 1772. His strategy was influenced by several factors: Bowles's influence on Carondelet's thinking; the resounding defeat the northern tribes inflicted on Arthur St. Clair's ragtag regulars and militia in the poorly conceived winter campaign of 1791; and, apparently, the suggestions of Indian leaders. From the evidence, St. Clair's defeat had led the baron to believe that the Indians, properly supported, were invincible. Neither the astute Indian diplomat Gayoso, who was serving as governor of the crucially strategic Natchez District, nor Carondelet's superiors endorsed his plans fully. On the other hand, no major objections were raised against his intention to pursue a more vigorous Indian policy, albeit one that fell short of provoking the United States into war.[2]

More immediately, Carondelet sought to restore uniform Spanish hegemony over the strife-ridden Creek and to gain the allegiance of the Cherokee to Spain. Accordingly, he solicited information on whether the continued involuntary absence of Bowles might provoke the Creek into attacking Spanish settlements. Carondelet cautioned his officers not to put any faith in the reports of Panton, Leslie employees because of McGillivray's association with the company, and because the company wanted it to appear that McGillivray had more influence over the Creek than he really enjoyed. Continuing Miró's earlier plans, Carondelet sent Lieutenant Pedro Olivier to the Creek as a Spanish agent.[3]

Olivier arrived in Little Tallassee in March 1792, for the ostensible purpose of assisting McGillivray with his many official duties. Actually, however, the Spanish officer had been instructed to keep a watchful eye

1. Whitaker, *Spanish-American Frontier*, 156–66; Nasatir, *Spanish War Vessels*, 9–15.
2. O'Callaghan, "Indian Policy of Carondelet," 8–9; Whitaker, "Spain and the Cherokee Indians," 255–56; Whitaker, *Spanish-American Frontier*, 163–66; Prucha, *Sword of the Republic*, 22–27; Las Casas to Carondelet, July 5, 1792, Lockey Papers.
3. Carondelet to Francisco Guesy [also Guessy], March 22, 1792; Carondelet to Folch, March 22, 1792, Kinnaird, *Spain in the Mississippi Valley*, 3:15–18; Carondelet to Floridablanca, February 4, 1792, AGI PC, leg. 633, West work cards.

on McGillivray and to preserve the Creek commitment to Spain. Shortly after his arrival, Olivier received additional instructions from Carondelet charging him to persuade the Creek not to permit the running of the Oconee boundary, either with or without McGillivray's support. To bring the Creek spokesman back into the Spanish fold, Olivier received authority to offer him full compensation from Spanish coffers for relinquishing his U.S. pension. Should McGillivray refuse, Olivier could inform him that arrangements would be made for Bowles's return.[4]

At the same time, Carondelet expressed amazement that Panton had stood idly by while his friend McGillivray made a land cession so inimical to their mutual interests. "Therefore as an Englishman, as a protectee of Spain, and as Mr. Panton," Carondelet wrote the merchant, "you ought to make every attempt" to block the fulfillment "of a treaty so contrary to the interests" of the Creek, Spain, England, and Panton himself.[5] Threatening the return of Bowles if McGillivray's connections with the Americans continued, the baron urged Panton to influence the Creek spokesman to oppose the treaty. The southern Indians would enjoy full Spanish support in defending their lands, Carondelet advised, and McGillivray could count on ample supplies of arms and ammunition to withstand any unilateral American attempt to seize the Oconee lands. If needed, the Cherokee, Chickasaw, Choctaw, and Shawnee would be enlisted as Creek allies.[6] Apparently, Carondelet either overlooked the fact that the Oconee lands had long since been settled, or he acted out of total ignorance.

Meanwhile, in Philadelphia, President Washington and Secretary of War Knox had monitored closely, and with great concern, Bowles's disruptive agitation among the Creek. The U.S. leaders were greatly relieved to discover that the adventurer enjoyed no official British support, that the Spaniards had no intentions of abetting his schemes, and that his removal had not caused an explosive upheaval. After St. Clair's defeat, the federal government's limited resources were committed to checking the aggressiveness of the British-backed northern tribes, through diplomacy if possible, but by arms if necessary. Concomitantly, the federal policy approach to the southern Indians had become conciliatory above all else by the end of 1791.[7]

4. Carondelet to Las Casas, March 22, 1792, *AGI PC*, leg. 1446; Caughey, *McGillivray*, 313; Carondelet to Olivier, March 30, 1792, Kinnaird, *Spain in the Mississippi Valley*, 3:21–22; O'Callaghan, "Indian Policy of Carondelet," 43.
5. Carondelet to Panton, March 24, 1792, *AGI PC*, leg. 214; Caughey, *McGillivray*, 316–17.
6. Caughey, ibid.
7. Wright, *William Augustus Bowles*, 79–80; Downes, "Creek-American Relations, 1790–95," 357–58.

When Congress created the Territory South of the River Ohio (the Southwest Territory) in May 1790, out of the western lands ceded by North Carolina the year before, the political presence of the United States in the Old Southwest became a reality. The previously remote authority of the federal government came into direct contact with the Cherokee and Chickasaw. In July 1791, Governor William Blount, in his ex officio capacity as southern Indian superintendent, concluded the Treaty of Holston with the Cherokee, which seemed to augur well for peaceful relations with even the unruly Chickamauga faction. Although the territorial provisions cost the Cherokee the lands lying between the Holston and French Broad rivers, this measure merely validated prior usurpations by the Franklinites. The treaty made the territorial loss more palatable to the Cherokee by providing as compensation an annuity of $1,000. This goodwill gesture was strengthened the following December when a Cherokee deputation, led by Bloody Fellow, visited "The City of Brotherly Love" and succeded in getting the annuity increased by 50 per cent. Washington and Knox feted the Cherokee visitors profusely, having in mind all the while the unsettled conditions north of the Ohio.[8]

In January 1792, President Washington followed up his successes with the Cherokee by naming Leonard Shaw as their temporary agent and by appointing James Seagrove of Georgia in the same capacity to the Creek. Two months later, James Robertson received a presidential appointment as temporary agent to the Choctaw and Chickasaw. The federal Indian agents received instructions to recruit warriors for service with the troops being assembled under Major General "Mad Anthony" Wayne and Brigadier General James Wilkinson against the northern tribes. Wilkinson had been curiously promoted from a lieutenant colonelcy, despite his known connections with the Spaniards. By enlisting southern tribes to fight against their northern brethren, Washington hoped to keep the two regions from coalescing into a unified force. To augment the efforts of the agents, Governor Blount received instructions to invite the Chickasaw and Choctaw to a conference at Nashville. Seagrove was charged with the additional duty of securing the consent of the Creek to run the Oconee boundary line, which had been delayed by the intrusion of Bowles.[9] All in all, the measures initiated by the Washington administration and by Carondelet in 1791 and 1792 set the respective Indian policies of the United States and Spain squarely on a collision course.

8. Cotterill, *Southern Indians*, 88–89; treaty is in *ASP IA*, I:124–25; John McDonald to Panton, June 7, 1792, *ANC F*, leg. 1, Exp. 5, no. 28; Prucha, *Sword of the Republic*, 45.

9. Cotterill, *Southern Indians*, 92–93; Secretary of War to Gov. Blount, April 22, 1792, and Secretary of War to James Seagrove, April 29, 1792, *ASP IA*, 1:252–55.

In January, before the capture of the Panton, Leslie store at St. Marks, Seagrove mistakenly expressed his pleasure to McGillivray that, because of his waning influence, the Creek would "soon be freed from so grand an impostor as Bowles."[10] The U.S. agent also informed the Creek leader that dispatches of the "utmost importance" had arrived from President Washington, and he requested an immediate conference at Rock Landing. McGillivray begged off, promising to meet Seagrove once the upheaval caused by Bowles had fully subsided. McGillivray surmised that Seagrove would insist on running the Oconee boundary and resigned himself to the completion of the task later in the spring.[11] Unusually heavy spring rains, however, postponed McGillivray's departure for Rock Landing long enough for Panton, thoroughly aroused by Carondelet's admonitions, to intervene.

Carondelet's chidings at first bewildered Panton, who felt it necessary to remind the governor-general that the Treaty of New York was the result of Spanish insistence on a U.S.–Creek peace settlement. That anyone should be amazed that a mere foreigner had refrained from countermanding clearly announced Spanish policy, Panton advised Carondelet, confused him. The merchant also suggested that the baron had overestimated Bowles's abilities to command the affection of the Creek. His success had stemmed from his artfulness in playing on Indian nostalgia for the British era, when expenditures for gifts and provisions averaged £20,000 in peaceful times and more than three times as much during war years. If Carondelet wished "to make [the Indians] equally attached to Spain," Panton observed, he should "be at the Same expence"—in which case all problems would melt away.[12]

Having set the record straight, Panton left Pensacola in April 1792 on an extended tour through the Creek and Chickamauga country to foment anti-American sentiment. He arrived at Little Tallassee on April 30, virtually on the eve of McGillivray's departure for Rock Landing. The Scottish merchant easily persuaded his associate to find a pretext to stall Seagrove and to go instead to New Orleans for discussions with Carondelet. Panton also prevailed on McGillivray to call an assembly of the principal chiefs so that Olivier could explain the new Spanish policy. Panton then hastily traveled northward for a visit with the Chickamauga.[13]

10. Seagrove to McGillivray, January 14, 1792, *AHN Indias*, leg. 21067, no. 507; Caughey, *McGillivray*, 303–4.
11. McGillivray to Seagrove, May 18, 1792, *ASP FR*, 1:287; McGillivray to Knox, May 18, 1792, *ASP IA*, 1:315–16; Olivier to Carondelet, April 10, 1792, *AGI PC*, leg. 25; Caughey, *McGillivray*, 303–4, 320–21.
12. Panton to Carondelet, April 16, 1792, *ANC F*, leg. 1, Exp. 5, no. 27, WP; Corbitt, "Georgia-Florida Frontier," 22:391–94.
13. Panton to O'Neill, May 28, 1792, *AGI PC*, leg. 39; Deposition of John Ormsbay, May 11, 1792, *ASP IA*, 1:297–98.

Panton arrived at the Chickamauga villages at the very moment when the Cherokee headmen had assembled at Coyatee with Governor Blount to receive the first annual payment provided for under the Treaty of Holston. The Scottish merchant called at the home of John McDonald, a trader and former British agent, and an acquaintance of Panton's from the war years. To the casually curious, Panton masked the true purpose of his visit by explaining that he had come to collect old debts and promote new business. Actually, he enlisted John McDonald as a Spanish agent and delivered Governor O'Neill's invitation to visit Pensacola to Chief John Watts, who had succeeded Dragging Canoe, and who was a defiant opponent of American expansion. There, Panton declared, Watts would find generous gifts of arms and ammunition waiting and, in addition to these, official offers of Spanish support and protection. Panton also warmly invited the Cherokee to become his customers.[14]

On Panton's departure, McDonald concentrated his efforts on breaking down the newly acquired affinity of Bloody Fellow for the United States. Meanwhile, Watts visited Pensacola with a large horse caravan. He returned with an abundant supply of munitions and with Governor O'Neill's encouragement that the Cherokee could expect firm Spanish support. The sporadic skirmishes against Cumberland, which had never completely ended, intensified, and McDonald escorted Bloody Fellow and other Cherokee leaders to Pensacola. From there, the deputation traveled to New Orleans for detailed discussions with Carondelet.[15]

On his return from the Cherokee, Panton stopped in the Upper Creek towns and later, en route to St. Marks and Pensacola, he called on the Lower Creek. Olivier also visited the two groups at about the same time. Both harangued the Indians, imploring them not to recognize the Oconee cession and to refuse to mark the boundary. They also emphasized Carondelet's determination to convert the southern Indians into a solid wall of resistance against American expansion, while Spanish diplomacy simultaneously and vigorously defended their territorial demands against the claims of the United States. In the meantime, ample supplies of arms for defense awaited them in Pensacola.[16]

14. Blount Coyatee "talk," May 23, 1792, *ASP IA*, 1:268-69; extract of James Carey's report to Blount, November 3, 1792, *ASP IA*, 1:327-29; deposition of James Leonard, July 24, 1792, *ASP IA*, 1:307-8; Blount to Secretary of War, July 4, 1792, Carter, *Territorial Papers*, 4:157-59.

15. Information of Richard Finnelson, November 1, 1792, *ASP IA*, 1:228-91; McDonald to Panton, October 6, 1792, *AHN Estado*, leg. 3898; information from Red Bird in letter of Blount, September 15, 1792, *ASP FR*, 1:284; Whitaker, "Spain and the Cherokee Indians," 257-58; Panton to Carondelet, November 6, 1792, *AGI PC*, leg. 203, doc. 28, WP; Corbitt, "Papers from the Spanish Archives," 28:133-34.

16. Seagrove to the President, July 5, 1792, *ASP FR*, 1:286-87; anonymous letter to

Panton also took this opportunity to publicize the impecuniousness of the U.S. government, alleging that it was in no position to lavish abundant gifts on the Creek. The Americans, he further contended, produced none of the trade goods desired by the Indians and depended entirely on English manufacturers to meet their own requirements. Panton therefore exhorted the Creek first to rob and then to expel all American traders who appeared in their midst.[17]

Impressed with the stirring eloquence of Panton and Olivier, the Creek prepared themselves for a fall conference at Pensacola with Carondelet. In the interim, when McGillivray visited the baron in New Orleans, the two worked out an agreement committing the Creek and Spain to a formal pact. Its provisions recommended that the Creek demand the withdrawal, within two months, of all Americans from Creek lands; it bound Spain to support the Creek, both offensively and defensively, in regaining their usurped territories; and it committed the signatories to mutual territorial guarantees. Although the treaty contained a proviso making its terms effective only after "his most gratious Majesty's pleasure should be known," it allowed time for the Creek to secure guns and ammunition distributed from Spanish magazines.[18] To avoid shortages, Carondelet commissioned Panton to procure an extraordinary shipment of 2,000 trade guns from New Providence.[19]

Warmly impressed by McGillivray's conduct in New Orleans, Carondelet believed that the Creek leader had left a "new man." Indeed, he should have, for Carondelet increased McGillivray's Spanish pension to $3,500 to ensure cooperation. Whatever else Carondelet had accomplished, by the end of summer 1792, the Treaty of New York was a dead issue. Furthermore, the Spanish governor saw in McGillivray an invaluable henchman to aid in forging the southern Indian confederacy into an effective instrument of Spanish policy. The harried McGillivray, however, actually was, at best, lukewarm to the idea.[20]

When McDonald reached Pensacola with Bloody Fellow and the Cherokee in November, Panton was on hand to give them a hearty welcome.

---

the Savannah *Gazette*, June 29, 1792, *ASP IA*, 1:309; deposition of James Leonard, July 24, 1792, *ASP IA*, 1:307–8.

17. Deposition of Leonard, ibid.

18. A copy of the treaty, dated July 6, 1792, is in *AGI PC*, leg. 2362; Caughey, *McGillivray*, 329–30.

19. Olivier to O'Neill, July 23, 1792, *AGI PC*, leg. 40, WP; Panton to Carondelet, September 7, 1792, *ANC F*, leg. 1, Exp. 5, no. 31, WP; Carondelet passport, September 3, 1792, *AGI SD*, leg. 2670, WP.

20. Information of Richard Finnelson, November 1, 1792, *ASP IA*, 1:288–91; Carondelet to McGillivray, July 6, 1792, *AGI PC*, leg. 205; Caughey, *McGillivray*, 330; Olivier to O'Neill, July 23, 1792, *AGI PC*, leg. 40, WP.

Panton sent McDonald off to New Orleans with a report that sentiment in favor of taking up the hatchet against the Americans had risen appreciably among influential elements within the Creek and Cherokee. Should Carondelet choose, Panton observed, the spring of 1793 "may Commense with as Bloody a War as ever the Southern States have experienced," but the Louisiana governor must receive the Cherokee warmly and give them firm promises of Spanish support. The impressions the Indians carried away from New Orleans, Panton prophesied, would decide their future course.[21]

The ferment created among the Indians during the summer of 1792 had not escaped the attention of U.S. observers along the southwestern frontier. Seagrove disbelieved McGillivray's relatively straightforward explanation, that Bowles had prompted Carondelet's interference in marking the Oconee boundary. Seagrove, doubtful of McGillivray's integrity, described him as a man with too many masters.[22] Caught between the interests of opposing powers, the forlorn Creek leader described himself as "a keeper of Bedlam, and nearly fit for an inhabitant."[23] The cares of a stormy decade of leadership were indeed pressing heavily on his shoulders.

As the full implications of Carondelet's policy became more clearly understood, Seagrove became convinced that Panton was more responsible for the heightened anti-American activity than Carondelet. The Scot, Seagrove observed, "from interest as well as inclination, is an inveterate enemy to the United States" and he declared that Panton wielded "more influence over Mr. McGillivray, than any person living."[24] Seagrove later suggested that the United States file a formal protest with the Spanish government against Panton, Leslie and Company. If the United States pushed the Spanish court hard enough, Seagrove wrote to the secretary of war, Spain would sacrifice Panton because it owed him nearly $200,000 for Indian supplies.[25] Nor did Panton escape notoriety in the reports of other American observers. Blount credited the Cherokee disturbances to both the Spaniards "and their instrument, Mr. Panton."[26] Georgians, enraged over Panton's activity in promoting Creek hostility, railed against the Scotsman "with the most inveterate enmity."[27]

21. Panton to Carondelet, November 6, 1792, *AGI PC*, leg. 203, doc. 28, WP; Corbitt, "Papers from the Spanish Archives," 28:133–34.
22. Seagrove to Knox, May 24, 1792, *ASP IA*, 1:296; Caughey, *McGillivray*, 323–24.
23. McGillivray to Seagrove, May 18, 1792, *ASP FR*, 1:287.
24. Seagrove to Knox, May 24, 1792, *ASP IA*, 1:296; see also Seagrove to Washington, July 27, 1792, *ASP IA*, 1:305–6.
25. Seagrove to Secretary of War, May 24, September 8, 1792, *ASP IA*, 1:296, 310–11.
26. Blount to Secretary of War, November 8, 1792, *ASP IA*, 1:325–27.
27. J. Leslie to Quesada, October 2, 1792, *EF* leg. 116L9; Caughey, *McGillivray*, 338–41.

In fact, throughout 1792 and well into 1793, rumors abounded that either the Georgians or the Indians, especially those who had been allies of Bowles, planned to even the score with Panton by looting the St. Marys store. Forrester specifically blamed John Galphin, Bowles's accomplice, and James Seagrove, for these threats. Nevertheless, Forrester continued to do a thriving business with the Indians. But in order to reach the store, the Indians necessarily passed through the lands and near the homes of residents on the St. Marys River, creating a near panic among them. As a result, the residents petitioned Governor Quesada to have the store moved up the river, beyond the farthest settler and nearer the Indian line.

Before Quesada received this petition, John Leslie had advised him that the Georgians were greatly upset by the reports of Panton's tour of the Creek nation. Leslie asked the governor for permission to close the St. Marys store because he feared that, in revenge, Georgian vagabonds might plunder company property and kill its employees. He also requested permission to open a new Indian trading post at Picolata or elsewhere on the St. Johns River.

Quesada at first refused Leslie's request, and the merchant made plans to remove the furs and some of the more expensive trade items to St. Augustine. However, the arrival of the petition from St. Marys residents helped change Quesada's mind, and in October 1792 the governor authorized Forrester to close the store. Although Forrester spent most of his time on the St. Marys until the following May, he had closed the trading post by March. Thus, the St. Marys store fell victim to the threats of Bowles's accomplices and of the Georgians. Within a few months, Forrester opened a new company Indian trading post, the Almacén de San Fernando de Pupo, on the west bank of the St. Johns River across from Picolata.[28]

Meanwhile, Panton had escaped personal embroilment in U.S.–Spanish diplomatic exchanges, but Lieutenant Olivier had not been so successful. Secretary of State Thomas Jefferson lodged an official complaint with José de Jáudenes and Josef Ignacio de Viar, the Spanish representatives in Philadelphia, concerning a Spanish agent who was intriguing on

28. Caughey, ibid.; inhabitants of the south of St. Marys River to Gov. Quesada, August 18, 1792; Andrés Atkinson to [Quesada], September 24, 1792; Quesada to John Forrester, November 6, 1792; Forrester to Quesada, October 1, 1792; March 13, 1793; *EF* leg. 122E10; W. Pengree to [Dr. Starling], April 28, 1793; Pengree, Forrester, Cook, and Gunby to [Gov. of East Florida], May 1, 1793; Forrester to Quesada, March 19, 1793, *EF* leg. 123F10; Howard to Quesada, March 8, 1793, *EF* leg. 24; Forrester to Quesada, April 20, 1793, *AHN Estado*, leg. 3895. On the new St. Johns store, see Forrester to Quesada, January 5, 1793, *EF* leg. 122F10; [Quesada] to [?] August 3, 1793, *EF* leg. 124G10. See also Ross and Chappell, "Diary of John Hambly," 62n7. Forrester located the new store on or near the site of the old Spanish fort, San Francisco de Pupo, built in 1734: TePaske, *Governorship of Spanish Florida*, 134–35 ff.

U.S. soil by inciting the Indians to break their treaty commitments. Such action, Jefferson complained, ran counter to all conventions governing the behavior of foreign representatives and must cease. Little more was said by the Spaniards in reply than that the Treaty of New York prejudiced Spanish claims to what was actually disputed territory. Although Jáudenes and Viar conceded that Spanish agents should refrain from interfering with Indians residing within the limits of the United States, they questioned whether the case of the Creek fell into that category. That matter remained to be settled in future boundary negotiations.[29]

When the Cherokee reached New Orleans in November 1792, they found themselves in the company of numerous representatives from the Chickasaw and Choctaw nations. These Indian delegations had appeared "spontaneously," so that Carondelet could lay the groundwork for a general Indian congress, which he proposed for the spring of 1793, to establish a southern Indian confederation. Reporting to the Conde de Aranda on the success of the preliminaries, Carondelet maintained that a strong intertribal alliance was "the only recourse that Spain has to hold the Americans within their boundaries."[30] Should Spain regain for the Indians their lost lands, either through diplomacy or, as Carondelet preferred, by supporting them in war, they would remain forever grateful. Since existing Spanish policy did not encourage his inclination to incite Indian warfare, Carondelet limited himself to encouraging the belief that Spain would assist diplomatically in restoring the disputed Indian boundaries. Meanwhile, the Indian visitors were urged to prepare their people to join together in a grand alliance against the United States.[31]

By the end of 1792, developments along the frontier had convinced Carondelet that the United States intended not only to eradicate Spanish influence with the Indians but also to sever the line of communications between lower and upper Louisiana.[32] The countermeasures he developed to thwart these supposed American designs annoyed Panton because they meant unwanted competition in the Choctaw and especially in the Chickasaw trade. Although interference in the company's Mobile monopoly had arisen before Carondelet's governorship, his assessment of the

29. Jefferson to Jáudenes & Viar, July 9, 1792; Jáudenes & Viar to Jefferson, July 11, 1792, enclosure no. 5 and 6 of Las Casas to Carondelet, September 24, 1792, *AGI PC*, leg. 152B, Lockey Papers; Jáudenes and Viar to Jefferson, October 29, 1792; Jefferson to Washington, November 2, 1792, *ASP FR*, 1:138-39.

30. Carondelet to Aranda, November 8, 20, 1792, Corbitt, "Papers from the Spanish Archives," 28:134-37.

31. Whitaker, "Spain and the Cherokee Indians," 258-59; Carondelet to the Cherokee Nation, November 24, 1792, and Carondelet to Aranda, November 28, 1792, Corbitt, "Papers from the Spanish Archives," 28:137-41.

32. Nasatir, *Spanish War Vessels*, 59-62; Carondelet to Aranda, January 8, 1793, WPA, "Despatches," 8:308-11.

mounting U.S. involvement in the Old Southwest hindered the company's ability to compete in the Indian trade.

In response to the colonizing threat raised by the South Carolina Yazoo Company, Gayoso, with Miró's approval, erected a Spanish fort in the spring of 1791 at Nogales, or, as the Anglo-Americans preferred to call it, Walnut Hills. To placate the Choctaw and Chickasaw, Gayoso instructed the commandant at Nogales, Elias Beauregard, to convince them of the advantages of locating a Spanish outpost in the vicinity. The fort would afford them greater security against their enemies and also would enhance the convenience of their trade because of its proximity to their best hunting grounds.[33]

Soon afterward, Nogales was opened for settlement to American emigrants, an action that drew complaints from the Choctaw. Located on a relatively narrow section of the Mississippi, Nogales had long served as a crossing for Choctaw parties bound for hunting in Louisiana (and, occasionally, lifting Caddo scalps). Chiefs Taboca and Franchimastabe protested vehemently against the unexpected infringement on Choctaw hunting rights, but they railed even more against Gayoso for having established a trading post at the site. Instead of returning home with deerskins, the chiefs complained, Indians now exchanged them at Nogales. The Nogales trade provided too easy an avenue for debt evasion and threatened ultimate ruin for Panton's traders, who by then exerted enormous influence over Choctaw headmen.[34]

In March, Gayoso dispatched an officer, Lieutenant Esteban Minor (Stephen Minor, formerly of New Jersey), on a diplomatic mission to soothe the Choctaw leaders, particularly Franchimastabe. Minor was instructed to impress the chiefs with the advantages of the Spanish presence at Nogales. The post served not only as a barrier to the United States but also gave the Choctaw a convenient alternative to trading at Mobile. Minor also was instructed to reiterate that the Spanish right to occupy Nogales had been established by virtue of conquest. The Indians had ceded the district to the British while West Florida was under their control.[35]

Minor enlisted the services of Turner Brashears and Ben James, trad-

33. Holmes, *Gayoso*, 145–46; "*Instrucciones reservadas para el comandante de los Nogales*," by Manuel Gayoso de Lemos, April 1, 1791, Serrano y Sanz, *España y los Indios*, 85–89 (see especially art. 17, p. 86); Whitaker, *Spanish-American Frontier*, 148.
34. Whitaker, *Spanish-American Frontier*, 158; instructions of Gayoso to Esteban Minor, March 13, 1792, Serrano y Sanz, *Documentos Históricos*, 407–14; Panton to Carondelet, April 16, 1792, WP; Corbitt, "Georgia-Florida Frontier," 22:391–94; Serrano y Sanz, *España y los Indios*, 44, 47; Gayoso to Carondelet, April 20, 1792, AHN Estado, leg. 3898; also in WPA, "Despatches," 8:12–16; Franchimastabe to Gayoso, March 28, 1792, ibid., 29–30.
35. Instructions of Gayoso to Esteban Minor, March 13, 1792, in Serrano y Sanz, *Documentos Históricos*, 407–14; Holmes, *Stephen Minor*, 1–3.

ers who had great influence with Franchimastabe. James, despite his earlier flirtations with William Davenport, had won Panton's confidence, if not McGillivray's, and had become a Spanish retainer while secretly maintaining contact with William Blount.[36] The traders agreed to gain the acquiescence of the Choctaw regarding the settlement of Nogales, but in return they demanded that the trading post be closed. In May, Gayoso ended the contention by agreeing to a generous distribution of gifts among the Choctaw, who claimed that the British had never compensated them for the Nogales lands, and by promising to discontinue the Nogales trade.[37]

The Choctaw chiefs had assumed, with some justification, that motives other than altruistic concern for Indian welfare lay behind Gayoso's support for the Nogales trade. Information obtained from Benjamin Fooy, a Dutch-born Natchez settler who traded at Nogales and who also served Gayoso as Indian interpreter, indicated that the Natchez governor had a personal interest in the venture.[38] In explaining the affair to Carondelet, Gayoso freely admitted that he had sent a small quantity of goods to Nogales. He added, however, that he intended no harm to Panton, who was deserving of confidence and consideration.[39] Gayoso also declared that he had told Brashears that the Nogales trade was intended more to free the Indians from extortion than to produce a profit. Nevertheless, the Natchez governor suggested to Carondelet that, because of Panton's acceptance among the Indians, he should be offered a post at Nogales, where he could establish a large warehouse with a wide variety of merchandise. Gayoso thought it imperative that Carondelet have an understanding with Panton since all of the Indian traders were under Panton's influence, and the traders in turn influenced and manipulated the Indian chiefs. Meanwhile, Gayoso said, he would continue to oversee the trade.[40]

Despite his declarations in support of Panton, Gayoso supplied Carondelet with disparaging information on the Pensacola merchant's activities. The Choctaw leader Taboca, Gayoso reported, had once asked him whether he thought the English would return. Replying negatively, the

36. "*Diario* of Estevan Minor, March 13–April 2, 1792," *AHN Estado*, leg. 3898, Exp. 5; also in Serrano y Sanz, *Documentos Históricos*, 418–36 (see esp. 422–29). This diary has been translated. See Ross and Phelps, "Natchez Trace," 252–73. Panton recommended James to Carondelet for a position as Spanish agent to the Choctaw: see Panton to Carondelet, September 7, 1792, ANC F, leg. 1, Exp. 5, no. 31. James was consorting with Blount at about the same time: James to Blount, June 30, 1792, *ASP IA*, 1:284.

37. "*Diario*," of Minor, in Serrano y Sanz, *Documentos Históricos*, esp. 421; Serrano y Sanz, *España y los Indios*, 47.

38. Gayoso to Carondelet, April 20, 1792, *AHN Estado*, leg. 3898; also in WPA, "Despatches," 8:12–16.

39. WPA, "Despatches," ibid.

40. Ibid.; Gayoso to Carondelet, April 14, 1792, *AHN Estado*, leg. 3898, Exp. 5; WPA, "Despatches," 7:455–59.

Spaniard inquired further to discover the basis of the Choctaw leader's query. Finally, pledging Gayoso to secrecy, Taboca intimated that Panton, without saying anything detrimental about the Spaniards, had told him that he would see his old friends, the English, once again.[41] Gayoso later informed Carondelet that he had won grudging approval by the pro–U.S. Chickasaw leader Piomingo for the Spanish fort at Nogales—but only after Gayoso told Piomingo that orders had been given to close the trading post there.[42] This did not necessarily prejudice Panton's request for trading privileges at the same location.

In April, meanwhile, Panton pressed Carondelet for permission to trade at Nogales, justifying his request on the grounds that it would permit lower prices, counteract U.S. influence, and prevent rivals from ruining his Choctaw-Chickasaw trade. Mather, Panton pointed out, had been granted the privilege of maintaining a post on the Yazoo near Nogales.[43] At the time, Carondelet thought it better to end the Panton, Leslie monopoly of the Indian trade. He therefore recommended declaring New Orleans a free port, open to the traders of all nations. The Indians could obtain all of their goods in that city and the Indian trade problem would be resolved.[44] While Carondelet awaited official reaction to his recommendation, competition for the Choctaw-Chickasaw trade continued and Panton, John Forbes, and a number of Choctaw traders registered strong protests with the baron.[45]

In October, Carondelet, somewhat softened by Panton's anti–U.S. exertions among the Creek and Chickamauga, declared to his superiors that if the court disapproved of his free trade recommendations, Panton should be allowed to locate at Nogales. A Panton, Leslie trading post at Nogales, he believed, would discourage the establishment of American trading posts among the Chickasaw and would destroy any posts already there. The Louisiana governor was now thoroughly alarmed over U.S. maneuverings among the Choctaw and Chickasaw and wanted no commercial penetration from that quarter.[46]

Meanwhile, in the spring of 1792, Governor Blount sent emissaries to

41. WPA, "Despatches," ibid.
42. Ibid.; Holmes, *Gayoso*, 148.
43. Panton to Carondelet, April 16, 1792, ANC F, leg. 1, Exp. 5, no. 27, WP; Corbitt, "Georgia-Florida Frontier," 22:391–94.
44. Carondelet to Floridablanca, March 22, 1792, *AHN Indias*, leg. 21067, no. 507; WPA, "Despatches," 10:80–84.
45. [Carondelet] to Panton, September 14, 1792, AGI PC, leg. 122A, doc. 1, WP; Panton to Carondelet, September 7, 1792, ANC F, leg. 1, Exp. 5, no. 31, WP; Corbitt, "Georgia-Florida Frontier," 23:78–79; J. Forbes to Carondelet, October 31, 1792, and including B. James to Forbes, September 28, 1792, AGI PC, leg. 203, WP; Corbitt, "Papers from the Spanish Archives," 28:129, 131.
46. Carondelet to Aranda, October 1, 1792, Corbitt, "Papers from the Spanish Archives," 28:129–30; Serrano y Sanz, *España y los Indios*, 77–78.

the Choctaw and Chickasaw to invite them to a conference at Nashville. The agents bore friendly messages from President Washington and expressed the pleasure of the United States at the goodwill the Indians had displayed since the negotiations at Hopewell. The president, the agents declared, wished to extend to the Indians a "well regulated & mutually advantageous Trade" as soon as circumstances permitted. Blount also assured the Indians of a warm welcome at Nashville, where an abundance of gifts and provisions awaited them.[47]

Carondelet, upset at the American overtures, assigned Juan de la Villebeuvre as permanent resident agent to the Choctaw and Chickasaw. He advised Aranda that the Americans had changed their plans. Convinced that it could not win by force of arms, the United States now had turned to a policy of attracting the Indians away from Spain through trade and presents. The creation of American trading posts from the Oconee to the Mississippi would ruin Panton, Leslie and Company. The Indians would come under the influence and direction of the United States, which could send those nations against the Spanish colonies. In addition to sending Villebeuvre as a Spanish agent, the governor also urged McGillivray to disrupt the American mission to the western tribes and to attack an American post rumored to have been built on the upper reaches of the Tombigbee. A U.S. post there, Carondelet wrote, "will shortly grow powerful and ruin Mr. Panton's trade."[48] Carondelet's urgings proved unnecessary; McGillivray explained that no such post existed, adding that the United States was actually interested in locating at Muscle Shoals.[49] A party of unruly young Creek, pretending to be drunk, appeared as unwelcome guests at the meeting between the U.S. commissioners and the Choctaw, dampening the latter's receptivity to American overtures. The meeting broke up because the Creek agitators, before taking their leave, warned the Choctaw against accepting the American invitation to Nashville.[50]

As a consequence, relatively few Choctaw, led only by minor chieftains, attended the Nashville conference in the summer of 1792. The Chickasaw, on the other hand, were well represented, especially the Pio-

47. Shaw, McClure, & Hampton to Choctaw Nation, April 13, 1792, Corbitt, "Papers from the Spanish Archives," 27:80–81; William Blount, "American Overtures to the Choctaw," May 10, 1792, Kinnaird, *Spain in the Mississippi Valley*, 3:7.

48. Carondelet to Aranda, October 1, 1792, Corbitt, "Papers from the Spanish Archives," 28:129–30; Carondelet to Las Casas, October 1, 1792, WPA, "Despatches," 8:187; Carondelet to McGillivray, July 18, August 19, 1792, AGI PC, leg. 205; Caughey, *McGillivray*, 331–32, 334–335. For a good summary of Villebeuvre's role as a Spanish Indian agent, see Holmes, "Juan de la Villebeuvre."

49. McGillivray to Carondelet, September 3, 1792, AGI PC, leg. 205; Caughey, *McGillivray*, 335–37.

50. McGillivray to Carondelet, July 22, 1792, AGI PC, leg. 2371; Caughey, *McGillivray*, 332–33; Cotterill, *Southern Indians*, 95.

mingo faction. Governor Blount pleased the Indians by disclaiming any interest on the part of the United States in acquiring Chickasaw and Choctaw lands. The governor also announced that the military campaign against the northern Indians had been postponed, so the services of Chickasaw and Choctaw braves would not be needed for the present. On the other hand, he pressed hard for their approval of a trading post at Muscle Shoals. Ugula Yacabe (Wolf's Friend), a rapidly rising war chief of the pro-Spanish faction, resisted the pressure with equal vigor, wary that the proffered post would lead to demands for land cessions. Piomingo, fearing the wrath of the Creek, also demurred.[51]

News of the Nashville conference, combined with other information, thoroughly unsettled Carondelet's already fragile composure. From Villebeuvre and Thomas Portell, the Spanish commandant at New Madrid, Carondelet received reports—apparently grounded only in the faulty expectations of Blount and other Tennesseans—that 1,500 troops would be detached from General Wayne's command for an assault against the Cherokee. Once the Cherokee were driven off, the United States intended to establish settlements at Muscle Shoals and at the Chickasaw Bluffs. Portell also anticipated an attack on New Madrid from Cumberland, whose settlers were enraged at Spanish support of the Cherokee.[52] Carondelet learned that General James Robertson intended to deliver supplies of corn to the drought-stricken Chickasaw at Chickasaw Bluffs in the spring of 1793—a plan the Louisiana governor believed was preparatory to erecting a permanent American fort at the site.[53]

Once the United States had won firm control of Muscle Shoals and Chickasaw Bluffs, Carondelet reasoned, it would command the Mississippi, its eastern tributaries, and the headwaters of the principal rivers flowing into the Gulf of Mexico. The Spanish position in Louisiana and West Florida would be rendered untenable. The United States could isolate at will New Madrid, Saint Genevieve, and Saint Louis and could launch attacks against Nogales, Natchez, New Orleans, Mobile, and Pensacola. The Spanish governor accordingly reinforced the defenses of New Madrid as best he could. He ordered Captain Pedro Rousseau, commander of the small Spanish galley squadron that patrolled the Missis-

51. Ibid.; Blount, Report on Cumberland Conference, August 7–11, 1792, *ASP IA*, 1:285–88; Gayoso to Carondelet, July 21, 1792, ANC F, leg. 2, Exp. 9; Corbitt, "Papers from the Spanish Archives," 27:87–90; Robert Welch to McGillivray, August 2, 1792, ibid., 95.

52. Carondelet to Aranda, January 8, 1793, WPA, "Despatches," 8:308–11; Portell to Carondelet, December 3, 1792, *AHN Estado*, leg. 3898; Nasatir, *Spanish War Vessels*, 59–62.

53. Nasatir, *Spanish War Vessels*, 65; Carondelet to Aranda, January 8, 1793, WPA "Despatches," 8:308–11.

sippi, to move northward from Natchez with armaments and munitions. He also instructed Rousseau to reconnoiter the Chickasaw Bluffs on his return voyage for the best site for a Spanish fort, a task he carried out on March 21, 1793, on his descent to New Orleans. Carondelet intended for Rousseau to return without delay to the Chickasaw Bluffs, in order to forestall their occupation by the United States, but the outbreak of war with France interrupted his plans.[54]

Requests made by Indians at the November 1792, conference also opened new possibilities in Carondelet's defensive planning. Bloody Fellow had asked for Spanish forts to be erected at Muscle Shoals and on the Tombigbee, from which the Cherokee could be conveniently supplied.[55] The elderly Chickasaw king (Taski Etoka), ever resentful of the Anglo-Americans for their lack of deference to his leadership, had asked Carondelet to permit John Turnbull to trade from a site on the Yazoo River convenient to the Chickasaw villages. At first, the Spanish officials refused to grant the request, but when the Chickasaw king vigorously protested, Carondelet agreed to license Turnbull to trade in Mobile.[56] Shortly thereafter, the baron realized that Turnbull might be useful as a stalking horse in securing the assent of the Chickasaw to the establishment of a Spanish fort on the Chickasaw Bluffs.[57]

Originally an inhabitant of the Natchez district during the British era, Turnbull participated in the abortive uprising of 1781 against Spanish control. He sought refuge in Cumberland after the insurgency was crushed, and from there he engaged briefly but unsuccessfully in the Indian trade. Returning to Spanish territory, Turnbull became a junior partner and clerk in the Mather and Strother trading venture in Mobile. In 1789, he angered McGillivray by sponsoring American settlers along the Tombigbee and Tensaw rivers, which caused the Creek leader to denounce him as an unalterable enemy of the Spaniards. In the summer of 1792, Turnbull moved to a plantation near Baton Rouge, where he apparently developed a relationship with Gayoso in the Nogales trade. The father of two half-Chickasaw sons, Turnbull kept close ties with the tribesmen of his offspring. This, above all other considerations, gained him Carondelet's favor.[58]

54. Nasatir, *Spanish War Vessels*, 62–68.
55. Whitaker, "Spain and the Cherokee Indians," 258–59.
56. [Carondelet] to Panton, November 21, 1792, *AGI PC*, leg. 122A, WP; see also Carondelet to McGillivray, December 14, 1792, *AGI PC*, 205; McGillivray to Carondelet, January 15, 1793, *AGI PC*, leg. 2363; Caughey, *McGillivray*, 349–53.
57. Carondelet to Gayoso, December 18, 1792, WPA, "Despatches," 8:300–303.
58. McGillivray to Miró, May 26, 1789, *AGI PC*, leg. 52, WP; Caughey, *McGillivray*, 234–35. For background data on Turnbull, see Williams, *Beginnings of West Tennessee*, 35n5; J. Forbes to Carondelet, October 31, 1792, *AGI PC*, leg. 203, WP; Panton to Carondelet, November 6, 1792, *AGI PC*, leg. 177; Corbitt, "Papers from the Spanish Archives,"

The Reverend William Leslie, 1748–1839. This painting hangs in the Parish Church of St. Andrews Lhanbryd. Courtesy of Rev. David Lunan, minister.

John Innerarity, 1783–1854. From copy in Special Collections Department, John C. Pace Library, University of West Florida.

Winning the friendship of Piomingo and Ugula Yacabe "at any price," Carondelet wrote to Gayoso in December 1792, was the key to thwarting the American menace.[59] With the Chickasaw firmly under Spanish control, not only would they join with the Cherokee in the vanguard of resistance against U.S. expansionism but they also would aid in building the anti-U.S. ardor of their southern neighbors, the Choctaw. Turnbull's services would be instrumental in dealing with the Chickasaw, and he could perhaps establish himself at Chickasaw Bluffs. Once this was accomplished, the trader could appeal to the Chickasaw to permit the Spanish to fortify the location as protection for the Chickasaw trade. Carondelet therefore opened the Chickasaw trade to Turnbull while, with cheerful assistance from Gayoso, he impressed the merchant with the prospect of losing the privilege unless he gained a foothold for Spain at Chickasaw Bluffs.[60]

Governor Carondelet reported to Panton, McGillivray, and John Forbes the pressure from Taski Etoka that had compelled the licensing of Turnbull to trade at Mobile. Denial of permission, Carondelet declared, would have meant losing the Chickasaw trade to Anglo-Americans, who were also promising the Chickasaw material support in the event of war with the Creeks. Turnbull would be subject to the same import and export duties as other colonists, while Panton's firm would still enjoy its official preference. Panton, however, was cautioned against harassing his new competitor and was warned to refrain from using his duty-exempt privileges to ruin Turnbull.[61]

Carondelet's explanation scarcely soothed Panton's irritation over his unwanted competitor. He petitioned again for a post at Nogales, making known his displeasure both candidly and vehemently. The irate Scotsman informed Carondelet that Turnbull had instigated the action of the Chickasaw king, and "for a Couple of shirts" he, Panton, could have gotten "any

---

28:132–33; Manuel de Lanzos to Carondelet, August 12, 1792, Kinnaird, *Spain in the Mississippi Valley*, 3:72–73. On the pecuniary self-interest of Gayoso, see LeGardeur and Pitot, "Memoir of Spanish Louisiana," 78–79 (esp. 79n32); Gayoso stood by Turnbull at the Chickasaw Bluffs even after Panton, Leslie and Company had won their concession there. See Coughlin, "Spanish Galleys," 404–6; Carondelet to Panton, August 15, 1797, FP, MPL. Carondelet advised Panton to satisfy Turnbull's complaints because Gayoso (now appointed governor) favored Turnbull and would not take kindly any reneging on Panton's part.

59. Carondelet to Gayoso, December 18, 1792, WPA, "Despatches," 8:300–303.

60. Ibid.; Carondelet to Gayoso, March 5, 1793; Gayoso to Carondelet, May 31, 1793, Corbitt, "Papers from the Spanish Archives," 33:62–63, 65–66; Gayoso to Carondelet, July 25, 1793, WPA, "Despatches," 9:10–13.

61. Carondelet to Panton, November 21, 1792, AGI PC, leg. 122A, doc. G, WP; Carondelet to Manuel de Lanzos, November 22, 1792, West work cards; McGillivray to Carondelet, January 15, 1793, AGI PC, leg. 2363; Caughey, *McGillivray*, 351–53. According to Caughey, this is the last letter written by McGillivray; he died a month afterward: ibid., 351n343.

chief in that Nation to say as much, or more" in his favor.[62] The haste with which Carondelet had approved Turnbull had prevented Panton from arguing against the proposal, and he added, "to my very great injury," the governor had broken the terms of the royal agreement.[63] Panton also pointed out the logical inconsistency of Carondelet's justification of the Turnbull concession. It was impossible for the Chickasaw to ally with the United States so long as the Creek and Cherokee forbade it; moreover, American traders faced too great a disadvantage in price competition. Panton continued that, should Carondelet confine Turnbull's trading activity strictly to Mobile, little harm would result. Should he be permitted to trade from his plantations at Tombigbee and Baton Rouge, however, he would provide too great an opportunity for Indians attempting to evade payment of Panton, Leslie and Company debts. Panton also warned Carondelet of Turnbull's untrustworthiness but predicted confidently, "keep him at Mobille and with Your assistance I will trounce him."[64]

Panton suspected Turnbull was merely serving as an agent for a "united force of the Merchants of New Orleans," who resented the royal privileges enjoyed by his firm.[65] These merchants, Panton learned, had petitioned Carondelet earlier to abolish the company's favored position. Interpreting the several royal orders that confirmed his company's status, the Scottish merchant noted that twelve months' prior notice was required before any alteration to the agreements between company and crown could be made. Presumably, Panton was referring to the twelve-month period of grace specified for withdrawal *in case of war*. Panton opined that "those orders, or Laws, Cannot legally be altered, suspended, or revoked, by any power on Earth, Short of the same authority that formed them."[66] Nevertheless, he presented terms on which his company would sell out to the complaining merchants and authorized Carondelet to convey the offer. They would have to secure the company in its outstanding debts and buy the company's fixed and movable assets at their fairly appraised value. They must also take the goods on hand at 30 per cent above prime cost; two-thirds of the purchase price must be in cash, but the balance could be arranged on time, provided that reasonable interest was paid and sound security was offered. The disgruntled merchants, Panton concluded, either could accept his terms or "be silent hereafter."[67]

62. Panton to Carondelet, December 17, 1792, *AGI PC*, leg. 122A, doc. H, WP.
63. Ibid.
64. Panton to Carondelet, January 1, 1793, *ANC F*, leg. 1, Exp. 5, no. 36, WP; Corbitt, "Georgia-Florida Frontier," 23:198–201.
65. Corbitt, ibid.
66. Ibid.
67. Ibid.

Turnbull, despite Panton's hopes, did not limit his trade to Mobile. Instead, he moved goods and rum up the Mississippi and, at Nogales, sent them up the Yazoo, deep into Chickasaw and Choctaw hunting lands. This action enabled him to obtain large quantities of pelts and deerskins that otherwise would have gone to pay debts owed to Panton's traders. The losses were not inconsequential to Panton, Leslie and Company, and both Panton and John Forbes consequently complained. The Choctaw and Chickasaw trade, Panton claimed, was of particular importance to company profits because it was free from American competition. Because the company charged the Choctaw and Chickasaw slightly higher prices to offset their lower earnings in dealing with the Cherokee and Creek, Panton hoped that Carondelet would order Gayoso to halt Turnbull's intrusions, which would remove all cause for further complaint.[68]

Panton apparently also induced Franchimastabe to visit Mobile for the purpose of lodging a formal complaint against Turnbull. The Indian chieftain, bemoaning the confusion created by the Yazoo commerce, reminded the commandant that Turnbull had received permission to trade only at Mobile. He should be made to comply.[69]

Turnbull, meanwhile, had failed to obtain permission from the Chickasaw to set up a trading post at Chickasaw Bluffs. Instead, they wanted him to remain permanently on the upper reaches of the Yazoo at a site more convenient to their villages. Turnbull was willing, but Carondelet was not. In May 1793, he ordered Turnbull's trade on the Yazoo halted immediately, on the grounds that it was prejudicial to Panton's interests and to the tranquillity of Spain's Indian allies. Carondelet also made clear that his bargain with Turnbull applied only to Chickasaw Bluffs. Moreover, since requests for funds to fortify the site had been rejected and the project had been postponed, Turnbull's disruptive tactics were no longer useful.[70] Carondelet temporarily abandoned Turnbull and the fort project. Panton had gained only a hollow victory, for Gayoso continued to make use of Turnbull's trade in working to establish a Spanish post at Chickasaw Bluffs.[71]

---

68. Panton to Carondelet, June 7, 1793, *ANC F*, leg. 1, Exp. 5, WP; Corbitt, "Georgia-Florida Frontier," 23:301–3; J. Forbes to Carondelet, October 31, 1792, *AGI PC*, leg. 203, doc. 26, WP; Corbitt, "Papers from the Spanish Archives," 28:131.

69. Franchimastabe "talk" of April 22, 1793; Lanzos to Carondelet, April 25, 1793, Kinnaird, *Spain in the Mississippi Valley*, 3:151–53.

70. Villebeuvre to Carondelet, March 8, 1793; Taskihatoka et al. to Villebeuvre, March 10, 1793, Corbitt, "Papers from the Spanish Archives," 30:96–98; Carondelet to Lanzos, May 7, 1793; Carondelet to Gayoso, July 25, 1793, *AGI PC*, leg. 20, West work cards.

71. Gayoso to Carondelet, October 18, 1793, Corbitt, "Papers from the Spanish Archives," 36:70–72; J. Forbes to Panton, May 15, 1793, *ANC F*, leg. 1, Exp. 9, no. 3, WP; Coughlin, "Spanish Galleys," 367–71.

In July, Carondelet offered Panton an opportunity to erect a trading post at Nogales. However, he must consent to pay 6 per cent on all imports and exports until the court decided whether to waive duties at the new site. The baron stated that he was powerless to offer Panton more; he could not summarily forbid Turnbull from trading either in Mobile or in Natchez. Panton accepted reluctantly, remarking that the extra expenses involved would in no way increase profits. Acceptance was the only way to forestall additional losses from Turnbull's activities.[72] The Franco-Spanish War, however, prevented Panton from acting on the offer, and the Walnut Hills plans were abandoned.

While Blount and Robertson were working at spreading their influence among the Choctaw and Chickasaw, from Georgia James Seagrove was attempting to restore the adherence of the Creek to the Treaty of New York. McGillivray, however, stirred to action by Carondelet and Panton, resisted Seagrove's attempts to fix the Oconee boundary on the pretext that a rash of minor border incidents along the Creek-Georgia frontier made conditions hazardous for such an undertaking. The Creek spokesman eventually yielded in part to Seagrove's request when the Lower Creek faced the prospect of famine due to a severe drought in the summer of 1792. He allowed Seagrove to schedule a meeting near the St. Marys for the purpose of distributing a large gift of corn and other goods made available by the United States for relief.[73]

A large number of Lower Creek, whose crops had been particularly hard hit by drought, met with Seagrove in November. McGillivray sent young Alexander Cornell as a trusted observer. Boundary discussions at the meeting led nowhere; nor were the Creek more than noncommittal to the American agent's trade proposals. Seagrove, with an eye toward personal gain, had earlier asked Secretary Knox for permission to license traders for the Creek. While Knox denied the request on the grounds that it violated the Treaty of New York, he fully approved Seagrove's plan to establish stores along the Georgia frontier. But to the chagrin of the Georgian, his Creek visitors showed little enthusiasm for his commercial overtures.[74]

---

72. Carondelet to Panton, July 27, 1793; Panton to Carondelet, August 18, 1793, *EF* leg. 116L9; Corbitt, "Georgia-Florida Frontier," 23:382-83.

73. McGillivray to Seagrove, May 18, 1792, *ASP FR*, 1:287; McGillivray to Knox, May 18, 1792, *ASP IA*, 1:315-16; Seagrove to Knox, May 24, July 5, 1792, *ASP IA*, 1:296-97, 303-4; McGillivray to Carondelet, November 15, 1792, *AGI PC*, leg. 205; McGillivray to Panton, November 28, 1792, *AGI PC*, leg. 204; Caughey, *McGillivray*, 344-49.

74. McGillivray to Panton, November 28, 1792, ibid.; Secretary of War to Seagrove, October 31, 1792; Seagrove to Secretary of War, July 5, 1792, *ASP IA*, 1:259-60, 303-4; McGillivray to Carondelet, January 15, 1793, *AGI PC*, leg. 2363; Caughey, *McGillivray*, 351-53; declarations of John Hambly and John Forrester, enclosures in Las Casas to

As the American campaign to soften Spanish influence among the southern Indians intensified, fate seriously damaged the capability of Carondelet and Panton to resist. Early in 1793, Alexander McGillivray traveled through inclement weather to Pensacola and arrived at Panton's house gravely ill. Late in the evening of February 17, he passed away. The "Poor fellow," Panton informed Carondelet, "left us at an untoward period." Panton took it upon himself to summon the Creek chiefs to Pensacola to facilitate the orderly transfer of Creek leadership. The Scot felt it imperative to forestall any advantage that the United States might gain from the death of McGillivray.[75]

In a subsequent letter, Panton suggested specific measures to Carondelet for filling the leadership vacuum among the Creek. To keep the Lower Creek in the Spanish orbit, the merchant suggested bestowing military titles and pensions on the half-Creek John Kinnard and on the Little Prince, a chieftain who had participated with Bowles in plundering the St. Marks store. In the interest of preserving his and Spain's hegemony, Panton was willing to embrace the "scoundrel." Regarding the loyalties of the Upper Creek, Panton expressed less concern. Carondelet might consider either pensioning three or four prominent leaders or investing McGillivray's brother-in-law, Milfort, as regent until the deceased leader's son, Aleck, came of age.[76]

Carondelet ignored Panton's suggestions on the Creek leadership crisis because more serious problems demanded his attention. These included the problem of colonial defense, in view of heightening Franco-Spanish tensions, but of more immediate concern was the imminence of Creek-Chickasaw hostilities. The prospect of Indian warfare not only threatened the baron's plans for forging a strong Indian confederation but also posed the possibility that the Chickasaw might be driven irreversibly into the American orbit. Since the preservation of peace among the Spanish treaty Indians took precedence over the question of designating McGillivray's successor, the mantle of Creek leadership passed without interference to Mad Dog, war chief of Tuckabatchee. Although Mad Dog had been a staunch supporter of McGillivray's policies, he proved to be less adept at holding together the Creek factions than his predecessor. He also was less pliable to Panton's control.[77]

Carondelet, January 16, 1793, *AGI PC*, leg. 152A, Lockey Papers; Smith, "James Seagrove," 45–46.

75. Panton to Carondelet, February 20, 1793, *AGI PC*, leg. 203, WP; Caughey, *McGillivray*, 354.

76. Panton to Carondelet, [February] 1793, *AGI PC*, leg. 178; Caughey, *McGillivray*, 355–56.

77. O'Neill to Carondelet, February 20, 1793, *AGI PC*, leg. 39, Stetson Collection;

Chapter 8

The brewing Creek-Chickasaw crisis had grown out of McGillivray's aggressive opposition to Piomingo's determination to gain access to U.S. trade. Animosity peaked in the summer of 1789 when a Creek war party ambushed a group of marauding Anglo-American frontiersmen above the Chickamauga villages. Among the victims were Piomingo's brother and nephew, who were returning home from a mission to the U.S. capital. The Creek, on examining the effects of their Chickasaw victims, discovered evidence that they had offered Congress a site for a permanent trading post at Chickasaw Bluffs.[78]

Encouraged by the Chickasaw overtures, President Washington and Secretary of War Knox decided to establish a U.S. post at Muscle Shoals instead of the proffered Chickasaw Bluffs. Once an American garrison was firmly established at the bend of the Tennessee, it would be in a position either to intimidate the Creek into submission or, if necessary, to launch a military campaign against them.[79] Thus, early in 1790, President Washington dispatched a small detachment of troops, under the command of Major John Doughty, up the Tennessee to Muscle Shoals. The expedition bore gifts and a presidential letter to Piomingo explaining that the party would settle a post at Muscle Shoals in conformity with the Treaty of Hopewell. The message also promised the Chickasaw gifts of ammunition for defense against their enemies. The Doughty party, however, was treacherously set upon in March by a party of Cherokee and Creek 230 miles up the Tennessee. Suffering eleven casualties and losing his baggage, Doughty retreated downstream. The Washington administration thereafter heeded Doughty's advice against attempting to occupy Muscle Shoals without consent of the Cherokee and Creek.[80]

Late in 1792, Piomingo's adherents obtained arms and supplies from General James Robertson. This assistance emboldened them into a retaliatory raid against the Creek, in which three youths, including a nephew and son of Mad Dog, were killed. McGillivray, determined not to let the attack go unanswered, had sent word to his warriors, many of whom were hunting, that they must return and strike the Chickasaw when the moon was full. The Chickasaw-Creek war continued in a somewhat desultory fashion through the winter. By spring McGillivray was dead, but Milfort

---

Carondelet to Las Casas, March 9, 1793, *AGI PC*, leg. 2353, Lockey Papers; Corbitt, "Papers from the Spanish Archives," 31:66–68; Cotterill, *Southern Indians*, 105–6.

78. McGillivray to Miró, June 24, 1789, *AGI PC*, leg. 202, doc. Q, WP; Caughey, *McGillivray*, 238–40.

79. Secretary of War to Governor St. Clair, December 19, 1789, Carter, *Territorial Papers*, 2:224–26.

80. Storm, "Up the Tennessee"; Washington to Hairlip King and Piomingo, December 17, 1789, *AGI PC*, leg. 203, doc. 12, WP.

planned a large-scale attack on the Chickasaw and ordered a 1,200-man Creek war party into the Chickasaw country, only to recall it a few days later when it became apparent that the Spaniards wanted the war ended.[81]

The drift toward full-scale hostilities had spurred Carondelet into action. He reiterated his earlier formal protests against U.S. interference in the affairs of the Choctaw and Chickasaw—tribes which he contended were bound under treaty to exclusive Spanish protection. He accused Governor Blount of deliberately inciting the Chickasaw to war for the purpose of acquiring rights to Chickasaw Bluffs. Carondelet also called on Gayoso, Panton, and the resident Spanish Indian agents to work toward an immediate restoration of peace.[82]

Panton took advantage of the conflict to reprove Carondelet's sponsorship of Turnbull. Permitting the interloper to make inroads among the Chickasaw, Panton argued, had weakened his own control over them, thus paving the way for closer ties with the United States.[83] He also gave concerted support to averting open warfare. Panton threatened to stop trade with the Creek and harangued them into realizing that the United States would be the principal beneficiary of war with the Chickasaw. These measures, together with the exertions of Carondelet and Milfort, halted the planned Creek offensive. Panton also sent "talks" to the Choctaw and Chickasaw, through the agency of Ben James, in favor of peace. These, combined with similar exhortations from Gayoso and Villebeuvre, persuaded Piomingo to embrace the opportunity to make peace.[84] By July

---

81. McGillivray to Carondelet, November 15, 1792, *AGI PC*, leg. 205; Caughey, *McGillivray*, 344–49; Cotterill, *Southern Indians*, 102; McGillivray to Panton, November 28, 1792, *AGI PC*, leg. 204; J. Forbes to Carondelet, November 7, 1792, *AGI PC*, leg. 203, Box 57, Stetson Collection; Piomingo and others to Carondelet, February 11, 1793, Corbitt, "Papers from the Spanish Archives," 29:154–55; Milfort to Carondelet, May 26, 1793, Caughey, *McGillivray*, 357–59; Mad Dog to Panton, April 20, 1793, *AGI PC*, leg. 208A.

82. Carondelet to Gayoso, March 5, 1793, *AHN Estado*, leg. 3898; Carondelet to Alcudia, February 28, 1793, ibid.; [Carondelet] to Olivier, February 28, 1793, *AGI PC*, leg. 214; Jáudenes and Viar to Jefferson, May 25, 1793, *AHN Estado*, leg. 3895, Exp. 1; Villebeuvre to Gayoso, June 8, 1793, Corbitt, "Papers from the Spanish Archives," 33:64–67; "Indian Speeches Made at Long Town," June 1, 1793, Kinnaird, *Spain in the Mississippi Valley*, 3:164–67; Carondelet to Las Casas, May 23, 1793, WPA, "Despatches," 8:400; Jáudenes and Viar to Jefferson, June 12, 18, 1793; *ASP FR*, 1:264–65; Jefferson to Short and Carmichael, June 30, 1793, *ASP FR*, 1:265–67.

83. Panton to Carondelet, June 7, 1793, *EF* leg. 116L9; Corbitt, "Georgia-Florida Frontier," 23:301–3.

84. Blount to Secretary of War, May 23, August 13, 1793, *ASP IA*, 1:454, 458; Carter, *Territorial Papers*, 4:259–61, 297–98; Villebeuvre to Gayoso, June 8, 1793, Corbitt, "Papers from the Spanish Archives," 33:64–67; Panton to Carondelet, October 15, 1793, Corbitt, "Georgia-Florida Frontier," 23:383–85; "Indian Speeches Made at Long Town," June 1, 1793, Kinnaird, *Spain in the Mississippi Valley*, 3:164–67. On peace efforts by the Spaniards, see also note 82 above.

1793, a reasonable semblance of tranquillity had been restored.[85] Panton's peacemaking efforts won the praise of the Spaniards. American observers were equally impressed by the powerful influence that the Scottish merchant wielded among the southern Indians, but not all believed Panton's motives to be laudable.[86]

General Robertson thought that Panton's real reason for wanting the war stopped was mercantile rather than humane. If the Indians stopped fighting among themselves and went to war against the United States, it would throw all of the Indian trade to Panton. Robertson could not understand how the Spaniards could "cherish and support, in the very bosom of their government, a refugee tory, (Mr. Panton) whose interest and inclination is to keep the Southern Indians, more or less, in a state of warfare against the United States, and whose influence and address put the gratification of both in his power."[87] Seagrove, never one to miss an opportunity to complain about Panton, charged that Panton's object in bringing peace to the Chickasaw and Creek was to destroy the American interest in those nations and to bring on a general war against the United States. Seagrove lamented that the seeds of the present troubles, planted by McGillivray and Panton, were now coming to maturity.[88]

With the return of peace, if not of complete harmony and trust, Carondelet resumed his preparations for a grand Indian congress. It finally got under way in October at Nogales, with Gayoso acting as the chief Spanish representative. The Choctaw, led by Franchimastabe, turned out en masse for the occasion. The increasingly pro-Spanish Ugula Yacabe led the Chickasaw delegation; Piomingo was conspicuously absent. With Mad Dog indifferent, at best, to an alliance with the Choctaw—much less with the Chickasaw—Coushatta chief Red Shoes led the small Creek delegation selected by Olivier. The Cherokee, temporarily engaged in skirmishing with Anglo-American frontiersmen, deputized the Creek representatives to act on their behalf. Later, however, the Cherokee, led by Bloody Fellow and John Watts, ratified the completed treaty.

On October 28, 1793, representatives of all interested parties signed the Treaty of Nogales. It bound together the southern tribes in an offensive-defensive alliance but fell short of meeting Carondelet's more belli-

---

85. Gayoso to Elias Beauregard, July 4, 1793, *AGI PC*, leg. 42, WP.
86. Gayoso to Carondelet, June 20, 1793, Corbitt, "Papers from the Spanish Archives," 33:72–75; Blount to Secretary of War, August 13, 1793, *ASP IA*, 1:458; Carter, *Territorial Papers*, 4:297–98.
87. Extract from General Robertson's Letter, Knoxville, May 23, 1793, *ASP IA*, 1:454; Coker, *Historical Sketches*, 41.
88. Coker, ibid., 41–42; Seagrove to Secretary of War, May 24, 1793, *ASP IA*, 1:387–88.

cose hopes. The baron had wanted a stipulation calling for concerted warfare against the United States in the event of American refusal to accede to tribal demands for a satisfactory boundary settlement. Gayoso prudently ignored Carondelet's wishes for the inclusion of such a dangerous proposal. The treaty also bound Spain to diplomatic support for Indian territorial pretensions, provided for an annual distribution of Spanish gifts at sites convenient to the Indians, and established permanent Spanish Indian agents. The provisions concerning gifts and agents were intended partly as a means of winning the acquiescence of the Chickasaw in the erection of a Spanish fort at Chickasaw Bluffs and another on the Tombigbee, at the site of a former French and British outpost. Although Villebeuvre had won Choctaw approval in May 1793 for Spanish occupancy of the Tombigbee site, Chickasaw consent was essential before work on the post could begin.[89]

Both during and after the Nogales conference, Gayoso, Turnbull, and other Spanish agents assiduously courted the favor of Ugula Yacabe. Cultivating his friendship was considered the key to winning a foothold for Spain at Tombigbee and at the strategic Chickasaw Bluffs. But Spanish diplomacy with the Chickasaw experienced many frustrations before its successful culmination.[90]

89. Cotterill, *Southern Indians*, 106–8; Holmes, *Gayoso*, 151–55; Nasatir, *Spanish War Vessels*, 11–12; Whitaker, *Spanish-American Frontier*, 168–69; Serrano y Sanz, *España y los Indios*, 91–92; Gayoso to Carondelet, December 6, 1793, AGI PC, leg. 42, WP.

90. For an overview of Spanish-Indian relations in this period, see DeFina, "Rivalidades y Contactos." A brief account is also in Mirat, *Las Floridas*, 61–109.

9

Beset by Friend and Foe Alike

*T*HE Montagnard-dominated French National Convention sent the hapless Louis XVI to the guillotine in January 1793. Within two months Spain and the French republic were at war. But the French foreign ministry, well in advance of the actual outbreak of hostilities, involved itself in numerous schemes to weaken Spain's foothold in North America. Late in February, on the eve of war, the youthful and ebullient Edmond Genêt, recently selected to represent France in the United States, set sail to execute his government's anti-Spanish designs.

Genêt's orders included conspiring with Kentuckians and other western settlers whose animosity toward Spanish domination of the Mississippi ran high and fomenting rebellion among the French-speaking colonists of Louisiana, thereby making that Spanish province ripe for conquest by disgruntled American frontiersmen. Genêt was also to pave the way for extensive French privateering activities through U.S. ports.[1] But President Washington's Proclamation of Neutrality of April 1793 rendered the attainment of these objectives impossible even for a seasoned diplomat. For Genêt, the proclamation set the stage for a fiasco of magnificent proportions.

Intentionally or otherwise, Genêt arrived in the United States not at

---

1. Jameson, "Genêt's Instructions," in *Annual Report*, 1:958–67; Turner, "Genêt's Projected Attack"; Jackson, *Privateers in Charleston*, 6–7.

Philadelphia but at Charleston, where many South Carolinians gave him a rousing welcome. There were numerous reasons for this tumultuous reception. Charlestonians of Huguenot lineage reveled in the ideals of *liberté, egalité et fraternité* that had so recently swept France. Many recalled with great bitterness the British occupation of Charleston during the American Revolution. Finally, land speculators and shipowners had a crasser yearning for gain at Spanish expense. Encouraged by his joyous reception, Genêt lost little time in divulging his plans to Governor William Moultrie, whose brother, Alexander, had been a prominent director of the South Carolina Yazoo Company. With Moultrie's encouragement, Genêt issued letters of marque to American privateers. He then plunged into the task of recruiting an army of southern backwoodsmen for an invasion of East Florida. With all plans proceeding smoothly, Genêt departed for Philadelphia to take up his ill-fated intrigues with George Rogers Clark against Louisiana; he left the French consul at Charleston, Michel Ange Bernard de Mangourit, in charge of the East Florida venture.[2]

Mangourit soon discovered that many Georgians were even more enthusiastic than the South Carolinians over the prospect of a military campaign against East Florida. The pro-French sympathies of Georgia frontiersmen were buttressed by bitter resentment against the Spanish for their support of the Creeks. Among the first Georgians attracted to Mangourit was Samuel Hammond, an officer in the state militia and a hero of the Battle of King's Mountain. Commissioned a colonel in the Revolutionary Legion of America, Hammond had principal responsibility for French military preparations against Florida.[3]

Pecuniary incentives added to Samuel Hammond's interest in the French intrigue. His brother, Abner, and his uncle, Leroy, were associated with the mercantile firm of Hammond and Fowler, a concern interested in expanding its meager Indian trade. The Hammonds saw in the French plans the ideal means of striking a blow at Panton, Leslie and Company, while at the same time gaining the lucrative business of supplying the French invasion force.[4]

Samuel Hammond convinced Mangourit that to succeed the expedition would require, if not the active support of the Creek, at least their tacit approval. It could be gained, Samuel judged, by reaching an agreement with certain Creek chieftains with whom he and Abner enjoyed in-

---

2. Jackson, *Privateers in Charleston*, 3–6, 25; Alexander Moultrie to McGillivray, February 19, 1790, *AGI PC*, leg. 203.
3. Murdoch, *Georgia-Florida Frontier*, 13–15; Northern, *Men of Mark*, 1:148–53.
4. Murdoch, *Georgia-Florida Frontier*, 25–26; Bennett, *Florida's "French" Revolution*, 148–49.

fluence. At a minimum, an accord would assure the invasion forces safe passage through Creek lands. The Hammonds held some hope for bringing the Creek into active support. If not, they could easily be persuaded to recognize French domination of East Florida by making the destruction of Panton, Leslie and Company's posts on the St. Marys and St. Johns the primary objective of the expedition. Once Creek trade had passed into the hands of Hammond and Fowler, complete control over the Indians would follow. Samuel Hammond informed Mangourit that funds for gifts with which to gain the interest of the Creek must be forthcoming.[5] Mangourit sent $1,500 to buy gifts through Hammond and Fowler, together with a draft of proposals for a French-Creek treaty.[6]

But plans for the invasion of Florida soon went awry. In August 1793, the U.S. government, enraged over Genêt's conduct, demanded his recall. Political control in France, meanwhile, had passed completely to the Jacobins, and Jean Antoine Joseph Fauchet had been sent to the United States to repair the damage Genêt had caused to Franco-American relations. Consequently, on March 2, 1794, Fauchet dismissed Genêt, and four days later in a public advertisement he forbade French nationals to violate U.S. neutrality and revoked French commissions issued earlier for that purpose. Mangourit, however, sensing the value of East Florida as an entrepôt and as a haven for French privateering operations, continued his preparations for the Florida campaign. On April 7, Citizen Fonspertuis arrived at Charleston to relieve Mangourit of his consular duties. The immediate invasion threat to East Florida collapsed.[7]

The abortive invasion scheme also had attracted the support of General Elijah Clarke. An inveterate opponent of the Treaty of New York because of its prescriptions against usurping Creek lands, Clarke had gathered a band of backwoods filibusterers for the invasion, promising them rewards of East Florida land grants. Determined not to be frustrated entirely in their filibustering ambitions, Clarke and his "army" marched northward from the St. Marys, crossed the Oconee north of Rock Landing, and raised a settlement on Creek land, which they proclaimed to be the "Trans-Oconee Republic." Governor George Mathews, equally embittered by federal Indian policy, at first ignored this open violation of the U.S.–Creek treaty.[8]

In July 1794, Panton received reports from his traders of Clarke's ac-

5. Bennett, *Florida's "French" Revolution*, 20–27; Hammond to Mangourit [n.d.], Turner, "Mangourit Correspondence," 595–96.
6. Murdoch, *Georgia-Florida Frontier*, 19–23, 27–28.
7. Jackson, *Privateers in Charleston*, 35–41.
8. Murdoch, *Georgia-Florida Frontier*, 50–56. Clarke's name is spelled both "Clark" and "Clarke."

tivities. The Scottish merchant passed the information on to Spanish authorities, adding that the Indians, low on arms and ammunition, were powerless to repulse the intruders. Furthermore, Panton warned, if left unopposed, the settlement would become "a rendezvous for all the vagabond French Americans on this Continent" and hence a serious threat to the security of the Floridas.[9] Conditions west of the Oconee remained unchanged through September, and Panton urged that the Creek, who were eager to drive the usurpers back into Georgia, be supplied with the arms needed for the task. Panton later intimated to Carondelet that a determined soldier might lead Spanish troops, supported by a body of Indians, in an attack against Clarke.[10] Such action, however, became unnecessary; pressure from Clarke's opponents in Georgia and threats from President Washington forced Governor Mathews to secure the abandonment of the trans-Oconee settlement. By late 1794, French-inspired threats against the Floridas and the trade empire of Panton, Leslie and Company had subsided.[11]

On the other hand, French privateers operating out of Charleston added to the company's mounting misfortunes. Although French corsairs had appeared occasionally in Charleston harbor before mid-1793, the port became crucially important to French privateering operations during the succeeding two years, for several reasons. The Federalist-dominated courts in the north, in contrast to Charleston, adhered more closely to principles of strict neutrality in admiralty cases. State officials in South Carolina, as well as federal customs agents, displayed a cooperative spirit in handling French prizes. Aside from the prevailing pro-French sympathy, the citizens of Charleston welcomed the economic benefits connected with privateering. Moreover, by mid-1794, British military and naval units, with the support of French royalists, had either seized or neutralized French ports in Saint Domingue and in the Lesser Antilles, making access to Charleston crucial to privateering.[12]

Three sea captains—Jean Baptiste Carvin of *L'Industrie*, Jean Bouteille of *La Sans Pareille*, and William Talbot of *L'Ami de la Pointe-à-Pitre*—dominated privateering operations out of Charleston. Carvin and Bouteille had sailed northward out of the French West Indies bearing letters of marque and reprisal early in 1793. Talbot, a native Virginian,

9. Ibid., 68; Jacob Townshend to Panton (extract), July 14, 1794; Panton to White [n.d.], ANC F, leg. 1, Exp. 5; Corbitt, "Georgia-Florida Frontier," 24:259–61.
10. Murdoch, *Georgia-Florida Frontier*, 66–67; Panton to Carondelet, September 30, 1794, Kinnaird, *Spain in the Mississippi Valley*, 3:346–47.
11. Murdoch, *Georgia-Florida Frontier*, 55, 69–70.
12. Jackson, *Privateers in Charleston*, 11, 17–20; Mahan, *Sea Power and the French Revolution*, 1:110–17.

had turned to privateering as a means of avenging losses inflicted by the notoriously venal vice-admiralty court in the Bahamas. In December 1793, he sailed the armed American schooner *Fair Play* to Guadeloupe, renamed the vessel and placed it under French registry, and became a naturalized French citizen.[13]

During the latter half of 1793, French privateers not only cruised the Florida passage but also patrolled the approaches to St. Augustine. In December, Bouteille and Carvin captured the *Aurora*, a Panton, Leslie and Company schooner under the command of Captain Dickie, and sent the prize to Charleston for condemnation proceedings. Although assessed at £4,000 by the British consul, the *Aurora*, when processed through the French consular court, somehow was purchased by James Penman and Company, a correspondent of Panton, Leslie and Company, for £150 and returned to Dickie's command.[14] Two months later, Bouteille again captured the *Aurora*, outward bound from Nassau to St. Augustine with a year's supply of trade goods for Panton, Leslie and Company's East Florida stores. The cargo was valued at £5,000. Subjected a second time to condemnation proceedings, the *Aurora* and its uninsured cargo sold for slightly over £3,800.[15]

In April, Captain Talbot captured a Panton, Leslie and Company frigate, the *Grenada Packet*. This vessel, bound for London out of Pensacola, carried a cargo of peltry valued at more than £13,800. Talbot dispatched this prize to Savannah, where it accidentally caught fire and burned, causing severe property damage along the harbor frontage.[16] The cargo, removed beforehand, brought the captors approximately £11,600. On learning of the fire, Panton declared that he could have borne his losses without regret if the *Grenada Packet* had been the means of burning Savannah to the ground.[17] While the cargo had been insured, the company had to absorb the loss of the vessel. Although Panton, Leslie and Company sustained no further direct losses to French cruisers, its insurance costs, depending on departure points and destinations, increased three- to sixfold. By mid-1794, Panton estimated company costs from losses and increased insurance premiums associated with the war at nearly $100,000.[18]

13. Jackson, *Privateers in Charleston*, 11–14, 52–55.
14. Extract of letter, [T. Forbes?] to Panton, September 10, 1793, Kinnaird, *Spain in the Mississippi Valley*, 3:203; Jackson, *Privateers in Charleston*, 17n26, 122, 130–31.
15. Panton to J. Forbes, June 4, 1794, GP; Panton to Carondelet, July 3, 1794, *AGI PC*, leg. 203, doc. 40, WP; Jackson, *Privateers in Charleston*, 17n26, 130–31.
16. Panton to J. Forbes, June 4, 1794, GP; Panton to Carondelet, July 3, 1794, *AGI PC*, leg. 203, doc. 40; Jackson, *Privateers in Charleston*, 55, 136–37.
17. Panton to J. Forbes, July 11, 1794, FP, MPL.
18. Panton to Carondelet, July 3, 1794, *AGI PC*, leg. 203, doc. 40. See table 3.

The effects of general warfare on European commercial patterns and practices also worked unfavorably against Panton, Leslie and Company's terms of trade. Indian goods, especially arms and ammunition, became scarce and costly, and the London fur market all but collapsed. Traffic with French fur buyers halted almost completely, while German, Russian, and English furriers and tanners bought only sparingly.[19] In the early 1790s, Panton, Leslie and Company, as suppliers of more than half the deerskins sold on the London market, occasionally had used its market power to maintain steady prices.[20] The war made this impossible. Although scarcities in trade items had abated by 1796, prices remained above their prewar levels. However, peltry prices rose only after 1800. As far as possible, the company shifted the burden of its cost-price squeeze to its Indian customers. The Indians, however, generally were unable to comprehend the underlying reasons why goods became at once costly and scarce and became suspicious and sullen.[21]

War with France also made it necessary for Spain to change the trade policies granted to Louisiana and West Florida in the royal *cédula* of 1782. Spain included East Florida in the new order. In fact, another reason for Spain's decision to issue the new trade regulations originated in East Florida. A cross section of the province's most prominent residents had complained about Panton, Leslie and Company's monopoly of trade there and its duty-free status. The new East Florida governor, Colonel Juan Nepomuceno de Quesada, endorsed their petition, which, some believe, had an important bearing on the issuance of the new Royal Order of June 9, 1793.

This directive completely revised Spanish commercial regulations for all three provinces. The new rules opened trade between Louisiana and Florida ports and all friendly nations in Europe and America which had commercial treaties with Spain. Foreign ships had been required to call first at either of two minor peninsular posts, Corcubión or Alicante, before proceeding to Louisiana and the Floridas, but in April 1794, this stipulation was removed. The decree imposed an import duty of 15 percent on goods from foreign sources; export duties remained at 6 per cent; and trade between Louisiana or Florida ports and those of other Spanish prov-

---

19. Phillips, *Fur Trade*, 2:101–2; Panton to Carondelet, April 4, 1793, *AGI PC*, leg. 203, doc. 36, WP; White to Carondelet, August 23, 1793, Kinnaird, *Spain in the Mississippi Valley*, 3:200–201; Panton to Carondelet, March 16, 1794, Corbitt, "Georgia-Florida Frontier," 24:83.

20. Panton to Miró, July 4, 1790, *ANC F*, leg. 1, Exp. 5, no. 14, WP; Phillips, *Fur Trade*, 2:198.

21. Diego de Vegas to Carondelet, June 7, 1794, Kinnaird, *Spain in the Mississippi Valley*, 3:295–96; Phillips, *Fur Trade*, 2:101, 217, 220.

inces was proscribed. But implementation and interpretation of the new regulations in East Florida entailed little change in the company's privileged status there. This practice alienated many persons and contributed to the problems experienced in East Forida during the so-called French revolution there in 1793–95.[22] Panton viewed the new policy as an opportunity for company expansion into Louisiana.

With the unusual alliance of Spain and Great Britain against France, Panton entertained thoughts of expanding his company's activities by taking advantage of the new commercial dispensation. Intimating to Carondelet that the decree of June 1793 would "produce much good" in promoting economic growth, Panton further inquired whether the governor wished for the company to open a "House in New Orleans."[23] With local price levels at least 100 percent above those prevailing in the United States, the proposal, which apparently went ignored, would have had highly lucrative results if acted upon.[24]

In London, meanwhile, preparations for war, orders-in-council restricting exports, and the Spanish regulations of June 1793 raised difficulties for Strachan and MacKenzie in filling orders for Panton, Leslie and Company. The growing European demand for guns made it difficult to acquire such items for the Florida Indian trade.[25] Although arms were obtainable in 1793, Strachan and MacKenzie were obliged to appeal to the Privy Council for special permission to export not just muskets but other strategic goods, such as pistols, gunpowder, ball, gun locks, saltpeter, sailcloth, cordage, certain ironware items, foodstuffs, and leather goods. For the duration of the Anglo-Spanish alliance, company requests for export privileges to Pensacola, New Providence, and St. Augustine met with approval but only under the lengthy stipulations laid down by the Privy Council. It required the inspection of muskets to ascertain that they were not adaptable to bayonets, the posting of bonds six times the value of exports, convoy travel for all Panton, Leslie and Company vessels outbound from England, and certification that the goods had arrived at the specified destination.[26] The convoy system frequently caused delays in departure,

---

22. Text in Whitaker, *Documents*, 176–85; extract in *ASP FR*, 1:273; see also Whitaker, *Documents*, 241n170. On the situation in East Florida, see Miller, *Quesada*, 77–94; Bennett, *Florida's "French" Revolution*, 21–22.
23. Panton to Carondelet, October 15, 1793, Corbitt, "Georgia-Florida Frontier," 23:383–85.
24. Pope, *Tour through the United States*, 41.
25. Panton to Carondelet, March 16, 1794, Corbitt, "Georgia-Florida Frontier," 24:83.
26. Privy Council, PROL, PC 2/138:590–92, 616–17; PC 2/139:78; PC 2/141:45–46; PC 2/142:66, 89–90, 313–14; PC 2/144:510–11; PC 2/146:130–31.

creating difficulties in getting peltry shipped from the Floridas before the warm season.[27]

The British requirement concerning convoy travel also forced Strachan and MacKenzie to ask Ambassador Campo for special dispensation from the Spanish rule on clearing through Corcubión or Alicante. To do so, the London merchants explained, would make it risky for Panton, Leslie and Company ships to rendezvous with the convoy, and if they fell prey to enemy cruisers, the bond as well as the vessel and cargo would be forfeit. Campo complied, but reluctantly.[28]

In 1793, while the French menace to Louisiana and the Floridas was strong, James Seagrove attempted to advance the American cause among the Creek in a determined, though less spectacular, manner. At first, the American agent shuddered upon hearing a rumor that on his deathbed McGillivray had chosen Panton as his successor, for Seagrove believed this would dash all hopes for peace. Subsequently, however, he became more optimistic. With McGillivray dead, Seagrove believed that the path to building U.S. influence among the Creek had finally been opened. He recruited Jack Kinnard and Timothy Barnard, who lived and traded among the Lower Creek, and they in turn cultivated the goodwill of such influential headmen as Mad Dog, Alexander Cornell, White Lieutenant of Okfuskie, and Hollowing King.[29]

Seagrove's efforts, however, were temporarily offset by a visiting delegation of Shawnee, who appeared in the Creek country late in 1792 bearing scalps taken from St. Clair's forces as well as entreaties for an anti-U.S. alliance. Although both Lower and Upper Creek councils spurned the invitation to join with the northern tribes, the Shawnee by themselves incited considerable anti-Georgian resentment—especially among those Lower Creek who had been recent adherents of Bowles. Reminded that American herders grazed cattle west of the Oconee with impunity and that American hunters indiscriminately slaughtered game in the same vicinity, early in March a band of Lower Creek visited the store of James's brother, Robert Seagrove, near Colerain and murdered the clerk and another American. Other massacres quickly followed. James Seagrove believed that Panton and the Spaniards had encouraged James Burges, a

---

27. Panton to Carondelet, March 14, 1795, *AGI PC*, leg. 203, docs. 43; Panton to Carondelet, December 14, 1793, *ANC F*, leg. 1, Exp. 5, no. 51.
28. Strachan and MacKenzie to Campo, September 24, 1793, May 30, 1794; Campo to Strachan and MacKenzie, September 26, 1793, *AGS Estado*, leg. 8137.
29. Seagrove to Secretary of War, April 19, 1793; Seagrove to Chiefs, etc. of Creek Nation, April 14, 1793; White Lieutenant, Alexander Cornell et al. to Seagrove, June 14, 1793, *ASP IA*, 1:378–79, 381, 396; Smith, "James Seagrove," 45.

trader who resided among the Lower Creek, to incite the massacres, particularly since the raiding party had carried off the account books. The American agent demanded that the Creek nation give satisfaction.[30]

Word of the "bloody plan at Trader's Hill," as Seagrove referred to the attack on his brother's store, reached John Forrester before he departed permanently from the St. Marys. Forrester hurriedly advised Governor Quesada that Seagrove, in retaliation, was inciting the Indians to fall upon the Spanish settlers on the St. Marys and to plunder the Panton, Leslie trading post. Fortunately for the company, Forrester had already closed the St. Marys store, and he soon left the area for the St. Johns River and the new trading post site at San Fernando de Pupo. Many of the other inhabitants also departed for safer locations, but those who took refuge on the St. Johns found their respite short lived. Although undoubtedly not inspired by Seagrove, the Indians, as Forrester had warned, swept through the St. Marys settlements and, not finding any Spaniards to molest, they killed or stole all of the cattle, horses, and Negroes they could find. Several bands moved south to the St. Johns to menace the settlers there. Forrester, in company with others on that river, appealed to the governor—Forrester hand-carried the letter to St. Augustine—for protection to prevent their total ruin and destruction and the depopulation of the district. They requested a detachment of soldiers and the erection of a blockhouse near the western limits of the settlements. They asked permission to form a body of scouts who would assist the military in their defense, and they strongly urged the governor to prohibit any but licensed traders to sell to the Indians. This last request might have seemed self-serving on Forrester's part, but unscrupulous traders often sold liquor to the Indians, and during times of stress the frontier did not need drunken Indians. Whatever the cause—a show of force, or the reaction of an unexpected ally, the Georgians—the St. Johns River settlers escaped the Indian threat unscathed.[31]

These border raids brought immediate retaliation from the Georgians. Despite Seagrove's admonitions, Governor Telfair activated the militia, and unruly detachments soon were making retaliatory raids. Despite the building tension, a general Creek council held at Tuckabatchee in June

30. Cotterill, *Southern Indians*, 100–103; Seagrove to James Holmes, February 24, 1793; Seagrove to Kings, etc. of Creek Nation, April 14, 1793; Seagrove to Secretary of War and enclosures, March 17, April 19, May 24, 1793, *ASP IA*, 1:373–74, 377–79, 381, 387–88; Panton to Carondelet, April 10, 1793, *AGI PC*, leg. 203, doc. 37, WP.

31. James Seagrove to Secretary of War, July 31, 1793, *ASP IA*, 1:399; Forrester to Quesada, March 13, 19, 1793, *AGS Estado*, leg. 8137; W. Pengree to Dr. Starling, April 28, 1793; Pengree, Forrester and others to [Governor of East Florida], May 1, 1793, *EF* leg. 123F10.

1793 invited Seagrove to visit the Creek nation and restore peace. A unit of the Georgia militia, however, ambushed the deputation sent to escort the U.S. agent to the Creek nation and brutally killed David Cornell, its leader. This incident, and subsequent forays by Georgia militiamen, delayed Seagrove's visit until November. Meanwhile, he sent the Creek profuse apologies, implored restraint, and emphasized that Georgia, not the federal government, had taken up the sword.[32]

Seagrove entered the Creek country with packhorses laden with gifts; he met a large Creek party at the Ocmulgee River and followed it to a rousing reception at the Lower Creek town at Cussetah. For some time before Seagrove's arrival, agents in his employ had resorted to the tactics Bowles had used with such telling effect: Barnard and Kinnard had intimated that Panton and his associates were guilty of exploiting the Indians. The tactic was quite successful. In October, at a meeting at Tuckabatchee, Joseph Cornell, McGillivray's father-in-law, not only denounced Panton but also impugned the loyalty of his own deceased son-in-law. On arriving at Pensacola, Cornell declared, Panton had promised to trade on the same terms as those that had prevailed during the British era. Afterward, however, the avaricious merchant had drawn McGillivray so completely into the interest of Panton, Leslie and Company as to make him a traitor. Thereafter, Cornell asserted, Panton had charged him double.[33]

Seagrove traveled to Tuckabatchee in late November to address a full Creek council. His reception was more guarded than that extended him at Cussetah; Tuckabatchee was the home of the slain David Cornell. Seagrove nevertheless succeeded in persuading the Creek to agree to peace with Georgia on the basis of a mutual return of hostages and plunder taken earlier in the year. The terms also included tentative provisions for blood satisfaction for the murders committed by both sides. The Creek deputized three principal chiefs to work with Seagrove in carrying out the terms, a task that detained the American agent in the Creek country until the following April.[34]

---

32. Smith, "James Seagrove," 48–52; Seagrove to Secretary of War, July 6, 31, 1793; Barnard to Seagrove (two letters this date), June 20, 1793; Seagrove to Alexander Cornell, July 5, 1793, *ASP IA*, 1:393–95, 398–99; Jacob Townshend to Maj. Gen. James Jackson [ca. July 7, 1793], in WPA, "Creek Indians," 1:327–28.

33. Smith, "James Seagrove," 53; Barnard "talk" to Cussetahs, March 22, 1793, *ASP IA*, 1:382–83; Milfort to White, October 19, 1793; White to Carondelet, November 11, 1793, Kinnaird, *Spain in the Mississippi Valley*, 3:221–22, 227–29. Joseph Cornell was the father of "one" of McGillivray's wives: Panton to Lachlan McGillivray, April 10, 1794, *Johnson et al. v. Innerarity, et al.*

34. Smith, "James Seagrove," 53–55; Seagrove to Secretary of War, November 30, 1793, *ASP IA*, 1:471–72; Durouzeaux to White, 1793, Kinnaird, *Spain in the Mississippi Valley*, 3:234–35.

Chapter 9

During his stay, Seagrove worked diligently to cultivate a strong following. He distributed gifts, rewarded his key supporters, spent heavily to ransom Georgian captives, and cast slurs against the "avarice" of Panton. At a March 1794 meeting at Tuckabatchee, Seagrove spoke on the causes of the widespread "nakedness" he had witnessed among the Creek. The primary cause, he asserted, stemmed from having placed their trade in one man's hands for ten years. To the south, the Creek dealt not with true friends but with impostors. To remedy this undesirable situation, General Washington, who wished to see the Creek warmly dressed, intended to erect trading posts along the frontier. At these new trading outlets, Seagrove promised, Indians would receive three blankets for the same price they currently paid for two. The agent closed his remarks with an exhortation to the Creek to throw open their trade and to do business with those who offered the better bargains.[35]

Panton quickly called Carondelet's attention to Seagrove's "ability in the Art of creating dissension"[36] and developed respect for the agent's effectiveness. Panton had good reason to regard Seagrove as a worthy antagonist. His labors apparently inspired the White Lieutenant, Mad Dog, and Alexander Cornell, all former McGillivray henchmen, to reprove Panton for giving the Creek "bad" advice. They also warned him against any further meddling in Creek affairs. After Seagrove's departure from Tuckabatchee, Panton expressed relief that some of the damage that Seagrove had caused had been repaired. In 1794, the Creek trade through Pensacola continued at normal levels, despite Seagrove's offer of low prices. Panton speculated that Seagrove was as yet unable to deliver on his promises of better trade terms. But Carondelet's parsimony in doling out Indian gifts, despite many indications of increasingly aggressive U.S. Indian policies, left Panton greatly concerned about the future.[37]

Meanwhile, in Philadelphia, President Washington had acted to give substance to Seagrove's trade promises. In his message to Congress of December 1793, the president said that the government's problems with the Cherokee and Creek were on a critical footing; the solution hinged on creating ties of interest between the tribes and the United States. After meting out justice to U.S. citizens who violated the rights of the Indians, Washington continued, "the establishment of commerce . . . was most

---

35. Milfort to Carondelet, March 20, 1794, *AGS Guerra*, leg. 7235, WP; Milfort to Carondelet, December 17, 1793, April 14, 1794, Kinnaird, *Spain in the Mississippi Valley*, 3:235–36, 266–68.

36. Panton to Carondelet, December 14, 1793. Corbitt, "Georgia-Florida Frontier," 24:79–80.

37. "Talk," White Lieutenant, Mad Dog, and Alexander Cornell to Panton, [May 1794], *EF* leg. 114J9; Panton to J. Forbes, June 4, 29, 1794, GP.

likely to conciliate their attachment." To be effective, however, the Indian trade "ought to be conducted without fraud, without extortion, with constant and plentiful supplies; [and] with a ready market for the commodities of the Indians" at fair prices. Private citizens, the president observed, would shun the Indian trade, "unless they be allured by the hope of profit." On the other hand, the government could conduct the trade without expectation of gain, so long as it incurred no losses. Washington concluded by recommending that Congress enact the necessary laws to make the Indian trade a government monopoly.[38]

Panton lost no time in bringing Washington's remarks to his associates' attention. This development, the Scot mused, when combined with the other misfortunes that had befallen the company, demanded a thorough reappraisal of the company's prospects. He decided that the Spanish authorities "must alter their Conduct to Indians and show a degree of Liberality superior to any thing I have seen in my time or all is lost."[39] The concerned Panton reduced his order for the 1795 season's supplies to the minimum and requested the backing of the Spanish government as a condition for continued operations. It had become impossible, Panton contended, for the private resources of the partnership "to hold out any longer against the purse of the United States and foes on every quarter."[40] If the Spaniards withheld assistance, Panton intended either to withdraw completely from the Indian trade or to continue perhaps on a limited basis, "in order the better to cover up my real intentions."[41] The nature of his "real intentions" is uncertain. Probably Panton hoped to capitalize on the commercial advantages afforded by the Royal Order of June 9, 1793.

On May 2, 1794, Panton formally petitioned Carondelet for Spanish assistance in coping with the U.S. Indian trade plan. Referring to Washington's December address to Congress, Panton declared it to be a great compliment to his company's success in attracting the southern Indian trade. Indeed, since American merchants could not compete effectively with Panton, Leslie and Company, the federal government (according to Panton) had been compelled to enter the fray. Based upon Seagrove's promises to the Indians, that they would soon be enjoying wholesale prices, Panton mistakenly assumed that Congress had acted positively on Washington's request for a government Indian trade monopoly.[42]

38. "Fifth Annual Address to Congress," December 3, 1793, Fitzpatrick, *Writings of George Washington*, 33:163–69; see also Harmon, "Benjamin Hawkins," 139–46.
39. Panton to J. Forbes, April 17, 1794, GP.
40. Panton to J. Forbes, February 3, 1794, GP.
41. Panton to Butler, March 30, 1794, GP.
42. Panton, Leslie and Company, memorial to Carondelet, May 2, 1794, *AHN Estado*, leg. 3888, Exp. 1.

Panton explained that, to preserve its own influence over the Indians, the Spanish government must accept one of two alternatives. The first, and most preferable to Panton, Leslie and Company, called for the Spanish government to buy out the company in both Floridas and to conduct the trade as a government monopoly. Spain would pay for the company's stocks, at cost plus handling charges, and purchase its fixed and movable assets at their fairly appraised value. The total amount involved was estimated at $400,000, which was to be deposited in London with Strachan and MacKenzie. Should the Spanish government select this alternative, Panton, Leslie and Company promised to act in London as its correspondents, thus assuring Spain of continued access to the company's experience and goodwill.[43]

The second alternative called for Spain to extend a ten-year, interest-free loan of $400,000, together with firm promises of indemnification should the company find it necessary to sell at a loss in competing with the United States. Under this plan, the petitioner stated, the partners stood to lose only their time and effort. The Spanish government, however, must buy all Indian presents from Panton, Leslie and Company exclusively, guarantee the concern a complete monopoly of the southern Indian trade, and allow the establishment of a duty-free post at Walnut Hills (the bitterness over Turnbull's activities had not subsided). Finally, the Spanish government must promise to adopt a more liberal Indian gift policy, one comparable to that employed by the British, because the Americans were sparing no cost to detach the Indians from Spanish control.[44]

Carondelet, even before receiving the Panton memorial, had agreed in principle to the need for official support of the company. Spain, by indemnifying Panton, Leslie and Company for its losses in underselling the U.S. government, could maintain the status quo. Within two or three years, Carondelet expected, the United States, having wasted its efforts, would abandon the enterprise. He also agreed on the expediency of heavily increased expenditures for Indian gifts.[45] In forwarding the memorial to the Spanish court, the Louisiana governor endorsed the first alternative, particularly since Panton agreed to train Spaniards in the intricacies of the business before leaving Pensacola. Spain, by buying out the company, could rid itself of overdependence on English influence in controlling the Indians—a significant consideration in the event of an Anglo-Spanish war. Moreover, the Spanish provinces in America would enjoy the eco-

43. Ibid.
44. Ibid.
45. Carondelet to Alcudia, April 9, 1794, Jameson, *Annual Report*, 1:1052–56.

nomic benefits of the arrangement in an economic area of overriding importance.[46]

On the other hand, Francisco Rendón, Navarro's belated replacement as intendant, favored the second alternative. The company's experience could then be retained, and, moreover, the Spanish government could expect repayment on a loan. The loan could be arranged in four annual installments and should be made in Florida rather than in London. Panton, Rendón suggested, should then be allowed to transfer funds from the provinces only as needed.[47]

Washington's plans for instituting a federally supported system of Indian trade matured slowly. In 1794, a House committee studied the president's recommendations of 1793, but Congress took no further action. This prompted Washington to repeat the recommendations in November. The following spring, Congress began deliberation on a bill to establish government-sponsored trade. Although the bill was defeated, in March 1795, Washington's supporters managed to obtain the passage of a compromise experimental measure authorizing the purchase of up to $50,000 in goods to be sold in the Indian trade as the president might direct.[48]

The War Department chose to use the limited appropriation to establish two government factories for trade with the Cherokee and Creek. Secretary Timothy Pickering allocated two-thirds of the funds to stock a government factory at Colerain on the St. Marys for the Creek; the remainder went to supply a Cherokee trading post at Tellico, in present-day Tennessee. The federal experiment, however, began under unauspicious circumstances. Before opening the factories, the government had to await the arrival of new shipments of Indian goods from London in the fall; American merchants had exhausted their supplies.[49]

Congress enacted a measure in May 1796 that gave permanency to the experiment of the preceding year. The act appropriated an additional $150,000 with which to maintain inventories for the Indian trade at prices that would cover the government's total costs. Supporters of the bill in the Senate justified government intervention in the Indian trade as the only means of supplanting British traders. Once the British were eliminated,

---

46. Carondelet to Alcudia, July 27, 1794, *AGI SD*, leg. 2670, WP; Carondelet to Las Casas, July 27, 1794, Lockey Papers.
47. Rendón to Gardoqui, April 25, 1795, *AGI SD*, leg. 2612.
48. "Sixth Annual Address to Congress," November 19, 1794; Fitzpatrick, *Writings of George Washington*, 34:36; Harmon, *Sixty Years of Indian Affairs*, 95–100; Way, "United States Factory System," 223–24; Prucha, *American Indian Policy*, 86–87.
49. Report, Secretary of War to Senate, December 12, 1795, *ASP IA*, 1:583–84.

the United States would withdraw. And Panton, Leslie and Company had earned a ranking position among those to be eliminated.[50]

Panton, meanwhile, futilely attempted to use American law to force the Spanish government to act favorably on the May 1794 memorial. Compared with U.S. activity in the field of Indian affairs, he cautioned, the Spanish court seemed "to have dropt into a slumber" from which he wished it might "awake in time to have any thing remaining worthy of contention."[51] Spanish ministers, however, were too preoccupied with more pressing wartime problems, and Panton's admonition passed unnoticed.

The removal of Genêt in March 1794 by no means had diminished the invasion threat from Kentucky and the Cumberland. Indeed, the French-inspired hue and cry for "natural rights" served to bolster the well-known particularism of the American frontiersmen, instilling in many greater resentment over the supposedly "callous" attitude of Washington and the Federalists toward the Mississippi question. General Clarke and his following continued to scheme for an attack on Louisiana, while General Robertson, Governor Blount, and other Cumberland settlers intrigued with the Chickasaw, especially after they resumed their warfare with the Creek in 1794. When General Wayne's army crushed the resistance of the northern tribes at Fallen Timbers on August 20, 1794, the removal of the threat of attack from that quarter further encouraged the aggressiveness of western backwoodsmen. Accordingly, Kentuckians and Tennesseeans, exasperated with endemic marauding by the Cherokee, ignored federal warnings and in September struck out heavily against the Indians. This action, plus a congressional increase of the annual subsidy to the Cherokee, eliminated the Cherokee menace for all practical purposes.[52]

In shoring up Louisiana's defenses, Carondelet frantically shuttled the flotilla of armed galleys and launches under Rousseau's command up and down the Mississippi, from the mouth of the Ohio to below New Orleans, in response to alternating rumors of American invasion from above and French seaborne invasion from below. The governor also renewed the intrigue with James Wilkinson and his associates in attempting to rekindle separatist sentiment among the westerners. To keep the silver pesos flow-

50. "Seventh Annual Address to Congress," December 8, 1795, Fitzpatrick, *Writings of George Washington*, 34:391–92. J. Meriwether to Headmen, etc. of Creek Nation, August 11, 1794, *ASP IA*, 1:496–97; Harmon, *Sixty Years of Indian Affairs*, 98–100; Way, "United States Factory System," 223–24.

51. Panton to Carondelet, August 1, 1796, Corbitt, "Georgia-Florida Frontier," 24:264.

52. Nasatir, *Spanish War Vessels*, 119–21; Whitaker, *Spanish-American Frontier*, 190–91; Cotterill, *Southern Indians*, 110–11; Prucha, *Sword of the Republic*, 35–37, 47–49.

ing in, Wilkinson kept the excitable Spanish governor duly alarmed over Clarke's activities.[53]

President Washington and General Knox were concerned that Genêt, and impatient westerners, might, by their meddling, wreck the diplomatic negotiations that the United States was conducting with the Spanish court and therefore ordered the refurbishment of Fort Massac, between the mouths of the Ohio and Tennessee rivers. Although the garrison had standing orders to dissuade would-be aggressors from moving down the river, Carondelet viewed the American presence at Fort Massac as the prelude to an advance on the Chickasaw Bluffs. He ordered Gayoso to incite the Chickasaw against Fort Massac—orders that Gayoso's more informed judgment led him to have countermanded.[54] At this juncture, however, the Georgia Assembly, yielding again to the overtures and bribes of speculators, parceled out its western claims to three new Yazoo companies for a pittance. Even Gayoso interpreted this as preliminary to the settlement of the Chickasaw Bluffs. Accordingly, in mid-1794, the Spaniards feverishly escalated their pleas to the Chickasaw for permission to occupy the strategic heights.[55]

By May 1794, Turnbull had resumed trading with the Chickasaw from an upstream location on the Yazoo. Gayoso simultaneously sent Benjamin Fooy to the lower of the bluffs to monitor both the site and the Chickasaw. Early in 1795, Gayoso, expecting the imminent arrival of an Anglo-American party at the Chickasaw Bluffs, ordered Rousseau, who was proceeding upstream from Los Nogales with reinforcements for New Madrid, to halt his ascent of the river at the lower bluffs. Rousseau was instructed to exercise vigilance against an American takeover, to distribute the annual presents to Ugula Yacabe and his following, and to implant once again in the Chickasaw chief's mind the desirability of locating a post at the site. This, it was hoped, would lead Ugula Yacabe to request a Spanish fort for Turnbull's protection.[56]

Panton, meanwhile, suspected Gayoso's complicity in Turnbull's enterprise but was reluctant to complain too severely. An overheated protest

---

53. Nasatir, *Spanish War Vessels*, 143–44; Whitaker, *Spanish-American Frontier*, 191–96.

54. Prucha, *Sword of the Republic*, 35–36; Secretary of War to Gen. Wayne, March 31, 1794, *ASP FR*, 1:458–59; Holmes, *Gayoso*, 158–59.

55. Rendón to Gardoqui, April 25, 1795, AGI SD, leg. 2612; Whitaker, *Spanish-American Frontier*, 213–15; Holmes, *Gayoso*, 166–67; Nasatir, *Spanish War Vessels*, 105–9.

56. Villebeuvre to Carondelet, May 7, 1794, Kinnaird, *Spain in the Mississippi Valley*, 3:280–82; Williams, *Beginnings of West Tennessee*, 54; Panton to J. Forbes, March 27, 1794, CP; Coughlin, "Spanish Galleys," 367–71.

might earn Carondelet's disfavor, and that could prove detrimental to the company's bid for Spanish financial support. Apparently, Panton also believed Turnbull and his backers were on the brink of insolvency.[57] For his part, Carondelet vacillated between supporting Panton or Turnbull. As late as March 22, 1795, the Louisiana governor instructed Gayoso to obtain the consent of the Chickasaw for either Panton *or* Turnbull to trade at the bluffs.[58]

Meanwhile, the uncertainty of Turnbull's future in the Chickasaw trade had become apparent. In January 1795, representatives of the contending firms appeared before Carondelet and drew up formal terms for Turnbull's retirement. The agreement stipulated that Turnbull was to continue trading on the Yazoo through 1795 but with goods consigned by Panton, Leslie and Company. This proviso was intended to enable Turnbull to collect back debts incurred among the Chickasaw. In October, Turnbull was to return all unused goods and was to sell his peltry receipts to the Panton firm at two reales per pound. At that time, Panton, Leslie and Company would also buy Turnbull's outstanding indebtedness for four thousand pesos, payable in two annual installments.[59]

In April, Carondelet instructed Gayoso to proceed to the Chickasaw Bluffs and to occupy them in the name of the Spanish crown, preferably with the consent of the Chickasaw but without it if necessary. Gayoso arrived at Rousseau's encampment on the west bank across from the lower bluff on May 20; there he learned that while Ugula Yacabe was favorably disposed to a fort and trading post, he intended to call a grand council before giving formal consent. Immediately afterward, Gayoso convinced Ugula Yacabe that formal consent could come after the fact; the dangers of Anglo-American intrusion were too great to permit further delay. On May 30, 1795, with construction finally under way, Gayoso formally took possession of the site and christened the fort San Fernando de las Barrancas, in honor of the heir apparent to the Spanish throne.[60]

Downriver, meanwhile, on March 31, Carondelet offered Panton, Leslie and Company the trading concession at the Chickasaw Bluffs. The terms of the concession permitted free transit of the Mississippi to and from the bluffs, an extension of duty exemptions to the bluffs, and the

57. Panton to Carondelet, May 1, 1794, *ANC F*, leg. 1, Exp. 5; Panton to Forbes, June 29, 1794, GP; Nasatir, *Spanish War Vessels*, 274n75.
58. Holmes, "Fort Ferdinand," 51–52 (Holmes cites Carondelet to Gayoso, March 22, 1795, *AGI PC*, leg. 22).
59. Panton, Leslie and Company–Turnbull and Sons contract, January 30, 1795, *AGI PC*, leg. 203, doc. 42, WP.
60. Coughlin, "Spanish Galleys," 372–79; "Diary of Departure for Natchez on *La Vigilante*," in Nasatir, *Spanish War Vessels*, 252–61.

privilege of trading—although not to the exclusion of others—with the northern tribes that frequented the area. Panton readily accepted and probably believed himself to be on the threshold of acquiring the lucrative Upper Louisiana trade. Panton sent Turner Brashears, with construction materials and a number of Negroes, to the site assigned by Gayoso. Gayoso described the location, about a mile south of the fort, as a "very beautiful site . . . on a hill above a good landing." Brashears completed the construction of his buildings by fall, when John Forbes arrived with trade goods and took charge.[61]

Gayoso resented the intrusion of Panton, Leslie and Company at Fort San Fernando, protesting to Carondelet that the Chickasaw had chosen Turnbull for the concession. Indeed, with Gayoso's support, Turnbull established himself at the bluff in competition with Panton, Leslie and Company, but the company won out after the appointment of Vicente Folch as commandant at San Fernando. The new commandant favored the Panton, Leslie cause, in open defiance of Gayoso.[62]

Panton, Leslie and Company eventually won back the Chickasaw trade from Turnbull. However, subsequent evidence of bad faith by Turnbull in collection of his past debts prompted Panton and John Forbes to declare the 1795 agreement null and void. Turnbull responded by pressing the Panton firm to meet its own obligations, but despite the admonitions of Carondelet, Panton resisted. The conflict was eventually settled through arbitration in March 1800, in favor of Turnbull.[63]

The establishment of Fort San Fernando climaxed Carondelet's defensive measures against the American westward advance. Early in 1794, Manuel de Godoy, Duque de Alcudia, who had parlayed his affair with Queen María Luisa into political power—he became the ranking minister

---

61. Panton to Carondelet, April 18, 1795, *AGI PC*, leg. 203, doc. 42; [Carondelet] to Panton, May 6, 1795, *AGI PC*, leg. 123, no. 7; Rendón to Panton, Leslie and Company, May 8, 1795, *AGI SD*, leg. 2670, WP; J. Forbes to Rendón, July 27, 1795, *AGI PC*, leg. 32, West work cards; Gayoso to Carondelet, July 29, 1795, *AGI PC*, leg. 198B; J. Forbes to Carondelet, May 29, 1795, *AGI PC*, leg. 203, Stetson Collection; Folch to Carondelet (two letters this date), October 8, 1795, *AGI PC*, leg. 52, WP; Nasatir, *Spanish War Vessels*, 274n75.

62. Coughlin, "Spanish Galleys," 405–6; Nasatir, *Spanish War Vessels*, 274n75. For a brief sketch of Forbes and other persons at the Chickasaw Bluffs store, see Coker, *Historical Sketches*, 20–21. By October 1797, Kenneth Ferguson was Panton's agent at the trading post, but little is known about his relationship with the company: Williams, *Early Travels in the Tennessee Country*, 380–81. Ferguson remained there until the spring of 1799, when he closed the trading post: William Simpson to John Forbes, March 1, 1799, GP.

63. J. Forbes to John Joyce, November 2, 1796, *AGI PC*, leg. 203, Stetson Collection; J. Forbes to John Joyce, November 15, 1796, *AGI PC*, leg. 203, doc. 50, WP; Carondelet to Panton, August 15, 1797, FP, MPL; decree of arbitration, J. Turnbull estate and Panton, Leslie and Forbes, March 28, 1800, IHP.

in the government of Charles IV—opted for a conciliatory settlement of the boundary dispute with the United States. As Spain's position in the war with France rapidly deteriorated, Godoy also opened secret discussions with the French Directory toward the establishment of peace, a peace that almost certainly would result in British enmity. The Franco-Spanish peace was concluded in July 1795 at Basle.[64]

With negotiations successfully completed, Godoy, now certain of British aggression and fully aware of John Jay's negotiations with the British government, immediately devoted his attention to a reconciliation of differences with the United States. Godoy had hopes of securing an anti-British alliance. If this proved impossible, he at least wanted to neutralize the United States in the event of an Anglo-Spanish war.[65] These considerations paved the way for Thomas Pinckney's successful diplomacy at San Lorenzo in the fall of 1795.

By the Treaty of San Lorenzo, Spain accepted the thirty-first parallel as the boundary of West Florida, opened the Mississippi to U.S. navigation, and provided for mutual cooperation in preventing Indian attacks along the Spanish-American frontier. However, in stipulating that the signatories would "endeavour to make the advantages of Indian trade common and mutualy beneficial to their respective Subjects and Citizens," the treaty allowed Panton, Leslie and Company the option of continuing its operations.[66]

William Panton considered the Treaty of San Lorenzo a prime example of Spanish duplicity, proclaiming that Spain had left his company "entirely abandoned to the mercy of the Americans," whom his firm had "highly exasperated." He also maintained that the collection of $200,000 in outstanding Indian debts had been seriously compromised and insisted on Spanish compensation for any losses the treaty might cause him. Without relief, Panton maintained, he and his partners must "either submit to absolute ruin or bow our knees to those whom we have much offended & endeavour to soften their resentment in the best manner we Can."[67]

Panton also suggested to his partners alternatives to avoid "more perplexity & loss." Believing it impossible to "contend with the purse of the United States," Panton suggested that they consider becoming "Americans and sollicit being the agents of Congress." If this move did not prove feasible, they should settle the company's affairs as quickly as possible. On

---

64. Whitaker, *Spanish-American Frontier*, 204–5.
65. Ibid., 206–7.
66. Bemis, *Pinckney's Treaty*, 343–62.
67. Panton to Carondelet, July 25, 1796, Corbitt, "Georgia-Florida Frontier," 24: 262–63.

the other hand, Panton suggested, the Americans might be bluffed into buying out the company rather than risking competition. Relief from the Spanish court seemed unlikely.[68]

Carondelet advised Panton to remain calm and expressed belief that Spain eventually would make up any losses. He even accurately predicted that his government would, after reconsideration, attempt to overturn its commitments to the United States. Panton accepted Carondelet's counsel, hoping to extract advantage from any possible source to salvage the company's misfortunes.[69]

Panton's fears regarding American competition were well founded. In the summer of 1796, Benjamin Hawkins headed a three-man U.S. commission, which entered into negotiations with the Creek at Colerain. President Washington had initiated treaty discussions at the request of Georgia, whose political leaders were interested in clearing titles to their most recent benefactions to Yazoo speculators. The federal government, of course, had no intention of abetting Georgia's interests. Instead, Hawkins used the occasion, with some success, to promote Creek interest in the newly adopted factory trading system. In its final version, the Treaty of Colerain reaffirmed the Treaty of New York, increased the annual Creek subsidy to $6,000 in gifts, and provided for the establishment of two government factories on the Creek frontier. The factory proviso formally confirmed a step the United States already had taken. The first and only government-sponsored Creek trading post began operations at Colerain in January 1796, with Edward Price serving as its first factor. In the summer of the following year, the Creek factory was relocated to the west side of the Oconee near Fort Wilkinson, a site considered more accessible to the Creek.[70]

At this juncture, both Spain and Panton, Leslie and Company grudgingly gave way to the inexorable American advance. In October 1796, the company began to settle its affairs with the Cherokee. In the spring of 1798, Spanish forces evacuated Los Nogales and Natchez, the last remaining Spanish strong points in U.S. territory. For some time, Panton hoped to transfer the company's Chickasaw Bluffs store to some new site in Upper Louisiana, but he received little official encouragement. The company finally closed its operations at Chickasaw Bluffs in 1799, in the face of U.S.-inspired harassment from the Chickasaw. At about the same time, it also drastically curtailed its operation at St. Marks. Despite Spanish

68. Panton to R. Leslie, July 18, 1796, FP, MPL.
69. Carondelet to Panton, July 4, 1796, GP.
70. "Letter Book of the Creek Trading House, 1795–1816, Introduction," NARG 75; *ASP IA*, 1:609–10; Harmon, "Benjamin Hawkins," 146–52.

procrastination and Creek opposition, a joint U.S.–Spanish commission completed its survey of the thirty-first parallel, the new West Florida boundary. Panton, Leslie and Company cooperated completely in this enterprise, even lending the hard-pressed Spanish officials sufficient funds to sustain the project.[71]

In December 1796, Benjamin Hawkins returned to the Creek country as the "principal temporary" U.S. agent to the southern Indians, to begin a long residency among the Creek. Hawkins and Panton eventually became good friends, but the American agent found it difficult to persuade the Scottish merchant that his fear of total ruin from U.S. trade competition was ill founded. As the years passed, Hawkins's counsel proved correct. At the turn of the nineteenth century, Panton, Leslie and Company still retained almost all of the Choctaw and Chickasaw trade and slightly over one-third of the Creek trade.[72] Hawkins strove to "domesticate" the Creek and thus made no serious attempt to undermine Panton's dealings. Furthermore, under U.S. policy, factories consistently sold to Indian and trader at the same price. The factory system also discouraged the use of credit in bartering with the Indians and did not allow cultivating the favor of influential chiefs with gifts. Since the United States bought its goods from domestic mercantile establishments at high prices, Panton retained a competitive edge.[73] The decline in trade suffered by Panton, Leslie and Company in the late 1790s arose principally from warfare between Great Britain and Spain, rather than from vigorous U.S. competition.

71. Whitaker, "Spain and the Cherokee Indians," 269n62; John Willet Booth to Panton, December 20, 1796, CP; [?] to Folch, September 16, 1797, *AGI PC*, leg. 56, WP; Carondelet to Panton, October 8, 1797, GP; J. Forbes to Panton, October 14, 1798, CP; William Simpson to J. Forbes, March 1, 1799, GP; J. Forbes to Panton, March 28, 1799, GP.

72. Hawkins to James McHenry, January 6, 1797; Hawkins to Panton, May 20, 1798, Grant, *Benjamin Hawkins*, 1:62–64, 194–95; Pound, *Benjamin Hawkins*, 203–4; J. Forbes to Folch, November 15, 1801, *AGI PC*, leg. 56, WP.

73. Hawkins to Edward Price, February 10, October 23, 1797; Hawkins to Barnard, March 7, 1797; Hawkins to Matthew Hopkins, April 22, 1798, Grant, *Benjamin Hawkins*, 1:66–67, 91–92, 133, 192; T. Pickering's instructions to Edward Price, November 26, 1795, "Letter Book of the Creek Trading House, 1795–1816, Introduction," NARG 75; Phillips, *Fur Trade*, 2:217–18; Pound, *Benjamin Hawkins*, 199–202.

10

War and Business

THE influx of French privateers into the Gulf of Mexico in the summer of 1796 perplexed William Panton. Reports circulated in Pensacola that Spanish ports in the West Indies had been declared open to the admission of British merchantmen taken as French prizes. Cruisers plying the waters adjacent to the Gulf coast had made it hazardous for Panton, Leslie and Company ships to enter or leave the harbors of Mobile and Pensacola. Panton fretted over rumors of French privateers operating out of New Orleans with Carondelet's knowledge—despite the fact that the company's ships and cargoes provided the prime attraction. This, the Scottish merchant observed cynically, was his "reward . . . for preserving these Provinces in peace & quietness for Eleven years past."[1]

But Panton scarcely could bring himself to believe accounts of an impending Spanish declaration of war against Great Britain. The king of Spain, Panton calculated, stood to lose much and to gain nothing by such action; kings usually behaved with more concern for their personal interests. But he erred in his assessment: in January 1797, news reached Panton that Spain had gone to war against Great Britain.[2] The declaration of war indeed propelled Spain into an alliance with France.

1. Panton to R. Leslie, November 8, 1796, FP, MPL.
2. Ibid.; Hawkins to Major John Habersham, February 9, 1797, GHS, *Letters of Benjamin Hawkins*, 9:76.

The French government lost no time in warning Spain about England and Panton. The French ambassador, the Marquis de Dominique Catherine, advised the Spanish government that England might try to capture Pensacola. If England were successful, France expected Pensacola to become a nest of privateers, which would devastate Spanish commerce in the Gulf of Mexico. The French also knew that Panton, Leslie and Company enjoyed a monopoly in the southern Indian trade. Panton had been careful to cultivate the friendship of the Indian chiefs and to keep the Indians loyal to the British. He had ulterior designs against which Spain should be advised, the ambassador warned. These warnings aroused concern about Panton, Leslie and Company at the highest levels in Spain. Minister of War Juan Manuel Álvarez, Secretary of the Treasury Pedro Varela y Ulloa, and even Manuel Godoy, the minister of state, all took an immediate interest in the company and in whether it posed a danger to the Floridas.[3] Fortunately for Panton, the French admonition had no discernible ill effect upon the company, which had other problems to be concerned about.

Indeed, the war presented Panton, Leslie and Company with some serious problems. The most immediate concern was to arrange for the safe disposal of furs on hand in West Florida. Not only was there need to safeguard the furs against capture, but in order to avoid losses from worm damage they had to be dispatched to markets before the warm season. Once these practical matters were resolved, the Spanish government would have to decide whether Panton, Leslie and Company would be allowed to continue in the trade.

At the time the war news reached Pensacola, a company brigantine, the *Sheerwater*, lay at anchor in Pensacola harbor. Panton quickly requested from Vicente Folch, now governor of West Florida, a safe-conduct pass for the vessel to proceed with part of the peltry on hand either to Charleston or to Nassau, where its captain would engage enough neutral ships to remove the balance of the stock. Panton justified the request under the twelve-month period of grace agreed to by the Spanish crown in 1790, which enabled the company, in case of an Anglo-Spanish war, to remove its effects from the Floridas by the most expedient means. Folch referred the petition to Gabriel Marín Pizarro, the customs officer at Pensacola, who declared himself powerless to comply under existing direc-

---

3. Pérignon to Prince of the Peace, March 6, 1797; extract of dispatch from French Vice Consul in New York to Minister of Foreign Affairs, March 6, 1797; Prince of the Peace to Pedro Varela, April 22, 1797; Varela to Prince of the Peace, April 27, 1797; Juan Manuel Álvarez to Prince of the Peace, May 1, 1797, *AHN Estado*, leg. 3888. See also V. du Pont to Minister of Foreign Affairs, June 3, 1797, Murdoch, "Correspondence of French Consuls," 77–79.

tives. Marín Pizarro pointed out that current policy permitted authorities at Pensacola to issue passports to the company for London only and that only the intendant at New Orleans could authorize voyages to Charleston or Nassau. Five days later, Panton, having fitted out the *Sheerwater* for sailing, asked for a passport to London. Marín Pizarro, with his suspicions justifiably aroused, reversed his earlier position and refused the passport. Panton, frustrated and fearful of losses from further delays, sent a trusted employee overland to New Orleans to expedite the necessary sailing permits.

Panton, meanwhile, also had placed the problems confronting the company before the Baron de Carondelet and Juan Ventura Morales, the interim intendant. The Scotsman again explained the necessity of removing the accumulated skins quickly to prevent loss, maintaining that the withdrawal privilege made this a matter of right. On the other hand, should the Spanish government wish Panton, Leslie and Company to continue in the Indian trade, it must permit certain innovations. Wartime restrictions, of course, prohibited direct commercial contact between West Florida and England. The Spanish crown must therefore allow neutral vessels, under U.S. registry, to call at West Florida ports with trade goods owned by American merchants. This arrangement would enable the company to barter skins for goods in Florida ports in order to replenish its stocks, thereby eliminating the risk of loss to privateers. Panton concluded that should the company be required to withdraw, he hoped the Spanish authorities would place no impediment in the way of salvaging the company's movable property. Justice and decency demanded as much, he contended, especially in light of the enormous losses suffered by the company in its service to the provinces.[4]

Unfortunately for Panton, however, Morales's sympathy for the company's plight was considerably less than that displayed by Carondelet. In his long and stormy career as a Spanish colonial official in Louisiana and West Florida, Morales earned a well-deserved reputation for contentiousness. His incessant quarrels with Spanish governors resulted in numerous but futile requests for his replacement. However, ministerial officials in Spain placed too great a faith in Morales's demonstrated zeal for resisting extravagance in colonial expenditures to allow his removal.[5]

In October 1796, before official notice of the Spanish declaration of

4. Panton to Folch, January 9, 1797; Folch to Contador, *Informe* of Contador, January 14, 1797; Folch to Marín Pizarro, January 14, 1797; Minutes of *Junta de Real Hacienda*, January 31, 1797, AGI SD, leg. 2670; Panton to Juan Ventura Morales, January 13, 1797, AHN Estado, leg. 3888, Exp. 1; Panton to Carondelet, January 26, 1797, AGI PC, leg. 213; Carondelet to Panton, January 26, 1797, IHP.
5. Holmes, "Dramatis Personae," 155–61.

war reached New Orleans, Morales had questioned Carondelet on the justifiability of Panton, Leslie and Company's privileged status. From the intendant's viewpoint, the Treaty of San Lorenzo, by allowing U.S. citizens trade access to the Indians, apparently obviated any further need for the services of the British firm. At least, Morales inferred, the company should lose its duty-free status. On this occasion, Carondelet, expecting a reversal in Spanish policy toward the United States, replied that secret reasons of state prevented any change in the company's privileges.[6]

Carondelet again supported Panton's interests in the disposition of his proposal of January 1797. The Louisiana governor agreed that the royally sanctioned one-year safe removal period precluded official interference with the company's prerogative to dispose of its trading posts, skins, and slaves. Carondelet then guilefully feigned disinterest, while convincing Morales of the expediency of allowing Panton—subject to later royal confirmation—to continue the trade on the terms requested. The company afforded the sole means of preventing the southern Indians (who were continually restless over the Treaty of San Lorenzo) from breaking into open hostility against Spanish settlements. Again, failure to cooperate with Panton, Leslie and Company might evoke enough resentment among the company's traders to cause them to incite the Indians to attack and plunder Spanish settlements. Should Madrid decide not to support the company, as it had requested in its memorial of May 1794, then a combination of prior losses and competition from American factories would in time cause Panton to retire voluntarily. The Indians, under such circumstances, scarcely could blame the Spaniards for the company's withdrawal.[7]

With Carondelet's counsels in mind, Morales called a meeting of the Junta of the Royal Treasury to consider Panton's petition in the light of the Indian problem. It agreed in principle to allow Panton, Leslie and Company to remain in the trade and to use American shipping and trade outlets; but it also approved Morales's earlier decision to bring the company's activities under closer scrutiny by customs officials. All company cargoes entering and leaving West Florida ports were to be checked carefully to see that only items directly related to the Indian trade received duty exemptions. Before sailing, all ships employed by the company were to obtain express approval from the intendancy.[8]

These restrictions countermanded many of the practices adopted by

---

6. Morales to Carondelet, October 28, 1796; Carondelet to Morales, November 3, 1796; Morales to Gardoqui, December 1, 1796, *AGI SD*, leg. 2614.

7. Carondelet to Morales, January 30, 1797, *AGI SD*, leg. 2670.

8. Morales to Folch, January 21, 1797; Folch to Panton, February 12, 1797, CP; Minutes of *Junta de Real Hacienda*, January 31, 1797, *AGI SD*, leg. 2670.

the company over the course of its operations in West Florida—practices which, Panton thought, had permanent official acceptance through usage. He promptly asked Morales to modify the directive to cover specific activities, so that the company's status would remain unchanged as far as wartime circumstances permitted.

Panton wished to know if the ruling prevented the company from transshipping goods and peltry between its Pensacola headquarters and its stores at Mobile, St. Marks, and Chickasaw Bluffs without first obtaining passports from New Orleans. In the past, the company had been required only to submit a list of goods to be shipped to the customs officer, who then compared the list against the freight. If no discrepancies were discovered, the customs officer authorized the shipment. If he were required to consult with the intendant each time the need arose to transship goods or skins, Panton contended, the company would suffer unnecessary inconvenience and costly delay. He asked Morales to waive this requirement.

The Scottish merchant also explained that a Royal Order obliged the company to procure from Havana the salt and rum used in the Indian trade. In the past, ships dispatched for these items had been permitted to carry as ballast, on a nondutiable basis, tar, pitch, and barrel staves produced in West Florida. This arrangement had helped defray expenses and had kept prices charged to the Indians low. Panton presumed Morales would continue this indulgence and also would dispense with the formality of applying to New Orleans for passports in these cases.

At times, Panton continued, the large quantities of salt demanded by the Indian trade had been unobtainable in Havana. Thus, the company had been permitted from time to time to acquire salt from neutral or friendly West Indian ports—where, incidentally, prices were lower. On these voyages, company vessels not infrequently had been allowed to export corn to exchange for salt. Because this practice also tended to lower selling prices, Panton presumed that it too would remain in effect.

Occasionally, in the past, the company had been granted the special favor of dispatching ships to Campeche for dyewood, a commodity ideally suited for ballast when combined with peltry shipments to England. Panton intimated that this concession, although favorable to the company, was not indispensable; dyewood could be obtained duty-free from British loggers in the Bay of Honduras. Panton hoped Morales would raise no objection to occasional summer voyages to Campeche for dyewood, since many of the company's smaller ships were not otherwise employed in that season.

Panton also requested that ox hides exported by the company be exempt from duty since the Indians also bartered small quantities of these; he also reminded Morales that the company enjoyed the privilege of importing free of impost a variety of goods intended for household consumption, as well as for sale to West Florida garrisons. The Scottish merchant concluded his requests with a recital of the numerous losses suffered by the company in the past, implying that he had continued to operate primarily at the request of Carondelet. Panton promised that the company would remain until the Spanish court perfected arrangements for a suitable replacement, as requested in the memorial of May 1794. Meanwhile, he earnestly hoped that Morales would offer the same encouragement and protection as his predecessors.[9]

Once more Carondelet supported almost every concession requested by Panton. But Morales's scrupulous application of royal directives prevailed. In this he enjoyed the support of the junta, which met for a second time to deliberate on the company's affairs.[10]

Morales, in communicating the junta's resolutions to Panton, began on a note of condescension. The delay in replying, Morales asserted, was due to Panton's practice of corresponding with the intendancy in English. If the Scottish merchant genuinely wished to avert future delays, he should communicate in Spanish, so as to make unnecessary the time-consuming task of translation. With respect to obtaining salt and rum from Havana, the company must use either Spanish ships commanded by Spaniards and manned by crews at least two-thirds Spanish, or it must resort to American ships and crews. No Englishmen were to be permitted access to such a strategically crucial port as Havana during the war. Ox hides could be shipped duty-free, but not tar, pitch, corn, or barrel staves. Although permitted in the past, this practice actually constituted an abuse of the privileges granted the company by the crown. Under no circumstances should Panton entertain the false notion that he was free to trade with British loggers in Honduras, either in peace or war. On the other hand, the junta might permit voyages to Campeche for logwood, but each case would be decided on its own merits. Panton might continue to sell goods to the West Florida garrisons to satisfy their immediate needs, but Morales warned that he would instruct the *subdelegado* in Pensacola to monitor such sales closely in order to prevent abuse. Passports from New Orleans to cover transshipments within the provinces were unnecessary; only ships clearing for foreign ports need carry passports issued by the inten-

9. Panton to Morales, February 15, 1797; Panton to Carondelet, February 15, 1797, *AGI PC*, leg. 214.
10. Carondelet to Morales, March 14, 1797; decision of *Junta de Real Hacienda*, March 17, 1797, *AGI SD*, leg. 2670.

dancy. Other than the required duties on tar, etc., Morales concluded, the revised regulations caused the Panton firm no harm and provided a framework in which the company must operate until His Majesty decided on the company's memorial.[11]

In compliance with a separate mandate from Carondelet, in March 1797, Panton and his employees promised under oath neither to interfere in the Spanish war effort nor to give aid and comfort to Spain's enemies. At the time, the company employed some eighty persons, all of whom were Protestant. But other than isolated instances of harassment and intimidation from residents of Pensacola—which caused Panton to observe that in wartime "the fittest Country for a Man to be in, is his own"—the company quickly adjusted to the greatly altered conditions of trade.[12]

Meanwhile, Panton worried that discussions of the company's status by Spanish officials in New Orleans might drag on into the summer and decided to dispose of the company's peltry on his own initiative. He dispatched a messenger overland to Savannah in February with instructions to a Charleston merchant, Henry Grant, to send American ships and what trade goods were immediately available to Pensacola. These were to be exchanged for Panton, Leslie and Company deerskins, which were to be consigned under Grant's name for shipment. An American schooner, the *Julius Pringle*, arrived in Pensacola on March 21 with a small cargo of trade goods consigned by Grant to Panton, Leslie and Company (under an arrangement made earlier). The *Julius Pringle* already had sailed from Charleston before Panton's new instructions arrived. Nevertheless, he persuaded the captain to agree to accept as payment a cargo of peltry, which was consigned to Grant.[13]

Much to Panton's consternation, however, Marín Pizarro, while permitting the trade goods to be unloaded, refused to sanction the *Julius Pringle*'s departure without approval from Morales. Panton then rushed John McQueen to New Orleans to obtain passports for the *Julius Pringle*, as well as for other American vessels expected momentarily at Pensacola.[14]

Panton's efforts to hasten the departure of peltry cargoes received little

11. Decision of *Junta de Real Hacienda*, March 17, 1797, *AGI SD*, leg. 2614; Morales to Panton, March 21, 1797, *AGI SD*, leg. 2670.
12. Declaration of neutrality of Panton and dependents, March 10, 1797, Stetson Collection; Francisco de Paula Gelabert to Carondelet, March 17, 1797, *AGI PC*, leg. 56; Panton to Carondelet, March 22, 1797, *AGI PC*, leg. 214. During the years 1796–1801, Panton employed an average of 75 persons in Pensacola: Coker, "Religious Censuses," 57.
13. Panton to Morales, March 22, 1797, *AGI SD*, leg. 2670; Hawkins to Ensign Thompson, February 9, 1797, *GHS, Letters of Benjamin Hawkins*, 9:75–76; Bill of Lading of the *Julius Pringle*, March 22, 1797, *AGI PC*, leg. 615.
14. Panton to Morales, March 22, 1797; Morales to Folch, April 1, 1797, *AGI SD*, leg. 2670.

sympathy from Morales. The intendant delayed action on the passport request for several days on the pretext that it had been presented in English, thus requiring translation. Moreover, he issued a passport for the *Julius Pringle* only. The other passports, he maintained, could be issued only after the vessels arrived. In fact, Morales reprimanded Panton for having acted independently in engaging ships before the junta had decided on proper procedures. The *Julius Pringle*, Morales asserted, should have been confiscated—or at least ordered out of Pensacola—without receiving permission to unload. But on this one occasion, Morales continued, he would overlook Panton's impropriety, since the latter was indispensable to the Indian trade. In the future, the intendant warned, Panton would do well not to arouse suspicion by flouting authority. The intendant also ordered Marín Pizarro to forbid the loading of the expected ships until proper passports were first obtained from New Orleans.[15]

Before Morales's tardy reply reached Pensacola, Panton and Folch had conspired to fabricate a pretext in order to clear the *Julius Pringle*, as well as two other small American vessels that had since arrived. Folch claimed to have had an urgent need for sending a bundle of dispatches to Havana without delay. Consequently, he approached Panton about renting a company schooner, the *Shark*, to carry the documents to their destination. Panton, however, had reportedly insisted on a guarantee of 1,500 pesos should the *Shark* fall prey to British privateers. He then allegedly had proposed that Folch clear the ships for Charleston, in return for which the dispatches would be delivered en route free of charge. Folch avowed that he had accepted because of the "importance" of the dispatches. Morales, after delivering a sharp rebuke, grudgingly accepted the fait accompli. Yet despite Panton's exertions, he complained that worm damage during the delay in shipping the skins had resulted in a substantial drop in the price received for the peltry and had nearly ruined him.[16]

The officious intendant next devoted his attention to correcting recently discovered minor discrepancies between bills of lading and the actual number of items transshipped from Pensacola to other company stores. Since receiving duty-exempt status in 1789, Panton had insisted on minimum formality in customs checks on the grounds that they were superfluous. Since no actual duties were involved, the Scottish merchant had resisted successfully the standard practice of customs agents of open-

15. Ibid.; Morales to Marín Pizarro, April 1, 1797; Morales to Pedro Varela y Ulloa, May 10, 1797, ibid.
16. Folch to Marín Pizarro, April 7, 1797; Panton to Folch, April 7, 1797, *AGI PC*, leg. 615; Folch to Morales, April 11, 1797; Morales to Pedro Varela y Ulloa, May 10, 1797, *AGI SD*, leg. 2670, WP; Panton to Gayoso, January 2, 1798, *ANC F*, leg. 1, Exp. 5; Corbitt, "Georgia-Florida Frontier," 25:375–76.

ing bundles and crates for an itemized count of the contents. He claimed that this practice only burdened the company with extra expenses in repackaging merchandise for protection against wear or for reconsignment to other stores. Spanish agents had consequently limited their inspections to comparing manifests against unopened packages while the company's ships were being loaded or unloaded. But Morales insisted that, henceforth, Spanish customs regulations, which required all items, dutiable or otherwise, to be inspected carefully, must be followed. He instructed Folch to see that Panton, Leslie and Company adhered strictly to all regulations.[17]

Marín Pizarro complained that the lack of a royal customhouse in Pensacola made compliance with Morales's new orders difficult. Indeed, to follow the directive properly, Panton must be made to arrange his goods for inspection in an empty company warehouse. Following customs examination, Panton could repack his goods for shipment or storage.[18]

Panton protested to Folch about the procedure, declaring it "oppressive and unnecessary." It contravened established practices and constituted an infraction of the agreement between the company and the crown. Before altering any company privilege, Panton insisted, the Spanish government was bound, by mutual agreement, to give twelve months prior notice. During this grace period, the company, if it chose, could withdraw. Panton further claimed that Marín Pizarro's idea would entail the expense of erecting "a new magazine and [keeping] it emptied for the accommodation of the *Contador*," as well as the additional costs of packing and unpacking. Panton insisted that Folch instruct Marín Pizarro to follow the former procedures and that he refused to comply except under express orders from the king.[19]

Panton earlier had appealed to the court, then, to Carondelet, then, to Gayoso, who replaced Carondelet as governor-general in August 1797, and finally, to O'Neill (who had been transferred to Mérida, in Campeche, in 1793) for assistance in curbing Morales's excesses. All but the Spanish court had agreed to help, leading Panton to believe that Morales soon would be made to "get upon the stool of repentance."[20] And in fact, following Panton's refusal to submit to the new customs regime, harassment by Morales abated.

17. Marín Pizarro to O'Neill, January 16, 1790; Miró to O'Neill, February 20, 1790, *AGI SD*, leg. 2670; [Morales] to Folch, March 21, 1797, *AGI PC*, leg. 615.
18. Marín Pizarro to Folch, August 18, 1797, *AGI SD*, leg. 2670.
19. Panton to Folch, October 8, 1797, *AGI PC*, leg. 615.
20. O'Neill to Panton, May 8, 1798; Gayoso to Panton, September 9, 1797, GP; Panton to J. Forbes, August 15, 1797, FP, MPL; Carondelet to Godoy, May 23, 1797, *AHN Estado*, leg. 3888.

At the same time that Panton had set in motion deliberation in New Orleans on the company's wartime status, he and his associates also had sought to clarify their status with the British government. The partners wished particularly to devise a safe means of evading condemnation proceedings in British prize courts. For this purpose, Panton, Leslie and Company solicited separate professional opinions from Sir William Scott and Sir John Nicholl, experts in British admiralty law. Both experts agreed that, should the partners remain in the Floridas and continue in the Indian trade, their cargoes, whether carried in neutral or British vessels, were liable to condemnation as legitimate prizes. Nicholl expressed the further opinion that, legally, the partners could be considered Spanish subjects. On the other hand, both also agreed that if the partners and their effects were captured while in the act of withdrawal from the Floridas, British admiralty courts most likely would order their property restored. In this case, restitution would be applicable if the partners' destination was a new location in either British or neutral territory. Both warned that evidence indicating intent by the partners to remain in Spanish territory would subject cargoes consigned in the company's name to valid seizure. This applied also to peltry that was exported directly to England to retire company indebtedness to British subjects.[21]

Potential and actual problems encountered in 1797 greatly discouraged Panton. He had anticipated correctly the adverse legal advice about attempting to maintain direct access to the London market. Yet, experience in procuring the types and quantities of items needed for the Indian trade from American sources proved to be not only expensive but almost impossible. Nor had American buyers demonstrated much enthusiasm for taking the company's enormous volume of peltry off its hands, except at reduced prices. Interference from the intendant further aggravated generally undesirable trading conditions, and rumors circulated openly of an impending transfer of the Floridas to France—an event that would, in all likelihood, result in the company's immediate ejection. There also remained the specter of ultimate ruin by attempting to compete with the U.S. government's trading factories.[22]

For an undetermined interval during 1797, Panton contemplated leaving the Floridas and notifying the Spanish to appoint a suitable replacement by May 1798. Perhaps Panton only feigned his intent to retire as a means of goading the Spanish court to take action on the company's re-

21. Admiralty opinions, April 20, 21, 1797, GP.
22. Panton to Gayoso, January 2, February 6, 1798, *ANC F*, leg. 1, Exp. 5; Corbitt, "Georgia-Florida Frontier," 24:375–77; Panton, Leslie and Company memorial to Charles IV, June 20, 1797, *AHN Estado*, leg. 3888.

quest for financial assistance. Private correspondence with relatives in England, however, indicates that Panton's sentiments likely were genuine. In any event, by 1798, Panton and his colleagues apparently had determined to hold on to their tenuous position as best they could, maintaining the trade by whatever means possible in the expectation of an imminent restoration of peace. The partners apparently hoped that the Spanish court might reward their tenacity with some form of compensation for prior losses. By 1798, prospects for obtaining the cooperation of the United States in settling the not-inconsequential indebtedness of the southern Indians also appeared good.[23]

In 1798, as an adjustment to the exigencies of wartime trade, Panton, Leslie and Company increasingly used the services of James Gairdner and Company of Charleston as correspondents. This business house acted as consignee for trade goods ordered from London by the Panton firm. Making use of the "broken voyage" ruse, Gairdner and Company then shipped the merchandise on its own account to Pensacola in U.S. vessels. Though it was costly, this practice partly offset the shortage of Indian wares that had been experienced the year before.[24]

On the other hand, in 1797, Panton had been unable to make satisfactory arrangements for disposal of the company's deerskins, a failure that prompted him to take a calculated risk early the following year. John Forbes, bearing Spanish letters of safe conduct, accompanied a cargo of deerskins carried by a company ship, *The Sisters*, bound for Charleston. Upon arrival, Forbes was to find an intermediary interested in dispatching the company's peltry, on a continuing basis, on to London. Should *The Sisters* be hailed by a British privateer, Panton believed that the presence of Forbes, together with his safe-conduct papers, would safeguard against an unfavorable decision in condemnation proceedings. As a partner in the firm, Forbes was to allege that he was engaged in removing the company's effects from Spanish possessions.[25]

The Sisters in fact fell prey to the *Plover*, a British privateer commanded by a Captain Newton, and was sent to Nassau for condemnation. The captor agreed to allow *The Sisters* to resume its voyage to Charleston after Forbes posted bond for the value of the cargo. Neither litigant stood to gain by subjecting the deerskins to the worm damage that would result from further delay. In Charleston, Forbes succeeded in reaching an agree-

---

23. Carondelet memorial to Prince of the Peace, July 1, 1797; John Innerarity, [Sr.] to Panton, January 8, June 2, 1798, GP; White to Panton, October 11, 1797, February 24, 1798; Panton to J. Forbes, November 9, 1797, CP; Cotterill, "Panton, Leslie," 276–77.

24. Panton to Gayoso, January 2, February 6, 1798, Corbitt, "Georgia-Florida Frontier," 24:375–77.

25. Panton to Gayoso, February 6, 1798, ibid., 24:376–77.

ment with James Gairdner and Company, who undertook to remove the remainder of the company's peltry from West Florida. Although the company lost no deerskins to British privateers thereafter, Forbes's delayed arrival at Charleston prevented the dispatch of American ships in time to reach West Florida before warm weather. The delay caused some loss of furs from worm damage.[26]

In March 1798, the vice-admiralty court at Nassau heard the case against the cargo of *The Sisters*. Witnesses formerly employed as ships officers by Panton, Leslie and Company gave incriminating testimony against the practices of the firm, asserting that company ships had sailed regularly under dual sets of registry papers—British and Spanish—and, more recently, American and Spanish. The deponents also divulged information on the connection between the Panton and Gairdner firms—and, even more damaging, one testified that in April 1797, Panton and all company employees in Pensacola had taken an oath of allegiance to Spain. The court ruled in favor of the prize captain, but Panton, Leslie and Company entered an appeal.[27]

Several months later, another privateer from the Bahamas captured the *Nancy* en route to Pensacola with trade goods shipped by Gairdner and Company. The vice-admiralty court also ruled this cargo a legitimate prize of war, probably on evidence of the Gairdner firm's connection with Panton's trading operations. Just when it appeared that the broken voyage ploy might be rendered useless, the British Board of Trade ruled that neutral ships could carry into enemy ports British manufactures (other than items expressly forbidden) on their own account. Under this technicality, broken voyages via Charleston were continued without further loss from British privateers, occasional molestation notwithstanding.[28]

An earlier decision by the Board of Trade was even more favorable to the interests of Panton and his associates. In November 1797, acceding to the demands of British manufacturing and commercial interests, the board opened Bahamian and Jamaican ports to ships from Spanish colonies traveling under licenses issued by appropriate British governors. Regulations governing this traffic permitted small Spanish vessels and British ships of any size to carry into the free ports specie and a variety of colonial products, including hides, deerskins, peltry, and logwood. These items

26. Panton to Gayoso, May 9, 1798, ibid., 24:379.
27. Depositions of William Fulford, March 21, 1798, *AGI PC*, leg. 216A; William Cooke, April 7, 1798, WP.
28. Panton to Gayoso, September 10, 1798, Corbitt, "Georgia-Florida Frontier," 25:71–72; "Liverpool's Rulings on Rights of Neutral Ships," December 28, 1798, GP; Panton to J. Forbes, October 23, 1800, and a "Draught of An Order of Council," [n.d.], GP; *FHQ* 14 (1936): 277–80; Panton to Gayoso, October 9, 1798, *AGI PC*, leg. 203.

could be exchanged for British manufactures, except for goods listed as contraband. Orders-in-council forbade British cruisers from capturing duly licensed ships engaged in this trade, whether Spanish or British.[29]

When he learned of the relaxation of British trade regulations, Panton immediately asked Gayoso and Morales for permission to trade through Nassau. The Louisiana officials hesitated to give their approval without the consent of the captain general of Havana. The matter was held in abeyance until October 1798, while they awaited his decision—a decision that never came. Since the British navy had brought communications between Cuba and New Orleans almost to a standstill, Gayoso finally consented, justifying his initiative on the grounds that poor trading conditions had reduced the Indians to desperation. Otherwise, he observed, they might have resorted to dealing with interlopers from the Bahamas.[30]

The favorable changes in British trade regulations greatly reduced the problem of maintaining open trade channels to and from London. The Panton firm used Nassau and Charleston alternately as intermediate ports for broken voyages. This practice, of course, added to the company's costs, as did continued losses from worm damage due to occasional delays in obtaining passports from New Orleans.[31]

The advantages gained by the diminution of the British threat were offset by a resurgence of French privateering activity, beginning in 1798. The *Cato*, a small vessel employed in the company's East Florida operations, fell prize to a French cruiser early in the year. A second company ship, the *Margaret Ann*, was taken as a French prize while carrying peltry out of Mobile in 1800. In the same year, two company brigs, the *Campbell* and the *Greenwood*, were lost at sea with all hands, which kept insurance premiums well above peacetime levels. In November 1801, the company reported that war-related costs in the form of higher insurance premiums—losses of uninsured cargo and ships to privateers and accidents at sea since the beginning of hostilities in 1793—had reached $400,000.[32]

Meanwhile, John Leslie had departed St. Augustine for England in

29. Nassau Free Port blank passports [n.d.]; additional instructions of George R. [n.d.], FP, MPL; Armytage, *Free Port System*, 96–101.
30. Panton to Gayoso, May 22, September 10, 1798, Corbitt, "Georgia-Florida Frontier," 24:71–72, 380–81; Gayoso to Panton, October 16, 1798, "Panton, Leslie Papers," *FHQ* 15 (1937): 250.
31. Gayoso to Panton, May 22, 1799, "Panton, Leslie Papers," ibid., 250–51; Panton to [Francisco Bouligny] October 9, 1799, Stetson Collection; J. Leslie to Panton, March 7, 1800, CP; J. Forbes to Marqués de Casa Calvo, February 5, 1801, WP.
32. Panton to Gayoso, February 6, 1798, Corbitt, "Georgia-Florida Frontier," 24:376–77; William Simpson to Panton, October 23, 1800, CP; Panton to J. Forbes, October 23, 1800, GP; J. Forbes to Folch, November 15, 1801, AGI PC, leg. 58.

Chapter 10

July 1798 to attempt to extricate the company from a number of its wartime difficulties. He was to seek special commercial concessions from the British government, represent the company in appealing the condemnation of the cargo of *The Sisters*, and clear up misunderstandings with Strachan and MacKenzie that had arisen since the onset of the war.[33]

By mid-1798, relations between the Panton firm and its powerful London correspondents, Strachan and MacKenzie, had been strained to the breaking point. Panton complained that Strachan and Mackenzie had been remiss in fulfilling his request that they seek official protection for the company while it withdrew from the Floridas. He believed the British government scarcely would deny such protection, for it had recognized from the outset the status of Panton, Leslie and Company in the Spanish Floridas. Panton also believed that the London firm had begun to act arbitrarily in handling routine business affairs: overcharging on commissions in the sale of peltry, procuring overpriced trade goods, and assigning insurance to underwriters on the basis of favoritism. In consequence, Panton had decided not to consign the 1797 peltry exports to Strachan and MacKenzie. Instead, he engaged the London firm of Penman, Shaw and Company as correspondent—an action which caused Strachan and MacKenzie a 2 percent loss on their insurance policy, inasmuch as they had already insured the 1797 shipment of peltry from Charleston to London.[34]

Strachan and Mackenzie retaliated by obtaining from the Lord Mayor's Court in May 1798 a writ of attachment against the property of Panton and his partners for alleged indebtedness in excess of £20,000. Thomas Forbes suspected that Strachan and MacKenzie also intended "to get their hands full" of the outstanding indebtedness of Panton, Leslie and Company and then to force a settlement. Forbes advocated resisting the demands of Strachan and Mackenzie since their own statements indicated that they had indeed been overpaid by Panton, Leslie and Company. As a member of a second partnership (Forbes and Munro), Forbes hoped to force a settlement in Nassau, where he wielded considerable influence. He believed that Strachan and MacKenzie would attach the cargo of the ship *Providence*, which was registered in his name, and that this would enable him to enter the lawsuit in Nassau, the home of Forbes and Munro.[35]

In April, before taking legal action against the Panton firm, Strachan and MacKenzie had obtained a special order-in-council that protected the

33. J. Leslie to Panton, July 6, 1798, IHP.
34. J. Innerarity, [Sr.] to Panton, January 29, June 2, 1798, GP; Panton to Gayoso, March 25, 1798, Corbitt, "Georgia-Florida Frontier," 24:378.
35. J. Innerarity, [Sr.] to Panton, June 2, June 16, 1798, GP; T. Forbes to Panton, July 25, 1799, CP.

property of Panton, Leslie and Company from seizure while it was actually being withdrawn from the Floridas to the Bahamas. The royally sanctioned directive, in fullfillment of Panton's earlier request, was carefully worded to cover not only property in the company's possession at the time war was declared but also property received in payment for goods that had been introduced into the Floridas before the war. These privileges were to remain in effect for two years.[36]

The two-year period of grace and the stipulation protecting property acquired in trade after the declaration of war undoubtedly were justified as necessary measures for settling company affairs and collecting back debts before evacuating the Floridas. Still, these provisions made the order-in-council flexible enough to protect the peltry exports received in exchange for goods procured *after* war had been declared. A sworn statement by any of the principals sufficed to verify that a given outgoing cargo was being removed as part of the overall process of withdrawal. Panton, of course, had requested these privileges before the Board of Trade had opened Nassau to commerce with Spanish colonies. And probably he had done so to comply with the expert legal opinions solicited in April 1797 regarding the company's status under admiralty law. At any rate, Panton was pleased that it had been granted; at the same time he doubted that the order-in-council would be retroactive, which would have saved the cargo of *The Sisters*. It could serve as an additional weapon in warding off rapacious British privateers; and he hoped that hostilities would cease before it expired.[37]

The order-in-council also may have been useful to John Leslie in effecting a reconciliation between Panton and his London correspondents. Leslie, for whatever reason, apparently bore less animosity toward Strachan and MacKenzie than did Panton. By October 1800, the London firm had at least partly resumed its services to Panton, Leslie and Company, but Penman, Shaw and Company also retained its connection with the Panton firm.

In 1799, both Panton and Leslie strove to acquire further concessions from the British government. Above all, they sought approval for direct trade between Pensacola and London, in British or neutral ships or both, especially for the highly perishable exports of peltry. Next in importance, the partners asked permission to import gunpowder, lead, saddles, and

36. Strachan and MacKenzie to Forbes and Munro, April 21, 1798, FP, MPL; see also Protection of British & Neutral Vessels Bringing British Property from East and West Florida, March 31, 1798, in PC 2/150:333, PROL; Permission for Panton, etc. to bring goods to the Bahamas, April 25, 1798, in PC 2/150:388–89, PROL.

37. Strachan and MacKenzie to Forbes and Munro, April 21, 1798, FP, MPL; Panton to Gayoso, October 9, 1798, *AGI PC*, leg. 203, WP.

nails—items expressly prohibited as contraband. Early in the following year, Penman, Shaw and Company won the approval of the Privy Council to employ neutral Swedish vessels in direct trade between London and West Florida. They also sought a two-year extension of the time allowed for withdrawal.[38]

The war had made the company's sources of supply extremely precarious for crucially important gunpowder and ball. Not even neutral vessels could carry gunpowder to the Floridas, under any pretext, without risking capture by British cruisers. Naturally, Panton's business acumen made him reluctant to advance trade goods to the Indians on credit unless the goods included ammunition—the wherewithal for obtaining the deerskins necessary for repayment. As early as February 1797, Panton had requested Carondelet's permission either to borrow or to buy gunpowder and ball from royal stores. The Spanish government, when convenient, had lent ammunition to the Panton firm, but not without Morales's insistence on undesirable terms. Panton had wanted the Spanish government to advance powder and lead at a price no higher than that charged the company's Indian customers. The firm, he stated, followed the practice of underselling American competitors appreciably in this line of merchandise, a tactic designed to foster goodwill and to assure successful hunting. But Morales had insisted on charging the company at New Orleans prices, which were nearly double Panton's selling price; Morales also had required the company to mortgage property as security for the loan.[39]

Panton, in supporting the company's request to the British government for special permission for direct trade and to import ammunition, argued that the concessions ultimately would benefit the Indians, who were "friends of Great Britain." It was good policy for the government to nurture the fondness of the Indians for the British by eliminating oppressive trading conditions—conditions that kept the Indians in a state of deprivation. Besides, since 1783 the company had kept open an important market for British manufactures, had created employment for British shipping, and had provided the British treasury with an estimated £217,600 in import duties and excises on finished buckskin products, all of which, Panton asserted, constituted "an advantage to our Native Country which [merited] some attention." Once lost, the advantage might never be regained.[40]

38. J. Innerarity, [Sr.] to Panton, March 12, 1799; Panton to J. Forbes, October 23, 1800, GP; J. Leslie to Panton, February 26, 1799, WP; Orders of the Privy Council, October 29, 1800, PC 2/156:77–83, February 27, 1800, PC 2/154:297–98, PROL.
39. Panton to Carondelet, February 15, 1797, AGI PC, leg. 214, WP; Panton to Gayoso, March 7, 1798, AGI PC, leg. 203, WP; Casa Calvo to Panton, March 5, 1800, IHP; Panton to [Bouligny], October 2, 1799, AGI PC, leg. 203.
40. Panton to Adam Gordon, July 24, 1799, GP.

In presenting Panton's views to Lord Liverpool of the Board of Trade, Adam Gordon represented Panton as "a Man of tried & unshaken Loyalty . . . to this, his native country." Panton's pleas, supported by the intercessions of Gordon and Leslie, brought a favorable response from the Board of Trade early in 1800. Panton, Leslie and Company received permission to import from Nassau just over half of its annual requirement of 10,000 pounds of gunpowder and 20,000 pounds of ball, as well as saddles, bridles and nails. The firm also obtained approval to ship deerskins directly to London.[41]

But in August 1800, the company lost its appeal of the condemnation of the cargo of *The Sisters*, a ruling that left John Leslie astonished. The counselors had advised against introducing evidence in support of the company's new-found favor with the Board of Trade. Such an imprudent course of action might have led to loss of the company's privileges, since relations were never very cordial between the commercially minded Board of Trade and the prize-minded naval commanders.[42]

The turn of events was once more favorable to the Panton company. In May 1800, Parliament enacted a measure granting British citizens the temporary right to import, in neutral vessels, products from enemy colonies in America. John Leslie was able to obtain permission for the company to engage in similar activities. The intent of the act was to promote the exchange of foreign colonial produce for British manufactures and to make the British Isles a wartime entrepôt for European colonial trade. Since Panton, Leslie and Company was ideally suited for this purpose, Liverpool could readily agree to grant the firm a special concession reaching beyond the letter of the law. Leslie received permission for the company to carry British goods on its ships directly to Spanish America. These could be exchanged for the equivalent value in colonial products, which then could be sent in company vessels to English markets.[43]

Panton and his partners valued this particular concession for reasons beyond facilitation of the Indian trade; it complemented separate negotiations which were under way with the Spanish court on the question of indemnification. As early as June 1797, Panton had appealed to the Spanish crown for a quick decision on his May 1794 memorial. It had been shunted along a tedious path through the Spanish bureaucracy, traveling

---

41. Orders of the Privy Council, February 27, 1800, PC 2/154:297–98, PROL; Adam Gordon to Earl of Liverpool, October 30, 1799, FP, MPL; Casa Calvo to López y Angulo, March 5, 1800, MC, Exhibit 2B; William Dowdeswell to Portland, August 10, 1800, GP.
42. J. Leslie to T. Forbes, August 22, 1800; "Liverpool's Rulings on the Rights of Neutral Ships," December 28, 1798, GP.
43. J. Leslie to Liverpool, April 15, 1800, GP; Thomas Lack to Gordon, April 26, 1800; "An Act to Permit the Importation of Goods and Commodities from Countries in America," May 1, 1800; Panton to J. Forbes, October 23, 1800, GP.

from the treasury to the war ministry before finally coming to rest at the ministry of state. Lack of funds, Spanish acquiescence in the westward advance of the United States, and more pressing considerations concerning national survival had all combined to hold the Panton, Leslie and Company memorial in abeyance. Panton, meanwhile, making use of the good offices of a John Savage of Madrid, had continued to press for favorable action.[44]

Panton reminded the court that the company had continued in the Indian trade despite the threat of competition from the United States, principally at the request of Carondelet. He had encouraged the partners to expect Spanish support, or at least compensation, for its higher insurance rates and losses to French privateers which, Panton informed the crown, had cost the company $185,059. Such costs, together with competition from the United States, would force the company to retire by May 1798. Panton therefore had asked Governor Carondelet to buy the company's property, arrange for a replacement, and allow the company to collect its debts before retiring. Debt collection had become a delicate matter in light of American competition. Undue pressure might drive the Indians into trading with the Americans. For these considerations, Panton observed, His Majesty should indemnify the company for its losses and also formally request the United States to assist in collecting the company's back debts. Furthermore, should France, as was rumored, gain control of the Floridas, the transfer agreement should, in justice, recognize explicitly the company's interests.[45]

Carondelet corroborated the truthfulness of Panton's appeal of June 1797 and further informed the court that the Indian trade was still very important in guarding the provinces against Indian depredations. A Spanish trade outlet, offering cheaper terms than those of the United States, also might keep the Indians secure in their lands, preserving their value as a buffer. Attesting that the past services of the company merited consideration as a matter of equity, Carondelet also promised to try to persuade Panton to extend his deadline for suspending the trade.[46]

Carondelet's firm endorsement encouraged the Scotsman to believe that the Spanish court, despite the Treaty of San Lorenzo, might agree to some form of support of the company—or at the least compensate it for losses. Panton advised Savage to emphasize in his dealings with the Span-

---

44. Savage to Panton, Leslie and Company, February 25, 1797, FP, MPL; Panton, Leslie and Company, Memorial to Charles IV, June 20, 1797, *AHN Estado*, leg. 3888.

45. Panton, Leslie and Company, Memorial to Charles IV, June 20, 1797; John Savage to Charles IV, September 9, 1799, *AHN Estado*, leg. 3888.

46. Carondelet Memorial to Prince of the Peace, July 1, 1797, GP.

iards the company's role in underselling the U.S. government, its mounting losses notwithstanding. In addition, he should impress upon the Spaniards that the Americans as yet had made "but little progress" in acquiring the Indian trade, "the object they Have long sought and contended for."[47]

By mid-1799, Savage's exertions on behalf of his British clients had still produced no results. The demands of war prevented the Spanish authorities from considering Panton's memorials. Moreover, should a favorable decision be forthcoming, Savage advised that Spain's lack of funds precluded any form of financial reimbursement in the settlement.[48]

Consequently, Panton altered the terms of the company's request. In lieu of monetary indemnification, the firm would accept commercial privileges with other Spanish colonies, as well as an Indian trading concession west of the Mississippi. As a basis for negotiations, Panton suggested that the company should be allowed to trade with Nassau and Charleston in dyewood from Campeche, as well as in sugar from Havana. The privilege should be made effective for two years beyond the duration of the war. The Spanish government also might consider permitting the Panton firm to conduct a general trade with certain other Spanish colonial ports, exchanging goods for local products.[49] These concessions could scarcely harm Spanish commerce, Panton reasoned, since the government already had opened its colonial ports to neutral shipping. The war indeed had caused the opening of Spanish colonial ports to neutral commerce, and U.S. vessels, since October 1797, had dominated the Spanish colonial trade.[50]

The efforts of Panton and Savage succeeded in arousing at least some interest in the company's problems in the Spanish ministry of state. In February 1800, Mariano Luis de Urquijo, who had succeeded Godoy as minister of state, instructed the governor of Louisiana, the Marqués de Casa Calvo, to submit a detailed report on the continued usefulness of Panton, Leslie and Company and on the merits of its claims. If the claims were indeed justified, Casa Calvo was to comment on the proper means of compensation.

After six months of investigation, Casa Calvo submitted his recommendations to the Spanish court. Panton, Leslie and Company must be preserved. Among the reasons given was that Panton's traders formed an important intelligence network among the Indian nations that kept the Spaniards informed about frontier events. Nobody suspected the traders,

47. Panton to Savage, August 12, 1797, GP.
48. Savage to Panton, May 26, 1799, GP.
49. Savage to Charles IV, September 9, 1799, *AHN Estado*, leg. 3888.
50. Whitaker, *Documents*, xlvii–xlviii; Clark, *New Orleans*, 240–44.

Table 3. Losses sustained by Panton, Leslie and Company from increased insurance premiums and vessels captured during the war between France and Great Britain, 1793–97.

Date	Sums insured £	Articles	Vessels' names	Voyage	Premium since the war	Premium before the war	Diff. of premium against us	Amount of the difference of premium
1793								
July	325	Goods	Santa Maria	Nassau to Pensacola	8 gs.	3 gs.	5 gs.	£17 1 3
September	11,170	Do	Esdaile	London to Pensacola	12	£3½	£9 2	1,016 9 4
November	1,640	Do	Brig Despatch	Havana to Pensacola	5	1½ gs.	3½ gs.	60 5 4
September	2,000	Ship	Esdaile	London to Pensacola	12	£3½	£9 2	182
1794								
February	730	Goods	Santa Maria	Nassau to Pensacola	8	3 gs.	5 gs.	38 6 6
Do	630	Do	Sheerwater	London to Nassau, thence to Pensac.	15	£3½	£11 10	72 9
July	—	Skins	Grenada Packet	Pensacola to London—captured, lost	—	—	—	3,602 9
Do	14,698	Ship & frght.	Esdaile	Pensacola to London	8	4	4 gs.	617 6 3
Do	3,000	Do	Do	Pensacola to London	8	4	4 gs.	126 10
September	4,600	Goods	Do	London to Pensacola	15	£3½	£12 5	563 4
November	1,475	Do	Sheerwater	Havana to Pensacola	5	1½ gs.	3½ gs.	54 16
Do	5,680	Do	Minerva	London to Pensacola	15	£3½	£12¼	695 2
Do	707	Do	Shark	Nassau to Pensacola	8	3 gs.	5 gs.	37 9 3
February	180	Do	Sheerwater	Nassau to Pensacola	8	3	5	9 16
December	675	Tar, &c.	Do	Mobile to Havana	5	1½	3½	24 1
Do	268	Goods	Reyna Louisa	Nassau to Pensacola	8	3	5	14 11 4
Do	1,125	Do	Hopewell	Pensacola to Philadelphia	6	3½	2½	29 1 7
December	725	Goods	Hopewell	Charleston to Pensacola	8 gs.	3 gs.	5 gs.	£38 2
1795								
February	400	Ship	Sheerwater	Nov. 21, 1794, to May 21, 1795	12	6	6	25 4 9
April	3,675	Goods	Mary	Virginia to Nassau and Pensacola	16	4	12	463 1 6
Do	10,585	Skins	Ann and Mary	Pensacola to Philada. and London	25	4	21	2,3 3 19
Do	350	Goods	Shark	Nassau to Pensacola	18	3	15	55 2 6
Do	956	Do	Do	Charleston to Nassau and Pensacola	25	4	21	210 15 11
Do	875	Do	Sheerwater	Havana to Pensacola	5	1½	3½	32 3 2
Do	3,700	Do	Rambler	London to Nassau, thence to Pensac.	26	5	21	815 17
June	1,250	Do	Mary	Nassau to Pensacola	7	3	4	52 10
August	2,800	Do	Esdaile	Pensacola to Yucatan	5	2	3	88 4
Do	345	Do	Shark	Nassau to Pensacola	10	3	7	25 7
Do	20,745	Skins	Minerva	Pensacola to London	25	4	21	4,574 6
Do	12,239	Goods	Do	London to Pensacola	15	£3½	£12¼	1,499 8
Do	1,000	Freight	Do	Pensacola to London	25	4 gs.	21 gs.	220 10
Do	2,000	Ship	Do	London to Pensacola	15	£3½	£12¼	245

Date	Qty	Type	Ship	Route				Total	s	d
September	2,760	Goods	Sheerwater	Pensa. to Philada. thence to London	25	4	21 gs.	608	11	6
October	245	Do	Rambler	Pensacola to Nassau	16	3	13	33	9	
Do	540	Do	Esdaile	Yucatan to Pensacola	5	2	3	48	10	
Do	2,500	Ship & frght.	Do	Pensacola to Yucatan and back	10	4	6	157	10	
November	1,495	Skins	Shark	Do. to Charleston, thence to London	25	4	21	329	13	
December	23,200	Goods	Catharine	London to Pensacola	18	£3½	£15 8	3,572	16	
1796										
January	24,970	Skins	Esdaile	Pensacola to London	25	4	21 gs.	5,505	17	8
Do	3,000	Ship & frght.	Esdaile	Pensacola to London	25	4	21 gs.	661	10	
February	12,185	Skins	Minerva	Pensacola to London	25	4	21	2,686	15	10
Do	3,000	Ship & frght.	Do	Pensacola to London	25	4	21	661	10	
March	1,345	Goods	Hope	Havana to Pensacola	5	1½	3½	49	8	7
July	220	Do	Shark	Nassau to Pensacola	18	3	15	34	13	
August	290	Do	Hope	Nassau to Pensacola	18	3	15	45	13	6
September	5,740	Do	Mary	London to Pensacola, via Philada.	18	£3½	£15 8	883	19	3
Do	915	Do	Sheerwater	Pensacola to Jamaica	18	4 gs.	16	153	14	5
October	860	Do	Do	Jamaica to Providence and Pensacola	20	4	16	144	9	6
Do	125	Do	Do	Nassau to Pensacola	18	3	15	19	13	9
Do	1,165	Do	Hope	Havana to Pensacola	5	1½	3½	42	16	3
Do	265	Do	Shark	Pensacola to Nassau	18	3	15	41	16	3
1797										
February	2,950	Skins	Sheerwater	Va. to London, via Charleston	25	4	21	650	9	6
April	1,555	Do	Shark	Do. do do	25	4	21	342	17	6
May	3,000	Do	Sheerwater	Do. do do	25	4	21	661	10	
Do	882	Goods	Shark	Do. to New York	20	4	16	138	2	
Do	20,000			Imports sent into St. Augustine for the Indian trade	14	3½	10½	2,105		
Do	20,000			Exports of skins from do	18	3½	14½	3,045		
				Loss of the Aurora, Capt. Dickie, from Nassau to St. Augustine, with a cargo of Indian goods, taken by the Sans Pareil				4,443	19	6
				Loss of 40 barriques of wine, per Kreps, schooner; from New Orleans to Pensacola, captured, at 30 drs. per br.				270		
								45,179	12	4

LESS

1795. Sept.	£ 8,934	2	6	Return for convoy per Minerva	at £7,	£ 625 8 9
1796.	23,200	0	0	Return for convoy per Catharine	at 9,	2,088 0 0
1793. Sept.	16,060	0	0	Return for convoy per Esdaile	at 5,	803 0 0
	830	0	0	Return for convoy per Minerva	at 3,	24 18 0

£ 41,638 5 7   3,541 6 9

                              41,638 5 7

Dollars at 4s. 6d. $185,059

PENSACOLA, July 24, 1797.

Source: Exhibit 42, *Mitchel et al. v. United States*, U.S. Supreme Court Records and Briefs, Pt. 1, 1832–60, Roll 3, Jan. Term, 1835, 1:370–72.

he said. More important, maintenance of the company's influence among the Indians served to counteract the ambitions of the United States. Spain must preserve, protect, and encourage Panton in order to keep the Indians independent; if trade and friendship with the Indians were lost, the province would be left exposed. Casa Calvo thought it might be necessary for the company to sell its goods below cost in order to compete with the United States. The crown, he suggested, should take such losses into consideration. To offset Panton's losses, Casa Calvo encouraged the court to allow trade by the company with Havana and Campeche on a limited basis. Other opportunities that might be extended to the company included a modified form of the *asiento*—a contract to furnish slaves. Panton, Leslie and Company could be granted an exclusive contract to import 4,000 new Negroes to the Mississippi duty-free and to export produce for a period of six years. He also suggested that the company be given twenty square leagues of land west of the Mississippi as indemnification for its losses, or, as Panton had already pleaded, a loan of $400,000 interest-free for ten years. Personally, Casa Calvo preferred a loan to the company rather than free trade and slaving. Casa Calvo insisted that control of the Indian trade continued to be indispensable to the security of the provinces, and if Panton, Leslie were forced to leave the Floridas, the company could not be replaced.[51]

Meanwhile, the Spanish court had suggested to Savage several possibilities for indemnifying his client along the lines suggested by Casa Calvo. Certain commercial concessions were involved which would permit Panton, Leslie and Company to trade for Spanish sugar and dyewood and to introduce slaves into Louisiana. By September 1800, however, Panton considered trade in Havana sugar and Campeche dyewood of no great potential advantage, especially since rumors of peace were in the air. He expected prices for these commodities to drop at the end of hostilities. The Louisiana slave trade would suffice only if granted as a monopoly (which Casa Calvo had recommended). Instead, Panton wanted the privilege of supplying British goods to Campeche duty-free, which likely explains his earlier interest in Campeche as a source of logwood ballast. Above all else, Panton would have preferred to sell the company to the Spaniards for $200,000.[52] He had become thoroughly weary of the stresses of the Indian trade.

Panton's negotiations with the Spanish and British governments, as

---

51. Urquijo to Governor of Louisiana, February 26, 1800, *AHN Estado*, leg. 3888; Casa Calvo to Urquijo, October 8, 1800, White, *New Collection of Laws*, 2:323–27; Coker, *Historical Sketches*, 43.

52. Panton to J. Forbes, September 22, 1800, GP.

well as his exertions to continue against all odds the war-strained trade, served similar purposes. Basically, he hoped to choose a proper time for the company to retire from the Floridas, while keeping intact as many of its assets as possible. His ability to close out the company's rapidly mounting credit among the southern Indians weighed heavily on the attainment of this greater objective. Success in this area depended to a large extent, in turn, upon the cooperation of the United States.[53] But before any substantial progress could be made in the settlement of Indian debts, William Augustus Bowles, the company's old antagonist, returned for an overdue reunion with his countrymen in the state of Muskogee—a compelling reason for a cautious approach to the debt settlement question.

53. Cotterill, "Panton, Leslie," 276–77; John Forbes to Carondelet, July 22, 1796, Corbitt, "Georgia-Florida Frontier," 24:266–67.

11

The Deaths of Panton and Bowles

*T*WO major problems confronted Panton, Leslie and Company during the years 1799–1803: the return to the Floridas of William Augustus Bowles and the settlement of the debts the Indians owed the company. These problems proved to be interrelated. Bowles opposed the company intensely and schemed tirelessly to bring about its downfall; he also took exception to the settlement of the Indian debts through land cessions. In the long run, solving the problems associated with Bowles, who proved himself a worthy adversary, turned out to be easier than collecting the Indian debts.

William Panton and John Forbes had sought assistance from the United States as early as 1796 in collecting Indian debts owed to the company. In July of that year, Forbes notified the Baron de Carondelet that he planned to go to Knoxville to see the federal agent there about an adjustment of the Cherokee debts, "which now become every day more doubtful from the proximity & cheapness of the American Supply."[1] Forbes met John McKee, U.S. agent to the Cherokee, on this visit. Though there is no record of their meeting, Forbes returned apparently satisfied with their discussions. McKee in turn followed up this initial contact in May 1797 with

---

1. Forbes to Carondelet, July 22, 1796, *ANC F*, leg. 1, Exp. 23, no. 1; Corbitt, "Georgia-Florida Frontier," 24:266–67.

a visit to Mobile and to Panton's Pensacola headquarters, although his appointment as Cherokee agent had ended in 1796.

Before McKee arrived in Pensacola, Panton compiled a list of Indian debts due the company. Total indebtedness at the five company trading posts amounted to $282,445. Panton estimated the amount due at Mobile and Chickasaw Bluffs at $160,000. When compared with a list of debts due by the four nations—the Cherokee, Chickasaw, Choctaw, and Creek—six years later, it appears that Panton may have considerably overestimated the Choctaw-Chickasaw (i.e., Mobile–Chickasaw Bluffs) debt. Nevertheless, whether the Indians owed the company $282,445 in 1797, or $173,141 in 1803, it was at that time, as General James Wilkinson exclaimed, "a monstrous sum."[2] By 1797, with the majority of the Indians indebted to Panton, Leslie residing in U.S. territory, there can be little doubt about the desire of Panton and Forbes to secure whatever assistance they could in the collection of their debts. Panton therefore probably greeted McKee at Pensacola with some degree of anticipation.

En route to West Florida, McKee visited Andrew Ellicott at Natchez and the Baron de Carondelet in New Orleans. He left the distinct impression with both men that he was involved in the Blount conspiracy to attack Spanish possessions in the lower Mississippi Valley by way of Canada. In fact, McKee so aroused Carondelet's suspicions that the baron ordered the commandant at Mobile to keep McKee under close scrutiny and to report his actions. The commandant notified Carondelet that from all that could be seen, McKee only wanted to become associated with Panton, Leslie and Company in the Cherokee-Chickasaw trade. But Governor Manuel Gayoso de Lemos, who succeeded Carondelet that summer, believed that the real purpose of McKee's visit was to secure Panton's aid in persuading the Indians to assist Blount. Gayoso even considered seizing

---

2. List of Outstanding Indian Debts Owing to Messrs. Panton, Leslie and Company, April 30, 1797, AGI PC, leg. 213. It is not difficult to prove that Panton's 1797 estimate of Indian debts was exaggerated, especially the Mobile-Chickasaw Bluffs debts, which included the Choctaw (Mobile) and the Chickasaw (Chickasaw Bluffs). For example, on December 31, 1799, the Choctaw traders and factors only owed the company $38,738. In 1803, the Choctaw owed $46,091, and the Chickasaw $11,178, for a combined total of only $57,269—a difference of more than $100,000 from the $160,000 claimed in 1797. Since neither nation had made an appreciable payment on their debts in those years, it is obvious that Panton had seriously overstated the Choctaw-Chickasaw debt. (See table 4.) Wilkinson to Henry Dearborn, Secretary of War, August 20, 1803, Letters Received by the Office of the Secretary of War Relating to Indian Affairs, 1800–1823, NARG 75; "List of Debts Due by the Traders and Half Breed Indian Factors of the Choctaw Nation to the House of Panton, Leslie & Co., of Mobille the 31st Day of December 1799," Adjutant General's Office, Miscellaneous Letters Received and Sent by the Secretary of War, 1799, NARG 94.

Table 4. Debts due Panton, Leslie and Company by Indian nations, 1797 and 1803

	Amount due	Comments
1797: trading posts		
Pensacola	$ 66,945-1 7/8[a]	Owed primarily by Upper Creek.
Apalachee–Wakulla River store	15,500	Lower Creek and Seminole debts.
St. Augustine	40,000	Estimated by Panton and probably including debts from the St. Marys store, abandoned in 1793. Upper and Lower Creek and Seminole debts.
Mobile and Chickasaw Bluffs	160,000	Estimated by Panton. Mobile debt largely Choctaw. Chickasaw Bluffs debt largely, if not exclusively, Chickasaw.
Total	$282,445-1 7/8	
1803: Indian nations		
Creek	$113,512-4 1/2	Included Upper and Lower Creek and Seminole debts.
Choctaw	46,091-2 1/2	
Chickasaw	11,178-5 3/4	
Cherokee	2,358-3 1/4	
Total	$173,141	

Sources: 1797, List of Outstanding Indian Debts owing to Messrs. Panton, Leslie & Co. of Pensacola, April 30, 1797, *AGI PC*, leg. 213; 1803, William Simpson, August 20, 1803, Letters Received by Sec. of War, Indian Affairs, 1800–1823, Microfilm M-271, Reel 1, NARG 75.

a. Monetary divisions of less than one dollar were given in reales and not in cents. Eight reales equaled one dollar.

McKee's and Panton's papers in order to discover what had transpired, but he decided not to do so for fear that it would alienate Panton, who, in retaliation, might turn the Indians against Spain. Gayoso lamented that he did not have either the arms or the money to risk the latter possibility.[3] He may have been closer to the truth than he realized, except that McKee's visit to Panton was not inspired by Blount.

McKee's visit to Panton may have been engineered by the Federalist war party. For two years, Spain had refused to surrender the territory north of the thirty-first parallel, in accordance with the Treaty of San Lorenzo of 1795. The United States contemplated taking the territory by force, if necessary. McKee made the trip to see Panton at the direction of Secretary of War James McHenry and with the knowledge and approval of

3. Gayoso to Conde de Santa Clara, September 24, 1797, *AGI PC*, leg. 1502B; Whitaker, *Mississippi Question*, 109, 125–26, 264; Secretary of State to Andrew Ellicott, August 30, 1798, in Carter, *Territorial Papers*, 5:42.

Secretary of State Timothy Pickering. Arthur Preston Whitaker suggested that it was incredible that the United States should send an agent to enlist the services of Panton, Leslie and Company. For nearly ten years the company had been "the chief agent of Spanish resistance to American influence among the Southern tribes," had encouraged the Indians to attack the Georgia and Tennessee frontiers, and "had stained its hands with the blood of American citizens." Before McKee left Pensacola, he assured Panton that the U.S. government would facilitate the company's efforts to collect its debts from those same Indians. In return, Panton would be expected to bring the Indians over to the side of the United States if war came.[4] Since the war did not materialize, Panton was not put to the test, but he and Forbes accepted McKee's promises of American support in the collection of the Indian debts. Later developments revealed that both McKee and Panton considered cessions of Indian lands an acceptable form of reimbursement.

Land payment by Indians as a means of retiring trading debts was in all likelihood a practice not unknown to Panton. During his years in the southern colonies, the British Indian department and the colonial governors had negotiated land settlements with the Creek and Cherokee.[5] Panton's decision to resort to the same method was not unusual. The very lands that Panton and his partners had exhorted the Indians to hold against U.S. encroachment they later sought for themselves—and Panton wanted American aid in obtaining them. Panton realized that the United States, under the aegis of Benjamin Hawkins, had embarked on a program of "civilizing" the southern tribes, especially the Creek. They were to be enticed away from hunting into the sedentary occupations of farming and raising livestock—pursuits that required considerably less territory.[6] Panton's decision to settle company arrears for land indicates his awareness that the American plan eventually would prevail. Hunting, and hence the fur trade, was doomed.

In 1798–99, Panton and Forbes worked assiduously through their agents, as well as those of the United States, in creating the proper climate for the Indian land cessions. Daniel McGillivray cautiously sounded out the Upper Creek for Panton and reported that those he had contacted opposed any such settlement. They did not wish to give their land away because they would soon have no land for hunting.[7] Panton wrote Ben-

4. Carter, ibid.
5. Sosin, *Revolutionary Frontier*, 16, 18.
6. Pound, *Benjamin Hawkins*, 164; Cotterill, *Southern Indians*, 124; Whitaker, *Mississippi Question*, 77–78.
7. McGillivray to Panton, April 24, 1798, CP.

jamin Hawkins soliciting his cooperation in the settlement of the Creek and Cherokee debts. He informed Hawkins that land was the only resource the Indians had with which to pay their debts. It was the best way, he wrote, "that Can be devised for extricating them from their embarrassments." He asked Hawkins to transmit the company's claims against the Indians to the seat of government. Panton believed that an investigation of his demands would result in approval by the United States of land cessions to liquidate the debts.[8]

Meanwhile, William Simpson, associated with the Panton, Leslie Mobile store and after 1803 a partner in the company, had talked with the Choctaw about paying their debts through land cessions and had received a favorable response. They "promised to use their utmost endeavours to convince the chiefs of the advantage it would be to their nations." Simpson also reported that, while the company had been forced to close its Chickasaw Bluffs trading post, General Wilkinson had authorized one of the company agents to remain there until the spring of 1800 to collect what debts he could from the Chickasaw.[9]

During the discussions, Forbes suggested that Panton inform Governor Gayoso of the company's intention to petition the United States for approval to accept land in payment of the Indian debts. Gayoso, Forbes surmised, could scarcely refuse without offering alternative forms of compensation. He reminded Panton that the company had been waiting in vain since May 1794 for the Spanish government to come forward with some remedy for the company's Indian debt problem. Furthermore, "like all Spaniards," Forbes continued, Gayoso was "ignorant of the value of Lands so circumstanced."[10]

Indeed, a month later, Forbes himself wrote Gayoso regarding the proposal. Gayoso readily acknowledged his personal awareness of the repeated sacrifices that Panton, Leslie had made on behalf of the Spanish government during the ten years in which Gayoso had lived in West Florida and Louisiana. He assured Forbes that he would not oppose the plan. Gayoso recognized that land cessions might be the only form of payment that the company would ever receive from the Indians.[11] Obtaining Span-

---

8. Panton to Hawkins, June 11, 1799, FP, MPL. The combined debts of the Cherokee and Creek nations amounted to $93,099 ¼ at the time Panton wrote to Hawkins. See "State of Claims," June 11, 1799, NARG 94.

9. Simpson to John Forbes, March 1, 1799, GP; John Forbes to Governor Folch, September 11, 1804, quoted in Folch to Someruelos, February 16, 1805, *AHN Estado*, leg. 3888, Exp. 1. Forbes told Folch that James Innerarity and William Simpson had been admitted to John Forbes and Company as partners.

10. Forbes to Panton, January 13, 1799, CP.

11. Gayoso to Forbes, February 21, 1799, MC, Exhibit OO.

ish acquiescence in the land cessions proved to be easier than securing American approval.

After leaving Pensacola, McKee went to Philadelphia, where he related his discussions with Panton to McHenry. But by then, the Spaniards were in the process of evacuating their posts north of the thirty-first parallel and the war scare was over. McKee reported that McHenry was too "indolent" to come to the company's assistance in the collection of the Indian debts, that the land business would require too much mental exertion. In spite of the lack of interest which he found in Philadelphia, McKee continued to support the idea of Indian land cessions to pay the company. The War Department sent McKee to the Mississippi Territory in the spring of 1799 as U.S. agent to the Choctaw. This location enabled McKee and Forbes to meet periodically to discuss the problem. McKee assured Forbes that he concurred fully with the plan and was convinced that sooner or later it would win government approval.[12] But the United States proved not to be the only obstacle to the company's plans. Other considerations, such as the restlessness of the Indians regarding trade shortages and high prices, the marking of the thirty-first parallel, and Bowles's return, made it expedient for Panton to defer action temporarily on the delicate matter of land cessions.

After escaping his Spanish captors in mid-1798, Bowles returned to London where he lingered for seven months, recuperating from his long imprisonment, pleading with the Pitt ministry for support in the capture of the Floridas, and seeking to interest former supporters (as well as new prospects) in the future of Muskogee. John Leslie, at first astounded at Bowles's presence, sought to have him arrested and prosecuted on criminal charges. But he had to abandon this plan, for no British court could claim proper jurisdiction in the plundering of the St. Marks store. The director-general departed for Barbados in February 1799 with official encouragement, if not full support, for his return to the Creek.[13]

After stopping involuntarily for several months in Bridgetown and then in Kingston, Bowles—accompanied by several new accomplices and carrying a small cargo of powder and bullets—reached Nassau aboard the sloop *Fox*, en route to the Florida coast. Bowles had not particularly wanted to stop at Nassau, though he still had friends there, including his former ally John Miller. Lord Dunmore had been recalled under less than favorable circumstances before Bowles arrived, and the new governor,

---

12. Forbes to Panton, April 30, 1800, GP. For the Jefferson administration's opposition to Indian land grants in U.S. territory to the company, see Cotterill, "Panton, Leslie," 278.
13. Wright, *William Augustus Bowles*, 94–108; John Leslie to William Panton, February 26, 1799, GP.

William Dowdeswell, was a friend of Panton. Thomas Forbes, now a member of the Bahamian council, enjoyed a close relationship with the new governor.

Eager to reach Florida and reestablish himself, Bowles intended to capitalize upon the Indians' suspicions of Panton, who had promised to send plenty of goods to the St. Marks store for them—but at higher prices, because of the war. While Bowles and Miller discussed ways of ending the Panton, Leslie monopoly, Thomas Forbes closely observed Bowles's activities and lost no opportunity to discredit him with the governor—including reports from Leslie in London that Bowles was out of favor there. At the same time, Bowles received assurances from a friend in London that all was well.[14] Only time and circumstances would reveal who was correct.

Bowles reached the mouth of the Ocklochonee only to be shipwrecked in a sudden storm on the eastern end of St. George's Island. Salvaging what baggage he could, Bowles and his small retinue made their way to the Lower Creek villages, to a joyful reception. Acclaimed again as "director general" by a small following of Lower Creek and Seminole, Bowles announced his intention of undoing the Treaty of San Lorenzo, denouncing the Spaniards for their abandonment of the Indians, and proclaiming the sovereignty of Muskogee. He also declared that he would send Panton off "in irons as a traitor" to Britain, all the while yearning for the sight of a British troop convoy appearing over the horizon of the sea.[15]

Meanwhile, Panton and the Spaniards, who for months had been well informed of Bowles's movements, prepared their defenses. Supplies were removed from the St. Marks store to the Spanish fort, and the company's cattle were herded to safer pastures. Spanish authorities dispatched armed galleys to patrol Apalachee Bay, with orders to capture Bowles and to intercept any supply vessel that might appear. To that end, Thomas Portell, commandant at St. Marks, announced that a price of $4,500 had been placed on Bowles, dead or alive.[16]

14. Wright, *William Augustus Bowles*, 108–12; Thomas Forbes to Panton, August 25, 1799, GP. John Forbes (no known relative of Thomas or John Forbes of Panton, Leslie and Company) succeeded Dunmore as governor of the Bahamas in 1796. Perhaps as an indication of Thomas Forbes's ascendancy in Bahamian politics, Governor Forbes nominated Thomas to the council and otherwise spoke highly of him. When the governor died on June 6, 1797, Thomas served as one of the executors of his estate: John Forbes to [?], no. 4, February 28, 1797, CO 23/35; John Forbes to [?], no. 7, June 1, 1797, CO 23/36; Thomas Forbes and Stephen Haven, letter re executors of the estate of John Forbes, late governor, June 8, 1797, ibid.; Thomas Forbes to Mr. Hall, June 6, 1797, CO 23/37, PROL. Dowdeswell was appointed governor on November 20, 1797: *Times* (London), November 22, 1797, 2c.

15. Wright, *William Augustus Bowles*, 114–19; Hawkins to Panton, October 9, 1799, AGI PC, leg. 216A, GP.

16. Edward Forrester to Panton, October 16, 1799, AGI PC, leg. 216A; Wright, *William Augustus Bowles*, 118–19.

Early in 1800, the "director-general" struck back at his antagonists. With three hundred Indians and less than a dozen white followers, he captured the St. Marks trading post and then sent a formal declaration of war to Commandant Portell, demanding the fort's surrender. When the Spanish officer refused, Bowles laid siege with his Creek and Seminole braves. In Pensacola, Folch and Panton, who perhaps could not conceive of Indians employing disciplined siege tactics, sent the company ship *Sheerwater* to St. Marks with supplies for the garrison and gifts for bribing away Bowles's army. Bowles, however, captured the *Sheerwater* as it sailed into the St. Marks River, thereby gaining plunder, supplies, and two small cannon with which to menace the garrison. Portell, though his command was not in imminent danger of being overrun, despaired of receiving any relief and surrendered. The arms of Muskogee had prevailed over Spain, following six weeks of action. The Spanish military later cashiered Portell for his surrender of the fort.[17]

Folch immediately organized land and sea forces to recapture the outpost. Assuming personal command, the Pensacola commandant embarked for St. Marks with three armed galleys and a contingent of troops. Following Folch's brief bombardment of the stone-walled fort, Bowles and his Indians retreated.[18]

Panton later reported the company's losses at $16,054.03, including a number of slaves carried away by Bowles. Yet what caused the harried Scotsman even greater concern was his belief that Folch might keep the recaptured *Sheerwater* and any company goods that Bowles had not carried off as spoils of war. Remonstrating against Folch, Panton insisted that such a step would be "a hardship indeed . . . were my property to be torn from me by my friends as well as my enemies." Since Bowles could be considered nothing more than "a robber by Sea, as well as by Land," justice required restitution.[19]

The St. Marks incident includes a certain tragic irony, since the seemingly indomitable Bowles, the first serious challenge to the trade empire of William Panton, was ironically also his last tormentor.

Almost perceptibly, the war had drained Panton's will to continue in the trade against such formidable odds. In fact, his complaints about his misfortunes had become more frequent and increasingly bitter. Fatigued from having played "a losing game for Eight years past," Panton earnestly

17. Wright, *William Augustus Bowles*, 127–35, 170; Marqués de Casa Calvo to Mariano Luis de Urquijo, August 8, 1800, AHN Estado, leg. 3889 bis, Exp. 10.
18. Wright, *William Augustus Bowles*, 134–36; Folch to Director General of the Muskogees, July 4, 1800, AHN Estado, leg. 3889 bis, Exp. 10; Manuel García to Casa Calvo, July 11, 1800, ANC F, leg. 2, Exp. 21.
19. Panton to Casa Calvo, July 24, 1800, ANC F, leg. 1, Exp. 5, no. 97; ASP PL, 4:162; Corbitt, "Georgia-Florida Frontier," 25:169–70.

Table 5. Losses sustained as a result of Bowles's capture of the St. Marks trading post, May 1800

Value of goods, houses, negroes, cattle, etc., existing in our possession at the time of the robbery, including the brig *Sheerwater*, which transported them from Pensacola			$16,549	06 3/4
Expenses in repairing the *Sheerwater* for the damage done to her while in possession of Bowles and his Indians	$ 672	07		
Detention of said brig from May 18 until November 11, 1800, during which time it was either in Bowles' possession or detained at Pensacola for repairing its damages, five months and twenty-four days, at $500/month	2,900			
A mulatto and a negro boy belonging to said brig, carried off by Bowles	800		4,372	07
			$20,922	05 3/4
To deduct the value of goods and negroes recovered at the retaking of Ft. St. Marks			4,868	02 3/4
Total loss			$16,054	03

Source: *ASP PL*, 4:162.

desired its end before "the last shilling" goes. He had begun to dream wistfully of retirement to his father's farm, the Mains of Aberdour overlooking the North Sea, the family home at the time of William's birth. By May 1800, John Forbes observed that his mentor no longer pressed the Spaniards for advantage with the same vigor as in the turbulent years before the Treaty of New York. Drained emotionally by the cares of the company and plagued by serious physical infirmities, Panton had become gravely ill by the end of 1800.[20]

On January 20, 1801, swollen and suffering from a dropsical condition, Panton was placed aboard the *Shark*, where, attended by his physician, Dr. Reeves Fowler, he departed hastily for Havana. Medical counselors had advised Panton that changing to a more favorable climate was absolutely necessary to save his life. That advice caused the *Shark* to depart before letters of recommendation from Casa Calvo to influential relatives in Cuba had arrived in Pensacola. Unfavorable winds made for a tedious three-week voyage, but Panton's low spirits improved as the *Shark* finally made her way past El Morro Castle.[21] The improvement was short lived,

---

20. John Innerarity [Sr.] to Panton, January 8, 1798; Panton to John Forbes, April 26, 1800; T. Forbes to Panton, January 3, 1801, GP; J. Forbes to Panton, May 30, 1800, CP.

21. Casa Calvo to J. Forbes, February 4, 1801, copy in MC, Exhibit OO; J. Forbes to

however, for Spanish authorities quickly delivered a blow to Panton's revived hopes. Though the governor was sympathetic, Panton, as an Englishman without letters of recommendation, was refused admittance, and the *Shark* was ordered to put out to sea.[22]

It was decided that the failing Panton would be moved to Nassau, but heavy seas en route forced the *Shark* to seek haven at Key West. An unsympathetic British naval officer detained her there for two days, while he weighed the merits of sending the schooner to Jamaica as a prize. Finally released, the *Shark* proceeded toward the Bahamas, but again she quickly encountered contrary winds and rough seas. William Panton, by this time emaciated and completely exhausted, died in his sleep on February 26. His death, Dr. Fowler reported, was the more tragic, because Panton's desire to live was so great. Buried at Great Harbour on Berry Island, Panton had fallen victim more to the antagonists whom he professed to serve than to natural causes.[23]

John Forbes thereafter emerged as leader of the firm. In April 1801, Forbes wrote the governor general of Louisiana and West Florida, explaining that he was now in charge of the company in the Floridas. He went on to ask for assurances from the Spanish officials that the company would be allowed to continue business on the same basis as before. His comment that these were troubled and chaotic times for conducting the Indian trade not only accurately described the company's recent history but also its future.[24] For the next two years, Forbes's principal problem was the company's old nemesis, William Augustus Bowles.

In addition to Miller, other merchants from Nassau supported Bowles in his efforts to drive Panton, Leslie and Company from the Floridas, particularly Joseph Hunter and John DeLacy. Hunter had used Bowles's influence with the Indians to set up a store in the Creek country, where he undersold Panton, Leslie. Although Bowles needed no prompting, it was Hunter who had urged him to take the Spanish fort at St. Marks so that Bowles's merchant friends would have a safe anchorage on the Gulf coast.[25]

DeLacy, on the other hand, had grandiose plans. He wanted to take over the entire southern fur trade at Panton, Leslie's expense. Specifically, he planned to establish a trading post on the Chattahoochee from which he could monopolize the Indian trade. To effect this plan, DeLacy

---

Casa Calvo, February 5, March 10, April 29, 1801, *AGI PC*, leg. 203; Dr. Reeves Fowler to J. Forbes, March 21, 1801, GP. On Dr. Fowler, see Parrish, "Southern Loyalists," 334-35.

22. Dr. Reeves Fowler to J. Forbes, March 21, 1801, GP.
23. Ibid.
24. John Forbes to Marqués de Casa Calvo, April 29, 1801, *AGI PC*, leg. 203.
25. Wright, *William Augustus Bowles*, 127, 132, 140, 142, 144-45, 154; Hunter to Bowles, March 5, 1800, GP; Folch to Casa Calvo, June 6, 1801, *AGI PC*, leg. 54.

made an extensive tour of the southeast, talking with many of the half-Indian and white traders employed by Panton, Leslie—traders whom he knew he must win over if his plan were to succeed. If he was successful, he optimistically anticipated a $4 million market for British manufactures. DeLacy also conferred with Bowles at length about how they were to accomplish their objective.

There appeared to be two possibilities for replacing Panton, Leslie and Company. If Britain reoccupied the Floridas to prevent France from doing so, Bowles maintained that he would become the British Indian superintendent and would replace the "half-Spanish" Panton, Leslie firm with DeLacy and his friends. Since reports were circulating that France had acquired Louisiana and might extend its control over West Florida to the Perdido (the boundary of French Louisiana prior to 1763) this possibility was not so far-fetched. DeLacy revealed an alternative plan to replace Panton, Leslie in a long letter to Bowles in December 1801, in which he noted that, for this, they must secure Spanish consent.[26]

DeLacy implied that since Governor Folch was deeply indebted to Panton, Leslie, he reluctantly did whatever the company desired of him. To extricate the governor from the company's grasp, DeLacy suggested that they lend Folch the amount of money he owed to Panton, Leslie. With Folch on their side, they could force the company out and take over the Indian trade for themselves. DeLacy, as well as Miller and Hunter, supported Bowles in the belief that in the end the state of Muskogee would be brought under the British sphere of influence.[27] But if the fur trade could be wrested from Panton, it mattered little to DeLacy or Hunter whether the trade was carried on under British or Spanish protection.

Continuing his denigration of his antagonists, DeLacy warned Bowles that Panton, Leslie and Company was the source of all their troubles: "the house of Panton, Leslie, Forbes & Co., have been and are the sole fomentors, abettors and promoters" of the war between Muskogee and Spain. Thomas Forbes in Nassau, he explained, had regularly informed his Florida partners whenever a rival company's ship left New Providence for the Florida coast. The members of the company in the Floridas would subsequently inform Spanish officials, who would then intercept the ships

26. Wright, *William Augustus Bowles*, 142–44; DeLacy to Bowles, December 9, 1801, Selkirk's Papers, Canada, MSS, ADD 27859, British Museum, London.
27. DeLacy to Bowles, December 9, 1801, Selkirk's Papers. It is not known how DeLacy learned of Folch's indebtedness to Panton. The records do not indicate any substantial sum owed to Panton by Folch, although in 1796 Folch had borrowed $600 from Panton to buy a brick kiln: Folch to Panton, November 9, 1796, GP. The company accounts reveal periodic charges to Folch through the years but only for small amounts.

wherever they could be found.[28] For example, in 1800, a Spanish galley had chased one of Hunter's ships, finally forcing it aground in Apalachee Bay. Hunter, who was aboard ship at the time, abandoned it and finally made his way back to Nassau.[29] In the summer of 1801, the galleys captured another of Hunter's ships, which was carrying a cargo of dry goods and a cannon.[30] Hunter laid blame for the capture of both his ships directly at the door of Panton, Leslie and Company.

As a way out of their troubles, DeLacy suggested to Bowles that they should, if possible, bribe the Spanish governors to allow their ships to pass, thus clearing the way to supply Bowles and his Indian friends with trade goods. For his part, Bowles was to insure that the Indians had furs ready to exchange for their merchandise.[31] It was probably obvious to Bowles, if not to DeLacy, that these proposals had little chance of success, and the "director general" returned to direct action.

Bowles even sent out Indian parties to steal the slaves of Spanish settlers in East Florida, where Forbes and his associates had a number of them employed on their cattle ranch. The company had already lost a number of slaves to Bowles and his Indian friends in the capture of the St. Marks store in 1800. On August 31, 1801, a party of sixteen Indians crossed the St. Johns River in canoes and stole thirty-eight blacks—eight men, eight women, and twenty-two children—from the plantation of Francisco Fatio. Governor Enrique White of East Florida advised Governor Folch that these same Indians, accompanied by others, had later appeared at the Forbes ranch looking for more slaves and cautioned Folch not to give them any gifts until they had returned the stolen blacks. In another instance, John Forrester, now in charge of the company's East Florida operation, complained that Indian raiding parties were so active in the St. Johns River area that planters were afraid to let their slaves go into the fields. He feared that there would be no one to harvest the cotton that fall. Forrester even sent a party of friendly Indians to recover the kidnapped slaves, but without success. He also claimed that the Indians, who should have been hunting by this time, had not done so because he had not been allowed to issue them the ammunition they needed.[32] Forrester despaired of protecting company property: "I know of no place of

28. DeLacy to Bowles, December 9, 1801, Selkirk's Papers; Hunter to Bowles, March 5, 1800, GP.
29. Ibid.
30. John Forbes to William Simpson, July 29, 1801, *AGI PC*, leg. 77.
31. DeLacy to Bowles, December 9, 1801, Selkirk's Papers; Wright, *William Augustus Bowles*, 144.
32. John Forrester to John Forbes, September 8, 1801, CP; Enrique White to Folch, September 12, 1801, *EF* leg. 114J9; Wright, *William Augustus Bowles*, 144–45.

Safty in this province to remove [our] slaves to where they could remain anyways in Safty, except to Augustine or the Islands. . . . The property of Cattel [we] have in this province I mean to endeavour to defend and keep together as well as I possibly can. . . . I shall move my family Immediately to town."[33] The following year, at a treaty conference with the Indians at St. Marks, Forrester managed to recover twenty-one of the stolen blacks and received promises that the others would be returned.[34] But by spring of 1803, the company still had not recovered all of its slaves from the Indians.

The succession of governors in the Bahamas after Lord Dunmore's departure—Forbes, Dowdeswell, and, in 1801, John Halkett—had done nothing to improve Bowles's standing there. Governor Halkett let it be known that he intended to rid himself of all remnants of Dunmore's gang, especially John Miller, whom the governor wanted removed from the council. Halkett soon took steps against Bowles's privateers, whom the Bahamian court ruled were nothing more than pirates. Judge John Kelsall, a close friend of Thomas Forbes, presided over the court which convicted Bowles's confederates and ordered them hanged. The Bahamas were no longer a haven for Muskogee privateers, and Governor Halkett also warned that if Bowles returned to the Bahamas he would be thrown in jail as well: "The political change in Nassau and the imprisonments and executions for piracy must have made [Panton] rest easier in his . . . grave." Yet Panton's partners were still alive, and their revenge was sweet.[35] Thomas Forbes remained on the Bahamian council, keeping the governor informed of Bowles's "real Character & the wickedness of his attempts to disturb the peace." The most important news item in Forbes's report was that St. Marks was again under siege by Muskogee's army.[36]

If, as Bowles intimated at the time, his fortunes seemed to improve in the Floridas, they continued to deteriorate for him elsewhere. In March 1802, England signed the Peace of Amiens, ending the war with France and Spain—an event that had a positive effect on Panton, Leslie and Company, and a bad effect on Bowles. The war's end enabled the company to send goods from London to Nassau and the Floridas with neither convoy escort nor the consequent charges for convoy expenses. Wartime insurance rates and freight charges were also reduced. More important, however, John Leslie could once again secure powder and ball for the Indian trade; because of the war, these items had been in extremely short

33. Forrester to Governor Enrique White, February 13, 1802, EF leg. 116L9.
34. Forrester to White, September 7, 1802, CP.
35. Wright, *William Augustus Bowles*, 156–57; Thomas Forbes to John Forrester and Philip Yonge, January 1, 1803, JIP, LSU.
36. Thomas Forbes to Governor Halkett, March 6, 1802, CP.

supply.[37] In a real sense, the war's end signaled the eclipse of Muskogee. Any hope that Bowles had for British support and cooperation in his war against Spain in the Floridas had vanished. Governor Halkett's stand clearly demonstrated the postwar policy toward Bowles and the State of Muskogee. Further, John Forrester helped to negotiate a treaty between the Seminole and Spain in August 1802, by which the Indians agreed to return the kidnapped slaves and to withdraw their aid and support from Bowles.[38]

Nevertheless, Bowles continued to have a substantial following among the Seminole and Lower Creek—a following that figured significantly in his future plans. In fact, this liaison afforded Bowles two possible methods by which he might obtain substantial support: a grand confederation of the southern Indian nations, under his leadership, and an alliance with the United States. On occasion, John Forbes and Governor Folch had fretted about the latter possibility and about the role played by U.S. Indian agent Benjamin Hawkins.[39] Their suspicions were ill founded, however.

Reports now and then reached Pensacola that Hawkins favored Bowles's plans, that he had encouraged the Upper Creek to join Bowles, or that he was following American policy by aiding Bowles in his war against Spain. In spite of these reports, Hawkins consistently opposed Bowles and vice versa.[40]

In January 1800, just three months after Bowles had returned to the Floridas, he warned one of his Creek allies, Little Prince, that Hawkins was a dangerous man and would cause much mischief. Bowles planned to seize Hawkins and to have him tried under Muskogee law.[41] The following year, Secretary of War Henry Dearborn warned Hawkins to be on his guard against Bowles, urging that Hawkins watch Bowles's every move, and that he counteract Bowles's intrigues among the Indians, using any means available. If Bowles were to appear in the United States, Hawkins was to exert every effort to apprehend him without compromising the peace.[42]

37. John Leslie to Thomas Forbes, October 16, 1801, CP. Although this letter is clearly dated 1801 the contents make it obvious that it should have been dated 1802.
38. John Forrester to Governor White, September 7, 1802, CP; Wright, *William Augustus Bowles*, 157; Holmes, "Spanish Treaties," 150–51.
39. John Forbes to Governor Folch, April 2, 1803; Folch to Forbes, April 2, 1803; Folch to Manuel de Salcedo, April 23, 1803, AGI PC, leg. 55.
40. Folch to Forbes, April 2, 1803; Folch to Manuel de Salcedo, April 23, 1803, ibid.; Pound, *Benjamin Hawkins*, 192.
41. Bowles to [John Reeves?], December 11, 1801, Selkirk's Papers; Pound, *Benjamin Hawkins*, 193.
42. Pound, ibid.

The reason advanced for this hostile attitude toward Bowles was that the United States wanted to secure valuable land cessions from the Indians—a plan that Bowles adamantly opposed.[43] Bowles's stand, however, failed to prevent the Creek from making two separate land grants to the United States in June 1802. In addition to other considerations, the United States paid the Creek $25,000 for the land, of which $10,000 was to be used to satisfy debts due the U.S. factory.[44] Forbes was not disturbed by the Creek land grants to the United States, but he did take exception to the $10,000 paid to the American factory, because these same Indians had made no effort to pay any of the huge outstanding indebtedness owed Panton, Leslie and Company—an indebtedness which Forbes had been trying to collect for several years.

In October 1802, Forbes met with the Creek to press them for payment of their debts, but all he received were promises that the Creek would eventually pay.[45] By the spring of 1803, as the southern Indians prepared to meet in council at the Hickory Ground, the Creek still had paid Forbes nothing on account. Bowles planned to attend this conference, hoping to emerge as the new king of a southern Indian confederation and to prevent any further Indian land cessions. Hawkins, for his part, intended to see that Bowles would be apprehended at the meeting and turned over to the Spaniards. Forbes, accompanied by Governor Folch's son, Estevan (Stephen), also planned to be there in order to present his claims against the Creek once again and to assist in whatever way he could to help to apprehend Bowles. The elaborate instructions provided to young Folch left no doubt about his mission. He was to encourage the Indians first to take Bowles prisoner, then to turn the prisoner over to him. If that plan failed, Folch was to have the chiefs order Bowles out of the nation, under a threat of death if he returned. Folch was to endeavor to get the assistance of Colonel Hawkins, but if that proved impossible, he was to carry out his mission alone.[46] The stage was set for a confrontation.

Since Bowles's status commanded much attention in the early days of the Hickory Ground conference, it was decided that the Creek would be asked to apprehend him. Hawkins sent Forbes a copy of the note he had

43. Bowles to [John Reeves?], December 11, 1801, Selkirk's Papers.
44. Royce, *Indian Land Cessions*, 2:660–62 and Map no. 15, two separate tracts each numbered 44; Records of the Bureau of Indian Affairs, NARG 75, Microcopy no. T-494, roll 1, Ratified Treaty no. 32, Treaty of June 16, 1802, with the Creek Indians.
45. "Talk" of John Forbes to the four nations of Creek, Cherokee, Choctaw, and Chickasaw Indians held at the Hickory Ground, May 30, 1803, HWP, LSU. For Forbes's reaction to the payment to the U.S. factory, see also entry of June 1, 1803, in Estevan Folch, "Journal of a voyage to the Creek Nation from Pensacola in the year 1803," May 5–June 3, 1803, *AGI PC*, leg. 2372.
46. Folch, "Journal," *AGI PC*, leg. 2372, esp. entry for May 12; Wright, *William Augustus Bowles*, 162–64; *Ynstrucciones á que deve ceñirse el cadete con funciones de*

written to one of the Creek chiefs, Hopoie Mico, asking that the Indians take Bowles prisoner. If they would not, Hawkins said, he would do so. Confidently, Hopoie Mico assured Hawkins that the Upper Creek chiefs would apprehend Bowles and that they could rely on the Cherokee, Chickasaw, and Choctaw for help if necessary. Amid doubt that he would appear, Bowles finally arrived with a body of his Seminole followers and met with the assembled Indians on the evening of May 24. Later that night, Bowles sent word to Forbes that all but four of the chiefs were with him, at the same time warning Forbes that plans to capture him might backfire. He also warned Forbes and Folch that they were ill advised in coming to the meeting, since Muskogee was still at war with Spain. But these warnings frightened neither Folch nor Forbes.

The following day, the chiefs questioned Bowles intently. Where was his commission and where were his papers? Bowles replied that he had come from a great prince, King George, to protect all the red people from having their lands taken away by the Americans and the Spaniards. But he could produce nothing in the way of a commission or other document to substantiate his claims. On the twenty-sixth, the Indians spent the day discussing what was to be done with Bowles. Forbes expressed surprise at how orderly the meeting went and how well the results of the Indian talks were kept secret. Finally, Big Warrior, chief of the Tuckabatchee, inquired of Colonel Hawkins how he wished Bowles disposed of. Hawkins replied that Bowles should be put under confinement immediately and properly secured until irons could be made; he should then be conducted, under guard, to Governor Folch. The next day, Big Warrior told Forbes that Bowles had been taken prisoner and had been confined in old Fort Toulouse, where he would remain until the irons were ready. Forbes and Folch, with several other white men, decided to pay Bowles a visit.

At their approach, Bowles turned pale and said, "he supposed his hour was come." He was informed that he had nothing to fear from them. The handcuffs finally were made ready and were ordered to be put on Bowles. As soon as the rivets were fastened the Indians put Bowles into a canoe and immediately left to deliver him to Pensacola. En route Bowles managed to escape from his Indian guard for a few hours, but he was recaptured and taken to Governor Folch. On the evening of Bowles's departure, a number of chiefs came to Forbes's quarters to talk with him about Bowles and to satisfy themselves that they had acted properly. Forbes recorded that, "they retired perfectly Satisfied & some jokes passed upon Bowles's friends who were Said to be crying in a corner."[47]

Abanderado Dⁿ Estevan Folch en la comisión á que se le destina, May 1, 1803, *AGI PC*, leg. 2355.

47. *Ynstrucciones . . . Folch*, ibid. "A Journal of John Forbes, May, 1803," GP, pub-

When Bowles arrived in Mobile, Spanish officials lost no time in sending him under guard to New Orleans and then to Havana. Imprisoned in the formidable Morro Castle, he died on December 23, 1805.[48] Thus ended the saga of William Augustus Bowles.

For John Forbes, Bowles's capture at the Hickory Ground was the accomplishment of the first of his two principal reasons for attending the conference. The second—how to collect the Indian debts owed to Panton, Leslie and Company—remained unresolved.

---

lished in the *FHQ* 9 (1931): 279–89; John Forbes's talks to the Creek Indians at the Hickory Ground, May–June 1803, in [John Innerarity] to William Simpson, June 18, 1803, Louisiana Historical Association Collection, Indian Affairs Papers, Howard-Tilton Library, Tulane University. John Forbes later charged the old firm of Panton, Leslie and Company $564 for expenses associated with his journey to the Hickory Ground. In June 1807, the bill was still pending and, with interest, amounted to $679: Account Current with the Existing Concern, John Forbes & Co., entry for June 30, 1807, GP.

48. Wright, *William Augustus Bowles*, 166–71.

12

Resolution of the Indian Debts

*T*HE discussion of the Indian debts and land cessions at the Hickory Ground proved to be just one more confrontation—albeit in the long run an important one—between the company and the Indians. Forbes planned to help Hawkins negotiate a large land grant between the Oconee and Ocmulgee rivers, on behalf of the United States, to complement the grant of 1802. If the negotiations were successful, Forbes expected to receive $100,000 in payment of the Creek debt. The debt, which included the Upper and Lower Creek and the Seminole, totaled $113,512, and took into account two robberies of the Wakulla River store, in 1792 and 1800. Unknown to Forbes until the meeting was nearly over, the Indians, especially the Cherokee, had come to the conference hoping to reach a common understanding: no more Indian land would be sold to anyone without the approval of the entire confederation. Only the Seminole were an exception to this consensus, and then only before the meeting was properly under way.

Shortly after Forbes's arrival, [Thomas?] Perryman, one of the Seminole chiefs, reiterated the Seminoles' previous offer to the company of a land grant on the Ocklochonee. Stephen Folch thought it a generous offer, "equal to a principallity." But Forbes refused to accept the grant on the grounds that the Indians wanted too much for the land and recommended that they keep it. He preferred instead that the Indians sell the lands between the Oconee and the Ocmulgee to the United States. Since he anticipated a cash settlement for the company if such a sale materialized, his preference for that option was understandable. But he did not rule out Perryman's offer and used it as the basis for a counteroffer. He proposed to pay the Seminole $30,000 for the Ocklochonee lands, provided the grant was extended eastward to the east branch of the Apalachee River (the present St. Marks River). But before the Seminole could seriously consider Forbes's proposal, the assembly delayed the question of land cessions and debts until the fate of Bowles, a vigorous opponent of any new land cessions by the Indians, was determined.

After Bowles's removal, Forbes addressed the assembled nations and presented his claims. Mad Dog, although retired as principal Creek chief, acknowledged that the Indians had gotten themselves into their predicament and that it was up to them to pay their debts. Hawkins also told the Indians that they were obligated to pay the company. He suggested that the Indians needed an additional annual income of at least $10,000, in order to continue their domestication program. This was a less-than-subtle plug for the Oconee-Ocmulgee grant which, in addition to the payment of the Forbes debt and other considerations, also included a $10,000 annuity. The Indians refused the bait but countered by promising to pay Forbes with wood and staves and a part of their current annuity, which amounted to about $4,000. Forbes replied that three times he had addressed the Indians regarding their debts, that each time they promised to pay him, and that all he had received were promises. These couldn't buy supplies or pay debts, he declared. He would not accept the wood and staves, nor would he take any of their annuity. The Indians were rich, not poor, he said. They had more land than they needed.

The Indians then accused Forbes of duplicity. Forbes had earlier refused to accept lands—the Ocklochonee grant offered by Perryman—in payment of their debts. But now, they charged, he wanted them to sell land. Forbes stated emphatically that he did not want their lands; he only wanted to be paid. He alluded to the earlier sale of lands to the United States, from which the Indians had paid the U.S. factory $10,000. Sell your lands, he told them, and then pay me. Hawkins again attempted to serve as intermediary but without effect. The meeting ended in an impasse. The Creek would not consent to the Oconee-Ocmulgee grant, nor would the Seminole respond to Forbes's counterproposal regarding the Ocklochonee lands. Forbes blamed his failure to secure the desired land cessions on Return J. Meigs, the Cherokee agent. The Cherokee, who were the most determined of all not to sell any more lands, had, at Meigs's urging, induced the Creek to thwart Forbes. As a result of the Cherokee stand, all four Indian nations resolved to sell no more lands without the consent of the entire confederacy. Before they left the Hickory Ground, the Upper and Lower Creek refused to accept financial responsibility for the St. Marks robberies, but they did promise Forbes that they would pay their debts.[1] Despite outward signs of failure, either to collect the debts or to secure the desired Oconee-Ocmulgee cession, the groundwork had been laid. Events would prove that the meeting was far from a failure.

In September, about three months after the Hickory Ground conference, Forbes met General Wilkinson on the Little River to discuss the Indian debts, land cessions, and company trade with the Indians in U.S. territory. Forbes promised Wilkinson that if the Choctaw and Chickasaw did not agree to the desired land cessions, the company would withhold supplies from them. Since both nations obtained nearly all of their supplies from the company ($40,000 worth annually) Wilkinson seemed convinced that Forbes's threats would result in land cessions that winter.

Wilkinson also thought it advisable that Forbes see Dearborn to explain his future plans to the secretary of war. Wilkinson believed that Forbes was being misrepresented in Washington, where he was suspected of having influenced the Spaniards to levy a tariff on goods going through Mobile to the U.S. government trading post at St. Stephens. The location of the government factory at St. Stephens had been dictated by the desire to block the company's trade with the Choctaw.[2] Wilkinson wrote Dear-

---

1. There are two journals of this meeting. That of Estevan Folch covers the period May 5–June 3, 1803. It supplements the journal of John Forbes, which does not begin until about May 12. Folch and Forbes spent several days with Hawkins, May 12–15, during which both merely wrote summaries of their discussions with Hawkins. Folch's journal resumes on May 15, but Forbes's does not start again until May 21. From May 21 to June 3, the two journals are similar enough to suggest that much of Folch's journal was copied from Forbes's. Forbes's journal of ca. May 12 to May 27 was published in *FHQ* 9 (1931): 279–89 (original in GP). The second half of this journal (May 27–June 3) was enclosed in a letter, probably from John Innerarity to William Simpson, Pensacola, June 18, 1803, Louisiana Historical Association Collection, Indian Affairs Papers. Folch's journal is in *AGI PC*, leg. 2372. Both journals leave no doubt about the Indians' stand against land cessions, contrary to what may have been written later about the meeting.

2. Cox, *West Florida*, 143–45. In 1800, the Marqués de Casa Calvo, Gayoso's successor as governor general of Louisiana and West Florida, expressed the strongest fears that the U.S. factory system would drive the company out of business. Opening the Mobile and Tensaw rivers to navigation by the United States would, Casa Calvo believed, cost the company not only the Chickasaw and Choctaw trade but the Upper Creek trade as well. After the Louisiana Purchase of 1803 and American claims to the area west of the Perdido, Spanish officials in Louisiana and West Florida feared that a buildup of American forces north of the thirty-first parallel would endanger the Spanish garrisons at such places as Mobile. Thus it was not merely their concern for Panton, Leslie and Company but a deeper concern for the safety of West Florida that caused Spanish officials to enforce rigorously the customs laws at Mobile. See Casa Calvo to Urquijo, October 8, 1800, Mississippi Provincial Archives, Spanish Dominion, Reel 6, Doc. 6, Ledger 7, pp. 277–319. A translated copy of this letter is in White, *New Collection of Laws*, 2:323–37. See Resolutions by the [Mississippi] Territorial

born that he found Forbes intelligent, cordial, and willing "to promote the views of Government in our Indian concerns, by every means in his Power." Because of the Indians' dependence on the company for supplies, Wilkinson reported, Forbes exercised almost complete control over the Creek and Choctaw. As yet, government supplies to the Indians amounted to only "a drop in the Bucket." Should the United States acquire the Floridas, Wilkinson predicted, Forbes would be indispensable in furthering American interests among the Indians, who in that event would be required to cede even more land to the United States.[3] Wilkinson also wrote a very complimentary letter of introduction on behalf of Forbes to Alexander Hamilton, former secretary of the treasury.[4] The reason is unknown, but Forbes delayed his trip to Washington until after the first of the year.

By the time of the Forbes-Wilkinson meeting, Wilkinson already knew that he was to occupy New Orleans and to assist in taking formal possession of Louisiana in December. In fact, he looked beyond that event to the cession of the Floridas to the United States, which he anticipated would soon follow. The acquisition of the Floridas and the two great seaports, Mobile and Pensacola, would usher in one of the most important states in the union, he predicted. Ownership of this new territory would necessitate additional land grants by the Indians, especially between the Chattahoochee and the Tombigbee rivers. Clearly, this early example illustrates that the avaricious appetite of American officials for Indian lands was not easily appeased.

During the month following his meeting with Wilkinson on Little River, Forbes had not been idle. He had indeed secured an agreement with several chiefs and warriors from the Upper Choctaw towns for a land cession on the Mississippi.[5] This decision to cede land on the Mississippi appeared to fulfill President Jefferson's plans to acquire that territory. Soon after they agreed to the land cession with Forbes, a delegation from the Choctaw went to Washington. There they offered to cede lands not on

---

Legislature, January 27, 1807, in Carter, *Territorial Papers*, 5:507-8; Judge Toulmin to the President, February 25, 1809, ibid., 705-8 ff.

3. Wilkinson to Dearborn, October 1, 1803, Letters Received by the Office of the Secretary of War Relating to Indian Affairs, 1800-1823, Microcopy 271, Roll 1, NARG 75.

4. Wilkinson to Hamilton, November 15, 1803, Alexander Hamilton Papers, vol. 84, Reel 35, LC.

5. Chiefs and Warriors of the Choctaw Nation to the President of the United States, September 20, 1803, Microcopy T-494, NARG 94; Wilkinson to Dearborn, October 1, 1803, cited in note 3 above. Before Wilkinson proceeded to New Orleans, he visited Pensacola, where he reached an agreement with the Creek to mark the boundary between the Alabama and Escambia rivers; John Forbes and James Innerarity witnessed this agreement: Boundary Agreement, October 26, 1803, Letters Received by the Office of the Secretary of War Relating to Indian Affairs, 1800-1823, Microcopy 271, Roll 1, NARG 75.

the Mississippi but on the Alabama and Tombigbee rivers. Since this was not the land that the United States desired (and that the Upper Towns had offered Forbes in September), the offer was refused.

Why had the Indians changed their minds? The only logical explanation is that when confronted separately—Upper Towns or Lower Towns—they often agreed to the demands of the moment, but once assembled as the Choctaw nation, they were not easily intimidated and chose to repudiate the earlier agreement. On several occasions, treaties had been concluded with a fraction of a nation, only to be repudiated later by the entire nation.[6] Had either Forbes or Simpson been in Washington, he might have been able to obtain the Mississippi lands; but neither was present.

While the Choctaw made their journey to the capital, Forbes continued his efforts to reach a settlement with the Seminole. With Bowles gone and no supplies coming from the Bahamas, the Seminole had little choice but to turn to the company. Yahulla Emathly, one of the Seminole chiefs, met Forbes in Pensacola, where they reached a general agreement on a tract of land to be ceded to the company, both in payment of their debts and in compensation for the St. Marks robberies. The proposed cession conformed to the changes that Forbes had suggested at the Hickory Ground the previous spring. Forbes sent William Hambly to explain the proposal to those chiefs who had not been in Pensacola. They approved the agreement and requested that a company representative meet them to complete the arrangements.

With Indian consent in hand, James Innerarity petitioned Governor Folch for permission to accept the grant and to send an agent to the nation to confirm it. Folch agreed, with one reservation: the company could not dispose of the land without the consent of the Spanish government. Because of his journey to Washington, Forbes was unable to attend the conference with the Indians, which took place in May 1804 at Chiskatalofa. Instead, James Innerarity and William Hambly completed the arrangements for the land grant to the company, while Forbes attempted to work out matters with the secretary of war on the general Indian debt problem.[7]

6. See Benjamin Hawkins to James Innerarity, Creek Agency, November 16, 1804, *AGI PC*, leg. 59, in which he advised Innerarity that the Creek had repudiated three treaties on the grounds that those signing the treaties were not authorized to do so: Doster, *Creek Indians*, 1:252.

7. "Talk" from Seminoles to Panton, Leslie and Company [December 1803 or early January 1804], GP; James Innerarity to Vicente Folch, January 5, 1804; Folch to Innerarity, January 7, 1804, MC, Exhibit OO; *ASP PL*, 5:331; Seminole Chiefs, Deed of Cession, May 25, 1804, ibid., 332. Chiskatalofa (variously spelled) was probably located on the Chattahoochee River in present-day Houston County, Alabama: Doster, *Creek Indians*, 1:248–49.

Forbes and Dearborn held several discussions in April and May 1804. Forbes offered to settle the entire indebtedness of the southern Indians— $173,000 plus $31,000 interest, a total of $204,000—in exchange for $150,000 to be paid by the U.S. government. He would accept $50,000, to be paid in three months, and the balance by Christmas of that year. Once the Indian debts were paid, Forbes announced, the company intended to withdraw from the Indian trade. But Dearborn was not interested in the lands offered by the Choctaw on the Alabama and Tombigbee rivers. The grant was insufficient to cover the amount owed. Consideration would be given to the grant only if it were extended significantly northward. The lands desired by the United States lay on the Mississippi River and were expected to be of such extent as to make the transaction worthwhile. Forbes offered no explanation for the Choctaw decision not to cede the Mississippi lands when they were in Washington. He expressed some surprise that the grant on the Tombigbee and Alabama rivers, which had been obtained only after much hard work on the company's behalf, was not acceptable. In fact, he indicated that he was not sure that the Mississippi lands still could be obtained. Yet he assured Dearborn that all possible effort would be exerted to do so.

Forbes further promised that William Simpson would be ready to negotiate with the Choctaw by August 30. He urged the secretary of war to appoint the U.S. commissioner to treat with the Indians and to determine as soon as possible the exact amount of land required in order that the work could be completed by the end of September at the latest. He knew, of course, that negotiations continued beyond that date would detain the Indians from their fall hunting. Moreover, since Forbes planned to go to London—he had lately learned of John Leslie's death—his brother Thomas in Nassau would be available upon request to come to Washington to complete the financial arrangements.[8]

In May 1804, with Louisiana now U.S. territory, one might question Dearborn's insistence on land cessions on the Mississippi and his apparent willingness to cooperate with Forbes in resolving the Indian debts. Since Forbes had announced his intention of withdrawing from the Indian trade after the debts were collected, Dearborn might have considered it worth the price to end the company's competition with the government factories. Indians then would no longer owe allegiance to a foreign company. But perhaps of more importance, the United States claimed that the Louisiana Purchase included all of West Florida from the Mississippi to the

8. Dearborn to Forbes, May 2, 1804; Forbes to Dearborn, May 3, 1804, copies in MC, Exhibits CC and 23X.

Perdido. If, as a result, the United States and Spain should go to war—as then appeared possible—Forbes might be useful in keeping the Indians neutral.

On the other hand, Forbes had not been entirely honest with Dearborn. While in Washington, Forbes had also visited the Spanish ambassador to the United States, Carlos Martínez de Irujo, the Marqués de Casa Irujo. Besides presenting a detailed physical description of the Spanish Floridas and declaring that West Florida could be converted into one of the most prosperous of all the Spanish colonies, Forbes had outlined plans designed to recover for Spain the allegiance of the southern Indians and to salvage the financial future of his company.

First, Spanish influence had to be reestablished among the Indians. At one time, Spain had predominance but had lost its control over the Indians when the United States established government factories to undersell Panton, Leslie and Company. Until 1794, Panton, Leslie had virtually absolute control over the Indians, which meant, in effect, that through the company Spain itself exercised such authority. But in 1804, that situation no longer existed.

Second, Indian title to the land was to be extinguished by first getting the Indians into debt and then "letting" them trade their land to pay their debts. Forbes admitted that the state of the company's business had forced him, reluctantly, to press the Indians into ceding land to the United States, thus enabling them to pay their debts to the company. Spain was to help the company reestablish its control over the Indians by advancing an interest-free loan of 400,000 pesos for a period of ten years. The company could then compete with the American factory system. In addition, if Spain treated the Indians generously, through presents and gifts to chiefs and other influential Indian leaders, force would never be required to secure their land.

Forbes's grand design contained yet a third feature. Immigrants were to be attracted to occupy the land obtained from the Indians and to make it profitable. Two groups came to mind for this purpose. First were the loyalists in the Bahamas, many of whom had lived in Florida under British rule and wanted to return. They had money to buy land but would have to be exempt from duties on goods which they would bring with them to Florida. Second were Europeans, such as the Swiss, Dutch, and Germans, who might be enticed to settle in West Florida. The Spanish crown probably would have to pay for the latter groups' transportation to Florida and also give each a cow and calf, along with land to cultivate. Slaves, likewise, should be sold on credit to the new settlers. Forbes stressed the need for Negro slaves, because he did not think that white

Chapter 12

men could perform hard, physical labor in the Florida climate without becoming ill. In addition, Forbes recognized that some land might not be suitable for farming, especially swamplands along the lower reaches of West Florida's rivers. However, these lands would make excellent rice plantations, he thought. As an additional inducement, he also stressed that religious tolerance was necessary to attract colonists. Conveniently, Forbes did not mention that the company was in the process of obtaining a huge land grant from the Seminole, which would be available for purchase by immigrants, as a final enticement.

To accomplish these objectives, the Spanish government would have to provide $15 million, the same amount of money which the United States had just paid for Louisiana. With this expenditure, Florida would again become extremely important to the Spanish crown.[9]

Casa Irujo forwarded Forbes's proposal to Madrid, but he was not disposed to endorse the ambitious role which Forbes recommended for the company. Accordingly, Casa Irujo suggested that some new plan for the Indian trade, and for control of the Indians, should be devised.[10] For these and many other reasons, the Spanish court never acted on Forbes's recommendations. Yet, from Forbes's discussions and correspondence with Dearborn and Irujo, it is obvious that he hoped to prosper with the help of both the United States and Spain. Forbes apparently never permitted allegiance to one country to interfere with company business and profits. After finishing his business in Washington, Forbes traveled to London to settle John Leslie's estate.

It was at about this time that the company underwent a name change. After Panton's death in 1801, John Leslie and Company took over the Panton, Leslie business in London, while the firm continued to operate in the Floridas under the old name. On July 30, 1803, the name "John Forbes and Company" appeared on the company's account books for the first time. Subsequently, during Forbes's visit to London in 1804, John Forbes and Company officially replaced John Leslie and Company. On September 11, 1804, Forbes wrote Governor Folch to advise him that John Forbes and Company had also supplanted Panton, Leslie and Company. In addition, he informed Folch that William Simpson and James Innerarity had been admitted to the company as partners. Folch forwarded the information to Spain and a Royal Order of December 20, 1805, approved the change.[11]

9. John Forbes to [Marqués de Casa Irujo]. April 28, 1804, *AGI SD*, leg. 2599. The original letter and the map accompanying it have never been found. The so-called Description has been translated, edited, and published: Coker, *John Forbes' Description*.

10. Casa Irujo to Pedro Cevallos, June 24, 1804; Cevallos to Prince of the Peace, August 15, 1804, *AGI SD*, leg. 2599.

11. *Registers of the Privy Council*, August 28, 1804, PC 2/165:634, PROL; entry of

Forbes did not return to the Floridas for nearly two years, during which time several of the company's employees, notably James and John Innerarity, William Hambly, William Simpson, and John Gordon, worked energetically—if not with complete success—toward liquidating the company's Indian debts. After Forbes returned in April 1806, he and another employee, Edmund Doyle, assisted by some of the others, continued their efforts to resolve the debt problem. The first of the negotiations involved the Seminole and Lower Creek.

Meeting with twenty-four Seminole and Lower Creek chiefs at Chiskatalofa on May 22, 1804, Hambly served as interpreter and company agent, together with James Innerarity, to receive the signed document formally ceding the lands to the company (approximately one million acres lying between the Apalachicola and Wakulla rivers). The grant, conforming roughly to that which Forbes had requested at the Hickory Ground the previous year, canceled a debt of $66,533.5 reales.[12]

En route to Pensacola to confirm the grant before Governor Folch, some of these Indians met General Wilkinson, who gave them a letter to deliver to Panton, Leslie and Company in Pensacola. Curious about its contents, they opened the letter and discovered to their consternation that Wilkinson wanted Forbes and Company to continue to press the Indians for land until Indian title to all lands east of the Flint River had been extinguished. But first, the company was to secure a cession of the lands east of the Apalachicola, the very grant which Hambly and Innerarity had just negotiated. Wilkinson expressed satisfaction in the letter about the prospects of negotiating with the Cherokee, Chickasaw, and Choctaw but anticipated trouble with the Seminole. The Seminole option seemed clear: cede their lands or go to war! Although very much upset by Wilkinson's letter, the Indians continued on to Pensacola, where Governor Folch confirmed the grant on June 22, 1804.[13]

All of the formalities concerning the Apalachicola land cession appeared to have been complete, but two months later, when James Innerarity met the chiefs and headmen at Prospect Bluff on the Apalachicola

---

July 30, 1803, Panton, Leslie and Company account books, HWP; Folch to Someruelos, February 16, 1805, *AHN Estado*, leg. 3888, Exp. 1; Folch to Ignacio Balderas, May 10, 1805, *AGI PC*, leg. 287; Someruelos to Cevallos, July 10, 1805, *AGI PC*, leg. 1737; Enrique White to Someruelos, May 21, 1807, *AGI PC*, leg. 1562; Folch to John Forbes and Company, January 7, 1807; Carlos Howard, proclamation of name change in Pensacola, May 21, 1807, *AGI PC*, leg. 1562; certified copies in MC, Exhibit 20U. See also Mirat, *Situación Histórica de Las Floridas*, 145.

12. Deed of Cession, May 25, 1804, printed in *ASP PL*, 5:332; copy in MC, Exhibit OO.

13. GHS, *Letters of Benjamin Hawkins*, 9:440–41; Doster, *Creek Indians*, 1:252–53. Cession verified by Vicente Folch, June 22, 1804, *ASP PL*, 5:332.

Table 6. Debts settled by the Creek-Seminole cession of the Apalachicola lands in 1804

Amount of the robbery committed on the store in Apalachy, January 16, 1792, as appeared by the statement on oath of Wm. Panton, before Don Vicente Folch, June 2, 1799, £2,681 01s., at 4s. 6d. per dollar		$11,915 06 ¼
Interest on said amount, at six percent yearly, from January 16, 1792, to August 22, 1804, at which date the chiefs agreed to sell and concede the lands to the house, twelve years seven months and six days		9,000 02 ½
Amount of the robbery on the store in Apalachy, in May, 1800, as appears by the statement made on oath by John Forbes and James Innerarity before Don Vicente Folch and two assistant witnesses, August 25, 1802		16,054 03
Interest on this sum, at six percent per annum, from May 31, 1800, until August 22, 1804		4,072 03 ½
Amount of debts due by different Indian dealers to the store, to the end of the year 1800, as appears by the statement taken from the books of said stores by James Innerarity, resident clerk at that time in Apalachy	$19,157.01	
Interest on this sum, at six percent per annum, from December 31, 1800, until the said August 22, 1804, three years seven months and twenty-two days	4,189 00	
		23,346 01
Expenses incurred on account of the different congresses held by the Seminoles, relative to the cession and sale of said land &c.		2,136 04 ¾
		$66,533 05
Errors and omissions excepted.		
		PANTON, LESLIE & CO.

Source: *ASP, PL,* 4:162–63.

to mark the boundaries, he discovered that several of the Indian leaders opposed the cession. The dissenters included a few chiefs who had not been present in May and June. Innerarity also discovered that others now opposed the grant because Benjamin Hawkins had insinuated that Forbes intended to populate the land with vagabonds from Georgia, which the Indians would bitterly resent. Innerarity assured them that immigrants were expected from the Bahamas, together with some other Englishmen, Spaniards, and Frenchmen. He assured them that whoever settled the land, only good men would be admitted.

Resolution of the Indian Debts 253

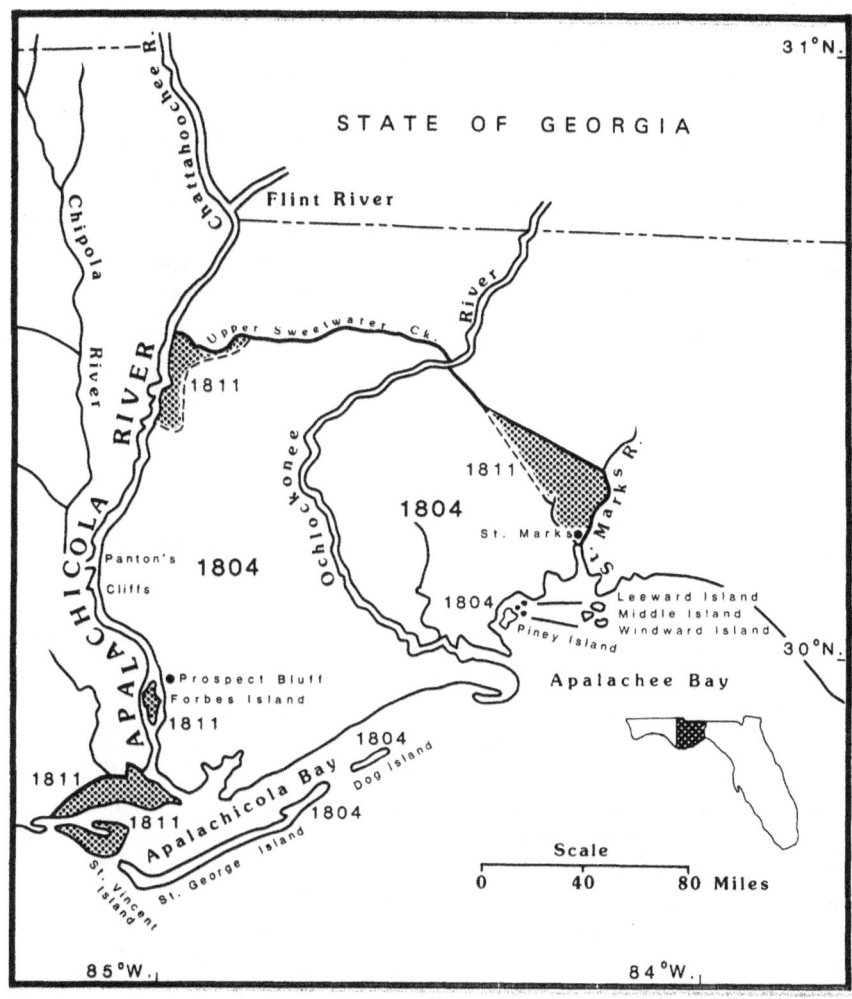

The Forbes Purchase, 1804-11

In spite of Innerarity's assurances, some opposition to the grant continued. Innerarity learned that Kinnard (variously spelled), a mixed-blood, who had taken over the Lower Creek–Seminole trade after Panton, Leslie had abandoned its store on the Wakulla, had begun an effort to annul the cession. Kinnard had realized a considerable profit in the trade, which he expected to lose when the company opened its new trading post. The last-minute arrival of Little Prince saved the day. Although a

Lower Creek chief, Little Prince had succeeded Mad Dog as the principal chief of the Creek. After Little Prince had harangued the opponents of the cession for an hour or two, Innerarity was advised that the Indians would go through with the cession ritual again.

This time the Indians insisted upon some changes to the boundaries, as stipulated in the earlier grant. Following more debate, an agreement was reached on the new limits. Innerarity later stated that it was the company's promises to establish a store on the Apalachicola and to provide a schedule of prices for goods and skins that persuaded the Indians to make the grant. Innerarity also claimed that it was only because of the grant that the company agreed to the new store, especially in light of the misfortunes suffered at the St. Marks trading post.

In a conference with the Indians, Innerarity made it clear that some new rules would govern the store, the most important being that the company would extend no credit whatsoever. After the conference, Innerarity and several designated Indians set out to mark a portion of the boundary, following which Innerarity returned to Pensacola. Thereafter, the company consistently represented the land as having been obtained from the Seminole only; yet an examination of the names on the deed of cession shows that parties from all three factions—Upper Creek, Lower Creek, and Seminole—approved the land cession, as they did four months later at Pensacola.[14]

The sequel to these events on the Apalachicola can be briefly told. Simpson visited Hawkins soon after Innerarity negotiated the final cession agreement for the Apalachicola lands. At that time, Simpson asked Hawkins if he had told anyone that Forbes planned to settle the lands with vagabonds from Georgia. Hawkins assured Simpson that he had not. Simpson then reported to James Innerarity that Hawkins seemed well disposed toward the company, and he was convinced that the company had nothing to fear from him. Simpson did warn Innerarity, however, that some of the Upper Creek chiefs were disappointed that the company had accepted the grant without consulting them. Privately, Simpson doubted that the cession would be considered binding without the signatures of several of the Upper Creek chiefs, especially The Singer and Big Warrior. Simpson therefore strongly recommended that those two chiefs be invited to Pensacola in order to get their signatures on the document. Hawkins concurred and warned of "problems" if *all* the Creek were not consulted

14. Deposition ceding the Apalachicola lands, August 22, 1804, MC, Exhibit OO; James Innerarity to Simpson, September 24, 1804, GP; also in *FHQ* 10 (1931): 102–8; cession verified by Vicente Folch, December 5, 1804, MC, Exhibit OO; Doster, *Creek Indians*, 1:252–65.

about the Apalachicola grant. He pointed out that the Creek had already repudiated three treaties, claiming that those who had signed them were not authorized to do so. Events transpired just as Simpson and Hawkins had predicted: the Upper Creek who had not signed the deed of cession later used it as pretext to refuse to pay their debts. Nevertheless, a formal survey of the grant was completed by August 1806, and, four months later, Governor Folch ratified the entire proceedings.[15]

While James Innerarity was busy with the Creek and Seminole, one of the other partners—probably William Simpson—returned to the Choctaw in an effort to get that nation to reconsider the cession of lands on the Mississippi. Again, the company successfully persuaded the Upper Towns to agree to the desired cession. In fact, the Upper Towns notified President Jefferson in the fall of 1804 that they could not pay their debts to Panton, Leslie and Company, but they offered as much land on the Mississippi as would be needed to satisfy the company debt. But the wheels of government turned slowly. In January 1805, Simpson traveled to Washington to try to discover what was delaying U.S. acceptance of the Mississippi grant and the payment to the company. Secretary of War Dearborn expressed to Simpson his sorrow for the delay but insisted that a formal treaty must be concluded between the United States and the Choctaw, at which time the exact amount of land to be ceded and the specific sum to be paid for the grant would be determined. The treaty must then be submitted to the Senate for ratification and the funds authorized by Congress before the company could be paid.[16]

Dearborn had instructed Silas Dinsmoor, the Choctaw agent, the previous October to make arrangements with the Choctaw for the treaty, but it was not until March 1805 that he actually appointed Dinsmoor and General James Robertson as commissioners to negotiate the land cession and provided them with the necessary instructions. Dearborn informed his two emissaries that the United States desired land on the Mississippi

---

15. [Simpson] to James Innerarity, November 16, 1804; [Benjamin Hawkins] to James Innerarity, November 16, 1804, *AGI PC*, leg. 59; deposition of the detailed description of the grant signed by eleven Seminole chiefs, August 2, 1806; John Forbes to Folch, November 28, 1806, and certificate of confirmation signed by Vicente Folch, December 3, 1806, MC, Exhibits NN and OO; Doster, *Creek Indians*, 1:238–40, 259. Cotterill, "Panton, Leslie," 285, stressed Hawkins's opposition to the Florida cession.

16. John Forbes and Company, memorial to the President of the United States, undated, Documents Relating to the Negotiation of Ratified and Unratified Treaties with Various Indian tribes, 1801–69, Microcopy T-494, NARG 94; Dearborn to Simpson, January 26, 1805, CP. Simpson also talked to President Jefferson, who informed him that the Louisiana Purchase included lands as far east as the Perdido and that he expected the negotiations then under way to result in cession of the Floridas to the United States: Simpson to Governor Folch, January 14, 1805, *AGI PC*, leg. 55.

between the mouth of the Yazoo and the Chickasaw line. If they were successful, the United States would pay Panton, Leslie and Company $46,091.02, or the amount of the Choctaw debt. Dearborn apparently anticipated a cession of between 3.5 and 4.5 million acres of land, for which the two commissioners were instructed not to pay more than two cents per acre. Dearborn informed his commissioners that the United States had only paid the Indians an average of one cent per acre during the preceding four years.[17]

Probably because of the difficulties of travel, Robertson was delayed in reaching the Choctaw nation, but he and Dinsmoor began their negotiations with the Choctaw in the early summer of 1805. As they proceeded, the two commissioners must have been surprised to learn that the Upper Towns now refused to make the cession on the Mississippi, apparently because such a large amount of land was being demanded at such a low price. The commissioners ultimately despaired of completing the treaty that summer, electing instead to travel north and treat with the Chickasaw. Blaming the conference's failure upon the Upper Towns, Dearborn instructed Dinsmoor to charge the entire expense of the meeting to the Indians.

The commissioners finally returned to the Choctaw in November and met with the nation's representatives at Mount Dexter, although the failure of William Simpson to attend the conference delayed the proceedings for a few days. Simpson had visited the Choctaw earlier in the fall, having at that time applied as much pressure as possible to secure a land cession. Now, in November, though the Choctaw still refused to grant any of their Mississippi lands, they did offer the commissioners a huge grant—in excess of four million acres—along the thirty-first parallel, between the old British grants. The offer also included lands at the fork of the Alabama and Tombigbee rivers. Despite the fact that no Mississippi River lands were included, Robertson and Dinsmoor accepted the Choctaw proposal, apparently pleased that the offer contained more land than the Choctaw had been willing to cede during the summer conference. In addition to other considerations, the treaty provided $50,500 cash, of which $48,000 was to be used to pay the Choctaw debts. Unfortunately for the company, when the treaty reached Washington, President Jefferson was so disappointed with it that he refused to submit it to the Senate for ratification.[18]

17. Dearborn to Dinsmoor, October 25, 1804; Dearborn to Robertson and Dinsmoor, March 20, 1805, Letters Sent by the Office of the Secretary of War, Microcopy no. 15, Reel 2:19 and 47, NARG 107.
18. Simpson to John Innerarity, June 5, 1805, GP; Dearborn to Dinsmoor, August 28, 29, 1805, Letters Sent by the Secretary of War, Indian Affairs, 1800–1824, Microcopy no. 15, Roll 2:101, 103, NARG 107; Simpson to James Innerarity, September 22, 1805, CP;

After Robertson and Dinsmoor left the Choctaw in the summer of 1805, they met in conference with the Chickasaw to negotiate a land cession with them. John Gordon, an employee from the Mobile store, also attended on the company's behalf. Before the meeting officially convened, Gordon met with Major George Colbert, a Chickasaw chief, who exercised great influence over the nation. Gordon read a letter to Colbert from William Simpson, which listed the Chickasaw debt to the company at $11,178. Colbert acknowledged the debt and promised that the Chickasaw would sell as much land as necessary to pay the debt, provided a suitable price could be agreed upon. Colbert further insisted that henceforth the company should do business only with persons who could be trusted to pay their debts. The commissioners and Gordon approved Colbert's proposal, even though certain Chickasaw debts required additional discussion. Gordon argued that some of these debts went back to 1792 and should bear interest. But, he said, Simpson would leave the matter up to the Indians. Though he acknowledged that the idea was sound, Colbert explained that Indians did not understand the concept of interest. Colbert subsequently offered to lend his assistance in resolving the debt but intimated that he would expect some "consideration" from Simpson and the United States for his services. After making his offer, Gordon retired from the meeting and the formal treaty conference began.

The commissioners had specified that the United States wanted lands along the Mississippi, but, like the Choctaw, the Chickasaw refused to consider ceding any of those lands. They countered by offering lands east of the Tennessee and Duck rivers, extending from the Ohio River into the northern part of Mississippi Territory (present-day Alabama). Chief Okoy proved to be the most outspoken opponent of the land cession, and within a few days the treaty seemed to be in jeopardy.

With the conference delayed, Gordon again conferred with the Chickasaw leader, Colbert. Gordon told Colbert of Simpson's high esteem for him and promised liberal rewards for his services. Colbert assured Simpson that the debts would be paid, after which the chief returned to the council. Nevertheless, considerable debate ensued. The debt schedule proposed by Gordon had been written two years previously, and the Indian nation objected to paying the debts owed by white traders. Gordon finally clarified the outdated debt schedule to Colbert's satisfaction and agreed that the company would assume responsibility for collecting debts

---

Extract from the Journal of the Choctaw Treaty, November 13, 1805, Documents Relating to the Negotiation of Ratified and Unratified Treaties with the Various Indian Tribes, 1801–69, Microcopy T-494, Roll 1:0152, NARG 94; DeRosier, *Removal of the Choctaw Indians*, 32; Kappler, *Indian Affairs*, 2:87–88.

from the white traders. Interested in his remuneration, Colbert then pressed Gordon to find out how much he would be paid for his efforts. Upon being informed that he would receive $400 for his work on behalf of the company, Colbert returned to the council and the land cession was completed. Still no land on the Mississippi was included in the grant—a circumstance that disappointed the commissioners, who agreed nonetheless to pay the Chickasaw $20,000, including the settlement of the Panton, Leslie debt. In addition, the treaty provided $1,000 apiece for Colbert and Chief Okoy for their services to the U.S. government. After the conference formally ended, Gordon sought to have Colbert sign an order for payment to the company. Colbert, however, dodged Gordon's request but wrote Simpson that the company would be paid soon after the purchase money arrived in the nation.[19]

The Chickasaw treaty upset the neighboring Cherokee: the Chickasaw cession included lands also claimed by the Cherokee, and the Cherokee still insisted that all of the southern Indians should form a confederacy and refuse to sell or trade any more land. This strategy was, of course, the same that the Cherokee had urged at the Hickory Ground in 1803—one that had contributed to Forbes's failure to secure the Creek cessions then.

The Cherokee, consequently, spent the summer and fall of 1805 in further efforts to form a confederacy. Though their efforts again delayed U.S. negotiation of the Ocmulgee cession from the Creek, the Cherokee were unable to protect their own nation from being caught in the land cession squeeze. Following its success in obtaining the Chickasaw lands, however, the United States tenaciously sought a treaty with the Cherokee, which, in addition to its call for more land, also included a quit-claim to the area in dispute with the Chickasaw. In spite of Cherokee resolve to the contrary, Return J. Meigs, the Cherokee agent, and Daniel Smith, serving as U.S. commissioners, secured a treaty with the Cherokee on October 25, 1805, in which the Cherokee relinquished their claims to the disputed lands. The United States agreed to pay the Cherokee $3,000 in

---

19. Journal of Commissioners to Treat with Choctaw and Chickasaw Indians, 1805, General James Robertson and Silas Dinsmore [sic], Microcopy no. T-494, NARG 94; [John Gordon], "John Forbes & Co., Successors to Panton, Leslie & Co., vs. The Chickasaw Nation: A Journal of an Indian Talk, July, 1805," *FHQ* 8 (1930): 131–42. At the time Gordon's journal was published, the editor was unaware of the author's identity. An examination of the handwriting in the journal—the original is in the Innerarity-Hulse Papers at the University of West Florida—leaves no doubt that it was written by Gordon. McKee's diary contains only a brief reference to his attendance at the Chickasaw conference: "Diary of Colonel John McKee, January 31, 1804–October 11, 1805," pp. 38, 41, John McKee Papers, Southern Historical Collection, University of North Carolina Library; Kappler, *Indian Affairs*, 2:79–80; Cotterill, "Panton, Leslie," 286–87; Gibson, *Chickasaws*, 104.

valuable merchandise immediately, $11,000 more within ninety days after ratification of the treaty, and an annuity of $3,000. Just when or how the Cherokee paid the Panton, Leslie company its debt of $2,358 is unknown, but presumably the money came from this treaty with the United States.[20]

Payment of the Cherokee debt thus presented no special problems, but the same could not be said about collection of the Creek debt, which, before it was over, became a nightmare for the company. At the Hickory Ground, in May and June 1803, Forbes had tried unsuccessfully to secure the highly desirable Ocmulgee lands for the United States. In a second meeting with the Creek in the aftermath of the Hickory Ground conference, General Wilkinson, Benjamin Hawkins, and Robert Anderson also failed to obtain those lands. The following April, Dearborn suggested that Hawkins again attempt to secure a treaty with the Creek and sent along General David Meriwether to assist in the negotiations. Discussions during the summer of 1804 were no more successful than on either of the two previous occasions. They were also unquestionably hampered by Wilkinson's letter to Panton, Leslie and Company, in which was expressed a desire that the company continue to pressure the Indians until all Indian land east of the Flint River belonged to the United States. Hawkins attempted to persuade a delegation of Creek chiefs to go to Washington for direct talks with the president and the secretary of war. But a series of sicknesses, deaths, and conflicts with the Cherokee—not to mention Wilkinson's untimely letter—caused the Creek to postpone the trip.

Finally, in November 1804, Hawkins met the Creek at the Flint agency and obtained a treaty despite a sharply divided Creek nation, many of whom obviously opposed the Ocmulgee cession (except at an exorbitant price). In short, this faction wanted payment of their debts, which may have been as much as $100,000, and a $500 annuity for each of the thirty-seven Creek towns. After discussing the Florida cession to Panton, Leslie and Company, this faction finally agreed to pay Forbes the debt owed the company from their annuity, but only after the price paid for the Florida lands was subtracted from the total purchase price. The meeting culminated in the Treaty of November 3, 1804, in which Hawkins went far beyond the anticipated purchase price, offering the Creek $200,000 in bonds at 6 percent interest, payable semi-annually, plus other considerations. Ironically, nothing in the treaty specifically provided for paying the Panton, Leslie debts. Because of its excesses, Hawkins correctly assumed

---

20. Fairbanks and Goff, *Cherokee and Creek*, 403–21; Cotterill, *Southern Indians*, 150–51. Cotterill, "Panton, Leslie," 287, refers to the Cherokee efforts to form a confederacy to oppose further land cessions, and to Cherokee agitation among the Creek. Cotterill's documentation for this has not been located; Kappler, *Indian Affairs*, 1:82–83.

that the treaty stood little chance of winning Senate ratification. The Senate indeed rejected the treaty, both because of the total amount to be paid and the manner of payment.[21] Nevertheless, Dearborn was still committed both to a treaty and to the payment of the Creek debts to the company.

Following Dearborn's instructions, Hawkins continued to work industriously among the Creek, attempting to raise a delegation to go to Washington. In Nassau, Thomas Forbes had followed the negotiations through the newspapers, and when he learned that a Creek delegation was finally en route to Washington, he wrote James Innerarity and William Simpson that someone from the company should be present in Washington to protect company interests. However, no one from the company made the trip, and it is doubtful that their presence would have made any difference in the final outcome. The Creek delegation of six chiefs had been carefully screened to ensure that only those chiefs who were "cooperative" made the trip. President Jefferson informed the chiefs, once they were in the capital, that the United States wanted a revised cession of the Ocmulgee lands at a lower purchase price. He also told them he wanted a road from the Ocmulgee through Creek territory to Fort Stoddart on the Mobile River.

At first the Creek refused to reconsider the grant, but finally, on November 14, 1805, they signed a treaty granting the road and again ceding their lands east of the Ocmulgee. In return, the United States agreed to pay them $206,000 in annuities over the next eighteen years. The Creek absolutely refused, however, to include a provision in the treaty calling for payment of the Forbes debts, although Dearborn had asked that they do so. Again, they claimed that a great part of their debt had already been paid by the land grant in the Floridas. Despite their refusal, however, they did indicate that they would take proper action to pay the balance.[22]

When Jefferson sent the treaty to the Senate in December 1805, he justified the purchase price by pointing out that it would require only $130,000 at an annual rate of 6 percent interest to pay the annuity. But, he added, if subtracted from the value of the road, the price would be only

21. Simpson to [James] Innerarity, February 22, 1805, CP; *ASP IA*, 1:690–93; Cotterill, "Panton, Leslie," 284–85; Doster, *Creek Indians*, 1:237–41; Pound, *Benjamin Hawkins*, 183–86; GHS, *Letters of Benjamin Hawkins*, 9:432–46; Cotterill, *Southern Indians*, 145–46.

22. Thomas Forbes to James Innerarity and William Simpson, July 18, 1805, FP, MPL; Simpson to James Innerarity, September 22, 1805, CP; Dearborn to Hawkins, February 12, June 28, 1805, Letters Sent by Office of Secretary of War Relating to Indian Affairs, 1800–1824, Microcopy M-15, Reel 2:41, 88, NARG 107; *ASP IA*, 1:698–99; Doster, *Creek Indians*, 1:241–43; Pound, *Benjamin Hawkins*, 186–87; Cotterill, "Panton, Leslie," 285, 287; Cotterill, *Southern Indians*, 152–53.

one-half that offered in the previous treaty. The Senate duly ratified the new treaty.[23]

When the Creek met in May 1806 to approve the treaty, there remained one problem. Forbes, who had returned from London the previous month, had sent John Innerarity to attend the conference and to urge the Creek to make provision for paying the company debt. Though Innerarity offered to give up the Florida lands for the amount that had been allowed for them, the Creek were not interested. When Innerarity failed to secure a concession of any kind from the Creek, Forbes again appealed to Dearborn.[24]

If the original Creek opposition against the Florida land grant to Panton, Leslie had not previously been clear, it became clear now. The opposition was based, in part, on divisions among the Upper Creek, Lower Creek, and Seminole—a schism not unlike the previously noted division among the Choctaw. When it was convenient, the Upper Creek always had considered the Lower Creek and Seminole to be part of the Creek nation. The Florida lands, belonging to the Creek nation, thus could not be given away by the Seminole without the concurrence of the other factions. Simpson and Hawkins had warned the company about this soon after the cession had been made.

Moreover, some of the Upper and Lower Creek were unwilling to admit the losses from the robberies committed by Bowles and his Seminole followers as a part of the company claims against the Creek nation. Their reasoning was not without basis, for of the $66,000 to be allowed for the Florida lands, $41,000 was charged against the robberies. If the Upper Creek faction could arrange for that debt to be disallowed, then the $41,000 would settle the other debts due the company—in which case, the entire Creek debt would be virtually eliminated.

But the question of how the company was to collect the amount due for the Seminole robberies remained unanswered. As far as the Upper Creek were concerned, collection was Forbes's problem. Yet Forbes's position also was clear: he had allowed $41,000 for the robberies and $25,000 for the other debts, including interest. Thus, the Creek nation still owed the company approximately $40,000 from the previous total of more than $100,000.[25]

The Creek enjoyed one advantage, Forbes another. The Upper and Lower Creek were no longer as dependent upon the company for their

---

23. *ASP IA*, 1:695; Kappler, *Indian Affairs*, 2:85–86.
24. Forbes to Dearborn, September 5, 1806, *ASP IA*, 1:750–51; Cotterill, "Panton, Leslie," 288.
25. Doster, *Creek Indians*, 1:246–47; *ASP PL*, 4:162–63.

supplies as were the Choctaw and Chickasaw, since the American factories were relatively close by and had sufficient goods to provide many of the Creek needs. The Florida lands, however, were in Spanish territory, and Forbes already had the approval of the Spanish government for the Seminole grant. Even with all this leverage, Forbes was unable to coax the Upper and Lower Creek into paying the balance of the debt, so he turned to Dearborn for advice.

Forbes reiterated the offer made by Innerarity to the Creek in May 1806: the return to the nation of the Florida lands for the $66,000 purchase price allowed for them, provided the rest of the debt could be collected. Dearborn soon replied that all his efforts to get the Creek to provide in the treaty for payment of debts to the company had been unsuccessful. Apparently, the Creek considered the land partial payment and informed the secretary of war that the Florida grant had paid a large part of their debt. Dearborn had been advised that the Creek did plan to take proper measures to pay the balance. But after so many frustrations, Dearborn's reply to Forbes was short and to the point, and even a bit sarcastic. "I hope no influence of your house," wrote Dearborn, "has been brought to bear on the free navigation of the Mobile."[26]

Predictably, Dearborn's letter disappointed Forbes. Accordingly, Forbes wrote the secretary of war that he considered the company's assistance in securing the Ocmulgee grant for the United States to be a fair price for the government's assistance in getting the company's debts paid. Previously, he had believed Dearborn's assurances of government influence to secure the debt. Without U.S. government pressure, Forbes contended, the Indians would never pay the company what they owed.

Again, Forbes implored Dearborn to have Hawkins determine the outstanding Creek debt and to assure its payment either through another land cession to the United States, or from current Creek revenues. He assessed the total debt at not less than $40,000. Forbes further informed Dearborn—apparently misinterpreting his sarcasm—that the company had had nothing to do with the thwarting of free navigation of the Mobile River and that until the king's pleasure on that subject was known, nothing could be done about it. Since the United States was exacting duties on company goods going overland by way of Mobile and Fort Stoddart to the Choctaw and Chickasaw country, Forbes decided to pressure Dearborn, informing him that he would advise the captain general in Havana about illegal duties being levied. This was a subtle hint that as long as the

---

26. Forbes to Dearborn, September 5, 1806; Dearborn to Forbes, November 12, 1806, *ASP IA*, 1:750–51.

United States charged duties on goods from Mobile, Dearborn could expect the Spanish to do the same with American goods passing through their territory.

Forbes ended his correspondence with Dearborn by declaring that the company had attempted to serve the best interests of both the United States and Spain. Admittedly, he wrote, the company was a political entity, which was nothing to be ashamed of. The company's operations might be reduced by circumstances, but its presence would always be important to the Florida trade. Forbes expressed disappointment; he had wanted for some time to withdraw from the province, but had been unable to do so because of his responsibility to secure the unpaid Indian debts. Nevertheless, Forbes's letter failed to move Dearborn, and there matters remained until 1808.[27]

Against this backdrop of frustration and political dealing, the international situation continued to deteriorate. Disagreements between Spain and the United States during the years 1803–8 had become critical by the beginning of 1808. Such problems as spoliation claims, expeditions into Spanish territory, and the Louisiana-Texas boundary dispute aside, the United States persisted in considering that portion of West Florida between the Perdido and Mississippi rivers as part of the Louisiana Purchase. By 1808, actual physical conflicts between such ruffians as the Kemper brothers and Spanish officials in West Florida had reached serious proportions.[28] As a result, President Jefferson took steps to secure ratification of the Choctaw treaty of 1805. According to its terms, the lands to be purchased, when added to the two previous land cessions along the thirty-first parallel, would extinguish Indian title to all land between the Mississippi and Mobile rivers. The time had come, Jefferson advised the Senate, to establish a strong militia along the West Florida frontier. The Choctaw, as well as their creditors, he added, were still anxious to sell those lands.

Subsequent ratification of the treaty and appropriation of funds for the purchase seemed to assure payment of the Choctaw debt to the company. Yet despite the imminent settlement of the debt, all did not go smoothly. In late February 1808, John Graham notified his acquaintance, Simpson, that the secretary of war intended to see that the company received drafts on the U.S. Treasury for the amount authorized by the chiefs (but not to exceed $48,000). Although Dinsmoor himself was temporarily out of the country, his agency was to notify the company when to attend the confer-

---

27. Forbes to Dearborn, February 7, 1807, *ASP IA*, 1:751.
28. Cox, *West Florida*, 152–324 passim; Cotterill, "Panton, Leslie," 289; Hatfield, *William Claiborne*, 237–58.

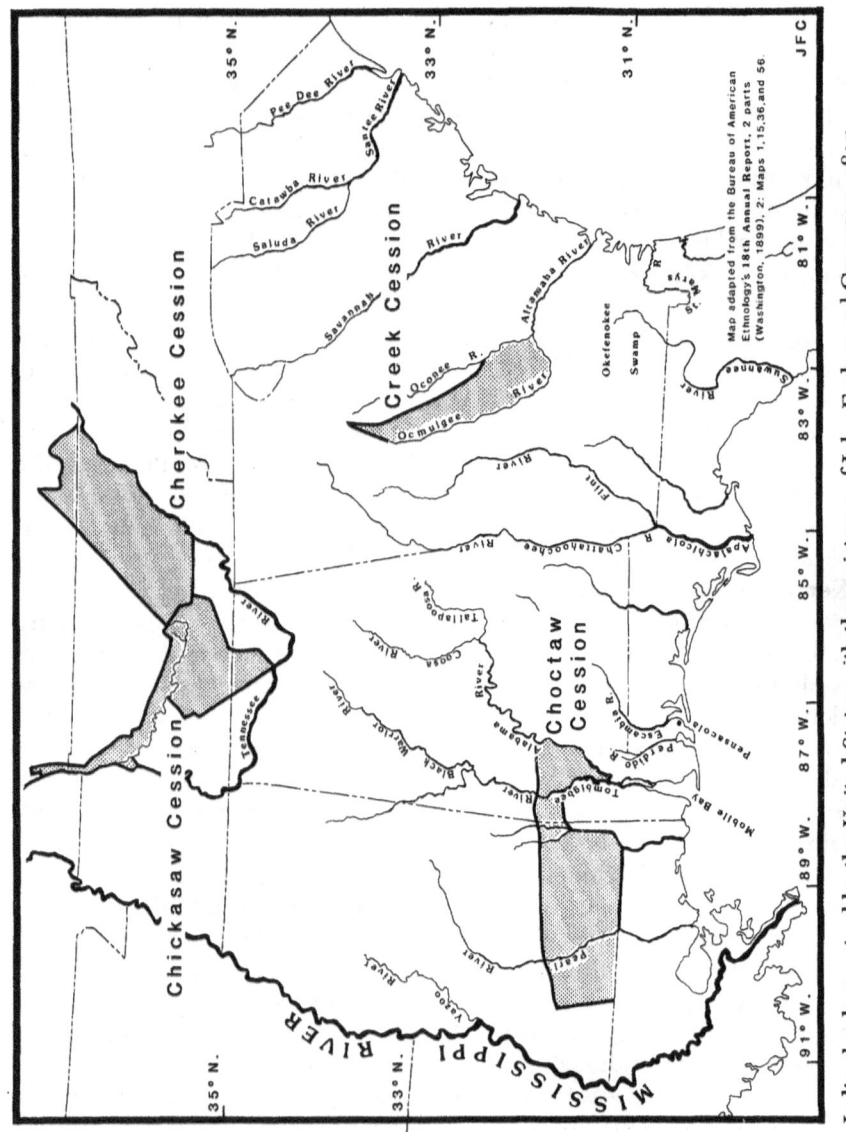

Indian lands acquired by the United States with the assistance of John Forbes and Company, 1805

Table 7. Indian land cessions to the United States influenced by John Forbes and Company[a]

Nation	Year of cession	No. acres sold to U.S.	Amount U.S. paid for land in money, goods, etc.[b]	Amount paid to Forbes & Co. for Indians' debts	Year paid
Choctaw	1805	4,142,720	$108,000	$41,787[d]	1805–9
Chickasaw	1805	345,600[c]	$22,000	$11,178	1805(?)
Cherokee	1805	1,209,600	$44,000	$2,358	1805(?)
Creek (Upper)	1805	2,225,194	$206,000	$21,916	1812–14

a. The number of acres in the Choctaw, Chickasaw, and Cherokee cessions and the sums paid by the United States are from *The New American State Papers: Indian Affairs, General* (Wilmington, Delaware: Scholarly Resources, Inc., 1972), 1:636. The number of acres in the Creek cession was kindly supplied by Marion Hemperley, Surveyor-General's Office, Georgia State Department of Archives and History, Atlanta.
b. Details of the amounts to be paid, such as annuities, payments to individuals, etc., are in Charles J. Kappler, comp. and ed., *Indian Affairs. Laws and Treaties* (Washington: GPO, 1904), 2:79–88. The figures given in Kappler are those contained in the treaties and were the amounts *to be paid*. The figures given in *The New American State Papers* (note a) are the amounts eventually paid.
c. There was some overlap in the Chickasaw-Cherokee land cessions. A portion of the Chickasaw cession was also claimed by the Cherokee. See Charles C. Royce, comp., *Indian Land Cessions in the U.S.*, in J. W. Powell, *Eighteenth Annual Report of the Bureau of American Ethnology* (Washington: GPO, 1899), part 2, pp. 668–69, and appropriate maps.
d. Only the Choctaw treaty specifically called for a certain sum, $48,000, to be set aside to pay debts owed the merchants, etc. (Kappler, *Laws and Treaties*, 2:87). The other nations knew that part of the money received from the sale of the land was to be used to pay their debts to the merchants, i.e., John Forbes & Co.

ence with the Indians. Graham assumed that the company would receive its money at this meeting.[29] But when Simpson appeared at the conference on October 17, he received only $26,000 from Dinsmoor. The Choctaw traders had paid the company $10,325 before the meeting, reducing the overall Choctaw indebtedness from $46,091 to $35,766. Dinsmoor refused to pay the company the remaining $9,765 because the company had already designated $5,462 as "bad" debts, and because of another suit which Forbes had brought against one of the traders in the Virginia courts for a debt of $4,304.

Simpson immediately protested Dinsmoor's arbitrary action. He pointed out that the Indians, after careful scrutiny, had already acknowledged the accuracy of the accounts. Similarly, the company had assigned some debts as "bad" because the persons owing the company had either died or gone broke in the trade and could not pay. Moreover, the principal reason for the company having worked so hard to secure the land cession for the United States, Simpson argued, was to obtain payment of those debts that were considered otherwise unrecoverable. The rest of the indebtedness, he wrote, they could eventually have recovered without ever having left their place of business. Without equivocation, Simpson informed Dinsmoor that the United States could not have obtained the land without the strenuous efforts of the company. Dinsmoor sent Simpson's letter on to Washington, whereupon Dearborn ordered Dinsmoor to pay the "bad" debts. Dinsmoor complied but still refused to pay the remaining $4,304, recovery for which had been filed in Virginia.[30]

The unpaid debt involved a trader, Ben James, and his son George. James had been doing business with the company for some years, but before paying the amount he owed, he had moved to Virginia. Finding that the company could not collect its money from the son who remained behind, Forbes had filed suit against James in the Virginia courts in 1804. In order to avoid payment, however, the father then denied the partnership with his son. By this time, and with the prospect of trouble both in securing the money from the nation and in prosecuting the case against Ben James, the company simply let the suit drop. Meanwhile, the elder James

---

29. President Jefferson to U.S. Senate, January 15, 1808, *ASP IA*, 1:748–49; John Graham to William Simpson, February 24, 1808, *FHQ* 16 (1937): 44.

30. Henry Dearborn to Silas Dinsmoor, May 16, 1808, Letters Sent by the Office of the Secretary of War Relating to Indian Affairs, 1800–1824, Microcopy no. 15, Reel 2:380, NARG 107; John Forbes & Co. to Silas Dinsmoor, Oct. 27, 1808; Dinsmoor to Secretary of War, December 8, 1808, Carter, *Territorial Papers*, 5:675–78; Dinsmoor to Simpson, [April 25, 1809]; Simpson to Secretary of War, October 19, 1810; Dinsmoor to Secretary of War, December 12, 1810, ibid., 6:123–27, 159–60; Secretary of War to Dinsmoor, October 23, 1810, ibid., 6:127–28; Cotterill, "Panton, Leslie," 289–91.

died. But his son did not accept responsibility for the debt. To evade payment of the James debt, Simpson charged, Dinsmoor encouraged another younger son of James, also named Ben, to enter a caveat against federal payment of the money to the company. The property inherited from Ben's father in Virginia, the son claimed, had been attached pending settlement of the case, which suggested that the company would someday be paid.[31] The company tried every avenue to force Dinsmoor to pay the amount held back to cover James's debt, but Dinsmoor persistently refused.

Feeling themselves cheated, John Forbes and James Innerarity filed suit against Dinsmoor in August 1809, in the U.S. District Court in New Orleans, contending that Dinsmoor owed them $4,304 for the James debt. To protect the complainant, the court required Dinsmoor to post $8,000 bail, which cost him $100. When the case failed to be settled because of a technicality, Dinsmoor immediately returned to Mississippi Territory where in retaliation he obtained an attachment against Simpson for $8,100. In December 1809, James Innerarity accused Dinsmoor of having invested the public money entrusted to him in plantations and other speculations. Innerarity claimed that was the reason Dinsmoor did not have the money to pay what he owed. Another suit against Dinsmoor followed in the Louisiana courts, where he was forced to appear for trial. But again a technicality permitted Dinsmoor to evade payment. Unsuccessful in the courts, the company sent William Simpson to Washington to complain directly to Secretary of War William Eustis, Dearborn's successor, about Dinsmoor's refusal to pay the company the James debt, as well as $437 in new debts incurred by the Choctaw. Simpson asked Eustis if it was consistent with the honor and dignity of a U.S. official to attempt to defraud the company by bringing suit in a "petty court in a remote Corner of the Mississippi Territory, where he hoped his personal and official influence might dictate the proceedings." Simpson further asked if it was proper for Dinsmoor to claim that the company actually owed him $8,100, merely because they had filed suit against him for half that sum.

Eustis subsequently presented Dinsmoor with the complaint and asked for an explanation. Dinsmoor replied that he had been justified in not paying the James debt; he repeated his contention that young Ben James's inherited property in Virginia had been attached by the court pending resolution of the case there and that the court had decided on those grounds that the debt was questionable. Subsequently, he explained, the company had unfairly brought suit against him in New Orleans. And since the additional $437 debt, he contended, had been in-

31. Simpson to Secretary of War, October 19, 1810, Carter, *Territorial Papers*, 6:123–26.

curred after the treaty, no funds were available to pay it. Furthermore, "John Forbes & Co. know it," he wrote.[32] In July 1812, James Innerarity complained that the case against Dinsmoor had not been resolved because of the slowness of the courts.[33] Apparently, the settlement of the Choctaw debt ended there, for the records do not reveal whether the company ever collected the James debt.

Difficulties encountered in collecting many Indian debts should have been sufficient reason for the company to stop extending credit to the Indians, but the nature of trade with the Indian nations made such a policy impracticable. This is shown by the brevity of Innerarity's company policy in 1804, which was to refuse further credit to those Indians trading at the Prospect Bluff store. The decision did not remain in effect long; by 1810 the Lower Creek and Seminole were again indebted to the company in the amount of $19,387.4½ reales.

Meeting at Chiskatalofa on April 10, 1810, Edmund Doyle, principal agent of John Forbes and Company on the Apalachicola, and William Hambly, who was both an interpreter and a representative of the company, secured from the Lower Creek and Seminole the cession of three tracts of land contiguous to their 1804 grant to the company. The cessions included the lands on the east side of the tract between the Wakulla and St. Marks rivers, a section on the northwest corner of the original grant, and an area on the southwest corner, including St. Vincent Island (see map). At the same time, the Lower Creek and Seminole ceded to John Forbes personally an island in the Apalachicola River, described as about seven miles long and one or more miles wide, and covering 6,000 to 8,000 acres. (A later survey revealed that this island actually covered 9,811.96 acres.) The Indians had given the island to Forbes in return for important services he had rendered them over the years, and because of the regard he had shown for them since 1785. Being a cautious man, from long dealings with these same Indians, and prompted by rumors that Spain planned to cede the Floridas to the United States, Forbes sent a runner to Big Warrior, requesting that he designate certain chiefs to assist in marking the boundary lines of the new grants. In addition, the company employed Daniel Blue to do the actual survey. The company also took steps to gain the assent to the grants from as many chiefs as possible.

To avoid the problems that earlier beset the company because too few

32. Ibid.; Dinsmoor to Secretary of War, December 12, 1810, ibid., 6:159–60; Secretary of War to Dinsmoor, October 23, 1810, ibid., 6:127–28; *John Forbes & Co. v. Silas Dinsmoor*.

33. James Innerarity to [Mr. Craik], July 11, 1812, GP; published in *FHQ* 10 (1932): 187.

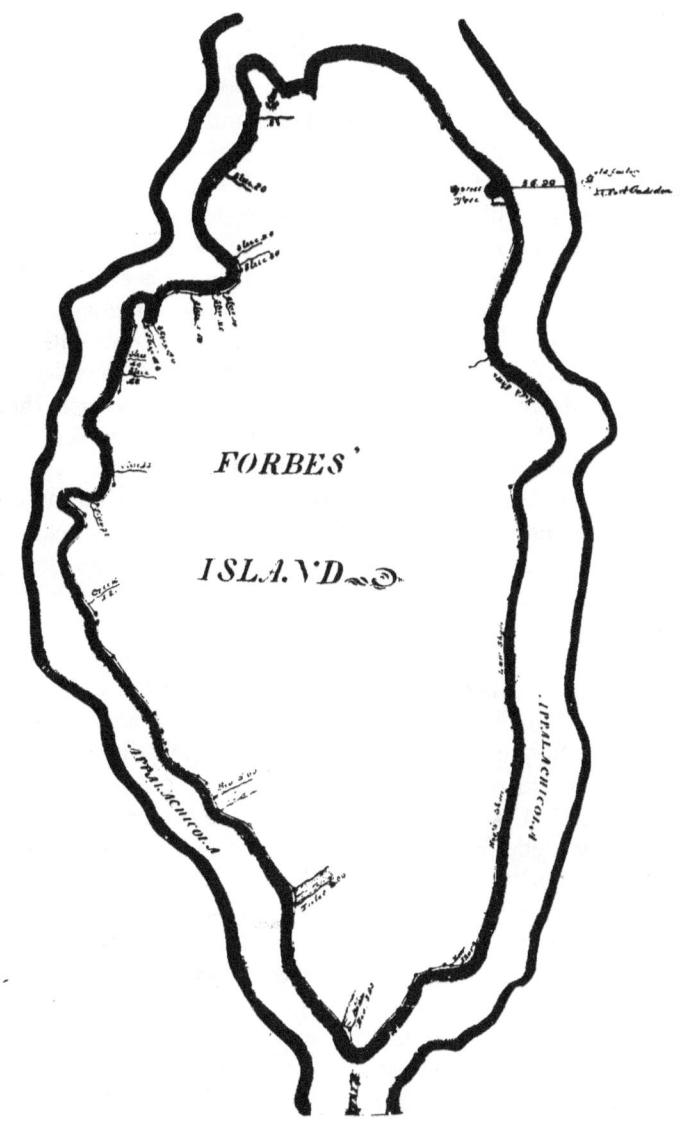

Survey of Forbes Island completed in 1839 by Robert B. Ker. Note "old factory," the Forbes trading post at Prospect Bluff. According to this survey, the island measured 9,811.96 acres. "Forbes' Survey," NARG 49.

chiefs had signed the grant, the company urged chiefs and headmen from many towns to assemble at Prospect Bluff on April 22 and at St. Marks on May 25 to confirm the cession. The records indicate that the cession was made at this time by the Lower Creek and Seminole. Yet Big Warrior, an Upper Creek, clearly was consulted: though he was unable to attend personally, he sent word that he approved the grant. John Innerarity formally applied to Governor Folch of West Florida on June 7 for confirmation of title, which Folch approved on June 15, with the same reservation that applied to the former cession: the land could not be sold or otherwise given away without the express approval of the Spanish government.[34]

The settlement of the Lower Creek and Seminole debts with the additional land cessions left only the Upper Creek debt to be collected. The Upper Creek had contacted Forbes in December 1807 to settle their debt through a land cession to the company, but nothing resulted from that contact. By the summer of 1812, the Upper Creek had made no payment on their account for years. Pursuing the settlement of this debt, John Innerarity finally made arrangements to meet the Upper Creek at Tallassee in October 1812, to work out a solution. After several days during which the chiefs discussed other matters, they invited Innerarity to present his list of debts, which totaled $40,000 including interest, of which $21,915.01½ was principal.

Innerarity had correctly anticipated opposition from the chiefs, who argued that the Florida lands had not been sold by agreement. A few drunken chiefs, they contended, had given it away. Furthermore, they refused to pay any interest on the debt. Referring to their meeting with John Forbes at the Hickory Ground in 1803, the chiefs commented that if Forbes had accepted their offers for payment at that time, no interest would have accumulated. They agreed therefore to pay only the principal, provided the company made certain concessions: the company must continue to trade with them, give them better prices for their skins, and lower the prices on goods they purchased. Innerarity agreed to the demands for lower prices but reminded them that Forbes had forewarned them at the Hickory Ground that the debt would grow larger if not paid. The interest, Innerarity said, was as sacred as the principal.

After much frustrating argument, Innerarity even offered to forgive 50 percent of the interest, but the Indians remained adamant. Trying a different ploy, Innerarity offered to forgive $10,000 of the interest. But again

---

34. All depositions and certificates pertaining to these grants may be found under the following dates: January 22, April 22, May 25, June 8, 15, 1811, copies in MC, Exhibits 1A, PP, and QQ; *ASP PL*, 4:159–69; Cotterill, "Panton, Leslie," 291; Doster, *Creek Indians*, 1:259–65. Forbes later gave Forbes Island to his goddaughter, Marianne Glennie: John Forbes's Will. For survey of Forbes Island in 1839, see "Forbes' Purchase," NARG 200.

Table 8. Summary of debts collected by John Forbes and Company, 1804–14

Nation	When paid	How paid	Amount
Debts incurred before 1803			
1. Seminole (Creek)	1804	Fla. land grant	$ 66,533[a]
2. Chickasaw	?	cash	11,178
3. Choctaw	1808	cash	26,000
4. Choctaw traders	by 1808	cash	10,325
5. Choctaw "bad" debts	1809	cash	5,462
6. Cherokee	?	cash	2,358
7. Upper Creek	1812–14	cash	21,916
Total			$143,772
Debts incurred after 1803			
8. Lower Creek–Seminole	1810	Fla. land grant	$ 19,387

Nation	I Debts out- standing, 1803	II Debts paid by 1814	III Unpaid debts, 1814	IV Unaccounted for
Creek	$113,512	$ 88,449 (1, 7)	$18,084[b]	$6,979
Choctaw	46,091	41,787 (3–5)	4,304[c]	
Chickasaw	11,178	11,178 (2)		
Cherokee	2,358	2,358 (6)		
Subtotal	$173,139	$143,772	$22,388	$6,979
Lower Creek–Seminole	19,387	19,387 (8)		
Total	$192,526	$163,159	$22,388	$6,979

Total cols. II–IV: $192,526

a. Reales not included.
b. Interest on Upper Creek debt canceled by John Innerarity.
c. James debt in courts (outcome unknown).

the chiefs refused and made plans to end the meeting. Left with no other alternative, Innerarity finally agreed to forgo all interest, depending upon how the debt was to be paid. When the Indians said the debt would take two or three years to pay, Innerarity objected but reluctantly accepted the offer.

The chiefs then signed an agreement authorizing a $5,000 draft against their current annuity and two subsequent drafts for the balance, to be paid on November 1, 1813, and November 1, 1814. At long last, an agreement had been reached for the payment of the Upper Creek debt.[35]

35. John Forbes and Company to Governor General, December 9, 1807, copy in MC, Exhibit 21V; John Innerarity, "The Creek Nation, Debtor to John Forbes & Co., Successors to Panton, Leslie & Co.: A Journal of John Innerarity, 1812," *FHQ* 9 (1930): 67–89; Doster,

Thus, by November 1812, nearly all of the outstanding Indian debts had been collected or arrangements completed for their payment.[36] The Lower Creek and Seminole debts had been canceled by land cessions in West Florida. Although the records do not reveal when or how, the Cherokee and Chickasaw debts had also been paid. Only that portion of the Choctaw debt that Dinsmoor had refused to recognize—the James debt of $4,304—remained unpaid. Ultimately, only $6,979 of the entire Indian debt of $192,526 remained unaccounted for.

In the long and often strained attempts to collect its debts, the company's relations with the Indian nations had suffered badly. Disagreements over the amount of the debts, haggling over the payment of interest, bickering about the location of the land to be sold or traded, the prices charged for trade goods, or the value of skins, and arguing over the establishment of government trading factories had all contributed to disaffection between John Forbes and Company and its customers. As the War of 1812 and the Creek War spilled over into the Floridas, the company faced difficult times.

Creek Indians, 1:260; Cotterill, "Panton, Leslie," 291. Many miscellaneous expenses of the company in securing the Apalachicola lands may be found in the account, "1807–1817 Apalachicola Land Purchase," FP, MPL.

36. Several authors have alluded to an indebtedness of $200,000 by the Spanish government to the company for Indian supplies furnished to Spanish officials in the Floridas. Evidence for this is found in a letter from James Seagrove to the Secretary of War, St. Marys, September 8, 1792, *ASP IA*, 1:310–11. Although the company did occasionally advance supplies and money on credit to local officers, no documentation has yet been found to substantiate a $200,000 debt. In fact, the amount of money owed to the company for such supplies was usually not more than a few thousand dollars.

13

The Company and the War of 1812

*T*HE location of Forbes's trading posts, in neutral Spanish territory throughout East and West Florida, should have prevented the company from becoming involved in the war, but flagrant violations of Spanish neutrality by the United States, Great Britain, and the Indians brought the war to the doorsteps of these stores.

In March 1812, for example, three months before its declaration of war against Great Britain, U.S. forces occupied Amelia Island and other sites in Spanish East Florida. As a pretext for this action, the United States claimed that it wanted to prevent Great Britain from occupying East Florida. Ironically, even though President James Madison soon repudiated the use of U.S. military forces in East Florida as a violation of Spanish sovereignty, troops remained on Amelia Island for more than a year.[1] Their presence, as it turned out, created the first major problem for John Forbes and Company.

While business at St. Augustine had declined over the years, Fernandina, on Amelia Island, had become an attractive and profitable port. Merchants and shippers used Amelia Island when they wanted to avoid

---

1. Patrick, *Florida Fiasco*, 83–127. Governor David B. Mitchell of Georgia commanded the American forces in East Florida during the spring and summer of 1812 and later wrote that U.S. troops were not withdrawn from the Spanish province in expectation of war with Great Britain: D. B. Mitchell to Major General Thomas Pinckney, December 1, 1813, Governors Letter Books 1809–14, pp. 83–84, Georgia State Archives.

273

the restrictions of the Jeffersonian embargo of 1807, or the 1808 prohibition on importation of slaves into the United States, or the Nonintercourse Act of 1809. At a considerable profit to those involved, goods and slaves were smuggled in both directions across the American-Spanish boundary at the nearby St. Marys River. The procedure was quite simple: When the "Moccasin Boys"—the name given to the smugglers—wanted to transport slaves or goods across the border, they spread rumors of an Indian attack to keep people out of the backcountry. If observed from the Georgia side, they simply turned their contraband back across the border into Spanish territory.[2]

With all this profiteering, it was not until 1811 that Forbes established a branch office on Amelia Island. In November of that year, William Lawrence, a long-time associate of the company, petitioned the Spanish government for a lot in Fernandina for the company office and warehouse. The government granted the company a choice lot facing the waterfront.[3] Though little is known about the details of the business under Lawrence's supervision, it is safe to assume that he stored and shipped American cotton and other goods to England, in addition to importing Negroes to be smuggled later into the United States via the "Moccasin Boys." Slaves performed the backbreaking work of loading and unloading the heavy cotton bales and other merchandise handled by Forbes and Company.

Apparently it was the company's involvement with slaves that first made it vulnerable to the war at this island outpost. On July 11, 1812 (about three weeks after the United States formally declared war on Great Britain), the U.S. military commandant on Amelia Island detained the Forbes company slaves on the pretext that John Forbes and Company was a British concern. Forbes applied for the return of the Negroes, but the commandant denied his request.[4]

Surprisingly, no accommodation was made for the return of the slaves during the ensuing months, even with so many company supporters at hand. For, in addition to William Lawrence, several close associates of Forbes lived at Fernandina. Philip R. Yonge, a former clerk, attorney, and one-time head of the St. Augustine branch of the firm, and his family

---

2. Patrick, *Florida Fiasco*, 42–47; Crider, "The Borderland Floridas," 67–68.

3. Lawrence to the Governor, November 20, 1811; Grant no. 115, "Memorials and Titles, Lots in Fernandina; Grants Town Lots 1-116-B, no. 355, 1809–1821," Land Records Section, BSL. The grant was one-half of Lot no. 10 in Block One and was seventeen *varas* in front and seventeen *varas* deep (a *vara* was about 32 inches). Henry Yonge purchased the lot from Forbes, May 8, 1815, ibid., Grant no. 90, May 18, 1815. On Lawrence, see Hartridge, *Letters of Don Juan McQueen*, 47.

4. Sebastián Kindelán to General Thomas Pinckney, April 26, 1813, CP; John Forbes to [Samuel] Craik, December 24, 1813, GP.

were prominent residents of Amelia Island.[5] George J. F. Clarke, Spanish surveyor-general for East Florida, who in 1786, at the age of twelve, had been apprenticed by his mother to Panton, Leslie and Company, also lived there.[6] Yonge and Clarke became spokesmen for the loyalist, or pro-Spanish faction. Captain Abraham Massias, the American officer-in-charge, depended upon their support during the ten months he remained on the island.[7] But all efforts by these men on Forbes's behalf were futile; by April 1813, the slaves were still in American military hands.

Forbes appealed at last to Governor Sebastián Kindelán y Oregón of East Florida to intercede. On his behalf, Kindelán wrote Major General Thomas Pinckney, commander of U.S. forces in East Florida, explaining that Forbes, a long-time resident of the Floridas, conducted his business under the protection of the Spanish crown. The United States, he insisted, had no right to seize the company's Negroes on neutral ground. Kindelán further expressed surprise that it had been done at all. He concluded that Forbes surely had made a mistake, because such an act in Spanish territory might compromise the harmony that existed between Spain and the United States. There was irony in Kindelán's criticism, because for more than a year the United States had occupied Spanish territory in East Florida in spite of every peaceful effort on the part of the governor to get the Americans out of the colony. Perhaps as a subtle retaliation, Kindelán felt obliged to request the return of the Negroes to Forbes and to permit him to claim compensation for the serious injury that he had suffered. Kindelán reminded General Pinckney that such matters had already been settled by the sixth article of the Treaty of San Lorenzo of 1795.[8]

Pinckney replied on May 6 that he had been told the Negroes were

5. On Yonge as attorney for Panton, Leslie and Company in August 1802, see *EF*, leg. 340S2. On Yonge at Amelia Island, see Patrick, *Florida Fiasco*, v, 87, 93–94, 99, 159, 163, 265; as head of the St. Augustine branch, see John Forbes to Rev. William Leslie, April 3, 1805, GP.

6. Hill, "George J. F. Clarke," 209–11. Clarke worked for the company for eleven years, including a seven-year apprenticeship. There is some doubt that he would have defended the company. John Leslie considered him a spy and tattler and got rid of him about 1797. Many years later, referring to Panton, Leslie and Company, Clarke wrote that he had "nothing to be individually grateful to them for, nor have I a hope or a fear connected with them": Clarke to Captain John R. Bell, St. Mary's, East Florida, August 15, 1821, *ASP IA*, 2:415. Robert Leslie did not like Clarke either: Robert Leslie to John Leslie, March 4, 1794, BSC, NYHS.

7. Patrick, *Florida Fiasco*, 163.

8. Kindelán to Pinckney, April 26, 1813, CP. On October 4, 1812, the secretary of war directed General Pinckney to inquire into the detention of Forbes's slaves and to take the proper steps; The results of the investigation do not appear in the records: Secretary of War to Pinckney, October 4, 1812, Records of the Secretary of War, Letters Sent, 1812–13, vol. 7, NARG 107.

the property of an Englishman residing in the Bahamas and that Forbes was intending to take them there at the time they were detained by the United States. He further suggested that when Forbes informed Pinckney that the slaves had been detained, he had not made clear his relationship with the Spanish government. Now that the matter had been cleared up, the general would order the officer on Amelia Island to return the slaves to Forbes's agent there. All this, Pinckney indicated, was in accordance with Article Six of the Treaty of San Lorenzo.[9]

No one knew the meaning of that treaty better than Pinckney, a fact that Kindelán was well aware of. Pinckney personally had negotiated the treaty between the United States and Spain in 1795. Under Article Six, property taken from a citizen of either country, if within the jurisdiction of the other, had to be returned, even if the two countries were at war.[10] Once the governor had established that Forbes was a Spanish subject by residence, Pinckney was forced to honor the treaty provision. In returning the slaves, the United States had treated Forbes far better than he would soon be treated by the British.

Just two days before Kindelán's letter to Pinckney, James Innerarity, now in charge of the company's Mobile business and property, had written Forbes that the United States had taken Mobile from the Spaniards on April 15, 1813. Anticipating such an event, James and his brother, John, had claimed Spanish citizenship by residence, obtaining a decree to that effect from the governor of West Florida at Pensacola. James suggested that Forbes should do likewise, after which, in order to protect the business in Mobile and Pensacola, he asked Forbes to send him a copy of the decree.[11] Though it was some months before he did so, Forbes finally sent Innerarity a copy of the letters written by Kindelán and Pinckney, in which he had been recognized as a Spanish citizen.[12] Thus, at almost the same time that Forbes had resolved his troubles in East Florida, further difficulties were about to begin in West Florida.

Intrigue and filibustering activity in West Florida dated back to the negotiations surrounding the Louisiana Purchase of 1803. Though some U.S. officials argued that West Florida and Mobile were part of the Louisiana Purchase, others disagreed. Some claimed that the purchase included

9. Pinckney to Kindelán, May 6, 1813, *EF*, leg. 110F9. Forbes later lodged a claim against the United States for $23,693 in losses sustained during the East Florida insurrection of 1812–13. In 1836, appraisers of Forbes's property certified that the claim was still pending. Complaint no. 27 in the case of *Thomas Dow et al. v. Venancio Sanchez, administrator of the Estate of John Forbes*. The claim was finally settled in 1838 (see chap. 17).

10. Bemis, *Pinckney's Treaty*, 348.

11. James Innerarity to John Forbes, April 24, 1813, GP.

12. Forbes to James [?] Innerarity, January 12, 1814, GP.

all territory east of the Mississippi to the Perdido River.[13] According to James Monroe, President Thomas Jefferson's envoy-extraordinary, who assisted in the negotiations with France, Mobile was included in the purchase, and he had so informed John Leslie in London in 1803. Leslie quickly advised his partners, therefore, that it might be expedient for some of them to become U.S. citizens in order to protect the company's property in Mobile.[14]

For the next seven years, West Florida was the object of conquest-by-filibuster from the United States. By 1810, the fear that West Florida would fall to the rebels was so real that Governor Vicente Folch offered to permit the United States to annex the disputed area, which would be kept in trust until a treaty between Spain and the United States could resolve the problem. Although James and John Innerarity seemed to be reasonably content with Spanish rule for themselves, the continued unrest was bad for business. Therefore, they thought that Folch's plan should be accepted by the United States.

James forwarded Folch's proposal to the American officials north of Mobile, while William Simpson, then living in New Orleans, attempted to secure support for the plan among U.S. officers there. John Innerarity believed that only intervention by the United States would prevent anarchy and prayed for the success of Simpson's efforts in New Orleans.[15] Folch soon repudiated his offer, but the United States annexed the area anyway, with the proviso that it be subject to later negotiation with Spain.[16] Until General James Wilkinson occupied Mobile in 1813, the United States controlled only that part of West Florida between the Pearl and Mississippi rivers, the area commonly known as the "Florida parishes" or, for a few days, the Republic of West Florida.[17]

Over the years a bond of friendship had grown between Forbes and

---

13. Napier, "Gulf Coast." Napier concluded that for the United States to gain West Florida "would take up to 16 years of both quiet and bellicose diplomacy, attempted bribery, border incursions, guerrilla warfare, establishment of a puppet revolutionary government, the lone star 'Republic of West Florida,' outright invasion, occupation, and a full-scale war to realize Jefferson's ambition" (113).

14. John Leslie to John Forbes, London, September 21, 1803, GP. Thomas Forbes also thought the United States would soon own Mobile, but he believed the United States would be willing to trade Louisiana west of the Mississippi River for the Spanish Floridas east of the river: Thomas Forbes to John Leslie, August 29, 1803, JIP, LSU.

15. Folch to Robert Smith, U.S. Secretary of State, Mobile, December 2, 1810, *ASP FR*, 3:398; John Innerarity to Mr. Sanderson, Pensacola, November 23, 1810, no. 31, Miscellaneous Papers Relating to Civil Commotions in West Florida . . . 1799–1827, West Florida Papers, Reel 5, LC; Cox, *West Florida*, 459–74.

16. "A Proclamation by the President of the United States of America," October 27, 1810, *ASP FR*, 3:397–98.

17. Cox, *West Florida*, 487–529.

Wilkinson, which was reaffirmed just two weeks before Wilkinson took Mobile. Captain James B. Wilkinson, the general's son, wrote James Innerarity on March 30, 1813, expressing regret about the problems Forbes was having with American officials in East Florida in regard to the company's slaves. He asked Innerarity to send his and his father's regards to Forbes, observing that his father had "a most exalted esteem & friendship for him."[18] Thus, General Wilkinson's presence in Mobile might have been to the company's advantage, if only Wilkinson had remained in the city for more than a few days.

On April 24, Innerarity wrote Forbes a letter about conditions in Mobile, in which he outlined anticipated problems with the new authorities but added that he expected no difficulty with the general himself. Innerarity lamented the loss of Wilkinson's power to confer any benefit on the company. Shortly thereafter, in mid-May, Wilkinson departed for New Orleans.[19]

Despite Innerarity's anticipation that the transition in Mobile from Spanish to American control would create problems for the firm, no harmful effect upon the company was noted. In fact, an examination of the records for 1813–14 indicates that the agents of the U.S. army quartermaster in Mobile purchased about one-third of their supplies from the company. For the most part, the items purchased were office supplies and building materials. Lumber, bricks, and tools bought from the company went into the renovation of Fort Charlotte and the construction of other posts, such as Fort Bowyer on Mobile Point. The army also rented warehouse space and several houses for its officers in Mobile from the company.[20] From the Pensacola branch, Captain Wilkinson even ordered a few scarce items, such as fish sauce and mustard, as well as four dozen black silk handkerchiefs. He advised John Innerarity to send the merchandise to him, indicating that he would pay the Mobile store the amount due.[21] Communication between Mobile and Pensacola does not appear to have been seriously hampered by differences between the United States and Spain.

But the American occupation of Mobile did hurt company business through the establishment of a customs office there under Addin Lewis.[22]

18. James B. Wilkinson to James Innerarity, March 30, 1813, HWP.
19. James Innerarity to John Forbes, Mobile, April 24, 1813, GP, James Wilkinson to General John Armstrong, May 15, 1813, Records of the Secretary of War, Letters Received, W-181(7) Inc. NARG 107; Mahon, *War of 1812*, 201–2.
20. U.S. Army Quartermaster Accounts, John Wirt, 1813–14 (Selected), NARG 94; Andrew Jackson to James Innerarity, April 20, 1815, GP.
21. James B. Wilkinson to John Innerarity, May 30, 1813, HWP.
22. Addin Lewis Letter Book, Sterling Library, Yale University.

Lewis opposed importation of Forbes and Company merchandise via the Perdido River or Bon Secour, insisting that the goods must come through Mobile where the duties were to be paid.[23] Of course, with the United States at war with Great Britain, the Mobile branch was not at liberty to violate U.S. prohibitions on trade with that country. Before the war, most of the Mobile store's goods had come from England. But with the Pensacola branch still under Spanish control and free to trade with the British, the worst effects of the trade restrictions on the company undoubtedly were avoided. It is known that goods received at Pensacola from British ports were smuggled into Mobile, but the records do not reveal the details. Thus, the imposition of U.S. customs laws and regulations were mostly an inconvenience for business.

A few months after the United States occupied Mobile, John Innerarity learned of the Indians' plan to attack the town, so he advised his brother to bring his family to Pensacola. The warning arrived too late, for the Battle of Burnt Corn Creek, the first battle of the Creek War, was fought on July 27, 1813, not far from Mobile—the same day that John had written his letter of warning to James.[24] The rest of the Creek War may be summed up as the culmination of the frustrations and hatred of some Indians toward the United States. The dissidents became known as "Red Sticks," symbolizing the hostility of this faction of the Creek toward the United States and the settlers who were encroaching upon their lands.[25]

At the outset of the war, in July 1813, Peter McQueen and High Head Jim, noted Red Sticks, with a band of about one hundred tribesmen, arrived in Pensacola and demanded guns, swords, and gunpowder from the Spanish governor, Mateo González Manrique. McQueen brought along a letter, written by an officer in the British forces in Canada to the governor at Pensacola, which the Indians interpreted as a demand that they be supplied with whatever guns and ammunition they required. When González Manrique refused, the Indians threatened the governor, accusing him of having two tongues and two hearts and saying that he was an American, not a Spaniard.

After the refusal of their demands by González Manrique, the Red Sticks turned to John Innerarity, crowding into his house and demanding ammunition and powder. They told Innerarity that there would be war

---

23. Addin Lewis to Messrs. John Forbes & Co., Mobile, June 17, 1814, ibid.

24. John Innerarity to James Innerarity [July 27, 1813], GP; printed in West, "Prelude to the Creek War."

25. Ibid., p. 248; Boyd, "Historic Sites," 260–61. For the origin of the term "Red Sticks," see Owsley, *Struggle for the Gulf Borderlands*, 13–14. Nuzum, *History of Baldwin County*, 58, gives an entirely diffferent origin of the name.

from the Gulf to Canada. Their shaker trembled, grinned horribly, and made convulsive movements, in an attempt to inspire terror in Innerarity, but he, like González Manrique, refused to be intimidated by their threats. Innerarity had discovered their real motives when he made a trip to see those same Indians the year before, to persuade them to settle their debts with the company. At that time, McQueen owed the company more than $700 and Josiah Francis owed more than $900. Innerarity explained in unequivocal terms that he had long expected the debts to be paid in cash. Further, he told the Indians that he was neither a king nor a governor, only a merchant, and that he could not give them presents. When Innerarity finally relented and gave them a few blankets, some tobacco, wampum beads, vermillion, and salt, he apparently aggravated their growing hostility. The trifling presents infuriated the Indians, who threw the vermillion in the sand and the beads in the air and trampled the blankets.

Apparently convinced that they could get no farther with Innerarity, the Indians again turned to the governor, who relented and offered the Red Sticks 1,000 pounds of powder and corresponding shot. At first, the Indians rejected the gift because it was not enough. They made threatening gestures, and only the immediate reaction of the Spanish garrison prevented what might otherwise have been a slaughter of the colonials. Innerarity would certainly have been one of the first objects of the Indians' wrath. But the confrontation passed, and the Indians departed.[26] However, word had reached the Americans, and they intercepted McQueen's party at Burnt Corn Creek. The Indians won that battle, but the Americans managed to capture some of the packhorses carrying the ammunition from Pensacola. The first shots of the Creek War had been fired.[27]

In spite of some successes, the first year of the war did not go well for the Red Sticks and culminated in March 1814, when General Andrew Jackson decisively defeated the Indians at Horseshoe Bend. Afterwards, more than a thousand Red Sticks sought refuge in the swamps of north-

26. West, "Prelude to the Creek War," 249–57. McQueen owed the company $734.1 ½ and Francis owed $905.2 ½: "List of Debts due . . . John Forbes & Co. . . . 1st Novemr. 1812," *FHQ* 9 (July 1930): 86. Paredes and Plante, "Subjugation of the Creek Indians," 140. The shaker was probably High Head Jim: Owsley, *Struggle for the Gulf Borderlands*, 15, 25.

27. As early as May 1813, the *Daily National Intelligencer* had credited "a considerable mercantile house in Pensacola," John Forbes and Company, for having used its influence to keep the Indians at peace and to pursue "those industrious and civilized habits so wisely introduced" by the U.S. government, May 24, 1813, 3:3. Obviously, the company's influence among the Indians had failed to prevent the war. Owsley, *Struggle for the Gulf Borderlands*, 30–33; Sugden, "Southern Indians," 277–79.

west Florida.[28] Anxious about the company's welfare and surrounded by enemies and debtors, John Innerarity had predicted that, should the Seminole join the Red Sticks, the situation would become critical. The company store on Prospect Bluff, which supplied the Lower Creek and Seminole, would be in jeopardy.[29]

The British took the Indians' defeat as an opportunity to enlist their aid as allies in the southern campaign against the United States. In May 1814, two British ships, the *Orpheus* and the *Shelburn*, anchored near the mouth of the Apalachicola River with a considerable supply of guns, ammunition, and other goods for the Indians. George Woodbine, brevet captain of Royal Marines, Sergeant Samuel Smith, and Corporal James Denny went ashore. They intended to assemble as many of the Red Sticks as possible for the proposed conflict. Woodbine established a commissary a half-mile below the Forbes Company store, on the east bank of the Apalachicola, twenty miles or so from the river's mouth.[30] The presence of Woodbine and a large band of hostile Indians so close to the trading post threatened the company employees, William Hambly and Edmund Doyle. At first, Doyle and Hambly willingly cooperated with Woodbine, who appointed Doyle storekeeper in His Majesty's service and employed Hambly as Indian interpreter. Doyle later complained that being forced to leave their own store unattended while working for Woodbine resulted in considerable loss to the company.

In addition to the store, the company had a herd of about 300 cattle at Prospect Bluff. Doyle attempted to send the cattle to Pensacola, out of harm's way; indeed, Hambly rounded up the herd and tried to get it under way, but the otherwise friendly Indian drovers declined to help for fear that the Red Sticks would attack them. Woodbine settled the matter when he refused to permit Hambly to move the herd and even retained it at Prospect Bluff to feed the Indians. The company suffered other losses as well: several horses were taken, and nine or more of the company slaves ran away and placed themselves under Woodbine's protection.

About a month after Woodbine arrived at Prospect Bluff, John Forbes

28. James Innerarity to John Forbes, February 17, 1814, GP; Sugden, "Southern Indians," 278; Owsley, *Struggle for the Gulf Borderlands*, 33–85; Mahon, *War of 1812*, 232–44.
29. John Innerarity to James Innerarity, [July 27, 1813], GP; West, "Creek War," 257.
30. Edmund Doyle to John Innerarity, May 25, 1814, warned of the arrival of the British. James Innerarity feared the consequences to company property on the Apalachicola: James Innerarity to Colonel John McKee, June 16, 1814, copies in Records of the Secretary of War, Letters Received, Unregistered, NARG 107; J. Wheeler to John Innerarity, June 6, 1814, CP; William H. Robertson to Brigadier General Thomas Flournoy, June 17, 1814, *ASP IA*, 1:859; Sugden, "Southern Indians," 281–84; Mahon, *War of 1812*, 341–43; Boyd, "Historic Sites," 266.

purportedly sent a letter to Doyle and Hambly in which he urged them to do everything in their power to prevent the Indians from joining the British, because, to his mind, it was impossible to succeed against the Americans. The Red Sticks intercepted the letter and became infuriated with Forbes. The chiefs sent twenty chosen warriors to St. Augustine either to kill Forbes or to kidnap him and bring him back to the Apalachicola. But Forbes remained safe in the Castillo de San Marcos at St. Augustine. Based on Forbes's letter, the Indians considered Doyle and Hambly to be in the American camp. Hambly was even accused of trying to enlist the Indians on the side of the United States. In retaliation, Doyle reported to John Innerarity that Woodbine would not let them drive their cattle to Pensacola.[31]

The Forbes letter played a significant part in the hostile attitude adopted by the Indians and some of the British officers toward John Forbes and Company. Did Forbes actually write such a letter? The British claimed that he did, and the Indians seemed convinced of it. But the only copy of the letter was lost.[32] Forbes himself never commented on it one way or the other. Doyle steadfastly accused Woodbine of having invented the letter to alienate the Indians from the company.[33] Yet the reasoning behind such an act is not immediately clear. The only logical explanation is that the Red Sticks had earlier convinced Woodbine they had been defeated by the Americans because Forbes and Company had refused to provide them with guns and powder. If that were not enough, word had reached Woodbine that ammunition and clothing delivered by the British to Innerarity in Pensacola, and intended for the Indians, had been purposely detained by Innerarity. In fact, Innerarity supposedly had hidden the supplies to keep their existence secret from the Indians.

Whether Woodbine was responsible for the letter or not, it accomplished its purpose. The Indians denounced the company, ultimately annulled the huge land cessions made to Forbes, and warned all company employees never again to set foot on their land. Doyle appealed to In-

---

31. James Innerarity to John Innerarity, June 24, 1814; Edmund Doyle to John Innerarity, July 4, 16, 22, 1814, GP; Doyle to Captain R. C. Spencer and Robert Gamble, April 6, 1815, FP, MPL; Doyle to [John Forbes], [April, 1816], *FHQ* 17 (January 1939): 238–42; Edward Nicolls to Sir Alexander I. Cochrane, undated [but ca. March 1816], WO 1/144:72–73, PROL.

32. Nicolls to Cochrane, ibid.

33. Edmund Doyle to [John Forbes], [April 1816?], *FHQ* 17 (January 1939): 238–42. In spite of Doyle's suspicions, Forbes probably did write the letter. Just a few months earlier, Forbes had expressed similar sentiments, saying that it was in the Indians' own best interests to maintain a strict neutrality: John Forbes to [?], Nassau, January 1, 1814, IHP.

nerarity to send something to "the Bluff" to appease the Indians because he feared for his life and Hambly's.³⁴

Woodbine traveled to Pensacola, arriving there on July 28, to determine for himself whether Innerarity was preventing supplies from being shipped to the Apalachicola.³⁵ There is no record of the meeting between Woodbine and Innerarity in Pensacola. Subsequent events, however, make it abundantly clear that Innerarity did not explain the matter to Woodbine's satisfaction, for on August 24, while Woodbine was still there, brevet Lieutenant Colonel Edward Nicolls of the Royal Marines and a detachment of officers and men reached Pensacola.³⁶

British strategy in the Floridas and Louisiana called specifically for Nicolls to gather and train the Red Sticks and as many American Negro slaves as would join the British cause. As enticement, the British promised the Negroes freedom, land, and transportation to one of the British colonies. Those who desired could join a West Indian regiment to fight the Americans. It was hoped that constant harassment by both the Indians and the newly enfranchised Negroes would encourage fear of an attack from the Floridas, forcing the United States to keep an army on the Florida frontier. American reinforcements for the Canadian campaign would be tied up in the South.

With the assistance of a large body of Indian and Negro auxiliaries, the British further planned to capture Mobile and New Orleans. To accomplish their objectives, they first had to capture Fort Bowyer on Mobile Point, which controlled access to Mobile Bay, in order to cut sea communications between the two cities. Nicolls hoped that the use of Pensacola as a base of operations would draw the U.S. Army out of Mobile and keep it engaged east of the Perdido while the British forces attacked Mobile.³⁷

After Mobile's proposed capture, and with as many additional Indians and slaves as they could gather, the British planned to march overland to Baton Rouge. There, they could prevent reinforcements and supplies

34. Edmund Doyle to John Innerarity, July 16, 1814, GP; "Chiefs of the Muscogee Nation . . . to our good Father King George," March 10, 1815, WO 1/143:65–66, PROL. The annulment of the land grants by the Indians did not affect the company's ownership of the land, which was subsequently sold to Colin Mitchel and Associates.

35. Doyle to John Innerarity, July 22, 1814, GP; Sugden, "Southern Indians," 287.

36. Sugden, ibid.; Mahon, *War of 1812*, 345–47. Mahon says, "Nicolls, 3 other officers, a surgeon, 11 non-commissioned officers, and 97 enlisted men landed and occupied Fort San Miguel." On August 30, 1814, Nicolls reported 139 officers, noncoms, and men, and 500 armed Indians with him in Pensacola: "Field Return of the Forces under the Command of Lieutenant Colonel Nicolls," August 30, 1814, *AGI PC*, leg. 221B.

37. Proclamations of Sir Alexander Cochrane, Bermuda, April 2, July 1, 1814, WO 1/143:31, 70; Memorial of the Services of Major Edward Nicolls, May 5, 1817, WO 1/144:196–97, PROL.

from reaching New Orleans from the north via the Mississippi River. With a British fleet blockading the entrance to Lakes Borgne and Pontchartrain to the east and denying access to the Mississippi River to the south, New Orleans would be effectively isolated. Realizing the danger of this strategy, General Andrew Jackson warned constantly that if the British successfully carried out their plans, New Orleans and the entire countryside would be easily conquered. Prize money was the incentive, as it had been in all amphibious operations recommended by the Royal Navy for the past two centuries; this time, New Orleans was the ultimate objective. The British expected to seize an estimated £4 million in commodities, including cotton, sugar, tobacco, hemp, lead, and ships.

But the consequences of a British victory on the Gulf coast would be more far-reaching than simply the winning of prize money. The United States already had annexed all of Spanish West Florida between the Perdido and Mississippi rivers under the pretext that it was included in the Louisiana Purchase of 1803. Since Great Britain and Spain were allies, the British were not expected to restore any of their conquests in West Florida to the United States but would return them instead to Spanish control. In a geographical sense, the fate of the Gulf coast was at stake, and Fort Bowyer on Mobile Point was the key to the British plans. If Fort Bowyer fell, the history of Fort Charlotte at Mobile indicated that it could not offer much opposition to an invading army. In fact, the vulnerability of the fort had forced the British to surrender it to the Spaniards in 1780, after only a brief bombardment. The Spaniards, similarly, had given it up to the United States in 1813 without a fight. Colonel Nicolls had received assurances in Nassau that John Forbes and Company would furnish many of the supplies needed for the Gulf coast compaign. After Nicolls reached Pensacola, John Innerarity promised to cooperate. But promises were all Nicolls ever received.[38]

As preparations for the attack on Fort Bowyer progressed, Nicolls virtually took over control of Pensacola from his Spanish hosts. He permitted no one to enter or leave the city without his authorization. He enforced this restriction with 500 Indians, who maintained a constant watch around Pensacola. As the day for the attack on Fort Bowyer neared, Nicolls confided his plans to Governor González Manrique, who shortly revealed

---

38. Nicolls to Cochrane, [ca. March, 1816], WO 1/144:72–73, PROL. Nicolls blamed the company's failure to cooperate on James Innerarity, who, Nicolls alleged, was mayor of Mobile and a colonel in the Mobile militia that had driven the British from Pensacola. The Mobile town commissioners elected James Innerarity their president on March 15, 1814, but there is no evidence to substantiate the charge that he was a member of the Mobile militia: Hamilton, *Colonial Mobile*, 388. He was not at Pensacola with General Jackson in November 1814. See also Coker, "Last Battle," 46–48.

them to his confessor, Father James Coleman. Coleman lost no time in relaying the information to Innerarity.

At this point, Innerarity feared for the safety of company property at Bon Secour, not far from Mobile Point, and the extensive company interests at Mobile managed by his brother, James. Innerarity also resented the treatment accorded company employees and property at Prospect Bluff earlier in the year by Captain Woodbine. Therefore, when Innerarity received the information from Father Coleman, he sent a rider named McVoy (in the style of Paul Revere) to warn Major William Lawrence, the commander at Fort Bowyer, that the British were coming. Nicolls soon discovered what Innerarity had done and quickly ordered several marines and a number of Indians, undoubtedly led by Captain Woodbine, to give chase. McVoy abandoned his horse in the swamps yet managed to reach Fort Bowyer ahead of his pursuers.

Despite the knowledge that their plans had been betrayed, the British decided to attack the fort anyway. The Indians, with Woodbine and some of the marines, marched overland to Mobile Point—crossing Spanish territory in serious violation of Spanish neutrality.

After he arrived at Mobile Point, Nicolls took full command of the land force and kept it until illness forced him back aboard ship. Command of the Royal Marines then fell to Captain Robert Henry, while Woodbine remained in charge of the Indians, who may already have been incorporated into the First Battalion, Royal Colonial Marines.

Four British ships bombarded the fort. In the exchange of cannon fire, *Hermes* received several hits, which so disabled her that her captain abandoned her and set her afire. Colonel Nicolls later charged that the loss of the *Hermes*, with its valuable lives, was entirely owing to the treachery of "that villain" Innerarity. Although outnumbered more than four-to-one, the Americans repulsed the British. Nicolls, with his command in disarray, was wounded several times and lost the sight of his right eye in the unsuccessful attack.[39]

On their retreat overland from Mobile Point, the Indians and their British allies sacked the Forbes Company store at Bon Secour, making off with all of the equipment, supplies, cattle, and horses and ten of the company's slaves. Company losses totaled $5,890. Captain Henry, who accom-

---

39. Coker, "Last Battle," 48–53; see Sugden, "Southern Indians," 291–92, for a slightly different version of the attack on Fort Bowyer; Nicolls to Cochrane, [ca. March 1816]; Memorial of the Services of Major Edward Nicolls, May 5, 1817, WO 1/144:72–73, 196–98, PROL; Juan Innerarity to Captain General, October 28, 1814, GP; "Narrative of the Operations of the British in West Florida in 1814/15," in the handwriting of John and James Innerarity [ca. January 1816], CP; Latour, *Historical Memoir*, 30–42. "McVoy" may have been William McVoy: *William McVoy v. J. McDavid*.

panied the land force on its retreat, reported that when he reached Bon Secour on September 17, a Lieutenant Castle and a detachment of Indians already were in possession of the site. Indeed, on September 12, Castle (also spelled "Cassals") and a band of seventy Indians surprised the inhabitants of Bon Secour, plundered the houses and the Forbes store, and took all of the company's slaves. They remained in the area until Henry and Woodbine arrived with their marines and Indians September 17. Henry's party killed two beeves and opened a couple of hogsheads of tobacco and several barrels of flour. When they marched out that afternoon, Henry added, ten black men told him that they belonged to a Mobile merchant and asked to accompany the British to Pensacola. The ten blacks obviously were the property of John Forbes and Company taken by Castle on the twelfth.

Innerarity accused Nicolls of illegally authorizing the pillage, charging that Nicolls knowingly misconstrued all territory west of the Perdido as belonging to the United States. Predictably, Nicolls denied Innerarity's charges as false and slanderous, "every line of which I will make him eat." He wished, Nicolls wrote, that "six times as much damage had been done to him, and his double faced concern," which had defied the British orders of blockade. Hoping to exacerbate the hostility between himself and Innerarity, Nicolls enlisted some Negroes found in U.S. territory—probably Forbes Company slaves—and so informed the Spanish governor. González Manrique also was told that Nicolls was not responsible to the Spanish governor for any acts committed outside Spanish jurisdiction. He added that if Innerarity wanted his property protected, he should keep it out of enemy territory. Nicolls laid the blame for the lost horses and cattle on some Indians who had taken the horses and sold them. Perturbed, Innerarity wrote the captain general in Havana that Nicolls had detained the company's Negroes in Fort San Miguel, in Pensacola. But even after such an appeal, Nicolls still refused to return company property.

After the British returned to Pensacola from Mobile Point, Captain Woodbine and several sergeants began to campaign to attract Negro slaves. They visited the Negroes' cabins, attended meetings, and in every possible way attempted to entice local slaves to join them. To comply, the slaves were required only to go to the fort, day or night, to be welcomed. Innerarity wrote John Forbes that the whole town was upset with Nicolls over this effort to seduce their slaves. Apparently because of his successful endeavors in wooing over more than a hundred Pensacola blacks to the British fort, in obvious violation of Spanish neutrality, Governor González Manrique ordered Woodbine to leave Pensacola.[40]

40. John Innerarity to Captain General of Cuba, October 18, 1814, GP; John Innerarity to John Forbes, November 2, 1814; Mateo González Manrique to Juan Ruiz de Apodaca,

As anticipated, the use of Pensacola as a British base of operations did not escape the notice of General Andrew Jackson at Mobile. Although it was neutral Spanish territory, Jackson intended to take Pensacola by force, thereby ending the problem. As Jackson neared Pensacola, however, rumors spread that he intended to permit his soldiers twenty-four hours of pillaging. Innerarity began moving everything possible, including his family and company records, on board the *Moscow*, a ship anchored in the harbor. He hoped that they would be safe aboard ship from the invading Americans and worked feverishly to accomplish the withdrawal, until he actually heard shots fired.

As Jackson approached, Commodore James Gordon, in charge of the British naval force at Pensacola, decided to abandon the city. The British, accordingly, commandeered many of the town's small craft and gathered the slaves belonging to Pensacola owners on the east side of the bay. Out of about 130 Negroes, twenty-five belonged to the company. They were to rendezvous with seven British armed ships standing by in the harbor. Once the Americans took the town and lowered the Spanish flag, the warships intended to level Pensacola.

Innerarity had been warned that the company's warehouses, which stood prominently on the waterfront, would be one of the main targets for the British guns. Yet though Innerarity complained later that cannonballs whizzed about his ears, the British decided not to destroy the town. Fortunately for him and the citizens of Pensacola, the British ceased bombardment after firing only a few shots. Instead, before leaving the harbor, they blew up the fort and powder magazine at Barrancas, which contained forty-six barrels of gunpowder belonging to the company. They also leveled the village of San Carlos de Barrancas and destroyed the fort on Santa Rosa Island.[41]

Colonel Nicolls and his men, accompanied by the Negroes, headed for

---

October 30, 1814, CP; Edward Nicolls to Matheo Gonzalez [Manrique], October 22, 1814, and a second letter (undated but after 22 October), FP, MPL; Addendum to the *Relación* by José Urcullo, February 28, 1815, signed by Mateo González Manrique, March 4, 1815; González Manrique to R. C. Spencer, March 11, 1815; Captain Robert Henry to Nicolls, Pensacola, September 20, 1814, Sir Alexander Cochrane Papers, MS 2328, NLS; Lackey, *Frontier Claims*, 25–28, 42–44; Owsley, *Struggle for the Gulf Borderlands*, 115–16; Sugden, "Southern Indians," 293–94. For more details on the problems at Bon Secour and the capture of William Ellis, U.S. customhouse officer there, see *Niles Weekly Register* 7 (1815, Supplement): 165–67.

41. On November 2, Nicolls warned the Spanish governor that if he did not turn over the fort and all Spanish soldiers to him to help defend Pensacola against Jackson's army, he would take his British soldiers and Indians and leave Pensacola to defend itself. Nicolls to Mateo González Manrique, November 2, 1814, AGI PC, leg. 221A. The Spaniards refused to forgo their neutrality by siding with the British, and the British abandoned Pensacola. John Innerarity to James Innerarity, Pensacola, November 10, 1814, GP; John Innerarity to John Forbes, Pensacola, May 22, 1815, FP, MPL; Andrew Jackson to Governor of Tennessee,

their rendezvous on Prospect Bluff. Soon after Nicolls reached the Bluff, he again pressed Doyle and Hambly into service.[42]

After the British withdrawal, Jackson did not tarry long in Pensacola. When he left, he mistakenly took one of John Innerarity's horses, thinking it had belonged to Colonel Nicolls. When Innerarity objected, he was told that since the general was already on the march, he would either return the horse or pay Innerarity $200 for it. Despite the "horse incident," General Jackson's engineer, Major A. Lacarrière Latour, claimed that the Americans had treated the Spaniards in Pensacola better than the British had treated them.[43]

With the British aggression over, John Innerarity soon wrote to his brother about the losses wrought at Bon Secour and Pensacola, which included a forty-five-foot pirogue, a smaller boat, and some sails, tackle and other stores, all valued at 665 pesos. He set the value of the ten Negroes from Bon Secour and the twenty-five from Pensacola at $25,900. All was not lost, however, because he had just received a shipment from Kingston with thirty casks of the best rum and a cargo of dry goods. If the customs collector at Mobile would permit it, and if they could somehow avoid the British blockade, John could supply the Mobile store with all of its wants.[44]

Nicolls's actions so angered James Innerarity that he wrote John, "Time was when the name Englishman was honorable, now it is synonymous with, nay it is a term to designate a man capable of everything that is low, vile, base, villanous, atrocious."[45] But James did not allow his anger to obscure his keen Scottish sense of business. He advised John that if his wife's Negro, Smart, was among those taken, the Pensacola store must pay for him. James said he would not have taken $1,000 for the Negro.[46]

November 14, 1814, Correspondence of West Florida, Series no. 881, NARG 59. According to the surveyor-general of West Florida, the British destroyed the "Military Post of Barrancas" and the "Fort of Santa Rosa" on the evening of 7 and the morning of 8 November, 1814: "*Plano de la Bahía de Panzacola y sus inmediaciones*," by Vicente Sebastián Pintado, Pintado Papers, LC; Sugden, "Southern Indians," 295–96; Pott, *Statement of Facts*, 4. See also Coker, "The Village on the Red Cliffs," 25.

42. Perhaps earlier, but possibly at this time, Nicolls appointed Hambly a first lieutenant in His Majesty's service, as head interpreter: Nicolls to Baker, British Chargé d'Affaires in Washington, June 12, 1815, WO 1/143:75, PROL.

43. Jackson arrived at Pensacola on November 6 and departed on November 9, 1814: John Innerarity to James Innerarity, November 29, 1814, *FHQ* 9 (January 1931): 130–33; Latour, *Historical Memoir*, 49. For a brief overview of the campaign against Pensacola, see Jackson to Governor of Tennessee, November 14, 1814, Correspondence Regarding West Florida, Series no. 881, NARG 59; Sugden, "Southern Indians," 296–97.

44. John Innerarity to James Innerarity, ibid.; "The War of 1812 . . . Some Florida Episodes," 330–31. The Forbes Company's losses at Bon Secour were carefully detailed in an addendum to the *Relación* of José Urcullo, February 28, 1815, signed by Mateo González Manrique, March 4, 1815, Cochrane Papers, MS 2328, folios 177–78, NLS.

45. James Innerarity to John Innerarity, Mobile, November 18, 1814, GP.

46. Ibid. James clearly refers to the Negro slave as "Smart," but he probably was really

The loss of their slaves and property to Colonel Nicolls so greatly upset the residents of Pensacola that they empowered a delegation to inquire about restitution. John Innerarity was a member of the delegation that called upon Vice Admiral Sir Alexander Cochrane, whose flagship, the *Tonnant*, had anchored near Pensacola in early December 1814. The delegation complained about the losses, asked for the restoration of their property, and remonstrated against Colonel Nicolls's conduct.

Luckily, Cochrane was in a good mood, filled with expectations of victory at New Orleans. While Innerarity dined with him that evening, the Admiral expressed surprise that Nicolls had taken the Pensacola Negroes. Nicolls's instructions, he recalled, were to enlist American Negroes, not those of its allies in Spanish territory. Cochrane promised that the slaves would be returned and gave Innerarity a letter ordering Colonel Nicolls to restore the Negroes taken from Pensacola residents. This favorable reception and resolution of the problem by the admiral greatly pleased Innerarity.[47]

Following the directions in Cochrane's letter, Governor González Manrique dispatched Lieutenant José Urcullo and several ships to Apalachicola to secure the Negroes. Innerarity sent William McPherson, an employee of Forbes and Company, with Urcullo. When the party reached the recently constructed British fort on Prospect Bluff, they learned that Colonel Nicolls was en route to join the fleet for the British attack on New Orleans. Captain Woodbine was also absent, having been ordered by Nicolls to go to East Florida to make contact with Admiral Sir George Cockburn, who was on station off the Georgia coast. In his place, Nicolls had left Captain Robert Henry in charge at the fort. With Nicolls gone, Captain Henry refused to do more than authorize the return of any Negroes who would go voluntarily. At the end of six weeks, the party returned to Pensacola with only four women slaves who belonged to the company.[48]

Governor González Manrique then dispatched Captain Vicente Se-

---

referring to a slave named "Sandy." In 1815, James filed a claim against the United States and valued Sandy at $600: Lackey, *Frontier Claims*, 42.

47. "Narrative of the Operations of the British in West Florida 1814/1815" [ca. January 1816], CP; John Innerarity to John Forbes, May 22, 1815, contains a summary of Innerarity's actions, Jackson's invasion of Pensacola, and subsequent British activities to the date of the letter: Mateo González Manrique to Admiral Cochrane, December 5, 1814; Admiral Cochrane to Nicolls, December 5, 1814, FP, MPL.

48. González Manrique to Nicolls, December 17, 1814; González Manrique to José Urcullo, December 17, 1814; José Urcullo to Mateo González Manrique, December 30, 1814, Janaury 23, 1815; John Innerarity to John Forbes, May 22, 1815, FP, MPL; Robert Henry to José Urcullo, January 8, 1815; Robert Henry to Governor of Pensacola, January 12, 1815, CP; *Relación* by José Urcullo, February 28, 1815, Cochrane Papers, MS 2328, folios 172–78, NLS. Sugden, "Southern Indians," 297, indicates that a "Lt. Christie" [Robert Chrystie Ambrister?] of the Royal Artillery supervised completion of the fort on the Apalachicola and built another at the juncture of the Chattahoochee and Flint rivers.

bastián Pintado, surveyor general of West Florida, to see Admiral Cochrane about the return of the slaves. Pintado also officially sought release for the Spanish garrison composed of black troops, who were reported to be in a state of misery, without shoes or clothing, after the British had taken them from Barranacas to Apalachicola. Pintado arrived at a bad time, however. The unsuccessful battle of New Orleans was over, and defeat and disappointment had changed the admiral's mood. Cochrane told Pintado that he could do nothing about the slaves, who were at that time among the Indians. If the Spanish government or the company wanted to recover the slaves, they would have to apply to the Indian chiefs for their restoration. Cochrane did, however, order a troop ship to Apalachicola to retrieve the Spanish Negro soldiers and to return them to Pensacola, but it arrived after the soldiers had already departed. At sunrise on April 26, 1815, fifty-six of these soldiers reached Pensacola, having walked from Apalachicola without proper clothing or arms. Meanwhile, somewhat softened in temper, Admiral Cochrane had sent Captain Richard Spencer of the Royal Navy to settle all outstanding accounts at Pensacola and to proceed to the Apalachicola to assist in the return of the slaves.[49]

Spencer opened a temporary office in the Forbes Company house at Pensacola, from which he advertised for and received claims against the British. In the settlement, John Innerarity received $18,000 in specie for supplies furnished from the company stores at Prospect Bluff and Pensacola. Pressing for full recovery, Innerarity even gave Spencer a bill amounting to $2,268 for the cattle killed by the Red Sticks at Prospect Bluff. Spencer told him that the bill could not be paid without a certificate from either Nicolls or Woodbine. In all, Spencer paid the company the total amount due, except for the gunpowder blown up at Barrancas and the Apalachicola cattle. For these acts, Innerarity reported that Captain Spencer had won the gratitude of Pensacola citizens. With accounts now settled at Pensacola, Spencer undertook his mission to the Apalachicola, with the thought that he could induce Innerarity's slaves to return because of their mild treatment from the company. Innerarity again sent McPherson to accompany the party and to act as company representative.[50]

49. Mateo González Manrique to Admiral Cochrane, January 25, 1815; Cochrane to González Manrique, February 10, 1815; González Manrique to Admirals Cochrane and Pulteney Malcolm, March 9, 1815; Malcolm to González Manrique, March 15, 1815, "Narrative of the Operations of the British in West Florida 1814/1815" [ca. January 1816], CP; Cochrane to Malcolm, February 17, 1815, WO 1/143:15–16, PROL; Citizens of Pensacola to Governor of West Florida, March 8, 1815, Cochrane Papers, MS 2328, NLS; John Innerarity to James Innerarity, May 15, 1815, FP, MPL; Crider, "The Borderland Floridas," 82.

50. John Forbes and Company to the Commissioners for Victualling His Majesty's Navy,

Meanwhile, following the Battle of New Orleans, Admiral Cochrane had ordered Nicolls to return to the fort on the Apalachicola and to gather a force of 3,000 Indians and 300–400 Negroes to continue the war if necessary.[51] So it was that when Spencer and McPherson arrived, Nicolls was once again in command at the Bluff. Nonetheless, Spencer made a genuine effort to persuade the slaves to return to Pensacola. Innerarity later lamented, however, that Nicolls craftily had undermined Spencer's every endeavor, and yet made it appear as though he was offering no obstacle to the Negroes' return. Openly, Nicolls told the Negroes that any who wanted to return could do so, but he gave sly assurances that they would enjoy permanent freedom if they remained with the British. He pledged that land would be available to them in Canada or Trinidad. The colonel further assured the Negroes that their former masters would be reimbursed by the British government for any losses suffered by their failure to return.

Since Nicolls's brevet commission as a lieutenant colonel was based upon the number of men under his command, Innerarity was convinced that Nicolls wanted to keep the Negroes in his colonial regiment so that he could retain his colonelcy. As a result of Nicolls's intervention, Spencer returned to Pensacola with only twelve Negroes, three of whom belonged to the company. Spencer recognized the substantial loss to the slave owners, yet he felt confident that the British government would reimburse them and offered to lend his services to assist in the matter. When asked, Innerarity told Spencer that the value of the slaves taken from Pensacola amounted to £20,000.[52] As the company worked for the return of their slaves from the Apalachicola fort, however, the British moved into the Georgia coastal area, making it even more difficult to recover any losses.

May 2, 1815; John Innerarity to the Commissioners for Victualling His Majesty's Navy, May 6, 1815; Captain R. C. Spencer and Robert Gamble to Messrs. Forbes and Company, May 6, 1815, CP; Statement re victualling by John Innerarity, May 6, 1815; John Innerarity to James Innerarity, May 15, 1815; James Innerarity to John Forbes, May 22, 1815, FP, MPL.

51. Cochrane to Major General John Lambert, February 3, 1815, WO 1/143:23–27, PROL.

52. John Innerarity to James Innerarity, May 15, 1815; John Innerarity to John Forbes, May 22, 1815, FP, MPL. For a good summary of Forbes and Company and the British in West Florida, see Boyd, "Events at Prospect Bluff," *THSA* 3 (1937).

14

The Aftermath of the War of 1812: Slaves and Negro Fort

*I*N January 1815, Admiral Sir George Cockburn occupied Cumberland Island, the southernmost of the Georgia sea islands and no more than a quarter-mile north of Amelia Island, which was Spanish and was the site of Forbes's earlier troubles in East Florida. At that time, Cockburn published Admiral Cochrane's proclamation of December 5, 1814, which was intended to woo slaves away from their American masters with promises of freedom, land, and transportation to new homes, or service in a British colonial regiment.[1] The admiral's unexpected appeal would produce even more problems for John Forbes.

Shortly after the British invaded Georgia, a number of slaves belonging to residents of Amelia Island fled to Cumberland Island. Although previous British proclamations were aimed at enticing American slaves away from their American masters, they appealed to slaves living in Spanish territory as well. Governor Kindelán, at St. Augustine, confronted Admiral Cockburn with hearsay evidence of British officers assisting Negroes to escape their bondage and promising them freedom in exchange for enlistment in His Majesty's service. Kindelán protested this activity, and asked for return of the slaves to their Spanish owners.

Cockburn acknowledged that some slaves from East Florida had taken

---

1. Sebastián Kindelán y Oregón to Rear Admiral George Cockburn, January 31, 1815, WO 1/144:31–32, PROL; Mahon, *War of 1812*, 370–71.

refuge on Cumberland Island but denied that any British officer had assisted in their flight. Cockburn retorted that, in his view, it was the responsibility of the Spaniards to prevent their slaves escaping from Spanish territory. He then authorized the owners to come to Cumberland Island, where they might try to encourage the Negroes' voluntary return. Cockburn, however, stipulated that he would force none of them to leave, nor would he prevent any of them from going. Since the British were in occupation of Cumberland Island, he informed Kindelán, the area would be governed by British law, which did not recognize slavery.[2] Such a policy certainly conflicted with the interests of Forbes, who in February 1815 employed approximately one hundred slaves on his St. Johns River plantation of San Pablo.

Apparently, the news of Cockburn's antislavery stance spread quickly to San Pablo, for on the night of February 23, sixty-two of Forbes's Negroes and four others belonging to Lindsay Tod, the Forbes plantation manager, stole a boat and fled. Anticipating that they were heading for Cumberland Island, Forbes followed, discovering that thirty-four of his slaves and the four belonging to Tod had taken refuge aboard HMS *Terror*. When first approached, the Negroes refused to leave voluntarily. Forbes then appealed to Admiral Cockburn for their return, on the grounds that he had been a resident of the Spanish Floridas for thirty years and was under the protection of the king of Spain. Forbes argued that the detention of the slaves was contrary to Spanish laws affecting property. Cockburn's reply to Forbes was the same as it had been to Kindelán: the slaves themselves must determine whether they wanted to return or not. Cockburn reiterated that he would not permit them to be forcibly taken. Yet he offered to return the stolen boat, provided Forbes could present proper proof of ownership.[3]

Cockburn's letters to Kindelán and Forbes left little doubt that the admiral considered himself on safe legal ground regarding the Negroes. Nevertheless, Cockburn soon requested that his superior, Admiral Cochrane, provide legal precedent for his position. He knew that a precedent existed in the Mediterranean, in which slaves escaping from a hostile shore and taking refuge on a British ship were protected. But Cockburn acknowledged that no legal precedent existed if the country was neutral, as was Spanish East Florida. Although no law was quite pertinent to the

---

2. Kindelán to Cockburn, January 31, February 18, 1815; Cockburn to Kindelán, February 13, 22, 1815, WO 1/144:31, 35–38, 106–7, PROL; John Greeves to John Innerarity, May 5, 1815, CP.

3. John Forbes to Rear Admiral George Cockburn, February 26, 1815; Cockburn to Forbes, February 26, 1815, WO 1/144:45–47, PROL.

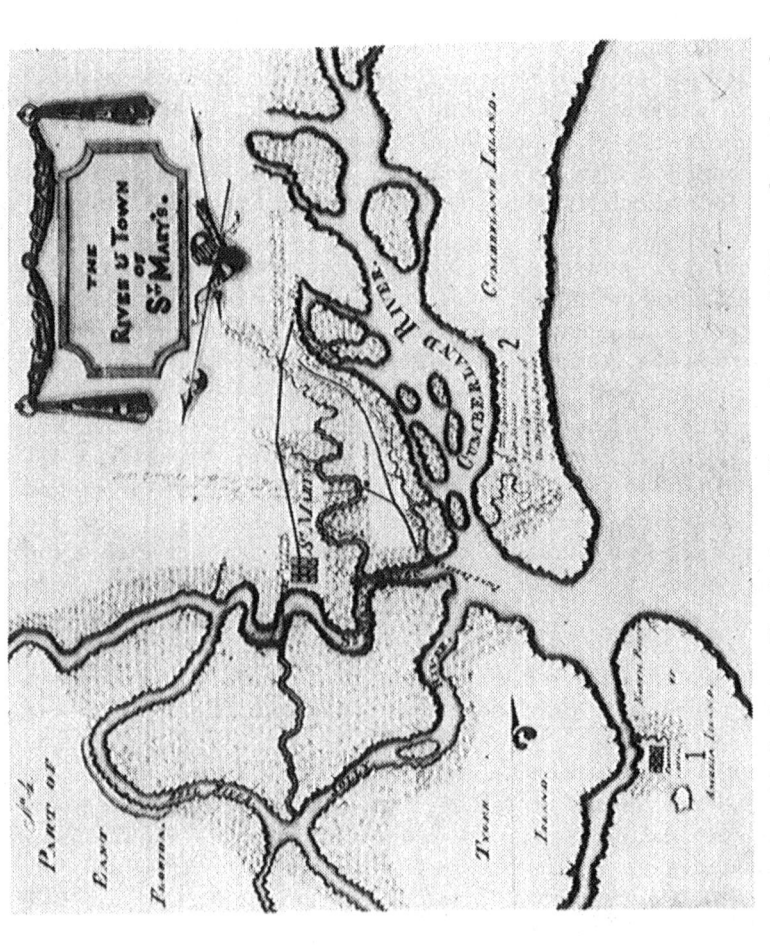

Locations of Forbes's East Florida slave problems, 1812–15. (1) Fernandina, where the United States detained company slaves in 1812–13. (2) Cumberland Island, where the slaves from Forbes's San Pablo plantation fled in February 1815. Plan courtesy Cartographic and Architectural Branch, NARG 77 N35.

matter, Cockburn continued to hold that even those slaves who escaped of their own free will in a friendly port, and reached a British ship, were entitled to protection. Spanish officials argued that such was not the case, as they considered slaves property, and property was to be returned when proof of ownership was presented. If the latter contention proved to be the relevant law, then a decision about the disposition of the slaves would have to be made by a duly authorized court.

Cockburn would not, however, consider the Negroes the absolute property of anyone. Florida itself, the admiral pointed out, had been at one time a haven for escaped slaves, until a treaty between the United States and Spain handled the matter differently. Cockburn genuinely did not believe that he had committed a hostile act, although he accepted Governor Kindelán's conservative view that he had done so. Turning the tables, Cockburn contended that Kindelán had first violated neutrality toward the British, by refusing His Majesty's ships permission to secure both fresh provisions in East Florida and pilots from Amelia Island to guide British ships into port. Moreover, Cockburn purported that shots fired from the Florida shore had killed persons aboard the British ships. Shrewdly, Cockburn had used this vaguely placed incident in his refutation, realizing that Kindelán exercised control only over St. Augustine and Fernandina. American marauders, who called themselves patriots, actually controlled the rest of East Florida. Kindelán was to be given no quarter in this matter as far as the British admiral was concerned. Cockburn concluded his clever defense of his position by reiterating that Cumberland Island, now subject to British law, did not recognize slavery; thus no person could legally be the property of any other person, and the Spanish laws affecting private property were negated. As a temporary protective measure, Cockburn intended to place all the Negroes on one ship while he awaited instructions.[4]

Soon after Cockburn had sent his request for instructions, he received word that the War of 1812 had ended. The question of the Negroes' status was soon settled by Cochrane, who ordered that all the Negroes be sent to the British island of Bermuda to await disposition of their cases. Having been informed of the order, Forbes lost no time in following the Negroes' ship, the *Albion*, to Bermuda, where he identified thirty-six of the Negroes as belonging to him. The rest of his Negroes were, however, not on the *Albion*. After cursory inquiries, he ascertained that some of them had

---

4. Cockburn to Cochrane, February 28, 1815, WO 1/144:23–30, PROL; Kindelán to Fernando de la Puente, January 11, 1815; Kindelán to Pedro Miranda, January 21, 1815; Kindelán to Cristobal Brabo, January 21, 1815, *ASP FR*, 4:488; Crider, "The Borderland Floridas," 121–22.

enlisted in a black regiment and that others had been sent along with American-owned Negroes to Halifax. For all his trouble, Forbes failed to secure the return of his slaves at Bermuda, where, after twelve months aboard another ship, the *Ruby*, the British had put them ashore and had employed them in His Majesty's dockyard.[5] Disappointed at his lack of success, Forbes launched a formal petition through Spanish diplomatic channels and advised his attorney in London, James S. Pott, to begin appeal there, through His Majesty's government.[6]

In reply to Pott's petition for the return of his slaves, Lord Bathurst, secretary of state for war and the colonies, wrote that orders had been sent to Bermuda for any of Forbes's slaves to be given the opportunity voluntarily to return with him. Forbes, however, would first have to put up a bond—plus penalties—that he would not mistreat the slaves, either for their escape or for any crime which they might have committed prior to their escape. By the time Bathurst's instructions arrived at Bermuda, Forbes had already departed, leaving no agent to act for the company. Fulfilling the British commitment, Commodore Andrew Evans, commanding officer at Bermuda, called the slaves before a board of officers and asked them if they wished to return to Forbes and Company. They unanimously refused.[7]

Even before these events took place, Forbes had assumed that the repatriation of his slaves was a lost cause. Naturally, this reversed the question of compensation for losses incurred. Apparently, the British were amenable to restitution. In January 1816, Rear Admiral Edward Griffith asked the new governor of East Florida, José Coppinger, to send him information regarding the number and value of the slaves who had escaped from East Florida during the war. In response, Forbes listed his losses as

---

5. Abstract of Forbes memorial to Governor of East Florida, July 4, 1815, sent by Governor of East Florida to Rear Admiral Edward Griffith, March 6, 1816; Commodore Andrew F. Evans to Mr. John Wilson Croker, Admiralty Office, November 24, 1815; Cochrane to Henry Goulburn, British Undersecretary of State, February 27, 1816; Cockburn to Croker, March 9, 1816; Griffith to Croker, April 11, 1816, WO 1/144:2-3, 19-21, 52, 88-89, 110-13, PROL; Catterall, *Judicial Cases*, 32-33. Some of the Negroes from the Floridas went to Nova Scotia and Trinidad as well as Bermuda: "Memorandum of a Gentleman of Respectability at Bermuda," May 21, 1815, *ASP FR*, 4:552; Pott, *Statement of Facts*, 4.

6. Abstract of Forbes memorial to Governor of East Florida, July 4, 1815, WO 1/144:110-12, PROL; Memorial of James S. Pott on behalf of Messrs. John Forbes and Company to Earl Bathurst, His Majesty's Principal Secretary of State for the Colonial Department, November 22, 1815, WO 1/143:80-81, PROL.

7. Pott to Goulburn, April 19, 1816; John Barrow to Henry Goulburn, May 21, 1816; Griffith to Croker, July 27, August 24, 1816, WO 1/144:84:85, 130, 152-54, 161-62, PROL. Although it did Forbes no good, at one point in the long-drawn-out controversy Lord Bathurst appeared to think that Forbes had a good case for the return of the slaves: [Bathurst] to John Barrow, January 17, 1816, WO 1/144:5-6, PROL.

sixty-two slaves but assigned them no dollar value. Based upon figures submitted by other slaveowners, Forbes's losses, including the loss of his slaves' labor, may be estimated at $30,000 for the East Florida slaves.[8]

In West Florida, the company estimated its losses to be much higher than those in East Florida; they reported at least forty-four slaves lost, including nine or eleven from the trading post at Prospect Bluff, ten from the Bon Secour store, and twenty-five from Pensacola. However, the value of lost labor, cattle, horses, boats, gunpowder, buildings, trade, and expenses incurred on behalf of the local government brought the company's West Florida losses to nearly $100,000. Although the company never assigned a dollar value to its loss of trade at Mobile, U.S. customs laws had doubtless hurt that establishment economically. We know, for example, that John Innerarity offered to supply the Mobile store with all of its wants, provided some way could be found to avoid the British blockade, and provided that permission could be obtained from Addin Lewis, the customs agent at Mobile. James Innerarity later complained that penalties imposed on goods from Pensacola prohibited him from taking advantage of John's offer. Worse, the war had practically eliminated the company's Indian trade, from which great profit had derived during its earlier years. In all, Forbes calculated company losses, because of the war, to be in excess of $100,000.[9] Yet merely determining the amount of the company's losses was not the same as getting an agreement from the British government to pay for them.

Losses in West Florida were significantly different from those in East Florida. No wholesale exodus of West Florida slaves followed the British departure from that province, although Forbes was later to accuse Captain George Woodbine of taking some slaves with him. For the most part, escaped West Florida slaves resided with the Indians, in the Negro villages on the Suwannee River, or at the British fort on the Apalachicola. By contrast, all the East Florida slaves left Cumberland Island on British ships. After Forbes's efforts to secure the return of the East Florida slaves failed, he asked the British government for compensation. Enlisting the aid of the Spanish ambassador in London, Carlos José Gutiérrez de los Tíos, the Count Fernán-Núñez, Forbes persuaded him to endorse the ap-

---

8. Griffith to Governor of East Florida, January 22, 1816; Governor of East Florida to Griffith, March 6, 1816, WO 1/144:179–82, PROL; Great Britain, *Reports of Cases Argued*, 2:448.

9. John Innerarity to James Innerarity, November 29, 1814, *FHQ* 9 (January 1931): 130–33; Juan Forbes to Don Pedro Antonio de Ayala, January 5, 1818, "Testimonio de las diligencias obradas á instancia Don Juan Forbes sobre reclamación de perjuicios del erario el año de 1818," ANC F, leg. 9, no. 7. A translation of this testimony is in MC, Exhibit DD, pp. 431–34.

peal for compensation in a letter written on the company's behalf. Predictably, Lord Bathurst politely informed the Spanish ambassador that the government did not feel compelled to reimburse Forbes, a reply that did not satisfy the count.

In December 1816, pursuing his quest, Count Fernán-Núñez reiterated Spain's demand that Forbes be compensated, blaming the slave losses on Admiral Cockburn's proclamation, which affected not only the slaves of Britain's enemy but those of her Spanish ally as well. The slaves, he contended, had been enticed to escape in boats stolen from their masters by His Majesty's officers. The ambassador concluded that Admiral Cockburn could not be censured for not forcibly returning the slaves but that just compensation was the only reasonable solution.[10] Fernán-Núñez's second appeal, however, had no greater success than the first.

The treatment that Great Britain gave Forbes and the other Florida slaveowners differed markedly from the way it treated American slaveowners. When the Americans first applied for compensation for their slave losses, which seemed to be covered by Article One of the Treaty of Ghent, the British government refused to pay. Interpretation of this article was then referred to the czar of Russia, who ruled that the slaveowners were entitled to compensation. Subsequently, Great Britain paid the American slaveowners but still refused to pay Forbes and the other inhabitants of the Floridas so much as a farthing for their losses.[11]

It is highly improbable that Colonel Nicolls influenced the government's decision not to reimburse Forbes. But after he returned to England, the colonel lost no opportunity to denounce both Forbes and the Innerarity. Before Nicolls left Prospect Bluff, the Indians, at Nicolls's urging, had taken formal action on several important issues. In February 1815, the Creek-Seminole Indians, in full assembly, revoked the land grants to John Forbes and Company for breach of contract. According to Nicolls, who denounced the company as sympathetic to the Americans, the Indians annulled the grants because the company had tried to prevent the alliance between the Indians and the British. A second reason for the Indians' revocation of the grants stemmed from charges that the company was selling land to Americans, in violation of its promises to sell the land only to Englishmen.[12]

More important to the future relations of the Indians with the United

10. Bathurst to Fernán-Núñez, October 19, 1816, WO 1/144:184–86; Fernán-Núñez to Viscount Castlereagh, December 13, 1816, WO 1/144:176–78, PROL.
11. Pott, *Statement of Facts*, 5.
12. Nicolls to Malcolm, February, 1815, Cochrane Papers, ms 2336, NLS; Crider, "The Borderland Floridas," 155; Alexander Arbuthnot to Governor of Havana, undated, *ASP FR*, 4:588–89.

States was Article Nine of the Treaty of Ghent. Nicolls maintained—and so convinced the Indians—that Article Nine of the treaty guaranteed to them the return of all lands taken from them since 1811. Nicolls called the Indians together in a formal ceremony attended by Hambly and Doyle where several chiefs accepted Nicolls's assurances that the land that they were forced to cede to the United States in the Treaty of Fort Jackson in August 1814 would be returned to them. Subsequently, however, the United States refused to accept this interpretation—a denial that set the stage for continued hostilities between the Indians and the Americans.[13]

Colonel Nicolls, Captain Woodbine, and the Red Stick chief Hillis Hadjo, also known as the Prophet Francis, together with his son, an interpreter, and a servant, set out from Prospect Bluff in May 1815. Nicolls left Hambly in charge of affairs on the Apalachicola, and wrote Benjamin Hawkins that he had instructed Hambly to communicate with Hawkins on any point relative to the Creek. Hambly was to do everything in his power to maintain the peace. Nicolls estimated that there were more than 3,500 Indian warriors, with perhaps another 1,800 in the Floridas, who still would rally to the British standard. He wanted to keep the communications and supply lines open with these Indians, so that they could be called upon for assistance against either Spain or the United States. Among other things, Nicolls hoped to be appointed Indian superintendent, which would enable him to share in the profits of the Indian trade and the sale of lands recently reclaimed from Forbes by the Indians.

If Nicolls did not return, the Indians were to realign themselves with the Spaniards and were to offer to recover the Pensacola slaves for their owners. In return, the Spaniards would make a commitment to protect them from the Americans. But the Indians preferred to place their hopes on the British, and instead of turning to the Spaniards they elected to await Nicolls's return.[14]

For his part, Hillis Hadjo went to England to secure a military and commercial alliance with the British which would enable the Indians to carry on the war with the United States until all of their lands had been restored to them. He also carried a memorial to the king which denounced John Forbes and Company and annulled the land cessions to the company.[15]

13. Crider, "The Borderland Floridas," 156–58; Nicolls to Cochrane (ca. March 1816), WO 1/144:72–73; see also WO 1/143:71–72, PROL; Nicolls to Hawkins, April 2, 1815, Bassett, *Correspondence of Andrew Jackson*, 2:208n1; Sugden, "Southern Indians," 303–8.

14. Crider, "The Borderland Floridas," 155–59; Sugden, "Southern Indians," 297–98, 306. See ibid., 298–99 for Nicolls's and Woodbine's attitudes toward the Indians.

15. Muscogee Chiefs to King George, March 10, 1815; Nicolls to Baker, June 12, 1815;

The British government, while sympathetic to the Indians' plight, refused to enter into a formal agreement either to supply or otherwise provide assistance for continuation of the war. Unfortunately, British officials failed to inform the Indians that they could not count upon His Majesty's government for support. Accordingly, the Indians continued to expect large-scale assistance, which never materialized.[16] For several years, however, Nicolls's efforts to secure such help also gave him additional opportunities to rail against Forbes and to lay the blame for all the Indians' misfortunes on the company.

Specifically, Nicolls blamed General Jackson's defeat of the Red Sticks on the treachery of Forbes and Company because it had refused to provide the Indians with ammunition. Nicolls also reiterated the charge that Forbes had written a letter to Hambly and Doyle in June 1814 advising them to do all in their power to prevent the Indians from joining the British. The colonel recalled that he had sent Captain Woodbine to make contact with Admiral Cockburn, who was known to be near Amelia Island. But Forbes had earlier persuaded the Spanish governor not to permit Woodbine to cross Spanish territory to meet Cockburn, on the grounds that it would be a violation of Spanish neutrality. Nicolls had planned to join the admiral with 3,000 men, but Forbes's efforts resulted in the cancellation of the plan. Nicolls complained that though the admiral had plenty to eat, he himself was starving at the same time. Nicolls also took exception to Pott's memorial on behalf of Forbes, which accused Admiral Cockburn of fault in the slaves' escape to Cumberland Island.

Forbes and Company, in one of its memorials to the British government, Nicolls wrote, had attempted to demonstrate its loyalty to the British cause in Florida. If loyalty consisted of betraying the English cause in every possible way, then, he contended, Forbes and Company had indeed been loyal. One British officer, whose name Nicolls did not divulge, called Forbes "a Snake in the Grass" who wanted the Americans to take the Floridas because such an act would make Forbes the richest man in the United States.[17] While Nicolls wrote his caustic reports to the British ministry, Forbes attempted to even the score with Woodbine.

Nicolls to P. Morier, September 29, 1815, WO 1/143:63–66, 68, 75–77; Nicolls to Cochrane (ca. March 1816), WO 1/144:72–73, PROL.

16. Crider, "The Borderland Floridas," 159; Secretary of State to George W. Erving, November 28, 1818, is an excellent overview of the entire affair: *ASP FR*, 4:539–45 (esp. 539–40); Sugden, "Southern Indians," 307–12.

17. Nicolls to Morier, September 29, 1815, WO 1/143:63–64; Nicolls to Cochrane, (ca. March 1816), WO 1/144:72–73, PROL. There is no evidence that Forbes influenced Governor Kindelán's decision to prevent Woodbine from meeting Admiral Cockburn. But Kindelán did warn Woodbine that he could not communicate with the British ships off the coast of

After Governor González Manrique ordered him to leave Pensacola, Woodbine went back to the British fort on the Apalachicola. Nicolls directed him to make contact from there with Admiral Cockburn on Cumberland Island. According to Nicolls, however, Forbes thwarted Woodbine's efforts to do so.

But contacting Admiral Cockburn was only one of the reasons for Woodbine's visit to East Florida. He had brought a number of Indians and Negroes to accompany him on the way to St. Augustine, where, as he told Governor Kindelán, he intended to use them against the American marauders who reportedly were overrunning East Florida. Kindelán, on the other hand, believed the Negroes had been brought to attract Spanish slaves to join the British cause. Woodbine denied any such intention, yet he admitted that he hoped to attract slaves from the United States, including those who had already escaped to East Florida to follow him.

Woodbine soon discovered that he was no more welcome in St. Augustine than he had been in Pensacola. How much credit Forbes deserved for his reception cannot be documented. In any event, Governor Kindelán soon ordered Woodbine to leave East Florida. Shortly thereafter, Woodbine departed with eighty slaves following, much to the distress of the East Floridians.[18] He returned to the Apalachicola, where he remained until he left with Colonel Nicolls. During that period, Woodbine disappeared for several months, and, though his actions cannot be verified, he apparently spent his time trying to recruit Indians and blacks for future operations in the Floridas.[19]

On October 11, 1815, John Forbes and John and James Innerarity brought suit against Woodbine in the Nassau General Court. They charged that Woodbine had slaves valued at £4,000 belonging to the company, which he had converted to his own personal use. Coincidentally, Woodbine arrived in Nassau on the same day, and on October 12 the police magistrate jailed him in lieu of £2,000 security. For several days, Woodbine tried unsuccessfully to regain his freedom. Finally, he managed to contact several persons who had been with him in Florida and to secure affidavits, including one from Robert Chrystie Ambrister, swearing that he had never had any of Forbes's slaves in his possession.

East Florida because it would violate Spanish neutrality: Woodbine to Kindelán, December 30, 1814; Kindelán to Woodbine, December 30, 1814, ASP FR, 4:491–92; EF leg. 198C16.

18. Woodbine to Kindelán, December 30, 1814, EF leg. 198C16; Kindelán to Woodbine referred to in Luis de Onís to Governor of East Florida, February 21, 1815, EF leg. 107C9; Kindelán to Apodaca, January 21, 1815, EF leg. 33G3.

19. Some of the East Florida Negroes who went to the Apalachicola with Woodbine were eventually returned to St. Augustine by Bowlegs, chief of the Seminole towns on the Suwannee River. As an inducement to the Indians, the governor of East Florida offered a

Woodbine then countercharged Forbes with "wilful and corrupt Perjury" in swearing to the affidavit against him. It was now Forbes's turn to put up a recognizance bond, backed by sureties. Charges and countercharges continued to be lodged first by one and then by the other.[20] A. H. Gordon, one of Forbes's associates in Nassau, claimed that he had seen documents proving that Woodbine had stolen Negroes and horses from St. Augustine and that he would be tried at the next court session.

Meanwhile, Woodbine was in Havana, busily "suborning witnesses." Gordon hoped that Forbes could catch Woodbine in Havana and have him tried and hanged there.[21] Although the Nassau court records fail to confirm the victory, John Innerarity wrote his brother: "Independent of how nearly it concerns us, I cannot express to you the glow of pleasure I feel, on Mr. Forbes' account, in his triumph over the hell-bred villany of Woodbine. Tho' nothing could affect the placid calm & serenity of his mind, yet he has need of this consolation."[22] Forbes later complained that the company had suffered great expense in its efforts to prosecute Woodbine, only to see him artfully escape the hands of justice.[23]

Forbes's failure to prosecute Woodbine successfully characterized the bad luck that the company had experienced since the end of the War of 1812. For example, the sequel to events at Prospect Bluff was far from favorable for the company. In August 1815, James Innerarity advised Forbes that the British had left the Negroes at Prospect Bluff in possession of a well-constructed fort, with plenty of provisions, arms, ammunition, and even cannon. Since the departure of the British, it was further reported, the Negroes had organized themselves, acquiring several well-armed vessels and turning to piracy.[24] John Innerarity wanted to reestablish the company store at Prospect Bluff but feared it was impossible until the "hornet's" nest of Negroes there was broken up.[25]

The reason for James's interest in reopening the Apalachicola store was not necessarily for any appreciable profit that the company might anticipate from the Indian trade. In fact, that store had been opened only because it was a condition that the Indians had attached to their earlier land

---

reward of 50 pesos for each adult and 25 pesos for each child returned: Juan José Estrada to Bowlegs, July 5, 1815, *EF* leg. 115K9.

20. Documents pertaining to these cases may be found in WO 1/144:74–82, PROL; General Court Minute Books, 1816–1817, SC/1/24, SC/1/25, SC/1/28, SC/1/29, SC/1/31, PRON.
21. A. H. Gordon to John Forbes, October 24, 1816, CP.
22. John Innerarity to James Innerarity, August 21, 1816, *FHQ* 12 (July 1933): 39.
23. Juan Forbes to Ayala, January 5, 1818, *ANC F*, leg. 9, no. 7.
24. James Innerarity to John Forbes, August 12, 1815, GP; *FHQ* 12 (1934): 128–29.
25. John Innerarity to John Forbes, May 22, 1815, FP, MPL.

grants to the company. From all accounts, the store had proven to be an unprofitable venture. But the recent wars had changed conditions considerably. James expected a large influx of white settlers into the area, who would avail themselves of the lands ceded to the United States in the Treaty of Fort Jackson. Meeting the needs of these new settlers would provide a lucrative business, and James expected the company to get a large share of the trade. He envisioned rapid growth for Mobile and the Apalachicola and Flint River areas, especially if Negro Fort were eliminated. None of the partners seemed concerned about the Indians' revocation of their land grants to the company but rather looked upon it as only a temporary nuisance, if that. As a last resort, the lands could be sold to the Americans, who would settle the land in spite of the Indians, the Negroes, or the English.[26]

Some of the Indians opposed the reopening of Forbes's store on the Apalachicola. Although Forbes was British, to the Indians he was no better than the Americans or the Spanish. They preferred to await Nicolls's return. Even Hambly appeared to oppose reopening the store.[27]

In June 1815, the commandant of Fort San Marcos de Apalache, Francisco Caso y Luengo, sent his commissary, Felipe Prieto, to Prospect Bluff for supplies. When he arrived, Hambly was temporarily absent, so Prieto left empty-handed. Even after Hambly had returned, he still could not satisfy the Spaniards' needs. He sent word to Prieto explaining his orders not to permit Spanish troops at St. Marks any food, since the Spaniards allegedly had permitted the Americans to enter Pensacola without a fight during Jackson's invasion the previous November. Hambly was determined to carry out Nicolls's orders and remained at Negro Fort, as it was now called, throughout the summer and fall of 1815. Doyle also had stayed on at the fort after Nicolls left, but he soon resumed his work for Forbes and Company. Unable to reestablish the store at Prospect Bluff, he went to Pensacola, where he obtained a boatload of supplies and headed for St. Marks.[28]

Doyle arrived at Apalachee aboard the *Henrique*, intending to open a trading post there at least temporarily and even to leave it functioning until he could return to the Apalachicola. This action apparently was

26. James Innerarity to John Forbes, August 12, 1815, *FHQ* 12 (1934): 127, 129.
27. Prieto to Doyle, September 17, 1815, CP; Crider, "The Borderland Floridas," 162–63.
28. Crider, "The Borderland Floridas," 159–61; John Innerarity to John Forbes, May 22, 1815; Prieto to Caso y Luengo, June 17, 1815, FP, MPL. Nicolls thought enough of Hambly's service to the British that he recommended him for a pension of £63.17.6 per annum, the half pay of a lieutenant: Sugden, "Southern Indians," 308.

strongly favored, for even the governor at Pensacola had supported the opening of a store there, hoping it would enable the Spaniards to rebuild friendly relations with the Indians while at the same time counteracting British influence on the Apalachicola. Accordingly, Doyle notified Hambly that he had brought supplies for him and also inquired about recovering the company's slaves known to be at Negro Fort.

Doyle's goals were to remain unrealized. One reason was that the commandant, Caso y Luengo, openly refused him permission to open a store for fear of the Indians' unfavorable reaction. The Spanish fort apparently was in no condition to resist an Indian attack. Also, there was the distinct possibility of an American and Indian attack on Negro Fort to recover the runaway slaves harbored there. Doyle, frightened by the prospect of open conflict all around him and equally fearful of the Indians, had received permission from the Spanish commandant to leave his goods at St. Marks, returning straightaway to Pensacola. Though he had left the goods specifically in Prieto's care, Caso y Luengo refused to allow his subordinate to sell any of the goods to the Indians either within or without the fort.[29] Thus, the company was stymied in its efforts to reopen a store at St. Marks or at Prospect Bluff during that summer and fall.

The first favorable break for the company on the Apalachicola came in September 1815. The escaped slaves at Negro Fort had become little more than brigands and pirates who would attack any ship except those flying a British flag. Hambly continued at least nominally as the officer in charge there until mid-September. But by then he had become convinced that the Negroes did not intend to return to more peaceful pursuits and announced that he wanted nothing more to do with the inhabitants of the fort, whom he termed "a band of rogues." His decision signaled a new cooperative attitude: he was now ready to help Forbes reestablish the company store on the Apalachicola.[30] But not everyone accepted Hambly's shifting loyalties at face value. One person accused him of covering all angles, hoping to be on the winning side no matter who won. Another admitted that he did not understand Hambly's intentions and planned to watch him closely. The only constant part of Hambly's behavior was his continuing correspondence with John Forbes and Company, whether he was employed by the company or not.[31] The company's efforts to reopen the Prospect Bluff store, even with Hambly's assistance, failed during the

29. Crider, "The Borderland Floridas," 160–62; Prieto to Francisco de Arroyo, July 14, 1815, CP.
30. James Innerarity to John Forbes, August 12, 1815, GP; Prieto to Doyle, September 17, 1815, CP.
31. Crider, "The Borderland Floridas," 175; General Edmund P. Gaines to Lieutenant Colonel D. L. Clinch, May 23, 1816, *ASP FR*, 4:558; Silver, *Edmund Pendleton Gaines*, 62.

remainder of 1815 and well into 1816. Negro Fort and its occupants apparently were the greatest deterrent to the company's plans.

By February 1816, Doyle had returned to St. Marks, with the approval of the governor of West Florida and the captain general of Cuba, to reopen the store there. The captain general looked upon this as perhaps the last opportunity to reestablish relations with the Indians as a counterweight to British influence there. Caso y Luengo, under this new policy, had little choice but to permit Doyle to open the trading post. The store may have been located within the fort compound, but if not it was much closer to the fort than the old Panton, Leslie trading post, which had been several miles north of the fort. In addition to opening the store, the governor of West Florida had authorized Doyle and Hambly, either separately or jointly, to meet with the Indians and arrange for the return of the Pensacola slaves.[32]

For a number of reasons, two separate meetings were held. Doyle met with some of the old Red Stick chiefs, including Kinache and Peter McQueen, at St. Marks. The meeting did not go well because of mistrust toward the Americans, who were known to be building a fort at the fork of the Chattahoochee and Flint rivers to protect some fifty American families who had settled on the banks of those rivers, on lands taken from the Creek in the Treaty of Fort Jackson. Consequently, Doyle made no headway in his talks with the Indians, who now viewed the inhabitants of Negro Fort as allies, thus ruling out any possibility of the Red Sticks assisting in the return of the Pensacola slaves.[33]

Hambly met with the Lower Creek at Chiskatalofa on April 17, where two factions were present: the Upper Towns, friendly to the Americans, and the Lower Towns, friendly to the British. Hambly, assisted by an Upper Town chief, The Prince, attempted to unite both factions in an attack on Negro Fort. Even Benjamin Hawkins had told The Prince that Negro Fort should be taken and the slaves returned to their masters. The Lower Town chiefs, however, reacted violently to this suggestion, leaving Hambly and The Prince fortunate to escape from the meeting with their lives. They both fled to Fort Gaines, on the Chattahoochee one hundred miles north of its juncture with the Flint, to the protection of the American soldiers there.[34]

Back in Apalachee, Doyle received the news of Hambly's disastrous

32. José de Soto to Doyle and Hambly, February 20, 1816, CP; Soto to Caso y Luengo, February 18, 1816, *AGI PC*, leg. 147A; Soto to Chiefs, Warriors, and Others of the Seminole Nation, February 17, 1816, IHP.
33. Caso y Luengo to Mauricio de Zúñiga, April 28, 1816, *AGI PC*, leg. 1796; Crider, "The Borderland Floridas," 165–66.
34. Clinch to Gaines, May 9, 1816, correspondence regarding West Florida, Series

meeting with the Indians and of his flight to the Americans. Fearing again for his own life, Doyle quickly packed his belongings and returned to Pensacola. Apparently, Doyle left the St. Marks trading post in the hands of Anastasio Montes de Oca, one of the supply officers at St. Marks. Unlike Prieto before him, Montes de Oca did manage to carry on a little trade with the Indians and the St. Marks garrison after Doyle departed.[35]

The meetings conducted by Doyle and Hambly in April 1816 represented the growing feeling among some elements of the population that Negro Fort must be eliminated. The Americans looked upon the fort as a haven for fugitive slaves and criminals and as a staging area for raids conducted across the border into the United States.[36] Mauricio de Zúñiga, now governor of West Florida, preferred that Spanish troops reduce the fort, both to rid the province of the nuisance it represented and to create an opportunity for the Spaniards to man the fort, thereby controlling American travel up and down the Apalachicola. But he recognized that he did not have the manpower for the job.[37] In fact, when General Andrew Jackson advised Governor Zúñiga in April that Negro Fort must be destroyed, Zúñiga indicated that if the destruction of the fort was of sufficient importance to warrant Jackson's presence, Zúñiga would be proud to serve under him. Zúñiga even suggested the possibility of calling upon Jackson directly for help in reducing the fort, if the captain general of Cuba did not furnish him with the necessary men and equipment to do so.

However, nothing came from this brief exchange. Since an American fort, Camp Crawford (later Fort Scott), was under construction on the west bank of the Flint River, a few miles north of its juncture with the Chattahoochee, General Edmund Gaines made it clear that he planned to destroy Negro Fort, should it offer opposition to the supply boats ascending the river.[38] Moreover, these American and Spanish officers were not alone in their determination to eliminate Negro Fort. John Innerarity also was determined to help to oust the blacks from the fort and to assist in the recovery of the Pensacola slaves. The company had already financed sev-

---

no. 881, NARG 59; General Edmund P. Gaines to Clinch, May 23, 1816, *ASP FR*, 4:558; Crider, "The Borderland Floridas," 167–68. See also Patrick, *Aristocrat in Uniform*, 28.

35. Caso y Luengo to Zúñiga, April 28, 1816, *AGI PC*, leg. 1796; Anastasio Montes de Oca to John Innerarity, December 12, 1816, CP; Crider, "The Borderland Floridas," 165–66, 175.

36. Secretary of State to George W. Erving, November 28, 1818, *ASP FR*, 4:540; Gaines to Commodore Daniel T. Patterson, May 22, 1816, *ASP FR*, 4:558–59.

37. Zúñiga to Apodaca, May 2, 1816, *AGI PC*, leg. 1796.

38. Andrew Jackson to Governor of Pensacola, April 23, 1816; Zúñiga to Jackson, May 26, 1816; Report of Captain Vero Z. Amelung to General Jackson, June 4, 1816; Gaines to Clinch, May 23, 1816, *ASP FR*, 4:555–58; Silver, *Edmund Pendleton Gaines*, 62; Fretwell, *This So Remote Frontier*, 191.

eral expeditions to the Apalachicola, and Innerarity elected to pay the cost of sending another one. Plans were made with several Seminole chiefs, who promised to see that the slaves were returned. Two ships and forty Spanish soldiers, commanded by Captain Benigno García Calderón and accompanied by Doyle, set sail in late July from Pensacola for the mouth of the Apalachicola, where they intended to prevent supplies from reaching Negro Fort from the south. Not only did García Calderón hope to retrieve the Pensacola slaves, but he also hoped to induce the Indians to destroy the fort.[39]

To the north, at Camp Crawford, Lieutenant Colonel Duncan L. Clinch prepared to attack Negro Fort. Clinch and 116 picked men left Camp Crawford on July 17, with Hambly serving as guide. Hambly had thoroughly briefed Colonel Clinch about the fort and the opposition he could expect. Supposedly, Hambly even furnished Clinch with a plan of the fort that included the location of the powder magazine. Since the fort contained no casemate or bombproof vault for the storage and protection of gunpowder, the magazine was the fort's most vulnerable point of attack, and Clinch presumably planned his strategy around Hambly's advice.

As Clinch descended the river, he was joined by a force of 150 friendly Indians led by Chief McIntosh of Coweta, who offered to assist in the capture of the fort. Clinch stopped just north of the fort to await contact with the U.S. Navy. Expected soon was Sailing Master Jairus Loomis, with several supply-laden transports and two gunboats, who was to rendezvous upriver with Clinch.

As he awaited word from Loomis, Clinch conferred with the Indians and completed his plans. When all was in readiness, the Indians surrounded the fort and opened fire on it. The defenders answered with cannon shot but did little more than frighten the Indians. It quickly became apparent that the fort could not be reduced without artillery.

By July 10, Loomis's flotilla had reached the mouth of the Apalachicola. While waiting to make contact with Clinch, Loomis decided to send a small boat with five men to reconnoiter the situation. As they headed upriver, a party of Negroes and Indians together opened fire on the boat, killing three and capturing one of the crew, Edward Daniels. One crewman managed to escape. Soon after this incident, Loomis and Clinch finally established contact, whereupon Loomis continued upriver and by July 25 reached a point four miles south of Negro Fort. Clinch wanted to install a battery of several 18-pound cannon on Forbes Island, across the

---

39. John Innerarity to James Innerarity, August 13, 1816, FP, MPL; Juan Forbes to Ayala, January 5, 1818, ANC F, leg. 9, no. 7; Crider, "The Borderland Floridas," 170–73.

river from the fort. But before the battery could be completed, the gunboats were brought up and anchored within cannon range of the fort.

The fort opened fire on the gunboats but caused no damage. The gunboats responded with cold shot. Finding the fort within easy range, Loomis decided to try heated shot, which they prepared in a makeshift furnace on one of the boats. The red-hot ball fell directly on the exposed powder magazine, and the resulting explosion destroyed the fort and killed nearly everyone within it.[40] Of 100 Negro men, 200 women and children, and 20 Choctaw, Loomis reported 270 killed and many of the others seriously wounded. Of the survivors, three escaped unhurt, and 25 prisoners were taken. Of the wounded left in Hambly's care, all except one woman were not expected to live. In a final retaliatory act, the Negro leader, Garçon, and one of the Choctaw chiefs were scalped and then hanged by friendly Indians, because they had tarred and burned alive the captured seaman, Edward Daniels.[41]

On August 2, as Doyle and the two ships from Pensacola were ascending the Apalachicola river, they encountered the gunboats coming back down and learned that Negro Fort had been destroyed. Doyle requested, but was refused, permission to go on to the fort to round up whatever Negroes he could find and to remove the wounded.[42]

Subsequently, the Negroes and the Red Sticks blamed Hambly for the loss of the fort and its personnel. Although Hambly had guided Clinch's army to the fort, it would be ridiculous to claim that the heated shot that struck the powder magazine was anything but accidental. As long as the gunpowder remained exposed, it was only a matter of time before one of the cannonballs landed on the site. If Hambly deserved any credit for the outcome, it would be merely that he accelerated the process.[43]

40. Clinch to Gaines, May 9, 1816, correspondence regarding West Florida, Series no. 881, NARG 59; Gaines to Clinch, May 23, 1816; Gaines to Patterson, May 22, 1816; Patterson to Crawley, June 19, 1816; Patterson to Loomis, June 19, 1816; Loomis to Patterson, August 13, 1816, ASP FR, 4:558–60; Patrick, Aristocrat in Uniform, 29–32; Doster, Creek Indians, 2:172–73. Alexander Arbuthnot's Journal, ASP FR, 4:609–10, is the most detailed accusation regarding Hambly's part in the affair. Since Arbuthnot wanted to put the blame for all of the Indians' and Negroes' troubles upon Hambly and Doyle, his comments must be interpreted accordingly. Arbuthnot had no firsthand knowledge of the Negro Fort situation and was only repeating what he had heard from the Indians and Negroes.

41. Loomis to Patterson, August 13, 1816, ASP FR, 4:559–60; Captain Benigo García Calderón to Zúñiga, August 8, 1816, AGI PC, leg. 1873. Reports on the number of personnel in the fort vary: Crider, "The Borderland Floridas," 172. Patrick refers to the Negro hanged as "Garcia," Aristocrat in Uniform, 32. See also Silver, Edmund Pendleton Gaines, 63, who states that there were 334 defenders in the fort, of whom 207 were killed instantly, while most of the rest died shortly thereafter.

42. García Calderón to Zúñiga, August 8, 1816, AGI PC, leg. 1873; John Innerarity to James Innerarity, August 13, 1816, FHQ 12 (1933): 37–39.

43. Alexander Arbuthnot's Journal, ASP FR, 4:609–10.

The Aftermath of the War of 1812

The attack on Negro Fort would have been inevitable under any circumstances. Many diverse interests—the United States, Spain, the Upper Town–Lower Creek, and John Forbes and Company—all had declared at one time or another their intent to do away with the fort. American officials, in fact, were extremely satisfied with the elimination of the problem. Governor Zúñiga similarly expressed relief that the menace had been removed at no expense to the Spanish crown. Naturally, however, those Pensacola residents whose slaves had been killed in the explosion bemoaned their financial loss.[44] Until then, they had hoped to recover their slaves alive, but dead slaves benefited no one. Some of the Forbes Company Negroes, of course, were among the killed or wounded.

Interestingly, several Negroes belonging to the company had escaped from the fort before the explosion. Six of them were returned to Pensacola, including Castalio, a Forbes slave. John Innerarity put the hapless Castalio in leg irons and sent him to the Public Works because he had prevented several other Negroes (perhaps members of his own family) from returning. Other company Negroes joined the blacks on the Suwannee; some fled as far south as Tampa. Over the next four or five years, the company attempted to recover the blacks in the Tampa area. In 1819, in fact, John Forbes received permission to go from Havana to Tampa for that purpose; it was reported that the blacks were living in a state of misery. If Forbes actually made the trip, he could have been only partially successful at best, for in 1821, James Innerarity reported that a number of their ex-slaves were no longer at Tampa but had moved south to the vicinity of Charlotte Harbor.[45]

Although the company lamented its losses following the War of 1812, the war merely presaged the ill fortune that awaited it during the First Seminole War. This conflict came hard on the heels of the company's earlier problems on the Apalachicola.

44. Zúñiga to Cienfuegos, August 22, 1816, AGI PC, leg. 1873. See also Hambly to Forbes, August 28, 1816, AGI PC, leg. 2356, for a different reaction in Pensacola.
45. John Innerarity to James Innerarity, August 13, 1816, FP, MPL. When Castalio left Pensacola with the British he was accompanied by his family: *Relación* by José Urcullo, February 28, 1815, Cochrane Papers, MS 2328, folio 172, NLS. The Pensacola house had purchased Castalio and his family (Harriet, Ned, and Rinah [also Rena]) from Forbes's East Florida plantation for $800 on June 11, 1811: Account in IHP, dated June 12, 1811. See also "War of 1812," 331; John Forbes to Captain General Juan Manuel Cagigal, November 16, 1819, AGI PC, leg. 1956; James Innerarity to John Innerarity, January 26, 1821, GP.

15

The First Seminole War Destroys Trade

*A*FTER the destruction of Negro Fort, the Americans continued to maintain several forts on the Chattahoochee and Flint rivers. By September 1816, John Forbes and Company anticipated an $8,000 monthly contract to supply these forts, provided some way could be found to avoid Spanish restrictions on trade north of the border.[1] Doyle already had returned to the Apalachicola in August to reopen the trading post there, in order to facilitate trade with the Americans. Although Hambly continued to correspond with Forbes and the Innerarity brothers, he opened his own store near Spanish Bluff, thirty-five miles north of Prospect Bluff, on the east bank of the Apalachicola, opposite Isla Verde. Hambly developed a good relationship with Colonel Clinch, and most of the supplies to the Americans were handled through Hambly's and Doyle's stores. In either case, John Forbes and Company supplied Doyle, who, in turn, provided Hambly with some trade goods. Doyle also supplied goods to Samuel Butler, the sutler at Camp Crawford.[2]

 1. John Innerarity to James Innerarity, September 12, 1816, FP, MPL.
 2. John Innerarity to James Innerarity, August 13, 1816, *FHQ* 12 (1933): 37–39; John Innerarity to James Innerarity, October 5, 1816, FP, MPL; D. L. Clinch to John Forbes, August 29, 1816, HWP; Doyle to John Innerarity, January 28, 1817, GP. For the location of Spanish Bluff (Loma Española), see Vicente Sebastián Pintado's map "Of the Possessions of Messrs. Forbes and Company," December 30, 1817, Manuscripts Division, Library of Congress. See also "Map of the Lands of Forbes Purchase," P. A. Mesier, NARG 200.

The company attempted to ship goods to the Apalachicola duty-free, claiming that they were intended for the Indian trade. Inspection by the treasury auditor, Miguel de Losada, of the cargo of one of the ships carrying goods to the Apalachicola revealed goods destined for American and not Indian consumption. Losada concluded that the company was abusing its privileges and that the Apalachicola store was merely a front for trade with the Americans. As a result, he decided that the company must pay duties on such goods. Actually, Losada wanted to close the Apalachicola River to trade entirely on the grounds that the Americans were the ones benefiting from the trade and not the Spaniards or Indians. He also questioned whether the company really had permission to establish a store there in the first place. He indeed believed that there was no need for it. Further, he believed that if a store really was necessary, Spanish traders would have been adequate to the task and would have welcomed the opportunity. Certainly, he argued, if Forbes and Company were entitled to duty-free privileges, so were other Pensacola merchants. The result, Losada feared, would be chaos and an empty treasury.

Of course, the company appealed Losada's decision to the captain general in Havana. Forbes argued that the Indians were eager to have the store at Prospect Bluff. During the war, the Indians had had little time to kill deer (deerskins being still their main trade item). But now that the war was over, hunting was better than ever. Forbes feared that if the company did not maintain a store on the Apalachicola, the Indians would take their skins to American traders north of the border. In addition, the British had alienated many of the Indians from Spain, and a number of new Indians had crossed the border into Spanish territory. Special efforts must therefore be made to win their friendship and allegiance. Nevertheless, as a result of Losada's ruling, Governor Zúñiga embargoed the ship and goods. Finally, however, he reconsidered and permitted the ship to depart, provided the duty was paid: the money was to be refunded if the company won its appeal to the captain general.[3]

While they awaited the captain general's decision, John Innerarity decided to have future goods shipped directly from New Orleans to the Apalachicola, thus avoiding problems with the contentious Losada. The goods were shipped on the *Italiano*, under U.S. registry, and were assigned directly to Hambly. Unfortunately, the ship had to put in at Pensacola because of heavy winds. Losada thought the vessel should be confiscated and its crew imprisoned because they had violated Spanish customs regula-

3. Crider, "The Borderland Floridas," 88–92.

tions. Colonel Francisco Maxmiliano de St. Maxent, again governor ad interim following Governor Zúñiga's recent death, overruled Losada as a matter of political expediency.

Although it took nearly two years, the captain general finally ruled that trade to the Apalachicola was to be entirely free of duty, not only to Forbes and Company but to all Spanish merchants based in Pensacola. He concluded that this policy would only continue in the spirit of all royal orders issued since 1788. Merchandise passing through Pensacola to other parts of the province would be assessed only 2 percent entry duty.[4] The captain general's ruling was still some months away, however, when the company began to experience difficult times.

In the fall of 1816, John Innerarity complained that the Pensacola market was depressed and that no money was circulating. His brother, James, at Mobile, however, saw some hope in the sale of blacks, tiles, and bricks, and in the collection of debts. Conditions were such that they believed the only real solution to the company's problems was the prospect that the U.S. Congress would approve the annexation of all of West Florida.[5] But American acquisition of the Floridas was still five years away.

A serious problem that the company faced during the years following the War of 1812 was the rapid turnover in Spanish governors of West Florida. Between February 1815, and May 1818, five different officers served as governor, or governor ad interim, of the province. While the company experienced reasonably good relations with four of these governors, it had difficulties with the fifth. The arrival of Governor José Masot, in November 1816,[6] was soon followed by an open break between his office and the company. Perhaps Masot's irritability was the result of the physical problems he had experienced before his arrival in Pensacola.

While serving as colonel and commandant-general of the Spanish army in Santo Domingo, Masot had developed cataracts which nearly blinded him. A subsequent operation cost him the sight of his right eye and so impaired the vision of his left eye that he retired in December 1814, after more than forty-one years of military service. Following his retirement, he settled in Havana. Although still nearly blind, by May 1816 he had regained enough sight in one eye to request recall to active duty. His request was approved, and he was appointed to the Pensacola post.[7]

4. Ibid., 94–95.
5. John Innerarity to James Innerarity, September 12, November 13, 1816; James Innerarity to John Innerarity, November 4, 1816, FP, MPL.
6. Holmes, "Commandants and Governors of Pensacola," 107.
7. Service record and file of Josef Tadeo Antonio Masot, *AGM*; Masot to Cienfuegos, November 29, 1816, *AGI PC*, leg. 1873.

At first, John Innerarity and the new governor appeared to get along very well. In December 1816, as evidence of their harmony, Innerarity contracted for the company to supply food for the hospital, the guard posts, and the fort. Because of a lack of storage space, Innerarity even turned over the company pavilion on Zaragoza Street to Masot for artillery stores.[8] But during an inventory of one of the warehouses, Losada discovered a shortage of thirty-seven barrels of flour supplied earlier by the company. The governor ordered Innerarity to deliver the missing flour or be fined. The local government, constantly in dire financial circumstances, was considerably indebted to the company, which had been furnishing goods and supplies on credit. Instead of delivering the flour as ordered, Innerarity informed the governor that the unpaid debts canceled the contract and that he had no flour to deliver. The incident ended any cooperation between Innerarity and Masot.[9] Thereafter, matters grew worse. Following his conflict with the governor, Innerarity had trouble, in turn, with the auditor of war and the treasury officials. The problems in Pensacola so affected trade with the Apalachicola that Doyle probably expressed the sentiments of all the members of the company when he wrote James Innerarity, "I hope the damned old blind Governor is by this time gone to the Devil—with a few more of his associates."[10]

Business on the Apalachicola continued to have its ups and downs throughout the remainder of 1816 and well into 1817. Hambly occasionally indicated a desire to rejoin the company and visited Doyle from time to time. He still purchased most of the goods for his store through Doyle, but nothing is known of the detailed financial arrangements between Hambly and the company. Finally, in December 1816, Hambly joined Doyle at Prospect Bluff. But a lack of trade goods, and Innerarity's order that they should extend no credit, seriously hurt business.[11]

For his part, poor Doyle felt trapped at Prospect Bluff. He complained of being surrounded by outlaws, murderers, and runaway slaves and feared constantly for his personal safety, reporting that he slept only briefly and fitfully. In addition, he warned John Innerarity that he expected the Indians to plunder the store at any time. He did attempt to

---

8. Masot to John Innerarity, December 30, 1816; January 3, 1817, CP; Masot to John Innerarity, January 2, 1817; John Innerarity to Masot, January 2, 1817, AGI PC, leg. 1928.
9. Crider, "The Borderland Floridas," 101–2.
10. Doyle to James Innerarity, August 17, 1817, FHQ 18 (1939): 140. For other problems between Innerarity and the Pensacola officials, see Crider, "The Borderland Floridas," 102–5, 109–14.
11. Doyle to John Innerarity, November 23, 1816; John Innerarity to James Innerarity, December 24, 1816, FP, MPL; James Innerarity to John Innerarity, December 13, 1816; Doyle to John Innerarity, January 28, 1817, GP.

secure those former Pensacola slaves still in the area and to return them to their owners, by promising them pardon and protection, yet he experienced little success in these endeavors. By June 1817, he anticipated business with the Americans to improve but was short of the necessary merchandise for trading with the Indians. Doyle remained at Prospect Bluff only until August, when he expressed a strong desire to leave. Indeed, he requested the company to send someone to take his place. Doyle had purchased a 640-acre plantation from John Innerarity at Spanish Bluff, adjacent to Hambly's. It was to obtain the land, Doyle said, that he had risked his life on the Apalachicola for seven years. Doyle had already made arrangements with a Mr. Hanna to work the plantation for shares.[12] He had other reasons for wanting to leave. Increasing trouble with the Indians along the border and the appearance of a serious competitor for the Indian trade portended grave danger for the company and for Doyle and Hambly.

Alexander Arbuthnot, a British merchant from Nassau, arrived in West Florida in February 1817 to open a trading post at the mouth of the Ocklochonee River. Arbuthnot's appearance sprang from his beliefs that the Indians had been ill treated by the United States and that the failure of the United States to return the lands taken in the Treaty of Fort Jackson was a clear violation of Article Nine of the Treaty of Ghent. Consequently, he intended to act as agent for the Indians in obtaining the aid of both the British and Spanish governments to see that justice was done. Of course, he also relied on the British government for arms, ammunition, and supplies to equip the Indians in the event war should come. There is no denying the sincerity of Arbuthnot's intentions; still, it also is obvious that he planned to wrest the Indian trade from John Forbes and Company and perhaps to acquire a sizable amount of land for himself in the process.

Arbuthnot communicated with Colonel Nicolls, British officials in the Bahamas and England, and the captain general of Cuba to complain of the encroachment of the Americans on Indian land. He also asked for help in forcing the United States to abide by the Treaty of Ghent. Losing no opportunity to lay the blame for many of the Indians' problems on John Forbes and Company, he proffered the opinion that the company had cheated the Indians by overcharging them for goods and by taking advantage of them in many other ways as well. Though Doyle received his share of the blame, Arbuthnot charged that Hambly was responsible for

12. Doyle to John Innerarity, June 3, 1817, *FHQ* 17 (1939): 315–18; July 11, 1817, *FHQ* 18 (1939): 136–37; June 17, 1817, GP; Doyle to James Innerarity, August 17, 1817, *FHQ* 18 (1939): 139; GP; Deed of sale from John Innerarity to E. Doyle for 640 acres on Apalachicola for $320, August 17, 1817, copy in MC.

the destruction of Negro Fort and the great loss of life there. He also accused Doyle and Hambly of persuading Americans to settle on Indian lands. Forbes and his associates had cheated the Indians out of their best lands under false pretenses. Instead of settling Englishmen on the lands, they were encouraging Americans to buy them. The anticipated cession of the Floridas—talks were already under way in Washington—had increased Florida land values by 300 to 400 percent. John Forbes and Company, Arbuthnot claimed, was making a fortune from land sales.[13]

A few months after Arbuthnot came to West Florida, Hambly, on behalf of a number of Creek chiefs, wrote to Arbuthnot suggesting that he withdraw from that little band of "outlaw" Indians—meaning those Red Sticks who had taken refuge in the Floridas. Hambly also implored Arbuthnot to stop inciting them to war against the Americans. At Arbuthnot's urging, Hambly wrote, the Indians had murdered at least twenty women and children and had stolen a hundred or more horses. Hambly warned Arbuthnot that doom awaited him at the hands of justice if he continued in his present course.[14] Arbuthnot countered Hambly's accusations by charging that it was the Americans who were causing all the trouble, by encroaching upon Indian lands, stealing their cattle, and murdering their people. The Indians were only retaliating when they caught Americans on their lands; furthermore, reports that they were raiding into American territory were false.[15] Doyle advised John Innerarity that Arbuthnot had warned Hambly that they would soon be driven off their lands.[16] Like Nicolls before him, Arbuthnot applauded the Indians' revocation of their land grants to Forbes and Company.[17] Since the Indians had revoked the grants, any land sales by the company were illegal, according to Arbuthnot.

While Arbuthnot's store on the Ocklochonee seriously affected business on the Apalachicola, he established yet a second trading post on the site of the old Panton, Leslie store on the Wakulla River. According to Montes de Oca, who was still acting on behalf of Forbes and Company at St. Marks, this store had completely taken over the trade with the Indians there, leaving him with only a few sales to the Spanish garrison at the

---

13. Secretary of State to George W. Erving, November 28, 1818, *ASP FR*, 4:540, 542; see also the many documents ibid., 4:577–92, 605–12. Certificate of Hambly signed at Washington, D.C., July 11, 1818, Correspondence Regarding West Florida, Series no. 881, NARG 59; *Niles Weekly Register*, May 31, 1817, p. 211; November 15, 1817, p. 182; December 12, 1818, p. 276. See also Sugden, "Southern Indians," 274–75, 301–7, 311.
14. Extract of a letter from W. Hambly to A. Arbuthnot, May 10, 1817, *ASP FR*, 4:579.
15. Arbuthnot to Hambly, May 3, 1817, *ASP FR*, 4:605–6.
16. Doyle to John Innerarity, June 3, 1817, *FHQ* 17 (1939): 315–18.
17. Crider, "The Borderland Floridas," 243.

fort.[18] Doyle was outraged to learn that Arbuthnot, who had no license to trade with the Florida Indians, had deposited a large supply of goods at St. Marks and that the commandant had done absolutely nothing about it.[19]

Arbuthnot lost no time in establishing even a third store—this one on the Suwannee—to absorb the trade of the Indian and Negro towns on the river. This intrusion upon Forbes's East Florida trade may have been the reason that the company closed its St. Augustine store before the end of 1817. Arbuthnot had made serious, if not fatal, inroads upon Forbes's trade in both East and West Florida.[20]

Throughout the fall of 1817, Arbuthnot continued to incite the Indians and to seek to convince them that Hambly and his friends were their principal enemies. Arbuthnot claimed that it was Doyle and Hambly who were providing the Americans with the pretext to attack the Indians in Florida by blaming the Indians for murdering Americans, stealing their cattle, and preparing for war against the United States. In particular, Arbuthnot was convinced that Hambly not only was responsible for guiding the American army to Negro Fort but also had been instrumental in blowing it up. Hambly had pointed out the location of the powder magazine so that the Americans could aim their cannon at it.[21] After almost a year spent in denouncing Doyle and Hambly, Arbuthnot finally decided it was time to bring them both to justice. At least, Hambly blamed their subsequent troubles on the Nassau merchant.

On December 13, 1817, a band of Indians led by Chenubby, a chief of the Fowl Town band, took Doyle and Hambly prisoner on their plantations near Spanish Bluff. Captured with them was Chief George Perryman, whom the Indians killed—allegedly for siding with the Americans. Others present included a farmer, Juan Guerra, and a free black, Carlos Noriega, and his wife, but they managed to escape. The Indians took virtually everything that they could carry away.

From the plantations, the Indians conducted their captives a few miles north to Ochechee Bluff, where they spent three days. During their stay there, the Indians were busy trying to prevent American transports from ascending the river. They were not far from the site where, only two weeks previously, the Indians had ambushed and massacred a party of American soldiers, women, and children, led by Lieutenant R. W. Scott.

18. Montes de Oca to John Innerarity, May 5, 1817, CP; Doyle to John Innerarity, June 17, 1817, GP; *FHQ* 18 (1939): 61–63.
19. Doyle to John Innerarity, June 17, 1817, GP.
20. Crider, "The Borderland Floridas," 38 (table 1, note d).
21. A. Arbuthnot to Governor of Havana, undated, *ASP FR*, 4:588–89; Arbuthnot's Journal, *ASP FR*, 4:610.

The Indians moved Doyle and Hambly east to Mickasuky, a Seminole town thirty miles north of St. Marks. Their next stop was the Suwannee, where Chief Kenhagee of the Mickasuky told them that Arbuthnot had ordered them captured and robbed. Arbuthnot had earlier ordered Doyle and Hambly brought to the Suwannee, where they were to be tried by him.

When captors and captives arrived, however, Arbuthnot was in Nassau. Kenhagee decided to send them to New Providence, thereby preventing their murder by the black survivors of Negro Fort, who were then living on the Suwannee. But before the chief could do so, Arbuthnot returned, whereupon he tried Doyle and Hambly and sentenced them to be tortured by some of the Choctaw survivors of the explosion at the fort, in revenge for the loss of their friends there. The charges against the two, Arbuthnot explained, were that they had sold Indian lands without the Indians' permission.[22]

During their imprisonment on the Suwannee, Doyle and Hambly became friendly with Peter B. Cook and a Negro chief named Nero. Cook was a former auctioneer's clerk in the Bahamas. Before coming to Florida as Arbuthnot's clerk, Cook had been jailed in the Bahamas for robbery and also for a short time at St. Marks for stealing from Arbuthnot, who on several previous occasions had threatened his life.

Obviously, Cook bore a grudge against Arbuthnot, and chose to work against him at every opportunity. Exactly how Cook and Nero managed it is unknown, but they did prevent the Indians from carrying out Arbuthnot's sentence against Doyle and Hambly.[23] At one point, Doyle and Hambly asked one of the Indian chiefs to prevail upon Arbuthnot to give them passage to New Providence on his schooner. Arbuthnot replied that if he was forced to take Doyle and Hambly, he would blindfold them and make them walk the plank.[24]

Unable to decide just what to do with their prisoners, the Indians fi-

22. Numerous spelling variations exist for the Indian bluffs and towns and for the names of the chiefs: W. Hambly's certificate, July 24, 1818; W. Hambly and E. Doyle to General Jackson, May 2, 1818, *ASP FR*, 4:577–78; see also Hambly's testimony, ibid., 4:583; Crider, "The Borderland Floridas," 183–87; Doster, *Creek Indians*, 2:211. There is a strong argument that Arbuthnot had nothing to do with Hambly's and Doyle's capture but that it was in retaliation for the American attack upon Fowl Town on November 21. Once captured, however, there is little doubt that Arbuthnot intended that they should be punished for their actions: ibid., 2:200–202; Parton, *Life of Andrew Jackson*, 2:465, 471–72.

23. Armbrister, "Recollections," 2:38; Cook to Carney, January 19, 1818, *ASP FR*, 4:605; Certificates of William Hambly, Washington, D.C., July 11, 1818, Correspondence Regarding West Florida, Series no. 881, NARG 59. These two certificates differ somewhat from that printed in *ASP FR*, 4:577; Arbuckle to Gaines, December 20, 1817, *ASP MA*, 1:690–91.

24. *The Trials of Arbuthnot and Ambrister*, 50.

nally returned them to Mickasuky. Kenhagee visited Caso y Luengo at Fort San Marcos, who agreed to keep Doyle and Hambly there under guard. They arrived at St. Marks on February 12, and while Caso y Luengo received them kindly, they were reminded that they were still prisoners. They discovered, much to their surprise, that most of the property taken from their plantations had been purchased by the soldiers and officers of the Spanish fort. Hambly also learned that the Indians frequently brought cattle stolen north of the border to the fort and sold them to the Spaniards. Because Hambly acted occasionally as interpreter, he discovered that the officers sometimes purchased the cattle even before they were stolen.[25]

Even though John Innerarity learned of Hambly's and Doyle's capture soon after it happened, he did not know where they had been taken. John wrote his brother, James, at Mobile, informing him of events on the Apalachicola. Rumors, John wrote, placed Woodbine among the Indians. He pleaded with James to ask General Gaines for help.[26] But John Innerarity could do little more than await whatever fate the Indians should decide for Doyle and Hambly.

Once Doyle and Hambly had been lodged at St. Marks, the commandant there permitted them some freedom of movement within the fort. Hambly even managed, through the aid of a friendly Indian, to send word to Pensacola of their situation. Innerarity quickly dispatched José Sarda, master of *Relámpago*, to Apalachee to rescue Doyle and Hambly. When Sarda reached St. Marks, Caso y Luengo did not object to Doyle and Hambly leaving, but he demanded that they agree never again to set foot in that country and not to communicate in any manner with the U.S. government or any of its officers. Both readily agreed, and they departed the fort on the night of March 28.

When the *Relámpago* reached Apalachicola Bay, it encountered two armed U.S. galliots and a provision ship under the command of Captain Isaac McKeever, who detained the *Relámpago* and its crew. Taking Doyle and Hambly on board his ship, McKeever continued to his destination, St. Marks. On arrival there, McKeever, not wishing to reveal the identity of his little fleet, flew the British flag. By then, Doyle and Hambly knew that General Jackson had invaded West Florida and that McKeever expected to meet him at St. Marks within a day or two.[27]

A Spanish officer from the fort visited McKeever and left believing that

25. Certificate of Hambly signed at Washington, D.C., July 11, 1818, Correspondence Regarding West Florida, Series no. 881, NARG 59. See also *ASP FR*, 4:577–78.
26. John Innerarity to James Innerarity, January 17, 1818, IHP.
27. Hambly's Certificate of July 24, 1818, *ASP FR*, 4:577; José Masot to Cienfuegos, April 2, 1818, *AHN Estado*, leg. 5563, Exp. 1.

the ships were indeed British. Several Red Stick chiefs, including Hillis Hadjo, back from his trip to England, and Homathlemico, who had led the attack on Lieutenant Scott's party, also visited McKeever under the impression that he and his "British" ship had brought them a cargo of arms and ammunition from Woodbine. Once they were aboard ship, McKeever took the Indians prisoner. Later, when several canoes approached the ship to find out why the two chiefs had not returned, McKeever ran up the U.S. flag and fired on the Indians, who quickly dispersed.[28]

Meanwhile, Arbuthnot had also arrived at the fort, where the Spaniards warned him that General Jackson, with an army of several thousand troops and Indians, was approaching to capture the fort and then to destroy the black population of the Suwannee. Arbuthnot quickly sent a letter to his son, John, and to Chief Bowlegs on the Suwannee, warning them of Jackson's approach. He advised Bowlegs that he should not attempt to resist and that they should take measures to avoid capture.[29] Arbuthnot seemed firmly convinced that Forbes and his associates were responsible for Jackson's invasion. If Jackson drove the Indians off the company's land, Forbes could confirm his claim and sell the land to American settlers at a huge profit.[30]

As expected—but before Arbuthnot could make his escape—Jackson and his army arrived at the fort. As soon as Jackson communicated with McKeever, he learned, through Hambly, that Arbuthnot was hiding in the fort. Hambly went ashore to act as interpreter for Caso y Luengo and Jackson, translating their letters and carrying messages back and forth between the two officers. Jackson lost no time in occupying the fort and in placing Arbuthnot under arrest, pending a formal hearing of charges that the merchant had incited the Indians to attack the Americans and had supplied them with arms and ammunition. Shortly afterward, McKeever delivered his two prisoners, Hillis Hadjo and Homathlemico, to the fort, where Jackson ordered them executed. Although Hillis Hadjo begged to be shot, Jackson decreed that he was to be hanged. Hambly, with vengeful justice in mind, reminded Homathlemico of the cruel and inhuman treatment which he had meted out to Lieutenant Scott and his party. As a result, General Jackson also refused to have Homathlemico shot; instead, he announced that he intended to disgrace him by hanging him like a dog. The executions were swiftly carried out. Afterward, the soldiers dragged the two bodies outside the fort and buried them.[31] With his work accom-

28. Parton, *Life of Andrew Jackson*, 2:454–57.
29. Arbuthnot to his son, John Arbuthnot, April 2, 1818, *ASP FR*, 4:584.
30. Arbuthnot to a Person of Rank in England, January 30, 1818, *ASP FR*, 4:607–8.
31. Parton, *Life of Andrew Jackson*, 2:457–59; General Jackson to Mrs. Jackson, April

plished at the fort, Jackson ordered the army to march to the Suwannee, unaware that Arbuthnot had warned the Indians and blacks there to flee.

Limited resistance on the march became stronger along the banks of the Suwannee, but after a brief struggle the Indians and blacks fled across the river. Efforts to pursue them were unsuccessful. The night before the army prepared to return to St. Marks, four men accidentally stumbled into the American bivouac: Robert Chrystie Ambrister, Peter B. Cook, and two Negroes. They were captured and searched. On one of the Negroes, the captors found Arbuthnot's letter to his son, which, according to Cook, Ambrister had read to the Indians and blacks, thus giving them the advance notice they needed to plan their escape. Hambly, who had accompanied Jackson on the march, informed the general about the activities of Cook and Ambrister.[32]

According to family tradition, after Ambrister left the British fort on the Apalachicola—the date of his departure is unknown—he returned to Europe with the British and was wounded at Waterloo in June 1815. Yet, he was back at the family home in Nassau by October 1815, when he presented an affidavit on behalf of Woodbine. Ambrister remained in British service until early 1817, when he fought a duel, for which he was suspended from the army. After his return to Nassau later that year, he again became associated with Woodbine and accepted a captain's commission in the force being raised by Woodbine and Gregor MacGregor. These two worthies planned to raise a small army in the Bahamas, and, with the help of the Indians and blacks, to wrest the Floridas from Spain. They arranged to rendezvous at Tampa Bay about May 1, 1818; from there they would march overland with the army to capture St. Augustine. It was in keeping with these plans that Ambrister arrived in East Florida in March 1818. He established a small settlement at Tampa Bay, then commandeered one of Arbuthnot's schooners and sailed for the Suwannee to organize and train the Indians and blacks for the coming campaign against the Spanish.

Ambrister succeeded in raising a force of about 300 blacks, including some from "the Bluff." Anticipating the American invasion, and accompanied by twenty-five blacks, he sailed for St. Marks, which he intended to capture and destroy in order to deny it to the Americans. He also hoped to secure a supply of arms and ammunition for his army. When he arrived at St. Marks, Ambrister found Captain McKeever already there. After siz-

---

8, 1818, Bassett, *Correspondence of Andrew Jackson*, 2:357–58; Crider, "The Borderland Floridas," 235–36.

32. Doster, *Creek Indians*, 2:206–11; Parton, *Life of Andrew Jackson*, 2:459–63.

ing up the situation, Ambrister slipped away to return to the Suwannee. Running their schooner aground, he plundered its cargo, and then he and his party, which now included Cook, headed for Arbuthnot's Suwannee store, which they likewise pillaged, distributing the booty among the blacks.

Ambrister decided at this point to return to Tampa, but upon reaching the schooner, he was told that the captain refused to sail because of inadequate supplies. Ambrister and Cook went back upriver to secure stores, and it was during this attempt to return to the Indian settlement on the Suwannee that Ambrister—wearing his captain's uniform—stumbled with his companions into Jackson's lines.[33] Vexed that the enemy had been warned and had fled, Jackson turned about and headed back for St. Marks, carrying his prisoners with him.

As soon as he reached the fort at St. Marks, Jackson ordered a general court-martial convened to try Arbuthnot and Ambrister. The charges against Arbuthnot included advising the Indians not to honor the terms of the Treaty of Fort Jackson: he also was accused of acting as a spy, of aiding, abetting, and comforting the enemy, and of supplying them with the means of war. The final charge against Arbuthnot accused him of inciting the Indians to kill Doyle and Hambly because they had actively attempted to maintain peace between Spain, the United States, and the Indians. Hambly and Cook, who were hardly impartial, were the most important witnesses against Arbuthnot. Although Doyle also attended the trial, he played only a minor role in the proceedings. With all this against him, the court still failed to find Arbuthnot guilty of the charge that he planned to have Doyle and Hambly killed, because such charges were outside the court's jurisdiction. Arbuthnot was, however, found guilty of the other charges, and the court sentenced him to be hanged.

In the case against Ambrister, there were two charges: aiding, abetting, comforting, and supplying the enemy with the means of war, and leading and commanding the Indians in war against the United States. Ambrister pleaded not guilty to the first charge and guilty with justification to the second. The court, however, found him guilty of both charges. They first sentenced him to be shot, but reconsidered, and sentenced him instead to fifty lashes and confinement with a ball and chain at hard labor

---

33. Armbrister, "Recollections," 2:2, 36, 38–41, 129. The accuracy of this manuscript as it pertains to Robert's military career after he left Florida is questionable. There is also a discrepancy regarding Robert's date of birth. In one place he is described as being born in 1797: ibid., 36; on p. 119, he was baptized on December 4, 1794. The year 1797 is probably correct since it is the date given by his father. See also *ASP FR*, 4:542–43, 604–5; Davis, *MacGregor's Invasion*, 68–69. Crider, "The Borderland Floridas," 230–46, includes a good overview of Ambrister and his Florida connection.

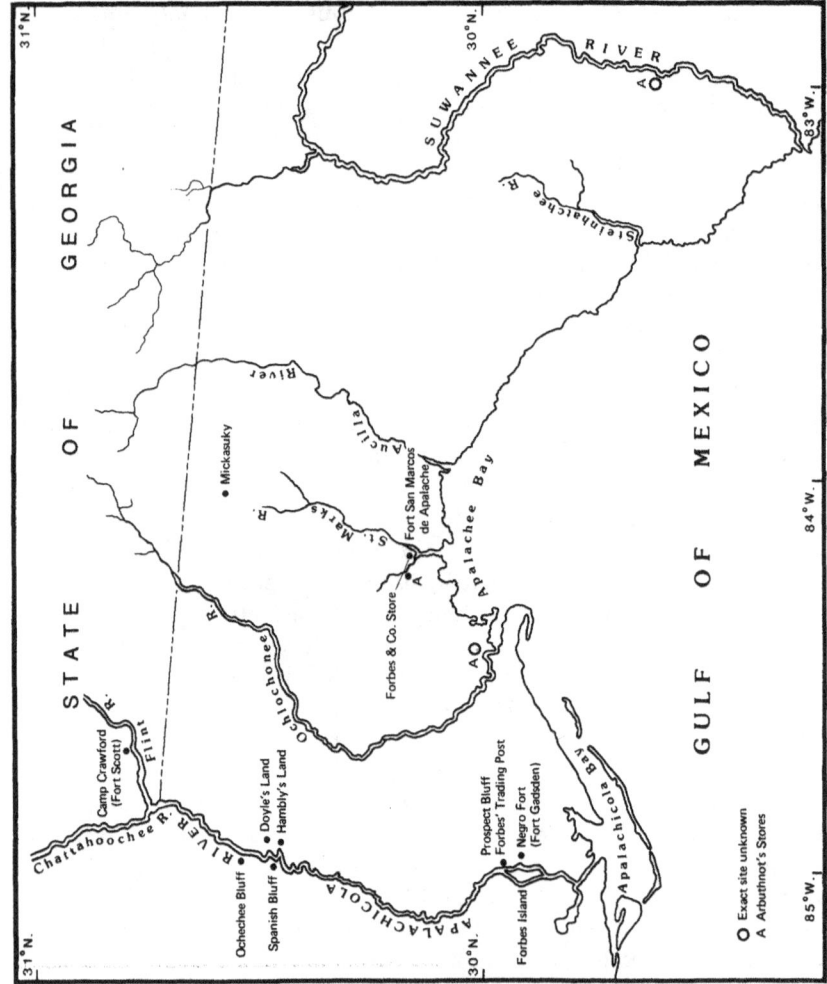

Apalachicola-Suwannee area, 1816–18

for twelve months. When Jackson reviewed the sentence, he disregarded the second recommendation and ordered Ambrister shot. On the morning of April 29, 1818, Arbuthnot was hanged from the yardarm of his own ship, the *Chance*, and Ambrister was shot by a firing squad.[34]

Some have wondered why the British government did not raise a hue and cry over the execution of two British subjects in neutral Spanish territory. Secretary of State John Quincy Adams, in the greatest state paper of his diplomatic career, not only justified Jackson's invasion of the Floridas but upheld the execution of Arbuthnot and Ambrister as well. Addressing the problem of the marauding Florida Indians and Negroes, Adams further asserted that Spain must either police the province or cede it to the United States. Lord Castlereagh, the British foreign secretary, acknowledged that Arbuthnot and Ambrister had encouraged the Indians to war and accepted their executions as justified under the circumstances. Besides, relations between the United States and Great Britain had improved remarkably since 1815. Thus, not wishing to jeopardize his peace policy, Castlereagh had unceremoniously withdrawn from the Florida intrigues and rivalries without informing either the Indians or their British advocates. Any act of retaliation against the United States over the Arbuthnot-Ambrister affair which might have been considered fell victim to the diplomatic talks then being conducted between the two countries.[35]

Following the execution of Ambrister and Arbuthnot, Jackson intended to leave the Floridas, his work there being done. The Indians and blacks had been dispersed, if not eliminated, and the two men considered most responsible for inciting them to war were dead. While still at St. Marks, Hambly informed Jackson of a rumor that a large number of Indians had gathered at Pensacola. José Sarda, captain of the *Relámpago*, reluctantly confirmed the information. When he sailed from Pensacola, Sarda related, there had been in the town about 450–500 Indians. They had been fed and armed and were committing depredations against Americans on the Alabama border and on Spanish subjects in West Florida.[36] Still undecided, Jackson returned to the newly constructed Fort Gadsden, built on the site of Negro Fort, on the Apalachicola. A letter from John Innerarity to Doyle, and conversations between Hambly and Juan de la Rua and Benito García, both recently arrived at Fort Gadsden with

---

34. *The Trials of Arbuthnot and Ambrister*, 1–80. Owsley, *Struggle for the Gulf Borderlands*, 185n, suggests that Hambly wanted to eliminate Arbuthnot because he had become a serious competitor for the Indian trade.

35. Bemis, *John Quincy Adams*, 325–29.

36. Jackson to Calhoun, February 5, 1819, Bassett, *Correspondence of Andrew Jackson*, 2:410–11.

goods from Pensacola, convinced Jackson that he must proceed to Pensacola to end the Indian problem there.[37] A variety of other reasons also influenced his decision.

John Innerarity had informed Jackson that Governor Masot had prohibited a shipment of goods destined for Fort Crawford to proceed via the rivers in Spanish West Florida. Jackson needed no further urging.[38] When Masot heard that Jackson was approaching Pensacola, he ordered the Indians out of town and provided them with food and powder for the journey. Hambly reached Pensacola on May 23, in advance of the army, and learned that Holmes, a noted Red Stick, and his party had left Pensacola for the Choctawhatchee the day before.[39] Jackson and his army arrived on May 24, finding Masot had left only a token force at Pensacola. The governor had retired to Fort San Carlos de Barrancas, nine miles from Pensacola, where he was prepared to defend Spanish honor in the event Jackson attacked. As events transpired, Jackson did not wish to deny Masot the opportunity. After a brief but determined effort on the part of Masot to defend the fort, marred by a near mutiny of his troops, the governor reluctantly surrendered. Nevertheless, Jackson's army had suffered far more casualties in the attack on the fort than Jackson ever admitted.[40]

Soon after his Pensacola visit, Jackson decided that several of the friendly Indians should receive, in Washington, compensation for their services and losses during the war. He therefore asked Hambly to accompany the Indians, sending with him a letter to the president. To the secretary of war, in another letter, Jackson wrote of Hambly, "You will find him an honest and faithful friend to our government, and valuable for the information which he can afford of Spanish policy and intrigue. He is well acquainted with all the transactions of foreign agents in this country, of their practices, etc., and how far encouraged by the Spanish authority, etc."[41] Jackson had, of course, left a force at Pensacola to maintain order until the Spaniards, whom he had shipped off to Cuba, could return.

Although the records of John Forbes and Company are not complete for this period, the company did supply the U.S. Army with some of its

---

37. Certificate of Hambly, June 2, 1818, *ASP FR*, 4:570; Bassett, *Correspondence of Andrew Jackson*, 2:410n2.
38. Crider, "The Borderland Floridas," 249.
39. Hambly's Certificate, June 2, 1818, and the sworn statements of a number of Pensacola residents, in *ASP FR*, 4:570–72.
40. Crider, "The Borderland Floridas," 249–54; Masot to Cienfuegos, Pensacola, June 6, 1818, in Papers Relating to the Yucatan (selected) mss. additional 42568 British Museum, London; Delson, "Andrew Jackson."
41. Parton, *Life of Andrew Jackson*, 2:503–4; President Monroe to Jackson, December 21, 1818, Bassett, *Correspondence of Andrew Jackson*, 2:404–5.

needs during the eight months it remained in Pensacola: oak oars, corn, hay, fodder, and coffee. But this was not unusual; the company had been supplying the American forces in Mobile and in the forts north of the thirty-first parallel for several years.[42]

Exactly when Hambly returned to the Apalachicola is unknown. One record shows that in November 1818, David Mitchell, former governor of Georgia but by then U.S. agent to the Creek, reported that Hambly had recovered his Negroes but had not yet submitted an account of his losses. Mitchell also reported that Doyle had notified him of his own losses to the Seminole.[43] By then, Doyle had disposed of his Spanish Bluff plantation to the Pensacola merchant, Juan de la Rua, for $2,000. Since Doyle had paid Innerarity only $320 for the land the previous year, he clearly made a substantial profit on the sale.[44]

Little is known of the subsequent activities of either Hambly or Doyle. It is certain that Doyle was still on the Apalachicola in 1821 when he wrote General Jackson about Indian problems in the area. Further records show that Doyle later moved to the area of present-day Tallahassee, where he died in 1831. In 1826, Hambly reportedly was an interpreter stationed at Fort Mitchell in Alabama. Later, he and his family may have migrated to the Indian Territory—present-day Oklahoma—during the period of Indian removal.[45]

John Innerarity's record of activities after 1818 is more vivid. Soon after the Spaniards returned to West Florida in February 1819, the new governor, Colonel José Callava, contracted John Innerarity's ship, the *Perdido*, to transport Spanish troops and supplies to regarrison Fort San Marcos de Apalache. At the same time, the governor sent Lieutenant Colonel Marcos de Villiers, John Innerarity's father-in-law, to command the fort. Colonel Villiers served thereafter also as the Forbes Company agent, reopening trade with the Indians in the area, although subsequently he re-

---

42. George Brooke to John Innerarity, October 30, 1818, CP; John Rogers to John Innerarity, May 2, 1818; George Brooke to John Innerarity, January 26, 1819, HWP. The Mobile store had been supplying the U.S. Army there since 1813, and the forts north of Mobile long before that.

43. David Mitchell to J. C. Calhoun, November 24, 1818, Ayer Collection, Newberry Library; Silver, *Edmund Pendleton Gaines*, 73n66.

44. Deed of Sale, Doyle to John de la Rua, June 27, 1818, copy in MC.

45. Doyle to Jackson, December 5, 1821, Jackson Papers, The Hermitage; White, "John Forbes Company," 179. According to Eddie Nesmith (Park Ranger at Fort Gadsden), Hambly's wife was Indian; Milly Francis, daughter of the Prophet Francis, reportedly met her on the Apalachicola and later at Muskogee, Oklahoma (Interview between Coker and Nesmith, 1978). If so, this would indicate that perhaps Hambly and his family did move to Oklahoma. On Milly Francis in the West, see Davis, "Milly Francis," 261–63. On Hambly as an interpreter at Fort Mitchell, see *ASP PL*, 4:455; this source locates Fort Mitchell in East Florida, but actually it was in Alabama on the Chattahoochee River.

ported that trade was poor. The colonel also engaged in the slave trade for himself and for John Innerarity.

Both of the Innerarity brothers, in fact, became heavily involved in slave trade during those years. They purchased some of their slaves in the Cuban slave market, preferring to buy families rather than individuals. These they sent to Hambly so that he could put them to work on the family's property on the Apalachicola.[46] For obvious reasons, no information is available on the number of slaves that they undoubtedly smuggled across the U.S. border during the years before the cession of the Floridas to the United States in 1821. Of more immediate concern to Forbes and the Innenaritys during those years was the buying and selling of land.

In December 1817, Forbes sold all of the Forbes Purchase (Forbes Grant I) to Carnochan and Mitchel, merchants of Savannah, for $66,666 2/3. Of the 1,427,289 acres in that tract, he reserved only 16,680 acres and Forbes Island, an additional 9,811 acres. The terms of payment provided for $16,666 to be paid in London on May 1, 1818. The balance of $50,000 was to be paid in four equal annual installments.[47] Shortly after he sold this land, Forbes became involved in another huge land grant in West Florida.

As a result of his failure to win compensation from the British government or from Woodbine in Nassau, Forbes despaired of ever being paid for the company's losses incurred during the War of 1812. On January 5, 1818, therefore, Forbes petitioned the captain general of Cuba, where Forbes resided at the time, for a grant of land between the Apalachicola and the Choctawhatchee rivers. The tract covered an estimated 1,500,000 *arpents* (1,275,000 acres) of land. Forbes informed the captain general that his losses in the Floridas to the Indians, and to the British during the war, plus the cost of arming and equipping the ships sent to recover the

46. Crider, "The Borderland Floridas," 296–97, 306–8; White, "John Forbes Company," 184–85.
47. Agreement signed by Forbes at Matanzas and by Colin Mitchell at Havana, December 4, 8, 1817, Exhibit A in case of *Innerarity Adm., etc. v. Trustees of Apalachicola Land Company*. There are also references to the sale of this land for $111,676.25. This is all part of a very complicated series of negotiations between Forbes and Carnochan and Mitchel, involving a second, spurious sale of the same property on May 29, 1819, which was intended to satisfy the heirs of Panton, Leslie, and Thomas Forbes. Leslie's heirs later contended that John Forbes could not speak for all of them and therefore contested the sale. It seems quite clear that Forbes bribed John and James Innerarity and Alexander Gordon, one of Leslie's heirs, to prevent their opposition to the sale of December 1817. For a detailed explanation, see *John Leslie Heirs v. The Trustees of the Apalachicola Land Company*. On the reserved 16,680 acres, see ibid., 55–57. In 1825, James Innerarity complained that John Forbes had appropriated £12,000 of the company funds for his own use: White, "John Forbes Company," 198–99.

Pensacola slaves and related company expenses on behalf of the Spanish government of West Florida, amounted to no less than $100,000. Since neither the Indians nor the British would compensate the company for its losses, he looked to the Spanish government alone for reimbursement. Accordingly, and with surprising speed, the king's assessor general in Havana approved the request, and on January 10, the captain general confirmed the grant. Governor Masot formally gave the company possession of the land on January 23, 1818.[48]

A year later, James Innerarity advised his brother, John, that they should sell their land in West Florida without delay. To accommodate the company, the new governor, Colonel José Callava, ordered the removal of anyone living in that area.[49] The disposition of the land had become urgent because of the expected cession of the Floridas to the United States.

During the treaty negotiations, the United States endeavored to force the Spanish government to annul all land grants made in the Floridas after August 11, 1802. Such a provision, naturally, would have put all grants to John Forbes and Company in jeopardy. The company therefore petitioned several parties, including Luis de Onís, the Spanish minister negotiating the treaty in Washington, as well as several American officials and the captain general of Cuba, to protect its interests. In spite of claims to the contrary, the company's petitions, ironically, had no influence on the final date selected—January 24, 1818—after which no land grants in the Floridas would be valid.[50] This date was finally settled on by the negotiators, Onís, and Secretary of State John Quincy Adams, only because Onís's letter to Adams (indicating that King Ferdinand VII of Spain had agreed to cede the Floridas to the United States) was dated January 24, 1818.[51] From all accounts, that date should have caused the company no problems, since all of their grants predated January 24. Yet, the grant later became the focus of a court case between the Innerarritys and the United States, even though it is not known how much land of Forbes Grant II had been previously sold by the company.

As these events unfolded, Forbes, discouraged by his experiences in the Floridas during the previous few years, withdrew from the firm and

---

48. John Forbes to Pedro Antonio de Ayala, January 5, 1818; Vicente Pintado to Intendant, January 10, 1818; Deed signed by Masot, January 23, 1818, MC, Exhibit DD, 431–39.

49. James Innerarity to John Innerarity, February 13, 1819, GP; Evacuation order by Callava, October 8, 1819, CP.

50. White, "John Forbes Company," 178–79; Crider, "The Borderland Floridas," 318. The date, August 11, 1802, was selected because it was the signature date of the convention between the United States and Spain, by which claims against Spain were to be decided by a joint commission: Brooks, *Diplomacy and the Borderlands*, 4.

51. Brooks, ibid., 147–48, 163.

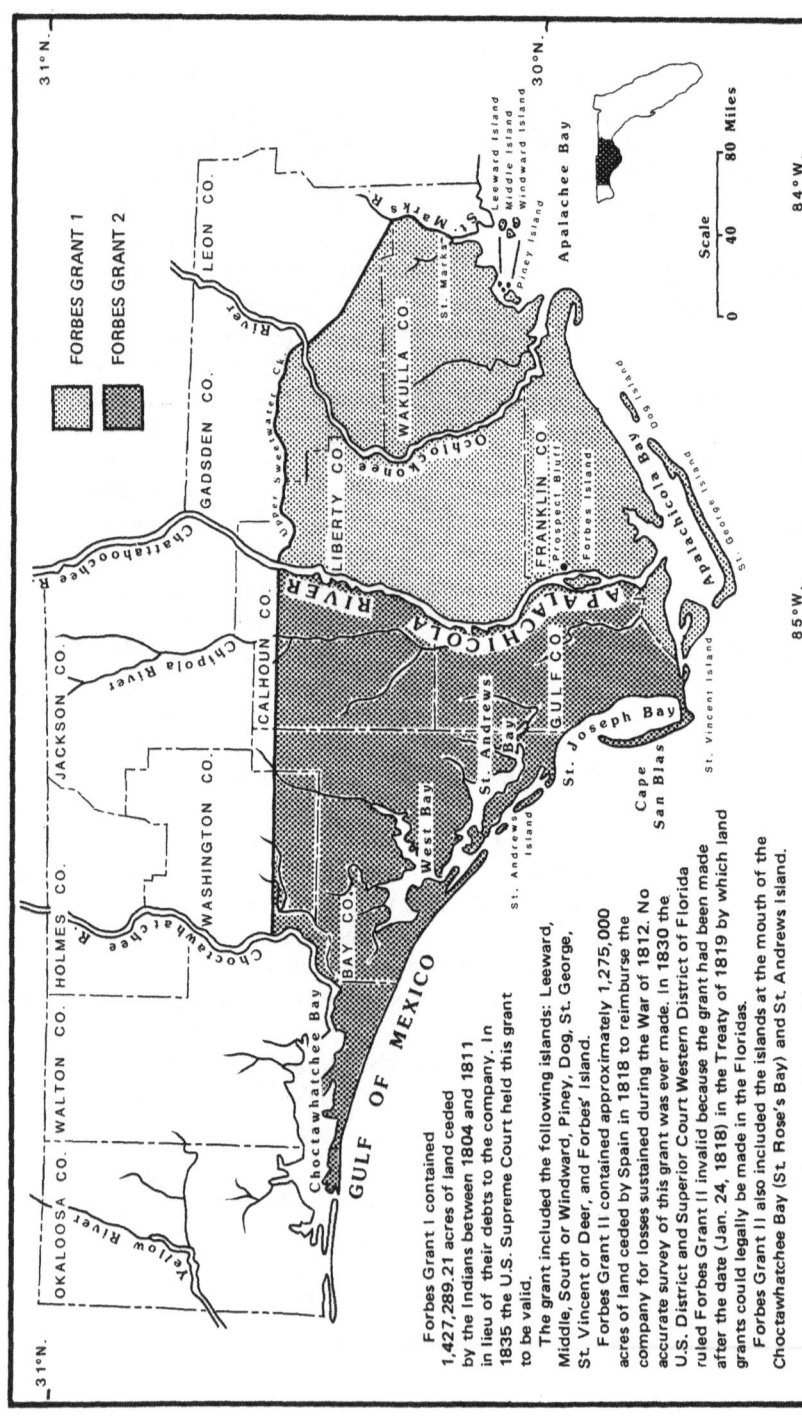

Land grants to Panton, Leslie and Company and John Forbes and Company, 1804–18

settled on a sugar plantation on the banks of the Canimar, in Matanzas Province, Cuba.[52] Until his death, on May 13, 1823, Forbes continued to be concerned with problems arising from the sale of Forbes Grant I and with the division of the estates of his former partners among their heirs.

Together, John and James Innerarity assumed control of John Forbes and Company in the Floridas. During this period, except for land speculation, the company's business was restricted largely to Mobile and Pensacola. John Forbes and Company ceased to operate in Pensacola in 1830, when John Innerarity purchased most of the company property there for his own use. This left James as the surviving partner. John Forbes and Company was on the tax rolls in Mobile until James died in 1847.

Although John Innerarity had been officially severed from the company since 1830, on May 16, 1854, just two months before he died, he renewed his efforts to secure compensation from the British government for the slaves and gunpowder lost during the War of 1812.[53] The last years of the lives of all three partners were a legal nightmare involving the Florida lands, claims against the company, and problems with numerous heirs.

52. The exact date of Forbes's withdrawal from the company is uncertain. Forbes had intimated his plans to withdraw from the company in early 1817: White, "John Forbes Company," 171. On January 30, 1818, Arbuthnot wrote that reports had reached him that Forbes had "withdrawn from all Indian concerns": *ASP FR*, 4:607. He may have picked up this information on his recent trip to Nassau, or from Hambly and Doyle while they were being held prisoners on the Suwannee.

53. White, "John Forbes Company," 198–99; Wright, "Diplomacy of Trade," 217; Greenslade, "John Innerarity," 94–95; U.S. Congress, *Report on John Forbes and Company*, 1836; John Innerarity, Power of Attorney, to James Pott, May 16, 1854, IHP.

On August 6, 1808, James Innerarity married Heloise Isabelle Trouillet in Mobile. They had five children, all born in Mobile between 1810 and 1820. Heloise died about 1820. James subsequently moved to Cuba, where he lived on his plantation, "Heloisa," in Canimar, Matanzas Province. There he met Laura Manuella Centeno and, apparently, five children were born out of wedlock to that union. The oldest, Frank, was born in Cuba in 1832, and the other four were born in Mobile between 1837 and 1843. When James died in 1847, he specifically excluded any children except those born to Heloise from receiving any part of his estate: James Innerarity's Will, September 14, 1847, Will Book 2, pp. 233–35, County Courthouse, Mobile; James Innerarity to John Innerarity, October 6, 1821, written from "Heloisa" Plantation, GP. Much of the genealogical information about James's family was supplied to the authors by Jean Innerarity Beattie and is on file in the Papers of Panton, Leslie and Company, UWF. James died October 4, 1847: *Funeral Book*, p. 258, Chancery, Diocese of Mobile.

16
The Vidal Case

*T*O end the history of the Panton, Leslie and John Forbes companies with the Spanish land grant of January 1818 would leave the impression that, eventually, everything worked out well for these companies. By 1818, virtually all of the Indian debts had been paid and the losses from the War of 1812 settled. But a cursory look at subsequent litigation reveals that everyone did not live "happily ever after." Although several volumes would be required to detail the numerous disputes in which members of these firms appeared before the bar, a close review of one crucial case is necessary. A few cases, such as those involving admiralty problems and the Choctaw debt, have been discussed; the records of these proceedings are a mine of information not found elsewhere, pertaining to the companies and the personalities associated with them.

One of the most interesting cases involving John Forbes and Company—and the most controversial for Andrew Jackson, the first American governor—came shortly after the change of flags in 1821. Governor Jackson formally received Pensacola and West Florida from Spain on July 17, 1821. Initially, Jackson acknowledged John Innerarity as one of Pensacola's leading citizens—not surprising, since Jackson had known Innerarity since the general first invaded Pensacola in November 1814. Indeed, on July 19, 1821, Jackson appointed Innerarity an alderman on the *cabildo*, or town council. Barely a month elapsed, however, before Henry M. Brackenridge—Pensacola's *alcalde*, notary, and keeper of the notarial archives—called Governor Jackson's attention to the plight of Mercedes (also Merced) Vidal, a free quadroon and long-time Pensacola resident.[1]

Mercedes and her sister, Caroline María, were the natural daughters of Dr. Nicolás María Vidal and a mulatto woman, Euphrozine Hinard, of New Orleans. Vidal had been lieutenant governor and, for a few days in 1799, temporary governor of Louisiana and West Florida. He later served as Spanish auditor of war for West Florida in Pensacola, where he died on May 25, 1806.[2] The exact date that Euphrozine and her daughters moved to Pensacola is not known, but Mercedes married Severino Palao there in 1811. By 1812, Euphrozine owned property in Pensacola and eventually engaged in buying and selling slaves.[3]

At the time of Vidal's death, no will was discovered among his papers. A month later, however, Cristobal de Armas arrived in Pensacola from New Orleans with a will, dated 1798, which named him executor and administrator of Vidal's estate. The local tribunal declared the will valid and issued letters of administration to Armas, who had the estate appraised and made preparations for its sale. Armas also examined and recognized as legitimate the notes, obligations, and accounts of Vidal's creditors.[4]

The records revealed that Vidal, at the time of his death, owed John Forbes and Company $3,361.4. This obligation included a note for $3,000, which he had borrowed from the company on December 14, 1805. The balance of $361.4 was for sundry merchandise which Vidal had purchased.[5] Vidal's estate included his personal property and a few slaves in Pensacola, twenty-odd boxes of furniture and personal effects deposited in the convent of the Ursuline nuns in New Orleans, and 16,000 arpents of land in the district of Baton Rouge.[6] In September 1806, John Forbes,

1. Carter, *Territorial Papers*, 22:131; *ASP M*, 2:811–12; Coker and Inglis, *Spanish Censuses of Pensacola*, 4.
2. Holmes, *Gayoso*, 266–67; *ASP M*, 2:811–12, 868. For brief biographical sketches of Dr. Vidal, see Holmes, "Dramatis Personae in Spanish Louisiana," 152–55; Holmes, "Vidal and Zoning in Spanish New Orleans, 1797," 172–75; Kerr, "Petty Felony, Slave Defiance, and Frontier Villainy," 39. Euphrozine Hinard's name is variously spelled. The spelling used here is from the administrator's sale of her property in 1866, File 1866-o-468, Escambia County Court Archives, Pensacola.
3. For a brief sketch of Euphrozine Hinard, see Sutton, *Women in Pensacola*, 68–69. For Mercedes Vidal's marriage see File 1821-29905, Escambia County Court Archives, Pensacola. At the same time that Mercedes was pressing for a settlement with John Innerarity, she also was involved in a separation suit with her husband which resulted in the public sale of their personal property: ibid.
4. *ASP M*, 2:868.
5. Ibid., 2:858. Where only one figure follows the decimal (e.g., $3,361.4), it represents reales. There were eight reales in one dollar. Thus, ".4" would be 50 cents.
6. *ASP M*, 2:849–50, 858–60. For the location of the 16,000 arpents of land and its sale at auction, see WPA, "Archives of the Spanish Government of West Florida," 12:260–67. For more on the sale of the land, see *ASP M*, 2:868.

on behalf of the company and the other creditors, petitioned for the sale of the land at Baton Rouge. Since Armas, the executor of the estate, was a resident of Louisiana, which was then foreign territory, the Pensacola court asked him to post security or a deposit. Instead, Armas applied to be relieved of his responsibility as executor, which the court granted. Forbes then petitioned the court to serve as depositary for the proceeds from the sale of the estate's property and to distribute the proceeds among the creditors.[7] Although never officially recognized as such, the company became the de facto executor of Vidal's estate.

It is not necessary to detail the sale of all of Vidal's property, only the portion that later figured prominently in the suit brought against the company. William Simpson, head of the New Orleans branch of John Forbes and Company, discovered Vidal's property in the Ursuline convent, and the sheriff subsequently sold it at auction. When all charges and commissions were paid, Vidal's New Orleans estate netted only $188.75. Included among the expenses was a payment of $200 to Edward Livingston, the company's New Orleans attorney, which had earlier been ordered by the court and paid to him by the sheriff. In addition, Simpson paid Terencio Le Blanc $209.2½ against a debt of $242 that Vidal owed to Le Blanc.[8] Eventually, John Forbes and Company collected $6,101, the total proceeds from the Vidal estate. Outstanding obligations amounted to $7,054.6½ and, when prorated among the creditors, left an unpaid balance of $953.0½. On its account, the company received $2,907.2 against a debt of $3,361.4, or 86.5 percent of the total due: the other creditors received a like percentage. Even so, the estate still owed the company $454.25. For her part, Euphrozine received $1,379 for her claim against Vidal of $1,590. According to the records, Forbes and Company neither claimed nor received any commission but served only as depositary for the funds of the insolvent estate.[9] On the surface, all seemed well.

In 1810, as the result of an auditor's report, a decree was issued requiring the company to produce $2,645.25, to be distributed among the creditors and heirs. This was the amount of assets, it was claimed, that the company still possessed which belonged to the estate. The basis for this decree apparently rested in part on the opinion that a proper accounting of the sale of the New Orleans property had not been made. Innerarity ignored the decree, and there matters rested until 1817.[10] On August 29 of that year, Caroline Vidal asked the Pensacola officials for records of the

7. *ASP M*, 2:868.
8. Ibid., 2:858–60, 868.
9. Ibid., 2:862, 868.
10. Ibid., 2:849, 868.

disposition of her late father's estate. A few days later, Governor Masot ordered that the papers be delivered to her. A search for the documents revealed that former Governor Mauricio Zúñiga had turned them over to Innerarity. When asked for the papers, Innerarity requested a week or so to find them. His bookkeeper, Innerarity reported, had hidden the papers when insurgents threatened Pensacola. By this, he may have been referring either to the visit of privateersman Job Northrup the previous December or to rumors that pirates from Galveston were about to attack the city. Again, in December 1817 and in February 1818, Caroline renewed her request for the papers, and Masot duly ordered Innerarity to produce them. But Innerarity now claimed that either they had been sent to Mobile in a trunk or that he may have returned them to the Pensacola archives, whence they were sent to Havana. In any event, Caroline did not get the documents she desired. In 1819, Mercedes joined the quest, repeating Caroline's demands for the records.

Colonel José Callava, by this time governor of West Florida, repeated the orders of his predecessor that Innerarity restore the records. True to form, Innerarity did not do so. After further procrastination, however, Innerarity finally "discovered" the papers "by a 'most extraordinary accident'" and turned them over to the Spanish officials.[11]

There followed, in the summer of 1820, a detailed audit of the accounts by Nicolás Santos Suárez, whose report indicated that the papers were "a confused mixture—a perfect labyrinth"—which may have resulted from "the malice of some individuals" or from the failure of the interested parties to have a lawyer advise them. As a result of this report, Colonel Callava directed Innerarity to make a deposit of $5,828 within five days and to provide within ten days "an exact and documented account" of the sale of Vidal's effects in New Orleans and of the 16,000 arpents of land at Baton Rouge. When the deadline was up, on July 10, 1820, and Innerarity still had not complied with his orders, Callava placed Innerarity's personal and real property under an interdict.[12] The governor's action notwithstanding, nothing was done until the summer of 1821.

A few days before the official change of flags at Pensacola, Mercedes again asked Callava for the papers. She was informed that she could have them copied a few at a time, but such a process proved costly; the testamentary papers covered more than 1,000 pages. No sooner had the government of West Florida changed hands than Mercedes applied to Alcalde

---

11. Ibid., 2:811–12, 816–18; Coker and Inglis, *Spanish Censuses of Pensacola*, 144n4; *The Floridian*, September 22, 1821, p. 2, col. d.
12. ASP M, 2:849–50.

Brackenridge to secure the papers before they were taken out of the country. Brackenridge and his associate, Richard Keith Call, served as attorneys for the Vidal heirs.[13]

According to Article Two of the Adams-Onís Treaty, all Spanish documents pertaining to property in the Floridas were to be turned over to U.S. officials. On July 17, when Jackson took possession of West Florida, many documents were surrendered to the new government. Obviously, not all papers were relinquished because the Spaniards kept the Vidal documents, among others. Because the Vidal papers related to the estate of a deceased Spanish officer, they were filed with the documents of the military tribunal. Still unanswered was the question of whether this was done intentionally, in order to spirit them out of the country, or whether they really were deposited with the other military records for the reason stated. No matter what the answer, since the papers did pertain to property, they should have been turned over to the United States. Mercedes managed to secure copies of a few of the pertinent papers, which she showed to Brackenridge. After inspecting them, Brackenridge notified Jackson that certain proceedings under the will should be set aside as "irregular and fraudulent." But first, the original documents must be obtained. Mercedes informed Brackenridge that Ensign Domingo Sausa had custody of those particular records, and he appealed to Jackson to secure them.[14]

Jackson sent George Walton, secretary of West Florida, and John Miller, clerk of the county court, together with Brackenridge, to see Sausa and to demand of him all documents relating to private property. After consulting with Sausa at his residence, they examined several boxes of documents and requested that Sausa turn over to them the papers in question. Sausa, however, refused to do so on the grounds that the papers had been entrusted to him for safekeeping. At the time, Richard Call was ill and did not accompany Brackenridge and the others to see Sausa. In reflection, Call later criticized his partner for not seizing the papers at that time: the result was the cause célèbre of Jackson's Florida governorship. Following Sausa's refusal to hand over the papers, Jackson ordered Sausa arrested and the documents brought to him, justifying his actions under Article 2 of the treaty.[15]

13. Ibid., 2:808; *The Floridian*, September 1, 1821, p. 3, col. a; Doherty, *Richard Keith Call*, 21.
14. *ASP M*, 2:808, 826; *ASP FR*, 4:805; Doherty, "Jackson vs. the Spanish Governor," 152. The spelling of Spanish names follows that in Callava, *Manifiesto*, and not the spelling in *American State Papers*.
15. *ASP M*, 2:802–4; Doherty, *Richard Keith Call*, 21.

But Sausa acted first. He decided to place the documents in Colonel Callava's care and delivered them to the former governor's house. Although Callava was not present, Sausa gave the two boxes of papers to Antonio de Follarate, Callava's servant. When Sausa was brought before Jackson, he admitted that the papers had been transferred to Callava's residence. Jackson declared that if Sausa secured the documents from Callava, he would not be detained. If not, however, he would be sent to jail. Sausa replied that a Spanish officer could not be put in prison. To which Jackson stormed that he would put them all in prison—Sausa, Callava, and Follarate—"for seven years, or until the papers should be forthcoming." Although directed to treat him with courtesy, Captain F. L. Dade took Sausa into custody and escorted him to see Colonel Callava. At the time, Callava was visiting the home of Colonel George M. Brooke, commanding the Fourth Infantry at Pensacola, where he and others (including John Innerarity) were dinner guests. Callava refused to permit Sausa to deliver any papers, either to Captain Dade or to Governor Jackson, even though he knew his refusal would result in Sausa's incarceration.[16]

The pace now quickened. Jackson ordered Colonel Brooke to send an officer, two NCOs, and twenty soldiers, all fully armed, to him for further orders. This detachment, commanded by Lieutenant G. W. Montz, was to accompany Jackson's emissaries, Colonel Robert Butler, Dr. James C. Bronaugh, and Brackenridge, to Callava's residence.[17] There they were to demand the Vidal papers from Callava and his servant Follarate. If they refused to surrender the papers, as requested, the two Spaniards were to be brought before Jackson to explain their failure. When the commission arrived at Callava's residence, they discovered that he was still at Colonel Brooke's home.[18]

The party left, but after waiting for half an hour, they returned to Callava's to find him still not at home. Brackenridge, who spoke Spanish, went to Colonel Brooke's where he called Callava, asking him to return home for a meeting with certain gentlemen who awaited him on important matters of business. Callava informed Brackenridge with considerable warmth that he had certain rights as commissioner of Spain. In effect, Callava claimed diplomatic immunity.[19] Nevertheless, the Spanish colonel, accompanied by several Spanish officers and Innerarity, soon de-

16. *ASP M*, 2:803–4, 824, 829.
17. Ibid., 805. For a brief description of Bronaugh and Butler, see Doherty, "Andrew Jackson's Cronies."
18. *ASP M*, 2:805–6, 808, 829.
19. Ibid., 829; Doherty, "Governorship of Jackson," 15.

parted Colonel Brooke's home and proceeded to Callava's. They were barely seated on the back porch when Brackenridge, Butler, and Bronaugh appeared to discuss the matter of the papers with Callava. After some preliminary sparring, Colonel Butler, through Brackenridge, explained that at Governor Jackson's orders they had come for certain papers—all of which was carefully translated for Callava by Brackenridge, assisted occasionally by Innerarity. Callava insisted on his rights but offered to give Jackson the papers, provided the request was made of him as commissioner or as late governor of West Florida. Otherwise, he refused to deliver them. He was then informed that if he did not produce the papers he would be required to appear before Jackson to answer certain questions. At this, as Jackson later wrote, Innerarity exclaimed, "the die is cast!" "Yes, he said truly the die was cast; for he must have clearly seen that the arts, the influence, the wealth, the power of no individual, not even of Innerarity himself, could any longer obstruct the pure channels of justice." In the continued conversation between Callava and Jackson's emissaries, the colonel finally offered to give up the papers, provided a written request specifying the exact documents desired was presented to him. Brackenridge noted that Callava this time omitted the prerequisite of receiving the request in his role as Spanish commissioner or former governor. The American party soon departed in order that Brackenridge could draw up a formal petition for the papers.[20]

When Brackenridge returned with the petition, Callava and his friends were feverishly packing boxes, as if everything that Callava possessed would be taken from him by force. Callava told Brackenridge that he was preparing a formal protest over the entire proceedings. After leaving the petition with Callava, Brackenridge said that Colonel Butler and Dr. Bronaugh would return for the papers in two hours.

At 9:00 P.M., Butler, Bronaugh, and Brackenridge, accompanied by their military escort, reappeared at Colonel Callava's residence. The house was dark, but the party unlatched the gate and proceeded to the front porch. Inside they heard what sounded like the rattling of arms. Brackenridge called out three times in Spanish to be admitted but received no answer. A guard had already been sent to the rear of the house, while a few soldiers remained in front. The rest now went to the rear, where some persons were observed on the back porch. When asked if Colonel Callava was at home, one of the persons on the porch replied that he did not know where the colonel was. Obtaining some candles, the party, with some soldiers, entered the house and began a room-by-room search. A candle was

---

20. *ASP M*, 2:801–2, 829; Callava, *Manifiesto*, 28.

found burning in one room, which turned out to be Callava's bedroom. There they found the colonel in bed, fully dressed except for his jacket. Callava expressed great surprise that his bedroom had been invaded at that hour of the evening. The papers were demanded of him, but he refused to give them up, even though the boxes containing the documents were in full view of everyone. Callava was now told that he must accompany the intruders to see Governor Jackson. To this he replied that they might murder or assassinate him, but he would not be taken from his home alive. At this point, Innerarity attempted to intervene on Callava's behalf but was ordered by the American officer to be silent. When the guard was commanded to prime and load, Callava offered no further resistance and, accompanied by Innerarity and some of his friends, he was conducted to Jackson. A corporal and three soldiers remained behind to guard the house and to ensure that the papers were not removed.[21]

There followed a heated discussion between Jackson and Callava. Since Callava spoke no English and Jackson no Spanish, Brackenridge served as interpreter. As Jackson and Callava screamed back and forth at each other, Brackenridge could not keep up with the translation and asked others, including Innerarity, to assist him. Jackson told Callava that the papers in question had been taken from the alcalde's office without a receipt being given for them. Further, he accused Callava of hiding the papers and of planning to take them to Cuba. More to the point, Jackson stated that the Vidal papers had been "stolen," but Brackenridge diplomatically declined to interpret the statement literally to Callava. Callava objected to the entire procedure, stating that he was answerable only to a *tribunal de residencia*. Brackenridge was unfamiliar with this term, but Innerarity explained it to him as a court specifically appointed to try provincial governors. Normally, an incoming Spanish governor conducted a *residencia* to inquire into the conduct of the retiring governor, who remained in "residence" during the investigation of his governorship. As the confrontation drew to an end, Jackson told Innerarity and others near him, "Gentlemen, you understand English; tell Colonel Callava, if he does not deliver up the papers, I will send him to the calabouse." Jackson next interrogated Follarate, Callava's servant, who admitted that the papers had been delivered to him by Sausa and were presently in Callava's house. Jackson then ordered Callava and Follarate to jail until the papers were produced.[22] Callava's friends could scarcely believe what they heard.

21. Callava, *Manifiesto*, 28–29; *ASP M*, 2:806–7, 829–30. Innerarity's efforts to intervene were later related by Callava: *The Floridian*, September 29, 1821, p. 1, col. e.
22. *ASP M*, 2:807, 824–31. Regarding the *residencia*, see Haring, *Spanish Empire*, 138–42.

Callava and Follarate soon joined Sausa in the local *calabozo*. The humor of the entire proceedings finally dawned upon Callava, who began laughing and mimicking Jackson. Bottles of champagne appeared, and, in company with his friends, Callava turned his stay in jail into a fiesta.[23]

Ever after Callava protested that neither the questions directed at him by Jackson nor his answers to them were faithfully translated, to which Innerarity, Father Coleman, and others agreed.[24] The Spanish officers who remained in Pensacola later issued a proclamation charging that none of the interrogatories and highly offensive accusations of Jackson, or Callava's replies to Jackson, had been faithfully translated. "*We shuddered at the violent proceedings exercised against our superior*," they declared. Jackson retaliated by insisting that the charge of misinterpretation was "a falsehood, invented and propagated by" Callava.[25] The evidence indicates two specific translation problems—Brackenridge's softening of Jackson's accusations that the documents had been "stolen," and Brackenridge's failure to understand the term tribunal de residencia—but there were others, too. There is little doubt, however, that Callava understood what was wanted of him, and, therefore, charges of failure to translate the questions and answers fully and accurately must be dismissed. If there was a valid charge to be made against Jackson in his confrontation with Callava, it was Jackson's insistence that Callava be treated as a private individual rather than as commissioner of Spain. Had Jackson done so, Callava's honor would have been preserved and, albeit unwillingly, he would undoubtedly have delivered the papers. As for the Spanish officers who issued the proclamation, the governor gave them four days to get out of the country, or be arrested. Among them were several who were related to Innerarity by marriage, including his father-in-law, Lieutenant Colonel Marcos de Villiers.[26]

Colonel Butler and Dr. Bronaugh reported on Innerarity's role in ad-

---

23. Parton, *Life of Andrew Jackson*, 2:632; James, *Life of Andrew Jackson*, 325.
24. Callava, *Manifiesto*, 25–32.
25. *ASP M*, 2:813–14, 828; *The Floridian*, September 29, 1821, p. 2, col. e, p. 3, col. a; October 8, 1821, p. 2, cols. d–e. Proclamation by Andrew Jackson, September 29, 1821, File no. 1821–25, Special Collections Department, University of West Florida. On September 29, Callava's version of his encounter with Jackson also appeared in *The Floridian*, September 29, 1821, p. 1, cols. c–e. Jackson's reaction to it differed little from his response to the proclamation of the Spanish officers: He called it "a tissue of falsehoods and distortion of facts from the commencement to the end—": ibid., p. 2, col. a.
26. Brackenridge admitted that he had softened some expressions in his translations and omitted others which tended only to "irritate and provoke": *ASP M*, 2:831. See also ibid., 2:813–14. In all, thirty-six officers, including Colonel Callava, remained in Pensacola, with the proviso that they must leave within six months: Doherty, "Governorship of Andrew Jackson," 10.

vising and defending Callava when they attempted to obtain the Vidal papers from the former governor. "We deem it an indispensable duty to recommend that your excellency will fill his [Innerarity's] place in the council with a character who will manifest a proper respect for the dignity of the laws and you their Executive." On August 23, the day after the Callava-Jackson meeting, Jackson removed Innerarity from the cabildo and advised him that he would be replaced by someone "better disposed to execute the laws and support its dignity." On the same day, Jackson ordered the removal of the Vidal papers from Callava's residence, and the order was carried out without further ado. Jackson prepared to release the Spaniards from jail, but before that could be done, Innerarity again intervened.[27]

Innerarity and several friends, including Father Coleman, called upon Eligius Fromentin, the recently appointed federal judge, and asked that he issue a writ of habeas corpus to secure Colonel Callava's release. Fromentin, as "a judge of the United States," believed that he had the jurisdiction to issue the writ.[28]

Apparently, Innerarity felt secure in approaching the judge. Fromentin, a former Catholic priest who had fled France during the Reign of Terror, eventually married into an influential family in the United States. Soon after moving to New Orleans he was admitted to the bar, and as early as 1807 he became active in Louisiana politics, serving in the U.S. Senate from 1813 to 1819. Upon returning to Louisiana, he became judge of the criminal court of New Orleans. In 1821, President James Monroe appointed Fromentin the federal judge for West Florida, ignoring Jackson's nominee, John Haywood. Once in Pensacola, Fromentin became fast friends with Callava and Innerarity. Among other things, Innerarity's command of the French language and the French heritage of his wife's family undoubtedly had much to do with his quick and close friendship with Fromentin.[29]

Although Fromentin offered to issue the writ of habeas corpus requested by Innerarity, he wanted security for Callava and the papers in

27. Jackson to Innerarity, August 23, 1821, Jackson Papers, The Hermitage; *ASP M*, 2:808–9, 834.
28. *ASP M*, 2:834–38.
29. *Biographical Directory of the American Congress*, 973. John Innerarity later served as French consular agent and British vice-consul in Pensacola. He corresponded with the French consul in New Orleans and with the government in France in excellent French, which he wrote in precise, minuscule handwriting. For Innerarity's appointment, see *Ministère des Affaires Etrangères, Archives Diplomatiques, Correspondance Consulaire, Nouvelle-Orléans*, 5:211. A number of letters in French by Innerarity are ibid., vols. 8–11 (1841–52). On his marriage and linguistic ability, see also Greenslade, "Innerarity," 92–94. On Haywood, see Bassett, *Correspondence of Andrew Jackson*, 3:150, 160; *ASP M*, 2:837.

his possession before setting the colonel free. Fromentin and Innerarity discussed the amount, and the judge suggested $40,000: $20,000 for Colonel Callava, and $10,000 each for two sureties. Innerarity and a Mr. Lama (Lara?) agreed to serve as sureties.[30] With that settled, and because there was no sheriff in town, Fromentin gave the writ to Dr. John Brosnaham, who delivered it to Lieutenant Mountz, the officer in charge of the jail. Mountz accepted the writ and turned it over to his superior, Captain Philip Wager, who in turn delivered it to Jackson.[31]

When Jackson received the writ, he exploded. He ordered Wager to inform the judge that the prisoners were confined for open contempt of his orders and decrees and would remain confined until he released them. Jackson also ordered Fromentin to appear before him and told him that his gubernatorial commission included jurisdiction as supreme judge in the Floridas. Fromentin was limited in his judicial powers to litigation concerning revenue laws and the importation of slaves. According to Jackson, not only had Fromentin exceeded his judicial authority, but he also had not followed proper form and procedure in executing the writ: he had issued the writ on an oral and not a written application, and the writ had been delivered by Dr. Brosnaham, a private citizen, and not by an officer of the court. When Fromentin agreed not to interfere again with Jackson's authority, Jackson treated it as an apology. Ironically, Fromentin later vehemently repudiated this inference. Nevertheless, Jackson had successfully nullified Fromentin's issuance of the writ of habeas corpus, and threatened to throw him in jail if he ever again interfered with the governor's authority.[32] But this was not Jackson's first unpleasant encounter with a judge over a writ of habeas corpus.

Following the battle of New Orleans, in January 1815, Jackson had continued martial law in that area for several months after the battle. On March 3, 1815, an article appeared in *La Courrière de la Louisiane*, written by Louis Louaillier, a member of the Louisiana state legislature, declaring that the war was over and that it was time to return to civil law. Shortly afterward, some troops mutinied and others refused to obey orders. Jackson immediately arrested Louaillier, but Judge Dominick Hall

---

30. *ASP M*, 2:834–36. While several persons with the name "Lara" can be found in the Escambia County Court Records, none have been discovered with the name "Lama."

31. Ibid.

32. Ibid., 2:810, 822–23, 836–38, 841–43; Doherty, "Governorship of Andrew Jackson," 14–19. Before Jackson declared martial law in New Orleans, he attempted, with the support of Governor Claiborne, to get the legislature to pass a law suspending the writ of habeas corpus. Louaillier headed the committee that reported the "measure as inexpedient": "War, Turmoil the First Police Jury," St. Landry Parish *Daily World*, November 3, 1955, p. 68.

issued a writ of habeas corpus to effect his release. Jackson then arrested Judge Hall for aiding, abetting, and inciting mutiny within his camp. On March 11, Louaillier was court-martialed on seven charges. The court, however, declared itself without jurisdiction in six of the seven charges and acquitted him of the seventh, that of being a spy. Jackson rejected the findings, sent Louaillier back to jail, and ordered Judge Hall escorted out of town. Official notice that the war was over soon reached New Orleans and Jackson lifted his martial law edict. Judge Hall returned to New Orleans and ordered Jackson before his court to show cause why he should not be held in contempt for his refusal to recognize the writ of habeas corpus in Louaillier's case. The trial was brief; Hall found Jackson in contempt and fined him $1,000 and costs.[33]

Perhaps the Pensacola incident gave Jackson an opportunity to avenge his earlier conviction by thwarting Fromentin's issuance of the writ. But, if that were not enough, Jackson looked upon Fromentin as a despised ex-priest—Jackson even called him an "apostate priest" twice in one letter. Nor had he been Jackson's choice as judge. Finally, he was a close friend of Innerarity and Callava.[34] All the furor over Callava's arrest and the issuance of a writ of habeas corpus were only preliminaries to the real issue: the case of *The Heirs of Vidal v. John Innerarity*.

A few days after the Vidal papers had been taken from Callava's house, Jackson wrote Secretary of State Adams that, although he was well aware of the corruption that existed in Spanish judicial proceedings, he still was not prepared "to expect such a scene of combined wickedness and corruption as has been brought to light by this investigation." Though his actions had been severe, he asserted, they were dictated by his desire to "save the unprotected orphan from being ruined by the most cruel oppression, by the most corrupt and wicked combination I ever investigated."[35]

In late August, Sheriff J. C. Craig delivered Jackson's order to Innerarity to appear before him to explain why he had not complied with Colonel

33. Parton, *Life of Andrew Jackson*, 2:58–62; James, *Life of Andrew Jackson*, 281–86.
34. Jackson to Call, November 15, 1821, Bassett, *Correspondence of Andrew Jackson*, 3:131. Jackson's attitude toward "apostate priests" was abundantly clear in this letter: "These perjured immorral monsters in society I allways did abhor, they never have or will be my associates": ibid. There were other reasons why Jackson disliked Fromentin, which are related in Hoffman, "Talleyrand," 56–58. On the other hand, Fromentin had defended Jackson's execution of Arbuthnot and Ambrister in 1818. Hoffman wrote, "Fromentin was a member of the tribunal before which that notable case was aired, 'I was found in the foremost ranks,' [Fromentin] stated, 'and, if not among the ablest, I am sure among the most zealous defenders of General Jackson'": ibid., 57. See also *ASP M*, 2:872.
35. *ASP M*, 2:801. On why Jackson supported Mercedes Vidal, see Doherty, "Andrew Jackson's Cronies," 10.

Callava's decrees to post bond and to render an account of the sale of Vidal's estate. Innerarity requested and Jackson granted him time to prepare his defense.[36]

During this respite in the Vidal case, Jackson and Innerarity clashed on other matters. In September, Jackson appointed a commission, consisting of Mayor George Bowie and Alcalde Brackenridge, which was instructed to interrogate various citizens in Pensacola, the exact purport of which is not entirely clear. When the two commissioners called upon Innerarity, he refused to answer their questions. Jackson summarily ordered Innerarity before him to answer the questions, warning Innerarity that failure to answer would be at his own peril. Innerarity complied with the demand.[37] The encounter left no doubt that Jackson would tolerate no opposition to his rule.

Pending the next formal hearing in the Vidal case, which had been delayed for several weeks, Innerarity and his attorney, Samuel Acre of Mobile, worked hard to prepare his defense. Innerarity attempted to obtain records from New Orleans and elsewhere to show that all of the money from the sale of Vidal's estate had been properly accounted for.[38] Acre also argued that the court did not have jurisdiction in the case.

Acre's arguments hinged on whether the Spanish Constitution of 1812 was or was not in effect in Pensacola at the time of the change of flags. If it were in effect at that time, it would have eliminated the judicial powers formerly enjoyed by the governor. Thus, Jackson would have been restricted in the judicial authority that he claimed. Although it could be proved that Colonel Callava had taken the required oath and that the constitution had been promulgated and sworn to in the "midst of rejoicings and illuminations, which lasted from the 26th to the 29th of May, 1820," Jackson and his advisors refused to acknowledge this act as binding. They contended that the transfer treaty should have been ratified in 1819, before the constitution was reinstated. According to their reasoning, the constitution never was in effect in Pensacola. Consequently, there was no legal basis for contending that Jackson did not have authority to hear the Vidal case.[39]

On September 17, Innerarity appeared before Jackson and John C. Mitchell, whom Jackson had appointed to sit with him in place of ailing

36. *ASP M*, 2:852–53.
37. Summons to John Innerarity, September 27, 1821, Jackson Papers, The Hermitage.
38. *ASP M*, 2:865.
39. *The Floridian*, September 15, 1821, 2e, 3a–c; *ASP M*, 2:846–48; See especially ibid., 814–16. Frederick Cubberly, a Jackson partisan, argued in "Andrew Jackson, Judge" that Jackson had jurisdiction in the case and that the decision rendered by the Jackson court was a proper one.

Justice David Shannon. The court, composed of Jackson and Mitchell, styled itself the "Supreme Court of Judicature of this Province."[40] They quickly settled the question of the court's authority simply by declaring that they had jurisdiction in the case. If Jackson had not already made clear his feelings about the case, the court's comments removed any doubt. "The defendant's inexplicable conduct, in keeping back the papers, and producing them at last on compulsion . . . does not incline the court to make any very violent presumptions in his favor." The court directed Innerarity to explain why Callava's decrees of July 1820 should not be carried out. Pending a final hearing, the court required Innerarity to post bond of $8,500 in real property. It also appointed Furguson H. Nisbet, Juan de la Rua, and William Davidson as auditors, to examine the accounts and to submit a report to the court.[41]

It was not until October 6 that the auditors made their report. It was a thorough and complete examination of all of the documents and accounts. Two of the auditors, Nisbet and Davidson, concluded that the $200 paid to Edward Livingston, Forbes's New Orleans attorney, should not be allowed. Two other payments were, in their opinion, questionable: the $432 paid to Miguel Eslava by the Mobile branch, for which there was no receipt, and the $209.2½ paid Terencio Le Blanc by William Simpson in New Orleans, which was not in Innerarity's account books and for which they could find no receipt. If these three payments were added to the $303.3 still on the books and the $70 reserved for future costs, Innerarity owed a total of $1,137.2½. If these payments were allowed, then the balance due the company from Vidal's estate, $454.25, should be credited to its account. Although he signed the audit, Juan de la Rua filed a separate report in which he argued that the payments to Eslava, Le Blanc, and Livingston should be allowed. All three auditors considered the administrative costs charged to the Vidal estate—$1,315.5—excessive. But John Forbes and Company was not accused of receiving any of these funds. In part because of La Rua's dissenting report, Innerarity requested that an umpire be appointed to rule on the disputed items. His request was denied and the court convened on October 8.[42]

Innerarity refused to acknowledge that any of the charges against him were true, disagreed with the conclusions of the auditors' report, and asserted that when all of Vidal's creditors were paid the estate was still indebted to the Forbes Company. The court held, however, that the auditors' report displayed "great skill and judgment, and the court are highly satis-

40. *The Floridian*, September 22, 1821, p. 3, col. a; ASP M, 2:852.
41. ASP M, 2:816–18.
42. Ibid., 2:861–63, 866–67.

fied with it," and ruled that the defendant's exceptions were not well taken. Accordingly, the court disallowed the payments to Eslava, Le Blanc, and Livingston. It also accepted the auditors' recommendations that the balance due John Forbes and Company, $454.25, be credited to the company's account. That left the company indebted to the Vidal estate in the amount of $683.06. But that was not all. Since the account should have been settled with the heirs in 1810, interest at the rate of 5 percent per annum from 1810 to 1821 was added, making the final amount due $1,027.19. Jackson and Mitchell charged all of the court costs to Innerarity—a sum that is unknown—and directed him to pay the total amount due to the alcalde within thirty days. All creditors were instructed to present their claims by November 30.[43] The appropriate response was to appeal the decision.

The court system of West Florida in 1821 was quite simple. There were only two courts: the county court and a court variously referred to as the supreme or superior court of West Florida, or, as noted earlier, the "Supreme Court of Judicature of this Province." Of course, Fromentin was a federal judge, but with limited powers and no appellate jurisdiction. The county court had jurisdiction in civil cases involving sums in excess of $20, and in all criminal cases. Appeal to the governor in his supreme judicial capacity could be made from the county court in civil cases of $500 or more, and no one could be executed without his approval. When Jackson and Mitchell heard the Vidal case, they were sitting as the supreme court of West Florida, from which the only appeal was a request for the governor to review the case. Innerarity knew that if the Vidal case was heard by the supreme court, he would have no avenue of appeal from its decision except to the governor himself. Small wonder then that before the trial began Innerarity requested that the case be tried in a court of first instance, which could only have been the county court.[44] The advantage to Innerarity was obvious. His case would be heard by the justices of the peace and not by Jackson. But Innerarity's request was ignored, if it was ever seriously considered and, as we know, the case was tried by the supreme court.

Two months after the Pensacola trial, the Vidal case was reviewed at Innerarity's request by the "Supreme Judicial Court of West Florida" in Mobile, Alabama. The decision of the Jackson-Mitchell court was care-

43. Ibid., 866–67; *The Floridian*, October 15, 1821, p. 3, col. e.
44. *ASP M*, 833–34, 865; Carter, *Territorial Papers*, 22:437, 437n8; see also ibid., 151; Doherty, "Governorship of Andrew Jackson," 12–13, 16, 18; Samuel Myers to George Walton [February 3, 1822], Jackson Papers, LC. This letter, also addressed to the "Supreme Executive Court of West Florida," is misdated; see Walton to Jackson, January 28, 1822, Carter, *Territorial Papers*, 22:347–48.

fully considered, point by point. Finally, on December 10, this court rendered an opinion which, on the surface, set aside the decision of the Pensacola tribunal. It declared that Innerarity did not owe the Vidal heirs anything and that the Vidal estate was, in fact, indebted to John Forbes and Company in the amount of $157.00. Further, the proper legal remedy, the opinion stated, was to grant Innerarity a new trial. The court's opinion was signed by Samuel Acre, Innerarity's attorney in the Vidal case. In effect, Jackson's decision had been overturned, or so it would seem from the documents printed in the *American State Papers*.[45] It would be fruitless to list the historians who have accepted that document as part of the legal record of the Vidal case. What was this "Supreme Judicial Court of West Florida"? Under what authority had it been constituted? Who had appointed Acre as the presiding judge? Why was it sitting in Mobile? Apparently, no one has ever raised these questions, much less attempted to answer them.

The proceedings in Pensacola after December 10, 1821, clearly show that the "Supreme Judicial Court of West Florida" was a title gratuitously given to the opinion rendered by Acre and requested by Innerarity. Such a "court" never existed as a body and Innerarity was absolutely right when he wrote that there was no appeal from Jackson's court. Fromentin categorically stated that the court created by Jackson in Pensacola was "a court without appeal."[46] But the general was not in Pensacola to be bothered by such legal problems. He and his family had departed for Tennessee on October 8. Interestingly, that is the date of Jackson's and Mitchell's decision in the Vidal case. George Walton, whom Jackson had appointed acting governor of West Florida, was left with the task of enforcing that decision.[47] Innerarity was busy managing, by one means or another, to prevent execution of the judgment against him until February 1822.

He first submitted Acre's "opinion" to Acting Governor Walton, asking that Walton review the case. But Walton paid no attention at all to Acre's opinion, indicating that he would proceed without delay to compel Innerarity to pay the judgment.[48] Meanwhile, perhaps for Acre's use, In-

---

45. *ASP M*, 2:873–75.
46. Ibid., 871.
47. Jackson to Monroe, October 5, 1821, Bassett, *Correspondence of Andrew Jackson*, 3:122. Traditionally, historians have concluded that Rachel and Jackson's family left Pensacola on October 8 and that Jackson followed a few days later: *The Floridian*, October 8, 1821, p. 3, col. d. A week later, the same paper reported that, contrary to its previous statement, Jackson *had* departed with his family "on Monday last," or October 8. It continued that they had been heard from at Claiborne, Alabama,—"all well": ibid., October 15, 1821, p. 3, col. d. For Walton's appointment, see Jackson to Walton, October [5], 1821, Carter, *Territorial Papers*, 22:229–31.
48. *ASP FR*, 4:800.

nerarity had obtained the case papers, for which he gave a receipt. When Walton called for the papers, Innerarity was "up to his old tricks." The acting governor threatened to throw him in jail "instantly" and to keep him there until he produced the papers. Innerarity quickly found the papers, but he had not yet given up.[49]

Innerarity hired new legal counsel, Pensacola attorney Samuel Myers, who in January submitted a long review of the Vidal case to Walton. Myers claimed that Innerarity had no remedy from the court under the existing judicial system of the province. Most of Myers's comments were similar to Acre's except that he contended that the Vidal heirs owed the company $158.25—$1.25 more than Acre had concluded they owed. Myers requested a stay of execution as well as a new trial, a rehearing, or a review of the case, contending that an injustice had been done.[50] Walton received the "Bill of Review," as he called it, but rejected it out of hand. He further advised Jackson that he had anticipated that Innerarity "would die hard, but die he must, and it only remains for the Sheriff to do his duty, perhaps the task would more properly belong to the hangman!"[51] Strong words for a $1,000 judgment!

While Innerarity was busy trying to get the case reviewed, his father-in-law, Lieutenant Colonel Marcos de Villiers, and a fellow officer returned to Pensacola from Havana early in January 1822. It should be recalled that Villiers had been ordered out of the country the previous September for his role in the defense of Colonel Callava. At the time of their departure, the officers had issued a farewell address which further infuriated Jackson. As a result, Jackson directed Walton to imprison them if they should return and to keep them in jail until he authorized their release. Villiers had returned to Pensacola because his wife was ill and also to settle his private affairs. He intended to remove his family to Cuba as soon as he was able. A few days after their arrival, Acting Governor Walton placed them under house arrest. Feeling that they were being unjustly discriminated against, the officers petitioned Walton for their release. Jackson, when he heard about the problem, wrote the secretary of state asking that Walton be directed to release them. Although it took several months for the communications to make the rounds, the president finally ordered their release. When advised about the furor he had created, Walton stated that he was only carrying out Jackson's orders in placing the officers

---

49. Ibid.
50. Samuel Myers to George Walton, [February 3, 1822], Jackson Papers, LC. On Myers's "Bill of Review," see note 44 above.
51. Walton to Jackson, January 28, 1822, Carter, *Territorial Papers*, 22:347–48.

under detention.[52] In retrospect, Walton's actions may have had a long-term good effect upon the Villiers and Innerarity families. Walton had directed Captain Henry Wilson, assigned to the Fourth Infantry at Pensacola, to bring Villiers before him for contempt and disobedience of Jackson's proclamation. Some have said that it was during this visit to Villiers's home that Captain Wilson met Mary, John Innerarity's teenage daughter. Six years later, in 1828, Henry Wilson and Mary Innerarity were married in Pensacola. One of the witnesses at the ceremony was Captain Philip Wager, who also had been intimately involved in the Callava-Vidal affair.[53]

Innerarity was not alone in his efforts to delay execution of the sentence against him. Judge Fromentin filled the mails to the secretary of state with continuing appeals on both his and Innerarity's behalf. He sent Adams a copy of Acre's opinion and argued at great length about Jackson's usurpation of power in Pensacola. In one of his many letters to Adams he wrote, "I regret it, sir—bitterly regret it, the Genius of American history will drop a tear in penning the page which is to record this single political phenomenon."[54]

Indeed, Innerarity shed more than a tear when the sheriff and his deputy arrived at his home on February 4, 1822, to demand that Innerarity pay the court's assessment. When told that if he failed to pay his slaves and household furniture would be taken, Innerarity attempted to soften their rancor, claiming that he was sick, and taking medicine. He further pleaded that he "was just going to puke. I shall puke now," he said, "wretching as if he was actually going to do so." Walton recorded that even "this climax of eloquence did not deter the Sheriffs, who proceeded to discharge their duty leaving Mr. Innerarity to puke, or do whatever else he might think proper." No sooner had the sheriff departed than Innerarity circled the town, complaining to all who would listen "of the

52. *ASP FR*, 4:800–801; Carter, *Territorial Papers*, 22:347–48, 369, 403–4; Doherty, "Governorship of Andrew Jackson," 29; Remini, *Andrew Jackson*, 416–17.

53. *ASP FR*, 4:801; Sutton, *Blacks and Slavery*, 8–9; Heitman, *Historical Register*, 1:1046. This was not Captain Henry J. Wilson's first visit to Pensacola. He served as regimental adjutant of the Fourth Infantry at Fort Barrancas in 1818–19 during the U.S. occupation of Pensacola. See Wilson to General D. Parker, Pensacola, June 29, 1818; Wilson to Major James M. Glassell, Pensacola, November 2, December [?] 1818; Wilson to Brigadier General Daniel Parker, Pensacola, January 10, 1819; Adjutant General's Office, Letters Received 1818–19, NARG 94. The twenty-eight-year-old Henry Wilson married twenty-year-old Mary Innerarity on May 15, 1828: Marriage Book "A," Escambia County Court Records; Coker and Inglis, *Spanish Censuses of Pensacola*, 104; No. 3 Papers Relating to Forbes Purchase, Henry J. Wilson's answers to interrogatories, September 8, 1840, pp. 190–91, Papers of Panton, Leslie and Company, UWF.

54. *ASP M*, 2:872–73.

cruel and tyrannical proceeding, and endeavoring to excite sympathy." When he returned home, he carefully walked on the far side of the square from where Walton lived in order to avoid "going by that house of persecution." Innerarity made no immediate effort to redeem his slaves and property, although Walton asserted that he could have paid ten times the amount due in an hour's time, had he so desired. It was all a design, Walton believed, to enable Innerarity to turn to the Spanish government, or to John Forbes and Company, and claim ten or twenty thousand dollars for losses on their behalf. Walton warned that if Judge Fromentin, who was continually at Innerarity's heels, attempted to issue an injunction to prevent the sale of Innerarity's effects, he would be sent to jail in irons.[55]

Here ends the record in the Vidal case. Notice of a sheriff's sale or public auction of Innerarity's slaves and furniture has not been found in the local newspaper. Since other such sales were published in *The Floridian*, it must be assumed that Innerarity finally redeemed his property.[56]

As for Callava, he hurried to Washington (after his release from jail) to complain to Adams about his treatment in Pensacola. Back in Havana, Callava issued a long and bitter manifesto on the same subject.[57] But his complaints were to no avail. Resolutions introduced in Congress to censure Jackson for his part in the affair died there.[58] In Pensacola, Dr. Bronaugh recorded one impression: "Among many of the old inhabitants here, the principal cause of astonishment was, that an ex-governor could be sent to prison, at the instance of two or three females, in the humblest walk of life."[59] A few months after the incident, the Jackson-Callava encounter was scarcely spoken of in Washington. In March 1822, *The Floridian* reported that the president would send the documents pertaining to the Vidal case to Congress in a few days: "They are very voluminous and will form a very interesting book."[60]

Secretary of State John Quincy Adams, in one of his ablest state papers, not only defended Jackson again, but managed (as only he could do) to lay the blame for the entire affair at the feet of the captain-general of Cuba and Colonel Callava.[61]

55. Walton to Jackson, February 4, 1822, Jackson Papers, LC.
56. For example, when Mercedes Vidal's and Severino Palao's property was sold at public auction, a note to that effect appeared in *The Floridian*, October 22, 1821, p. 3, col. d. A receipt for $10.20 to John Innerarity from the Executive Court of West Florida, dated March 1822, is in the Greenslade Papers. But it is obvious from the contents that the amount paid the court was for filing fees and for copies of the documents, etc., and did not represent the total court costs of the Vidal case.
57. Remini, *Andrew Jackson*, 415–16; Callava, *Manifiesto*.
58. *The Floridian*, April 13, 1822, p. 1, col. e.
59. Ibid., October 8, 1821, P. 2, col. b.
60. Ibid., March 4, 1822, p. 3, col. d.
61. *ASP FR*, 4:802–7.

Some historians have ended their discussion of the Vidal case with Acre's "opinion," that is, that the Vidal heirs owed Innerarity $157.[62] Others have qualified that conclusion by suggesting that appeals prolonged the final settlement without ever indicating the outcome.[63] Just how many creditors ever filed claims to share in the small windfall created by Innerarity's payment has never been determined. It is doubtful, however, that the heirs ever received so much as a penny from the money Innerarity was obliged to pay.

Thus, while Jackson's intentions were laudable, he had in fact created an international incident with the imprisonment of Colonel Callava, destroyed the credibility of the only U.S. judge in West Florida, humbled John Forbes and Company together with its Pensacola partner, and netted the Vidal heirs little or nothing.

The Vidal case, which received so much publicity, was merely one of a series of court cases involving John Forbes and Company and those associated with it. While the Vidal case involved only a modest sum of money, some of the other litigation involved thousands of dollars and millions of acres of land. Several of these cases reached the U.S. Supreme Court. But none of the other cases ever achieved the notoriety of *The Vidal Heirs v. John Innerarity*.[64]

62. Parton, *Life of Andrew Jackson*, 2:639.
63. James, *Life of Andrew Jackson*, 832n15; Remini, *Andrew Jackson*, 415.
64. Another case in which John Forbes and Company was accused of withholding money due a Spanish military officer was that of Joaquin Osorno and his wife; it included suspected collusion between John Forbes and Governor Vicente Folch y Juan. See White, "John Forbes Company," 193–95.

17
Years of Litigation

*T*HE lawsuits selected for review in this chapter may be divided into three principal categories: continued efforts to secure compensation for the company's wartime losses, extended litigation over land grants, and a series of suits brought by the numerous heirs of individuals connected with the company. The Vidal sisters were not alone in believing that John Forbes and Company had cheated them out of their rightful inheritance. The heirs of William Panton, John Leslie, Thomas Forbes, and even Alexander McGillivray began pressuring John Forbes not many years after Panton's death for a settlement. Some of the heirs were relentless in pursuing their claims. Likewise, John Forbes did not relent in his efforts to win compensation for his East Florida losses, despite the fact that the British government had refused to pay him anything.

Supposedly, the Spanish land grant, Forbes Grant II, had reimbursed the company for its losses during the War of 1812, but apparently Forbes considered the grant compensation for only his West Florida losses and expenses. Thus, he elected to bring suit against the British officers involved for the loss of his East Florida slaves. Forbes sued Admirals Cochrane and Cockburn in the London Court of Common Pleas for enticing the slaves to escape and for detaining them after the officers certainly knew the slaves belonged to Forbes. In 1822, the court awarded Forbes £3,800 in damages. In rejoinder, the two admirals appealed the decision, but it was two years before the Court of King's Bench ruled on the appeal.

Meanwhile, on March 12, 1823, Spain and Great Britain signed a convention by which it was believed Forbes would be compensated, no matter what the Court of King's Bench decided in his case against Cochrane and Cockburn. In part, the convention provided that just claims of British or Spanish subjects for losses incurred during and after the War of 1812 would be paid by one or the other of the two governments. Claimants against the British government in East and West Florida hurried to complete detailed statements of their losses, which they subsequently registered with the mixed commission appointed to review their cases.

The following year, 1824, the Court of King's Bench reversed the decision against Cochrane and Cockburn, ruling that British law did not recognize slavery on British soil, or on British property, as in the case of His Majesty's ships. Forbes had no property rights in the Negroes after they came under British jurisdiction and protection; therefore, the admirals owed Forbes nothing. In 1858, a leading abolitionist ranked the Forbes case second only to the celebrated Somerset case of 1772 as the most important case in British slave law history. Yet, in 1824, when the court reversed the decision in the Forbes case, the emancipation of slavery throughout all of the British empire was still a decade away; slavery existed in the British West Indies until 1833. In sharp contrast to the treatment given Forbes, the British Emancipation Act provided £20 million for compensation of its citizens for their financial losses. The adverse ruling of the Court of King's Bench in 1824 did not cause Forbes's London attorney, J. S. Pott, undue concern. After all, the Convention of 1823, between Spain and Great Britain, ensured that fair compensation would yet be paid.

By 1828, the mixed commission had accomplished nothing. In that year the British claimants against Spain, convinced that they would never be paid, persuaded the British government to negotiate a new convention with Spain. The new agreement, known as the "Convention of 1828," included a complicated reciprocal financial agreement which provided that Spain would pay Spanish claimants against England, the category into which Forbes fell. During the convention negotiations, these claimants had repeatedly requested the British government to avoid such an arrangement, inasmuch as they did not believe that Spain, which was bankrupt, would ever pay them anything. Since Spain had already given Forbes more than a million acres of land in compensation for his losses, Forbes's heirs, by this date, probably had little hope of any additional compensation. It is easy to understand why they preferred to plead their case in London. Nevertheless, Pott pressed the case in Madrid.

As anticipated, he failed to secure any money, but so did all of the other claimants.[1] The company heirs had twice failed to gain compensation for the East Florida slaves. But a new question now surfaced: Did the company still own Forbes Grant II, which it had received for its wartime losses?[2]

The Forbes grants each exceeded one million acres, and no law existed to provide for the settlement of such enormous claims until 1828. In that year, Congress passed a law by which grants of such large size could be adjudicated by the judge of the Superior Court of the district in which the land lay, upon petition of the claimant.[3] But there were those, most prominently Richard Keith Call, who believed, for one reason or another, that these large grants were fraudulent.

Call, who had played only a minor role in the Vidal case, remained in Pensacola for several years as an attorney. During this time, he became deeply involved in the land litigation. He also became something of a land speculator and, among his many dealings, he even became a partner of James Innerarity in the purchase of 800 arpents of land on Santa Rosa sound. In 1825, after a term as territorial delegate to Congress, Call was appointed by the president to be receiver of public monies in the General Land Office in Tallahassee. As a result of his experience in Pensacola and Tallahassee, Call became an expert on Spanish land grants in Florida. Call had also maintained a close relationship with Andrew Jackson. Consequently, in several large land claims soon to be before the courts, including both Forbes grants, Jackson, now president, appointed Call assistant counsel for the United States to handle these cases.

One of the major problems facing the government, as Call saw it, was the claimants' submission of copies rather than the original documents to prove their ownership of the land. A trip to Havana confirmed Call's suspicions that Spanish officials were being bribed to alter copies, to make them conform to the provisions of the Treaty of 1819, as well as to the requirements of U.S. laws. Such copies would pass inspection, but the originals would not. Accordingly, one of the primary reasons for Call's trip to Cuba was to secure the original documents to Forbes Grant II, a mission which he accomplished.[4]

1. Great Britain, *Cases of King's Bench*, 2:448–73; Giddings, *Exiles of Florida*, 32; Woodward, *Age of Reform*, 369–73; Wilson, *Emancipation*, 16–20; Pott, *Statement of Facts*, 5–12. British claims against Spain stemmed from the Peninsular War in Europe, 1808–14, and were not connected with the War of 1812 in the Floridas.
2. There is no question that Forbes Grant II was intended to fully compensate John Forbes and Company for its losses during the War of 1812: White, *New Collection of Laws*, 2:352–53.
3. WPA, "Spanish Land Grants," 1:xlix–li.
4. Doherty, *Richard Keith Call*, 24–62.

The Innerarity brothers, wasting little time, had made efforts to sell Forbes Grant II. But few, if any, sales in the grant had taken place before they filed suit in the Superior Court in Pensacola in 1828, seeking to confirm title to that land. Their efforts were abruptly halted in 1830, when the court heard the case. At that time, Call produced the original document, showing the actual date of the grant to be March 10, not January 10, 1818. A line had been drawn through "March" and the word "January" written above it on the original document. By contrast, the copy submitted to the court by John Innerarity showed only January 10, 1818. This evidence nullified Forbes Grant II, since, as noted previously under Article Eight of the Treaty of 1819, Spain could legally make no land grants in the Floridas after January 24, 1818. Therefore, the Innearitys lost their bid for title to the land.[5] Obviously, neither Forbes nor the Spanish officials in Cuba were aware at the time of the cession that a provision in the treaty ceding the Floridas to the United States would invalidate the grant. Thus, by a matter of only forty-five days (January 24 to March 10), the company lost the land grant that compensated it for its wartime losses. Since the alteration of the original document was so obvious, the Innearitys did not appeal.[6] The loss was devastatingly complete, for any further compensation for the loss of the Forbes II land grant through a comparable Spanish land grant elsewhere was no longer possible.

During the negotiations between Spain and the United States over the Floridas, Onís had suggested the possibility of replacing any Florida land grants invalidated by the January 24, 1818, deadline with lands in Texas.[7] In the case of Forbes Grant II, no such substitution was possible in 1830. Even if Spain had been willing to make the switch, by 1830 Texas belonged to Mexico, whose government would never have agreed to any such arrangement.

Although John Forbes had sold Forbes Grant I to Carnochan and Mitchel in 1817, some lands had been reserved in the grant. By 1828, when the owners filed suit to confirm the grant, James Innerarity still claimed 1/30th, or about 40,000 acres, of the tract and was thus officially involved in the litigation.[8]

    5. *James and John Innerarity and the heirs of John Forbes, dec'd. Petitioners, v. The United States.* Escambia County Court Case 1830–2637, Historical Documents Section, Judicial Building, Pensacola, copy in Papers of Panton, Leslie and Company, UWF. The Pensacola *Gazette* (November 6, 1830, 2:3–5, 3:1) published Judge Brackenridge's decision in this case.
    6. Doherty, *Richard Keith Call*, 64.
    7. Brooks, *Diplomacy and the Borderlands*, 163.
    8. It is not known under what circumstances James Innerarity still continued to claim his 1/30th: *John Leslie's Heirs v. The Trustees of the Apalachicola Land Company.* See "Forbes Purchase," copy in care of Mr. Jay Shuler, attorney at law, Apalachicola, Florida;

Again, Call figured prominently in the government's efforts to overturn the Forbes I grant. Call based his arguments against the claim on three major premises: The Indians did not own the land that they ceded to Forbes because title to the land was vested in the Crown; the governor of West Florida did not have the power to ratify Indian grants; and the lands were in East Florida and thus out of the jurisdiction of the governor of West Florida.[9]

The Superior Court of Middle Florida, which heard the case, held the grant to be invalid and illegal because Governor Folch, who had confirmed the grants, did not have authority to confirm land grants east of the Apalachicola River. Those lands, the court contended, being located in East Florida, were out of his jurisdiction. On appeal, the case reached the U.S. Supreme Court in February 1831.[10]

At Call's urging, the Supreme Court delayed hearing the case until 1835. In the interim, the government sent Jeremy Robinson to Havana to obtain documents to support the government's arguments. Fully briefed by Call, Robinson spent two years in Havana locating and identifying documents, but he died in 1834 before any of these papers were sent to Washington. Nicholas Philip Trist succeeded Robinson and uncovered forty-five documents in Havana, which the Supreme Court refused to admit as evidence.

In 1835, the Supreme Court refused to delay the hearing any longer, despite Call's request for more time. Chief Justice John Marshall wrote the final opinion in the case, in which he showed that the governor of West Florida had often exercised jurisdiction as far east as St. Marks. Hence, the Supreme Court overturned the lower court's decision and upheld as perfectly legal the land grants to John Forbes and Company, tacitly validating its subsequent sale of the lands to Carnochan and Mitchel.[11] Since this was Marshall's last case as chief justice, both the attorney general and Call felt free to criticize Marshall for gratuitously including Forbes Island in his decision, when the island had not been mentioned in the original suit.[12] In fact, Forbes Island was the subject of a case being heard in Florida at the time.[13] Even though the owners had regained title to the land, further problems lay ahead of them.

United States of America to Colin Mitchel, and Others, Patent, June 9, 1842, recorded in vol. 470:174–188, General Land Office, copies in Papers of Panton, Leslie and Company, UWF.

9. Doherty, *Richard Keith Call*, 64.
10. MC; 9 Peters 711, 715, 738; 11 Curtis 539–40, 552–53.
11. 9 Peters 723–24; Doherty, *Richard Keith Call*, 64–69.
12. 9 Peters 738–43; Doherty, *Richard Keith Call*, 67–68.
13. Doherty, *Richard Keith Call*, 68.

The history of Forbes Grant I through 1835 is far more complicated than has been indicated. For one thing, John Forbes and Company had not received payment in full for the land by the terms of the sale in December 1817. On October 9, 1820, Octavius Mitchel, Colin Mitchel's brother, gave John Forbes a mortgage on the land for the last two installments of $12,500 each still owed on the purchase. These two payments had originally been due on December 8, 1820, and December 8, 1821— dates for payment that were extended to March 9, 1821, and March 9, 1822, respectively. Unfortunately for Forbes, Mitchel and Carnochan failed to meet either of these payment schedules, even though three payments were later made. In October 1823, William Henry Forbes, Thomas's son, accepted a payment of $7,841.01. In May 1823, James Innerarity received $2,680.81, and in February 1825 he received an additional $2,080.87 on behalf of William Panton's heirs. Without considering interest or penalties, this still left a balance due of $12,397.31. John Forbes's heirs in Cuba refused to accept any payment for the land, apparently fearing involvement in litigation over the land sale. For a variety of reasons, no further efforts were made by the purchasers to make additional payments.

The firm of Carnochan and Mitchel became insolvent, and in 1822 they assigned the lands they owned in Forbes Grant I to their creditors— especially to one creditor, William Christie, who quickly advertised his lien on the property and warned against any sales or mortgages on the Carnochan and Mitchel lands. Nothing more was done until the Supreme Court validated the title of the property in 1835. On November 28, 1835, the owners and creditors formed the Apalachicola Land Company for the express purpose of promoting land sales. The formation of the company renewed the interest of several heirs, notably John and James Innerarity and William Henry Forbes.

On July 5, 1836, John Innerarity obtained letters of administration for the estate of John Forbes in Florida. Shortly thereafter, Innerarity began to pressure the Apalachicola Land Company for payment of the money still due on the land. Having been unsuccessful in his efforts, Innerarity filed suit on August 19, 1839, to foreclose on the mortgage, which, with penalties and interest, he claimed now totaled $57,790.18. The mortgage in question was that given John Forbes by Octavius Mitchel in 1820. The case was heard in Pensacola in 1841, and the court adjudged the balance due on the mortgage to be $50,159.60. Naturally, the trustees for the Apalachicola Land Company appealed. The Court of Appeals for the Territory of Florida, in its January 1844 term, decreed the amount due to be only $28,500. Both parties then appealed this decision to the U.S. Supreme Court. The trustees took exception to the judgment on the grounds that the interest was improperly computed and that certain credits should have been applied to the amount due.

One of the credits was a payment of $13,357.73, made in 1840 to Thomas M. Blount, president of the Bank of Pensacola. Also an attorney and agent of John Innerarity, Blount had gone to New York on behalf of Innerarity, where he exceeded his instructions in negotiations with the trustees. Because he acted on his own in accepting the money, Blount was repudiated by Innerarity. In fact, when Blount returned to Pensacola, Innerarity curtly refused to accept the money from Blount and notified the trustees accordingly. To remain ethical, Blount deposited the money in his bank. The following year, matters worsened: both Blount and his bank were found insolvent, and even this money was lost.

The Supreme Court did deal with the exceptions noted earlier by the trustees in their appeal, declaring their arguments to be invalid. In December 1847, the court affirmed the decree of the Appeals Court that the trustees owed the Innearitys and the other heirs $28,500.[14] Four years later, on February 22, 1851, John Innerarity filed suit against the trustees in the Supreme Court of the State of Florida for having failed to comply with the order of the U.S. Supreme Court.

During the twelve years between 1839, when Innerarity first filed his suit against the trustees, and 1851, when he sued to have the Supreme Court decision enforced, Florida had undergone significant political changes. The territory of Florida had become the state of Florida in 1845. The federal superior court and the court of appeals, which had heard Innerarity's case, were only territorial courts. Now, the Florida Supreme Court was a state court. On the grounds that Innerarity's case was heard by the territorial (i.e., federal) courts in Florida and not the state courts, the Florida Supreme Court denied its authority to give Innerarity the relief he requested and to which he seemed to be entitled and advised him to seek redress elsewhere. According to John Leslie's heirs, Innerarity and the trustees finally settled the matter in 1851. No details of the transaction are available, but the intimation is that the settlement did not involve payment of the amount due.[15]

14. *Curtis and Griswold Trustees of the Apalachicola Land Co., Appellants v. John and James Innerarity, Appellees.*

15. *In re John Innerarity, Administrator of John Forbes Deceased v. Curtis and Griswold, Trustees of the Apalachicola Land Company;* 4 Florida Reports 175–91; *John Leslie's Heirs v. The Trustees of the Apalachicola Land Company,* pp. 43, 60. The Leslie heirs, Alexander Gordon excepted, did not learn the details of the sale of Forbes Grant I until 1851. They later filed suit to recover one-third of the money received, which they argued should have been reserved for John Leslie's estate. Although the outcome of the suit is

The 1851 decision of the Florida Supreme Court was not the last legal action in the state courts concerning the Panton, Leslie and Forbes companies. More was yet to come—all having originated with John Forbes many years earlier. Three of the original Panton, Leslie and Company partners—William Panton, John Leslie, and Thomas Forbes—each named John Forbes as one of the executors of their respective wills. Panton died in 1801, Leslie in 1803, and Thomas Forbes in 1808. Out of the proceeds of their estates, John Forbes reserved $62,000, which he agreed to invest, less commission and expenses, in public stocks and bonds in Great Britain, to be used to settle the accounts with the heirs of Alexander McGillivray.

By December 15, 1813, Forbes had settled with all of the heirs except McGillivray's. But Forbes had not yet invested the $62,000, and in 1814, in Nassau, he signed a formal contract with various heirs by which he promised to invest the money as stipulated and to draw up a trust setting forth the details for their benefit. He further agreed that once he had settled with McGillivray's heirs, the residue of the money would be equitably distributed among the others.

Before Forbes could send the money to England for investment, however, he indicated that he wanted a legal opinion from the Lord Chancellor. In the same year, 1814, Forbes returned to the Spanish government 15,000 acres of land in East Florida, now in St. Johns and Putnam counties, which had been granted to Panton, Leslie and Company in 1799. In exchange, Forbes received a grant of 10,000 acres of land on Little St. Marys River and in nearby Cabbage Swamp, in present-day Nassau County. It seems clear that the 15,000 acres which Forbes had traded away should have been divided among the Panton, Leslie and McGillivray heirs, if they were entitled to a share of the company's assets.

As for the McGillivray heirs—his two daughters, Lizzy and Margaret—a suit had already been initiated to secure anything due them by Roswell Post Johnson, a former bookkeeper for John Forbes and Company. In October 1806, Johnson had made an entry in the company accounts which indicated that the company owed the girls $53,000. Since Thomas Forbes had not yet died, this amount could only have been sums set aside from the Panton and Leslie estates by John Forbes.

On August 5, 1810, in a further complication, Daniel W. Johnson of Savannah and George Edwards of Charleston purchased from Lizzy and Margaret the right to any money to which they were entitled from Pan-

---

unknown, it did not affect the sale, nor does it appear that the Leslie heirs ever received anything for their efforts.

ton, Leslie and Company and its successor firm, John Forbes and Company. Daniel Johnson and Edwards acquired the consignment of the inheritance to themselves for $18,000. Whether they actually paid Lizzy and Margaret anything, then or later, remains unknown. We know nothing about the relationship of Roswell Post Johnson to Daniel Johnson or Edwards or what commission he may have received from them for his information. There is no doubt that he expected to share in any money received.

In Charleston, in December 1810, these gentlemen brought suit against John Forbes, William Simpson, and others for the sum of $63,600. This amount apparently included the principal of $53,000 plus interest accrued since 1806, when Johnson noted that sum on the company books. Unsuccessful in Charleston, Johnson and Edwards filed similar suits in Mobile in 1816 and again in 1818. In all three cases, they charged, Forbes and Company had artfully avoided a decision.

By 1823, contrary to his promises of 1814, John Forbes had not invested the money set aside for the McGillivray heirs. Nor had he prepared the trust document. Before he died, and apparently because of the failure of Johnson and Edwards to win any of their three suits against the company, Forbes became convinced that the company did not owe the McGillivray heirs anything. In fact, from the money set aside for them, John Forbes had already settled with Alexander Gordon, a Leslie heir, for $6,000. Francisco Dalcourt, husband of Forbes's daughter, Sophia, was appointed executor of Forbes's estate in Cuba. No one was appointed at the time to settle Forbes's Florida estate. Forbes's death in 1823 probably triggered the fourth suit by Johnson and Edwards on behalf of Lizzy and Margaret.

Convinced that there still was something to be gained, Johnson and Edwards filed suit in New Orleans in 1823 against John and James Innerarity, the surviving partners of John Forbes and Company. The complainants claimed that the company owed the McGillivray heirs $130,000—the original $53,000 plus interest—and an additional $200,000, which they claimed for the sale of Forbes Grant I. To add to their other inconveniences, the New Orleans court attached 16,816 arpents of land belonging to the Innenaritys and the company in Feliciana Parish until the case was resolved. The Innenaritys denied that they, as successors to the firm of John Forbes and Company, had assumed any indebtedness or other financial responsibility to the McGillivray heirs.

At this juncture, Roswell Post Johnson appeared on the scene as an attorney in his own right and pursued the case in the Louisiana courts until 1830. The lower court decided the case against Johnson on the grounds that he had not and could not show proof of the assignment of the contract between Lizzy and Margaret McGillivray, and Daniel Johnson and Edwards, to himself. Roswell Johnson appealed, and in 1830 the Louisiana Supreme Court also decided the case against him but for a different reason. The court held that McGillivray had no interest or part in the "new" Panton, Leslie and Company, established on September 1, 1792. Any claims on the part of the McGillivray heirs were against the original partners of Panton, Leslie and Company, referred to as the "old" company, of which McGillivray had been a partner. The documents in the case clearly showed that Alexander McGillivray had declined any share in the profits of the firm as early as 1788.[16] Thus, Roswell Post Johnson lost his bid to participate in the division of any profits due Lizzy and Margaret McGillivray.

As soon as the heirs of Thomas Forbes—Mary Sophia, William Henry, and John Gordon Forbes—learned that the suit on behalf of McGillivray's heirs had been decided adversely, they filed suit in the Spanish court in Matanzas, Cuba, to obtain their part of the $62,000 set aside by Forbes. Meanwhile, Dalcourt had divided the money between himself and Forbes's other son-in-law, Edmund DePestre. In 1836, to cloud the transaction further, the Matanzas court decided in favor of Thomas Forbes's heirs and awarded them one-third—their share, $10,333 2 ½ reales—out of the one-half of the $62,000 from Dalcourt. The court also gave them liberty to sue DePestre for the same amount, $10,333 2 ½ reales. DePestre refused to admit any liability to the heirs. If Thomas Forbes's heirs ever sued DePestre—and it is assumed they did—no record of the case has been discovered. Perhaps when it is possible to examine the Cuban court records, the suit against DePestre may be found.

In the same year that Thomas Forbes's heirs recovered their share of the money set aside by John Forbes, the St. Johns County Court in Florida appointed John M. Fontaine and James S. Sanchez appraisers of the goods and chattels of John Forbes in Florida. On May 28, 1836, Fontaine and Sanchez certified that John Forbes had no property in Florida. They did discover a claim against the United States for $23,693 by Forbes for a

16. For details, see *Johnson et al. v. Innerarity et al.; John Forbes and Company v. D. W. Johnson; John and James Innerarity v. R. Post Johnson*. On the 10,000 acres of land, see *ASP PL*, 4:695:97. In August 1815, James Innerarity informed John Forbes that he expected Roswell P. Johnson to renew his attack on them in Mobile. James wrote, "I observed simply, that he had made the attempt before at Charleston, & had thought prudent to withdraw & that if he renewed it he would most certainly burn his fingers." J. P. Kennedy, Innerarity's Mobile attorney, had advised him "that Johnson could not recover, as being an interested person, & having no evidence but his own": James Innerarity to John Forbes, August 12, 1815, GP.

"store and plantation plundered, etc.," which had resulted from the insurrection in East Florida in 1812. William Travis, administrator for the estate of John Forbes, on September 11, 1834, had filed this claim under Article Nine of the Treaty of 1819. In 1837, Judge Robert R. Reid reported the claim as valid but for some reason disallowed $3,913, leaving a balance of $19,780. During the hearings, the judges took under consideration compensation for the lost use of the property. At the time, the average interest rate in the United States was 5 percent, and the judges used this figure to arrive at "fair compensation." Under this formula, Forbes's losses, computed from May 10, 1813, amounted to an additional $24,466. But the secretary of the treasury, Levi Woodbury, chose to consider the fair compensation as "interest," which he refused to pay. The government, subsequently, issued a warrant for the payment of the $19,780 on February 1, 1838, to the Hon. C. Downing, as attorney for the Forbes estate.[17] What Downing did with the money paid to him is not known. Presumably, he turned it over to some of Forbes's heirs, less fees.

Fontaine's and Sanchez's report made no mention of the 10,000 acres which Forbes had acquired in 1814. On July 13, 1824, George Murray, acting as attorney on behalf of John Forbes and Company, submitted a claim for the land, which the land commission recommended for confirmation. But the land commission could not validate a claim in excess of 3,500 acres. To confirm the 10,000 acres, a suit was filed with the superior court of that district. On September 9, 1838, the superior court confirmed the land claim for the heirs of John Forbes.[18] Exactly who received the 10,000 acres and what happened to it subsequently still has not been determined. To be sure, the heirs of William Panton did not share in the division of this land.

In 1845, nine years after Fontaine and Sanchez filed their report, Venancio Sanchez, for some unexplained reason, was appointed administrator of John Forbes's will in Florida. Some years later, Sanchez testified that Forbes had no property in East Florida except a claim against William Travers for $260. Sanchez stated that most of that sum was used for expenses and costs in pursuing the case. He said nothing about the 10,000 acres, and there matters rested until 1876.

17. *Thomas Dow et al. v. Venancio Sanchez* [see also 23 Florida Reports 445–54]. U.S. Congress, *Report of the Secretary*, 34–35. Hartley, "Florida Claims," furnished the authors with the details of this claim.
18. *ASP PL*, 4:406, 571; WPA, "Spanish Land Grants," 3:130–32. Although the confirmation stated that the 10,000 acres were located on the Nassau River, the surveys showed that 7,000 acres were on Little St. Marys River near Spell's Swamp and 3,000 acres were in Cabbage Swamp, on or near an arm of the Little St. Marys: *ASP PL*, 4:695–97. The land was located a few miles south of Kings Ferry in present-day Nassau County, Florida.

In that year, the heirs of William Panton—the sons and daughters of his sisters, and their offspring—learned about the $62,000 set aside by John Forbes in 1814 for the McGillivray heirs. Neither they nor their attorneys were aware of the division of the John Forbes estate in Cuba and the distribution of the $62,000 by the Matanzas court. Through their attorney, the Panton heirs sued Venancio Sanchez, as administrator of Forbes's will, for the sum of $2,202,049—having arrived at that figure by claiming that if Forbes had invested the $62,000 on January 1, 1814, as he had agreed to do, the principal plus interest would have amounted to that sum. In addition, they demanded either the value of the 15,000 acres Forbes had traded for the 10,000 acres in 1814, with compound interest, or his 10,000 acres in settlement. By 1876, Sanchez was an old man. He denied that he had in any way profited from the Forbes estate in Florida and claimed to have little more than the clothes on his back. Nevertheless, Judge R. B. Archibald decided the case in favor of the Panton heirs and ordered Sanchez to pay the more than $2 million out of any property belonging to the Forbes estate. Sanchez appealed to the Florida Supreme Court.

It was 1887 before the State Supreme Court finally delivered its opinion, which reversed the lower court ruling. The higher court held that too much time had elapsed since the division of the estate. The heirs had made no legal move in more than forty years to recover their share of money or land. Therefore, the court concluded, their claim was "stale" and thus was barred by the lapse of time.[19] The courts finally had heard the last bid by the heirs to share in whatever residue remained of the Panton, Leslie and Forbes estates. But one last question regarding Forbes Grant I remained to be answered.

In 1923, the Apalachicola Land and Development Company brought suit against the Florida commissioner of agriculture and the shellfish commissioner. The company sought to prevent the commissioners from leasing or using for planting and cultivating oysters the submerged lands between the mainland and the islands granted to John Forbes and Company. The company argued that the submerged lands were included in the Indian land grants to John Forbes and Company and now belonged to the Apalachicola Land and Development Company. After a comprehensive review of the lands granted to John Forbes and Company, and of the private and public ownership of submerged lands, the Florida Supreme Court ruled that private ownership of lands bordering on navigable waters extended only to the high-water mark. The submerged lands belonged

19. *Thomas Dow et al. v. Venancio Sanchez.*

to the state and not under Spanish, U.S., or Florida law had they ever belonged to John Forbes and Company.[20] A century had passed after John Forbes had been laid to rest before the same could be said of the litigation involving the company which he once headed.

"What a tangled web we weave" would aptly describe the sequence of events surrounding the dealings of Forbes and the Inneraritys with the three "superpowers" of those times—Spain, England, and the United States. Though the records of these transactions may seem dry, their implications generate fascinating insights into the relations of free-market business pioneers on the Gulf coast and the shifting power of political entities going through a period of major change.

20. *The Apalachicola Land and Development Company, et al. Appellants. v. W. A. McRae, Commissioner of Agriculture of The State of Florida, and T. R. Hodges, Shell Fish Commissioner of The State of Florida, Appellees*; 98 Southern Reporter 505–28; 86 Florida Reports 393–465.

Summary and Conclusions

*T*o evaluate the long history of the companies requires consideration of four topics: the different partnerships, the companies' varied accomplishments, the methods behind their accomplishments, and the events leading to their decline. With regard to the first topic, it should be observed that the individual partners were involved in several different companies over the years, but this study focuses only on Panton, Leslie and Company and its successor firm, John Forbes and Company. Occasionally in the text, Panton, Leslie and Company is referred to, alternatively, as both the "old" and the "new" company, but for convenience and to avoid confusion we will consider them all as one company.

There were three sets of partners: the members of the "old" company, 1783–92; the members of the "new" company, 1792–1804; and the members of John Forbes and Company, 1804–47. Of the first or "old" Panton, Leslie and Company, there were five original partners: William Panton, Thomas Forbes, John Leslie, William Alexander, and Charles McLatchy. In addition to these men, Alexander McGillivray remained a silent partner until 1788, though we do not know exactly when in 1784 he joined the company.

All of these men had been directly involved in the American Revolution, during which they used their experience, resources, and connections to supply the British in East Florida. Having overtly helped Great Britain during the war, at its close two of the partners thought it prudent to move permanently to the Bahamas, the others choosing to remain in the Floridas. In retaliation for their support of the British, the United States confiscated their property in states that had been American colonies. The new government also refused to permit the company's collection of any debts owed them there and warned the partners that an attempt to return to Georgia or South Carolina would endanger their lives. Little wonder that the partners harbored deep and bitter resentment toward the United States, determining to prevent its expansion at all costs and interdicting trade between the Indian nations and American merchants.

In 1792, when John Forbes, John Forrester, and Robert Leslie became partners, only three of the original anti-American partners were still active in the firm, William Panton, John Leslie, and Thomas Forbes. Of course, the three new members had worked for the "old" company before they had been admitted as junior partners. Moreover, the new members had suffered neither confiscation of their property nor threats upon their lives by the United States. Thus, while vigorously opposed to American traders in the Indian nations, they were not as bitter opponents of the United States as were the older partners. Still, the new partners were not strangers to controversy, facing such new and unusual problems as William Augustus Bowles, on the one hand, and French intrigues, on the other.

Between 1798 and 1804, three of the original partners died and one withdrew from the company, leaving only John and Thomas Forbes. But by 1804, two new partners had joined John Forbes and Company: William Simpson and James Innerarity. John Innerarity, James's brother, did not become a partner until 1812, yet he played a major role in company affairs from the time he arrived in Pensacola in 1802. Thomas Forbes died in 1808, leaving only the newer and younger members as partners.

By the early 1800s, the company was spending much of its time and energy on the collection of Indian debts. As the company acquired more and more land in settlement of Indian debts, the question of the disposition of the land became important. The partners—especially John Forbes—developed colonization and settlement plans, but little came of these projects. Although the company continued to trade with the Indians after 1804, its interests had expanded to include trade with the Spanish colonists and garrisons, as well as with the Americans living north of the thirty-first parallel. After the Indian debts were resolved in 1812, the partners' energies were absorbed by problems created by wars in Europe, the Creek War, and the War of 1812. By 1812, all of the older members were gone, and the Indian trade, upon which the company had made its fortune, was no longer its principal source of income. Thereafter, the

Table 9. Panton, Leslie and Company and John Forbes and Company Stores and Trading Posts[a]

Store or trading post	Years of operation	Other data	Code[b]
St. Augustine	1783–1817		P-L and F
Lower Store [Spalding's]	1783–1790s?	Stokes Landing, St. Johns R.	P-L
Upper Store [Spalding's]	1783–?	Volusia, St. Johns R.	P-L
Wakulla River	1783–1800	Near St. Marks	P-L
Nassau	1783–1821?	New Providence Island, Bahamas	P-L and F
Pensacola	1785–1830		P-L and F
Mobile	1790–1847		P-L and F
St. Marys River	1791–93	Near Kings Ferry	P-L
San Fernando de Pupo	1793–?	St. Johns R.	P-L
Picolata	1790s–1800s?	St. Johns R.	P-L and F?
Chickasaw Bluffs	1795–99	Memphis	P-L
Prospect Bluff	1804–14 and 1816–1820s?	Apalachicola R.	F
New Orleans	1807?–13		F
Fernandina	1811–15?	Amelia Island	F
Bon Secour	1813–14	Bon Secour Bay	F
San Marcos de Apalache	1816–21	St. Marks	F

a. See endleaves for locations of symbols in note b.
b. P-L = Panton, Leslie and Company ✦
F = John Forbes and Company ■
P-L and F = both companies ▲

Indian trade continued to decline as land sales, speculation, and trade with the Americans occupied an increasing amount of the company's attention. By 1821, in fact, the company's trade had been restricted largely to Mobile and Pensacola. Thus, it might not be facetious to suggest that litigation became the partners' most important occupation after 1821.

In the more than forty years between 1778 and 1821, what was accomplished or contributed by the various partners and the company? The first major contribution of the partners was their support of the British in the Revolutionary War. After being formed in either late 1782 or early 1783, Panton, Leslie and Company was tarred by the brush of "loyalism" because its partners had assisted in the supply of the British Loyalists in East Florida during the Revolution. Panton and his partners also had served British Governor Tonyn during the Revolution by handling the Indian trade, which had at that time assumed considerable strategic importance. Members of the company assisted the British in many other subtle ways, confirming that it was not for lack of their support that the British lost the war. Beyond mere politics, however, it was their perseverance that enabled the Loyalists in East Florida to escape much of the misery that a lack of supplies would have produced.

In another sector, the company furnished Indian gifts and trade goods on credit to the Spaniards when they arrived in the Floridas, filling a definite commercial need for the newcomers. From such a propitious beginning, the company had acquired, in just a few years, a virtual monopoly in the trade of the southeastern Indians. It meant that the company controlled a great dependency that could be used for political purposes. Between 1783 and 1795, in effect, the company had made of the Indian nations a great human barrier to buffer the Spanish provinces from the United States. At the same time, the company helped to curb internal friction among the Indian nations and continued to supply them during the transitional period after 1795. Further, the company prevented the Indians from joining the Americans in menacing both East and West Florida during and after this period. The company also assisted in thwarting French plots against the Floridas in the 1790s. Similarly, the company played an important, perhaps even a key, role in defeating the plans of William Augustus Bowles and assisted in his capture. Withal, the political posture assumed by the company at any given time consistently reflected the overriding interest of its partners—that of maximizing profits and minimizing losses.

Loyalty to purse rather than to flag also explains the willingness of the partners to work closely with U.S. officials in pressuring the Indians to sell land to the United States. It offered the most certain means for paying off their otherwise uncollectible past indebtedness to the company. In West Florida, where the Spanish government posed no objections to the Indians extinguishing their debts to the company through a direct land cession, the Forbes Purchase (Forbes Grant I) made the company the largest landowner in the Floridas during the second Spanish era.

Similarly, the partners' assessment as to which side most benefited its interests determined to some extent the company's stance during the War of 1812. While it cannot be given total credit for the British defeat in the southern campaign, the company clearly exerted a positive influence for the United States. John Forbes unquestionably orchestrated the poor reception accorded British forces in East Florida, and John Innerarity proved less than cooperative with them in West Florida. Colonel Nicolls, in fact, blamed him for the British defeat at Fort Bowyer in 1814. British incitement of the company's slaves to seek their freedom, and British efforts toward alienating its Indian clientele, went far toward impelling the company along its anti-British course.

The lingering British-inspired animosity continued to influence the company's behavior in the aftermath of the War of 1812. John Hambly and Edmund Doyle, long-standing associates of the company, were involved in the destruction of Negro Fort by U.S. forces. Many Indians, whether correctly or not, laid the entire blame for the fort's destruction at the company's doorstep.

Continuing its penchant for promoting its self-interest, the company played a significant role in the First Seminole War, 1816–18, particularly in the arrest and trial of Arbuthnot and Ambrister. The company assisted in the defeat of Nicolls's and Arbuthnot's plans to gain hegemony over the Florida Indians and also undermined the intrigues of Woodbine, McGregor, and Ambrister to wrest the Floridas from Spain. Clearly, Hambly, Doyle, and John Innerarity were, in large measure, directly responsible for Jackson's capture of Pensacola in 1818. Although difficult to evaluate precisely, this event—which demonstrated to Spain just how vulnerable the Floridas really were—had an important bearing on Spain's decision to cede the Floridas to the United States. Thus, while the company can be credited with helping to maintain Spanish sovereignty in the Floridas for many years, it also was responsible to some degree for the acquisition of those provinces by the United States.

Merely listing the company's chief accomplishments leaves unexplored its far more interesting machinations, that is, why and how this mercantile enterprise was able to do what it did. Both companies—Panton, Leslie and Company and John Forbes and Company—were notable exceptions not only to the mercantilist theory but also to the common practices of the Spanish crown. Although there were exceptions, such as the *asiento*, or slave trade monopoly, nowhere in its empire did Spain ordinarily permit a foreign company to engage in trade with its subjects, much less allow foreign interests to acquire a virtual monopoly in that trade. For the most part, the company acquired its trade goods in British ports and colonies, another exception to the standard practice of requiring such companies to purchase their supplies through Spanish channels. To be sure, the crown occasionally permitted trade with other friendly or neutral countries, but such was not normal practice. Thus, from the beginning, there was nothing normal about the relationship of the company with the Spanish government and its colonial officials. These differences explain, in part at least, why the company was so successful. But there were additional reasons why the company was able to succeed where others failed.

Not much needs to be said about the partners' contributions to Great Britain during the American Revolution. They were all loyalists who depended upon British trade goods. Certainly, they were available at the right time and place to provide what assistance they could to the British in East Florida. This aid was later reciprocated by Governor Tonyn's willingness to lend the company such scarce items as gunpowder, and to enter pleas on its behalf with both the British and Spanish governments—which helped the company.

The company's contributions to Spain, however, differed markedly from its involvement with either Britain or the United States. When the Spaniards arrived, they did not have either the desired trade goods or the traders. The company befriended the Spanish officials by extending goods to them on credit, thus securing the grateful support of Governor Zéspedes of East Florida. Since there were no Spanish merchants to replace Panton, Leslie and Company, it retained its East Florida monopoly by default.

The situation in West Florida was markedly different from that in East Florida. Maxent's fall from grace as Indian agent for Louisiana and West Florida had given the company the opportunity to expand into West Florida. Also, the company's intimate connections with such Indian leaders as Alexander McGillivray had given it spokesmen who advocated the establishment of the company there. Once entrenched, the company was provisioned by its London factors when other companies—Mather and Strother, for example—could not obtain the necessary quantities of trade items. So it was that two competing companies failed before Panton, Leslie and Company acquired the Indian trade of all of West Florida. Of course, since McGillivray and several Spanish officials, including Miró and Navarro, shared in the company's profits during the early years, there was every reason for its success in West Florida. Later, this vested interest continued when still other Spanish officials deposited their money with the company and received a good return on their investment.

To further enhance its trading monopoly in West Florida, the company acquired tax-free status on the importation of goods for the Indian trade. Goods for Indians and colonists alike came into the province under this privilege, making it impossible for other companies to compete successfully with Panton, Leslie and with Forbes. Although the other merchants complained about the practice, many years passed before they were put on an equal footing with the Forbes company. A limited amount of trade competition survived throughout the entire period in East and West Florida, but for all intents and purposes it was more annoying than harmful until the War of 1812.

Over the years, the company entertained the right people lavishly (at least for a frontier trading firm) and saw to it that these gentlemen received gifts according to their ability to help the company. These officials, more often than not, returned the favor by pleading the company's cause with the Spanish government, by permitting the company to evade customs regulations, and by assisting it in other ways in its never-ending feud with officious intendants. The governors extended extraordinary privileges, convinced that the security—and perhaps even Spanish sovereignty over the provinces—depended upon the influence of the company among the Indians. With so many factors contributing to the company's success, what could cause its eventual decline?

The year 1793 often is referred to as the "epic" or watershed year in the company's history. Alexander McGillivray died in February, and, although Panton claimed to have made McGillivray who he was, the Creek leader had been invaluable to Panton. He was the key to the Creek trade and was one of the persons most responsible for the company's early success.

Again, the outbreak of war in Europe in 1793, with Spain and England allied against France, seriously hurt the company. Its supply of munitions was drastically reduced, and company ships were seized and cargoes lost. After Spain withdrew from the war with France and became involved in war against the British, supplies and shipping suffered even more than previously.

Further, the rise of a strong federal government in the United States after 1789 was a portent of serious trouble for the company. The United States adopted an aggressive Indian policy, and as early as 1793 President Washington urged Congress to establish the Indian trading factories specifically to challenge Panton's Indian trade monopoly. When the Treaty of San Lorenzo, in 1795, placed most of Panton's customers in U.S. territory, the die was cast. Panton appealed to the Spanish government for financial assistance, but Spain declined to come to the company's support. Although not crucial at the time, the efforts of William Augustus Bowles to take the Indian trade away from Panton were very annoying. Bowles's capture and looting of the St. Marks store on two occasions were costly to the company. The constant pressure from Anglo-American and French sympathizers was particularly bad for business in East Florida, where trade patterns were disrupted and the Indians were kept in a constant state of turmoil. The result of all this was a serious decline in the number of Indian customers. Offers to sell out to Spain and to train Spanish merchants to take the company's place failed to interest the Spanish government.

Even before Panton's death, the problem of collecting the huge outstanding Indian debts greatly concerned the partners. Slowly but surely over the years, the partners expended more energy on pressuring the Indians to sell or trade their lands than they expended in trade with the Indians. They concentrated more on collecting Indian debts and less on expanding the business. And, with the deaths of Panton and John Leslie, the new partners—especially John Forbes—devoted much of their time to the problems of settling the Panton and Leslie estates. One positive factor stands out: The Louisiana Purchase of 1803, which delivered a devastating blow to Spain and West Florida, helped rather than hurt the company, for after that year, much of the company's business and trade was conducted through New Orleans.

The most serious blow sustained by the company came during the War of 1812. It suffered huge losses in slaves, property, and business, and during the war it alienated many of its prewar Indian customers. Thus, at the war's end, the company had considerable difficulty in reestablishing its stores on the Apalachicola and at St. Marks. The attitude of the Indians and the inroads of Arbuthnot so affected the already declining state of trade in East Florida that the trading post at St. Augustine, the only remaining company store in East Florida, closed in 1817. Even the fur trade was no longer as profitable as it once had been. But the company seemed more concerned about compensation for its wartime losses from Britain and Spain than it did about rebuilding the Indian trade, and Forbes's efforts were spent on those problems rather than on the resumption of trade. At the same time, there was a further shift away from trading and the sale of trade goods to a concern with land and land sales. Continuing problems with the intendants, as well as distrust and competition, all had a part in the diminishing role the company played among the Indians, which left Spain without an effective Indian policy or an agency in the Floridas.

The pro-American inclinations of the partners became more pronounced after 1817, when the company closed the East Florida branch and lost its privileged status in West Florida. In fact, the partners' interests lay more with the growing American market than with the near-defunct Indian trade. Furthermore, few doubted that the Floridas would soon be a part of the United States, and it was obvious to the partners that their future rested there and not with Spain.

What we have chronicled in this study is the struggling birth of an entrepreneurial enterprise: the vigorous, rapid, and successful rise—followed by the eventual decline—of a truly representative frontier trading company. In the annals of Spanish borderlands history, no other mercantile operation generated so much important social, political, psychological, legal, and economic activity.

Appendix: The Papers of Panton, Leslie and Company

*I*N the spring of 1972, James A. Servies, director of libraries at the University of West Florida, suggested that the university sponsor a project to collect all of the documents pertaining to the Panton, Leslie and the Forbes companies. Servies's suggestion had great merit, for Pensacola had been the "headquarters" for both companies from 1785 to 1830. In addition, the Innerarity-Hulse Papers, an important resource, were then on deposit in the university's John C. Pace Library. Of the principals, John Innerarity, William Panton's nephew, had arrived in Pensacola in 1802, later becoming a member of John Forbes and Company, in 1812. On the other side, Dr. Isaac Hulse, a U.S. Navy surgeon stationed at the Pensacola Navy Yard, married Melanie Innerarity, John's daughter. From these two families a rich collection of documents accrued. The Innerarity-Hulse Papers became the nucleus for the larger collection of papers pertaining to these companies.

His proposal, having received the favorable endorsement of James R. McGovern, chairman of the History Faculty, and Alfred B. Chaet, then provost of Gamma College, was subsequently approved by Vice-President for Academic Affairs Arthur H. Doerr and finally by President Harold Bryan Crosby. William S. Coker, professor of history, was appointed director in 1972, and the project was formally under way. The director has been aided immeasurably by these strong supporters of the project and the narrative history for the past twelve years. Without such support neither this history nor the documentary project would ever have been completed.

In 1973, the Florida Historical Society and the University of Florida also entered into sponsorship of the project. In particular, Samuel Proctor, Gustave A. Harrer, and Elizabeth Alexander of the University of Florida graciously lent their endorsement and support, as did Jay Dobkin and Paul Camp, former and present directors of the Florida Historical Society, together with the society's officers and board of directors. Once the project had the official blessing of these organizations, a grant request for financial support was submitted to the National Historical Publications and Records Commission (NHPRC). From the recommendation of the executive director, Fred Shelley, the commission then funded the grant request. Subsequent funding from the NHPRC received the support of the new executive director, Frank G. Burke, and his staff, including Roger A. Bruns and George L. Vogt. Over the years from 1974 to 1983, the NHPRC has provided more than $160,000. These funds were utilized for the identification and collection of the documents and for the administration of the project office.

The Spanish-American Bicentennial Commission, chaired by Ramón Bela Armada of the Instituto de Cooperación Iberoamericano, Madrid, provided some much-appreciated financial support for William Coker's research in Spain in 1973–74. Dr. Bela, Dr. Francisco Morales Padrón, and their colleagues on the commission are due a note of thanks for such welcomed assistance.

Since 1972, more than 200,000 pages of documents—copies of the original documents for the most part—have been collected from archives, libraries, and depositories throughout the United States, Canada, France, Great Britain, Mexico, and Spain. (See William. S. Coker, "The Papers of Panton, Leslie and Company," Journal of the USF Library Associates *Ex Libris* 2 (Fall 1978): 13–15, for more on the collection phase and some of the other major collections acquired.) NHPRC staffers Richard N. Sheldon, Mary Guinta, and especially Sara Dunlap Jackson assisted in the collection phase in Washington, D.C. When copies of the documents were received in the project office, they were processed, calendared, and filed in anticipation of the microfilming of the collection, the final preparation and carrying out of which is scheduled to be completed in 1985. A detailed description of the collection and related matters is reserved for inclusion in the published guide to the microfilm edition, including the names of many other persons who proved helpful during that phase of the project.

The following persons, all of whom worked in the UWF project office at one time or another, deserve mention for their contributions to the documentary project. While listed in alphabetical order, the names of those serving directly as office manager or who, in some substantial way, contributed significantly to the project have asterisks following their names:

Alina Franco Atwell*	Ann Ruebush Graybiel*
Gladys Bibb	Tamara West Harrell*
Daniel J. Buker	Gary N. Ives*
Vicki Burchem	Beatrice Lindeman*
Vicki D. Butt*	María del Carmen MacDonald*
Susana Duran	Ileana Martinez*
Joyce Lee Durbin*	Robert Merlano
Richele J. Falkenstein*	Patricia A. Reyes
Mario Cyrano Fernández	Sally Savage*
Judy Forsha*	Diane Culver Wells
Mirta Gonzalez*	Mary Ellen West*
Patricia Ann Gonzales	

The staff of the John C. Pace Library assisted the project in many ways. Among those who have made a contribution are:

Cyndi Denham	Frances M. Land
Frances A. Eubank	Jeannette Light
Bodil H. Gilliam	Robert W. Perdue
Lois C. Gilmer	Paula J. Thomas
Josephine R. Kinder	Peggy Toifel

From the Pace Library's Special Collections Department, others deserve mention. Marion Viccars, now deceased, served for a number of years as head of that department, always having been helpful in many ways. In addition, we acknowledge the assistance of the present head, W. Dean DeBolt, and Elizabeth M. Baggett and Marie B. Scroggs. The John C. Pace Library Fund provided welcome financial assistance in the acquisition of documents, books, and other such materials.

Dr. Chaet, now associate vice-president for research and sponsored programs, and his staff, helped in the preparation of grant requests.

John G. Martin, vice-president for administrative affairs, helped in financial matters, and in the controller's office David L. Reinhardt and Eleanor G. Settle handled the "books" on the project's finances.

It would be gratifying to be able to say that we have copies of all important documents pertaining to these companies, but we know that we do not. We believe that we have a large percentage of such materials, perhaps as much as 95 percent. While we have utilized many of the documents that we have collected in writing the history of the companies, by no means has that subject been exhausted. Hardly any part of their history has had the last word written about it. We encourage those whose interest may have been whetted by our efforts to continue the search. The documentary collection "The Papers of Panton, Leslie and Company" is a good place to start.

Bibliography

Foreign Sources
Bahamas
Nassau, New Providence Island.
  Christ Church.
    Baptism Register, 1791–1840.
    Baptism and Marriage Register, 1733–1805.
  Lands and Surveys Department.
    Grant Books A–C, I, K, Z.
  Office of the Registrar General.
    Books M, Z.
  Public Records Office.
    William Alexander's Will, September 30, 1796.
    F. W. D. Armbrister, "Recollections." Manuscript, 2 vols.
    Journal of General Assembly and Minutes and Journal of the Council, 1789–1810.
    "Plan of Town of Nassau," by Captain Andrew Skinner, 1788.
    General Court Minute Books, 1816–17. SC/1/25 to SC/1/31 (selected vols.) (*see* "Court Cases" in Bibliography).

Cuba
Havana
  Archivo Nacional de Cuba.
    Florida Correspondence
      Legajo 1 (1785–1800).
      Legajo 2 (1780–1807).
      Legajo 9 (1784–1830).
    Cédulas y Ordenes 286 (1780–85).

France
Paris
> *Ministère des Affaires Etrangères.*
> *Archives Diplomatiques: Correspondance Consulaire, Nouvelle-Orléans.* 22 vols. 1804–1901.

Great Britain
London, England
> British Museum, Additional Manuscripts
> > Papers Relating to the Yucatan, H2568.
> > Selkirk's Papers, Canada, 27859.
>
> Public Record Office.
> > Audit Office, AO 1/1261, East Florida; AO 13/36,100, Loyalist Records.
> > Board of Trade, BT 5/2, Minutes.
> > Chatham Papers, 30/8/344, Correspondence of the first Earl of Chatham and of his son, William Pitt.
> > Colonial Office, CO 5/546, 550, 552, 556–61, 572, East Florida; CO 23/27–28, 35–37, Bahamas, Original Correspondence; CO 37/23, Bermuda.
> > Privy Council, PC 1/41, Papers (mostly unbound); PC 2/130–65 (selected vols.) Registers.
> > Probate Records, PROB 6/181 (1805); PROB 11/1411 (1804).
> > Treasury, T 77/1, Loyalist Records (claims) 1787–89.
> > War Office, WO 1/143–44, In letters—Expedition to the Southern Coasts of North America, 1814–17.

Edinburgh, Scotland
> General Registry Office.
> > Old Parish Registers, 141/2 Rothes; 169/1 Aberdour; 223/1 Montquhitter.
>
> National Library
> > J. B. Brown Papers.
> > Alexander Cochrane Papers, MS2328 and MS2336.

Elgin, Scotland
> County Library
> > *Churches of the Parish of St. Andrews/Lhanbryd-Cramond.*
> > Sasines Elgin Forres 1781–1860, 294 and 629.
> > Scottish Collection. *Miscellaneous Contents in a Bound Volume.*

Spain
Madrid
> *Archivo Histórico Nacional.*
> > Sección Estado.
> > > *Legajos* cited: 3885–88, 3895, 3898, 3901. These *legajos* are calendared chronologically in Miguel Gómez del Campillo, *Relaciones Diplomaticas.*
> > > *Legajo* 5563, Expediente 1. General Andrew Jackson's invasion of West Florida, 1818.
> >
> > Consejo de Indias.
> > > *Legajo* 21067, No. 507. The case against the adventurers William Bowles and William Cunningham.
> > > *Legajo* 21225, No. 628. The *residencia* of Arturo O'Neill.

Segovia
> *Archivo General Militar.*
> > Service record of Colonel Josef Tadeo Antonio Masot.

Sevilla
> *Archivo General de Indias.*
> > *Papeles de Cuba.* 98 *legajos* cited. All are fully identified, with a summary of contents, in Hill, *Descriptive Catalogue.*
> > *Audiencia de Santo Domingo.* Seven *legajos* cited: 2543, 2559, 2612, 2613, 2665, 2667,

Bibliography 377

2670. These *legajos* are calendared in Peña y Cámara, et al., *Catalogo de Documentos*, which also contains a "Technical Preface" (pp. xxxv–xxxviii) describing the section (*Sección Quinta*) in which these *legajos* are found.
Simancas
　Archivo General de Simancas.
　　Secretaria de Estado, Embajada de Inglaterra.
　　　Legajos 8137–38. *Expedientes y correspondencia sobre . . . Florida.*
　　　Legajo 8148. *Correspondencia con la Corte.*
　　　Legajos 8183–84. *Correspondencia de cónsules, vicecónsules y varios.*
　　Secretaria de Guerra.
　　　Legajo 7235. *Generalidad de Indias. Invasión de Luisiana y Florida por los franceses.*

Newspapers

Bahama Gazette, 1784–85. Nassau, New Providence Island, Bahamas.
Daily National Intelligencer, 1813. Washington, D.C.
Daily World, 1955. St. Landry Parish, Louisiana.
Elgin Courant, 1839. Elgin, Scotland.
The Floridian, 1821–22. Pensacola, Florida.
Georgia Gazette, 1764–98. Savannah, Georgia.
London Times, 1797. London, England.
Niles' Weekly Register, 1815 Supplement, 1817. Baltimore, Maryland.
The Royal Gazette, 1781. Charleston, South Carolina.
Royal Gazette of Georgia, 1779–82. Savannah, Georgia.

Sources in the United States

Alabama
Mobile
　Chancery, Diocese of Mobile
　　Funeral Book.
　Mobile County Courthouse
　　Will Books 1 and 2.
　Mobile Public Library, Rare Books and Special Collections Department
　　John Forbes Papers

California
Berkeley
　Bancroft Library, University of California
　　Documentos relativos a la Luisiana, 1767–1816.
　　Estevan Rodríguez Miró Papers.

Connecticut
New Haven
　Sterling Library, Yale University
　　Addin Lewis Bound Letter Book, Lewis Family Collection.

Florida
Apalachicola
　"Forbes Purchase" land (title), property of Mr. Jay Shuler.
Gainesville
　P. K. Yonge Library of Florida History, University of Florida.
　　East Florida Papers (microfilm copy).
　　Joseph Byrne Lockey Papers.
　　John B. Stetson Collection.
　　Elizabeth Howard West Papers.

Pensacola
  Escambia County Court Archives, Historic Documents Section
    (See "Court Cases" in Bibliography.)
    Marriage Book "A."
  Pensacola Historical Society, Old Christ Church
    William Panton's Will.
  University of West Florida, John C. Pace Library, Special Collections Department
    Innerarity-Hulse Papers (66–1 and 66–3)
    Murphy Family Papers (68–2)
    Papers of Panton, Leslie and Company (includes copies of most of the documents cited in this volume).
St. Augustine
  Cathedral Basilica of St. Augustine
    Baptisms (White), 1784–99.
    Deaths (Infant White), 1784–1826.
    Deaths (White), 1784–1826.
  St. Augustine Historical Society
    Eugenia Price Letters.
    Spanish Censuses of St. Augustine, 1786, 1793.
Tallahassee
  Bureau of State Lands
    Land Records, 18th and 19th centuries
  Florida State Supreme Court
    (See "Court Cases" in Bibliography.)
Tampa
  Florida Historical Society, Library, University of South Florida
    Heloise H. Cruzat Papers, 1788–1859.
    Marie Taylor Greenslade Papers, 1764–1900.

Georgia

Atlanta
  Office of the Secretary of State
    Surveyor General Department
      "Grants, Register of 1772–1775," Books L, M.
    Department of Archives and History
      Governors' Letter Books, 1809–14.
      "Unpublished Letters of Timothy Barnard, 1784–1820." Manuscript.
      Works Progress Administration. "Creek Indian Letters, Talks, and Treaties, 1705–1839." 4 parts. Manuscript.
East Point
  Federal Records Center, National Archives.
    (See "Court Cases" in Bibliography.)
    "Letter Book of the Creek Trading House, 1795–1816." Manuscript, NARG 75.

Illinois

Chicago
  Newberry Library
    Ayer Collection.

Louisiana

Baton Rouge
  Library, Louisiana State University
    John Innerarity Papers.
    Henry Wilson Papers.
New Orleans
  First Judicial District
    (See "Court Cases" in Bibliography.)

Louisiana Supreme Court
  (*See* "Court Cases" in Bibliography.)
Howard-Tilton Library, Tulane University.
  Indian Affairs Papers. Louisiana Historical Association Collection.
  Works Progress Administration. "Despatches of the Spanish Governors of Louisiana"
    (*see* WPA in Bibliography).
New Orleans Public Library
  Estevan Miró Papers, 1784-94.
  (*See* "Court Cases" in Bibliography.)

Michigan
Ann Arbor
  William L. Clements Library, University of Michigan.
    Thomas Gage Papers.

Mississippi
Jackson
  Mississippi Provincial Archives, Spanish Dominion. 9 vols. 1759-1820.

New York
New York City
  New York Historical Society
    Buckingham Smith Collection.

North Carolina
Chapel Hill
  University of North Carolina, Library, Southern Historical Collection
    John McKee Papers.

South Carolina
Columbia
  South Carolina Department of Archives and History
    Charleston Wills, vol. 21.
    Index to Land Surveys or Plats, vols. 9, 11.
    Judgment Rolls, 1770, 1776, 1783.
    Land Survey or Plat Books, vols. 8, 10, 16.
    Memorial Book, vols. 6, 10.
    Miscellaneous Records, vols. KKK, PP, YY, ZZZ.
    Mortgages, vols. FFF, HHH.
    Royal Grants, vol. 21.

Tennessee
Hermitage
  Andrew Jackson Papers.

Texas
Fort Worth
  Federal Records Center, National Archives
    (*See* "Court Cases" in Bibliography.)

Washington, D.C.
U.S. Library of Congress
  East Florida Papers. Twenty *legajos* cited: 21H2-340S2. These papers have been calendared by Bruce Chappell; a copy of the calendar is available at the P. K. Yonge Library of Florida History, University of Florida, Gainesville.
  Andrew Ellicott Papers.
  Alexander Hamilton Papers.
  Andrew Jackson Papers.

Miscellaneous Papers Relating to Civil Commotions in West Florida, . . . 1799–1827, West Florida Papers.
Vicente Sebastián Pintado Papers.
U.S. National Archives and Records Service
(see also Federal Records Centers, East Point, Georgia, and Fort Worth, Texas). Only general records group number and title are given here. See individual entries in the notes for specific subsection within the records group. See NARS, *Guide to the National Archives of the United States* (Washington: National Archives and Records Service, General Services Administration, 1974), for a general discussion of each records group.
    NARG 59, General Records of the Department of State.
    NARG 75, Records of the Bureau of Indian Affairs.
    NARG 94, Records of the Adjutant General's Office.
    NARG 107, Records of the Office of the Secretary of War.
    NARG 200, National Archives Gift Collection.
    NARG 267, Records of the Supreme Court of the United States.

Wisconsin
Madison
  Wisconsin Historical Society
    Archivo Nacional de Cuba, Legajos 1, 2, 9 (typescripts). See Cuba.

Court Cases

The following court cases are cited in this study. Some have been recorded in the appropriate printed records of the states and the federal government, others are in manuscript only. Even when the cases appear in print, they usually do not contain the many exhibits found in the manuscript copies. It is often in the exhibits that important letters and documents are discovered that are vital not only to the history of the case but to the larger history of the companies and the persons associated with them. Many of these documents are not found elsewhere. Copies of most cases are also in the papers of Panton, Leslie and Company (PLP), John C. Pace Library, University of West Florida, Pensacola, Florida.

The Apalachicola Land and Development Company et al., Appellants v. W. A. McRae, Commissioner of Agriculture of the State of Florida, and T. R. Hodges, Shell Fish Commissioner of the State of Florida, Appellees, 98 So. 505–28; 86 Fla. 393–465.
Catterall, Helen Tunnicliff, ed. *Judicial Cases Concerning American Slavery and the Negro.* Vol. 1, *Cases from the Courts of England, Virginia, West Virginia, and Kentucky.* New York: Octagon Books, 1968.
Lewis Curtis et al. v. John and James Innerarity. See *Lewis Curtis and George Griswold, Trustees of the Apalachicola Land Company, Appellants v. John and James Innerarity, Appellees;* 6 Howard 146; Case file no. 2459, Records of the Supreme Court of the United States, NARG 267, Microcopy no. MNP 165, Roll no. 2; Papers relating to Forbes Purchase, Federal Records Center, East Point, Georgia. Reel 75, PLP.
Thomas Dow et al. v. Venancio Sanchez, Administrator of the Estate of John Forbes. Circuit Court, 4th Judicial Circuit, St. Johns County, State of Florida, File no. 0575, Florida Supreme Court, Tallahassee, Reels 92 and 237, PLP. See also *V. Sanchez, Administrator, Appellant v. Thomas Dow et al., Appellees,* 23 Fla. 445–54.
John Forbes v. George Woodbine. General Court Minute Books, 1816–17. SC/1/28, PRON. Copy in PLP.
Barnewell, Richard Vaughan, and Cresswell, Cresswell. *John Forbes against Sir Alexander Inglis Cochrane, Knight, and Sir George Cockburn, Knight.* 1824. Great Britain, Court of King's Bench. *Reports of Cases argued and determined in the Court of King's Bench. With tables of the names of the cases and the principal matters.* London: Butterworth & Son, 1823–32. Cases in Michaelmas Term. 2 B & C 448–73. Copy in PLP.

John Forbes and Company v. D. W. Johnson. See *John Forbes & Co., Plaintiff versus D. W. Johnson.* Case no. 1999.
John Forbes & Co. v. Silas Dinsmoor. Case no. 296, filed August 11, 1809, New Orleans Circuit and District Courts, FRC #449440, Acc. 70–A–6, Federal Records Center, Fort Worth, Texas. Reel 104, PLP.
John Forbes et al. v. George Woodbine. General Court Minute Books, 1816–17. SC/1/25, PRON. Copy in PLP.
John Forbes & Co., Plaintiff v. D. W. Johnson. Case no. 1999, Dk. 3, filed June 12, 1823, New Orleans Circuit and District Courts, FRC #449468, ACC. 70–A–6, Federal Records Center, Fort Worth, Texas. Reel 104, PLP.
John G. Forbes et al. v. Apalachicola Land Co. December 28, 1882. Florida Supreme Court, Tallahassee. Reels 100 and 224, PLP.
Great Britain, Court of King's Bench. *Reports of Cases.* . . . See *John Forbes against Sir Alexander Inglis Cochrane, Knight.*
Euphrozine Hinard, Sale of Estate, File no. 1866–0–468, Historic Documents Section, Judicial Building, Pensacola. Not in PLP.
James Innerarity v. Roswell P. Johnson. Case no. 6694, filed June 13, 1825. First Judicial District Court, New Orleans Public Library. Reel 465, PLP.
In re. John Innerarity, Administrator of John Forbes Deceased v. Curtis and Griswold, Trustees of the Apalachicola Land Company, 4 Fla. 175–91.
John and James Innerarity v. R. Post Johnson et al. Case no. 2080, filed December 13, 1823, Cases of the United States Circuit Court, New Orleans, FRC 449469, Acc. 70–A–6, Federal Records Center, Fort Worth, Texas. Reel 104, PLP.
John and James Innerarity & the Heirs of John Forbes v. the United States. Case no. 1830-2637, Historic Documents Section, Judicial Building, Pensacola. Copy in PLP.
D. W. Johnson & George Edwards, to the use of R. Post Johnson v. John Forbes & Co. See *John Forbes & Co., Plaintiff v. D. W. Johnson.* Case no. 1999.
D. W. Johnson & George Edwards, to the use of R. Post Johnson v. James and John Innerarity, Surviving Partners of John Forbes & Co. Case no. 5955, filed February 23, 1824. First Judicial District Court, New Orleans. Copy in PLP.
D. W. Johnson & George Edwards v. John & James Innerarity & Alexander Gordon. Case no. 6701, filed June 20, 1825. First Judicial District Court, New Orleans Public Library. Reel 465, PLP.
D. W. Johnson et al., Appellants v. James Innerarity et al., Appellees. Case no. 1156, filed April 11, 1825. Louisiana State Supreme Court, New Orleans. Reels 234–35, PLP.
The King v. John Forbes. General Court Minute Books, 1816–17. SC/1/24, SC/1/28, PRON. Copies in PLP.
The King v. George Woodbine. General Court Minute Books, 1816–17. SC/1/24, SC/1/28, SC/1/29, SC/1/31, PRON. Copies in PLP
John Leslie Heirs v. The Trustees of the Apalachicola Land Company. Brief & Exposition of the Bill of Exhibits, Circuit Court, Middle Circuit, Florida. J. B. Brown Papers, MS 3276, National Library of Scotland, Edinburgh, Reel 447, PLP.
William McVoy v. J. McDavid. Cases no. 1821-8 and 1823-169, Historic Documents Section, Judicial Building, Pensacola.
Colin Mitchel et al. v. The United States, 9 Peters 711; 11 Curtis 539. There exist at least three manuscript copies of this case that contain copies of pertinent documents (exhibits) not found in the foregoing citations. One copy is at the Federal Records Center, East Point, Georgia. Order no. 260NNFL-75(697). Reel 105, PLP. A second copy, listed as "No. 1, Miscellaneous Papers Filed Prior to the Civil War," is entitled *Colin Mitchel et al. v. The United States.* Decree of Leon Superior Court, 1830, and is also in the Federal Records Center, East Point, Georgia. Reel 75, PLP. A third copy, *Colin Mitchel et al. v. The United States.* Case no. 1671, is in Records of the Supreme Court of the United States, NARG 267, Microcopy MNP 165 (Roll no. 2). Reel 449, PLP. A printed copy of this case (but with some exhibits missing) is in the Law Library, Library of Congress; U.S.

Supreme Court, Records and Briefs, Part One, Vol. I (January Term 1835 to January 1836), Shelf LL-043, Reel no. 3; Reel 510, PLP. See also Myers, *History of the Supreme Court of the United States,* 340–54.

Moses v. Alexander. 401A-3B, 401A-3² F&B, 401A-6 F&B, South Carolina Department of Archives and History, Columbia. Copy in PLP.

Myers, Gustavus. *History of the Supreme Court of the United States.* New York: Burt Franklin, 1968 [1912].

V. Sanchez, Administrator, Appellant v. Thomas Dow et al., Appellees; 23 Fla. Reports 445–54.

V. Sanchez, Appellant v. T. Dow, et al., Appellees. Filed January 13, 1880. Florida Supreme Court, Tallahassee. Reel 223, PLP.

Somerset v. Stewart. See Catterall, *Judicial Cases concerning Slavery,* 14–18.

The Trials of A. Arbuthnot & R. C. Ambrister charged with Exciting the Seminole Indians to War against the United States of America, from the Official Documents which were Laid by the President Before Congress. London: Printed for James Ridgway, Piccadilly, 1819. Copy in Special Collections Department, John C. Pace Library.

Trustees Apalachicola Land Co. v. John Innerarity, Adm. of Jno Forbes. Record on file at Federal Records Center, East Point, Georgia. Reel 75, PLP.

The Vidal Heirs v. John Innerarity. The pertinent documents are in "Transactions in the Floridas under Governor Jackson," *American State Papers, Miscellaneous* 2:799–875.

Merced Vidal, File 1821–29905, Historic Documents Section, Judicial Building, Pensacola. Not in PLP.

George Woodbine v. John Forbes. General Court Minute Books, 1816–17. SC/1/25, PRON. Copy in PLP.

Books, Articles, and Manuscripts

Abernethy, Thomas Perkins. *From Frontier to Plantation in Tennessee: A Study in Frontier Democracy.* Chapel Hill: University of North Carolina Press, 1932; rep. University: University of Alabama Press, 1967.

Alden, John Richard. *John Stuart and the Southern Colonial Frontier. A Study of Indian Relations, War, Trade, and Land Problems in the Southern Wilderness, 1754–1775.* New York: Gordian Press, 1966.

"Alexander McGillivray's Oath of Allegiance to the United States." *Gulf Coast History Magazine* 1 (July 1902): 47–48.

"America's First Millionaire." *Wentworth's Magazine* 4 (April 1944): 3, 8–9.

Armbrister, Mary K. "Henrietta my Daughter." Manuscript, compiled by Mary K. Young. Old Greenwich, Conn., August 1970.

Armbrister, P. W. B. "Recollections." 2 vols. Manuscript, Public Records Office, Ministry of Education and Culture, Nassau, New Providence, Bahamas.

Armytage, Frances. *The Free Port System in the British West Indies: A Study in Commerical Policy, 1766–1822.* London: Longmans, Green, 1953.

Avery, Isaac Wheeler. *The History of State of Georgia, 1850–1881, Embracing the Three Important Epochs: The Decade before the War of 1861–5; The War; The Period of Reconstruction, with Portraits of the Leading Public Men of the Era.* New York: Brown and Derby, 1881.

Barr, Ruth B. "Panton, Leslie and Company." Manuscript, U.S. Federal Writers Project, Florida. Florida Historical Society, Pensacola, 1937. Copy in Florida Historical Society, Florida Collection, University of South Florida Library, Tampa.

Bartram, William. "Observations on the Creek and Cherokee Indians, 1789." 3 parts. *Transactions of the American Ethnological Society* 1 (1853) 1–81.

———. "Travels in Georgia and Florida 1773–1774: A Report to Dr. John Fothergill." Edited by Francis Harper. *Transactions of the American Philosophical Society* n.s. 33 (1943): 121–242.

———. *The Travels of William Bartram*. Edited by Francis Harper. New Haven: Yale University Press, 1958.
———. *Travels through North and South Carolina, Georgia, East and West Florida*. Reprint edition. Savannah: Beehive Press, 1973.
Bassett, John Spencer, ed. *Correspondence of Andrew Jackson*. 6 vols. Washington: Carnegie Institution of Washington, 1926–35; rep., New York: Kraus Reprint, 1969.
Beerman, Eric. "Arturo O'Neill: First Governor of West Florida during the Second Spanish Period." *Florida Historical Quarterly* 60 (July 1981): 29–41.
Bemis, Samuel Flagg. *John Quincy Adams and the Foundations of American Foreign Policy*. New York: Knopf, 1965.
———. *Pinckney's Treaty, America's Advantage from Europe's Distress, 1783–1800*. New Haven: Yale University Press, 1960.
Bennett, Charles E. *Florida's "French" Revolution, 1793–1795*. Gainesville: University Presses of Florida, 1981.
Born, John Dewey, Jr. "British Trade in West Florida, 1773–1783." Ph.D. diss., University of New Mexico, 1963.
Boyd, Julian P., ed. *The Papers of Thomas Jefferson*. 20 vols. Princeton: Princeton University Press, 1950–.
Boyd, Mark F. "Events at Prospect Bluff on the Apalachicola River: An Introduction to Some Letters of Edmund Doyle, Trader." *Tallahassee Historical Society Annual* 3 (1937): 82–102.
———. "Events at Prospect Bluff on the Apalachicola River, 1808–1818." *Florida Historical Quarterly* 16 (October 1937): 55–96.
———. "Historic Sites in and around the Jim Woodruff Reservoir Area, Florida-Georgia." In *River Basin Surveys Papers*, edited by Frank H. H. Roberts, Jr., 199–314. Bureau of American Ethnology Bulletin 169. Washington: Smithsonian Institution, 1958.
Brackenridge, Henry Marie. *Judge Brackenridge's Letters to the Public, 1832*. Washington: N.p., [1832].
Brooks, Philip Coolidge. *Diplomacy and the Borderlands: The Adams-Onís Treaty of 1819*. Reprint edition. New York: Octagon Books, 1970.
Brown, J. A. "Panton, Leslie and Company Indian Traders of Pensacola and St. Augustine." *Florida Historical Quarterly* 37 (1959): 328–36.
Burnett, Edmund C., ed. "Papers Relating to Bourbon County, Georgia, 1783–1786." *American Historical Review* 15 (1910): 66–111, 286–353.
Callava, Coronel Don José. *Manifiesto sobre las tropelías y bejaciones que cometió el gobernador americano de Panzacola Andres Jackson, contra la persona y representación del comisario de la España Coronel Don José Callava nombrado para la entrega de la Florida occidental á los Estados-Unidos de América*. Habana: Imprenta del Comercio de D. Antonio María Valdés, calle del Teniente-rey, casa número 81, 1821.
Candler, Allen D., ed. *The Revolutionary Records of the State of Georgia*. 3 vols. Atlanta: Franklin Turner, 1908.
Candler, Allen D., and Knight, Lucien Lamar, eds. *The Colonial Records of the State of Georgia*. 26 vols. Atlanta: [state printers], 1904–16.
Carter, Clarence Edwin, ed. *The Territorial Papers of the United States*. 26 vols. Washington: U.S. Government Printing Office, 1934–62.
Catterall, Helen Tunnicliff, ed. *Judicial Cases Concerning American Slavery and the Negro*. Vol. 1, *Cases from the Courts of England, Virginia, West Virginia, and Kentucky*. New York: Octagon Books, 1968.
Caughey, John Walton. *Bernardo de Gálvez in Louisiana, 1776–1783*. Berkeley: University of California Press, 1934; rep., Gretna, Louisiana: Pelican Publishing Co., 1972.
———. *McGillivray of the Creeks*. Norman: University of Oklahoma Press, 1938.
Chestnutt, David R. See Hamer, Philip M.
Claiborne, J. F. H. *Mississippi as a Province, Territory, and State*. Jackson, Miss.: Power & Barksdale, 1890; rep., Baton Rouge: Louisiana State University Press, 1964.
Clark, John Garreston. *New Orleans, 1718–1812: An Economic History*. Baton Rouge: Louisiana State University Press, 1970.

Clark-Genêt Correspondence. See Jameson, J. Franklin.
Cline, Howard F. *Florida Indians: Notes on Colonial Indians and Communities in Florida 1700–1821*. 2 vols. New York: Garland Publishers, 1974.
Coker, William S. *Historical Sketches of Panton, Leslie and Company*. Pensacola; University of West Florida, 1976.
———. "The Last Battle of the War of 1812: New Orleans. No, Fort Bowyer!" *Alabama Historical Quarterly* 43 (Spring 1981): 42–63.
———. "The Papers of Panton, Leslie and Company." Journal of the USF Library Associates: *Ex Libris* 2 (Fall 1978): 13–15.
———. "The Religious Censuses of Pensacola, 1796–1802." *Florida Historical Quarterly* 61 (July 1982): 54–63.
———. "Una compañía privilegiada (John Forbes), en La Florida española durante la guerra de 1812." *Revista de Indias* 159–62 (January–December 1980): 219–54.
———. "The Village on the Red Cliffs." *Pensacola History Illustrated* 1, no. 2 (1984): 22–26.
———, ed. *John Forbes' Description of the Spanish Floridas, 1804*. Pensacola: Perdido Bay Press, 1979.
——— and Inglis, G. Douglas. *The Spanish Censuses of Pensacola, 1784–1820: A Genealogical Guide to Spanish Pensacola*. Pensacola: Perdido Bay Press, 1980.
——— and Rea, Robert R., eds. *Anglo-Spanish Confrontation on the Gulf Coast during the American Revolution*. Pensacola: Gulf Coast History and Humanities Conference, 1982.
Coleman, James Julian, Jr. *Gilbert Antoine de St. Maxent: The Spanish-Frenchman of New Orleans*. New Orleans: Pelican Publishing House, 1968.
Coleman, Kenneth. *The American Revolution in Georgia, 1763–1789*. Athens: University of Georgia Press, 1958.
Cook, Warren L. *Flood Tide of Empire: Spain and the Pacific Northwest, 1543–1819*. New Haven: Yale University Press, 1973.
Corbitt, Duvon C., ed. and trans. "Papers Relating to the Georgia-Florida Frontier, 1784–1800." *Georgia Historical Quarterly*. Corbitt's translation of Spanish documents appeared in vols. 20–25 (1936–41).
Corbitt, Duvon C., and Corbitt, Roberta, eds. and trans. "Papers from the Spanish Archives Relating to Tennessee and the Old Southwest, 1783–1800." *East Tennessee Historical Society Publications*. The Corbitts' translations began in vol. 9 (1937) and appeared in many subsequent volumes.
Corkran, David H. *The Cherokee Frontier: Conflict and Survival, 1740–62*. Norman: University of Oklahoma Press, 1962.
———. *The Creek Frontier, 1540–1783*. Norman: University of Oklahoma Press, 1967.
Cotterill, Robert S. "A Chapter of Panton, Leslie and Company." *Journal of Southern History* 10 (August 1944): 275–92.
———. *The Southern Indians: The Story of the Civilized Tribes before Removal*. Norman: University of Oklahoma Press, 1954.
———. "The Virginia-Chickasaw Treaty of 1783." *Journal of Southern History* 8 (November 1942): 483–96.
Coughlin, Frances Ellen. "Spanish Galleys on the Mississippi: 1792–1797." Master's thesis, Claremont College, 1945.
Covington, James W. *The British Meet the Seminoles*. Contributions of the Florida State Museum. Social Sciences, no. 7. Gainesville: University of Florida Press, 1961.
Cox, Isaac J. *The West Florida Controversy 1789–1813*. Baltimore: John Hopkins Press, 1918; rep., Gloucester, Mass.: Peter Smith, 1967.
Crane, Verner W. *The Southern Frontier, 1670–1732*. Ann Arbor: University of Michigan Press, 1929; rep., 1956.
Crider, Robert Franklin. "The Borderland Floridas, 1815–1821: Spanish Sovereignty under Siege." Ph.D. diss., Florida State University, 1979.
Cubberly, Frederick. "Andrew Jackson, Judge." *American Law Review* 56 (October 1922): 686–701.

Davenport, Frances Gardiner and Paullin, Charles Oscar, eds. *European Treaties Bearing on the History of the United States and its Dependencies.* 4 vols. Reprint edition. Gloucester, Mass.: Peter Smith, 1967.

Davis, T. Frederick. *MacGregor's Invasion of Florida, 1817. Together with an Account of His Successors Irwin, Hubbard and Aury on Amelia Island, East Florida.* Jacksonville: Florida Historical Society, 1928.

———. "Milly Francis and Duncan McKrimmon: An Authentic Florida Pocahontas." *Florida Historical Quarterly* 21 (January 1943): 254–65.

Debo, Angie. *The Rise and Fall of the Choctaw Republic.* 2d ed. Norman: University of Oklahoma Press, 1961.

De Fina, Frank Paul. "Rivalidades y Contactos entre España, Norte América y las Naciones Indias Chactas, Chicasas, Cherokis y Criks en la segunda mitad del Siglo XVIII." 2 vols. Ph.D. diss., University of Madrid, 1962.

Delson, L. A. "Andrew Jackson and the Battle of Pensacola, May 1818: A reappraisal based upon the documents of Governor José de Masot." Manuscript, September 1982. Special Collections Department, John C. Pace Library, University of West Florida.

De Pauw, Linda Grant, et al., eds. *Documentary History of the First Federal Congress, 1789–1791.* 2 vols. Baltimore: Johns Hopkins Press, 1972–74.

DeRosier, Arthur H., Jr. *The Removal of the Choctaw Indians.* Knoxville: University of Tennessee Press, 1970.

DeVorsey, Louis, Jr. *The Indian Boundary in the Southern Colonies, 1763–1775.* Chapel Hill: University of North Carolina Press, 1966.

Doherty, Herbert J., Jr. "Andrew Jackson's Cronies in Florida Territorial Politics: With Three Unpublished Letters to His Cronies." *Florida Historical Quarterly* 34 (July 1955): 3–29.

———. "Andrew Jackson vs. the Spanish Governor, Pensacola, 1821." *Florida Historical Quarterly* 34 (October 1955): 142–58.

———. "The Governorship of Andrew Jackson." *Florida Historical Quarterly* 33 (July 1954): 3–31.

———. *Richard Keith Call, Southern Unionist.* Gainesville: University of Florida Press, 1961.

Doster, James Fletcher. *The Creek Indians and Their Florida Lands 1740–1823.* 2 vols. New York: Garland Publishers, 1974.

Downes, Randolph C. "Creek-American Relations, 1782–1790." *Georgia Historical Quarterly* 21 (June 1937): 142–84.

———. "Creek-American Relations, 1790–1795." *Journal of Southern History* 8 (August 1942): 350–73.

Fairbanks, Charles H., and Goff, John H. *Cherokee and Creek Indians: Ethnographic Report on Royce Area 79: Chickasaw, Cherokee, Creek.* New York: Garland Publishers, 1974.

Fitzpatrick, John C., ed. *The Diaries of George Washington, 1784–1799.* 4 vols. Boston: Houghton Mifflin, 1925.

———. *The Writings of George Washington from the Original Manuscript Sources 1745–1799.* 39 vols. Washington: U.S. Government Printing Office, 1937–44.

Forbes, John. See "A Journal of John Forbes," May, 1903.

Fortier, Alcee. *History of Louisiana.* 2 vols. New York: Manzi, Joyant and Co., 1904.

Fretwell, Mark E. *This So Remote Frontier: The Chattahoochee Country of Alabama and Georgia.* Tallahassee: Rose Printing Co., 1980.

Genêt-Clark Correspondence. See Jameson, J. Franklin.

Genêt's Instructions. See Jameson, J. Franklin.

Georgia Historical Society. *Letters of Benjamin Hawkins 1796–1806.* Collections of the Georgia Historical Society, vol. 9. Savannah: Georgia Historical Society, 1916.

Gibson, Arrel Morgan. *The Chickasaws.* Norman: University of Oklahoma Press, 1971.

Giddings, Joshua R. *The Exiles of Florida.* Facsimile reprint of 1858 edition. Introduction by Arthur W. Thompson. Gainesville: University of Florida Press, 1964.

Giraud, Marcel. *Histoire de la Louisiàne française.* 3 vols. Paris: Presses Universitaires de France, 1953–66.

———. *A History of French Louisiana. The Reign of Louis XIV, 1698–1715.* Translated by Joseph C. Lambert. Baton Rouge: Louisiana State University Press, 1974.
Gold, Robert L. "Politics and Property during the Transfer of Florida from Spanish to English Rule, 1763–1764." *Florida Historical Quarterly* 42 (1963–64): 16–34.
Gómez, Canedo Lino. *Los Archivos de la Historia de América, Período Colonial Español.* 2 vols. Mexico, D.F.: Instituto Panamericano de Geografia e Historia, 1961.
Gómez del Campillo, Miguel. *Relaciones Diplomaticas entre España y los Estados Unidos: Segun los Documentos del Archivo Histórico Nacional.* 2 vols. Madrid: Consejo Superior de Investigaciones Científicas, Instituto Gonzalo Fernández de Oviedo, 1945.
Gordon, John. "Journal of a Council . . . between U.S. Government, Chiefs of Indian Tribes and Panton, Leslie Co." Manuscript, Innerarity-Hulse Papers, University of West Florida, Pensacola. Printed in "John Forbes & Co., Successors to Panton, Leslie & Co., vs. The Chickasaw Nation: A Journal of an Indian Talk, July, 1805." *Florida Historical Quarterly* 8 (January 1930): 131–42.
Grant, C. L., ed. *Letters, Journals and Writings on Benjamin Hawkins.* 2 vols. Savannah: Beehive Press, 1980.
Great Britain. Court of King's Bench. *Reports of Cases Argued and Determined in Court of King's Bench,* by Richard Vaughan Barnewall and Cresswell Cresswell. 10 vols. London: J. Butterworth & Son, 1823–32.
Great Britain. Historical Manuscripts Commission. *Report on American Manuscripts in the Royal Institution of Great Britain.* 4 vols. Reprint edition. Boston: Gregg Press, 1972.
Greenslade, Marie Taylor. "John Innerarity, 1783–1854." *Florida Historical Quarterly* 9 (1930): 90–95.
———. "William Panton." *Florida Historical Quarterly* 14 (1935): 107–29.
Greenslade, Marie Taylor, and Cruzat, Heloise Hulse. "The Panton-Leslie Papers." *Florida Historical Quarterly.* A series of letters and documents from the collections of Greenslade and Cruzat appeared in the *FHQ,* vols. 9–17 (1930–39). The papers have since been deposited with the Florida Historical Society as the "Greenslade and Cruzat Papers."
Hamer, Philip M., Rogers, George C., Jr., and Chestnutt, David R., eds. *The Papers of Henry Laurens 1724–1792.* 9 vols. Columbia: Published for South Carolina Historical Society by University of South Carolina Press, 1968–81.
Hamilton, Peter J. *Colonial Mobile: A Historical Study Largely from Original Sources of the Alabama-Tombigbee Basin from the Discovery of Mobile Bay in 1519 until the Demolition of Fort Charlotte in 1821.* Boston: Houghton Mifflin, 1897.
Haring, C. H. *The Spanish Empire in America.* Reprint edition. New York: Harcourt, Brace, 1963.
Harmon, George D. "Benjamin Hawkins and the Federal Factory System." *North Carolina Historical Review* 9 (April 1932): 138–52.
———. *Sixty Years of Indian Affairs. Political, Economic, and Diplomatic 1789–1850.* Chapel Hill: University of North Carolina Press, 1941; rep., New York: Kraus Reprint, 1969.
Harper, Francis, ed. *The Travels of William Bartram.* New Haven: Yale University Press, 1958.
Hartley, Howard K. "Florida Claims." Manuscript, Special Collections Department, John C. Pace Library, University of West Florida.
Hartridge, Walter Charlton, ed. *The Letters of Don Juan McQueen to His Family.* Published for the Georgia Society of the Colonial Dames of America. Columbia: Bostick and Thornley, 1943.
Hatfield, Joseph T. *William Claiborne.* Lafayette: University of Southwestern Louisiana Press, 1976.
Hayne, Isaac. "Records Kept by Colonel Isaac Hayne." *South Carolina Historical and Genealogical Magazine* 9 (1910): 27–38.
Heitman, Francis B. *Historical Register and Dictionary of the United States Army.* Reprint edition. Urbana: University of Illinois Press, 1965.

Higgins, W. Robert. "Charles Town Merchants and Factors Dealing in the External Negro Trade, 1735–1775." *South Carolina Historical Magazine* 65 (1964): 205–17.
Hill, Louise Biles. "George J. F. Clarke, 1774–1836." *Florida Historical Quarterly* 21 (January 1943): 197–253.
Hill, Roscoe R. *Descriptive Catalogue of the Documents relating to the History of the United States in the Papeles Procedentes de Cuba deposited in the Archivo General de Indias at Seville.* Washington: Carnegie Institution of Washington, 1916; rep., New York: Kraus Reprint, 1965.
Hoffman, M. M. "Talleyrand: An American Copy." *Catholic World* 157 (April 1943): 54–60.
Holmes, Jack D. L. "Commandants and Governors of Pensacola: 1781–1821." In *Colonial Pensacola*, edited by James R. McGovern. Pensacola: Tom White, 1974.
―――. "Dramatis Personae in Spanish Louisiana." *Louisiana Studies* 6 (Summer 1967): 149–85.
―――. "Fort Ferdinand on the Bluffs; Life on the Spanish-American Frontier, 1795–97." *West Tennessee Historical Society Papers* 13 (1959): 38–54.
―――. *Gayoso. The Life of a Spanish Governor in the Mississippi Valley 1789–1799.* Baton Rouge: Louisiana State University Press, 1965.
―――. "Juan de la Villebeuvre and Spanish Indian Policy in West Florida, 1784–1797." Paper read at the Western History Association, San Diego, California, October 19, 1977.
―――. "Notes on the Spanish Fort San Esteban de Tombecbé." *Alabama Review* 18 (1965): 281–90.
―――. "Spanish Treaties with West Florida Indians, 1784–1802." *Florida Historical Quarterly* 48 (1969): 140–54.
―――. *Stephen Minor.* Vol. 1, Spanish Borderlands Biographical Series. Birmingham: Louisiana Collection Series, 1983.
―――. "Vidal and Zoning in Spanish New Orleans, 1797." *Louisiana History* 14 (Summer 1973): 171–82.
Humphreys, Frank L. *The Life and Times of David Humphreys.* 2 vols. New York: G. P. Putnam's Sons, 1917; rep., St. Clair Shores, Mich.: Scholarly Press, 1973.
An Impartial Account of the Late Expedition Against St. Augustine under General Oglethorpe. Facsimile reproduction of 1742 edition. Introduction and indexes by Aileen Moore Topping. Gainesville: University Presses of Florida, 1978.
Innerarity, John. "The Creek Nation, Debtor to John Forbes & Co., Successors to Panton, Leslie & Co.: A Journal of John Innerarity, 1812." *Florida Historical Quarterly* 9 (October 1930): 67–89.
Jackson, Harvey H. "Button Gwinnett: Whig to Excess or Scoundrel?" *American History Illustrated* 16 (August 1981): 19–24.
―――. *Lachlan McIntosh and the Politics of Revolutionary Georgia.* Athens: University of Georgia Press, 1979.
Jackson, Kenneth T., and Adams, James Truslow. *Atlas of American History.* Rev. ed. New York: Scribner, 1978.
Jackson, Melvin H. *Privateers in Charleston, 1793–1796.* Smithsonian Studies in History and Technology, no. 1. Washington, D.C.: Smithsonian Institution Press, 1969.
James, Marquis. *The Life of Andrew Jackson.* Indianapolis: Bobbs-Merrill, 1938.
Jameson, J. Franklin, et al. "Selections from the Draper Collection in the Possession of the State Historical Society of Wisconsin, to Elucidate the Proposed French Expedition under George Rogers Clark against Louisiana, in the Years 1793–94." In *Annual Report of the American Historical Association for the Year 1896*, 1:930–1107. 2 vols. Washington: U.S. Government Printing Office, 1897.
Jenkins, Charles Francis. *Button Gwinnett: Signer of the Declaration of Independence.* Garden City, N.Y.: Doubleday, Page, 1926.
Jensen, Rhiner Christan. "Panton, Leslie, and Company: 1770–1801." Master's thesis, University of Southern California, 1959.
Johnson, Cecil. *British West Florida, 1763–1783.* New Haven: Yale University Press, 1942; rep., Hamden, Conn.: Archon Books, 1971.

Jones, Charles C., Jr. *The History of Georgia.* Boston, 1883; rep., Spartanburg, S.C.: Mifflin Reprint, 1965.
"A Journal of John Forbes, May, 1803." *Florida Historical Quarterly* 9 (1931): 279–89.
"Journal of the Second Council of Safety." *Collections of the South Carolina Historical Society.* Vol. 3. Charleston: South Carolina Historical Society, 1859.
Kappler, Charles J., comp. and ed. *Indian Affairs, Laws and Treaties.* 7 vols. Washington: U.S. Government Printing Office, 1904; facsimile ed., New York, 1972.
Kerr, Derek Noel. "Petty Felony, Slave Defiance and Frontier Villainy: Crime and Criminal Justice in Spanish Louisiana, 1770–1803." Ph.D. diss., Tulane University, 1983.
Kinnaird, Lawrence. "American Penetration into Spanish Louisiana." In *New Spain and the Anglo-American West*, edited by George P. Hammond, 1:211–37. 2 vols. Lancaster, Pa.: Lancaster Press, 1932.
———. "American Penetration into Spanish Territory, 1776–1803.' Ph.D. diss., University of California, 1928.
———. "International Rivalry in the Creek Country: The Ascendency of Alexander McGillivray, 1783–1789." *Florida Historical Quarterly* 10 (October 1931): 59–85.
———. "The Significance of William Augustus Bowles' Seizure of Panton's Apalachee Store in 1792." *Florida Historical Quarterly* 9 (January 1931): 156–92.
———. *Spain in the Mississippi Valley 1765–1794. Translations of Materials from the Spanish Archives in the Bancroft Library. Annual Report of the American Historical Association for the Year 1945*, parts 1–3. 4 vols. Washington: U.S. Government Printing Office, 1946–49.
Knight, Lucien Lamar. *Reminiscences of Famous Georgians.* 2 vols. Atlanta: Franklin-Turner Co., 1907–8.
Krakow, Kenneth K. *Georgia Place-Names.* Macon, Ga.: Winship Press, 1975.
Lackey, Richard S., comp. *Frontier Claims in the Lower South . . . During the War of 1812.* New Orleans: Polyanthos, 1977.
Latour, A. Lacarrière. *Historical Memoir of the War in West Florida and Louisiana in 1814–1815.* Facsimile reproduction of 1816 edition. Gainesville: University of Florida Press, 1964.
LeGardeur, Rene J., Jr., and Pitot, Henry C. "An Unpublished Memoir of Spanish Louisiana, 1796–1802." In *Frenchmen and French Ways in the Mississippi Valley*, edited by J. F. McDermott. Urbana: University of Illinois Press, 1969.
Leslie, William. *An Account of the Antiquities, Modern Buildings, and Natural Curiosities, in the Province of Moray, Worthy of the Attention of the Tourist; with an Itinerary of the Province.* Edinburgh: Printed by Michael Anderson for I. Forsyth, 1813; 2d ed., 1823.
———. *General View of the Agriculture in the Counties of Nairn and Moray, with Observations on the Means of Their Improvement.* London: Printed for Richard Phillips, 1811.
———. *A Letter to William IV on Church Patronage.* Elgin, 1833.
"A Letter of James Innerarity on William Panton's Estate." *Florida Historical Quarterly* 10 (April 1932): 185–94.
Lewis, Addin. Letter Book. Sterling Library, Yale University, New Haven, Conn.
Lewis, Kenneth Edmund, Jr. "The History and Archaeology of Spalding's Lower Store." M.A. thesis, University of Florida, 1969.
"A List of the Officers of His Majesty's Province of Georgia and their Present Places of Residence." *Collections of the Georgia Historical Society* 3:251–53. Savannah: Georgia Historical Society, 1873.
"List of Debts Due by the Traders & Factors of the Upper Creek Towns to the Firm of Messrs. Panton, Leslie & Co., and John Forbes & Co. of Pensacola, adjusted to 1st Novemb. 1812." *Florida Historical Quarterly* 9 (October 1930): 86.
Lockey, Joseph Byrne. *East Florida 1783–1785.* Berkeley: University of California Press, 1949.
Lovell, Caroline Couper. *The Golden Isles of Georgia.* Boston: Little, Brown, 1932.
M'Call, Hugh. *History of Georgia.* 2 vols. Savannah: Seymour Williams, 1816; rep., Atlanta: Cherokee Publishing Co., 1969.

Bibliography 389

McDermott, J. F., ed. *Frenchmen and French Ways in the Mississippi Valley*. Urbana: University of Illinois Press, 1969.
McDonnel, John. "Parish of Forres." *The Statistical Account of Scotland*. Edinburgh: William Creech, 1796.
McDowell, William L., Jr., ed. *Colonial Records of South Carolina: Documents Relating to Indian Affairs, 1754–1765*. Columbia: South Carolina Archives Department, 1970.
McReynolds, Edwin C. *The Seminoles*. Norman: University of Oklahoma Press, 1957.
McWatt, Alexander. "Parish of Rothes." *The New Statistical Account of Scotland*. Edinburgh: William Blackwood and Sons, 1845.
Mahan, Alfred Thayer. *The Influence of Sea Power upon the French Revolution and Empire, 1793–1812*. 2 vols. Reprint edition. St. Clair Shores, Mich.: Scholarly Press, 1969.
———. *The Influence of Sea Power upon History, 1660–1783*. Boston: Little, Brown, 1918.
———. *Sea Power in Its Relations to the War of 1812*. Reprint edition. New York: Greenwood Press, 1968.
Mahon, John K. *The War of 1812*. Gainesville: University of Florida Press, 1972.
"Mangourit Correspondence." See Turner, Frederick J.
Milfort, Louis LeClerc. *Memoirs*. Translated and edited by Ben C. McCary. Savannah: Beehive Press, 1959.
Miller, Janice Borton. *Juan Nepomuceno de Quesada: Governor of Spanish East Florida, 1790–1795*. Washington: University Press of America, 1981.
Mirat, Elena Sánchez-Fabrés. *Situación Histórica de las Floridas en la Segunda Mitad del Siglo XVIII (1783–1819)*. Madrid: Ministerio de Asuntos Exteriores, 1977.
Mohr, Walter H. *Federal-Indian Relations, 1774–1788*. Philadelphia: University of Pennsylvania Press, 1933.
Morris, Richard B. *The Peacemakers: The Great Powers and American Independence*. New York: Harper and Row, 1965.
Mowat, Charles Loch. *East Florida as a British Province 1763–1784*. Facsimile reprint edition. Gainesville: University Presses of Florida, 1964.
Murdoch, Richard K. "Correspondence of French Consuls in Charleston, South Carolina, 1793–1797." *South Carolina Historical Magazine* 74 (1973): 1–17, 73–79.
———. *The Georgia-Florida Frontier, 1793–1796. Spanish Reaction to French Intrigue and American Designs*. Berkeley: University of California Press, 1951.
Napier, John Hawkins III. "The Gulf Coast: Key to Jeffersonian Empire." *Alabama Historical Quarterly* 33 (Summer 1971): 98–115.
Nasatir, Abraham P. *Borderland in Retreat: From Spanish Louisiana to the Far Southwest*. Albuquerque: University of New Mexico Press, 1976.
———. *Spanish War Vessels on the Mississippi 1792–1796*. New Haven: Yale University Press, 1968.
Nimnicht, Randy Frank. "William Panton: His Early Career on the Changing Frontier." Master's thesis, University of Florida, 1968.
Northern, William J., ed. *Men of Mark in Georgia*. 7 vols. Reprint edition. Spartanburg, S.C.: Reprint Company, 1974.
Nuzum, Kay. *A History of Baldwin County*. 3d ed. Fairhope, Ala.: Eastern Shore Publishing Co., 1971.
O'Callaghan, Mary A. M. "The Indian Policy of Carondelet in Spanish Louisiana." Ph.D. diss., University of California, 1942.
O'Donnell, James H., III. "Alexander McGillivray: Training for Leadership, 1777–1783." *Georgia Historical Quarterly* 49 (June 1965): 172–86.
———. *Southern Indians in the American Revolution*. Knoxville: University of Tennessee Press, 1973.
Omand, Donald, ed. *The Moray Book*. Edinburgh: Paul Harris, 1976.
Otis, D. S., and Prucha, Francis Paul, eds. *The Dawes Act and the Allotment of Indian Lands*. Norman: University of Oklahoma Press, 1973.
Owen, Thomas McAdory. *History of Alabama*. Reprint edition. Spartanburg, S.C.: Reprint Company, 1975.

Owsley, Frank Lawrence, Jr. *Struggle for the Gulf Borderlands: The Creek War and the Battle of New Orleans, 1812–1815.* Gainesville: University Presses of Florida, 1981.
The Oxford English Dictionary. 13 vols. Oxford: Clarendon Press, 1933, 1961.
Palacios Zuasti, María Concepción. "La Casa Panton y Leslie y El Comercio de Pieles en las Floridas, en el Siglo XVIII." Master's thesis (*Tesis de Licenciatura*), University of Madrid, 1966.
Panagopoulos, E. P. *New Smyrna: An Eighteenth-Century Greek Odyssey.* Gainesville: University of Florida Press, 1966.
Paredes, J. Anthony, and Plante, Kenneth J. "Economics, Politics, and the Subjugation of the Creek Indians." Manuscript, Department of Anthropology, Florida State University, Tallahassee, October 1975.
Parrish, Lydia Austin. "Records of Some Southern Loyalists: Being a collection of manuscripts about some 80 families, most of whom emigrated to the Bahamas during and after the American Revolution." Manuscript, Harvard University Library, Cambridge, 1940 (1953).
Parton, James. *Life of Andrew Jackson.* 3 vols. New York: Mason Brothers, 1860–61.
Patrick, Rembert W. *Aristocrat in Uniform, General Duncan L. Clinch.* Gainesville: University of Florida Press, 1963.
———. *Florida Fiasco: Rampant Rebels on the Georgia-Florida Border, 1810–1815.* Athens: University of Georgia Press, 1954.
Peña y Camara, José de la, et al., eds. *Catálago de Documentos del Archivo de Indias.* 2 vols. New Orleans and Madrid: Loyola University and Dirección General de Archivos y Bibliotecas, 1968.
Peters, Thelma. "The American Loyalists in the Bahama Islands; Who They Were." *Florida Historical Quarterly* 40 (1961–62): 226–40.
Phillips, Paul Chrisler. *The Fur Trade.* 2 vols. Norman: University of Oklahoma Press, 1961.
Pickett, Albert James. *History of Alabama and Incidentally of Georgia and Mississippi from the Earliest Period.* Birmingham, Ala.: Webb Book Co., 1900; rep., Spartanburg, S.C.: Reprint Company, 1975.
Pickman, Susan Lois. "Life on the Spanish-American Colonial Frontier: A Study in the Social and Economic History of Mid-Eighteenth Century St. Augustine." Ph.D. diss., State University of New York at Stony Brook, 1980.
Pitot, James. *Observations on the Colony of Louisiana from 1796 to 1802.* Translation and introduction by Henry C. Pitot. Baton Rouge: Louisiana State University Press for New Orleans Historic Collection, 1979.
Pope, John. *A Tour through the Southern and Western Territories of the United States of North America. The Spanish Dominions on the River Mississippi, and the Floridas; the Countries of the Creek Nations and Many Uninhabited Parts.* Richmond: John Dixon, 1792; rep., New York: Arno Press, 1971.
Pott, J. S. *A Plain Statement of Facts, in which Appears a Question of International Law of Great Importance to Colonial Proprietors, Arising out of the Claims of the Inhabitants of East and West Florida on the British Government, for Aggressions Committed by the British Forces during the War with the United States of America in 1814; Shewing also their Subsequent Treatment under the Conventions with Spain of 1823 and 1828.* London: Cunningham and Salmon, 1838.
Pound, Merrit B. *Benjamin Hawkins—Indian Agent.* Athens: University of Georgia Press, 1951.
Pratt, Julius W. *A History of United States Foreign Policy.* Englewood Cliffs: Prentice-Hall, 1965.
Prucha, Francis Paul. *American Indian Policy in the Formative Years: The Indian Trade and Intercourse Acts, 1790–1834.* Cambridge: Harvard University Press, 1962; rep., Lincoln: University of Nebraska Press, 1970.
———. *The Sword of the Republic: The United States Army on the Frontier, 1783–1846.* London: Collier-Macmillan, 1969.

Reilly, Robin. *The British at the Gates: The New Orleans Campaign in the War of 1812.* London: Cassell & Co., 1974.
Remini, Robert V. *Andrew Jackson and the Course of American Empire, 1767–1821.* New York: Harper & Row, 1977.
Roberts, William I. III. "The Losses of a Loyalist Merchant in Georgia during the Revolution." *Georgia Historical Quarterly* 52 (June 1968): 270–76.
Robinson, W. Stitt, Jr., ed. *Richard Oswald's Memorandum on the Folly of Invading Virginia, The strategic Importance of Portsmouth, and The Need for Civilian Control of the Military.* Charlottesville: University of Virginia Press, 1953.
Rogers, George C., Jr. *A South Carolina Chronology, 1497–1970.* Columbia: University of South Carolina Press, 1973.
Romans, Bernard. *A Concise Natural History of East and West Florida.* New York: The Author, 1775; rep.; New Orleans: Pelican Publishing Co., 1961.
Ross, Daniel J. J., and Chappell, Bruce S. "Visit to the Indian Nations: The Diary of John Hambly." *Florida Historical Quarterly* 55 (July 1976): 60–73.
Ross, Edward Hunter, and Phelps, Dawson A., trans. and eds. "A Journey over the Natchez Trace in 1792: A Document from the Archives of Spain." *Journal of Mississippi History* 15 (1953): 252–73.
Royce, Charles C., comp. *Indian Land Cessions in the United States.* In *Eighteenth Annual Report of the Bureau of American Ethnology*, by J. W. Powell. Washington: U.S. Government Printing Office, 1899.
Schoolcraft, Henry. *Information Respecting the History, Condition and Prospect of the Indian Tribes of the United States, Collected and prepared under the direction of the Bureau of Indian Affairs, March 3, 1817.* 6 vols. Philadelphia: Lippincott, 1851–57.
Scott, Hew. *Fasti ecclesiae scoticanae; the Succession of Ministers in the Church of Scotland from the Reformation.* 8 vols. Edinburgh: Oliver and Boyd, 1915–50.
Scott, Michele. "International Intrigue on the Florida Frontier: The Panton, Leslie Company, 1783–1805." Master's thesis, University of South Florida, 1976.
Serrano y Sanz, Manuel, ed. *Documentos Históricos de la Florida y Luisiana.* Madrid: Librería General de Victoriano Suárez, 1913.
———. *España y los Indios Cherokis y Chactas.* Sevilla: Tip. de la "Guia Oficial," 1916.
Sherlock, John V. "Panton, Leslie and Company." Master's thesis, Florida State University, 1958.
Sherwood, Adiel. *A gazette of Georgia; containing a particular Description of the State: its resources, Towns, Villages, and whatever is usual in Statistical works.* Macon, Ga.: S. Boykin, 1860.
Siebert, Wilbur Henry. *Loyalists in East Florida, 1774–1785.* 2 vols. DeLand: Florida State Historical Society, 1929.
Silver, James W. *Edmund Pendleton Gaines: Frontier General.* Baton Rouge: Louisiana State University Press, 1949.
Sinclair, John. *The Statistical Account of Scotland, Drawn up from the Communications of the Ministers of the Different Parishes.* Edinburgh: William Creech, 1793.
Smalley, A. S., Jr., comp. *Marriage Notices in the South Carolina and American General Gazette.* Columbia: South Carolina Historical Society, 1914.
Smith, Daniel M. "James Seagrove and the Mission to Tuckaubatchee, 1793." *Georgia Historical Quarterly* 44 (March 1960): 41–55.
Smith, Josiah. "Josiah Smith's Diary, 1780–1781." *South Carolina Historical and Genealogical Magazine* 33 (April 1932): 76–116.
Sosin, Jack M. *The Revolutionary Frontier, 1763–1783.* New York: Holt, Rinehart and Winston, 1967.
Spalding Club. *List of Pollable Persons within the Shire of Aberdeen 1696.* 2 vols. Aberdeen: William Bennett, 1844.
Stacy, Pheriba Kay. "8Wa39, a Panton, Leslie and Company Trading Post Site: History, Ethnohistory, and Archaeology." Master's thesis, Florida State University, 1967.

Starr, J. Barton, *Tories, Dons, and Rebels: The American Revolution in British West Florida.* Gainesville: University Presses of Florida, 1976.
Stephen, Sir Leslie, and Lee, Sir Sidney, eds. *The Dictionary of National Biography.* 21 vols. Reprint edition. Oxford: Oxford University Press, 1964-65.
Storm, Colton, ed. "Up the Tennessee in 1790: The Report of Major John Doughty to the Secretary of War." *East Tennessee Historical Society Publications* 17 (1945): 119-32.
Sugden, John. "The Southern Indians in the War of 1812: The Closing Phase." *Florida Historical Quarterly* 60 (January 1982): 273-312.
Sutton, Leora M. *Blacks and Slavery in Pensacola, 1780-1880.* Pensacola: Privately printed, 1977.
―――. *Women in Pensacola, 1765-1965.* Pensacola: Privately printed, 1977.
Swan, Caleb. "Position and State of Manners and Arts in the Creek, or Muscogee Nation in 1791." In *Information Respecting the History, Condition and Prospects of the Indian Tribes of the United States. . . .* compiled by Henry Schoolcraft. 6 vols. Philadelphia: Lippincott, 1851-57.
Swanton, John Reed. *Early History of the Creek Indians and Their Neighbors.* Washington: U.S. Government Printing Office, 1922.
Tanner, Helen Hornbeck. *Zéspedes in East Florida, 1784-1790.* Coral Gables, Fla.: University of Miami Press, 1963.
TePaske, John J. *The Governorship of Spanish Florida, 1700-1763.* Durham, N.C.: Duke University Press, 1964.
Thomas, Alfred B. *Governor José Callava and General Andrew Jackson: The Callava Papers on the Delivery of West Florida, July 17, 1821.* Pensacola: Historic Pensacola Preservation Board, 1971.
Thomas, David Yancy. *A History of Military Government in Newly Acquired Territory of the United States.* Reprint edition. New York: AMS Press, 1967.
The Trials of Arbuthnot and R. C. Ambrister, charged with Exciting the Seminole Indians to War against the United States of America, from the Official Documents which were laid by the President Before Congress. London: James Ridgway, 1819.
Turner, Frederick Jackson. "The Mangourit Correspondence in Respect to Genêt's Projected Attack upon the Floridas, 1793-94." *Annual Report of the American Historical Association, for the Year 1897,* 569-679. Washington, D.C.: U.S. Government Printing Office, 1898.
―――. "The Origin of Genêt's Projected Attack on Louisiana and the Floridas." *American Historical Review* 3 (July 1898): 650-71.
―――. *The Significance of Sections in American History.* New York: Henry Holt & Co., 1932; rep., Gloucester, Mass.: Peter Smith, 1959.
Upchurch, John C. "Aspects of the Development and Exploration of the Forbes Purchase." *Florida Historical Quarterly* 48 (October 1968): 117-39.
U.S. Congress. *American State Papers, Documents, Legislative and Executive of the Congress of the United States.* 38 vols. Washington, D.C.: Gales & Seaton, 1832-61.
―――. *Biographical Directory of the American Congress, 1774-1971.* Washington, D.C.: U.S. Government Printing Office, 1971.
―――. House Committee on Private Land Claims. *Report on John Forbes and Company to Accompany Bill H.R. No. 747.* 24th Cong. 1st sess., 1836.
―――. Senate. *Report of the Secretary of the Treasury and the Attorney General.* S. Exec. Doc. 82. 33d Cong. 1st sess., 1854.
U.S. National Archives and Records Service, *Guide to the National Archives of the United States.* Washington, D.C.: U.S. National Archives and Records Service, 1974.
U.S. Works Progress Administration. "Archives of the Spanish Government of West Florida." Translations and transcriptions. 18 vols. Microfilm copy (no. 285), UWF Library.
―――. "Creek Indian Letters, Talks and Treaties, 1705-1839." 4 vols. Manuscript, Department of Archives and History, Atlanta, 1939.
―――. "Despatches of the Spanish Governors of Louisiana, 1766-1798." 1766-1791, 5 books (25 vols.); 1792-1798, 11 books. Manuscript, Baton Rouge, 1937-41.

———. *South Carolina: A Guide to the Palmetto State.* New York: Oxford University Press, 1941.
———. "Spanish Land Grants in Florida." 5 vols. Tallahassee: State Library Board, 1940.
Wagstaff, Henry McGilbert, ed. *The John Steele Papers.* 2 vols. Raleigh: Edwards and Broughton Printing Co., 1924.
"The War of 1812 . . . Some Florida Episodes," *Louisiana Historical Quarterly* 1 (April 1918): 330-32.
Washington, Henry A., ed. *The Writings of Thomas Jefferson.* 4 vols. New York: John C. Riker, 1854.
Watson, Thomas D. "Continuity in Commerce: Development of the Panton, Leslie and Company Trade Monopoly in West Florida." *Florida Historical Quarterly* 54 (April 1976): 548-64.
———. "Merchant Adventurer in the Old Southwest: William Panton, the Spanish Years, 1783-1801." Ph.D. diss., Texas Tech University, 1972.
———. "A Scheme Gone Awry: Bernardo de Gálvez, Gilberto Antonio de Maxent and the Southern Indian Trade." *Louisiana History* 17 (Winter 1976): 5-17.
———. "Strivings for Sovereignty: Alexander McGillivray, Creek Warfare, and Diplomacy, 1783-1790." *Florida Historical Quarterly* 58 (April 1980): 400-414.
Watson, Thomas D., and Wilson, Samuel, Jr. "A Lost Landmark Revisited: The Panton House of Pensacola." *Florida Historical Quarterly* 60 (July 1981): 42-50.
Way, Royal B. "The United States Factory System for Trading with the Indians, 1796-1822. *Mississippi Valley Historical Review* 6 (1919-20): 220-35.
Webber, L. Marbel, ed. "Thomas Elfe Account Book." *South Carolina Historical and Genealogical Magazine* 35 (1934): 96-105, 153-65; 38 (1937): 131-36; 41 (1940): 147-56.
West, Elizabeth Howard. "A Prelude to the Creek War of 1813-1814." *Florida Historical Quarterly* 18 (April 1940): 248-60.
Wheeler, Roderick Paul (O.F.M.). "El Comercio Indio de Panton, Leslie & Co.: Su Influencia en la Historia de la Segunda Dominación Española de las Floridas. (1783-1819)." 2 vols. Ph.D. diss., University of Madrid, 1940.
Whitaker, Arthur Preston. "Alexander McGillivray, 1783-1789." *North Carolina Historical Review* 5 (1928): 181-203.
———. *The Mississippi Question, 1795-1803.* New York: American Historical Association, 1934.
———. "The Muscle Shoals Speculation, 1783-1789." *Mississippi Valley Historical Review* 13 (December 1926): 365-86.
———. "Spain and the Cherokee Indians, 1783-1798." *North Carolina Historical Review* 4 (July 1927): 252-69.
———. *The Spanish-American Frontier: 1783-1795. The Westward Movement and the Spanish Retreat in the Mississippi Valley.* Reprint edition. Lincoln: University of Nebraska Press, 1969.
———, trans. and ed. *Documents Relating to the Commercial Policy of Spain in the Floridas with Incidental Reference to Louisiana.* DeLand: Florida Historical Society, 1931.
White, David Hart. "The John Forbes Company: Heir to the Florida Indian Trade, 1801-1819." Ph.D. diss., University of Alabama, 1973.
———. *Vicente Folch, Governor in Spanish Florida—1787-1811.* Washington: University Press of America, 1981.
White, George. *Historical Collections of Georgia: Containing most interesting Facts, Traditions, Biographical Sketches, Anecdotes, etc.* New York: Pudney & Russell Publishers, 1855; rep., Baltimore: Genealogical Publishing Company, 1969.
White, Joseph M. *A New Collection of Laws, Charters and Local Ordinances of the Governments of Great Britain, France and Spain Relating to the Concessions of Land in Their Respective Colonies: Together with the Laws of Mexico and Texas on the Same Subject.* 2 vols. Philadelphia: T. & J. W. Johnson, 1839.
Willett, William. *A Narrative of the Military Actions of Colonel Marinus Willett, Taken chiefly from his own Manuscript.* New York: G. & C. & H. Carvill, 1831.

Williams, Samuel Cole. *Beginnings of West Tennessee in the Land of the Chickasaws, 1541–1841.* Johnson City, Tenn.: Watauga Press, 1930.
———. *Dawn of Tennessee Valley and Tennessee History.* Johnson City, Tenn.: Watauga Press, 1937.
———. *Early Travels in the Tennessee Country 1540–1800, with Introductions, Annotations and Index.* Johnson City, Tenn.: Watauga Press, 1928.
———. *History of the Lost State of Franklin.* Rev. ed. New York: Press of the Pioneeers, 1933; rep., Philadelphia: Porcupine Press, 1974.
Wilson, John B., and Hays, Louise Frederick. "Unpublished Letters of Timothy Barnard, 1784–1820." Manuscript, Department of Archives and History, Atlanta, 1939.
Wilson, Joseph T. *Emancipation: Its Course and Progress, from 1481 B.C. to A.D. 1875.* . . . Reprint edition. New York: Negro Universities Press, 1969.
Woodward, E. L. *The Age of Reform, 1815–1870.* Oxford: Clarendon Press, 1938.
Wright, Homer E. "Diplomacy of Trade on the Southern Frontier: A Case Study of the Influence of William Panton and John Forbes, 1784–1817." Ph.D. diss., University of Georgia, 1971.
Wright, J. Leitch, Jr. *Anglo-Spanish Rivalry in North America.* Athens: University of Georgia Press, 1971.
———. "British Designs on the Old Southwest: Foreign Intrigue on the Florida Frontier, 1783–1803." *Florida Historical Quarterly* 44 (April 1966): 265–84.
———. "Creek-American Treaty of 1790: Alexander McGillivray and the Diplomacy of the Old Southwest." *Georgia Historical Quarterly* 51 (December 1967): 379–400.
———. *Florida in the American Revolution.* Gainesville: University Presses of Florida, 1975.
———. "Lord Dunmore's Loyalist Asylum in the Floridas." *Florida Historical Quarterly* 49 (April 1971): 370–79.
———. "The Queen's Redoubt Explosion in the Lives of William A. Bowles, John Miller and William Panton." In *Anglo-Spanish Confrontation on the Gulf Coast during the American Revolution,* edited by William S. Coker and Robert R. Rea, 177–93. Pensacola: Gulf Coast History and Humanities Conference, 1982.
———. *William Augustus Bowles: Director General of the Creek Nation.* Athens: University of Georgia Press, 1967.

Index

Acre, Samuel: attorney for John Innerarity, 342; and Vidal case, 345–46
Adams, John Quincy (secretary of state): and Andrew Jackson, 341; and execution of Arbuthnot and Ambrister, 323; and treaty negotiations with Spain (1818), 327; and Vidal case, 347
Adams-Onís Treaty (1819), 334
A. Glennie, Son & Co., 21
Alabama, Indian raids on, 323
Alabama Indians, 4; raids on Tensaw-Tombigbee settlements (1788), 123; tariff agreement with Spain (1784), 59
Alabama River, 5, 256; and Indian cessions, 247; and proposed Choctaw cession to U.S., 248
Alachua, Bowles at, 119
Albion (ship), and escaped Forbes slaves, 295
Alexander I (czar of Russia), 298
Alexander, Georgiana Sally Leslie, 44
Alexander, Hunter Dick, 44
Alexander, Col. James, 113
Alexander, Louisa Janet, 44
Alexander, Mary, 44

Alexander, Mary (Cleland), 44
Alexander, Rachel Louisa, 44
Alexander, Theodore George, 44
Alexander, William, 15, 24, 31–32, 36, 40; and Alexander & Leslie Co., 39; in Bahamas, 43–44; in East Florida, 23; life of, 21, 41, 44–45; and Panton, Leslie, 44, 363
Alexander, William Keith, 44
Alexander & Leslie (company), 39–40, 42
Alicante, 189
Allwood, Phillip, 12
Almacén de Nuestra Señora de la Concepción. *See* Concepción
Almacén de San Fernando. *See* St. Johns River: Panton, Leslie store at
Altamaha River, Georgian claims to, 80, 111, 138–39, 140, 143
Álvarez, Juan Manuel (Spanish minister of war), and Panton, Leslie, 204
Ambrister, Robert Chrystie, 320; and attempted attack on Fort San Marcos (1818), 320; capture of, by Andrew Jackson, 320–21; court-martial of, 321; in East Florida, 320; execution of (1818), 323; fili-

395

Ambrister, Robert Chrystie (*continued*) bustering activities of, 367; and George Woodbine, 301; and John Forbes & Co., 367; at Suwannee, 321

Amelia Island, 292, 295, 300; John Forbes & Co. at, 273–74; pro-Spanish faction at, 275; U.S. occupation of (1812), 273

American Revolution: and loyalty of southeastern Indians to Great Britain, 26–27; and Panton, Leslie support of Great Britain, 363–67

Anderson, Robert, 259

Apalachee Bay, 88, 118, 149; Spain in, 107, 232, 237

Apalachee River, 244

Apalachicola Bay, U.S. Navy at (1818), 318

Apalachicola Land and Development Co., 361

Apalachicola Land Company, 355–56

Apalachicola River, 2, 149–50, 268, 308, 318, 320; area of (1816–18), map 322; British fort at, 297, 301; Edmund Doyle and his store at, 310, 314; Forbes store at, 254, 281, 302–4, 307, 370; George Woodbine at (1814), 301; Indian cession to John Forbes & Co. on (1804), 251, 254–55; John Forbes & Co. trade at, 309, 311, 313, 325; John Hambly at (1815), 299; land grant to John Forbes & Co. on, 326; Panton, Leslie store on, 50–51; Pintado at, 290; Red Sticks at, 282–83; Richard Spencer at, 290; slaves smuggled to, 326; Spanish fort at, 303–4; Spanish grants on, 354; U.S. navigation rights on, 306; U.S. settlers at, 303

Aranda, Conde de, and Barón de Carondelet, 166, 170

Arbuthnot, Alexander, 320; arrest of, 319; and captain general of Cuba, 314; court-martial of, 321; and destruction of Negro Fort, 316; and Edmund Doyle, 316, 317; and Edward Nicolls, 314; and establishment of store at Ochlockonee (1817), 314–15; execution of, 323; at Fort San Marcos, 319; and Indian trade competition with John Forbes & Co., 314, 316, 367; and John Hambly, 314–16, 317; and Peter Cook, 317; and Red Sticks, 315; and southeastern Indians, 314–16, 370; and Spanish Indian trade, 316; and store at Ochlockonee, 314–15; and stores at St. Marks and Suwannee, 316, 321

Arbuthnot, John, 319

Arbuthnot, Marriot, 37

Archibald, R. B. (judge), and suit against John Forbes's estate, 361

Armas, Cristobal de, and Vidal estate, 331–32

Aurora (schooner), capture of, 186

Bahamas, 214–15; "Conch" faction in, 115; and filibustering activities in East Florida, 320; Loyalist refuge, 114–15, 249, 364; and Panton, Leslie in, 217; and salt trade, 133–34; and southeastern Indian trade, 110, 116, 126, 132–34, 247; Spanish conquest of, 37; Thomas Forbes in, 45

Bailie, George, 28

Bank of Pensacola, 356

Barnard, Timothy, 189, 191

Barrancas, 287, 290

Bartram, William, 34

Bathurst, Lord (secretary of state for war and the colonies): and Count Fernán-Núñez, 298; and escaped Forbes slaves, 296; and John Forbes's demand for compensation, 298

Baton Rouge, 172, 174; British threat to, 283; Vidal lands at, 331–33

Battle of Burnt Corn Creek (1813), 279–80

Battle of Fallen Timbers (1794), 196

Battle of Horseshoe Bend (1814), 280

Battle of New Orleans (1814), 290–91, 340

Bay of Honduras, 207

Beauregard, Elias (Spanish commandant at Nogales), 167

Bellenger, George, 29

Bermuda, escaped slaves sent to (1815), 295–96

Berry Island, 235

Bertucat, Capt. Luis de, commandant at St. Marks fort, 102

Big Warrior (Upper Creek chief): and cessions to John Forbes & Co., 254, 270; and imprisonment of Bowles, 241

Bloody Fellow (Cherokee chief): and Indian congress at Nogales, 180; and John McDonald, 162–63; and proposed Spanish

fort at Muscle Shoals, 172; relations with U.S., 162; visit to Philadelphia (1791), 160
Blount, Thomas M., 356
Blount, William (governor of Georgia): and Ben James, 168; at Cayotee (1792), 162; and Cherokee, 74, 164; and Chickasaw, 176, 196; and Chickasaw Bluffs, 179; and Choctaw, 176; and conspiracy against Spanish territorial claims, 227; and Creek-Chickasaw hostilities, 179; and Indian conference at Nashville (1792), 169–71; and John McKee, 227; and Spanish Indian policy, 164; and Treaty of Holston (1791), 160; and William Panton, 164
Blue, Daniel, 268
Bon Esperance (plantation), 44
Bonnamy, Broomfield: attack on Panton, Leslie stores by, 118; in Bahamas, 115; and Lord Dunmore, 115; and McGillivray, 117; and southeastern Indian trade, 119
Bon Secour River, Forbes's store at: British plundering of (1814), 285–86, 288; and Forbes's Indian trade, 279, 285; losses at, 297
Bourbon County, Georgia: affair at (1785), 77–78, 83, 141; creation of, 77
Bouteille, Jean (French privateer), 185–86
Bowie, George (mayor of Pensacola), and Andrew Jackson, 342
Bowlegs (Seminole chief): and escaped slaves, 301n; at Suwannee (1818), 319
Bowles, William Augustus, 114–15, 242; and Alexander McGillivray, 112, 116–17, 120, 124, 148–150, 154; and Anglo-Spanish relations, 148; and Arturo O'Neill, 120; and Bahamas, 124, 149–51, 154; in Barbados, 231; and Barón de Carondelet, 151, 154, 156, 158–59, 164; and Benjamin Hawkins, 239; and Bernardo del Campo, 148; and Chickamauga, 148, 150, 154; and Chief Perryman, 149; at Coweta, 150; and Creek, 112, 115, 116, 117, 118–19, 120, 150–51, 153, 154, 156, 231, 240, 241 (*see also* Lower Creek; Upper Creek); and declaration of war on Spain by, 233, 239, 241; escape from Spanish custody, 231; and Esteban Rodriguez Miró, 120; and Estevan Folch y Juan, 241; and execution of associates for piracy (1802), 238; exile to Philippines, 156; and George Wellbank, 151, 153; in Havana, 156, 242; and Hickory Ground conference (1803), 240–41, 244; hope for Spanish alliance, 153–54; and Hopoie Mico, 241; imprisoned in Spain, 156; and Indian cessions to U.S., 240, 244; and John DeLacy, 235–37; and John Forbes, 241; and John Galphin, 119; and John Halkett, 238–39; and John Leslie, 231; and John Miller, 118, 149, 231–32, 235; and José de Hevia, 153; and Joseph Hunter, 235; and Little Prince, 239; in London, 125, 148; and Lord Dunmore, 115–16, 118, 120; and Lower Creek, 148, 150, 189, 232, 239; at Ochlockonee River, 232; and Oconee cession, 160; and Panton, Leslie, 116–17, 118–20, 124, 149–51, 177, 226, 232, 235, 366, 369; and Panton, Leslie store at St. Marks, 151–53, 233, 235, 238, 261, 369; and Panton, Leslie store at St. Marys, 32; and Peace of Amiens (1802), 238; and proposed alliance with U.S., 239; and proposed British capture of the Floridas, 231; and proposed grand Indian alliance, 149–50, 239; in Quebec, 125; raids by, 237; and Seminole, 150–51, 232, 239, 241, 247; slave-stealing by, 233, 237; and southeastern Indians, 237; and Spanish government of Florida, 150–51, 153, 232; and "state" of Muskogee, 148–49, 154, 225; and Thomas Forbes, 149, 232; and Treaty of New York (1790), 148–49; and Upper Creek, 150; and William Cunningham, 151; and William Grenville, 148; and William Panton, 112, 121, 151–52, 154, 161, 232
Brackenridge, Henry M. (alcalde of Pensacola): and Andrew Jackson, 330, 337–38, 342; and José Callava, 335; and Vidal estate, 333–36
Brailsford, Samuel, 25
Brashears, Turner: and Choctaw trade, 167; at Chickasaw Bluffs, 199
Bridgetown, 231
British army: in Georgia (1815), 291; and plundering of Forbes store at Bon Secour (1814), 285–86; recruitment of slaves by, 289–91, map 294, 301

British-Creek Treaty (1773), 80
British Emancipation Act (1833), 351
British Indian trade, 7–8
British loyalists, 249
British navy: at Fort Bowyer (1814), 285; at New Orleans, 284; at Pensacola (1813), 287; sanctuary for escaped slaves, 293; and theft of Forbes slaves, 287; use of escaped slaves, 296
Bronaugh, Dr., and Vidal estate, 336, 338
Brooke, Col. George M., and Vidal estate, 335–36
Brosnaham, Dr. John, and Callava, 340
Brown, Col. Thomas, 55, 112, 119; and Indian congress at St. Augustine (1783), 49–50; and McGillivray, 53–54; and Spanish Indian trade, 63
Bruin, Col. Peter Bryan, and S. C. Yazoo Co., 142
Burges, James, and Seagrove's store, 189
Butler, Col. Robert, and Vidal estate, 335–36, 338
Butler, Samuel (sutler at Camp Crawford), and Doyle, 310

Cagigal, Juan Manuel de, 12
Cain, John, 47
Call, Richard Keith, 327, 334, 352, 354
Callava, José (governor of West Florida): arrest of, by Andrew Jackson, 337–38; and Brackenridge, 335; and demand for trial by tribunal de residencia, 337; and Domingo Sausa, 335; and Eligius Fromentin, 339; and George M. Brooke, 335; and John Innerarity, 333; and Marcos de Villiers, 346; as Spanish commissioner at Pensacola (1821), 335–38; and Spanish regarrisoning of Fort San Marcos de Apalache (1819), 325; and Vidal estate records, 333, 336–43; writ of habeas corpus for, 339–40
Campbell, John, 37
Campbell (brig), captured, 215
Camp Crawford, 306
Campeche: and dyewood trade, 207–8, 221; and logwood trade, 134; Panton, Leslie trade with, 224; and Spanish Indian trade, 207–8
Campo, Bernardo del (marqués; Spanish ambassador to Great Britain), 51–52; and convoy shipping system, 189; and Esteban Rodriguez Miró, 132; and memorial to Spanish court (1788), 109; and Panton, Leslie, 104; and royal order (1789), 129–30; and southeastern Indian trade, 89–92, 106, 110, 127, 134; and Spanish commercial rivalry with Great Britain, 87–88; and Strachan & MacKenzie, 130–32; and William Augustus Bowles, 148; and William Panton, 130
Canada: and slaves recruited into British army, 291; U.S. operations in (1814), 283
Candler, William, 25
Carnochan & Mitchel, and Forbes Grant I, 326, 353–55
Carondelet, Barón de (Francis Luis Hector) (governor of Louisiana): as administrator, 157; and Alexander McGillivray, 151, 156, 161, 163, 170, 173, 176, 177; and Arthur St. Clair, 158; and Cherokee, 158, 166; and Chickasaw, 166, 170; and Choctaw, 166, 170; and Conde de Aranda, 166, 170; and Creek, 158–59, 163; and Creek-Chickasaw hostilities, 179; and French privateers in Gulf of Mexico (1796), 203; and Indian conference at Nashville (1792), 171; and Indian trade concession at Chickasaw Bluffs, 198; and James Wilkinson, 196–97; and John Forbes, 173, 226; and John McKee, 227; and John Turnbull, 174, 175, 176, 198; and Juan de la Villebeuvre, 171; and Juan Ventura Morales, 205–6; and Manuel Gayoso de Lemos, 168–69, 175, 198; and Oconee cession, 159, 164; and Panton, Leslie, 153, 158, 198, 205–6, 209, 220; and Pedro Olivier, 159; and proposed grand Indian alliance, 163, 166, 180; and southeastern Indians, 158–59, 161, 163, 166–67, 170; and Spanish-Creek relations, 156, 163; and Spanish Indian policy, 161, 164; and Spanish Indian trade, 163, 192, 194; and Spanish occupation of Chickasaw Bluffs, 198; and Thomas Portell, 171; and threat of invasion of Louisiana, 196; and U.S. expansionist policy, 158, 162, 171–73, 199; and U.S. Indian trade, 170, 194; and U.S. presence at Fort Massac, 197; and U.S.

relations with southeastern Indians, 181; and U.S.–Spanish relations, 161, 166–67, 181; and U.S. threat to Spanish territory, 171–73; and wartime trade regulations, 208; and William Augustus Bowles, 151, 154, 156, 158–59, 164; and William Panton, 151, 154, 156, 159, 161, 164, 169, 171–74, 176, 177, 185, 188, 192–94, 201, 205, 211, 218, 220
Carvin, Jean-Baptiste (French privateer), 185–86
Casa Calvo, Marqués de (governor of Louisiana): and Panton, Leslie, 221, 224; and Spanish Indian trade, 221; and U.S. factory system in southeastern Indian trade, 245; and William Panton, 234
Casa Irujo, Marqués de (Carlos Martínez de Irujo), 249–50
Casa y Luengo, Francisco (commandant of Fort San Marcos de Apalache), 303–4, 305, 318
Castillo de San Marcos, John Forbes at (1814), 282
Castle, Lt., and Forbes slaves, 286
Castlereagh, Lord (British foreign secretary), and Arbuthnot and Ambrister, 323
Cato (ship), captured, 215
Cayotee, Cherokee conference at, 162
Chance (ship), and Arbuthnot, 323
Charles III (king of Spain), 8, 10, 11–12
Charles IV (king of Spain), 200
Charleston, 23, 357–58; British capture of (1780), 39; and British Indian trade, 7; British withdrawal from (1782), 49; and French privateers, 183, 185–86; Panton, Leslie trade with, 221; and southeastern Indian trade, 204
Charlotte Harbor (East Florida), escaped Forbes slaves at (1821), 309
Chattahoochee River, 5, 114, 306; and Indian cessions, 246; proposed DeLacy trading post at, 235; U.S. fort at, 305, 310; U.S. settlers at, 305
Chenubby (chief of Fowl Town), capture of Doyle and Hambly by, 316
Cherokee: attack on Doughty expedition (1790), 178; and Barón de Carondelet, 158, 166; as British auxiliaries, 49; cessions to U.S. (1805), 258–59; debts to

John Forbes & Co., 272; debts to Panton, Leslie, 227, 230, 243, 259; and Georgian expansionist policy, 79; and Hopewell treaties (1785), 84; and Indian congress at Nogales (1793), 180; and Panton, Leslie, 175, 201; and proposed grand Indian alliance, 258; and proposed U.S. trading post at Chickasaw Bluffs, 178; raids against Cumberland settlements, 162; raids on Kentucky and Tennessee by, 196; relations with Chickasaw, 173–74; relations with Creek, 159; relations with Spain, 68, 79, 162; relations with U.S., 75, 79, 141, 160, 164, 192, 195, 196, 251; resistance to land cessions among, 244; and "state" of Muskogee, 148; territory of, 5, 258; visit to New Orleans by (1792), 166; and William Augustus Bowles, 241; and William Blount, 164
Chickamauga, 178; and French Indian trade, 95; and proposed grand Indian alliance, 150; relations with U.S., 99, 160; territory of, 5; and U.S. expansionist policy, 75; war with Georgia, 122; and William Augustus Bowles, 148, 150, 154; and William Panton, 161–62, 169
Chickasaw: and Barón de Carondelet, 166, 170; and Benjamin Fooy, 197; as British auxiliaries, 49; cessions to U.S., 85, 258; and conference at Yazoo River (1786), 100; and Coushatta, 101; and Creek, 73, 83, 85; debts to John Forbes & Co., 258, 272; debts to Panton, Leslie, 227, 230; and Fort Massac, 197; and Georgian expansionist policy, 78–79; and Hopewell treaties (1786), 85; and Indian conference at Nashville (1792), 170; and Indian congress at Nogales (1793), 180; influence of John Gordon on, 257; and James Robertson, 176, 196, 256–57; and John Forbes & Co., 262; and John Turnbull, 197; and lands on Mississippi River, 257–58; and Manuel Gayoso de Lemos, 197–98; and Panton, Leslie, 90, 105, 146, 175, 245; and proposed cession to U.S. (1805), 257–58; relations with Cherokee, 173–74; relations with Choctaw, 173; relations with Creek, 159, 174, 177–79, 196; relations with Spain, 59, 68, 78, 79, 85–86,

Chickasaw (*continued*)
101, 102; relations with U.S., 75, 101, 141, 160, 169, 171, 173, 177, 178, 179, 251; and Silas Dinsmoor, 256–57; and Spanish occupation of Chickasaw Bluffs, 197; territory of, 4; and U.S. Indian trade, 99; and U.S. land policies, 75, 79, 101, 142; and Virginia, 78; visit to New Orleans (1792), 166; and William Augustus Bowles, 124, 241; and William Blount, 176, 196; and William Panton, 142–43, 179

Chickasaw Bluffs, 75, 198; Panton, Leslie at, 199, 201, 207, 227, 230; proposed U.S. trading post at, 178; Spanish fort at, 172, 175, 181; Spanish occupation of, 197; Turnbull trading post at, 175; U.S. settlement at, 171, 197; U.S. trading post at, 101

Chickasawhay River, 4

Chiskatalofa, Indian conferences at: 247, 251 (1804); 268 (1811); 305–6 (1816)

Choctaw: and Barón de Carondelet, 166, 170; as British auxiliaries, 49; and British fur trade, 50; and Chickasaw, 173; and conference at Yazoo River (1786), 100; and Creek, 73, 83, 159, 180; and Georgian expansionist policy, 78; and Hopewell treaties (1786), 85; and Indian conference at Nashville (1792), 170; and Indian congress at Nogales (1793), 180; and James Robertson, 176, 256–57; and John Forbes, 246; and John Forbes & Co., 255, 262, 263, 266–68, 330; land cessions to British (1765), 77; land cessions to U.S., (1786) 85, (1805) 263, 266; and Manuel Gayoso de Lemos, 168; as a nation, 247; at Negro Fort, 308, 317; and Panton, Leslie, 90, 105, 146, 175, 227, 230, 245–46, 256–57, 262; and proposed cession to U.S. (1804), 248, 256; raids on settlements (1788), 123; and relations with Spanish, 59, 68, 78, 86; and relations with U.S., 141, 160, 169–70, 171, 179, 246–47, 251, 255; and Silas Dinsmoor, 256–57; Spanish trade with, 85–86, 101; territory of, 4, 77; and Upper Choctaw, 246; and U.S.–Indian trade, 99; and U.S. land speculation, 142; and U.S. settlement at Nogales, 167–68; visit to New Orleans (1792), 166; and William Augustus Bowles, 241; and William Blount, 176; and William Panton, 142, 179; and William Simpson, 230, 248, 255–56

Choctawhatchee: land grant to John Forbes & Co. at, 326; Red Sticks at (1818), 324

Christie, William, and Carnochan & Mitchel, 355

Christmas, Nathaniel, and Bourbon County, 77

Clark, George Rogers, 77; and Edmond Genêt, 183

Clarke, Elijah (general): and Creek Indian trade, 56; and filibustering in East Florida, 184–85; and George Mathews, 184–85; and Georgia-Creek relations, 82, 113; and Louisiana, 196; on Ogeechee River, 76; opposition to Treaty of New York (1790), 184; and proposed French invasion of East Florida, 184; and "state" of Franklin, 75; and "Trans-Oconee Republic," 184; and William Panton, 184

Clarke, George J. F. (surveyor-general for East Florida), and Panton, Leslie, 275

Clinch, Lt. Col. Duncan L., and Negro Fort, 307–8

Cochrane, Vice Admiral Sir Alexander, 291; and black Spanish troops, 290; and British military recruitment of slaves, 292–93; and Forbes slaves, 289, 350–51; and John Forbes, 350–51; and John Innerarity, 289; proclamation by (1814), 292

Cockburn, Admiral Sir George: and British military recruitment of slaves, 292–93; and Cochrane's proclamation, 298; and Cumberland Island, 292, 301; and escaped Forbes slaves, 300, 350–51; and George Woodbine, 289; and John Forbes, 293, 300, 350–51; and sanctuary for escaped slaves, 293, 295, 298; and Sebastián Kindelán y Oregón, 293, 295

Colbert, Maj. George, 257–58

Coldwater Creek, French trading post on, 95

Coleman, Father James: and arrest of José Callava, 338–39; and John Innerarity, 284–85

Colerain: Robert Seagrove's store at, 189; and U.S.–Indian trade, 195; U.S. trading post at, 201

Concepción: attack by Bowles on, 118–19; Panton, Leslie store at, 34
Continental Congress. See United States: Continental Congress
Conventions of 1823 and 1828, 351
Cook, Peter B.: and Doyle and Hambly, 317; and Andrew Jackson, 320–21
Coosa River, 5
Coppinger, José (governor of East Florida), and escaped slaves from East Florida, 296
Corcubión, 189
Cornell, Alexander, 176, 189, 192
Cornell, David, 191
Cornell, Joseph, and Panton, 191
Court of Appeals for the Territory of Florida, and Apalachicola Land Company case (1844), 355–56
Coushatta: and Chickasaw, 101; and Indian congress at Nogales (1793), 180; raid on U.S. trading post by (1786), 101
Coweta (Lower Creek town), 116
Cow Ford, 27, 33
Craig, J. C. (sheriff), 341
Credit, necessity of, in southeastern Indian trade, 254, 268
Creek: and Barón de Carondelet, 158–59, 163; and Benjamin Hawkins, 202, 229, 259; and British, 27, 49, 50; and Cherokee, 159; and Chickasaw, 85, 159, 174, 177–79, 196; and Choctaw, 73, 159, 180; Cumberland district, expedition against (1788), 97; and Doughty expedition, attack on (1790), 178; and Edward Nicolls, 298–99; and France, 95, 183, 184; and Hammond & Fowler, 184; and Hickory Ground conference (1803), 240–41; independent commercial port for, 117–18, 136, 138; independent state proposed for, 139–40; and Indian congress (Nogales, 1793), 180; and James Innerarity, 255; and James Seagrove, 176; and John Forbes, 240, 246; and John Forbes & Co., 254, 260–62, 280, 282, 298; and John Hambly, 315; and Lord Dunmore, 116, 118; and Mobile, attack on (1813), 279; Oconee River, attack on settlements by, 80; and Panton, Leslie, 35, 175, 227, 229–30, 240, 242, 243, 245–46, 255, 259–61, 369; Red Stick faction of, 279–81; resistance to land cessions, 244; and Shawnee, 159; in South Carolina, 53; and "state" of Muskogee, 148; territory of, 4, 55–56, 76–77, 79–80, 136, 138–39, 166; and Treaty of Colerain (1796), 201; and Treaty of Fort Jackson (1814), 305; and Treaty of New York (1790), 143; and William Augustus Bowles, 112, 115–16, 150, 154, 156, 231, 240, 241; and William Panton, 152, 161, 163, 165, 169, 179. See also Creek War; Lower Creek; Red Sticks; Upper Creek
—and Georgia, 53, 164; border warfare with, 176; and Georgia's expansionist policies, 74–76, 78–79, 113; cession of lands to Georgia by, 80 (1786), 143 (1790); Georgia treaty commission to (1786), 83; and peace negotiations with (1793), 191–92; relations with, 112, 126, 135–36; war against Georgia by (1786–87), 80–83, 96–98, 115, 117, 120, 122–23
—and Spain: memorial to (1785), 79; military support of, by Spain, 76, 80–82, 94, 96–98, 107, 111, 120–21, 123–24, 159, 163, 183; Pedro Olivier as Spanish agent to, 158–59, 163; relations with, 125, 143–44, 147; siege of Spanish fort at St. Marks by (1800), 233; and Spanish-Indian trade, 122; and tariffs, 58, 60, 68; and trade with, 56, 58, 107, 123; and treaties, 58, 67 (1784), 163 (1792)
—and U.S.: cessions to U.S. by, 240, 243, 255, 258–60, 262; delegation to Washington, 260; hostility to U.S., 99; proposed cessions to U.S. by, 243, 255, 258–60, 262; proposed U.S. trading post at Chickasaw Bluffs, 178; relations with, 135, 142–46, 178, 189, 192, 305; trade relations with, 195; and treaty, 261 (1805); U.S. attempt to convert to agriculture, 229; and U.S. expansionist policy, 53, 55–56, 73, 79, 115, 121, 164; and U.S.–Indian diplomacy, 56; and U.S.–Indian trade, 171, 201; and U.S. peace missions to, 79–80 (1785), 98–99 (1788); and U.S. subsidy to, 201; and U.S. trade commission to (1796), 201; and U.S. treaty commission to, 135–38; and war against U.S. by (1813–14), 279–81
Creek War (1813–14), 272, 279–80, 364

Cuba, 1, 215; captain general of, and Alexander Arbuthnot, 314; and duty-free status of Pensacola merchants, 312; John Forbes's retirement to, 329; and John Forbes & Co., 311, 326, 327; slave trade in, 326

Cumberland Conference (1792). *See* Nashville, Indian conference at

Cumberland district, 95, 112, 172; Cherokee raids against, 162; and Creek expedition against (1788), 97; and Creek war against Georgia, 83; French influence on, 196; North Carolina's claims to, 74; settlements in, 162

Cumberland Island, Georgia: British occupation of (1815), 292–93, 295; escaped Forbes slaves at, 297, 300

Cumberland River, 74

Cunningham, William, 151, 154

Cussitah, Fat King of. *See* Fat King of Cussitah

Dade, Capt. F. L., 335

Dalcourt, Francisco, 358–59

Daniels, Edward (seaman), at Negro Fort, 307

Dartmouth, Lord, 27

Davenport, William, 85, 101; and Ben James, 168; and creation of Bourbon County, Georgia (1785), 77; and Creek war against Georgia, 83; as Georgia's agent to Choctaw and Chickasaw, 78; and Indian conference at Yazoo River, 100; and U.S.–Indian trade diplomacy, 99–100

Davidson, William, and Vidal case, 343

Davis, Strachan & Co., and southeastern Indian trade, 35

Dearborn, Henry (secretary of war): and Benjamin Hawkins, 239; and Indian debts to John Forbes & Co., 263, 266; and Indian debts to Panton, Leslie, 256, 260; and John Forbes, 248–50, 261–63; and proposed Indian cessions to U.S. (1803), 245, 256, 260; and Silas Dinsmoor, 255–56, 266; and U.S. desire for Indian lands on the Mississippi River, 248; and William Augustus Bowles, 239; and William Simpson, 255

Deerskins, importance in southeastern Indian trade, 8, 35, 52, 58–60, 187, 219, 311

DeLacy, John, 235–37

Denny, Corp. James, and Red Sticks, 281

DePestre, Edmund, and John Forbes's estate in Cuba, 359

Dickie, Capt., 186

Dinsmoor, Silas (Choctaw agent): and Ben James's debt to John Forbes & Co., 267–68, 272; and Choctaw debt to John Forbes & Co., 263, 267; and Henry Dearborn, 255–56, 266; and James Robertson, 255–56; lawsuits against by John Forbes & Co. (1809), 267; and negotiations with Chickasaw (1805), 256–57; and negotiations with Choctaw (1805), 255–57; and William Eustis, 267; and William Simpson, 266, 267

Dominique Catherine, Marquis de (French ambassador to Spain), 204

Donelson, John, and Treaty of French Lick (1783), 78

Doughty, Maj. John, and U.S. expedition to Muscle Shoals (1790), 178

Dowdeswell, William (governor of the Bahamas), 232, 238

Downing, C., attorney for John Forbes's estate, 360

Downing, Rebecca, 47

Doyle, Edmund, 325; and Alexander Arbuthnot, 316, 317; and Andrew Jackson's capture of Pensacola (1818), 367; and British relations with southeastern Indians, 300; capture and imprisonment of, 316–18; at Chiskatalofa Indian conference (1811), 268; and fear of Indian attack, 304–6; and Francisco Caso y Luengo, 305, 318; and Indian conference (1815), 299; and Indian conference at St. Marks (1816), 305–6; and Indian debt negotiations, 251; and Indian debts to John Forbes & Co., 251; and James Innerarity, 313–14; and John Forbes, 282; and John Forbes & Co., 268, 281, 303, 305–6, 310, 314; and John Hambly, 304, 310, 313–16; and John Innerarity, 282–83, 315, 323; and Kinache, 305; and losses to Seminole, 325; at Negro Fort (1815), 303, 308, 367; and Peter B. Cook, 317; and Peter Mc-

Queen, 305; at Prospect Bluff (1814), 288, 313–14; and Red Sticks, 305; relations with U.S., 316; and Samuel Butler, 310; and store at Apalachicola (1816), 310, 314; and supplying of U.S. forts, 310; and "trial" of, 317; and U.S. settlers in West Florida, 315; and U.S.–Spanish relations, 321
Dragging Canoe (Cherokee chief), and U.S. expansionist policy, 162
Duck River, 257
Dunmore, Lord (former governor of Virginia), 231; and Broomfield Bonnamy, 115; and Creeks, 116, 118; and feud with Panton, Leslie, 48, 115, 120; as governor of Bahamas, 238; and John Miller, 119–20; and "state" of Muskogee, 149; and William Augustus Bowles, 115–16, 118, 120, 149; withdrawal to Bahamas (1787), 45
Dutch, as possible immigrants to West Florida, 249
Dyewood, 207, 221, 224

East Florida: and American Revolution, map 40; and blacks, legal rights in, 41; and British Loyalists, sanctuary for, 26, 31–32, 365–66; British possession of, 1, 7; cession of, to Spain (1783), 1, 43, 50–51, 61n, 139; Commons House of Assembly of, 41; escape of slaves from (1812–15), 296; filibustering expedition into (1794), 184; "French revolution" in (1783–95), 188; John Forbes & Co. in, 273, 297, 316; neutrality of, 292–93; Panton, Leslie trade concession in, 368; revision of commercial regulation in (1793), 187–88; Robert Chrystie Ambrister in (1818), 320; and smuggling to Georgia, 274; supply of Indian trade goods in, 9, 14, 35; U.S. invasion of (1812), 273–75, 301; William Augustus Bowles's raids in, 273
Edwards, George, and McGillivray estate, 357–59
Elbert, Samuel (governor of Georgia), 53; and Creek Indian trade, 56; and Georgian encroachment on Creek territory, 76; and U.S. congressional peace commission to Creek (1785), 79

Elfe, Thomas, 17
Ellicott, Andrew, and John McKee, 227
Elliott, Grey, and John Gordon, 16
Emistisiguo (Creek chief), 53
Eslava, Miguel, and Vidal estate, 343–44
Euchee Indians, 4
Eustis, William (secretary of war), 267
Evans, Commodore Andrew, and escaped Forbes slaves, 296
Ezpeleta, José de (captain general of Cuba), 121

Fair Play (schooner), 186
Farley, Samuel, 25
Fatio, Francisco, 237
Fat King of Cussitah, 75, 80, 83, 84
Fauchet, Jean Antoine Joseph, 184
Favre, Simon (Spanish Indian agent), and Indian conference at Yazoo River (1787), 100
Federalist Party, and Mississippi question, 196
Ferdinand VII (king of Spain), and cession of the Floridas to U.S. (1821), 327
Fernandina (Amelia Island, Georgia), 295; as port for John Forbes & Co., 273–74; and recruitment of slaves by U.S., map 294
Fernán-Núñez, Count (Spanish ambassador to Great Britain), and John Forbes, 297–98
Firearms, in southeastern Indian trade, 188
First Seminole War (1816–18), and John Forbes & Co., 309, 367
Fish, Jesse, 16
Flint River, 2, 5; and U.S. expansionist policy, 251, 259; U.S. fort at, 305, 310; U.S. settlers at, 303, 305
Florida: British operations in (1814), 283; Creek War in, 272; decline of Indian trade in, 365; fraudulent land claims in, 352; French activities in (1790s), 366; French threat to (1793), 189; Great Britain in, during American Revolution, 363; judicial authority of governor of, 344; jurisdiction of county courts of, 344; ownership of submerged lands in (1923), 361–62; possible French acquisition of, 212; possible U.S. acquisition of, 246; rumored Spanish cession of, to U.S. (1811), 268; as sanctu-

Florida (continued)
    ary for escaped slaves, 295; slaveowners in, and Great Britain, 298; supply of Indian trade goods in, 70; U.S. annexation of (1821), 303, 326–27, 330, 333–34, 367; U.S.–Spanish negotiations over, 353; War of 1812 in, 272
Florida, East. See East Florida
Florida, West. See West Florida
Floridablanca, Conde de, 4, 8; and royal order (1789), 129; and southeastern Indian trade, 110–11, 127; and Spanish-Indian trade, 87, 91; and Spanish–U.S. relations, 122; territorial claims by, 2, 5
Florida Commissioner of Agriculture, suit against (1923), 361
Florida Superior Court, and Forbes Grant II (1828), 353
Florida Supreme Court, 356, 361
Folch y Juan, Estevan, 240; and Hickory Ground conference (1803), 240–41, 245; and proposed Seminole cession to Panton, Leslie (1803), 243; and William Augustus Bowles, 241
Folch y Juan, Vicente (commandant at Mobile and at Fort San Fernando; governor of West Florida): and Alexander McGillivray, 121; and Enrique White, 237; and Forbes Grant I, 354; and James Innerarity, 247; and John Forbes, 239, 250; and John Forbes & Co., cessions to, 251 (1804), 255 (1804), 270 (1811); and Juan Ventura Morales, 210–11; and Marín Pizarro, 211; and Panton, Leslie, 199, 204, 236, 247; and Spanish-Creek relations, 121, 123–24; and Spanish fort at St. Marks, 233; and West Florida, possible U.S. annexation of (1810); 277; and William Augustus Bowles, 239; and William Panton, 210, 233
Follarte, Antonio de, and Andrew Jackson, 335, 337–38
Fontaine, John M., and estate of John Forbes in Florida, 359–60
Fooy, Benjamin, 168, 197
Forbes, Anne, 21
Forbes, Elizabeth Ann (Yonge), 46
Forbes, James Grant, 41

Forbes, John, 21, 329, 358; and Alexander Gordon, 358; and Alexander McGillivray's heirs, 357–58, 361; and Andrew Jackson's invasion of West Florida (1818), 319; and Barón de Carondelet, 173, 226; and Ben James, lawsuit against (1804), 266; and Benjamin Hawkins, 240, 243; and British in East Florida in War of 1812, 366; British land grants to in East Florida, 35–36; at Castillo de San Marcos (1814), 282; and Chickasaw trade, 169; and Choctaw, 169, 246, 247; and claims against U.S. (1812), 359; and Creek, 240, 245–46, 249, 261, 282; and Creek debts to Panton, Leslie, 240, 259, 261; and Daniel W. Johnson and George Edwards, suits by (1810–18), 358; and deerskin trade, 213–14; and demand for British compensation for losses in War of 1812, 297; and Edmund Doyle, 282; and Edward Nicolls, 298, 301; and escaped Forbes slaves (1815), 293, 295–97, 309; estate of, settled (1887), 361; and Esteban Rodríguez Miró, 133; executor, estates of William Panton, John Leslie, and Thomas Forbes, 357; and Forbes Grant I, sale of (1817), 353; Forbes Island, cession to (1811), 268; and George Woodbine, 300–302; and heirs of William Panton, John Leslie, Thomas Forbes, and Alexander McGillivray, 350; and heirs of Panton, Leslie partners, 357; and Henry Dearborn, 248–50, 261–63; and Hickory Ground Indian conference, 240–41, 245, 251, 270; and Indian debt negotiations, 243–45; and Indian debts to Panton, Leslie, 245, 247–48; and James Innerarity, 276, 278; and James Wilkinson, 245–46, 278; John Forbes & Co., withdrawal from (1817), 327, 329; and John Hambly, 247, 282; and John Innerarity, 261, 286; and John Leslie's estate, 250, 270, 358; and John McKee, 226, 231, 299; and John Turnbull, 175, 199; in Knoxville (1796), 226; and land sales, 326; and Lord Chancellor of Great Britain, 357; Lower Creek and Seminole cessions to (1811), 268; and Manuel Gayoso de Lemos, 230; and Marqués de Casa Irujo, 294–50; and Octavius Mitchel, 355; and Panton, Leslie, leader

of, 235; and Panton, Leslie, partner in, 364; and Red Sticks, 282; and Return J. Meigs, 244; and salt trade, 133; and Seminole, 244, 247, 262; and Silas Dinsmoor, suit against (1809), 267; and Sir Alexander Cochrane, suit against (1822), 350–51; and Sir George Cockburn, suit against (1822), 350–51; as slaveholder, 293; and slavery in Florida, 249; and slaves lost to British Navy, 350; and Spanish control of navigation on the Mobile River, 262; and Spanish government, relations with, 235; and Spanish Indian trade, 111, 275–76; as Spanish subject, 275–76, 293; and Thomas Forbes's heirs, 359; and U.S. assistance in collecting Indian debts, 226; and U.S. Indian trade, 246; and Vicente Folch y Juan, 239, 250; in Washington (1804), 246–50; and West Florida, U.S. settlers in, 315; and William Augustus Bowles, 239, 241–42; and William Panton, 21, 229–30, 234, 370; and William Simpson, 248; and Yahulla Emathly, 247
Forbes, John (governor of the Bahamas), 45, 238
Forbes, Rev. John, 41
Forbes, John Gordon, 46, 359
Forbes, Mary Sophia, 46, 359
Forbes, Munro & Co., 46
Forbes, Sophia, 21, 358
Forbes, Thomas, 15, 21, 24, 27, 34, 59; in Bahamas, 43–45, 115, 238; in Charleston (1783), 23; death of (1808), 46, 357, 364; in East Florida Commons, 41; will and estate of, 357, 359–61; heirs of, and estate of John Forbes in Cuba, 350, 359; and James Innerarity, 260; and John Gordon's estate, 23; and John Kelsall, 238; law practice of, 41; as Loyalist refugee, 32; in Nassau (1783), 45, 72; at New Providence Island (1787), 91; and Panton, Leslie, 216, 363–64; and prisoner exchanges, 36–38; and proposed Indian cessions to U.S., 248, 260; and southeastern Indian trade, 236; and Spanish government, 51–54, 236; Spanish war preparations, report on (1781), 37; and William Augustus Bowles, 149, 232; and William Dowdeswell, 232; and William Panton, 25; and William Simpson, 260

Forbes, Thomas Irving, 46
Forbes, William Henry, 46, 355, 359
Forbes & Munro, 216
Forbes family in Scotland, 21
Forbes Grant I, 366; James Innerarity's interest in, 353; legitimacy of, 354–55; litigation over, 354, 361; sale of (1817), 326, 353, 355, 358
Forbes Grant II: and John Forbes & Co. losses in War of 1812, 350–53; litigation over, 352–53; sales of, 327, 353
Forbes Island, 326, 354; and attack on Negro Fort (1816), 307; cession of, to John Forbes (1811), 268; survey of, 268, map 269
Forbes Purchase. See Forbes Grant I
Forrest, Capt. Matthew, 90, 109–10, 130
Forrester, Edward, 151–52, 165
Forrester, John: and Juan Nepomuceno de Quesada, 190; Panton, Leslie partner, 364; and Panton, Leslie store at St. Marys, 32, 153, 190; at St. Johns River, 32; and southeastern Indians, 237; and Spanish-Seminole treaty (1802), 239; and treaty conference at St. Marks (1802), 238; at St. Johns River, 32; and William Augustus Bowles's raids at St. Johns River, 237
Fort Bowyer, 278, 283–85, 366
Fort Charlotte, 278, 284
Fort Crawford, 324
Fort Gadsden, on site of Negro Fort (1818), 323
Fort Gaines, 305
Fortier, Miguel, 11
Fort Massac, 197
Fort Mitchell, Alabama (1826), 325
Fort San Carlos de Barrancas, 324
Fort San Esteban de Tombecbé, 124. See also Tombigbee River
Fort San Fernando de Pupo, 32
Fort San Francisco de Pupo, 32
Fort San Marcos de Apalache, 303, 318–20, 325
Fort San Miguel, Forbes slaves at, 286
Fort Scott. See Camp Crawford
Fort Stoddart, 260, 262
Fort Toulouse, 241
Fort Wilkinson, 201
Fowler, Reeves, 234–35
Fowl Town (Indian settlement), 316

Fox (sloop), 231
France: Anglo-Spanish alliance against (1793), 188; Creek, proposed treaty with (1793), 184; Directory, 200; the Floridas, possible acquisition by, 212; in the Floridas (1790s), 366; Great Britain, war with, 238, 369; Louisiana, acquisition by, 236; and Panton, Leslie, 204; and privateers, 182–83, 185–86, 203; Spain, alliance with (1797), 203–4; Spain, war with, 172, 176–77, 182–87, 200, 369; and Spanish Indian trade, 128; U.S., covert operations in, 182; U.S. frontier, influence on, 196
Franchimastabe (Choctaw chief), 100, 102, 168; and Creek war against Georgia (1787), 83; and Georgia, 78; and Indian congress at Nogales (1793), 180; and John Turnbull, 175; and U.S. Indian trade, 99; and U.S. settlement at Nogales, 167
Francis, Josiah, 280
Franklin, "state" of, 74–75, 78, 151, 160
Frederica (St. Simons Island, Georgia), 15, 33
Free Port Act (1787), 148
French Broad River, 160
French Revolution, 182
Fromentin, Eligius (U.S. federal judge), 339; and Andrew Jackson, 340–41; and John Innerarity, 339–40; and José Callava, 339, 340–41; judicial authority of, 340, 344–45; and Vidal estate, settlement of, 347
Fur trade: European decline in, 126–27; importance of, 8; Spanish inhibitions to, 10–11

Gaines, Gen. Edmund, and Negro Fort, 306
Galphin, John: and Panton, Leslie, 165; and William Augustus Bowles, 119
Galphinton, U.S. congressional peace commission at (1785), 79–80
Galveston, pirates operating from (1816), 333
Gálvez, Conde Bernardo de, 2, 8, 10, 13, 37, 65, 92; and Creek war against Georgia, 81; and Georgia's western territorial claims, 77; and the Hopewell treaties (1785), 85; and military support to Creek, 76–77; and southeastern Indian trade, 54; as viceroy of New Spain, 67
Gálvez, José de, 2, 8, 12, 91–92; and Panton, Leslie store at St. Marks, 86; and Spanish commercial rivalry with Great Britain, 87–88
García, Benito, and John Hambly, 323
García Calderón, Capt. Benigno, and Spanish expedition to the Apalachicola (1816), 307
Garçon (leader at Negro Fort), 308
Garçon, Juan (Creek interpreter), 96
Gardoqui, Diego de (Spanish chargé d'affaires), 107; and Indian memorial to Spanish crown (1785), 79; and James O'Fallon, 141; and John Jay, 122; mission of, to U.S., 77; and Spanish–U.S. relations, 122; and U.S. land speculation, 141
Gayoso de Lemos, Manuel (governor of Louisiana), 157, 211; and Benjamin Fooy, 197; and Barón de Carondelet, 168, 169, 175, 198; and Chickasaw, 167, 197–98; and Choctaw, 167–68; and Creek-Chickasaw hostilities, 179; as governor of Natchez district, 158; and Indian congress at Nogales (1793), 180; and John Forbes, 230; and John McKee, 227–28; and John Turnbull, 172, 197; and Nogales, 168; and Panton, Leslie, 199, 230; and Piomingo, 169; and proposed Spanish fort at Chickasaw Bluffs, 175; and Spanish Indian trade, 168, 215; and Spanish occupation of Chickasaw Bluffs, 198; and Taboca, 168–69; and Turner Brashears, 168; and Ugula Yacabe, 181; and U.S. settlement at Chickasaw Bluffs, 197; and William Panton, 168, 197, 215, 227–28, 230
Genêt, Edmond: dismissal of (1794), 184, 296; and French covert operations in U.S., 182; and George Rogers Clark, 183; and George Washington, 197; and Henry Knox, 197; and proposed French invasion of East Florida, 183; and U.S. government, 184; and William Moultrie, 183
George III (king of Great Britain), 148, 241
Georgia: and American Revolution, map 40; and Apalachicola Indian cession to John Forbes & Co. (1804), 254; British evacua-

tion of (1782), 49; British invasion of (1815), 291–92; and British Loyalists, 31; and Creek, 76–77, 93–95, 112, 126, 135–36, 164, 176, 190–92; Creek lands ceded to, 55, 75, 80; Creek war against (1787), 80–83, 97–98; and land speculation, 201; Loyalist Commons House of Assembly, 38, 39; and Michel Ange Bernarde Mangourit, 183; Oconee River lands ceded to (1790), 143, 154; and Panton, Leslie, 165, 364; pro-French sympathies in, 183; and proposed French invasion of East Florida, 183; Provincial Congress, 26; and smuggling from East Florida, 274; and southeastern Indian trade, 105, 109, 176; and Treaty of New York (1790), 147; and U.S. Congress, 79–80; and U.S. Indian trade, 106; western territorial claims of, 74–76, 94, 96, 113, 126, 137–38, 140–41, 147, 176; and William Panton, 27–28, 164

Georgia Assembly: and Creek territory, 76; and Creek war (1787), 82–83, 97; and land speculation, 141, 197; protest to Spanish government by (1786), 82; treaty commission to Creeks (1786), 83; and western territorial claims, 197

Georgia Council of Safety, and William Panton, 28, 30

Germain, Lord George, 28, 35, 37

Germans, possible immigrants to West Florida, 249

Glennie, Alexander, 21

Godoy, Manuel de (Duque de Alcudia), and U.S.–Spanish boundary dispute, 199–200

González Manrique, Mateo (governor of West Florida): and British attack on Fort Bowyer (1814), 284; and British military recruitment of slaves, 286; and Edward Nicolls, 286; and George Woodbine, 286, 301; and Red Sticks, 279–80; and restoration of stolen Forbes slaves, 289

Gordon, A. H., and George Woodbine, 302

Gordon, Alexander, and John Leslie estate, 358

Gordon, Commodore James, and British abandonment of Pensacola (1814), 287

Gordon, John, 15, 41; in Charleston, 23; Florida land claims by, 16; and George Colbert, 257–58; and Grey Elliott, 16; and Indian debts to John Forbes & Co., 251; influence among Chickasaw, 257; and John Stuart, 24; in slave trade, 16; and William Simpson, 257

Gordon & Netherclift (company), 16

Graham, John, and William Simpson, 263

Grand Pré, Carlos de (commandant at Natchez), 123

Grant, Henry, and William Panton, 209

Great Britain: and ban on export of weapons (1790), 132–33; and Baton Rouge (1814), threat to, 283; Board of Trade, 214, 217, 219; and colonial revenue bills (1775), 26; and Conventions of 1823 and 1828, 351; Court of Kings Bench, 350–51; and execution of Arbuthnot and Ambrister (1818), 323; the Floridas, operations in (1814), 283; Fort Bowyer, threat to and attack on (1814), 283–85; and France, war with, 238, 369; and John and James Innerarity, 362; and John Forbes & Co., 276, 300, 327, 351; John Forbes and the Lord Chancellor, 357; John Forbes's suit against Cochrane and Cockburn (1822), 350–51; and lawsuits for recovery of losses in War of 1812, 351; Louisiana, operations in (1814), 283, 284; military use of slaves by, 283; Mobile, threat to (1814), 283–84; and Navigation Acts, 87–88, 90; neutral shipping, use of, 218, 219; New Orleans, threat to (1814), 283–84; and Panton, Leslie, 218, 363–67; Parliament, 219; possible acquisition of the Floridas by, 236; privateers of, 214; Privy Council, 188, 218; and sea otter trade, 125; slavery laws of, 351; trade regulations in wartime, 214–15. *See also* British army; British navy

—and southeastern Indians: British military support of, 314; land settlements with, 229; loyalty to Britain in American Revolution, 26–27; proposed alliance with (1815), 299–300; relations with, 299–300, 311; restrictions on arms trade with, 219; support of British by, 299; and trade, 194

—and Spain: alliance with (1793), 188, 284, 369; commercial rivalry with, 1, 7, 9, 10, 13, 87–88, 110, 125, 132; importance of Spanish, in Indian trade, 52, 62, 367; relations with, 107, 122, 125, 144, 148; threat of war with (1790), 131–32; violations of Spanish neutrality by, 273; and wartime trade with Spanish colonies, 214, 219; war with, 203–6, 209, 238, 369
—and U.S.: British use of Creek allies against, 283; commercial rivalry with, 143, 145; relations with, 323; and U.S. Indian trade, competition with, 195; and U.S. slaveowners, 298; war with (1812–15), 273–91, 295
Green, Thomas, and creation of Bourbon County, Georgia, 77
Greensville, Georgia, burnt by Creek (1787), 97
Greenwood, William, 16, 23, 27
Greenwood (brig), captured (1800), 215
Grenada Packet (ship), captured (1794), 186
Grenville, William, 148
Griffin, Cyrus, U.S. treaty commissioner to Creek (1789), 135, 137, 139
Griffith, Rear Admiral Edward, and escaped slaves from East Florida, 296
Guadeloupe, 186
Guerra, Juan, captured by Indians (1817), 316
Gulf of Mexico, French privateers in (1796), 203
Gunpowder, in southeastern Indian trade, 35
Gutierrez de los Tios, Carlos José. *See* Fernán-Núñez, Count
Gwinnett, Button (president of Georgia), 29

Halifax, Nova Scotia, escaped slaves sent to (1815), 296
Halkett, John (governor of the Bahamas), 238–39
Hall, Dominick (judge), and Andrew Jackson, 340, 341
Hallowing King (Creek chief), 94, 189
Hambly, John: and Alexander Arbuthnot, 314–16, 317; and Andrew Jackson, 319, 324; at Apalachicola, 299, 325; and attack on Suwannee (1818), 320; and Benito García, 323; and British relations with southeastern Indians, 300; capture of (1817), 316–17, 318; and capture of Pensacola (1818), 367; at Concepción (1788), 119; and Creek, 315; and Creek-Seminole cession to John Forbes & Co. (1804), 251; and Duncan L. Clinch, 307; and Edmund Doyle, 304, 310, 313–16; and execution of Hillis Hadjo and Homathlemico (1818), 319; and Felipe Prieto, 303; at Fort Gaines (1816), 305; and Francisco Caso y Luengo, 318; at Indian conference (1815), 303–4; and Indian conferences at Chiskatalofa, 247, 251, 268, 305–6; in Indian territory (1830s?), 325; and John Forbes, 247, 282; and John Forbes & Co., 251, 281, 303–4, 311, 313–14; and John Innerarity, 283; and Juan de la Rua, 323; and Lower Creek, 305; and Negro Fort, 303–4, 308, 315–16, 367; and Panton, Leslie, proposed Indian cession to, 247; at Pensacola (1818), 324; and Peter B. Cook, 317; at Prospect Bluff (1814), 288, 313; relations with U.S., 316; and slave smuggling, 326; at Stokes Landing (1787), 34; as U.S. army interpreter (1826), 325; and U.S.–Spanish relations, 321; at Washington (1818), 324
Hambly, María, at Stokes Landing (1787), 34
Hamilton, Alexander, and James Wilkinson, 246
Hammond, Abner, 183
Hammond, Leroy, 183
Hammond, Samuel, 183
Hammond & Fowler (company), 183–84
Hancock, John, and George McIntosh, 29
Handley, George (governor of Georgia), and Creek war, 98
Havana, 37–38; George Woodbine at (1816), 302; imprisonment of Bowles at, 242; Panton, Leslie trade with, 224; and Spanish Indian trade, 124, 129, 133, 149, 207–8; and sugar trade, 221; and Vidal estate records, 333
Hawkins, Benjamin: and Apalachicola cession to John Forbes & Co. (1804), 254–55; and Creek, 202, 229, 259; and Creek debts to John Forbes & Co., 262; and David Meriwether, 259; and Edward

Nicolls, 299; and Henry Dearborn, 239; and Hopoie Mico, 241; and Indian debts to Panton, Leslie and Company, 230, 244; and John Forbes, 240, 243; and Negro Fort, 305; and proposed Creek cession to U.S. (1804), 259; and proposed U.S. alliance with Bowles, 239; and Upper Creek, 239; as U.S. agent to Creek, 202; and U.S. congressional peace commission to Creek (1785), 79; and U.S. trade commission to Creek (1796), 201; and William Augustus Bowles, 239; and William Panton, 202, 229–30; and William Simpson, 254

Haywood, John, 339
Hector, Francis Luis. See Carondelet, Barón de
Heirs of Vidal v. John Innerarity, 341–42
Henrique (ship), 303
Henry, Capt. Robert, 285–86, 289
Hermes (ship), 285
Hevia, Ensign José de, and Bowles, 153
Hickory Ground, Indian conference at (1803), map 22, 240–41, 243–45, 247, 251, 258–59, 270
Higginson, William, 16, 23, 27
High Head Jim (Red Stick leader), 279
Hillis Hadjo (Red Stick chief), 299, 319
Hinard, Euphrozine, and debts to N. Vidal, 331–32
Hitchiti (Indians), 4
Hiwassee River, 2
Holmes (Red Stick), 324
Holston River, 160
Homathlemico (Red Stick chief), 319
Hopewell treaties (1785–86), 84–85, 99–102, 141, 170, 178
Hopoie Mico (Creek chief), 241
Hopton, John, 25
Houston County, Georgia, 75, 141
Houstoun, John (governor of Georgia), and Creek, 76
Houstoun, Patrick, 28
Howard, Capt. Carlos, 119–20
Huguenots, 183
Hume, James, 36
Humphreys, David, U.S. treaty commissioner to Creek (1789), 135, 137–39
Hunter, Joseph, and Panton, 235–37

Indian River, 112, 118, 149–50
Indians, southeastern, map 6; and Alexander Arbuthnot, 316, 370; Anglo-Spanish war, effects on, 204; and attacks on U.S. settlers in West Florida, 315; and Barón de Carondelet, 158–59; conference of (1815), 299; congress at St. Augustine (1793), 49–50; debts to John Forbes & Co., 251, 263, 330, 364, 370; debts to Panton, Leslie, 213, 225–30, table 228, 240, 243–44, 247, 248, 249, 369; Edward Nicolls, meeting with (1815), 299; and firearms, shortage of, 237; and fur trade, 8, 13, 187; and George Woodbine, 318; and John Forbes & Co., 299, 302–3, 314, 315; and John Forrester, 237; land cessions, resistance to, 243–44; life-styles of, 5, 7; and Panton, Leslie, 204, 206, 245–46, 249, 366; and proposed grand Indian alliance, 158, 166; and raids against Alabama, 323; and restrictions on arms trade, 218; and slaves, 237–38, 297; trade, importance for political control of, 145; trade, type of merchandise, 34–35; and treaty conference at St. Marks (1802), 238; and Treaty of Fort Jackson, 314; and Treaty of Ghent (1815), 314; and William Augustus Bowles, 237
—and Great Britain: British military support of, 314; land settlements with British Indian Department, 229; loyalty to, 26–27, 204, 299; proposed alliance with (1815), 299–300; relations with, 299–300, 311, 362
—and Spain: hostility to Spanish settlements by, 206; raids against, in West Florida, 323; relations with, 249, 299, 304–5, 311, 362; and Spanish Indian trade diplomacy, 11–14, 180–81; Spanish intelligence-gathering among, 221; violations of Spanish neutrality by (1812), 273
—and U.S., 168–69; cessions to U.S., 240, map 263, table 265, 303; raids against, 323; relations with, 311, 314, 316, 362; and U.S. diplomacy during American Revolution, 26; U.S. enlistment of, against northern Indians, 160; and U.S. expansionist policies, 49, 51–53, 158, 240
Indian trade, decline of, in the Floridas, 365

Innerarity, James: and Apalachicola Land Company, 355; and cessions to John Forbes & Co., 251, 254; and Creek, 255; and Daniel W. Johnson and George Edwards, suit by (1823), 358; and economic depression in West Florida (1816), 312; and Edmund Doyle, 313–14; and Edward Nicolls, 288, 298; and Forbes Grant I, 353; and Forbes Grant II, 353, 355; and Forbes stores, 285, 302; and Indian conference at Chiskatalofa (1804), 247, 251; and John Forbes, 276, 278; and John Forbes & Co., 250, 251, 329, 364; and George Woodbine, suit against (1815), 301; and McGillivray heirs, 358; marriage, 329n; at Mobile, 276–78, 318; on Negro Fort, 302; and possible U.S. annexation of West Florida (1810), 277; and proposed Seminole cession to Panton, Leslie, 247; at Prospect Bluff (1804), 251; and Richard Keith Call, 352; and sale of Florida lands (1819), 327; and Seminole, 255; and Silas Dinsmoor, 267–68; in slave trade, 326; and southeastern Indian trade, 268; as Spanish subject, 276–77; and Thomas Forbes, 260; and U.S. customs regulations, 297; and U.S. settlers in West Florida, 303; and Vicente Folch y Juan, 247; and William Panton, 18–19

Innerarity, John, Jr., 18n, 288, 329; alderman of Pensacola (1821), 330; and Andrew Jackson, 324, 330, 337, 339, 341–42; and Apalachicola Land Company, 355; and British in West Florida in War of 1812, 366; and captain general of Cuba, 286; and capture of Edmund Doyle and John Hambly (1817), 318; and Creek attack on Mobile (1813), 279; and Daniel W. Johnson and George Edwards, suit by (1823), 358; and economic depression in West Florida (1816), 312; and Edmund Doyle, 282–83, 315, 323; and Edward Nicolls, 284, 286, 291, 298; and Eligius Fromentin, 339–40; and Father James Coleman, 284–85; and Forbes Grant II, 353; and Forbes slaves at Negro Fort, 306; and Forbes stores, 302, 307, 311; and Fort Bowyer, British attack on (1814), 284–85; and George M. Brooke, 335; and George Woodbine, 283, 301, 302; Great Britain, relations with, 362; and Indian debts to John Forbes & Co., 251, 270–71, 280; and John Forbes, 261, 286, 355; and John Forbes & Co., 270, 329, 364; and José Callava, 333, 338, 339–40; and José Masot, 313; and McGillivray heirs, 358; and Negro Fort, 306; and Pensacola, British at (1814), 284, 287, 290; and Pensacola, Jackson at, 287 (1814), 367 (1818); and Red Sticks, 279–80; and sale of Florida lands (1819), 327; and Sir Alexander Cochrane, 289; in slave trade, 325–26; Spain, relations with, 362; and Spanish bureaucracy of West Florida, 313; as Spanish subject, 276–77; and Thomas M. Blount, 356; and U.S., relations with, 362; and U.S.–Creek war, 281; and U.S. customs regulations, 297; and Vidal estate, 333, 336–37, 342, 343–47; and William Hambly, 283; and William Panton, 18, 19

Innerarity, John, Sr., 18–19
Innerarity, Mary, marriage to Henry Wilson (1828), 347
Innerarity family genealogy, 329n
Isla Verde, 310
Italiano (ship), 311

Jackson, Gen. Andrew: and Antonio de Follarte, 337–38; and Battle of New Orleans (1815), 340; and capture of Cook and Ambrister (1818), 320–21; and Dominick Hall, 340, 341; and Domingo Sausa, 334–35, 358; and Eligius Fromentin, 340–41; and Fort San Carlos de Barrancas, capture of (1818), 324; at Fort San Marcos (1818), 319–20; and George Bowie, 342; and George Walton, 346; and Henry M. Brackenridge, 330, 342; and Isaac McKeever, 319; and John C. Mitchell, 342; and John Hambly, 319, 324; and John Innerarity, 300, 324, 330, 339, 341–42; and John Quincy Adams, 341; and José Callava, 337–38, 340; judicial authority of, 342, 343; and Louis Louaillier, 341; and Marcos de Villiers, 338, 346; and martial law in Louisiana (1815), 340; and Mauricio de Zúñiga, 306; and Negro Fort, 306; at Pensacola, 287–88 (1814), 303 (1814), 330 (1814), 324 (1818), 330 (1821); and Red Sticks, defeat of (1814), 300; Suwannee, attack on (1818), 320; Tennessee, return to (1821), 345; and U.S. annexation of the Floridas (1821), 334; as U.S. territorial governor of Florida, 330; and Vidal estate, 334–37, 341, 342–44, 347; and West Florida, invasion of (1818), 318–19, 323

Jamaica, 126, 214

James, Benjamin: and Choctaw trade, 167; and Creek-Chickasaw hostilities, 179; and Creek war against Georgia, 83; and Indian conference at Yazoo River, 100; and William Blount, 168; and William Davenport, 168; and William Panton, 168

James Gairdner & Co., and Panton, Leslie (1798), 213–14

James Penman & Co., and Panton, Leslie, 186

Jáudenes, José de (Spanish representative at Philadelphia), 165, 166

Jay, John: and negotiations with Great Britain, 200; and negotiations with Spain (1786), 122

Jefferson, Thomas (secretary of state; president): and Alexander McGillivray, 144; and Creek cession to U.S. (1805), 260; and Indian debts to Panton, Leslie, 255; and José de Jáudenes, 165; and Josef Ignacio de Viar, 165; and proposed Choctaw cession on Mississippi River, 246; and rejection of proposed U.S.–Choctaw cession treaty (1805), 256; and Spanish-Creek relations, 166; and Spanish Indian policy, 165–66; and Treaty of New York (1790), 144; and U.S.–Creek relations, 144; and U.S.–Spanish relations, 165–66

John Forbes & Co.: and Addin Lewis, 297; and Alexander Arbuthnot, 314; and British admiralty courts, 330; and British theft of property, 288–89; and captain general of Cuba, 311; and Chickasaw, 258, 262; and Choctaw, 262, 330; and Creek, 260–62; Creek-Seminole cessions to, 254, 298; and collection of Indian debts, 312; duty-free status of, 311–12; and East Florida Indian trade, 316, 350; and Edmund Doyle, 310, 314; and Edward Nicolls, 300; and escaped slaves of, at Negro Fort, 304–5, 309; and First Seminole War, 309; Florida land grants to (1818), map 328, 330; Great Britain, relations with, 300; and Indian cessions, 302–3, 315; and Indian trade at Apalachicola, 313; and Indian trade competition with Arbuthnot, 316; and John Hambly, 304, 313–14; James and John Innerarity as leaders of (1817), 329; and John Innerarity, withdrawal from (1830), 329; John Leslie & Co. succeeded by (1804), 250; and José Masot, 312, 313; losses at Pensacola (1814), 288, 290; losses in War of 1812, 297, 309, 326–27, 329–30, 350; Marcos de Villiers as agent of, 325; and Miguel de Losada, 311; and Negro Fort, 303–5; Panton, Leslie succeeded by (1804), 250; and proposed Chickasaw cession to U.S. (1805), 257; proposed Seminole cession to (1805), 262; and Red Sticks, Jackson's defeat of (1814), 300; slaves stolen from, 289–91; southeastern Indians, relations with, 251, 254, 299, 314; and Spanish Indian trade, 262, 297, 302, 311; and Spanish trade restrictions, 311; store at Apalachicola, 302–3, 307, 309, 311, 325; store at Bon Secour, 279, 285–86, 288, 297; store at Mobile, 297, 343; store at Prospect Bluff, 290, 297, 302–4; store at St. Augustine, 316; store at St. Marks, 303–6, 315; supplier to Spanish troops, 303; supplier to U.S. army, 324–25; supplier to U.S. forts, 310–11; and Upper Creek debts, 255; U.S., relations with, 261–62; and U.S. customs regulations, 297; and U.S. occupation of Pensacola, 303; and Vidal estate, 331–32, 343; in West Florida, 326–27, and West Florida Indian trade, 316; withdrawal from Pensacola (1830), 329

John Gordon & Co., and William Panton, 15

John Leslie & Co., 250. See John Forbes & Co.; Panton, Leslie & Co.

Julius Pringle (schooner), 209–10

412 Index

Juzan, Pedro (Spanish Indian agent), and Indian conference at Yazoo River, 100

Kelly, John, 95
Kelsall, John (judge), 46, 238
Kelsall, Roger, 33–34
Kemper brothers, 263
Kenhagee (chief of Mickasuky), 317, 318
Kentucky, Cherokee raids on, 196
Kerlérec, Louis Billouart de, 9
Key West, 235
Kinache (Red Stick chief), 305
Kindelán y Oregón, Sebastián (governor of East Florida): and British military recruitment of Spanish slaves, 292–93; and George Woodbine, 301; and Sir George Cockburn, 293, 295; and Thomas Pinckney, 275–76
Kings Ferry, 153
Kingston, Jamaica, 231, 288
Kinnard, Jack, 191; and U.S.–Creek relations, 189; proposed successor to McGillivray, 177
Knox, Henry (secretary of war): and Cherokee, 160; and Creek, 143, 159; and Creek war, 98; and Edmond Genêt, 197; and Fort Massac, 197; and James Seagrove, 176; and proposed U.S. military post at Muscle Shoals, 178; and U.S.–Creek relations, 140; and William Augustus Bowles, 159; and William Panton, 144

La Clède Liguest, Pierre, 9
Lake Borgne, 284
Lake Pontchartrain, 284
Lama, —, and release of Callava, 340
L'Ami de la Pointe-à-Pitre (ship), French privateer, 185
Lane, Timothy, 111–12, 121
Lang, Richard, 32
La Roche, Isabel, 9
La Sans Pareille (ship), French privateer, 185
Las Casas, Luis de (captain general of Cuba), 156
Latour, Maj. A. Lacarrière, and U.S. occupation of Pensacola (1814), 288
Lawrence, Maj. William: and British attack on Fort Bowyer (1814), 285; and John Forbes & Co., 274
Le Blanc, Terencio, and estate of N. Vidal, 332, 343–44
Leslie, Alexander, 19
Leslie, Anna, 47
Leslie, Anna (Duff), 19
Leslie, Elizabeth (Cain), 46–47
Leslie, Elizabeth Rose, 47
Leslie, Helena, 47
Leslie, John, 15, 19, 24, 40, 43, 120, 215; abandonment of West Florida trade by, 86–87; and Alexander & Leslie Co., 39; and Alexander McGillivray, 117, 145; and British Board of Trade, 219; and British prize courts, 219; death of, 47n, 248, 357, 370; in East Florida, 23; estate of, 250; will and heirs of, 350, 356, 357; and James Monroe, 277; and John Forbes, 250, 350; and Juan Nepomuceno de Quesada, 165; law practice of, 42; and memorial of loyalty (1776), 32; and Panton, Leslie, 36, 363–64; in St. Augustine, 46, 72, 129, 132; at St. Marys, 32; and Spanish-Creek relations, 117; and Spanish Indian trade, 63; and Strachan & MacKenzie, 217; supplier of arms for southeastern Indians, 238; and use of neutral shipping, 219; and wartime trade regulations, 216; and William Augustus Bowles, 231
Leslie, Robert, 46, 152; and Panton, Leslie, 18, 19, 364
Leslie, Rev. William, 19–21
Leslie family, in Scotland, 19
Lewis, Addin (U.S. customs officer at Mobile), and John Forbes & Co., 278–79, 297
Lincoln, Gen. Benjamin, U.S. treaty commissioner to Creek (1789), 135, 137–40
L'Industrie (ship), French privateer, 185
Little Exuma Island, and salt trade, 133
Little Prince (Creek chief): and attack on Panton, Leslie store at St. Marks, 177; proposed successor to McGillivray, 177; and renegotiation of Creek cession to John Forbes & Co. (1804), 254; and William Augustus Bowles, 239
Little River, 245

Little St. Marys River, Spanish grant to John Forbes on (1799), 357
Little Tallassie, map 22, 96, 143; William Panton at (1792), 161
Liverpool, Lord, 219
Livingston, Edward, and Vidal estate, 332, 343–44
Logwood trade, and Campeche, 134
London: and direct trade with Pensacola, 217–18; and southeastern Indian trade, 205
London Court of Common Pleas, and Forbes's suit against Cochrane and Cockburn (1822), 350
Long, Nicholas, 77
Loomis, Jairus (sailing master), and attack on Negro Fort (1816), 307
Losada, Miguel de (Spanish treasury auditor), and John Forbes & Co., 311–12
Louaillier, Louis (Louisiana state legislator), 340, 341
Louisiana: acquisition by France, 236; acquisition by U.S. (1803), 246, 248; boundary dispute with Texas, 263; British operations in (1814), 283; and Creek, 74; defenses of, 157, 196; French in, 182, 189; Georgian encroachment on, 77; martial law in (1815), 340; Panton, Leslie's opportunities in, 188; rebellion in (1768), 9; revision of commercial regulations in (1793), 187; and Spanish Indian trade, 58, 62, 127; Spanish possession of, 1, 9,; supply of Indian trade goods in, 9, 13; and U.S., 166, 196; U.S. immigration into, 156; West Florida included in boundaries of, 248
Louisiana Purchase (1803), 245, 285; boundaries of, 263, 276–77; and John Forbes & Co., 370; Mobile considered part of, 276–77; West Florida considered part of, 276
Louisiana Supreme Court, and McGillivray heirs, 359
Louis XVI (king of France), 182
Lower Creek, 95–96; and Alexander McGillivray, death of, 177; and cessions to John Forbes & Co., 251–54 (1804), 268, 270 (1811); and Creek cession to U.S. (1805), 261; debts to trading companies, 243, 245, 268, 270, 272; drought among (1792), 176; and Indian conferences at Chiskatalofa, 241 (1804), 268 (1811), 305 (1816); and James Seagrove, 176, 191–92; and John Forbes & Co., 281; and John Hambly, 305; opposition to Negro Fort by, 309; and Pedro Olivier, 162; and proposed grand Indian alliance, 150, 189; and proposed Seminole cession to John Forbes & Co. (1806), 262; Robert Seagrove's store, attack on, 189–90; territory of, 4–5; and Timothy Barnard, 189; and William Augustus Bowles, 124, 148, 150, 189, 232, 239; and William Panton, 162
Loyalists, British, in East Flordia, 365–66
Ludlow, Henry, 12

McDonald, John, and Panton, 162–64
McGillivray, Aleck, 177
McGillivray, Alexander (Creek chief), 53; and Alexander Cornell, 176; appointed U.S. brigadier general, 146; and Arturo O'Neill, 55–56, 121; and Barón de Carondelet, 151, 156, 161, 163, 170, 173, 176; and Bourbon County, Georgia, affair (1785), 78; British commissary to Creek, 53; and Broomfield Bonnamy, 117; bounty on, 84; and cession of Creek lands to U.S. (1783), 55; in Charleston, 24; and Chickasaw trade, 57; and Choctaw trade, 57; and Creek-Chickasaw hostilities, 178; as Creek chief, 53; and Creek trade, 57; and Creek treaty with Spain (1792), 163; and Creek–U.S. relations, 146; and Creek war against Georgia (1787), 76–77, 80–83, 95–97, 120; death of, 177, 189, 369; and Esteban Rodriguez Miró, 113, 117–18, 121, 123, 136–37, 140, 147; and Fat King of Cussitah, 75; and George Washington, 144; Georgia, relations with, 147; heirs of, 350, 357–58, 361; and Hopewell treaties (1785–86), 85; and independent commercial port for Creek, 117–18, 138–40, 144; and independent Creek state, 139; and James Mather, 61, 65, 68; and James Seagrove, 164; and James White, 93, 139; and John Forbes, 350,

McGillivray, Alexander (*continued*)
357–58, 361; and John Leslie, 117, 145; and John Miller, 117; and John Turnbull, 172; lands of, in Georgia, 146; and Marinus Willett, 142; in New Orleans (1792), 163; in New York (1790), 142–43; oath of allegiance to U.S., 146; and Panton, Leslie, 56–57, 62, 113, 140–45, 158, 191, 358, 359, 363, 368; and Pedro Olivier, 159; and Piomingo, 178; and raids on Tensaw-Tombigbee settlements (1788), 123; and Spain, 144; Spanish agent to Creek, 59, 69, 113; and Spanish-Creek relations, 113, 120–21, 124, 136, 138; and Spanish-Creek treaty (1784), 58; and Spanish government of Florida, 55–56, 69, 96–97, 120–21, 124, 146; and Spanish Indian policy, 164; and Spanish Indian trade, 56–58, 61, 68, 73–74, 112, 116–17, 122, 127, 140, 144; and Spanish pension, 163; and Tame King of Tallassie, 75; and Treaty of Augusta (1783), 75; and Treaty of New York (1790), 143–45, 146, 149; and U.S., relations with, 180; and U.S. congressional peace commission (1785), 79–80; and U.S. expansionist policy, 53–54, 73–74, 115; and U.S. Indian trade diplomacy, 94–95; and U.S. peace mission (1788), 113; and U.S. treaty commission to Creek (1789), 137–39; and Vincente Manuel de Zespedes, 63, 64, 69–70, 87, 97, 140; and West Florida trade, 86–87; and William Augustus Bowles, 112–13, 116–17, 120, 124, 148–50, 154; and William Panton, 54, 57, 59, 61, 65, 68, 86, 88, 97, 121, 123, 136–37, 139, 142–45, 150, 152, 161, 176–77, 189, 369; and William Seagrove, 161

McGillivray, Daniel, 229
McGillivray, Rev. Farquhar, 53
McGillivray, Lachlan, 24, 53
McGillivray, Lizzy, 357–59
McGillivray, Margaret, 357–59
McGillivray, Sehoy (Marchand), 53
McGregor, Gregor, filibustering activities in East Florida (1818), 320, 367
McHenry, James (secretary of war), and John McKee, 228, 231
McIntosh (chief of Coweta), 307

McIntosh, George, 28, 29, 30
McIntosh, Lachlan, 29
McKay, Donald, and southeastern Indian trade, 33
McKee, John: agent to Cherokee and Choctaw, 227, 229, 231; and Andrew Ellicott, 227; and Arthur Preston Whitaker, 229; and Barón de Carondelet, 227; and James McHenry, 228, 231; and John Forbes, 226, 229, 231; and Panton, Leslie, 227; and proposed Indian cessions to Panton, Leslie, 231; and Timothy Pickering, 229; U.S. Choctaw agent (1799), 231; and U.S. Federalist party, 228; and U.S. War Department, 231; and William Blount, 227; and William Panton, 229, 231
McKeever, Capt. Isaac, at St. Marks, 318–20
McKenzie, Colin, 36
McLatchy, Charles, 15, 21, 47, 97; and abandonment of West Florida trade, 86; in East Florida, 23; and Panton, Leslie, 36, 43, 50, 57, 65, 69, 363; and Spalding-Kelsall trading posts, 34
McLeod, Mary (Alexander), 44
McLeod, William, 44
McMurphy, Daniel, 82, 84
McPherson, William, representative of John Forbes & Co., 289–90
McQueen, Ann, 16
McQueen, Gordon & Co., 15
McQueen, John, 15, 16, 209
McQueen, Peter (Red Stick chief), 279, 280, 305
McVoy, —, and British attack on Fort Bowyer (1814), 285
Mad Dog (Creek war chief of Tuckabatchee), 189, 254; and Creek-Choctaw relations, 180; debts to Panton, Leslie, 244; and James Seagrove, 192; successor to McGillivray, 177–78; visit to Arturo O'Neill (1786), 76; and William Panton, 177, 192
Madison, James (president), and U.S. forces in the Floridas, 273
Mangourit, Michel Ange Bernarde (French consul at Charleston), 183–84
Margaret Ann (ship), captured, 215
Marín Pizarro, Gabriel (customs officer at Pensacola), and William Panton, 204–5, 209–10

Marshall, John (chief justice): and Forbes and Vicente Folch, 211; and Forbes Grant I case (1835), 354
Martin, Joseph, 78–79
Martín, Corp. Mateo, at Concepción, 119
Masot, José (governor of West Florida): and John Forbes & Co., 312, 313, 327; and John Innerarity, 313; and U.S. shipments to Fort Crawford, 324; and Vidal estate records, 333
Mather, James: and Alexander McGillivray, 61, 65, 68; and military support to Creek, 124; and southeastern Indian trade, 85; and Spanish Indian trade, 58, 61–62, 67–71, 86, 88–90, 126; and — Strother, 90; and William Panton, 86, 131–32; on Yazoo River, 169
Mather & Strother (company): and John Turnbull, 172; and Panton, Leslie, 368
Mathews, George (governor of Georgia), 97, 184–85
Maxent, Francisco Maximiliano de St. (governor of West Florida), 312
Maxent, Gilberto Antonio de, 8–9, 10–14, 56–57, 368
Maxent, María Felicitas, 10
Maxent, María Isabel, 10
Maxwell, John, 47–48
Mediterranean, escaped slaves in, 293
Medway River, 28
Meigs, Return J. (U.S. Cherokee agent): and Cherokee, 258; and John Forbes, 244
Memphis (Chickasaw Bluffs), 75
Meriwether, David, 259
Mickasuky (Seminole town), Doyle and Hambly captives at (1817), 317–18
Milfort, Louis Le Clerc de, 154; and Creek-Chickasaw hostilities, 178–79
Miller, John: and Alexander McGillivray, 117; and Creek trade, 120; and John Halkett, 238; as Loyalist refugee in the Bahamas (1788), 115; and "state" of Muskogee, 149, and William Augustus Bowles, 118, 149, 231–32, 235
Miller, John (clerk of county court), and Vidal estate records, 334
Minor, Esteban. See Minor, Stephen
Minor, Lt. Stephen, and Choctaw, 167
Miranda, Francisco de, 12

Miró, Esteban Rodriguez (governor of Louisiana), 13–14, 57–59, 61–62, 67–68, 70, 157, 167; and Alexander McGillivray, 108–9, 113, 117, 121, 123, 136–37, 140–41, 147; and Antonio Valdés y Bazán, 126; and Bernardo del Campo, 132; and Bourbon County, Georgia, affair (1785), 78; and Creek–U.S. relations, 137, 141; and Creek war against Georgia (1787), 77, 80–81, 96, 98; and the Hopewell treaties (1785–86), 85; and independent commercial port for Creek, 140; and Indian conference at Yazoo River, 100; intendant of Louisiana (1789), 128; and James Mather, 104; and James O'Fallon, 141; and James Wilkinson, 139; and John Forbes, 133; and military support to Creek, 76, 96–97, 121, 123–24; and Panton, Leslie, 71–72, 125–26, 368; and southeastern Indian trade, 127–28, 133–34; and Spanish-Creek relations, 108–9, 120–21, 124, 147; and Spanish fur trade, 13; and Spanish Indian trade, 86–87, 89–91, 99, 100–102, 104–7, 136; and — Strother, 104; and U.S. Indian trade, 107, 147; and U.S. land speculation, 141; and William Augustus Bowles, 120; and William Panton, 108–9, 112, 125–26, 133, 140, 142
Mississippi, Federalist party and, 196
Mississippi River, 75, 77, 141, 167, 175, 221, 224–25, 267, 284; as boundary of Louisiana Purchase, 277; and boundary of West Florida, 263; Chickasaw lands on, 257–58; navigation rights on, 2, 4, 122, 129, 198, 200; proposed Choctaw cession on, 246–47; proposed Creek cession to U.S. on, 255; and Spanish domination of, 182; Spanish galleys on, 172, 196; U.S. and, 171; U.S. desire for Indian lands on, 248, 255–57
Mississippi Territory, 231, 257, 267
Missouri River, French Indian trade on, 9
Mitchel, Colin, and Forbes Grant I, 355
Mitchel, Octavius, and Forbes Grant I, 355
Mitchell, David B. (governor of Georgia): and U.S. invasion of East Florida (1812), 273n; as U.S. Creek agent, 325
Mitchell, John C., 342–44
Mobile, 121, 172, 175–76, 358; British

Mobile (continued)
  threat to (1814), 283–84; Choctaw at, 167; considered part of Louisiana Purchase, 276–77; Creek attack on (1813), 279; economic depression at (1816), 312; and French Indian trade, 7; and French privateers, 203; and fur trade, 8, 71; importance to U.S. as seaport, 246; James Innerarity at (1818), 318; John Forbes & Co. office at, 279, 285, 288, 297, 343, 365; Panton, Leslie store at, 129, 207, 227; and southeastern Indian trade, 85, 99–102, 104–5, 126, 129; Spanish-Choctaw-Chickasaw meeting at (1784), 78; Spanish conquest of, 49; Spanish customs duties paid at, 245; and Spanish Indian trade, 59, 61–63, 65, 109, 131–33, 260, 262; U.S. army at, 283 (1814), 325 (1818); U.S. customs at, 288; and U.S.–Florida smuggling, 279; U.S. occupation of (1813), 276–79; U.S. settlers at, 303; U.S. threat to, 171; and Vidal estate records, 333; William Augustus Bowles at, 242
Mobile Bay, 283
Mobile Point, 284–86
Mobile River, Spanish control of navigation on, 262
"Moccasin Boys," and smuggling at St. Marys River, 274
Mollinedo, Francisco, and southeastern Indian trade, 110–11
Monroe, James (president), 277, 339
Montes de Oca, Anastasio, 306, 315
Moore, Philip, 36; and partnership with William Panton, 24–26
Morales, Juan Ventura (intendant of Louisiana): and Barón de Carondelet, 205–6; and Panton, Leslie, 205–6, 209–11, 218; and Spanish Junta of the Royal Treasury, 208; and Vicente Folch y Juan, 210–11; and wartime trade regulations, 206–8; and William Panton, 207–10, 215
Morgan, Pat, 90–91, 126
El Morro castle (Havana), 37, 242
Moscow (ship), and John Innerarity's withdrawal from Pensacola (1814), 287
Moultrie, Alexander, and South Carolina Yazoo Company, 142, 183
Moultrie, William (governor of Georgia), and Edmond Genêt, 183
Mount Dexter, U.S. treaty commission at (1805), 256
Mountz, Lt. G. W., 335, 340
Murray, George, attorney for John Forbes & Co., 360
Muscle Shoals, 83, 95; Chickasaw cession at, 85; Doughty expedition to (1790), 178; John Sevier and, 75; proposed Spanish fort at, 172; proposed U.S. military post at, 178; U.S. colonization attempt at, 75; U.S. trading post at, 99, 170–71
Muskogee (independent "state"), 154, 156, 231, 233, 238, 241; and Bahamas, 148; and Cherokee, 148; and Creek, 148; decline of, 239; and Great Britain, 149; and independent commercial port for Creek, 148, 151; and John Halkett, 239; and Lord Dunmore, 149; war with Spain, 236; and William Augustus Bowles, 225; and William Grenville, 148
Myers, Samuel, and Vidal case, 346

Nancy (ship), captured, 214
Nashville, Indian conference at (1792), 170–72
Nassau, 235; Alexander Arbuthnot at (1817), 317; Ambrister at, 320; Panton, Leslie trade with, 221; and southeastern Indian trade, 102, 130, 132, 134, 204, 314; and Spanish Indian trade, 70; Thomas Forbes in, 216, 260; and trade with Spanish colonies, 214–15, 217; as wartime free port, 215
Nassau County, Florida, 357
Nassau General Court, suits against George Woodbine in (1815), 301
Natchez, 168, 172, 176; evacuation of Spanish forces from (1798), 201; U.S. immigration to, 124; U.S. threat to, 171
Natchez District, 4, 77, 122
Navarro, Diego Joseph, and Thomas Forbes, 38
Navarro, Martín (intendant of Louisiana), 9, 61–62, 67, 109; and James Mather, 104;

and Panton, Leslie, 71–72, 368; resignation (1788), 106; and southeastern Indian trade, 127; and Spanish commercial rivalry with Great Britain, 87–88; and Spanish Indian trade, 58, 68, 86, 89–91, 99, 105, 128; and — Strother, 104

Negro Fort: destruction of, by U.S. (1816), 308–10, 315–16, 367; escaped Forbes slaves at, 304–7; Indian attack on (1816), 307–8; and John Forbes & Co., 303–5; John Hambly at (1815), 303–4; location at Prospect Bluff, 302; and piracy, 302, 304; possible Indian attack on (1815), 304; possible U.S. attack on (1815), 304; Spanish opposition to, 306; site of Fort Gadsden (1818), 323; survivors of, and capture of Doyle and Hambly (1817), 316; U.S. opposition to, 306, 309

Nero (Negro Seminole chief), and capture of Doyle and Hambly (1817), 317

Netherclift, Thomas, 16–17, 23, 24, 25

Netherclift & Co., and John Stuart, 24

New Madrid: Pedro Rousseau at (1795), 197; U.S. threat to, 171–72

New Orleans, 81, 172, 174, 196, 212, 215, 343, 358; Battle of (1814), 290–91; British attack and defeat at (1814), 289; and British navy, 284; British threat to (1814), 283–84; Eligius Fromentin at (1807), 339; French privateers at, 203; John Forbes & Co. at, 311, 370; martial law ended in (1815), 341; occupation by James Wilkinson (1803), 246; Panton, Leslie at, 129; proposed as free port, 169; and southeastern Indian trade, 102, 104; and Spanish Indian trade, 58, 70–71, 163–64; U.S. threat to, 171; Vidal estate sale, 331–32; William Augustus Bowles at (1803), 242

New Providence, 188, 236; Doyle and Hambly to be sent to (1817), 317; and southeastern Indian trade, 149

New Providence Island, 89, 91, 110, 112

New Smyrna, Florida, 16

Nicholl, Sir John, 212

Nicolls, Lt. Col. Edward, 290, 291; and Alexander Arbuthnot, 314; and Benjamin Hawkins, 299; and British at Pensacola (1814), 284, 287; and British attack on Fort Bowyer (1814), 285; and British military recruitment of slaves, 291; and Creek, 298–99; and George Woodbine, 300; at Indian conference (1815), 299; and James Innerarity, 288, 298; and John Forbes, 298, 301; and John Forbes & Co., 284, 298, 300, 367; and John Innerarity, 284, 286, 291, 298; and Mateo González Manrique, 286; at Nassau, 284; at Pensacola, 283; at Prospect Bluff (1814), 288; and Red Sticks, 283; and Robert Henry, 285; and Seminole, 298; and theft of Forbes property at Pensacola (1814), 288–89; and theft of Forbes slaves, 286, 298; and Treaty of Fort Jackson (1814), 299; wounded at Fort Bowyer (1814), 285

Nisbet, Furguson H., and Vidal estate, 343

Nogales, 172, 175; evacuation of Spanish forces from (1798), 201; Indian congress at (1793), 180–81; location of, 167; Panton, Leslie at, 169, 173, 176; Pedro Rousseau at (1795), 197; Spanish fortification of, 167, 169; U.S. immigration to, 167–68; U.S. threat to, 171

Nonintercourse Act (1809), 274

Nootka Sound, Canada, British-Spanish confrontation at (1790), 125, 131–32, 134, 144–46

Noriega, Carlos, escaped from Indians (1817), 316

North Carolina: and Creek war against Georgia, 98; sale of Cherokee lands by (1783), 74; western territorial claims of, 74–75, 160

Northrup, Job (privateer), 333

Nova Scotia, and southeastern Indian trade, 126

Oak Forest (plantation), 36

Ochechee Bluff, 316

Ochlockonee River, 150–51, 243–44, 314–15

Ocmulgee River, 243–45, 258–60, 262

Ocochappo River, 85

Oconee lands: boundaries of, 164, 176; Creek cession of, to Georgia, 148, 154, 159–60

Oconee River, 55, 76, 83, 96, 99, 184–85,

Oconee River (*continued*)
189, 243–45; Georgian claims to, 94, 136, 138–40; U.S. trading post at, 170, 201
O'Fallon, James, 141
Ogeechee River, 75–76
Oglethorpe, James, 32
Ohio River, 2, 4, 105, 160, 196–97, 257
O'Keefe, James, 111–12
Okfuskie (Creek town), 189
Okoy (Chickasaw chief), 257–58
Olivier, Lt. Pedro: and Alexander McGillivray, 159; and Barón de Carondelet, 159; and Creek, 163; and Indian congress at Nogales (1793), 180; and Lower Creek, 162; as Spanish agent to Creek, 158–59; and Spanish Indian policy, 161; and Upper Creek, 162; and U.S. expansionist policy, 162
O'Neill, Arturo (governor of West Florida), 8, 58, 63, 70, 162; and Alexander McGillivray, 55–56, 79, 106–8, 112–13, 121; and Creek, 56–57; and Creek raids on Georgia, 76; and Creek war against Georgia (1787), 81–82, 98; and Indian trade diplomacy, 94–95; and Spanish-Creek relations, 108, 113; and Spanish Indian trade, 65, 68–70; and Spanish military support of Creek, 96; and supply of military stores to Panton, Leslie, 133; and U.S. congressional peace commission to Creek (1785), 79–80; and William Augustus Bowles, 120; and William Panton, 107–8, 111–13, 211
Onís, Luis de (Spanish minister), 327, 353
O'Reilly, Alejandro, 9–10
Orpheus (ship), 281
Oswald, Richard, 59, 61n
Otis, Samuel (U.S. Senate clerk), 140
Oxhides, in Spanish Indian trade, 207–8

Pacific Ocean. *See* Nootka Sound, Canada
Palatka, Florida, 34
Panton, Barbara (Wemyss), 17
Panton, Catherine, 18
Panton, Christian, 17
Panton, Forbes & Co.: formation of (1775), 26; and Lower Creek trade, 35; merchandise traded by, 34–35; ships owned by, 36
Panton, Henrietta, 18
Panton, John, 17
Panton, John, Jr., 18–19
Panton, Leslie & Co., 24; abandonment of West Florida trade by, 86–87, 110–11; and Alexander McGillivray, 54, 56–57, 62, 68–69, 107–8, 113, 140, 144–45, 158, 191; and American Revolution, losses in, 42–43; and Anglo-Spanish war (1793), 188; and Antonio Valdés y Bazán, 91; and Barón de Carondelet, 158, 198, 205–6, 209; and British Honduras, 208; and British privateers, 210, 213–14; and British prize courts, 212–14; and cession of the Floridas to Spain, 43–44, 51; and Cherokee, 175, 201; and Chickasaw, 105, 126, 146, 173, 175, 202; and Choctaw, 105, 126, 146, 175, 202; and convoy shipping system, 188–89; and Creek trade, 88, 139, 175, 202; and European mercantile systems, 186; formation of (1782?), 36, 40, 43; and France, 204; and French privateers, 185–86, 215; Georgia, relations with, 147; and Georgian trade competition, 81–82; and Hammond & Fowler, 183–84; and Indian fur trade, 14; and Indian trade concession by Spain, 73; and James Penman & Co., 186; and James Seagrove, 164; and James Wilkinson, 147; and John Galphin, 165; and John Leslie & Co., succeeded by (1801), 250; and John Turnbull, 173–75, 198–99; and Juan Manuel Álvarez, 204; and Juan Ventura Morales, 205–6, 209–11; and Lord Dunmore, 48, 115, 120; and Louisiana, commercial opportunities in, 188; and Manuel de Godoy, 204; and Manuel Gayoso y Lemos, 199; and Pedro Varela y Ulloa, 204; profits of, 42, 104–6, 108–9; and royal order, 131–33 (1789), 187 (1793); at St. Marks, 86, 88; and salt trade, 133–34; and shortage of Indian trade goods (1797), 212–13; and Sir John Nicholl, 212; and Sir William Scott, 212; and southeastern Indian trade, 50, 94, 124–25, 175, 206; and Spain, 51, 52, 68, 70–71, 107, 109–10, 201; and Spanish customs and duties,

126–27, 129, 210–11; Spanish garrisons in East Florida, trade with, 134; and Spanish Indian trade, 64, 65, 67, 69–70, 86–89, 90–91, 98, 105, 110, 116, 122, 126–27, 134, 140, 173–75; and Spanish Indian trade concession, 56–57, 72, 187; Spanish military stores, use of, 133; stores in East Florida, 32–33; and Strachan & MacKenzie, 129, 131; and Tensaw-Tombigbee settlements, 133; and U.S.–Creek relations, 144; and Vincente Manuel de Zéspedes, 63–65, 68, 86–87; and William Alexander, 44; and William Augustus Bowles, 116, 118, 120, 124, 149–50
Panton, Magdalene, 18
Panton, Robina, 18
Panton, William 15, 17, 24, 41, 43, 78; abandonment of West Florida trade by, 103, 105, 118, 125–27; acquisition of Spalding-Kelsall trading posts, 33; and Alexander McGillivray, 54, 57, 59, 61, 65, 68, 86, 88, 97, 103, 106, 121, 123, 136–37, 139; and Arturo O'Neill, 107–8; in the Bahamas (1788), 115; and Bernardo del Campo, 130; and Charles McLatchy, 86; in Charleston, 17, 24; and Chickasaw trade, 90; and Choctaw trade, 90, 109; and Creek-Spanish relations, 136; and Creek trade, 81, 109; in East Florida, 27, 35–36; and Esteban Rodriguez Miró, 108–9, 112, 125–26, 130–33, 140; and George McIntosh, 28–30; in Georgia Assembly, 38–39; Georgia lands of, 25; and Georgians, 81; and James Innerarity, 18–19; and James Mather, 86, 131–32; and James White, 94; and John Forbes, 21; and John Gordon, 23; and John Gordon & Co., 15, 17; and John Innerarity, 19; and John Leslie, 86; as Loyalist refugee, 32; and memorial of loyalty (1776), 31–32; and memorial to Spanish court (1788), 106, 109, 125; and military support to Creek, 124; in Nassau, 47, 65; and Philip Moore, 24–26; and revenue bills, 26; and royal order (1789), 130; at St. Marks store, 59; in slave trade, 24; and southeastern Indian trade, 85, 111; and Spanish-Creek relations, 108, 112–13, 116–17, 120, 123; and Spanish Indian trade, 61, 63, 70–74, 91, 100–103, 105, 107, 108–9, 112, 118, 125; and Thomas Forbes, 25; and U.S.–Creek relations, 136; U.S. embargo against, 27–28; and U.S. expansionist policy, 74; and U.S. Indian trade diplomacy, 95; and William Augustus Bowles, 112, 121
Panton & Forbes, 42
Panton family, in Scotland, 17–18
Pascagoula River, 4
Peace of Amiens (1802), 238
Pearl River, 277
Penman, Shaw & Co., 216–18
Pensacola, 108, 110–11, 113, 120–21, 124, 188, 239, 311, 338, 342; Andrew Jackson at, 288, 324, 330, 367; black Spanish troops return to (1815), 290; as British base of operations (1814), 283–87, 289; British bombardment of (1814), 287; British threat to, 204; and Creek trade, 96, 191–92; damage claims against British at (1815), 290; economic depression at (1816), 312; Forbes slaves at, 327; and French privateers, 203; and fur trade, 8, 71; George Woodbine at (1814), 301; importance to U.S. as seaport, 246; Indian raiders gathered at (1818), 323–24; John Forbes & Co. office at, 276, 279, 290, 329, 365; lack of royal Spanish customhouse at, 211; London, direct trade with, 217–18; and Negro Fort, 309; and Panton, Leslie, 129, 207; Red Sticks in (1813), 279; and southeastern Indian trade, 86–87, 89–91, 102, 104, 106–7, 125, 128, 130–34; Spanish attack on (1780), 37; Spanish conquest of (1781), 37, 49, 114; Spanish-Creek congress at (1784), 58; and Spanish Indian trade, 59, 61–63, 65, 67, 69–71, 81, 208, 312; U.S. army at (1818, 1821), 324–25, 335, 347; U.S.–Florida smuggling, 279; U.S. occupation of (1814, 1818–19), 288, 303; U.S. threat to, 171; and Vidal estate records, 333
Perdido (ship), 325
Perdido River, 236, 249, 283–84, 286; as boundary of Louisiana Purchase, 277; as boundary of West Florida, 263; and Forbes Indian trade, 279

Perroneau, John, 29
Perryman (Lower Creek chief), 316; and Bowles, 149
Perryman, Thomas (Seminole chief): and Bowles, 114; and proposed Seminole cession to Panton, Leslie (1803), 243–44
Philadelphia, 165
Philatouchy (Lower Creek chief), 149
Pickens, Gen. Andrew, and peace commissions, 79, 98–99, 106
Pickering, Timothy (secretary of state), 195, 229
Picolata, Florida, 32, 165
Pinckney, Thomas, 200, 275–76
Pintado, Vicente Sebastián (surveyor general of West Florida), 289–90
Piomingo (Chickasaw war chief): and Alexander McGillivray, 178; and Creek-Chickasaw relations, 179; and the Hopewell treaties (1786), 85; and Indian congress at Nogales (1793), 180; and John Sevier, 78; and Manuel Gayoso de Lemos, 169; and Spanish Indian trade, 102; and U.S. Indian trade, 99; and U.S. threat to Spanish territory, 173; and U.S. trading post at Muscle Shoals, 171; and Virginia, 78
Pirates: at Galveston (1816), 333; at Negro Fort, 302, 304
Pitt, William (prime minister), 231
Plover (ship), as British privateer, 213
Portell, Thomas (Spanish commandant at New Madrid and St. Marks): and Barón de Carondelet, 171; and William Augustus Bowles, 232–33
Pott, James S.: and escaped Forbes slaves, 296, 351; representative of John Forbes & Co., 300
Powell, Robert, 25
Price, Edward, 201
Prieto, Felipe, 303, 304, 306
Prince, The (Creek chief), 305
Privateers, 183, 185–86
Prophet Francis (Red Stick chief). *See* Hillis Hadjo
Prospect Bluff, 310; British fort at, 289; Edmund Doyle at, 288, 313–14; Edward Nicolls at, 288, 298; escaped slaves at, 313–14; Forbes store at, 281, 285, 290, 297, 302–4; George Woodbine at, 299; Indian conference at (1810), 270–71; James Innerarity at, 251; John Hambly at, 288, 313; location of Negro Fort at, 302; Red Sticks at, 290; Robert Henry at, 289; threat of Indian attack at, 313
Providence (ship), 216
Putnam County, Florida, 357

Quesada, Juan Nepomuceno de (governor of East Florida): and James Seagrove, 190; and John Forrester, 190; and John Leslie, 165; and royal order (1793), 187; and seizure of Panton, Leslie store at St. Marks (1792), 153

Ravago, Francisco Fernando de, 12
Red Shoes (Coushatta chief), and Indian congress at Nogales (1793), 180
Red Sticks (Creek war faction): and Alexander Arbuthnot, 315; as British allies, 281; defeat of, 280, 300; demand for Spanish arms by, 279–80; and Edmund Doyle, 305; and Edward Nicolls, 283; and George Woodbine, 281–82; and John Forbes, 282; and John Innerarity, 279–80; and Negro Fort (1816), 308; at Prospect Bluff (1815), 290; retreat to West Florida (1814), 280–81; and Seminole, 281; and U.S., 279–80. *See also* Creek
Reid, Robert R. (judge), and John Forbes's estate (1837), 360
Reid, William (captain), 90
Relampago (ship), at Apalachee (1818), 318
Rendon, Francisco (intendant), 195
"Republic of West Florida," 277
Revolutionary Legion of America, 183
Robertson, Gen. James, 180; and Chickasaw, 171, 176, 178, 196, 256–57; and Chickasaw Bluffs, 75; and Choctaw, 176, 256–57; and Creek, expedition against (1787), 95; and Silas Dinsmoor, 255–56; and Spanish–U.S. relations, 122; as treaty commissioner to Choctaw (1805), 255; as U.S. agent to Choctaw and Chickasaw, 160
Robinson, Jeremy, 354
Rochemore, Vincent de, 9
Rock Landing, 184; Georgians at, 139; In-

dian conference at (1792), 161; U.S. treaty commission at (1789), 137, 140
Rousseau, Capt. Pedro, 153, 171–72, 197
Rua, Juan de la, 323, 325, 343
Ruby (ship), and Forbes slaves, 296
Rum, in Spanish Indian trade, 207–8

St. Augustine, 14, 23, 29, 32, 34, 112, 118, 188, 190, 215, 295; and filibusters, 320; and French privateers, 186; George Woodbine at, 301–2; Indian congress at (1783), 49–50; John Forbes & Co. at, 273, 316, 370; Red Sticks at (1814), 282; sanctuary for Loyalists, 26; and southeastern Indian trade, 103; and Spanish Indian trade, 61, 63, 70, 91, 124, 132, 149, 165; William Panton at (1783), 41
St. Clair, Gen. Arthur, 158–59, 189
Saint Genevieve, U.S. threat to, 171
St. Johns County, Florida, 356, 359
St. Johns River: attempted Creek raids at (1793), 190; British trading post at, 13, 23; James Spalding store at, 34; John Forbes plantation at, 293; Panton, Leslie store at, 32–33, 43, 65, 69, 98, 118–19, 165, 184, 190; raids by William Augustus Bowles at, 237; Spanish settlers at, 190
St. Louis, 9, 171
St. Marks: Arbuthnot's store at, 316; as Creek port, 117; Edmund Doyle at, 316, 318; Forbes store at, 303–6, 315, 370; Indian conference at, 270 (1811), 305–6 (1816); Isaac McKeever at (1818), 318–20; John Hambly at, 318; Spanish at, 303, 306
—, Panton Leslie store at, 50, 57, 59, 61, 63, 65, 69, 71, 86, 88, 91, 98, 102–3, 107, 110, 118, 129, 149, 177, 201, 207, 231–32; Bowles's capture of, 233, 235, 237, 238, 261, 369; closing of, 165; Indian attacks on, 245, 254; losses at, table 155; robbery of, 247; William Cunningham's seizure of (1792), 151, 154, 161
St. Marks (fort), 88; Panton, Leslie trade at, 129, 184; Spanish garrisoning of, 67, 102–3
St. Marks River, 233, 244, 268, 354
St. Marys, Panton, Leslie store at, 32, 190
St. Marys River, 80, 140, 143, 176, 184, 195; closing of Panton, Leslie store at, 32; Creek raids on settlements at, 190; Georgian claims to, 138–39; Spanish settlers at, 190; U.S.–Spanish smuggling at, 274
St. Stephens, U.S. factory at, 245
St. Vincent Island, ceded to John Forbes & Co., 268
Salt, trade in, 133–34, 207–8
San Carlos de Barrancas, British destruction of (1814), 287
Sanchez, James S. and Venancio, and Forbes estate, 359–61
San Fernando de las Barrancas. *See* Chickasaw Bluffs
San Fernando de Pupo, 32, 190
San Francisco de Pupo, 32
San Pablo (Forbes plantation), 293, map 294
Santa Rosa Island, 287
Santa Rosa Sound, 352
Sarda, Capt. José, 318, 323
Sausa, Ensign Domingo, 334–35, 338
Savage, John, and William Panton, 220–21
Savannah, 23, 326, 357; British at, 38, 49; and French privateers, 186
Scott, Lt. R. W., 316, 319
Scott, Sir William, 212
Seagrove, James: and Alexander Cornell, 192; and Alexander McGillivray, 161, 164; and Creek, 176; and Creek-Chickasaw hostilities, 180; and Georgia-Creek hostilities, 191; and Henry Knox, 176; and Juan Nepomuceno de Quesada, 190; and Lower Creek, 176, 191–92; and Mad Dog, 192; and Oconee cession boundary, 160–61; and Oconee settlements, 176; and Panton, Leslie, 164; and Spanish-Creek relations, 164; as U.S. agent to Creek, 160; and U.S.–Creek relations, 189; and U.S. Indian policy, 164; and U.S. Indian trade, 176, 193; and White Lieutenant, 192; and William Panton, 164, 180, 192; and Zéspedes, mission to, 98
Seagrove, Robert 189–90
Seminole, 149; and Creek cession to U.S. (1805), 261; and Edward Nicolls, 298; and Edmund Doyle, 325; and Indian conferences at Chiskatalofa, 251 (1804), 268 (1811); and James Innerarity, 255; and John Forbes & Co., 251, 254, 262, 268,

Seminole (*continued*)
270, 272, 281, 298; and Negro Fort, 307; and Panton, Leslie, 102, 243–44, 250; part of Creek nation, 261; and Red Sticks, 281; resistance to land cessions among, 244; siege of Spanish fort at St. Marks by (1800), 233; and Spain, treaty with (1802), 239; territory of, 5; and Treaty of New York, 143; and U.S., relations with, 142; and William Augustus Bowles, 150–51, 232, 239, 241, 247. *See also* First Seminole War

Sevier, John: and Muscle Shoals, 83; and Piomingo, 78; and Spanish–U.S. relations, 122; and "state" of Franklin, 74

Shannon, David (judge), 343

Shark (schooner), 210, 234–35

Shaw, Leonard, U.S. agent to Cherokee, 160

Shawnee, 4, 159, 189

Sheerwater (brigantine), 204–5, 233

Shelburn (ship), 281

Shoulderbone Creek, Creek-Georgian meeting at (1786), 83–84

Simpson, William: and Ben James, 267; and Benjamin Hawkins, 254; and Chickasaw, 257, 258; and Choctaw, 230, 247, 248, 255–56, 267; and Henry Dearborn, 255; and John Forbes, 248; and John Forbes & Co., 250, 251, 254–55, 257, 263, 364; and John Gordon, 257; and John Graham, 263; and Johnson and Edwards' suit against (1810–18), 358; and Panton, Leslie, 230, 257; and Silas Dinsmoor, 266, 267; and Thomas Forbes, 260; and Vidal estate, 343; in Washington (1805), 255; and West Florida, possible U.S. annexation of (1810), 277; and William Eustis, 267

Singer, The (Upper Creek chief), 254

Sisters, The (ship), and British admiralty courts, 213–14, 216–19

Slaves: British military recruitment and use of, 283, 290–92, 296, 301; in Pensacola, 286; trade in, 325–26; U.S. prohibition on importation of (1808), 274

Smith, Daniel, and Cherokee, 258

Smith, Sgt. Samuel, and Red Sticks, 281

Smuggling: in Louisiana and West Florida, 128; in Mobile and Pensacola, 279; in West Indies, 87–88, 90–91, 110, 127–28

Somerset case (1772), and British slavery law, 351

South Carolina: and American Revolution, map 40; and British departure from (1782), 49; and Creek war against Georgia (1787), 98–99; and land speculators, in Franco-Spanish war (1793), 183; and Panton, Leslie, 346; and William Panton, 27–28

South Carolina Council of Safety, and William Panton, 28

South Carolina Yazoo Company, 141–42, 147, 150, 167

Southwest Territory, U.S. creation of (1790), 160

Spain: and Cherokee, 162; and constitution of 1812, 342; and Conventions of 1823 and 1828, 351; and Creek, military support to, 76, 80–82, 94, 96–98, 107, 111, 120–21, 123–24, 159, 163, 183; East Florida, ceded to (1783), 43, 50–51; and the Floridas, land grants in, 350–51; and the Floridas, unrest in, 323; and Indian trade diplomacy, 11–14, 54, 56, 58, 193; and John and James Innerarity, 362; and John Forbes & Co., 250, 327, 351–52, 361–62, 366, 367; Junta of the Royal Treasury, 206; mercantile system of, 10–11, 54–55, 88–92, 128, 367; merchant guilds in, 91, 127–28; Negro Fort, opposition to, 306, 309; North American territorial claims of, 227; in northern Pacific, 125; and Panton, Leslie, 187, 193–94, 201, 206, 230, 249–50, 357, 366–68; royal order of 1789 and Indian trade, 128–29, 187; and Seminole, treaty with, 239; "state" of Muskogee, war with, 236; Supreme Council of State, 127–28; and Treaty of New York, 143, 147; and Treaty of San Lorenzo, 228; West Florida, investment in, 250; and William Augustus Bowles, 233

—and Creek: and Creek–U.S. relations, 137; military support to, 76, 80–82, 94, 96–98, 107, 111, 120–21, 123–24, 159, 169, 183; relations with, 125, 143–44,

147; treaty with (1784), 58–60, 67, 70, 100, 129; treaty with (1792), 163
—and France; alliance with (1797), 203–4; peace treaty with (1795), 200; Supreme Council of State and French Revolution, 128; war with (1793), 172, 176–77, 182–87, 200, 369
—and Great Britain: alliance with (1793), 188, 284, 369; commercial rivalry with, 1, 7–8, 10, 13, 87–88, 105–7, 110, 125–27, 132; relations with, 107, 122, 125, 144, 148; war with, 203–6, 209, 238, 369
—and southeastern Indians: relations with, 166, 249, 299, 304–5, 311; trade with, 7, 50–52, 54, 58, 61–63, 65, 67–68, 70, 88, 90–93, 102–11, 116–17, 127–29, 166, 181, 187, 194
—and U.S.: boundary dispute with, 3, 166, 199–200, 228; cession of the Floridas to, 268, 353, 367; commercial rivalry with, 2, 13, 62, 73–74, 88, 90, 99–100, 132, 143–45, 170; and filibustering in U.S. territory, 263; Louisiana boundary, possible war over, 249; relations with, 148, 158, 160–66, 206, 263, 274–77, 321, 366; and trade restrictions on U.S., 310–11; treaties with, 122, 295; and U.S. expansionist policy, 162, 201, 220, 224; and U.S. Indian policy, 160
Spalding, James, 23, 33–34
Spanish Bluff, 310, 316
Spanish Bluff (plantation), 325
Spanish neutrality, violations of, 273, 285–86
Spencer, Capt. Richard, 290–91
Stokes Landing, stores at, 33, 34
Strachan, James, 90–91, 109–11
Strachan, MacKenzie & Co., 98; and Anglo-Spanish alliance (1793), 188; and Bernardo del Campo, 130–32; and convoy shipping system, 189; and John Leslie, 217; and Panton, Leslie, 21, 129, 131, 188, 194, 216–17; and *Providence* (ship), 216; and smuggling, accused of, 130; and Spanish Indian trade, 129
Strother, —: and James Mather, 90; and southeastern Indian trade, 85; and Spanish-Chickasaw relations, 104; and Spanish-Creek relations, 104; and Spanish Indian trade, 62, 67–68, 71, 99, 103–4, 109, 126
Stuart, John (British superintendent of Indian affairs), 24, 26, 27, 33
Suárez, Nicolás Santos, and Vidal estate records, 333
Sugar trade, 221, 224
Sunbury, Georgia, 28
Superior Court of Middle Florida, and Forbes Grant I, 354
"Supreme Judicial Court of West Florida" (Mobile), and Vidal case (1821), 344–45
Suwannee River: Ambrister at (1818), 321; Arbuthnot's store at, 316, 321; area of, map 322; Doyle and Hambly at (1817), 317; escaped slaves' settlements at, 297; U.S. attack on (1818), 319, 320
Swiss, possible immigrants to West Florida, 249

Taboca (Choctaw chief), 99–100, 167, 168–69
Talbot, Capt. William, 185–86
Tallahassee, Doyle at (1831), 325
Tallapoosa River, 5
Tallassee (Creek town), John Innerarity at, 270
Tame King of Tallassie, 75, 113; and Georgia, 80, 84,; at Shoulderbone Creek (1786), 83
Tampa, escaped Forbes slaves at (1819), 309
Tampa Bay, and filibustering in East Florida (1818), 320
Taski Etoka (Chickasaw king), 100, 172–74
Telfair, Edward (governor of Georgia), 83, 190
Tellico, Cherokee trading post at, 195
Tennessee, Cherokee raids in, 196
Tennessee River, 2, 4–5, 74–75, 85, 178, 197, 257
Tensaw River, 115; U.S. settlements on, 122–24, 133, 136, 172
Terror (ship), and escape of Forbes slaves, 293
Texas, and boundary dispute with Louisiana, 263
Thomas Forbes & Co., losses in American Revolution, 42–43

Tod, Lindsay, 293
Tombigbee River, 4–5, 141, 170, 174, 256; and Indian cessions, 246–47, 248; Spanish fort at, 172, 181; U.S. settlements at, 122–24, 133, 136, 172
Tonnant (ship), at Pensacola (1814), 289
Tonyn, Patrick (governor of East Florida), 28–30, 42–43, 59; and Commons House of Assembly of East Florida, 41; and Indian congress at St. Augustine (1783), 49; and Indian diplomacy during American Revolution, 27; and memorials of loyalty, 31, 32; and Panton, Forbes & Co., 36; and Panton, Leslie, 56, 365; and prisoner exchanges, 36–38; and southeastern Indian trade, 35, 50; and Spanish government, overtures to, 51, 54; and Spanish Indian trade, 63; and William Panton, 26, 365
"Trans-Oconee Republic," 184–85
Travers, William, and debts to John Forbes, 360
Travis, William, administrator of John Forbes's estate, 360
Treaty of Augusta (1783), 55–56, 75–76, 80 83, 136
Treaty of Colerain (1796), 201
Treaty of 1819, 352–53, 360
Treaty of Fort Jackson (1814): and Edward Nicolls, 299; and Indian cessions to U.S., 299, 303, 305; provisions of, 305, 321; and U.S. annexation of Creek lands, 305, 314
Treaty of French Lick (1783), 78
Treaty of Galphinton (1786), 80, 83, 136
Treaty of Ghent (1815), 298, 299, 314
Treaty of Holston (1791), 5, 160, 162
Treaty of Hopewell. *See* Hopewell treaties
Treaty of New York (1790), 146, 149, 161, 163, 166, 176, 201, 234; denunciations of, 147; opposition of Elijah Clarke to, 184; provisions of, 143–44; U.S. ratification of, 145
Treaty of Nogales (1793), 180–81
Treaty of Paris (1783), 2
Treaty of Pensacola (1784), 75, 80, 107, 137, 147
Treaty of San Lorenzo (1795), 206, 220, 228, 232; and Panton, Leslie, 200, 369; and U.S.–Spanish relations, 275–76

Treaty of Shoulderbone Creek (1786), 83, 84, 136
Tribunal de residencia, and José Callava, 337
Trinidad, and British recruitment of slaves, 291
Trist, Nicholas Philip, and Forbes Grant I, 354
Trouillet, Heloise Isabelle, marriage to James Innerarity (1808), 329n
Truetlen, John A., 29
Tuckabatchee (Upper Creek town), 76, 80, 177, 190–91
Turk's Island, and salt trade, 133
Turnbull, John, 172–76, 179, 181, 194, 197–99

Ugula Yacabee (Chickasaw war chief), 171, 173, 180, 181, 197–98
Ulloa, Antonio de (governor of Louisiana), 9
United States: and Alexander McGillivray, 180; Amelia Island, occupation by (1812), 273; Articles of Confederation, management of Indian affairs under, 93; Canada, operations in, 283; and Chattahoochee-Flint settlement, 305; and Chickamauga, 160; Constitution, federal lands under, 141–42; Continental Congress, and George McIntosh, 29–30; District Court at New Orleans, suit brought by John Forbes & Co. in (1809), 267; and Edmond Genêt, 184; expansionist policy of, 1–3, 49, 51–56, 71, 99, 122, 158, 162–63, 171–73, 182, 199, 201, 220, 224, 240, 244–46, 248–49, 251–59, 262, 364, 369; and factory system in Indian trade, 201–2, 245, 248–49, 262, 272; Federalist party, and John McKee, 228; filibustering activities in West Florida by, 276–77; Flint River, desire for Indian lands east of, 251; and the Floridas, annexation of, 246, 303, 312, 326–27, 330, 333–34, 367; and Florida slave trade, 274–75; and immigration to Indian cessions, 249; Indian and Negro raids against, 323; Indian cessions to (1805), map 264, table 265, 299; and Indian diplomacy in American Revolution, 26; Indian policies of, 369; and Indian

trade, 93, 99–100, 102, 159–61, 162, 163, 191–93; invasion of East Florida by (1812), 273–74, 301; and John and James Innerarity, 362; and John Forbes & Co., 261–63, 266, 267, 274–76, 278, 327, 364, 366, 370; John Forbes's claims against (1812), 359; and Louisiana, 166; and Louisiana Purchase, 246, 248, 276; and Mississippi River, 171, 200, 255–57; and Mobile, occupation of (1813), 277–79; and navy, 307, 318; and Negro Fort, 306–8, 309, 310, 316; neutrality of, in Franco-Spanish war, 182, 185; and Panton, Leslie, 192, 194, 200–202, 212–13, 226–31, 248, 250, 256, 364; and Pensacola, occupation by (1814), 288; Proclamation of Neutrality (1793), 182; and proposed Indian cessions to, 249; and proposed military post at Muscle Shoals, 178; and proposed trading post at Chickasaw Bluffs, 178; and Senate, 140, 255, 260, 261; settlement at Chickasaw Bluffs (1795), 197; and southeastern Indians, 164, 169, 311, 314, 316; and southeastern Indian trade, 51–52, 56, 71, 73, 90, 93, 99, 100, 105–6, 126–27, 168–69, 180–81, 201–2, 245, 248–49, 262, 272; Southwest Territory, creation of (1790), 160; Supreme Court, 354–56; Suwannee, attack on (1818), 319; trading post at Muscle Shoals, 171; and Treaty of Ghent (1815), 314; and Treaty of New York (1790), 142; and Treaty of San Lorenzo (1795), 228; War Department, 195, 231; and West Florida, Indian attacks on settlers in, 315; and West Florida, occupation of (1813), 284; and West Florida, possible annexation of (1810), 277; and William Augustus Bowles, 239–40

—army of: and Camp Crawford, construction of (1816), 306; Fourth Infantry, at Pensacola (1821), 335, 347; garrisons at Mobile and Pensacola, 324–25; and John Forbes & Co., 274, 278, 324–25; at Mobile (1814), 283; and Negro Fort, destruction of (1816), 315, 367; seizure of Forbes slaves by (1812), 274–76

—and Cherokee: cession to U.S. (1805), 258; Congress and Cherokee subsidy, 196; negotiations with (1804), 251; relations with, 141, 160, 192; trade relations with, 195

—and Chickasaw, 169; cession to U.S. (1805), 258; and Creek-Chickasaw hostilities, 179–80; military support to, 173, 178; negotiations with (1804), 251; proposed Chickasaw cession to (1805), 257; refusal to cede Mississippi lands to U.S. (1805), 257–58; relations with, 141, 160, 171, 177, 179, 210; and trade, 173–74

—and Choctaw, 169–70; cession to U.S. (1805), 263, 266; and Choctaw debts to Panton, Leslie, 256; negotiations with (1804), 251; and proposed Choctaw cessions, 248, 256; and proposed treaty with (1805), 255; refusal to cede Mississippi lands (1805), 256; relations with, 141, 160, 171, 179

—and Congress: and Bourbon County, Georgia, affair (1785), 77; and Cherokee subsidy, 196; and Creek, peace commission to (1785), 79–80, 98–99; and Creek war with Georgia (1787), 97–98; and Georgian western territorial claims, 79; and Indian trade monopoly, 195; and Spanish land grants in the Floridas, adjudication of, 352; and "state" of Franklin, 74; and William Panton, 200

—and Creek, 305; Congressional peace commission to (1785), 79–80, 98–99; Creek cession to, 240 (1802), 258–60 (1805); and Creek-Chickasaw hostilities, 179–80; and Creek-Spanish relations, 138; and drought among Lower Creek (1792), 176; negotiations with (1804), 251; proposed Creek cession to (1805), 243–45; protection of Creek villages by, 143, 146; relations with, 135, 140, 142–46, 178, 189, 192; subsidy to, 201; trade with, 195, 201–2; treaty commission to (1789), 139; treaty with (1805), 261; U.S. attempt to convert to agriculture, 229; war with (1813–14), 279–81

—and Great Britain: British operations in the Floridas (1814), 283; commercial rivalry with, 143, 145; competition with

British Indian trade 195; relations with, 323; and U.S. slaveowners, 298; war with (1812–15), 273–91, 295
—and Spain: adjudication of Spanish land grants in the Floridas, 352; boundary dispute with, 3, 166, 199–200, 228; commercial rivalry with, 2, 3, 62, 73–74, 90, 99–100, 105–7, 126–27, 132, 143–45, 170; negotiations over the Floridas, 353; possible war over Louisiana boundary (1804), 249; relations with, 148, 158, 160–66, 206, 263, 277, 321, 366; Spanish cession of the Floridas to, 268; and Spanish customs and duties, 262–63, 288, 297; and Spanish grants to John Forbes & Co., 327; and Spanish Indian policy, 160; and Spanish Indian trade, 145, 174, 176–77, 310–11; as threat to Spanish territory, 171–73; treaty concerning escaped slaves, 295; treaty negotiations with (1786), 122; violations of Spanish neutrality by (1812), 273
Unzaga y Amezaga, Luis de, 10
Upper Creek, 95, 113; and Apalachicola cession to John Forbes & Co. (1804), 254–55; and Benjamin Hawkins, 239; and Creek cession to U.S. (1805), 261; debts to trading companies, 243, 245, 255, 270–71; and Pedro Olivier, 162; and proposed grand Indian alliance, 150, 189; and proposed Seminole cession to John Forbes & Co. (1806), 262; territory of, 4; and William Augustus Bowles, 150, 241; and William Panton, 162
Urcullo, Lt. José, 289
Urquijo, Mariano Luis de (Spanish minister of state), and Marqués de Casa Calvo, 221

Valdés y Bazán, Antonio, 110; and Miró, 126; and Panton, Leslie, 91, 125; and Spanish Indian trade, 104, 109
Varela y Ulloa, Pedro (Spanish secretary of treasury), and Panton, Leslie, 204
Vera Cruz, 104
Viar, Josef Ignacio de (Spanish representative at Philadelphia), 165–66
Vidal, Caroline María, 331, 332, 333

Vidal, Mercedes, 331–34
Vidal, Nicholas Maria (lieutenant governor of Louisiana and West Florida): debts to Euphrozine Hinard, 331–32; debts to John Forbes & Co., 343–45; debts to Terencio Le Blanc, 332; estate of, 331–47
Villebeuvre, Capt. Juan de la (Spanish agent to Choctaw and Chickasaw): and Barón de Carondelet, 170–71; and Chickasaw, 102; and Creek-Chickasaw hostilities, 170; and Indian conference at Yazoo River, 101; and Spanish fort on Tombigbee River, 181
Villiers, Lt. Col. Marcos de, 325, 338, 346
Virginia, suit brought by John Forbes in (1804), 266

Wager, Capt. Philip, 340, 347
Wakulla River, 251; cession to John Forbes & Co. on (1811), 268; Panton, Leslie store at, 50, 243, 315
Walnut Hills, 141, 167, 194
Walton, George (secretary and acting governor of West Florida), 334, 345–47
War of 1812: end of (1815), 295; in the Floridas, 272; and John Forbes & Co., 302, 364, 366, 367, 368; losses of John Forbes & Co. in, 309, 326–27, 329–30, 350–51, 370. See also Great Britain, war with U.S.; U.S., war with Great Britain
Washington, George (president): and Alexander McGillivray, 144; and Cherokee, 143, 159–61; and Creek trade, 192; and Creek-U.S. relations, 140–43, 145; and Edmond Genêt, 197; and enlistment of southeastern Indians against northern Indians, 160; and Fort Massac, 197; and Georgian western territorial claims, 140; and independent commercial port for Creek, 140; and Indian conference at Nashville (1792), 170; and Indian trade, 145, 192–95, 201; message to Congress (1793), 192–93; and Proclamation of Neutrality (1793), 182; and proposed U.S. military post at Muscle Shoals, 178; and South Carolina Yazoo Company, 142; and Spanish Indian trade, 145; and U.S. Indian policy, 160, 369; and U.S. land speculation, 141, 142; and U.S. treaty commis-

sion to Creek (1789), 135–36, 138; and William Augustus Bowles, 159; and William Panton, 144
Washington, Tom, and South Carolina Yazoo Company, 142
Washington, D.C.: Choctaw delegation at (1804), 246–47; John Forbes at (1804), 250
Watts, John (Cherokee chief), 162, 180
Wayne, Maj. Gen. Anthony, 160, 171, 196
Wellbank, George, 151, 153, 154
Wells, John, 46
West Florida: Anglo-Spanish War, effects of, 204; boundaries of, 2–3; boundary settlement (1795), 200, 202; British cession to Spain (1783), 1–2, 43; British possession of, 1, 7; climate of, 250; and Creek, 55–56; defenses of, 157; description of, 249–50; escape of slaves from (1812–15), 297; exports of, 133–34; government of, and relations with trading companies, 236–37; governors of (1815–18), 312; immigration to, 249–50; Indian raids against Spanish in, 323; Indian trade in, 204; invasion of, by Andrew Jackson (1818), 318–19, 323; John Forbes & Co. in, 273, 297, 316, 326, 327; judicial system of (1821), 344; and Louisiana, subordination to, 67–69; and Louisiana, U.S. acquisition of (1803), 248, 276; Panton, Leslie expansion into, 368; possible U.S. annexation of (1810), 277; Red Stick retreat to (1814), 280–81; religious tolerance in, 250; revision of commercial regulations in (1783), 187; slavery in, 249–50; Spanish customs duties in, 310–12; Spanish governor of, and jurisdiction in East Florida, 354; Spanish investment in, 250; supply of Indian trade goods in, 57, 68–69; supreme court of, 344; and Treaty of San Lorenzo (1795), 200; U.S. annexation of (1813), 284, 312; U.S. filibustering activities in, 276; U.S. immigration into, 157; U.S. settlers in, 303, 315
Whitaker, Arthur Preston, 229
White, Enrique (governor of East Florida), 237
White, James, 111, 122, 140; and Alexander McGillivray, 93, 139; and mission to Creek (1787), 93–96; and U.S. Indian trade diplomacy, 93–94
Whitefield, George, 99, 106
White Lieutenant (Creek chief), 189, 192
Wilkinson, Brig. Gen. James, 122, 160; and Alexander Hamilton, 246; and Barón de Carondelet, 196–97; and Indian debts to Panton, Leslie, 227, 230; and John Forbes, 245–46, 278; and Miró, 139; and occupation of New Orleans (1815), 246; and Panton, Leslie, 147, 251, 259; and possible U.S. annexation of the Floridas, 246; and proposed Creek cession to U.S. (1804), 259; and proposed Indian cessions to U.S., 245–46; and U.S.–Creek relations, 139; and U.S. expansionist policy, 246; and U.S. occupation of Mobile (1813), 277–78
Wilkinson, Capt. James B., 278
Willett, Col. Marinus, 142–43
Wilson, Capt. Henry, 347
Woodbine, Capt. George, 290, 319, 326; accusations against (1816), 320; and British military recruitment of slaves, 286; in East Florida, 289, 301; and Edward Nicolls, 300; and escaped Forbes slaves, 281, 301; and filibustering activities in East Florida (1818), 320, 367; and González Manrique, 286, 301; in Havana (1816), 302; and Hillis Hadjo, 299; and John Forbes, 300–302; and John Forbes & Co., 281; and John Innerarity, 283; and Kindelán, 301; lawsuits against (1815), 301; in Nassau (1815), 301; in Pensacola (1814), 283, 301; and Red Sticks, 281–82; and retreat from Fort Boyer, 286; and Robert Chrystie Ambrister, 301; in St. Augustine (1814), 301–2; and southeastern Indians, 318; and theft of Forbes slaves, 297
Woodbury, Levi (secretary of the treasury), and John Forbes's estate (1837), 360

Yahulla Emathly (Seminole chief), 247
Yazoo River, 4, 14, 77, 169, 172, 175, 197, 256; Georgian land speculators on, 201; Indian conference at (1787), 100
Yeats, David, 42
Yonge, Henry, 46

Yonge, Philip R., 274

Zéspedes, Vincente Manuel de (governor of East Florida), 119–20; and Alexander McGillivray, 64, 69–70, 87, 97, 140; and civil marriages, 42; and Creek war against Georgia (1787), 81, 98; and Indian trade diplomacy, 63–65; and James O'Fallon, 141; and Panton, Leslie, 34, 63–65, 69, 86–87, 368; and southeastern Indian trade, 127; and Spanish Indian trade, 68, 102–3; and U.S. land speculation, 141

Zúñiga, Mauricio de (governor of West Florida), 312; and Andrew Jackson, 306; and Negro Fort, 306, 309; and Spanish trade restrictions on John Forbes & Co., 311; and Vidal estate records, 333